JAPAN IN CRISIS

D1564154

MICHIGAN CLASSICS IN JAPANESE STUDIES
NUMBER 20

CENTER FOR JAPANESE STUDIES
THE UNIVERSITY OF MICHIGAN

JAPAN IN CRISIS

ESSAYS ON TAISHŌ DEMOCRACY

Edited by

Bernard S. Silberman
and
H. D. Harootunian

Contributors

GAIL BERNSTEIN
JAMES B. CROWLEY
H. D. HAROOTUNIAN
AKIRA IRIYE
YOSHIO IWAMOTO
SHŪICHI KATO
TAKAYOSHI MATSUO
TETSUO NAJITA
JAMES I. NAKAMURA
BERNARD S. SILBERMAN
GEORGE O. TOTTEN
ANN WASWO
KOZO YAMAMURA

CENTER FOR JAPANESE STUDIES
THE UNIVERSITY OF MICHIGAN
ANN ARBOR, MICHIGAN

Reprinted in 1999 with the permission of Princeton University Press by
the Center for Japanese Studies, The University of Michigan,
202 S. Thayer St., Ann Arbor, MI 48104-1608

Library of Congress Cataloging-in-Publication Data

Japan in crisis : essays on Taishō democracy / edited by Bernard S.
  Silberman and H.D. Harootunian ; contributors, Gail Bernstein . . .
  [et al.].
      viii, 469p. 23cm. — (Michigan classics in Japanese studies ; no. 20)
    Reprint. Originally published: Princeton, N.J. : Princeton University
  Press, 1974.
    Includes index.
    ISBN 0-939512-97-1 (pbk. : alk. paper)
    1. Japan—History—Taishō period, 1912–1926—Congresses. 2.
  Japan—Politics and government—1912–1926—Congresses. I.
  Silberman, Bernard S., 1930– . II. Harootunian, Harry D., 1929– .
  III. Bernstein, Gail Lee. IV. Series.
  DS886.J36   1999
  952.03'2—dc21   99–31074
                                                                         CIP

The paper used in this publication meets the requirements of the
ANSI/NISO Standard Z39.44-1992 (Permanence of Paper for
Publications and Documents in Libraries and Archives).

Printed in the United States of America

T HE CONFERENCE on Taishō Japan was held at Quail Roost, North Carolina, in January 1970. Altogether, nineteen Japanese and American scholars participated in the conference. In addition to the writers of the papers that make up this volume the following scholars were also present: Hugh Borton, Columbia University; David Abosch, State University of New York at Buffalo; Arthur Tiedemann, City College of the City University of New York; Joseph Spengler, Duke University; Eugene Soviak, Washington University, St. Louis; Fred Notehelfer, University of California at Los Angeles. Serving as commentators and devil's advocates, they contributed immeasurably both to the discussions and the quality of the papers. The editors and the authors wish to express their gratitude for these contributions.

The editors would also like to thank the Conference on Modern Japan, the Association for Asian Studies, and Duke University for providing, in equal amounts, the funds for support of the conference and the preparation of the papers. There are a number of people in these organizations to whom the editors would like to extend special thanks: John W. Hall and Robert E. Ward of the Conference on Modern Japan; Charles O. Hucker and David Steinberg, past secretaries of the Association for Asian Studies; Craufurd Goodwin and Marion Salinger of Duke University.

Finally, the editors wish to make clear that the views expressed in the introduction with regard to the meaning of the conference and the papers are theirs alone. Although indebted to the authors and the discussants for their insights the views expressed in the introduction and conclusion do not necessarily represent those shared by any or most of the participants in the conference.

Bernard S. Silberman
H. D. Harootunian

Contents

JAPAN IN CRISIS

Introduction:
A Sense of An Ending
and the Problem of Taishō

I T IS probably easier to describe the end than the beginning of an epoch. Participants in historical eras always seem to have a sharper sense of an ending than of a beginning. But hindsight is more secure than foresight; reflection more acceptable than the expression of new impulses. Perhaps to see a break in the line, an epochal disjunction, or to conceive of epochs as unities, is to do violence to the experiences left to us from more distant times.

Perhaps this is the way it should be. We have learned that if it is easier to sense an ending and describe it, we might also divine something about what is beginning. Hegel thought so, and modern historical writing has been founded on this single premise. But we have also discovered—only recently—that something might end and not be followed by a beginning. In any case, the important questions always relate to when epochs end, what passed into history, and why we ask such questions in the first place. Of course, there is rarely any agreement among contemporaries who try to answer the substantive questions concerning the end of an epoch, or among later historians who, in trying to reach some sort of consensus, comfort themselves with the knowledge that they have moved historical studies a step ahead. Perhaps this knowledge is another fiction. But if in studying endings we have come no closer to actually knowing what things have ended and why, we have, nevertheless, provided a fascinating disclosure of historical consciousness. For in the very act of selecting such questions, whatever they are, we have revealed what is historically important to us at this time. The interest in a discontinuous time says more about our own condition and historical consciousness than it does of those times we seek to redeem historically. But history can never be dissociated from the perception of it.

The end of the Meiji period and the establishment of the Taishō era is a reminder that the problem of endings and beginnings

3

still prevails and that the questions such problems raise are very much a part of contemporary historical consciousness.

Officially, the Meiji period ended in 1912, when Meiji was succeeded by a son who took the reign name of Taishō. But few observers (then and now) would accept this change as anything more than a chronological convenience. Although the year 1912 signifies simply a changing of the guard, we must also note that this change had already been preceded by contemporary expressions of the knowledge that an era was coming to a close. Indeed, these expressions revealed a growing agreement that the goals of an earlier time had been reached, the symbols of an age had become tarnished. Even the Japanese government acknowledged this fact and worried about vanished ideals. Its response was to interpret the emerging social protest in the first decade of the twentieth century as a sign of moral failure. In its effort to stem change as moral failure (a very good Confucian perception), the government issued an Imperial Rescript in 1908 (*Boshin no chokusho*) which attempted to retrieve older guidelines of ethical behavior. Yet such a rescript itself was an open acknowledgment that one conception of society was giving way to another, a process that *did not* involve only the simple change from traditional to modern. Far from it. Japan was, by the first decade of the twentieth century, a "modern" society. An older model of society, which had achieved its goals, was failing to satisfy new demands, new needs, and to accommodate new social constituencies which the success of earlier policies had now made possible.

Meiji society had created the conditions for its own disconfirmation. What the vague and unformulated stirrings of the early twentieth century showed was the emergence of a new model of society in which class, social order, and state would stand in a relationship of clear counterpoint and tension to each other. In what proved to be the closing years of Meiji the vague contours of what was to be Imperial Japan began to surface with regular frequency. Some of the details of what this model of society was and what it sought to accomplish are examined in the several papers in this volume. Rather than rework this terrain, I would like to establish a point of view comprehensive enough to account for the depth of analysis and the varieties of perceptions offered here. Yet I should also add that such a point of view is made possible by the suggestiveness of the vast range of problems raised and perceptions yielded in these papers. In this foreword I should

4

like to present a view of what ended with the Meiji, and how this ending might have affected the spiritual life of Imperial Japan.

The death of Emperor Meiji in 1912 stunned the nation. The philosopher and social critic Miyake Setsurei has described the mood of the evening on which the emperor died. "The moon was covered by clouds, and just as it began to rain heavily, we received news of the emperor's death. The crowd of people (outside the Imperial Palace), which numbered approximately 70,000, lamented in unison. The numbers who stayed through the night without sleep were considerable." Almost immediately the nation was treated to another shock. "Completely unexpectedly, we were surprised by the news of the suicide of General Nogi Maretsuke and his wife." Yet, Miyake noted in his journal, it was news which also won the nation's praise.[1] Natsume Sōseki dramatized this elegiac moment in his novel *Kokoro* (1913), when he has his reluctant hero, Sensei, take his own life on hearing the news of the death of the emperor and the double suicide of General and Mrs. Nogi. For Sensei the deaths represented the end of an era. Raised in a different kind of society, and believing that the "Spirit of Meiji" had passed into history, Sensei confessed that he no longer wanted to live in the new era.

Perhaps the suicides of General and Mrs. Nogi were more symbolic. The Meiji Emperor had ruled for forty-five years. He had—metaphorically—led Japan into the modern world. By the time of his death Japan ranked as an equal partner in the international comity of nations. Independence, power, and wealth had all been realized during his rule. Meiji reminded the nation of the success of the Restorationist Revolution of 1868 (*Ishinteki kakumei*).[2] In the contemporary photographs of him, draped in military dress, seated erect on a white horse, looking stern and determined, Meiji revealed something of the purpose and charisma which had characterized the political leadership of his day. But the photographs were deceptive. At one level this charisma was impersonal inasmuch as it was associated with the imperial office. Yet Meiji's larger-than-life persona added a personal dimension to it. At still another level Meiji symbolized the charisma of the revolutionary leadership which led Japan to its present position as a world power in the early twentieth century. But the charisma which had

[1] Miyake Setsurei, *Dōjidaishi* (Tokyo, 1953), IV, 141-142.
[2] I am indebted to Tetsuo Najita for this phrase.

been so generously deployed in the Meiji period was doomed to routinization. Just as the leadership would be succeeded by a formal bureaucracy, which hereafter would make impossible the kind of leaders who brought off the Restoration, so Meiji would be succeeded by men who could not possibly duplicate his personality. After Meiji no Emperor could exceed, by sheer personal energy, the impersonal limits of the office. Taishō was mentally incompetent, and the timid Shōwa Emperor, Hirohito, has remained virtually indistinguishable from the institution of the imperial system. But even if either man had been personally vigorous, it would not have changed the style of the institution.

Meiji's successor, Yoshihito, was crowned at the age of thirty-four. Two men could not have been more different. Meiji (Mutsuhito) had ascended the throne at fifteen, during the turbulent years of the 1860's. His accession marked an imperial restoration; his rule a sustained epiphany. During his reign the institution of Emperor, which had been consigned to an "existence beyond the clouds" since the Middle Ages, was refashioned into a dynamically human role and reconsecrated into a divine office. Meiji satisfied the requirements of both with consummate skill, often, it seemed, improvising on his own, dramatizing both the human and divine aspects of the new concept of emperorship. He was human for all to see. Yet his enactments were larger than life. In his time it was believed that he was a "living deity" who was able to talk with Amaterasu Ōmikami at the Grand Shrine of Ise. When he became ill, his doctors, it has been reported, were disinclined to touch his body. They were able to examine him only when he was asleep.[3] Another story is that when Meiji bathed, he would immerse only the lower half of his body in hot water; attendants splashed water on the upper half. The apparent reason for maintaining this division was to prevent the upper half from being polluted by the dirt of the lower half for it was believed that deity (*kami*) dwelt in the upper half of the Emperor's body.

Meiji's appetite in drink, food, and women was also "divinely" prodigious. One story reports how Meiji ate nearly a pound of rice and fifteen or sixteen sweet fish (*ayu*)—the large variety caught early in autumn—at one sitting. Five years before his death he suffered—not surprisingly—from a severe kidney disorder, following which chronic illness became his steady com-

[3] As reported in Nezu Masashi, *Nihon gendaishi* (Tokyo, 1966), I, 21-33.

panion. But even in illness Meiji could consume a bottle of French wine at a sitting. One can only guess at the dimensions of his sexual appetite.

The death of Meiji, then, was the death of a hero. A heroic time had ended. Neither the charisma nor the heroism could be repeated again. Nogi's death, which most clearly symbolized this sense of an ending, was praised in the press and popular literature as an act of "samurai sincerity and pure loyalty."[4] But it also revealed that the years of magic and heroism were over. Japan had come of age. Mushakoji Saneatsu hailed the event as an outstanding example of "*bushidō* seeking its end" and the passing of the Spirit of Meiji. Others were not so enthusiastic. But all saw in the peculiar expression of *junshi*—the warrior's taking his own life after his master had fallen—the military sense of determination and achievement that had characterized the Meiji period. Yet if *bushidō* had been completed and the Spirit of Meiji had reached its end, something had also begun. The stirrings had been sighted long before the death of Meiji and Nogi.

By comparison the new Taishō emperor appeared as a parody of his illustrious father. If he failed to match Meiji's style, his own style was matchless in its inconsistency and incompetence. Meiji's personality fitted the needs of a heroic age; Taishō would not affect the office he occupied. It was in his reign, it should be remembered, that the effort was made to make the Emperor into an instrument. By the time of his reign the institution of Emperor was larger than any man could be. Never a robust man, Taishō had suffered from meningitis early in youth, and the illness was to mark him for life. The German physician to the Japanese court, Erwin Baelz, noted in his diary in 1900 how Prince Yoshihito had declined since his childhood illness and how little attention was paid to his mental capacity. Ten years later his condition had visibly worsened. His performance as a student at the Peers School (*Gakushū-in*) had been a failure and the subject of a good deal of gossip. Court attendants, recognizing his limitations, devised a program that consisted of "three parts learning, seven parts physical education." Ultimately he was withdrawn from the school in the interest of secrecy and respect for the imperial office. It was believed that the Crown Prince's performance might dam-

[4] On the metaphorical meaning of Nogi's death there is a large literature, but see Hashikawa Bunzō, *Rekishi to taiken* (Tokyo, 1968), pp. 182-203.

age the carefully contrived image of an institution which could
not suffer human failure. Even the knowledge of his origins had
been withheld from him and it was only after he reached adult-
hood that he learned that he was the son of a concubine. Despite
his spectacular antics—insulting the Korean crown prince, speed-
ing to his father's funeral and shouting outrageously all along the
way, "Get out of the way, get out of the way,"⁵—men held
great hopes for the new period.

A rescript which solemnly proclaimed to the nation that "We
have encountered a sudden and unexpected sorrow. We have
reached the extreme of bereavement," announced that the new
reign name would be Taishō (great rectification, reform). Authentication of the promise was provided by the *I Ching*. In accordance with the precedent established by the Meiji revolutionaries,
the name was inspired by an auspicious passage selected from this
classic of divination: "To bring about great adjustments (*taishō*)
is received from the Way of Heaven." Yet, as if to cover all bets,
the allusion to "great adjustments" could also be found in the
Confucian *Ch'un-ch'iu kung-yang chüan* (The Kung-yang Tradition of the Spring and Autumn Analects), where it is stated that
the "superior man (*kunshi*) is one who adjusts greatly."

Simultaneously, the government changed all stamp issues, and
after 1913 established the Emperor's birthday (August 31) as a
national holiday. (It was changed to October 31, owing to the
mid-summer holidays [*kyūka*].) As if to diminish the heroic and
revolutionary achievements of the Meiji, the Taishō period was
pledged to "correctness," "rectification," and "adjustments." Institutions, political style, and modes of social behavior were fixed,
and all that would be required hereafter was "adjustment."

While "adjustment" and "correctness" pledged the government
to order, it inspired others to seek radical political and social
change. Maruyama Kandō declared in the January, 1913 issue of
Nihon oyobi Nihonjin that something new was occurring. "Even
though there is no rational reason to draw a line in national
thought between Meiji and Taishō," he wrote, "we still feel, perhaps unconsciously, the signs of a new period." He compared this
sense of newness to the airplane, which appeared at about the
same time, and what it represented for the future. "We felt like
demonstrating the advent of a new civilization against old social
conventions and habits." The "signs of a new period" were made

⁵ *Ibid.*, p. 21.

8

more explicit in an editorial written in the wake of the august new beginning and appearing in the liberal newspaper *Ōsaka Asahi.* The September 27, 1912, editorial was entitled "The New Politics of Taishō," and argued that while there was the politics of Meiji in the Meiji period, in the Taishō period there must be the politics of Taishō. "To measure the politics of Taishō by that of Meiji is the ideology of those who are captive of the Meiji period. . . . It is more essential to nourish the strength of the people than it is to enlarge the army with two additional divisions. Until today the people have been deceived and we have walked the road of military politics." More, the editorial saw in the "new Taishō period" a "great incentive" which, it was hoped, would stimulate all to "expel the reactionary and conservative indolence which have cast a pall over the people." If the article was not actually calling for revolution, it was saying that the new era offered the occasion for fundamental political change.

This argument was amplified in the journal *Yorozu chōhō* at about the same time. After observing how the ideograph for *tadasu* (*shō* in the compound *Taishō*), contained both the character for high and low, and since both are united in this context, the essayist announced that the "reign name offers a new ideal" which will promise to unify all opposites. But, the writer warned, echoing Tokutomi Sohō more than a generation earlier, "We are not the men of Meiji. We are the men of Taishō." (Ironically, we are reminded today that the men who control Japan are the "men of Taishō, whose mark on contemporary history has been significant, if not profound.) "Our stage is Taishō," he declared, and a new stage required a new scenario. "In the old Meiji period it was held that *bushidō* was everything but in the new Taishō . . . if military politics or *bushidō* appears, it must never be permitted." Although it was possible to "fill old bottles with new wine," the old notables—what he called the "Meiji inheritance," Yamagata, Katsura, Inoue, Matsukata and Saionji—had outlived their usefulness. In remaining alive after the death of the Emperor Meiji, he charged, they were being "disloyal." But sweeping aside old politicians was not enough. It was necessary to develop a new political consciousness. "In antiquity the people stood outside the orbit of politics. Those who filled the ranks of the Restoration movement were recruited from the lower samurai class (*ashigaru made de atta*) but the enterprise of Taishō must add to it ordinary peasants and merchants." To make the kind of "adjustment of

9

politics" required by the new age, "we must open up a politics of democratism (*minshushugi*) which is founded on the idea of the Emperor." This was what was meant by "adjusting mightily."

Yet this very call for a liberation from the recent past and the establishment of a new political consciousness dramatized for many what in fact had been lost. Tokutomi Soho, who a generation earlier had denounced the "Old Men of Tempō" for smothering revolutionary impulses, complained in 1916 that a great illness was sweeping society and threatened to damage the structure of the Empire itself. "The greatest single illness of our times is the loss of state ideals and national purpose," he announced in a work which sought to restore the vanished ideals of his youth and to stir the "youth of Taishō" in a manner he had realized in the 1880's. Here, he called upon the generation of Taishō to establish a new vision in which national aspiration and personal hope might once more be merged in common purpose. Society lacked the "great principle that should activate people to cooperate with each other." And he condemned the youth of his day for being uninterested in the state, for a general "unrelatedness to the times, which is common to all these days." Worse, he charged, "they are all divided between disinterested, colorless youth and despairing youth who worry about the problems of life, between success-oriented youth carried off by the fever of rising in the world (*risshin shusse*) and examples of youth without ambition. These are the youth of Taishō."[6] What Tokutomi failed to acknowledge is that with the ideals of the past he was trying to reach an audience with very different ideals. In this effort he tried to formulate a theory of patriotism which would revivify the bland principles of the *Boshin chokusho*. He summoned the traditional ideal of "loyalty to the lord, love of the nation" (*chūkun aikoku*) as the basic principle upon which to construct a new vision aimed at securing cooperation among high and low. In earlier times, he recalled, people had voluntarily shared in the implementation and realization of the great goals of *fukoku kyōhei* (rich country, strong army) and *bussan kōgyō* (commerce and industry), not for personal profit but for the advancement of the nation. These ideals had been imparted as a sacred trust to all Japanese, regardless of class and status and their acceptance had made possible the intellectual and spiritual unity of the Meiji period.

[6] Quoted in Sumiya Mikio, "Kokuminteki būijon no tōgō to bunkai," in *Kindai Nihon shisōshi kōza* (Tokyo, 1960), v, 14.

Despite Tokutomi's atavism his assessment of contemporary social conditions was essentially correct. The youth of Taishō, the nation itself, had indeed lost the ideals that had served society so well during the Meiji period. But what Tokutomi failed to acknowledge about these goals, and why his pronouncements fell on deaf ears, was that such goals had been promoted by the government. They had not been initiated by the people. Success during the Sino-Japanese and Russo-Japanese wars had catapulted the nation into the ranks of the great imperial powers of the world. Independence and strength had been achieved. The wars had represented a realization of national goals; the final result of self-sacrificing "perseverance and determination" (*gashin shōtan*) and realization resulted in their dissolution. While there was widespread disagreement over whether a "rich country" had indeed been realized, it was apparent to Tokutomi and his critics that national purpose was sliding away into new expressions of individual self-interest. Tokutomi and the government failed to see in the frequent expressions of self-interest the aspirations of social constituencies and the emergence of a new model of society. In response to the loss of "state ideals," the government issued the *Boshin* imperial rescript in 1908. The rescript was a phantom from the past; it sought to reify values which had served a different kind of social order in a different time in history.

In selecting the word *boshin* the government consciously sought to invoke the authority and spirit of the Meiji Restoration itself (the Boshin War of 1868). A good deal had happened since the war with China in 1895, and the new rescript acknowledged publicly the crisis in national ideology and the growing sense of confusion which, its drafters believed, the masses were experiencing. In response to this failure of nerve and, of course, the very real threat of social disorder and widespread protest, the rescript called for a unification of high and low, in heart and mind. The unification was to be achieved by fruitful work and a forswearing of all pleasures and entertainment. To counter the excesses of "private activity," the rescript sought to re-establish the structure of officially sanctioned behavior (*ōyakegoto*) and a sustaining national morality (*kokumin dōtoku*) as the pledge and guarantee of its realization. The government saw in the social unrest of the early 1900's a continual reminder of uncontrolled "private behavior"; what it failed to perceive is that such private behavior was not the expression of the simple urge of self-interest.

11

Selfishness had traditionally been associated with private activity, and was permissible as long as it did not interfere with the performance of public duties. It was the product of social differentiation in a traditional society; it held no meaning for emerging social classes who sought in protest a means by which to dramatize their aspirations. What worried the government was the belief that an excessive display of private interest usually spilled over into political activity. Strikes, disorder, labor and tenant disputes, and urban riots, provided confirmation that public expectation was being abandoned and that people, as evidenced by the numbers pouring into the cities, were following private impulse and selfish desire. Yet the same evidence attested to the emergence of new social classes demanding a greater share in the distribution of national wealth and a larger role in the disbursement of social power. The reified equation between public and private could only reject the datum of the present for the security of an idyllic, orderly, and altogether imaginary pre-industrial past. Thus, to offset the apparent collision of claims, and the pressure of the past against the aspirations of the present, the government sought to reinstate the primacy of public values over private choice as a means of containing the corrosive effects of the new individualism. But ironically, I should add, the new individualism was produced by the same set of historical conditions which had given expression to statism.

Despite the romantic impulse to reject the present for an orderly and undifferentiated moral past, and years before the proclamation of the bright new promise of Taishō, the *Boshin* rescript revealed that Japanese society was undergoing profound structural changes and beginning to experience a genuine crisis of culture. The causes of the change and crisis were far more complex and fundamental than the simple desire to establish a democratic polity. What the rescript disclosed in its archaic language and anxious admonitions was the end of Meiji civilization (*bummei*) and the emergence of an unmediated individualism as a basic unit of social action. Recently, the Japanese social historian Kamishima Jirō has equated the end of Meiji with the formation of individualism and privatization.[7] Yet Kamishima has argued

[7] Kamishima Jirō, "Meiji no shūen," in Hashikawa Bunzō and Matsumoto

that individualism and privatization, as they developed in the late Meiji period, were different from the historical variety found in the modern West. Although there are natural similarities, there is also a fundamental divergence: the "competitive" type and the "gathering-in" type of individualism. What distinguishes them is what differentiated Japan from the West in the late Meiji period. Whereas in the West individualism was formed by gathering-in a slice of private space from the social environment, a kind of colonization of public space, in Japan it was sliced off from the natural environment. In the West, according to Kamishima, the private world is created or made possible by gathering-in openly, publicly; the sense of individualism resulting from this gathering-in is intimately united to the world of public space. Since the Japanese variety has developed from the natural environment, "the realization of individualism (*kotai*) is confined to this fact," and since it stems from "non-self"—that is, the natural environment—it is not related to or mediated by the world of the public self. In the West individualism leads to a kind of "possessive individualism," reflecting the arrangement of market relationships; in Japan it leads to excessive competition promising exclusive possession. Moreover, both models were available to the late Meiji experience. The choice was revealed in the transmutation of Kitamura Tōkoku's concern for inner conscience into Takayama Chogyū's defense of private interest.

While such hair-splitting distinctions are important to Japanese, still searching for residual differences, they are probably less instructive than dramatic. Even though Kamishima has sought to reduce individualism to irreducible metaphysical categories, both models are still products of a bourgeois ideology. In the West the "balance" of individual interests promised by the mediating function of politics was more illusory than real. In Japan the dissolution of such a promise early exposed the real separation between public and private and the constant conflict raised by competing interests. Whether one model was more competitive and possessive than the other is hard to say. Yet individualism in both societies reflected what Marx called an "infinite dissipation of interests" and the very atomization of life which forms the central metaphor in liberal political thought and action. To critics of

Sannosuke (eds.), *Kindai Nihon seiji shisōshi* (Tokyo, 1971), I, 384-386; also Kamishima, *Kindai Nihon no seishin kōzō* (Tokyo, 1967), pp. 177-194.

twentieth-century Japanese society before World War II, who have seen in the Taishō experience either the failure of democracy or its aberration or both, the wrong questions are being asked.[8] If Taishō culture possessed any meaning distinct from Meiji civilization, it is to be found in the development and triumph of that conception of private interest and atomized individuality which is at the heart of the liberal political and social creed. In short, it is to be found in the transformation of the distinctively political into the social.

Kamishima has also argued that in Japan's encounter with the nations of the West in the late nineteenth century, and its exposure to Great Power politics, it was this kind of competitive individualism that was refracted through the Japanese lens. After the Russo-Japanese War, the perception of the international arena as one of quarrelling nations, each competing with the other for exclusive possession of resources or superior economic advantage, was transmuted within Japanese society into that of a competitive quarrel among the populace. Yet, again, I think that the archetype for international rivalry was the arrangement of possessive market relationships in which competition, unlike that in the simple market in products, was viewed as a means by which men, and by extension nations, who want more may convert more of the powers of others to their use than others convert of theirs.[9] If, in any case, the Russo-Japanese War had any meaning for Japanese society it was to lend confirmation to this principle of

[8] For a recent reminder, see E. O. Reischauer, "What Went Wrong," in James Morley, (ed.), *Dilemmas of Growth in Prewar Japan* (Princeton, 1971), pp. 489-510. The question has a timelessness to it, but it also discloses the attempt of liberal historians to explain certain episodes, which do not conform to the normal flow of history, as aberrations or departures from what is considered an established course. Something of this view has also informed historians of modern Germany, who have treated the Nazi movement as a departure from the course of modern German history. Yet in both cases, Japan and Germany, this liberal effort to locate a true course has until recently prevented us from seeing such episodes as the Hitlerite movement or the drift to militarism in the 1930's in the larger perspective of modern history. Specifically, this view has distracted us from seeing that Shōwa militarism, for example, was something more than an aberration, that it indeed reflected or disclosed some of the central elements of Japan's modernist experience.

[9] C. B. MacPherson, *The Political Theory of Possessive Individualism* (London, 1962), pp. 55ff. A truly brilliant work essential for the understanding of modern society.

14

possessive individualism which was to find expression in the drive for success and careerism (*risshin shusse*).[10]

In fact, the term "culture" (*bunka*) was used on a wide scale for the first time in the Taishō period, in contrast to the associations raised by the description of Meiji Japan as *bummei kaika* (civilized and enlightened). Meiji civilization summoned purpose and goal—self-sacrifice and nationalism (*fukoku-kyōhei* and *bussan kōgyō*)—whereas Taishō culture, as it was conceived, evoked new associations related to the nuances of consumers' life, to individualism, culturalism (*bunkashugi*), and cosmopolitanism. The transfer from *bummei* to *bunka* also marked profound changes in modal personality types, from what the men of Meiji celebrated as *shūgyō* (education) to what the men of Taishō cherished as *kyōyō* (cultivation). The former meant a commitment to discipline, practical education and self-sacrificing service; the latter, a Japanese gloss on the German conception of *allgemeine Bildung*, stressed personal self-cultivation and refinement. The idea of *shūgyō* enjoined men to act publicly and to serve goals larger than themselves; *kyōyō* required men to operate in the private sphere and to serve only themselves; the former subordinated private choice to public expectation, while the latter subordinated public to private considerations. Yet in both cases there was an effort to obliterate essential identities. Moreover, the promise of a political balance of interests, promoted by Meiji liberals, would dissolve into middle-class apoliticality and mass consumerism—to precisely that dissipation of interests and atomization of life which characterized Japanese society in the interwar years.

The possibility of establishing politics as a form of mediation between public and private would give way to either political indifference or violence; action would be replaced by behavior. This identification between individualism and culture was even more real than apparent, yet was acknowledged early by writers and intellectuals as the distinguishing feature of the new era. In a reminiscence of Tsubouchi Shōyō and a group at Waseda University (*Bunka jigyō kenkyūkai*), for example, we have an early account of this concern for culture and what it came to mean for many contemporaries. After identifying *bunka* with the German *kultur* the group announced that the purpose of "culture (*bunka*)

[10] Mita Munehide, *Gendai Nihon no seishin kōzō* (Tokyo, 1965), pp. 57-71.

15

is to show the intent of self-discipline, training, refinement, and cultivation (*kyōyō*)."[11]

The implications of this commitment to culture for Imperial Japan were profound; its consequences were, perhaps, frightful, yet enduring as a central metaphor in the national experience. Moreover, it is important to suggest that this commitment rarely strayed from the idealist associations which had inspired the idea of *Kultur* in its German setting—often providing the same justifications for the establishment of a specific class *Lebensgefühl*, and expressing in coherent fashion the inchoate aspirations of the new Japanese middle class. Above all, culture meant a reverence for the diverse creations of the spirit, for the mystery of the arts which, to so many Japanese, possessed a power and beauty greater than life itself.

Yet such a conception of culture was founded on a set of unfortunate dichotomies—between culture and civilization, life and the spirit, between, as Thomas Mann wrote of Germany and the West in World War I, "soul and society, freedom and politics, art and literature; and culture, soul, freedom, art—that is Germanism and not civilization, society, politics, and literature." But in Taishō Japan the larger dichotomy between the spirit (culture) and politics, embraced all other antinomies. In opposing culture (*bunka*) to civilization (*bummei*), which meant the world of Meiji materialism, rationalistic and shallow spiritual planning and the leveling of existence, Japanese intellectuals and writers were confusing—dangerously I think—spirit with power, and art with life, and making the erroneous assumption that culture itself was a more than adequate substitute for politics. In any case, conviction of the moral superiority of culture lent confirmation to the indispensability of education. However, it was an education which through the humanistic cultivation of mind would lead to individual self-perfection and self-refinement (*kyōyō*), as Takayama Chogyū had urged at the turn of the century in his call for the creative personality.

Yet this conception of culture presupposed another, equally important opposition. Middle-class intellectuals, on whom the idea of *bunka* and *kyōyō* conferred aristocratic values and elite status, pitted culture and refinement against the threatening

[11] Reported in Ikimatsu Keizō, *Gendai Nihon shisōshi* (Tokyo, 1971), IV, 86.

claims of mass culture—consumption and consumerism, and the feared "secularization" and democratization of cultural life itself which the emergence of new classes in the Taishō period had promised to promote. The high-minded cultural aspiration of Taishō intellectuals was to defend *bunka* before the onslaught of debasement which the masses promised to bring in their wake, and to translate this conviction into a common set of pieties and a shared posture promoting the rejection of politics as the surest defense of culture. Ironically, this belief in the fundamental incompatibility of culture and democracy seeped into the ideological pronouncements of social reformers and supporters of democratism, and explains why so many Taishō ideologues and rural populists (*nōhonshugisha*) like Yoshino Sakuzō, Kawakami Hajime, and Kita Ikki, were able to dramatize the social problem but failed to link it to the broadening of political consciousness.

Finally, this commitment to culture—its veneration and exaltation—led to a redefinition of individualism. Part of this redefinition presupposed the important transition from "inner conscience" to the defense of "private interest," which had marked late Meiji intellectual consciousness. Yet the belief in the perfectibility of the aesthetic and rational faculties of the individual (*kyōyō*) independent of political conditions, forged a new conception of personality in Taishō Japan. It is interesting to note that the Japanese in the Taishō period substituted an earlier (Tokugawa-Meiji) belief in the perfectibility of the moral faculties of the individual (public) for the aesthetic perfectibility of the individual (private). What *kyōyō* meant here in contrast to *shūgyō* was self-fulfillment of the individual in the private realm, without the necessity to perform publicly to achieve a non-personal goal. The promise of Takayama Chogyū's creative personality's transcending the contemporary to realize himself in the making of culture found expression in Taishō individualism, now draped in aesthetic-aristocratic values, and imposing a distance between the new middle class and the rest of society. The resulting rejection of politics implicit in this twin veneration of culture and the creative personality produced profound political consequences which led not simply to indifference, but to the deployment of culture as a surrogate for politics.

Against the social moralism which mass society made urgent, Taishō intellectuals insisted upon the isolation and self-centeredness of the aesthetic man, as revealed in Nishida Kitarō's search for the pure and unmediated experience and Kuji Seizō's disclosure of style (*iki*) and sensibility as the central elements in culture. This aesthetic vision transformed what necessarily was into an ethic, and demanded a wholeness of being in which all moral clashes were contained and surpassed. The ethics of the Taishō intellectual were thus, largely an ethics of being, rather than a morality of doing, which had characterized the requirements of *shūgyō*. He would, of necessity, appear to others as one concerned with himself alone, as the narrator of Abe Jirō's *Santarō no nikki* or countless confessional novels suggest. But this was an illusion occasioned by the fact that the aesthetic man could not have any serious concern for or involvement in the arbitrary fluctuations of social and political problems. In reality, however, the improvement of all else would follow upon the transformation of the self. The Taishō liberal Ōyama Ikuo was not far from the truth when he complained (in 1916) that "the majority of people . . . do not think politics has anything to do with them . . . politics does not shape the content of their lives."[12]

If individualism as cultural consciousness marked off Taishō Japan from what came before, and culture from civilization, the conditions for its development and the resulting associations were determined by the experiences of late Meiji society. "Not since the dawn of history," Ukita Kazutami announced in the influential magazine *Taiyō* in 1910, "have we seen throughout the world such a reverence for the development of individualism as it has been revealed today in the pursuit of material well-being."[13] Perhaps Ukita was exaggerating the mood of the times, but his announcement disclosed a commonly shared perception. Although individualism owed its beginnings to the 1880's and 1890's, by the time of the Russo-Japanese War it was beginning to reach the level of popular consciousness. What had been closely identified with art and literature was eventually expanded to include other, less lofty modes of activity and consciousness.

Something of this popularization of individualism was disclosed in the linkage of success (*seikō*) to self. Originally, the term *risshin shusse*, which came to convey the sense of success in one's

[12] Quoted in Peter Duus, "Ōyama Ikuo and the Search for Democracy," in Morley, p. 429.

[13] Quoted in Oka Yoshitake, "Nichiro sensōgo ni okeru atarashii sedai no seichō," *Shisō* (Tokyo, 1966, 1967), p. 137. I have relied heavily on this very informative article relating to the transition to the Taishō period.

career, had been used to signify the name of the family or one's native place: to succeed was to simply honor one's family or region. Often success in a career was restricted to the acquisition of high government office, as early dramatized in Futabatei Shimei's novel, *The Floating Cloud.* Yet even as early as this work there were already suggestions that advancement to high governmental office was achieved through shallow contrivance. The first half of the Meiji period, Tokutomi Sohō observed in 1906, was a time of "bureaucratic prosperity." But today the sentiment of "revering the bureaucracy, despising the people" had been reversed so that people "revere money and despise the bureaucracy."[14] Closely linked to *seikō*, the idea of *risshin shusse* came to express the pursuit of the self alone in the private interest, a self no longer limited by concerns for family name or honoring one's native place. Though individual success was expressed most dramatically in the acquisition of wealth, it was unrestricted in its application. What is important is that the idea of success was identified with the self, with the individual pursuit of private interest, whether in art or in the accumulation of wealth. Success was adequate to its method. Only this kind of atomized pursuit of private interest could be justified by the appeal to a higher purpose, such as "for the sake of the country." In the absence of even the illusion of an agency balancing conflicting interests, all that was left to conceal private interest and possessive competition was the hollow litanies of a collectivist statist morality. However, it is important to note that this kind of individualism was consistent with the Meiji conception of *shūgyō*.

Thus, magazines abounded in stories of successful people, the rules and short-cuts leading to success and what really constituted the good life. Tokutomi complained about the frequency of discussions about success which he apparently saw everywhere in the mass media. "A perusal of magazines and newspapers today shows that all are filled with conversations and real-life experiences of so-called successful men. . . . Why be successful? For what reasons does one pursue success?" he asked rhetorically.[15] Tokutomi already knew the answer. His major grievance was over the expression of private interest and the total failure to link success to some higher sense of responsibility. Another writer, Kuroiwa Ruikō, noted that the major aim of all this activity and

[14] *Ibid.*   [15] *Ibid.*, p. 138.

knowledge concerning success was to permit others to "develop new and novel methods." Their purpose was to "find short-cuts" in their solitary journey, and to "reach the shores of success in one leap."[16]

If the pursuit of individual success had few limitations, it was not purposeless. For beyond the cynical appeal to patriotic service, success authenticated the self. The experience of "making it" validated the quest of the individual and, for some, came to represent individualism itself. Yet individualism and success also offered new choices of life-styles and new modes of criticism of the existing arrangement of things. Success, according to its critics, led to the shameless pursuit of pleasure, which was contrasted to the single-minded purpose that apparently had informed the activity of youth in the early Meiji period. Writers as different as Ishikawa Takuboku, Tokutomi Sohō and Taoka Reiun called attention to the excessive display of "individualistic dissipation," the "preoccupation with carnal desire," and the general celebration of luxury.

How different contemporary youth were, complained Taoka Reiun, from the *shosei kishitsu* of an earlier time, known for their "rustic character, seriousness," their devotion to study and hard work.[17] Yet this plunge into pleasure represented a form of dandyism which did not simply summon traditional associations of the Tokugawa *tsu* and merchant culture but represented a repudiation of the social conformism which government in the late Meiji period was trying to re-establish. It brings to mind Baudelaire's famous defense of dandyism as the "best element in human pride," which, in its struggle with social conformism, signals the need "to combat and destroy triviality." The youth of today, another critic charged in this connection, were clothes horses, effeminate, and morally unregenerate. But pleasure may have served, in fact, to affirm the self against the official claims demanding "self-sacrifice, perseverance and determination" (*gashin shōtan*) in the realization of national goals. If the Russo-Japanese War confirmed the nation in its new international style, it also symbolized for many an end to the years of self-sacrifice. The time for working together in a collective effort to achieve some larger national purpose was over; the meaning of self-sacrifice and group effort was trans-

[16] *Ibid.*

[17] Taoka Reiun, "Meiji hanshinden," in *Taoka Reiun zenshū* (Tokyo, 1969), I, Preface.

muted into the promise of the self seeking its own goals; public interest became private interest.

Much of this sentiment was expressed in the mood of despair and disbelief. True, despair and disbelief had been earlier identified with romantic longing. But the new mood represented a rejection, albeit a passive one, of the official effort to see private success as public necessity. Miyake Setsurei, writing in *Nihonjin* (1906), argued that this kind of individualism, draped in personal despair and disbelief, actually constituted an attack on the state. He also believed that it might yield a new conception of society. One of the distinctive features of this individualism in the late Meiji period was that in rejecting the established conception of a family state, it sought to find expression in new modes of activity which, it was hoped, might reveal a new model of social order. It was in this way that individualism was associated with such movements as women's liberation and free love, and why it was linked with literary naturalism and political socialism. Both Ishikawa Takuboku and Taoka Reiun, committed late Meiji socialists, saw individualism as the true promise of socialism. Tokutomi Sohō worried about the political consequences of individualism. In the past, he wrote in an article in the *Kokumin shinbun* (1905), "youth were strong and brave," and not nearly so "aware of individuality." They were willing to "throw themselves into fire and water for the state." Yet, that "they were willing to give up their lives for such a purpose was not because of any religion of martyrs." The state was the "religion of the Japanese people," and "contemporary youth have lost their faith." An awareness of the state had given way to an awareness of the self.[18]

The tension between *embourgeoisement* and the statist claims of Imperial Japan resulted in the transformation of the distinctively political and the emergence of the concept of society as an autonomous structure. The political became identified with a narrow set of institutions devoted to what Marx called "national housekeeping"; society was increasingly conceived of as an entity distinct from political arrangements and as the symbol of all worthwhile endeavor. Not only was this the meaning of Taishō *bunka*, but it also is what most distinguishes the modern from the pre-modern. The conception of an "unpolitical" society, what Marx referred to as the "socialization of man," was the informing belief common to a variety of disparate and competing ideologies,

[18] Oka, p. 140.

such as social democratism (*minshushugi*), conservatism, social-ism, humanism (*jindōshugi*), socialism, statism, and managerial-ism. Meiji liberal theorists like Kitamura Tōkoku, Nakae Chōmin, and Kuga Katsunan had already set the stage in their effort to model the political order after society. Yet the attempt to recap-ture the spontaneity, naturalism, and peaceful satisfaction of needs in a political setting sprang from a romantic impulse to summon a nonpolitical order. It also disclosed a chronic hostility toward, and indeed a rejection of, politics, which could be pla-cated only by the installation of a conception of society as a distinct and self-subsistent entity. In Imperial Japan this substi-tution of the political for society was manifested in an individual-ism which, as suggested earlier, sought expression in art; which permitted release from political bonds in the ideology of the left; which sought to substitute administration for politics as the main method for handling social problems.

The search for artistic expression led to bizarre experiments in utopianism (Taoka Reiun's call for a William Morris variety of aesthetic socialism and the later New Village movement of the *Shirakabaha*, to mention the best-known examples), to lifeless humanism and culturalism; the introduction of new administra-tive methods led to attempts to reform society so that it might spontaneously generate its own life. Social democrats, socialists, Marxists, and anarchists, not to mention National Socialists, all shared the belief that politics and the political order existed be-cause of social conflict, which originated in outmoded forms of organization. Once such forms were removed, cleavages would vanish and struggle would cease, and the necessity for political order would die. The conflict in Taishō Japan was not between state and individual, but rather between authority and concep-tions of community.

The social ramifications of the maturation of Japanese capital-ism served also as the condition for an ethos which found expres-sion in a nonpolitical and aesthetic conception of life. It is inter-esting to observe that just as the Japanese bourgeoisie, armed with an aesthetic ethos (resulting from the curious marriage between liberalism and idealism), withdrew from the world of politics, so their withdrawal marked a cosmopolitan opening up to the wider world. For as liberals they had already abandoned politics and authority in the name of liberty in order to surrender themselves to society; and as custodians of culture they were on constant call to prevent the ever-threatening corruption of spirit and culture by politics. Moreover, it was this surrender which explains why so much of Taishō thought and action appeared to reject the political and why so much else inclined to cosmopolitanism. This nonpoliticality or "unpoliticality" was also true of all those doctrines which claimed to have discovered the masses. It was discovered that the masses were less (if at all) a political constituency than the location of a social problem.

In this process the government enunciated a cultural policy which, while seemingly repressive, was actually consistent with middle-class aspirations about politics and culture. The greatest effect of this cultural policy was to separate politics from culture. Official anxiety over cultural affairs was disclosed as early as the 1890's. In 1897 the so-called *Tetsu gakkan* incident involved a clash between academic freedom and governmental interference in philosophical discourse. Ultimately the government ruled to remove the special power of Middle Schools and Normal Schools to grant certification without an examination. In 1906 the government issued (under the auspices of the Minister of Education Makino Shinken) a set of principles regulating student behavior and curbing academic freedom (*Gakusei shisō torishimari ni kungi*). Specifically, the purpose was to stem the intellectual activity which was raising important and threatening questions in society in the years after the war. The drafters of the document located the source of the peril in the publication of books in recent years. "Some," rang the edict shrilly, "display theories of violence and danger, others explain philosophies of oppression, while others yet portray the basest conditions." After denouncing the state of contemporary literature, the document urged the necessity to "investigate the contents of books which students are reading."[19] If, in the interest of a "healthy intellectual life," the Regulations sought to inhibit students from being seduced by reading books on socialism, revolution, and violence, the Great Treason Trial of 1910-1911 affirmed the government's determination to raise the stakes and exterminate "dangerous thinking" altogether.

Kōtoku Shūsui's imprisonment and subsequent execution stunned the intellectual world. Yet, unlike the Dreyfus affair in France or the Sacco-Vanzetti case in the United States, the Kōtoku incident failed to inspire a massive response among intellectuals

[19] Miyagawa Torao, "Kokuminteki bunka no keisei (2)," in *Iwanami kōza, Nihon rekishi* (Tokyo, 1963), xviii, 319-320.

and writers. Only a few raised their voices, and those who did, like Tokutomi Roka or Kinoshita Naoe, expressed their disapproval of the government's arbitrary and swift action in the most muted tones. No real evidence was ever offered by the government to link Kōtoku directly to an alleged anarchist plot to assassinate the Meiji Emperor. Yet as a harassed revolutionary who had had several skirmishes with the government, and as a theorist of violence, Kōtoku was held responsible for incendiary writings, and condemned as an accomplice in the plot. In executing Kōtoku the government delivered an unprecedented blow against political individualism. It was clear to most that any attempt to cause the state to liberate the individual from accountability to public expectation—in the interest of "private affairs," conscience, and personal rights—must be total and violent. The poet-turned-socialist Ishikawa Takuboku described the incident in elegiac tones and registered surprised dismay at the way the "government makes practical use of its police powers in the intellectual and literary world," and the earnestness and swiftness which prompted such action. "This measure," he despaired (writing about Kōtoku's execution), "left little doubt that the will of the government might eventually eradicate all new thought." Elegiac, perhaps, but in a fit of outrage he also provided Imperial Japan a fitting epitaph: *"Nihon wa, dame da!"*—"Japan, it's hopeless."

In July of 1910, while the trial was still being argued, Kawada Shiro's *The Woman's Problem* (*Fujin mondai*) became the object of "intellectual management," because it threatened to undermine the family system. It "spontaneously went out of print" and speedily slipped into obscurity. Five months after Kōtoku was executed in 1911 Okamura Tsukasa, a professor of civil law at Kyoto Imperial University, found himself in the middle of a conflict with the government over academic freedom and the freedom of expression. Okamura had delivered a lecture on the family system before an educational society in Saga prefecture, which he criticized as unmodern and socially stifling. More, he denounced the civil code and its basic premises as a violation of individual rights. His punishment was slight, a fact that reveals, I think, the ambivalence over the question of academic freedom in a government school. That he was punished, however, suggests that the government was unwilling to overlook the question.

Throughout the first decade of the twentieth century the government sought to realize a measure of "intellectual management" by a series of reforms in the educational system and by imposing greater control over the content of textbooks. This issue was dramatized by the famous controversy over the question of legitimacy between the Southern and Northern courts in the fifteenth century (*Nambokuchō seijun mondai*). More than most, this incident showed how far the government was willing to go to enforce educational orthodoxy and to suppress free inquiry, thought, and learning. The issue arose in 1911, when a conservative member of the House of Representatives protested the treatment of the Southern-Northern court problem in the revised edition of the official textbook on Japanese history for primary schools. Prime Minister Katsura Tarō entered the controversy, and pacified what appeared to be a growing attempt to discredit his government over this issue by deflecting responsibility to Kida Teikichi, one of the authors of the text, who ultimately was obliged to resign from his post on the textbook committee. Katsura promised his critics to have the textbook revised, and the incident was soon forgotten. Yet before its disappearance it had not only inspired vociferous criticism in the press and the establishment of an organization pledged to defend the *kokutai*, as well as the effort to seek official support for recognition of the legitimacy of the Southern court, but also threatened to topple the Katsura government itself. After the smoke had cleared, the appropriate sections of the text had been revised, the legitimacy of the Southern court had been validated and the title: "The Period of the Southern and Northern Courts" was changed to the "Period of the Yoshino Court." The Northern court and its claims were expunged from official history.[20]

In 1911 a petition was presented to the 27th Diet calling for the promotion of national morality and education (*Kokumin dōtoku kyōiku shinkō no kengi*). Its purpose was to respond to the reaction which some imagined the Kōtoku incident had inspired. The intent of the petition was to re-establish the great principle of loyalty and filiality (*chūkō*); its function was to prevent any further challenge to national morality. A year later the government drafted the *Sankyō gōdō*—the "Union of the Three Religions" (Buddhism, Shintō, and Christianity)—which required a written vow of loyalty to the state from adherents of the three religions. But the real purpose of the loyalty oath was to blunt Christian energies, which had exploded as a leading anti-govern-

[20] *Ibid.*, p. 323.

ment force in the late 1890's and early 1900's. Art and literature also fell, in stages, under official regulations. As early as 1907, for example, the government inaugurated a regular series of "official exhibitions" (*kanten*) with the opening of the Ministry of Education's exhibition hall. And in literature, which had successfully escaped official scrutiny, the government ultimately moved to reinforce its own principles of aesthetics. In response to the naturalist threat the government placed prohibitions on the number of books for sale. To exercise closer control over literature at the source of creativity, even before the Kōtoku trial, the Ministry of Education (led by Komatsubara Eitarō) proclaimed the official establishment of a literary board. The apparent purpose of this bureaucratization of literary taste was to enforce the separation between politics and culture, to curb the excesses of individualism, and to inhibit writers from dealing with subjects of a social and political nature. Although at one level the Treason Trial had raised important questions about politics and political behavior, at another level it was intimately linked to the world of ideas and culture. Even Mori Ōgai, the staunchest supporter of governmental authority among Japanese writers at the time, affirmed the necessity to keep politics separated from culture, yet defended the social right of the individual writer to speak and write about cultural matters. Ironically, one of the first acts of the new Literary Board was to issue a prohibition against Ōgai's novel *Vita Sexualis*, and in a short story called *Shokudō* (1911) he answered, perhaps meekly, in his defense that anarchists "will not increase in numbers, if the leadership holds the reins of government firmly, if it steers the rudder skillfully."

In short, Ōgai, despite his belief that the government's decision to execute Kōtoku was an attempt to "guide humanity into the proper path," recognized that the incident was not simply a political matter. Since it was also an intellectual incident it involved politics and culture. Even if the government's decision was not oppressive from a social psychological viewpoint, it raised doubts in his mind from the intellectual viewpoint. He was not sure of the salutary effects of intellectual guidance, and his own recent skirmish with government censorship spurred him to suggest that political management and cultural policy were really two different things. Ōgai hoped, again limply, to see the reintroduction of culture into politics as a moderating agent, but he never explained how this might be achieved.

Ishikawa Takuboku shared Ōgai's belief that political management and cultural policy represented different things; he also believed that cultural policy should be separated from the making of culture. In a sense he attempted to resolve the question which Ōgai left hanging: how to reintroduce culture into politics as a moderating force? In order to hasten the achievement of a genuine culture of humanity, Takuboku proposed the establishment of a new magazine. He hoped the new magazine would avoid proscription but "would not turn its back to the name of literature," that it would "clarify the consciousness of contemporary youth" and the "internalized movement of national life." In it Takuboku proposed to propound a philosophy of youth for what he called the next period, the new society. Once these cultural ideals were worked out, after a few years, the magazine would politicize its purpose and begin to promote practical movements calling for universal suffrage, woman's liberation, the universalization of the Roman alphabet (*romaji*), etc.

The Treason Trial induced in Takuboku's thinking a two-stage theory of culture: a cultural movement as a future ideal and a political movement which, beginning with the trial, was pledged to bringing about these future ideals.[21] (Ōsugi Sakae's later *Kindai shisō* was in fact the magazine Takuboku had hoped to start, and Sakae's theory of mass culture the philosophy he had hoped to initiate.) Despite differences, Ishikawa Takuboku and Mori Ōgai each tried to find a connection or bond between politics and culture. Yet underlying this pursuit was the view of politics and culture as having separate sources, rather than the Meiji view which bundled the two together. What Ishikawa and Mori objected to most was not so much the separation of politics and culture, but the government's systematic effort to neutralize culture completely, to subsume it under principles of political management. The government's cultural policy had not just stripped culture of its political and social purpose, it had robbed it of its central significance. In a sense the government banalized culture, narrowing its scope of neutrality to such things as pleasure, entertainment, geisha, saké, historical romance, and the love of the solitary self.

With characteristic ambivalence Natsume Sōseki argued that the "development of literature . . . presupposes the existence of society to the extent that it welcomes literature." The new literary

---

[21] *Ishikawa Takuboku zenshū* (Tokyo, 1929), v, 532.

commissars of the *Bungei i-in kai,* insteàd of fostering and promoting literature, have "hastened its decline." The reason is simple. "The Literary Bureau has encouraged only works which are
satisfactory from the administrative standpoint, and suppresses
all others."[22] Yet Sōseki, unlike either Ōgai or Takuboku, offered
no real plan for rescuing literature from its narrow domain and
re-establishing a role for culture in the conduct of state and society. He called vaguely for the establishment of a literary association (*kumiai*), a group similar to a writers' organization, that
would make "agreements with bureaucrats," since writers "had to
eat." Perhaps the poet Takamura Kōtarō who, in accepting this
division between politics and culture, set the tone for Taishō
bunka when he wrote in 1910 that in the "psychological conditions of creativity there is only the humanity of one individual."
Politics was unimportant. Only culture, manifested in the universalization of beauty, could claim the serious attention of the artist.

However, it was precisely this separation of politics and culture
which enabled writers like Takamura to celebrate the universalization of beauty as the highest cultural ideal, transcending both
domestic political differences and national boundaries. The separation also dramatized the shift to a conception of an unmediated
aesthetic self and privatized individualism, Takamura's "humanity of one individual," and the final completion of the meta-
morphosis of *shūgyō* into *kyōyō*.

[22] Natsume Jun'ichi (ed.), *Sōseki zenshū* (Tokyo, 1928), xiv, 224-230.
"*Bungei-i in wa nan no suru ka.*"

Some Reflections on Idealism in the Political Thought of Yoshino Sakuzō

T HE LACKLUSTER image of Taishō history is not easy to overcome. In contrast to the "brilliance of Meiji," the phrase "Taishō things" (*Taishō mono*) certainly does not stir the historian's imagination. Yet it is becoming increasingly evident that the Taishō period was of basic importance to Japan's modern development. For those concerned with political and intellectual development in a rapidly industrializing non-Western society, one item stands out among others in that broad historical landscape. After having "constitutionalized" (by the Meiji Constitution of 1889) the process of massive industrial transformation in politically non-monolithic terms, Japan was still unable to incorporate party government as the primary political instrument to regulate that process of transformation within the general legal framework. It was in Taishō Japan, well *after* industrialization was a fact, that this problem took on crucial significance for her subsequent development. How, within the legal framework, could a pragmatic form of government run by powerful competitive parties be legitimized, with theoretical or ideological certainty, as being best for the political future of the nation?

If this question fails to add luster to Taishō history, it is neither academic nor unimportant to historians. An entire generation of university students and intellectuals committed themselves to a political ideology called "Taishō democracy." Although this ideology was antipathetic to violent and revolutionary modes of political action, and akin to Western liberal democracy in certain significant respects, it nonetheless was unable to function as a stable underpinning to the party and parliamentary government that developed within the confines of the constitutional order. Admittedly there is no simple explanation for this crucial and complex pattern of development, but some clues can be gathered by examining the governing concepts of Taishō democracy. It is in this general context that this essay analyzes the thought of Yoshino

Sakuzō (1878-1933),[1] the tireless and prolific writer and speaker who has been acknowledged by students and critics of his day and by subsequent historians as the key voice of Taishō democracy and to whom intellectuals in Japan still turn as a source of ideas in their quest for ideological legitimation of Diet politics.

This essay contends that certain features of Yoshino's conception of liberal democracy were extremely difficult to reconcile with the actual process of exercising power through the Diet system, outlined in the Meiji Constitution and viewed by and large as an acceptable legal framework by Yoshino. His political assumptions often were so different from those of men directing party development that one might well argue the inevitability of steady erosion in the relationship between ideology and parliamentary government, and of a serious decline in the effectiveness of Taishō democracy as the ideological underpinning for party government in the crucial decades of the 1920's and 1930's. Some may object that such a generalization belies the historian's sense of certainty in the outcome of a sequence of events and does not explain why another pattern might not have been generated. For objections of this kind to be cogent, it seems to me, an assumption must be made that the ideology of Taishō democracy, primarily Yoshino's, had in it a legitimizing potential. Furthermore, it must be assumed that the ideology had such a potential because Yoshino's political thought was "liberal," "utilitarian," and "moderate left," those general characteristics usually associated with ideologies supportive of party and parliamentary government.

But these usual characterizations of Yoshino's political thought are misleading; they tend to obscure some of his governing ideas and convey the idea that Taishō democracy indeed possessed the legitimizing potential suggested above. Passages from his famous essay on "government based on the people" (*minponshugi*),[2]

---

[1] Bernard S. Silberman has presented a clear and concise exposition of Yoshino's view on democratic government in "The Political Theory and Program of Yoshino Sakuzō," *Journal of Modern History*, xxxi, 4 (December, 1959), 310-324. Henry D. Smith has written on the long-term influence of Yoshino and his colleagues on Japanese intellectuals down into the post-war period in "The Shinjinkai (1918-1921): The Making of an Intelligentsia," *Papers on Japan* (Harvard East Asian Research Center, 1965), iii, 162-229. And Takeda Kiyoko has written a fine, sympathetic essay, "Yoshino Sakuzō," *Japan Quarterly*, xii, 4 (October-December, 1965), 515-524.

[2] Yoshino Sakuzō, "Kensei no hongi o toite sono yūshū no bi o nasu no michi o ronzu," *Minponshugiron: Yoshino Sakuzō Hakushi minshushugi*

which discuss democratic procedures in government under the general rubric "function," make Yoshino appear as an advocate of liberalism and utilitarianism; and his support of democratic socialism in the 1920's can categorize him as moderate left. Such characterizations are not erroneous, but they do not reveal the central theme in his political thought. An examination of some of Yoshino's major writings indicates a use of certain definitions, assumptions, and political vocabulary and imagery that must be understood in a theoretical context other than those suggested by the above terms. Despite a changing emphasis at different points in his career, Yoshino's thought was based on idealistic philosophy, and, as critical political expression, it both supported and undermined existing parliamentary institutions, including party government. He conceived of democracy as a pure metaphysical ideal, and it was idealism that led him, toward the end of his life, to deny in sweeping fashion the democratic potential of organized political activity—a denial which a supporter of liberal or social democracy in the West at that time would have found difficult indeed to uphold.

The essay first examines briefly some of the bases of Yoshino's thought, and then explores his plea for and defense of parliamentary government. Throughout, the focus has been restricted to continuities in Yoshino's arguments and, accordingly, descriptive biographical data have been compressed or deleted.

Throughout his career, Yoshino never placed himself squarely in the tradition of pragmatic utilitarianism and logical empiricism. The foundations of his political thought militiated against it. Thus, one does not find an unequivocal endorsement of parliamentary systems based on political utility, although he was a frank admirer of British parliamentary government as perhaps the highest expression of democracy at work. Such a political position is not so inconsistent as it may appear.

Yoshino and other intellectuals of the twentieth century inherited two disparate intellectual legacies from the Meiji period

ronshū (Tokyo, 1948), I, 1-130. Translated portions of this essay are included in Ryūsaku Tsunoda, William Theodore deBary and Donald Keene (eds.), *Sources of the Japanese Tradition* (New York, 1964, paperback edition), II, 217-239. See also George O. Totten (ed.), *Democracy in Prewar Japan, Groundwork or Facade?* (Boston, 1965), pp. 36-49.

(1868-1912). One legacy, derived primarily from the 1870's, presumed that men and nations developed toward universal ends, which Yoshino and others often referred to as the goals of "enlightenment." The central feature of this line of thought was its theoretical justification of Japan's transformation in politics and economics. On the premise that societies were comparable in terms of certain universal constants, the distinctions between Europe and Japan could be blurred, the economic and cultural isolation of the previous 250 years discarded, and the introduction of new ideas and institutions defended with intellectual certainty. However, the second legacy, drawn from the 1880's, flatly denied as *a priori* the notion of comparabilities between cultures based on universal norms. It contended instead that each society was a unique entity, the product of a distinctive history. In this view, therefore, the purpose of acquiring the outward trappings of wealth and power from the West was not to establish a more cogent basis of relatability between societies but to protect a vital and distinct history. This "historicist" conception of development constituted the real foundation of Japanese nationalism in the twentieth century, and virtually all scholars and serious political critics were influenced by it to varying degrees. Yoshino was not an exception to this generalization. Yet, throughout his career, he believed that the two legacies were reconcilable, and his conception of political democracy in Taishō Japan was, I believe, an attempt to realize a synthesis of the two contending theoretical positions he inherited.[3]

More important was the sequence in which Yoshino arranged these two positions. His point of departure was grounded in the historicist assumptions of the 1880's, and he retained some of their key definitions and premises in his political vocabulary. But from that starting point, he turned to revive the universalistic ideals of the 1870's and to incorporate them into the political life of twentieth-century Japan. With able support from colleagues at Tokyo University his scholarly effort still stands as a monument of that conviction.[4] Yet, despite his desire to restore "prenational-

[3] See Moriya Masamichi, "Yoshino Sakuzō," in Inoue Kiyoshi (ed.), *Nihon jimbutsushi taikei* (Tokyo, 1960), VII, 103-137. Also, Yoshino, "Meiji bunka no kenkyū ni kokorozeshi dōki," *Meiji bunka kenkyū: Yoshino ronshū*, VIII, 1-10.

[4] This is the famous *Meiji bunka zenshū* (Tokyo, 1929 and republished, 1955). Twenty vols.

ist" ideals, he retained as his operating intellectual framework the nationalistic logic with which he started.

This view of Yoshino can be contested. It may be argued that although his early political rhetoric was laced with nationalistic jargon, his ideals were basically Christian. Indeed, shortly after entering high school, Yoshino was baptized into the Presbyterian Church, and there exists a story that his "mission" was to organize men like himself from the northeast part of Japan—"the Scotland of Japan"—to lead a spiritual transformation of the country.[5] No doubt his life-long commitment to humane government reflected his Christian training, a point certainly worthy of emphasis, to which this essay will return. But of greater importance, because his Christian beliefs took on political significance within it, was his baptism into another faith while he was a student at Tokyo University—German philosophic idealism.

Yoshino's graduate thesis for the Department of Legal Studies (Hōgakubu) at Tokyo University, "The Foundations of the Legal Philosophy of Hegel,"[6] was written under the direction of Hozumi Nobushige, a leading conservative legal scholar at the time, completed in 1904, and published the following year. Although he later discarded many of the conservative and authoritarian implications of his study of Hegel, its imprints on his thought were lasting. From the outset, he argued for national ends with idealistic terminology. As he put it, "the acheivement of ideal national goals must be based on a set of moral norms common to all," and moreover, "these norms are derived from the ideal objective of the nation."[7]

Of greater importance to Yoshino, perhaps, was the influence of Hegel's view of history. Faithful to Hegel, he saw the dynamics of history as dialectic, a constant process of contradiction and transcendence of contradiction. All things, he noted, were "self-contradictory" in the sense that they possessed simultaneously an identity and the "potential" of becoming "something else." The dynamic movement from one identifiable state of being to another he described as "overcoming a state of contradiction," as achieving a higher and more "rational" form of human existence. More-

[5] Hayashi Shigeru, *Kindai Nihon no shisōkatachi* (Tokyo, 1958), pp. 107-160, especially p. 111.

[6] Yoshino Sakuzō, "Hegeru no horitsu tetsugaku no kiso," in the journal *Horironsō*, XII (1905).

[7] Moriya, "Yoshino," 118-119.

over, the process of development from one distinct state to another must be linked by a logical relationship assuring causal
identity in a particular sequence. Thus, equally as important as
the logic of historical transformation was the concept of "becoming," a view that led Yoshino to emphasize heavily the preservation of historical continuity.[8]

Here is, no doubt, the logical basis of Yoshino's political moder-
ation: change, though dialectical, must be gradual, leading to a
better society. It was this point of view, rather than an acceptance of utilitarian precepts, that predisposed Yoshino to value
highly the workings of the parliamentary system in Great Britain.
It likewise explains his consistent opposition to radical attack on
social and political institutions along lines of class dynamics, a
fact that separated him, in the 1920's, from Marxist scholars and
many of his students. The expectation of total transformation, he
warned, was unwarranted and impractical because it disrupted
relationships of identity in the process of change, thus triggering
uncontrollable patterns of events.[9] Yoshino, in short, did not use
dialectics as an "algebra of revolution," as Herzen once put it,
but as the basis of gradual and controlled progress.

Yoshino's emphasis on historical identity was closely related to
his definitions of social and political organization. Society was
never an abstraction but a concrete historical product—a complex
configuration of ethnic, ethical, ideological and political forces
bequeathed by the past. Those who denied this, he felt, tended
to commit one of the following fallacies. One was to see social and
political change as purposeless, governed by unpredictable contingencies, by the joker in a deck of cards. Another was to believe
that the flow of history could be disrupted violently, a view that
would surely breed anarchy and loss of direction. And still another was to see society uncritically as a static "reality as it is."[10]
None of these views, he held, was either accurate or constructive.
He insisted that society was descriptive of an identifiable historical whole and took on meaning as it embodied a distinctive
"spirit" or "popular will" (*kakujin kyōtsū no ishi*).[11] Fashioned by
a country's history and beliefs, this spirit held individuals to-

[8] See Tanaka Sōgoro, *Yoshino Sakuzō* (Tokyo, 1958), pp. 69-75. This
work by Tanaka is the most complete biography of Yoshino to date.

[9] This is a theme scattered through Yoshino's writings. See especially his
essays in *Minshushugi seiji kōwa: Yoshino ronshū*, II.

[10] Moriya, "Yoshino," 103-105.   [11] *Ibid.*, p. 117.

gether in a comprehensive social whole, giving them their objectivity. By the same token, the spirit was not a mere abstraction since it was embodied concretely in social and political organizations from which no person could exempt himself. Thus, "Men cannot live in isolation; their actions in both economic and social matters take place within the framework of *national* society."[12]

From this standpoint, Yoshino accepted the theoretical derivative that human personality was "social," not "natural," its essential spirit one and inseparable from the comprehensive "will of organization" (*dantai no ishi*). This will, moreover, determined or controlled all aspects of the internal and external aspects of a person's life. In its most widely applicable sense, he noted, it could be thought of as the "national spirit."[13] As with Hegel, in short, political organization was an equivalent of nation-state, possessing spiritual sovereignty over and beyond the pragmatic and legal power to regulate conflicting interests.

Despite Yoshino's view of the will of organization as having a determining force on human personality, he intended it to be a non-absolute force. Although this may seem curiously contradictory, Yoshino believed that the preconditioning forces of history must not be underestimated, for to do so would lead to exaggerated expectations for change. To impute, however, perfect rationality in external structure, as he believed Hegel tended to in the nation-state, was equally unrealistic.[14] Thus, while the possibility of change was preconditioned by the past, history was also a dynamic process in which there was no logical end to men's quest for a more rational form of existence. In this sense, the individual must never be subordinated absolutely to historical constructs or national will. He later raised this belief to the level of unshakeable dictum, giving a ring of genuine conviction to his view that the aim of government was personal welfare. Indeed, rather than insubordination, he saw the individual in constant engagement with national institutions, in a relationship he described in 1919 as "confrontation, conflict, resolution."[15]

How then might the individual retain a critical stance to "confront" institutions? Yoshino's answer to this question changed with

[12] *Ibid.*, p. 114.
[13] *Ibid.*, pp. 114-115, and Tanaka, *Yoshino*, 64-65.
[14] Tanaka, *Yoshino*, p. 72 and *passim*.
[15] See his "Kokkachūshinshugi to kojinchūshinshugi ni shikō no tairitsu-shotosu-chōwa," *Yoshino ronshū*, I, 167-226.

his assessment of the political order. In his earlier, more optimistic years, he placed his defense on men's intellectual capacity to understand historical process. Men could take an independent stance by understanding that history was not natural, but secular and purposeful in the sense that men built and created culture in terms of governing ideals perceived at a particular time.[16] Precisely for this reason, men could gain an awareness of the inevitable direction in which history was moving. Men therefore reconstructed the past so that they could predict and control the process of change. They grasped essential guidelines and staked out the future. The very best among them perceived ideals on the basis of which they made judgments of value and threw light on the "necessary" course of historical development. Institutions were reshaped, reformed, to accord with this course, and, in this manner, abstraction became concrete.[17]

This line of reasoning reveals a significant trait in Yoshino's thought, characterized by the juxtaposition of a particular historical process and the perceived ideal. It points to a tendency in thought in which the ideal as universal truth steadily superseded distinctive national history in importance. The "light" he spoke of was to show the inevitable development of national into universal history. Indeed, to him this was the essence of modernization. This tendency in his thinking can be discerned in his early polemical writings during the Russo-Japanese War (1904-1905), when nationalism still held sway in his thinking.

Joining forces with nationalistic writers, he wrote a series of essays attacking opponents of the war. Christian pacifists (e.g., Kinoshita Naoe) and atheistic socialists (e.g., Kōtoku Shūsui) both misunderstood the significance of the war. Rather than being meaningless or a conflict between imperialist powers pure and simple, the war was Japan's defense against the threat of Western bureaucratic penetration of the country. Moved essentially, he felt, by a blind prejudicial fear of "the yellow peril," the West had determined to destroy Japan's cultural autonomy. But, by refusing to capitulate to this threat, Japan had asserted its right to preserve its distinctive national spirit. This spirit, moreover, was not something manufactured by a few selfish politicians, but was fashioned by history and shared by all Japanese. Therefore, the war was, by definition, popular.

Arguments to the contrary did not move him. For example,

---

[16] Yoshino, "Meiji bunka kokorozeshi," *Yoshino ronshū*, VIII, 6-7.
[17] *Ibid.*, pp. 1-10.

Kinoshita, perhaps the most eloquent of Yoshino's opponents in this debate, denied the concept of a spiritual connection between the people and men in power. Such a notion, he argued, was seductive in the extreme; it was a myth, concocted by a selfish elite in government to preserve its status and power. Defending the war in terms of national spirit, therefore, was to advocate a "national religion" which would preserve the political status quo and turn into a detriment for the people. But Yoshino replied firmly and unequivocally that society was a unified spiritual whole transcending inequities in distribution of power or wealth. Without popular commitment to that unifying spirit, Japan would be neither a nation nor a people and could not expect to develop in a creative fashion.[18]

Having stated his position in these nationalistic terms, Yoshino then proceeded in a direction unacceptable to most nationalists. The war was not merely a defense of a unique culture against the West. There was broader significance to it. The war was a major turning point in world history, leading to the convergence of different races and cultures in a new process of world history contributing mightily to the incorporation of Japan and all Asia into a new world order. Because of Japan's preservation of its cultural integrity, Asia now would have a voice in that order. Although most nationalists would have agreed with Yoshino on this point—indeed, it was an integral part of the rhetoric of national "mission" beyond Japanese expansionism[19]—they could not accept Yoshino's definition of a new world order. To Yoshino, it meant the beginning of universal history in which self-centered nationalism would decline in significance and all nations would be united by a common idealistic concern to maximize the spiritual and intellectual development of all human beings.[20] The ideal, he noted, was "government centered on the people" (*shiminshugi*). We need not labor over the obvious non sequitur in Yoshino's reasoning. Of significance was his desire to redirect his logic toward universal ideals, and avoid the irrational propensities implicit in the language of nationalism.

Yoshino's evaluation of the Russo-Japanese War in terms of its

[18] Moriya, "Yoshino," 107-109.

[19] See Matsumoto Sannosuke's excellent article, "Kokuminteki shimeikan no rekishiteki hensen," in *Sekai no naka no Nihon*, VIII, *Kindai Nihon shisō-shi kōza* (Tokyo, 1961), pp. 83-136.

[20] See Yoshino, "Minshuteki jiiundō o ronzu," *Gendai no seiji* (Tokyo, 1916), pp. 1-57, especially 46-47. Also, Moriya, "Yoshino," 109-119.

dual significance sums up the main features and tendencies of his thought that he would develop more fully in his subsequent career. Basically, the outline of his ideas can be characterized in the following manner. He arranged two sets of opposites in intersecting axes. One axis posed the polarities of the universal and the particular, the former representing ideal ends toward which history moved, the latter the preconditioning forces generated by a distinctive historical sequence. The other axis posed the individual against the collective. The "individual" stood for the critical personality that grasped the trends of universal history and refashioned reality into a "better form," and the "collective" represented popular national union, a "people" (*minzoku*), held together by a unique spirit inherited from the past. These opposites were not mutually exclusive, each being essential components of a logical whole. It is clear that Yoshino sought to balance these opposing elements in such a way that the individual and the universal would take precedence over the collective and the particular. Yet it must also be noted that the latter constituted the framework within which universalistic ideals were worked out. This was logically necessary for Yoshino since he placed heavy emphasis on the maintenance of historical identity in the process of transformation. Thus, though Yoshino abhorred the excesses of nationalistic attitudes, his position was actually quite tolerant of nationalist arguments, much more tolerant certainly than of conceptions of class dynamics or utilitarian politics. Within Yoshino's theoretical frame, in short, some could stress individualism and universalism as the new "tide of history," a phrase used repeatedly in this period, while others could stress with logical justification the collective and particular as essential for dynamic development. And despite different uses of the same paradigm, both could and did speak out with one another in seductive unison in the 1910's against the corrupt politics of the oligarchy and extol the virtues of government centered on the people and, in turn, of popular participation in national politics.

Yoshino's early thought is an essential guideline for understanding the ideas articulated in his more mature years. He did not relinquish that logical frame; hence his arguments of the 1910's and 1920's must be assessed within it. In this regard, his conception of parliamentary government was an institutional format to synthesize the various polarities he had begun to identify during the Russo-Japanese War as intrinsic to modern political life.

Following a study tour of Europe (1910-1913), Yoshino revised the phrase "government centered on the people" to read "government based on the people" (*minponshugi*). This marked an important shift from his earlier paternalistic view of government to one fully supportive of popular participation. The earlier phrase connoted governmental guarantee of certain essentials required by the people. The later phrase implied popular control of politics based on the principle of the unlimited capacity of individuals to develop into critical personalities. It was obviously in this latter sense that Yoshino understood the new "ideal" of the modern world.[21]

Some doubts have been raised as to whether Yoshino meant democracy by the phrase "government based on the people." For example, the phrase was used by nationalistic theoreticians such as Inoue Tetsujirō in the 1890's and more recently by Uesugi Shinkichi, one of Yoshino's principal antagonists in the 1910's. Some noted that he could not have meant democracy in a basic sense because he rejected the natural-right theory of popular sovereignty, this theory being, in his view, logically untenable and contrary to the preamble of the Meiji Constitution.[22] Although these doubts may be justifiable, it must be emphasized that Yoshino gave to the phrase the meaning of popular control of politics absent in earlier uses of it by nationalist thinkers. More important, he did not view popular sovereignty and democracy as equivalents, or the former as a necessary condition for the latter. For him, the British case provided ample justification for distinguishing between the two. By "government based on the people," he quite clearly understood democracy within constitutional monarchy, in which the people would have the right to select leaders and render ultimate judgment over governmental policy. Furthermore, as noted above, he understood the proper aim of this policy to be the enhancement of the right of each individual to realize to the fullest his capacity for intellectual and moral growth. Thus, although he avoided rendering *minponshugi* as "democracy" in the early 1910's to describe the politics he had in mind, he freely used the phrase "the spirit of democracy" and from the early 1920's on simplified it to "democracy" (*minshu-*

---

[21] Yoshino, "Minshuteki jiiundō . . . ," *Gendai* . . . , 46-47; and Moriya, "Yoshino," 119-120.

[22] See Hayashi, *Kindai shisōkatachi*, 117-128.

Najita

shugi).[23] Of greater significance in the context of this essay, however, was his continuing use of the logical premises of his earlier years despite a profound shift of emphasis in his thinking. It is the relationship between those premises and his new conception of democracy that require clarification.

Yoshino's plea for popular government was pinned to the argument of historical necessity. As indicated earlier, men perceived inevitable trends in history and gave them concrete form. As consistent with this view of history, he pointed to similar patterns of political development abroad and at home which shared a common characteristic that was not mere happenstance. Everywhere, without reference to particular history or racial make-up, all societies had begun to coalesce into a broad and unified movement toward political democracy. The workings of European, and in particular British, parliamentary institutions and the rise of labor movements he felt were inevitable and part of a single historical development held together by a common spirit of democracy.[24] He further noted certain developments on the domestic scene reflecting that same irresistible spirit which the ruling elite in Japan could not prevent. Thus, with the certainty of one convinced of the emergence of democracy, he went on to suggest that the main political issue in Japan was not whether democracy was inevitable but who would provide the best direction leading toward that form of government. The "new politician" of Taishō, therefore, must be one who perceived that inevitable trend and acted accordingly in the processes of government.[25]

From this somewhat amorphous reasoning (which, incidentally, created great difficulty for him in the 1920's when the inevitability of democracy in world history no longer seemed certain) Yoshino went on to develop a case for the compatability between Japanese history, the particular, and democracy, the universal ideal. Relying on a vocabulary drawn from his earlier years, he wrote: "Those who argue that democracy is not compatible with the national spirit believe in the anachronistic and erroneous notion that the Emperor and people are mutually exclusive of each other."[26] Such a belief was repugnant to the essen-

[23] See his essays in *Yoshino ronshū*, II.

[24] Yoshino, "Kensei no hongi . . . ," *Yoshino ronshū*, I, 4-5; and also, Hayashi, *Kindai shisōkatachi*, 114-115; Moriya, "Yoshino," 103-119; Tanaka, *Yoshino*, 122-138.

[25] Yoshino, "Taishō seikai no shinkeikō," *Gendai . . .* , 162-182.

[26] Yoshino, "Minshuteki jiiundō . . . ," *Gendai . . .* , 14 and *passim*.

40

tial symbolic value of the Emperor in modern Japan. The modern transformation of Japan was possible precisely because the Emperor stood simultaneously for two seemingly contrasting phenomena: a distinctive history and a current transformation that was leading to new modes of economic production and political expression. Along with virtually all political critics of his day, he used the imperial pledge of 1869 as a reference to support his assertion. The pledge confirmed the modern principle of public discussion as the basis to settle all affairs of state. Moreover, it recognized the right of equal opportunity for each individual, regardless of previous status or geographical origin, to maximize his potential in a field of his choice. Both these items in the pledge indicated that the Emperor's position was legitimized less by divine sanction requiring unquestioning submission by his subjects than by his total symbolic commitment to guarantee the satisfaction of the wishes and aspirations of his people. Moreover, these items in the pledge pointed to the fact that the Emperor did not transcend, but took on significance within history and nation, which, by definition, were popular in content in the sense of being manifestations of a will common to all. Thus, the Emperor ought not to be separated from the people by divine distance, hedged in by artificial barriers erected by the oligarchs to protect their narrow political interests. He should be unified intimately with the people. Indeed, he "belonged to the people" (*kokumin no tennō*, as rendered by two Japanese scholars in a recent work),[27] and therefore the politics of the nation also belonged to the people.[28] Regardless of status and wealth, everyone had the right to serve the nation loyally. This included, among other things, the right to participate in government and help shape a destiny in which all would share. The concept of democracy, he concluded, was utterly compatible with the national spirit.[29]

Although the point of view just outlined was rejected by conservative legal theorists such as Uesugi Shinkichi, who continued to speak rigidly of the Emperor as sovereign and as synonymous

[27] See the stimulating work by Kunō Osamu and Tsurumi Shunsuke, *Gendai Nihon no shisō* (Tokyo, 1956), 144-160 and *passim*; also, Imai Seiichi, "Seiji shidōsha no shisōteki yakuwari," in *Shidōsha to taishū: Kindai Nihon shisōshi kōza*, v (Tokyo, 1960), 61-103, especially 61-62.

[28] See Yoshino's "Gendai seiji shikō," *Yoshino ronshū*, ii, 1-92, especially p. 9.

[29] Yoshino, "Minshuteki jiiundō . . . ," *Gendai . . .* , 13-15 and *passim*, and "Kensei no hongi . . . ," *Yoshino ronshū*, i, 12-25, 38-39, 49.

with the nation, it reflected the views of many important nationalists representing different shades of thought. Some, such as
Miyake Setsurei, used it to define the Emperor as the pure expression of the unique spirit of the Japanese people, while others,
such as Kita Ikki, used the same paradigm to devise a radical
program for social monarchy. Yoshino, however, did not emphasize popular cultural unity as Miyake did, assuming it generally
as a given historical fact without further need of romanticization,
and he flatly rejected the idea of an active popular monarchy.[30]
To him, the union of Emperor and people as in Great Britain
could be achieved best in the framework of parliamentary government. Within it, the egalitarian principle imbedded in the
Imperial pledge of 1869 would cease to be an abstraction, as it
had been throughout much of Meiji history, and become concretely politicized in such a way that all people could take part
in government and help shape their common future.[31]

According to Yoshino, the development from the abstract to
the concrete was well under way in Japan. The promulgation of
the Meiji Constitution in 1889 was one evidence of this. In this
document, he noted, the principle of limitation of power was
explicitly stated. It was tantamount to a public concession by the
Emperor and men in power at the time that absolutism was inconsistent with modernization. And as part of this admission, the
constitution specifically guaranteed civil liberties and the right
of commoners to take part in party and Diet politics. Despite im-
perfections, which Yoshino admitted were numerous, the over-all
significance of that document should not be overlooked. In sum,
it had redefined and constitutionalized the national spirit in terms
of a body of legal and political theory that had universal significance and it had created a new form of institutional outlet
for that spirit in a Diet system. Thus, while the national spirit
could still give a particular constitution a distinct flavor, it was
now more fundamentally regulated by an abstract principle of
constitutional government that had its own unifying spirit. As an
ideal, this spirit was a universally valid principle (*genri, hongi*)
of humanity and justice. In the concrete, it stood for democratic
politics or government based on the people.[32] Yoshino believed

[30] Yoshino, "Minshuteki jiiundō . . . ," *Gendai* . . . , 13; and "Gendai
shikō," *Yoshino ronshū*, ɪɪ, 12-15.

[31] Yoshino, "Minshuteki jiiundō . . . ," *Gendai* . . . , 1-57.

[32] *Ibid.*, pp. 13-15. See also, Yoshino, "Kensei no hongi . . . ," *Yoshino
ronshū*, ɪɪ, 16-17, 26-28, 49-61; and Moriya, "Yoshino," 118-120.

the Meiji Constitution embodied this principle, and that it there-fore should be viewed and evaluated in that positive light, as having marked a decisive turning point in the concrete realiza-tion in Japan of the democratic ideal of the enlightenment.[33]

Yoshino's assessment of the Meiji Constitution was closely tied to his optimistic view of another development which to him also pointed to the unfolding of the spirit of democracy on the domes-tic scene. The Japanese, he felt, had begun to emerge as a politi-cally conscious people possessing a significant aptitude for criti-cal protest. Yoshino observed unprecedented numbers of people taking to the streets in movements and demonstrations of protest such as in riots against the Portsmouth Treaty of 1905, the Move-ment for Constitutional Government in 1912-1913, the protest against naval corruption in 1914, and the rallies against high con-sumption taxes throughout these years. And he felt the momen-tous transformation of political consciousness among the people to be the central theme of these demonstrations. Thus, in his essays of 1914-1915, his first and in many respects most impor-tant, he heralded the demonstrations as marking the dawn of a new era. "It cannot be doubted," he wrote, "that from late Meiji and early Taishō, a new trend has begun to emerge in conspicu-ous fashion. . . . One aspect of this new trend is the steady decline of the elder statesmen, the other is the powerful growth of public opinion."[34] For the first time the people had begun to recognize the serious discrepancy between existing politics and their own image, however vague it still was, of a better life for themselves and their society. As a consequence, they denounced government by a narrow oligarchy and demanded the establishment of elected party cabinets responsive to the material and moral needs of the people. In this sense, Yoshino noted, the spirit of democ-racy was no longer a distant ideal but an operational ideology understood by broad segments of the public. He concluded that the central demand of the people that their voices be heard and their influence felt in the political process could not be denied them much longer by the ruling elite.[35]

Yoshino, of course, was not alone in imputing a democratic potential in the popular demonstrations. Indeed most of the crit-ics of the time made similar evaluations, although some, such as

[33] Yoshino, "Kensei no hongi . . . ," *Yoshino ronshū*, II, 27-28, 38-39.
[34] Yoshino, "Taishō seikai no shinkeikō," *Gendai* . . . , 162.
[35] *Ibid.*, pp. 32-57, 162-185. See also, Ishida Takeshi, *Kindai Nihon seiji-kōzō no kenkyū* (Tokyo, 1956), 131-246, *passim*.

43

Tokutomi Sohō, viewed the trend with considerable alarm. For the most part, however, the demonstrations were viewed with optimism. The influential critic Maruyama Kanji, for example, referred to them as the beginning of a new political and cultural movement against anachronistic political custom.[36] Ukita Kazutami, editor of the widely read journal *Taiyō*, whom Yoshino acknowledged as having had a major influence on him, spoke of the possibility of realizing at last the "fundamental principle" of politics based on public opinion.[37] Although Yoshino's view coincided with those of Maruyama and Ukita, what set him apart from these other critics was his deep sense of personal mission to give over-all intellectual direction to seemingly disconnected series of protests—to help define and sharpen the popular self image of a new and better world. Such a task obviously would require a clear logical statement, articulated in terms understandable to the bulk of society. Thus, although he temperamentally abhorred popular violence and continued to believe in intellectual elitism, he minimized the significance of violence in the demonstrations and, suppressing his disdain for the general level of intelligence of the masses, spoke in ringing terms of the new protest movements as cause for much rejoicing.[38]

Two interrelated concepts are crucial for understanding Yoshino's pattern of thought directed to the people. One of these was his notion of custom, the other, function. Both these terms had special meanings which, perhaps misrepresented by his simple style, have eluded critics of the time and historians subsequently. Often these terms have been used to characterize Yoshino's "utilitarianism," a view that is misleading because it distorts the logical frame of reference Yoshino relied on. Indeed, a case can be made that Yoshino was fundamentally anti-utilitarian in his thinking despite certain obvious leanings toward party politics within a parliamentary system.

Yoshino's argument for custom can be described in the following manner. Law and politics were distinguishable categories. Law rationally defined the limits of politics but did not determine its content. Politics, on the other hand, was the arena in which

---

[36] See Maruyama's "Minshuteki keikō to seitō," *Nihon oyobi Nihonjin*, 597 (January 1, 1913), 72-76.

[37] See Ukita's "Rikkenseiji no kompongi," *Taiyō* (April, 1913), 2-11; and also, "Taishō ishin wa kore," *Taiyō* (December, 1912), 25-27.

[38] Yoshino, "Minshuteki jiiundō . . . ," *Gendai* . . . , 3-4, 8-9.

the creative process of history took place, leading to higher levels of rational existence. Quite obviously, custom was born, nurtured, sustained, or changed, within politics. Thus, he noted, government based on the people is a political and not a legal concept.[39] Pointing more concretely to the Japanese legal system, Yoshino argued there was ample room politically to create the custom of government based on public opinion and popular participation. The constitution did not preempt the possibility of party government. On the contrary, since the Emperor as a matter of custom did not rule directly but entrusted politics to his servitors (which to Yoshino meant the people at large), responsible, elected party government was possible and not repugnant to the letter and spirit of the law.[40]

There was, however, a troublesome aspect to his argument. Others could, and in fact did, use that same framework of discourse to defend the opposite of popular government—namely, transcendental government controlled by a small group of leaders—precisely because it transcended the interests of partisan groups, such as political parties, and hence was the most representative of the wishes of the Emperor, nation, and people at large. Yoshino conceded that such an arrangement for politics might well have been valid historically, but it was now an anachronism. It was old custom and must be broken decisively and replaced by the new custom of popular politics within the same legal framework.[41] In the sphere of politics, in short, custom was not sacrosanct—it could be made and unmade in the creative process.

This was strange use of the term "custom." The explanation lies partly in the fact that Yoshino rejected violent attack against legal structures and wished to extend limits of law as far out as possible in order to maximize the arena of political give-and-take. Yoshino, however, was using "custom" in two ways: as historical custom (or historical ideal) and potential custom (or futuristic ideal) with the latter taking precedence as far as he was concerned.[42] In British utilitarianism, by way of contrast, both

[39] *Ibid.*, pp. 15-16; and Yoshino's "Kensei no hongi . . . ," *Yoshino ronshū*, II, 57.

[40] Yoshino, "Minshuteki jiiundō . . . ," *Gendai* . . . , 46-60 and *passim*; and his "Kensei no hongi," *Yoshino ronshū*, I, 60-72.

[41] See Hayashi, *Kindai shisōka*, 128-145.

[42] See Yōshino, "Minponshugi no igi o toite futatabi kensei yūshū no bi o nasu no michi o ronzu," *Yoshino ronshū*, I, 131-166, especially 158.

45

historical and potential custom was attacked and discarded theoretically as inadequate guides to political action. Custom was displaced by the criterion of utility, the calculated satisfaction of human personality by government at specific points in time without regard to abstract metaphysical questions of idealistic principle. Yoshino, however, was doubtful of this essentially materialistic and pragmatic definition of politics.[43] To him, politics ought to be guided by an idealistic norm, which for him increasingly took on the flavor of a universally valid category of reality, a principle outside time and, in the Kantian sense, prior to experience itself.[44] Thus, he observed, politics required an ultimate norm, an ideal, to counter the "utilitarian conception of gauging immediate advantage and disadvantage."[45] And although such a universally valid ideal could never be fully achieved in reality, so that men must settle for an approximation to it, still it ought to be the critical goal toward which men strove. Politicians, therefore, should be philosophers (in Plato's sense, he suggested) who subjectively perceived absolute truth and sought to lead the country accordingly.[46] Those politicians who continued to believe in the possibility of an algebraic, scientific, calculation of utility were in fact opportunists. In this context, one of the values of a two-party system was that it provided a framework in which considerations of utility could be rectified by a subjective ideal.[47] In short, his critique on "old custom" and of pragmatic Diet politics, was pinned not to utilitarianism but to philosophic idealism, a view of politics as a creative struggle toward the realization of a timeless ideal. This metaphysical conception of politics was explicitly rejected in early utilitarianism in Great Britain, as it was also by John Stuart Mill in his sophisticated reformulations of that tradition in his essays on liberty and empirical logic.

Yoshino's notion of function closely followed the above pattern of reasoning. Although he used the term to describe the actual workings of parliamentary government and identified and supported such concrete items as universal manhood suffrage, representative party government based on two major alignments, and

[43] *Ibid., passim,* and Yoshino, "Minshuteki jiiundō . . . ," *Gendai . . . ,* 8-16.

[44] Moriya, "Yoshino," 120; and see the postscript in *Yoshino ronshū,* II, 344-346.

[45] Yoshino, "Minponshugi futatabi . . . ," *Yoshino ronshū,* I, 254.

[46] *Ibid.,* pp. 257-258.   [47] *Ibid.,* pp. 258-260.

civilian and Lower House control over the House of Peers and the military, he did not place primary emphasis on the pragmatic manipulation of legal institutions to achieve concrete ends. He argued repeatedly that achieving "something better" within parliamentary government meant not the selection and execution of the best policy available at a given time, but the creation of the best possible situation in which ideal could become concrete.[48]

The ideal could become concrete, however, only within the framework of the nation, an idealistic collectivity of individuals. This he felt was a truism of modern political life that had not been adequately accounted for in the utilitarian scheme of individual happiness culminating in the greatest happiness for the greatest number. His government based on the people, he therefore argued, would harmonize both individual interest and national well-being. Yet, it is quite certain that in his thinking the ideal of nation superseded individual utility as the more valid of the two principles. Indeed, the individual took on significance within the nation, as he had argued in 1905, and, precisely for this reason, each individual should share in the responsibility of shaping the nation's future. Thus, the function of Yoshino's political man was not to determine concrete personal needs (as, for example, economic well-being to protect individual autonomy, a point central to utilitarianism) while striving within an organized format to influence the processes of government. It was primarily the "right" and moral commitment of each individual to serve the nation by helping to determine what was ideally best for the entire country.[49] To contribute in this fashion, however, each person must have an abstract ideal standard (the valid options being historical or futuristic in his view) which superseded concrete considerations of individual needs and which served to gauge the over-all political situation.[50] To Yoshino, therefore, "function" connoted, as Professor Matsumoto Sannosuke has aptly suggested, an idealized philosophy of action.[51] Politics led, as Yoshino himself put it, to the "idealistic union between the struc-

[48] *Ibid.*, pp. 238-260. See also his essays in *Yoshino ronshū*, II, 1-169, 319-326, *passim*.

[49] Yoshino, "Kensei no hongi . . . ," *Yoshino ronshū*, I, 88-89.

[50] Yoshino, "Minponshugi futatabi . . . ," *Yoshino ronshū*, I, 254-260.

[51] Matsumoto Sannosuke, "Minponshugi no rekishiteki keisei," *Seijigaku nempō* (Tokyo, 1957), 109-131, especially 114-115.

ture of power and value."[52] It was entirely consistent with his idealism that Yoshino should become increasingly dissatisfied with political studies of institutional and organizational dynamics and of legal problems of sovereignty. The proper focus of political research, he concluded succinctly in 1920, was the study of *ethical* value at all levels of society.[53]

At first glance, it may seem as if Yoshino sought to revive a Confucian approach to politics such as was being attempted by the famous party leader Inukai Tsuyoshi.[54] His emphasis on moral over "legalistic" concern with political apparatus, and similarly his strategic use of terms such as "the way" of government, "humanity," "principle" (rendered in characters having prepotent value for Japanese readers), indeed have a ring reminiscent of Confucianism. This view, however, is misleading and clouds Yoshino's main concern. His de-emphasis of political structure belied the fact that he retained in his theoretical baggage the definition of national organization as sovereign, as embodiment of "collective will." His emphasis on ethics, therefore, was not actually a "Confucian" de-emphasis of structure, but a modern recognition of the might of sovereign political structure. Ethical ideal, in this context, constituted a theoretical basis (and for him a practical one as well) from which to blunt, without denying its logical validity, the argument of nation-state as embodiment of "value"—a view he traced in Japan to the writings of Katō Hiroyuki.[55]

The ambiguity is clearly evident in his critique of 1916 on the "Emperor-centered" view of the nation propounded by conservative legal theorists such as Uesugi Shinkichi.[56] First he denied the general thesis that the nation transcended the individual as an absolute principle. He then explained that Hegel, from whom that thesis was drawn, actually did not speak of a nation as being the absolute ideal towards which men strive. Although Hegel

[52] See Moriya, "*Yoshino*," 120-137; and also, Yoshino, "Gendai shikō," *Yoshino ronshū*, II, 1-92 *passim*.

[53] Yoshino, "Seijigaku no kakushin," *Yoshino ronshū*, II, 327-333.

[54] See my short essay, "Inukai Tsuyoshi: Some Dilemmas in Party Development in Pre-World War II Japan," *The American Historical Review* (December, 1968).

[55] Yoshino, "Seijigaku no kakushin," *Yoshino ronshū*, II, 327-333; and his "Minponshugi futatabi . . . ," *Yoshino ronshū*, I, 238-240.

[56] Yoshino, "Kokkachūshinshugi to kojinchūshinshugi," *Yoshino ronshū*, I, 168-225.

wrote of the nation as the structural expression of a people and, as such, the framework within which the individual exists and develops, he intended this to mean a nation for the people.[57] As is well known, Hegel was ambiguous on this point, signifying to some the importance of maximum moral development along highly individualistic lines despite (even in defiance of) the external arrangement of institutions, while indicating to others the nation state as the ultimate form of rational existence. What matters in the context of this discussion, however, is that Yoshino used his interpretation of Hegel as sufficient reason to reaffirm the polarities of individual and collective will as logical complements. Thus, he affirmed again the validity of defining collective organization as nation—as "organic body (*yūkitai*) composed of persons having common cultural norms."[58] Similarly, he once again defined the individual as a concrete social entity, inextricably tied to conditions of history and political constructs. As part of society, moreover, this individual shared with the nation a common fate, took part in a common effort. It was because of this fact, Yoshino affirmed, that it was ethically consistent to grant participant rights to the people and incorporate them into the national political life according to the principle of democracy.[59] What is striking in Yoshino's thinking is not that he directed his logic toward democracy, but that he restated definitions that could be and, indeed, were construed as significant theoretical concessions to the nationalist position.

Yoshino complicated his case further by injecting a relativistic criterion by which to determine the primacy of the individual over the collective at a given time. All modern countries emphasized one or the other according to time and circumstance.[60] However, in modern and enlightened societies, the shifting emphases between those poles took place naturally because conscious political action was natural. Thus a debate in these societies over the primacy of individual or collective was academic. But in Japan this debate was crucial because the country's organic structure had not yet reached a phase of rational exist-

[57] *Ibid.*, pp. 194-195.

[58] *Ibid.*, pp. 170-173. See also Yoshino's "Gendai shikō," *Yoshino ronshū*, II, 33 and *passim*.

[59] Yoshino, "Kokkachūshinshugi to kojinchūshinshugi," *Yoshino ronshū*, I, 170-176, 197.

[60] *Ibid.*, p. 173.

ence. And since this was the case, there was no real alternative but to stress unequivocally the individual over the collective, thereby avoiding the irrational tendencies of nationalism.[61] This admission of backwardness, of course, was not limited to Yoshino; nationalists made the same admission grudgingly. The implication, however, that the emphasis on the individual was dictated less by logical consistency than by historical circumstance tended to weaken his over-all case for democratic government.

Yoshino's foes, and potential foes, used the same criterion to argue in opposite directions. Some, for example, argued that circumstances did not warrant the incorporation of democratic principle in Japan, not because such a course was theoretically impossible, but because it would tear the fabric of society apart, undermining its organic historical unity by nurturing a divisive cult of personal success. The times dictated the restoration of social cohesion and of national direction in the growing social uncertainty brought on by industrialization and tension on the international scene. Others, less hostile to Yoshino's position, agreed on the efficacies of parliamentary government, but they also denied that such a form of government should be used to buttress the principle of individualism. Rather, parliamentary institutions were useful as instruments to help regain and crystallize social solidarity. Yoshino did not reject this latter position. To him, however, it was aimed in the wrong direction. National unity was a historical fact in Japan; hence it had little need of emphasis. Local interests were similar throughout the country so that regional divisions were minimal, and racially, religiously, and emotionally, Japan was a homogeneous country.[62] Indeed, because this unity existed, the *nation* could be used as an *instrument* to incorporate the higher ideal of democracy. To nationalists, however, the legacy of spiritual cohesion had begun to lose its vitality in industrial Japan. There was every reason to emphasize collective union. National solidarity was essential, parliamentary government the device to achieve and protect it.

Despite differences between Yoshino and nationalists over what was essential, and what was the device, their disagreement was less on grounds of logic and more on grounds of relative

[61] Yoshino, "Seishinkai no Taishō ishin," *Sekai heiwashugi, Yoshino ronshū*, vII, 1-17.
[62] Yoshino, "Minshuteki jiiundō . . . ," *Gendai* . . . , 68-73.

interpretive assessments of Japan's development and needs in the twentieth century. Yet out of this difference in subjective assessment, the voices behind Taishō democracy, seemingly unified in the 1910's, began to fall into disarray in the 1920's. Time and circumstance cruelly undermined Yoshino's certainty regarding the inevitable course of history. But once again Yoshino reworked his logical apparatus into a defense of parliamentary government for Japan.

Political developments at home and abroad in the late 1910's seemed to vindicate Yoshino's belief in the inevitable unfolding of democracy throughout the world. On the domestic scene popular movements persisted unabated. Indeed they took on a greater degree of sophistication in the movement for universal manhood suffrage. Moreover, the realization of party government within the Meiji constitutional order was no longer a hypothetical goal but a fact. On the international scene, Wilson's idealism reinforced Yoshino's faith in a new democratic world order, and he publicly endorsed it. Recalling his evaluation of the Russo-Japanese War, he assessed World War I as the triumph of democracy, which Wilson epitomized, over authoritarian politics.[63] Yet these political developments took a cruel turn for Yoshino. The Soviet model for revolutionary change and Mussolini's rise to power both clearly militated against the prospects for a new democratic world order. At home, moreover, party government seemed to point not toward political democracy but to pork-barrel politics and corruption on an unprecedented scale. Despite these ominous trends, Yoshino continued to believe that the spirit of democracy would emerge triumphant. Although the confidence with which he had spoken in the earlier decade steadily declined in the 1920's, he was convinced that the rise of totalitarian regimes in Europe—he did not differentiate clearly between the Russian and Italian modes of government—was at best ephemeral, an aberration from the true course of modern history. Japan, therefore, should not lightly abandon the principle of democracy and parliamentary government. Both the Marxist conception of class conflict and the ultranationalist glorification of uniqueness and

[63] Yoshino, "Kokka seikatsu no isshin," *Yoshino ronshū*, IV, 17-86, and "Seishinkai no ishin," *Yoshino ronshū*, IV, 1-16.

expansionism tended to encourage this, but the violent course of action implicit in these views would produce social chaos, the prelude to political despotism itself. Avoidance of this development, in Yoshino's view, depended substantially on the capacity of legal parliamentary institutions to incorporate rapid change and retain at the same time the spirit of democratic interchange between contending points of views. In this way, he added, the aims of socialism could be incorporated into the spirit of democracy in fact as it was in theory.[64]

Much of Yoshino's concern in the 1920's, therefore, was to explain why parliamentary government, in contrast to totalitarianism, was vital for Japan's development. What is perhaps most striking about his arguments, however, was the growing ambiguity in his thought. Early in the decade, he argued that parliamentary government in Japan could be transformational; toward the end he virtually denied this possibility.

In his early essays on behalf of democracy, he depicted democracy in Japan as an ideology caught in a seemingly insoluble predicament and identified two distinguishable attitudes, both apolitical in his view, that had caused this predicament and the consequent dissipation of support for democracy.[65] One of these was a completely negative attitude of rejecting political organization altogether; by definition, organization precluded the possibility of democracy. According to Yoshino, men holding this attitude tended to sever connections with political affairs and withdraw into their private worlds. The second, and for Yoshino more important, attitude was the theoretical rejection of parliamentary institutions, especially those in Japan, as being neither democratic nor potentially democratic. This position he identified with the Marxist scheme of overthrowing existing political institutions on the basis of the revolutionary theory of class conflict. Yoshino severely criticized this program of direct action by an alienated proletariat because it was anarchistic and barren of constructive proposals for a new political order, and could only produce a political situation vulnerable to selfish demagogues. Both Russia and Italy, he pointed out, had in fact gone through

[64] Yoshino, "Gendai seiji no ichi jūyō gensoku," *Yoshino ronshū*, II, 323-324.
[65] Yoshino, "Itabasami ne natteiru demokurashii no tame ni," *Yoshino ronshū*, II, 303-305.

this process leading to totalitarianism, despite romanticized claims of direct popular action and control.[66]

Yoshino conceded that both positions opposing parliamentary government had made important contributions to political thought. Both rightly pointed to the key fact that the political environment of the 1920's was dominated by "bourgeois culture."[67] The recognition of this phenomenon, however, did not in his view warrant either withdrawing from political affairs or violently attacking institutions. Both attitudes were essentially romantic because they overlooked the fundamental fact that society is a complex network of institutions and organizations bequeathed by history that neither individual nor groups of individuals could escape.[68]

Using familiar vocabulary, Yoshino flatly denied that an individual or a people could be conceived of in terms of the abstractions of revolutionary theory. Politics, he stated, was an all-inclusive term for social existence within the confines of an objective structure.[69] This structure, moreover, was a system of external controls imposed on men, thus rendering every aspect of human existence political. And, finally, the most comprehensive of objective structures in the modern world was the nation-state. Unlike other organizations, it was absolute and unconditional, admitting no sovereignty above or outside it. The nation-state constituted the external manifestation of a culturally unified people (*minzoku*) whose bonds had been forged by history. The destruction of that order or escaping from it were both seductive ideas that would prevent the possibility of realizing "freedom." They were synonymous with cynical rejection of the masses of the people.[70]

Despite his insistence on this set of assumptions, Yoshino countered it, as he had done before, by pointing out that the individual nonetheless need not, indeed must not, sacrifice his autonomy within the framework of sovereign political structure. Rather, the individual finds his autonomy *within* it. Such an assertion was not contradictory in his view. A theoretical acceptance of the neces-

[66] Yoshino, "Gikai seidō no hontō no ummei," *Yoshino ronshū*, II, 309-318, especially 310.

[67] Yoshino, "Itabasami . . . ," *Yoshino ronshū*, II, 303-305.

[68] *Ibid.*

[69] Yoshino, "Gendai seiji shikō," *Yoshino ronshū*, II, 2.

[70] *Ibid.*, pp. 3-7; and "Itabasami . . . ," *Yoshino ronshū*, II, 303.

sity of institutions did not constitute a denial of the principle of unlimited self-development generic to men. Acceptance of external organization, therefore, was not to be construed as simple reconciliation of the self with institutions as they exist.[71]

Of crucial importance to Yoshino in this regard was his theory, drawn from his early studies of Hegel, that political institutions were external manifestations of internal convictions. Stated in another way, the structure of sovereignty was never static because it was externalized, or objectified, as Hegel put it, into a hierarchy of command. This phenomenon, he noted, was inseparable from the process of history itself, from ancient times to the present. In the ancient world, normative standards of political action were perceived by a few individuals, whom he called sages, and transposed by them into a structure of authority. Yet the fact that men recognized sages indicated that the people perceived in their wisdom a self better than their own.[72] In modern times, this recognition of a qualitatively superior self had become an aspiration of all men, regardless of country, historical background, and the like. This theme in modern times, he noted, was best captured in Alexander Pope's adage, "Man never is but always to be bless'd."[73] This deceptively simple truism, Yoshino went on to note, was not mere craving for material comfort or upward mobility. It indicated modern man's conscious recognition that the rational external order was generically related to the self and that it stood for one primary purpose, which was to enhance man's quest to realize his true self (*shinjitsu no jiga*).[74] And in this sense, that external order, or institutionalized self, was being constantly reshaped in a dialectical and dynamic reality by true and potential self. Was it not in this conceptual context, he asked rhetorically, that men exercised doubt, inquiring as to whether or not the external order was rational in the sense of reflecting true self?[75] The ability of men to exercise this doubt, Yoshino explained, would determine a nation's capability to realize its comprehensive potential (*zenkanōsei*).[76] It would determine, furthermore, the quality of the objective order as a framework to synthesize "in an organically related process of

---

[71] Yoshino, "Itabasami . . . ," *Yoshino ronshū*, II, 303-305.

[72] *Ibid.*; and also Yoshino's "Gendai shikō," *Yoshino ronshū*, II, 26.

[73] Yoshino, "Gendai shikō," *Yoshino ronshū*, II, 41-42.

[74] *Ibid.*, pp. 18, 24-26.   [75] *Ibid.*, pp. 31-38.

[76] *Ibid.*, p. 41, *passim*.

development,"[77] self and structure, free will and institutional imperative, historical and potential self. In sum, Yoshino argued that the acceptance of external organization in no way implied capitulation to it, but rather that it was a necessary first step in man's quest to forge a better, more rational world.[78]

If this position was theoretically sound, it was not entirely effective as a logical tool to stave off growing distrust of parliamentary institutions in Japan. The question that loomed larger on the horizon as the 1920's proceeded was not so much whether parliamentary institutions could be explained theoretically as whether they could be defended in the concrete. Could they achieve the quality of rationality implied in his scheme of thought? In 1922 Yoshino was cautiously optimistic on this point.[79] Admitting that there was considerable room for pessimism, he still believed the Diet system outlined in the Meiji Constitution to be viable. Discarding it would constitute a severe setback. Party and parliamentary government, therefore, must be transformed from within and made to accord with the feelings and aspirations of the people by continuing to rely on the enlightened principle of majority rule. He noted that a temporarily "bad" majority was always better than permanent control by a dictator or oligarchy. By preserving the principle of numbers, he concluded, the people could select leaders—specialists—through a formalized process of politics and entrust them with the extremely intricate task of operating the government, a task the people could not do themselves. Hence, it was far more reasonable to retain the right to elect leaders than to dismantle the legal structure.[80]

Despite Yoshino's apparent affirmation of party government, even if run by a bad majority, his attitude toward party politics was quite ambiguous. He conceded that party government within the constitutional framework had been realized with great difficulty, and that legal restrictions of one kind or another had forced the parties to pursue a highly pragmatic course of development. They had concentrated on penetrating the legal structure wherever possible and then had driven hard bargains with

[77] *Ibid.*, pp. 26-29, 31-35, 41-42.
[78] *Ibid.*; also, Yoshino's "Gendai seiji gensoku," *Yoshino ronshū*, II, 322-325.
[79] Yoshino, "Itabasami . . . ," *Yoshino ronshū*, II, 307, and "Gikai seidō no ummei," *Yoshino ronshū*, II, 310-318.
[80] Yoshino, "Gendai seiji gensoku," *Yoshino ronshū*, II, 322-325, "Gendai seiji no kompon mondai," *Yoshino ronshū*, II, 102-104, and "Gendai shikō," *Yoshino ronshū*, II, 59-70.

the oligarchs for a favorable redistribution of power. In short, he was fully aware of the obstacles the parties faced in their quest for party cabinets. As he noted, parties in Japan could not build a strong political base first and then demand power on the basis of numbers. Consequently, their struggles were "truly delicate" from the very beginning.[81]

Yoshino's recognition of the practical problems party men had to solve explains his ambivalent appraisal of Hara Kei, builder of the powerful Seiyūkai and prime minister of the first party cabinet (1918-1922). Yoshino despised Hara's pork-barrel politics, his bargaining for positions of power which he used to cultivate regional bases for the party. Yet he noted that Hara had surpassed all other party politicians in manipulating an essentially restrictive legal structure and bending it to favor party growth. As Yoshino grudgingly put it, "Hara had overcome obstacles in a rather fine way."[82]

Despite this brief and cryptic appraisal of Hara, Yoshino's attitude toward parliamentary government in Japan veered sharply, from the mid-1920's on, toward extreme pessimism. He now doubted seriously that the Diet system could be internally transformed under the leadership of party men. While still acknowledging the necessity for politicians to engage in struggles for power in order to seek out policy alternatives, he concluded that these struggles had enmeshed party men so thoroughly in "connections of interest"[83] that it had become virtually impossible for them to be critical about the institutions within which they operated. In their use of economic and political coercion to cultivate electoral bases they had made the Diet system perpetuate a corrupt majority and the inequities of bourgeois culture.[84] The use of the majority principle in Japan, therefore, had not yielded Yoshino's expected fusion of power and morality: it had yielded the "custom" of moral decadence in politics. In sweeping fashion, Yoshino then concluded that politicians in general could not be expected to transform a Diet system from within because their main concern was, through "contrivances," to build organized bases of power and select the best policy alternatives that existed

[81] Yoshino, *Gendai seikyoku no tembō* (Tokyo, 1930), p. 15; also his "Minshuteki jiiundō . . . ," *Gendai . . .* , 62.

[82] Yoshino, *Gendai tembō . . .* , 13-15, 99-100.

[83] Yoshino, "*Gendai kompon . . .* ," *Yoshino ronshū*, ɪɪ, 96.

[84] *Ibid.*, pp. 93, 110-111, 310.

at a given moment. By definition, they were committed to a static reality and hence were intellectually incapable of improving the political life of the country.[85]

This conclusion of Yoshino had far-reaching implications for his conception of the individual's relationship with politicians and political institutions. If politicians could not transform the Diet system from within, the source of change obviously must come from outside. As already indicated, however, Yoshino rejected the strategy of revolutionary attack on existing institutions. He thus sought to de-emphasize the interconnected nature of all individuals in society, which earlier he had defined as the source of collective organization. He now hypothesized that individuals could disengage themselves completely from external institutional constructs. Men, he argued, were totally autonomous spiritual entities, separated from any external organization and its will.[86] Thus, they could liberate themselves from the culture of money and power, as well as from the forces of economic production and class identity. Environmentalist theories of human personalities, be they used for conservative, liberal, or radical purposes, were outmoded ideas because changes in the environment did not necessarily produce changes in human personality. Men, he concluded, were by nature spiritual, and as such they created their own personalities from within, and, in turn, fashioned culture around them.[87]

Yet throughout his career, and even at this time, Yoshino held to the theoretical position that human personality was social, that people were by and large not creative, that the structure of sovereignty was more than a legal apparatus—it was a spiritual force as well, that shaped the personalities of men. To those who doubted him, he often cited the example of the impact of the Imperial Rescript on Education of 1890.[88] It was from this position that he had earlier rejected the natural-rights theory as logically untenable. And it was likewise from this premise that he had advocated universal manhood suffrage: men should be allowed to vote because everyone was united by the national spirit; and that as a unified people, "the acts of every individual no

[85] Yoshino, "Gendai shikō," *Yoshino ronshū*, II, 81.
[86] *Ibid.*, pp. 81-83.
[87] *Ibid.*, p. 57; also Yoshino's "Gendai kompon . . . ," *Yoshino ronshū*, II, 162.
[88] Yoshino, "Gendai shikō," *Yoshino ronshū*, II, 25.

matter how inconsequential they may seem, are interrelated with the destiny of the nation."[89] Since this was indeed the case he had argued that men should transcend individual and class biases and participate in the political life of the country.

This idealistic argument for popular government was quite distinguishable from his new form of idealism, which posited a realm of pure moral ideal intrinsic to personalities of men and separate from the social environment. Yet because Yoshino was convinced that transformation could not come from within the structure of sovereignty, he glossed over ambiguity in theory and spoke with certainty of the politics of a pure idealism residing entirely outside existing organizations which would, on the basis of an essential moral faith, produce higher levels of rational existence (*gōriteki sonzai*).[90] All men ought to sever connections with "the politics of the politicians," with all political organization, be they complex structures or simple associations, organizations at the local level, intermediate regional groupings centering on prefectural assemblies, or national parties in the Diet. The only admissible relationship between individual and political organization must be nonpolitical, "a relationship of pure morality" [*junzentaru dōtoku kankei*].[91] This prescription followed his reading of parties and the Diet system as irretrievably corrupt. To partake in their political workings would be corruptive of human nature itself.

Morally autonomous individuals, then, would coalesce into a new popular movement to overcome the politics of corruption by selecting men of moral rectitude. Such a movement was possible even without careful planning or organization because all men had the innate capacity to make moral judgments. Thus, even though individuals by and large could not create a new political order, or run governments, they could choose what was qualitatively good.[92] By maintaining a strict posture of moral autonomy, the people then could begin to exercise popular control (*kokumin no kantoku*) over government.[93]

---

[89] Yoshino, "Futsūsenkyō no shomondai," *Yoshino ronshū*, II, 169-292, especially 170-179, 201.

[90] Yoshino, "Gendai shikō," *Yoshino ronshū*, II, 34-35, 59-87.

[91] Yoshino, "Gendai kompon . . . ," *Yoshino ronshū*, II, 110-111, and 93-114 *passim*.

[92] Yoshino, "Gendai shikō," *Yoshino ronshū*, II, 57-59.

[93] Yoshino, "Futsūsenkyō . . . ," *Yoshino ronshū*, II, 204.

Yet quite obviously Yoshino's program of popular control—the politics of the people—was structureless. He envisioned a natural coalescence of moral men into a movement held together by a common moral faith.[94] In denying, as a nonrevolutionary, that political organization could be penetrated and transformed from within, he had placed the burden of political change almost exclusively on the shoulders of autonomous and moral individuals stripped of organizational links with the political world. Contrary to his earlier view, all men should vote, he now argued, because they were spiritually autonomous. And since the bulk of the male population had not yet voted (the first election under universal manhood suffrage came in 1928), and hence were uncorrupted by organized politics, manhood suffrage would constitute a new moral force on the political scene.[95] As can be surmised, manhood suffrage did not produce the results Yoshino had anticipated. Rather than unifying politics and morality it further separated them. Corruption reached unprecedented levels as more new voters were trapped by the workings of organized interest politics. As this process continued unabated and his pessimism regarding organized politics deepened, Yoshino's idealized political individual resembled far more closely than he perhaps realized the apolitical personality of the withdrawal-type he had criticized earlier in the decade. He had actually depoliticized his earlier conception of the political individual expressing himself within critical movements of protest. In this sense, his last form of idealism was an indication of his failure to fulfill his ambition of providing intellectual leadership over the emerging political consciousness of the people he had observed with spirited optimism in the early 1910's. Indeed, might not the sudden decline of mass movements of protest in the late 1920's and 1930's, as contrasted to earlier decades, be attributable in part to that failure?

Yoshino's tendency to think of moral idealism along highly individualistic lines stands in contrast to the efforts of his British counterparts to defend the principles of liberalism and utilitarianism from an idealistic point of view. For example, L. T. Hobhouse (who thought of himself as a liberal socialist) argued as

[94] Yoshino, "Gendai shikō," *Yoshino ronshū*, II, 58-59, "Gendai kompon . . . ," *Yoshino ronshū*, II, 110, "Futsūsenkyō . . . ," *Yoshino ronshū*, II, 237.
[95] Yoshino, "Futsūsenkyō . . . ," *Yoshino ronshū*, II, 236-283.

Yoshino did that a strict environmentalist definition of human personality was untenable. Progressive development, in his view, was created by the spiritual self, not out of personal adjustment to the social environment. But Hobhouse denied the meaningfulness of political action along strictly individualistic lines and affirmed the importance of organization as a channel for political expression. To him, political and social organizations—local, intermediate, national—were essential also in acting as buffers for the individual against the otherwise crushing weight of governmental and industrial bureaucracies. And in the sense that organization minimized the individual's psychological uncertainties in the modern world, it helped to maximize his creative potential.[96]

This difference in conceptions of organization can be extended further to the over-all role of government in a democratic society. Yoshino tended to see government as essentially a passive agent—or perhaps permissive, in the sense of autolimitation of sovereignty, is more apt. But unlike Hobhouse and his predecessor T. H. Greens, Yoshino did not emphasize the desirability of enlightened interventionism to curb the power of privilege. It is true that on occasion he spoke of governments "pulling up" (*hikiageru*) the people,[97] implying, as advocates of popular nationalism such as Kuga Katsunan had done as early as the 1890's,[98] that active governmental intervention was a necessary corrective to economic and political inequities. Despite tentative suggestions in this direction, he held by and large to the view that government should be passive. This was logically consistent with his views both that the legal structure should be as unrestrictive as possible, and also that capturing or toppling the government could not produce a truly new society. Although this view reflected in part his consistent opposition to revolutionary strategy, it also reflected, particularly in the 1920's, his declining faith in the transformational capacity of government and political organization in general. If his rejection of radical political strategy was akin to the attitudes of idealistic liberals in the West, his pessimism regarding government certainly was not.

Indeed, as already mentioned, Yoshino ended his career de-

[96] See L. T. Hobhouse, *Liberalism* (New York, 1964, first edition, 1911), 116-119, and *passim*.

[97] Yoshino, "Gendai shikō," *Yoshino ronshū*, II, 34.

[98] Kuga Katsunan's key essay in this regard is his "Kinji seiron kō," *Seijihen*, III, *Meiji bunka zenshū* (Tokyo, 1958; first edition, 1929), 459-526.

emphasizing a positive role for government and believing instead in the capacity of individuals, acting independently, to transcend political constructs and ethnic identity on the basis of what he called the "new idealism" (*shinrisōshugi*).[99] Yoshino readily admitted that the concept of autonomous men striving individually to perfect themselves in the light of transcendent ideals was Kantian. But for him it was also Christian. His belief that Christianity stood for a composite of universalistic values remained with him throughout these years. Christianity played the role of reconciling his commitment to universal ideals and acceptance although he was a member of Japanese society, historically non-Christian. Christianity reconciled, in short, things as they are and things as they should be (*de aru—to naru*). To Yoshino, therefore, Christianity did not mean primarily an organization of churches, a community of believers. Although he continued to be a Presbyterian, Christianity for him was a set of principles transcendent of organization, and, in this sense, his view resembled Uchimura Kanzō's "churchless" (*mukyōkai*) Christianity. When Yoshino spoke of man's essential nature (*honrai*) as being spiritual, and when he spoke of the ultimate aim of government as humaneness, he meant by those terms not Confucian political ethics, but Christian values. For him these had been stated best in secularized vocabulary by Kant and, on occasion, Saint-Simon in his "new christianity."[100]

Yet it is in this equation of Christian values and ideal metaphysical imperative that one detects Yoshino's shortcomings as a voice for political democracy. While de-emphasizing the role of pragmatic organization in democracy, he retained the somewhat awkward position that Christianity (in the sense noted above) was a prerequisite for democracy. His syllogism ran as follows: most democratic countries are Christian; the most thoroughly Christian countries are the most democratic—it is "natural" that this was so; therefore, Japan must become Christian before it could become truly democratic.[101] Realities in the West and at home plainly defied that logic. Quite aside from the fact that some Christian countries in the West were not democratic, it was

[99] Yoshino, "Gendai kompon . . . ," *Yoshino ronshū*, ɪɪ, 161-162 and *passim*.

[100] Yoshino, "Demokurashii to kuristokyō," documented in Takeda Kiyoko (ed.), *Kuristokyō*, vɪɪ, *Gendai Nihon shisōtaikei* (Tokyo, 1964), pp. 236-241.

[101] *Ibid.*

obvious that Japan was neither Christian nor about to become Christian, thus precluding the possibility for democracy in Japan. Japan's national spirit, after all, came from different sources, as nationalists friendly to party government such as Inukai explicitly pointed out and as Yoshino himself repeatedly agreed by noting that the Japanese would not be a people without that spirit. His plea that the people ought to be educated in the new values of Christianity, furthermore, flew in the face of the fact that the educational system was primarily in the hands of the government, about which Yoshino had grown steadily more pessimistic. The outcome of this dilemma was Yoshino's tendency to speak of political man in abstract terms in spite of his comments to the contrary. Thus, his "new idealism" did not produce a new political personality but tended to foster the development of the "privatized" intellectual, of whom scholars in Japan have become increasingly aware in recent years.[102] On the other hand, for his predominantly non-Christian audience, his prescription of maintaining only the tie of pure morality with the political order meant reaffirming the moral values of history. Autonomous moral man, aside from the intellectual elite, was still national man, inextricably tied to a set of normative ethical values common to all—tied, in short, to the national spirit.

By identifying the transcendent democratic ideal as Christian, and at the same time admitting the logical validity of the conception of nation as an idealistic organic union, Yoshino's net impact was not to Christianize the country but to reaffirm the moralism of national ethics. Although Yoshino most certainly did not intend that his ideas reinforce nationalist attitudes, friends of his, such as Kinoshita Naoe, had warned him back in 1905 of this tendency in his thinking.

Yoshino's political thought lends strength to the often-quoted adage, originally Hegel's, that ideological liberalism is always certain to be defeated by concrete politics—those struggles between partisan economic and political interests that militate against the idealistic quest for individual freedom in a constitu-

[102] See Maruyama Masao's, "Patterns of Individuation and the Case of Japan: A Conceptual Scheme," in Marius Jansen (ed.), *Changing Japanese Attitudes Toward Modernization* (Princeton, 1965), pp. 489-531.

tional order. For ideological reasons Yoshino's liberalism could not function as the long-term "empowering"[103] basis for the organized pursuit of partisan, oligarchic interests. At the same time, on theoretical grounds it denied the efficacy of attacking the legal order that sustained those interests. The legal order, therefore, tended to persist, pointed in directions that advocates of ideological liberalism such as Yoshino found repugnant but could not correct. Such would seem to have been in part the fate of ideological liberalism as it developed within the framework of the Meiji Constitution.

Conceived in highly pragmatic and instrumentalist terms by Itō Hirombuni and his advisers, the Meiji Constitution was pinned to the assumption that rationally conceived laws could mediate between contending economic and political oligarchies in the modern developmental process. It established a framework, in short, that defined Japan's modern development as essentially non-monolithic yet controlled in a reasonably predictable manner by a set of fundamental laws. It was this highly pragmatic conception of the legal order that the parties incorporated into their strategy of expanding their power. The parties manipulated the available legal instruments to construct nationwide organizations of partisan interest and emerged in the 1910's and 1920's as major political forces in the land. Yet it was this very process developing within the confines of the Meiji Constitution that was tested by Yoshino and found woefully unsatisfactory, and it is not difficult to see why such a serious discrepancy should develop between ideology and concrete politics, resulting in the end in the failure of Yoshino's political thought to function as ideological underpinning for party and parliamentary government in pre-World War II Japan.

The political dynamics emerging from the constitutional order were being assessed by Yoshino and others on the basis of a set of assumptions that had not been essential to the men who designed the legal framework. Although both drew their ideas from German political theory, there was substantial difference between Itō, who tended to see law as the embodiment of practical reason, and Yoshino, who saw it as the permissive confines within

[103] This is a term used by Harold Lasswell. See his essay "Power and Personality," in Heinz Eulau, Samuel J. Eldersveld, and Morris Janowitz (eds.), *Political Behavior* (Glencoe, 1956), pp. 90-103.

which men realized ideal goals. While such a distinction might seem moot, since there were significant areas of overlap, still the degree of commitment to one or the other position tended to produce two distinguishable attitudes and approaches to politics in Japan as in Germany. One stressed the utility of manipulating legal instruments to achieve certain concrete strategic aims. In practice, this position was epitomized by the party leader, Hara Kei, in scholarship by the legal theoretician, Minobe Tatsukichi, as indicated particularly in his view of government as the rational and positive application of law. The other, however, tended to de-emphasize the efficacy of law, to push its boundaries as far out as possible, and to stress instead the role of "politics" as constant criticism of and protest against certain legal institutions and political procedures on grounds of perceived ideals—"things as they are not and ought to be." Clearly, Yoshino espoused this latter position, as is indicated in the explicit distinction he made between "original cause," the guiding assumptions underlying the Meiji Constitution, and "dynamic reality," the politics of Taishō democracy.[104] This reality was separated from the original cause, in his view, by time and the process of change, and was determined less by original cause than by the "dialectical" transformation toward a better world. The central aim of Yoshino's ideology, seen in this perspective, was to impute the possibility of transformation measured against an ideal criterion, into a constitutional order designed to maintain institutional stability through legalistic mediation. In this respect, it might well be that idealistic liberalism was an ideological burden for the constitution. Perhaps more important, it severely restricted alternative courses of action that liberals might have taken.

The transformation of legal institutions from a nonrevolutionary conception of "process" and "identity" required that they be penetrated and then, from within, be directed toward desired ends. At the outset, Yoshino accepted this strategy of manipulating political organization from within but later concluded that this approach was self-defeating. In the concrete, men would be corrupted by the prerequisites of acquiring power, which he admitted is essential to the life of politicians. In theory, partaking in organized politics was ipso facto corruptive of the ideal. In his defense of parliamentary government, he drifted to the position

[104] Yoshino, "Gendai shikō," *Yoshino ronshū*, ii, 31-32.

that all organizations, simple associations as well as complex political structures, precluded the possibility of democracy since they were by nature conservative. Yoshino's "new idealism" must be understood in the context of this theoretical truism. And, as we have seen, the irony of his view of moral protest along individualistic lines was that, despite its theoretically being aimed against extreme nationalism, it dovetailed, much more closely than he probably realized, with the view of some prominent nationalists of his day who also viewed rational organization with disdain, as corruptive of the individual's moral worth, and who urged protest based on the traditional intuitionist theory of the absolute moral autonomy of all individuals.[105]

Such then are some interpretive implications that seem consistent with an analysis of Yoshino's basic logical assumptions, his reasoning behind popular government, and his defense of parliamentary government in terms of idealistic individualism. Far from being a utilitarian or a liberal concerned with concrete institutional procedures, Yoshino was fundamentally committed to idealistic philosophy. His conception of nation as a popular multi-class union held together by historical spirit, his definition of democracy as a universally valid principle or absolute standard of historical development, and his view of political man as inextricably tied to a transcendent ideal all seem to point to this general conclusion.

There is much in Yoshino to admire, and his high-mindedness and his commitment to a quest for a better world are traits for which he is still remembered and respected, although less than enthusiastically by Marxists. From the angle of vision adopted in this essay, however, his central historical significance is that he brings into view the painful dilemma which idealistic liberals like him faced in the 1920's and from which they were unable to disengage themselves. Resembling their liberal counterparts, such as the roughly contemporary Hu Shih in China, they could neither reconcile themselves to the concrete processes of government nor could they attack, by using revolutionary ideology and strategy, the constitutional order that provided mediation and hence tended to protect those processes. Thus, Yoshino and men

[105] I have written briefly on this theme in "Nakano Seigō and the Spirit of the Meiji Restoration in Twentieth-Century Japan," in James Morley (ed.), *Dilemmas of Growth in Prewar Japan* (Princeton, 1972).

of his persuasion found themselves increasingly separated from, and unable to influence, contending oligarchies that used the legal instruments provided by the Meiji Constitution for such practical ends as economic gain, the acquisition of power, and the stabilization of strategic interests in Asia.

A Note on the Political Thought of
Natsume Sōseki in His Later Years

THE TWELFTH election of representatives to the National Diet, held on March 25, 1915, is a well-known event in Japan's modern history. It was marked by a campaign which flaunted the democratic pose of Prime Minister Okuma Shigenobu; by Home Minister Ōura Kanetake's forceful interference in the election at the demand of the elder statesman Yamagata Aritomo; and, as a result, by the irretrievable defeat of the Seiyūkai which, as the "perennial party in power," had since its establishment continuously maintained a majority position. Buried in the records of this singularly tumultuous election is this entry: Tokyo, 11 seats and 27 candidates; defeated, and second from the bottom, with 32 votes, Baba Katsuya. Furthermore, an examination into the circumstances surrounding this small and altogether forgotten fact turns up an unexpected phenomenon in the history of Japanese literature: a tide of democracy flowing swiftly into the literary world, and the figure of Natsume Sōseki in his last years, poling in the vanguard of that current.

Baba Katsuya, whose real name was Baba Kocho, was the younger brother of Baba Tatsui, a left-wing disputant in the democratic "People's Rights Movement." He attended Meiji Gakuin with the writer Shimazaki Tōson, was a member of the *Bungakkai* literary group, and was a professor at Keio University after the Russo-Japanese War. He was best known, however, as a critic with a deep interest in political and social problems. During the "winter" of socialism following the Great Treason (Daigyaku) incident, for instance, he did not hesitate to associate with socialists, and was on familiar terms with the members of the *Baibunsha* (a socialist fraternity whose "chief" was Sakai Toshihiko). Moreover he was in sympathy with the movement for the emancipation of women.

Kocho presents his convictions in the opening paragraph of his "Reasons for Candidacy":

The ascendancy of a people must depend on the fulfilling activities of each individual who is an element of that people. The politics of a nation must take place on a foundation of these activities. The beginning of the people's activities should begin with each individual's self-awareness as a member of the nation. Therefore, the laws of a country should not be such that they inconvenience or obstruct the individual's self-awareness or legitimate activities.[1]

He goes on to present the following reform measures: widespread extension of the franchise; women's suffrage (within certain limitations); the establishment of civil control over the military; armaments reduction; unqualified opposition to the formation of two additional army divisions (a major issue in this election); reduction of the length of military service; the establishment of a legal system which would prevent violations of human rights by police and magistrates; revision of newspaper laws for the sake of freedom of speech and thought; the abolition of the Public Peace Police Law, which prohibited students and women from even listening to political speeches, and which essentially prohibited unions and labor strikes; the repeal of business, travel, and other irrational taxes; administration and financial readjustment.

Arising in the anti-peace movement of the Russo-Japanese War, Taishō democracy directly confronted the major problem of imperialism and the expansion of armament.[2] With the abolition of irrational taxes as its economic slogan and the dissolution of clan government, along with the establishment of a party cabinet system as its political slogan, it overthrew the third Katsura cabinet in 1913 and the first Yamamoto cabinet in the following year. Faced with this danger to the ruling system, however, Okuma Shigenobu, who was bearing the brunt of the attack as the final trump in the *genrō* hand, used the outbreak of World War I— "the divine aid of Heaven"—to enforce military expansion. Although the Seiyūkai had been against increases in the army, this position had never been more than political strategy. Popular sentiment, which had been diverted to external political concerns, at this time left the Seiyūkai and its long-time policies of compromise with clan government, and was attracted to the camp

[1] *Hankyō*, 2, 3 (1914).

[2] Matsuo Takayoshi, "The Development of Democracy in Japan," *The Developing Economies*, IV, 4 (1966).

of the democratic *poseur* Okuma. It was at this juncture that Baba Kocho again raised demands which had been made by democratic factions since the end of the Meiji period, and presented them together with the new order being urged by democrats of a new era—provisions for women's suffrage and the protection of human rights, the acquisition of freedom of speech and labor rights. He was the only candidate to wave such thoroughly progressive banners. Not even Kayahara Kazan, another candidate and the editor of the magazine *Daisan teikoku* (once called the *terakoya* or *doyen* of people's rights by the noted anarchist Ōsugi Sakae) was anxious to urge universal suffrage for men during this campaign. Baba Kocho's position was at this time in the very forefront of the tide of Taishō democracy, and his backers were the people of *Hankyō*, a unique magazine of political, religious, and art commentary practically unknown even by historians of literature.

Hankyō was founded on April 16, 1914, just after the Siemens incident caused the dissolution of the Yamamoto cabinet, as a joint enterprise of two of Sōseki's followers who had been friends since their high-school days, Ikuta Chōkō and Morita Sōhei. The magazine was financed by a priest of Aichi prefecture, Andō Gankei, who was associated with Itō Shōshin's journal *Mugaen*; it began with its main strength in men like Abe Jirō, Watsuji Tetsurō, Komiya Toyotaka, Abe Yoshishige, and other disciples of Sōseki, then added the naturalist writers Iwano Hōmei and Chikamatsu Shūkō. As men associated with the *Kindai shisō* and *Seitō* groups were included (for example: Baba Kocho, Sakai Toshihiko, Yasunari Sadao, Itō Noe, and Ikuta Hanayo), *Hankyō* was gradually transfigured into a magazine of radical criticism similar to *Seikatsu to geijutsu* (whose editor was Toki Zemaro, a friend of Ishikawa Takuboku) and *Daisan teikoku*. The man leading and controlling this change was Ikuta Chōkō, who had been editor from the outset; Morita Sōhei was the business manager.

Chōkō insisted from the beginning that the magazine's criticism should be politically oriented and necessarily partisan. Time and again he affirmed the following two beliefs as the core of this partisanship:

It is only by improving oneself that society can be improved; and it is only by improving society that one can improve himself.

69

If the truth—the facts—are not known, there can be no improvement in either private or social life—I suppose this is
common knowledge. In this regard I have yet another belief:
that it is only when one desires to improve something that he
knows the truth.

This emphasis on the relationship between social and self-
improvement, as well as on both action and speculation, was in
opposition to the naturalists, who had acquiesced in current political conditions. These same ideas came to be directed against
Sōseki's intellectuals, who were then making an appearance in
one corner of the literary world. Chōkō did not avoid a battle
with even those closest to him: Abe Jirō and Abe Yoshishige, who
held self-improvement to be their major aim, were the earliest
objects of his criticism.[3]

By "social improvement" Chōkō meant the democratization of
Japan's modern society, which was characterized by an overlap-
ping of the contradictions of capitalism with the vestiges of a
feudal system. The mere sight of the words Imperial Rescript on
Education (*kyoikuchokugo*) or Emperor (*Tennō*) excited in him
both fierce animosity toward, and fear of, the emperor system. He
declared publicly the "necessity for a surgical operation" on the
problem of the widening gulf between poverty and wealth.[4] He
sought supporters for his reforms among amateurs rather than
professionals, and roused the intellectuals with "we amateurs now
holding some ground . . . [in the art world] . . . must raise our
bamboo spears and flags and make further inroads into the religious world, the political world, and all other societies besides
these."[5] Although Chōkō distinguished between himself and the
socialists ("I'm not yet ready to be placed on the scaffold."), he
associated with them of his own accord, sought manuscripts for
Hankyō from Sakai Toshihiko, and even maintained a friendly
relationship with Ōsugi Sakae. What is more, Morita Sōhei in no
way opposed Chōkō's tendencies.

Hankyō's support of Baba Kocho stemmed from the magazine's
stress on the relationship between self-improvement and social
improvement, and its advocacy of the expulsion of professionals

[3] *Hankyō*, "Saikin no shimbun zasshi kara," 3 (1914); "Iwayuru ichidaiji
to wa nanizoya," 9 (1914) and *Yomiuri shimbun*, "Abe Yoshishigekune,"
February 24 and 25, 1915.

[4] *Hankyō*, "Sakai Toshihiko ni kotaefu," 4 (1914).

[5] *Hankyō*, "Fushojiki naru chinmoku," 1 (1914).

by amateurs in the political world. Kocho was still undecided until Sakai Toshihiko, after consulting with him[6] and with his own colleagues, inserted the following notice in the January 23 edition of the newspaper *Yorozu chōhō*: "We recommend as candidate for member of the House of Representatives Kocho Baba Katsuya." This endorsement provided an incentive which swelled the ranks of those urging Kocho's decision. Subsequently, on February 12, Chōkō, Sōhei, and Yasunari Sadao met at Kocho's home to accept his declaration of candidacy.

These men then organized an association for the support of Baba. The campaign abandoned door-to-door canvassing and relied exclusively on an "English-style" speech campaign. They planned to finance their activities by taking contributions of manuscripts from acquaintances of Baba and *Hankyō* associates, publishing them as a collection, and using the profits from its sale. The Baba family had close relations with the Mitsubishi *zaibatsu*, and Kocho's niece was the wife of Toyokawa Ryōhei, a prominent personality in the Mitsubishi group. Yet Kocho chose to have no ties whatsoever with the *Rikkendōshikai*, a political party linked to Mitsubishi. He was determined to wage the campaign as an individual man of letters. The company chosen to publish the collection was the *Jitsugyō no Seikaisha*, whose president, Noyori Hideichi, was known for his propaganda in favor of the emperor system and against communism, especially after the Second World War. From at least the end of Meiji to the Middle of the First World War, however, although he was an ardent nationalist, he showed his hostility to clan bureaucracy as well as to privileged capital. He was associated with the liberalist bourgeoisie of the *Kojusha* group on the one hand and, on the other, with the fading socialists. He sympathized with Chōkō's criticism of the intellectuals and had already become thoroughly familiar with Kocho's views and personality. His support of Baba, he said, was "I believe, the realization of one of my ideals," and he agreed to accept the publishing job.

The campaign activities of the supporting association were the distribution by mail of an outline of Kocho's political views with a letter of endorsement, and the holding of speech meetings. The endorsement was signed by 20 people, beginning with Natsume Sōseki. Nakazawa Rinsen, Hasegawa Tenkei, Morita Sōhei, and Yosano Tekkan were among those who spoke at the group's two

[6] Baba Kocho, *Meiji bundan kaiko* (Tōkyō, n.d.), p. 176.

meetings. Meanwhile, the printing of the collection was completed in an exceptionally short time, and on March 12 the large volume (1,127 pages) comprising manuscripts contributed by 81 authors appeared as *Kocho Baba Katsuyashi rikkōhōkoen gendaibushū* (A modern collection in support of the candidacy of Kocho Baba Katsuyashi).

In the introductory remarks to the *Gendaibunshū* it is pointed out that there were a number of people who, although they approved of this enterprise, did not have the time to make a contribution.[7] The names of the contributors nevertheless constitute a surprisingly colorful array of personalities: disciples of Sōseki,[8] the naturalists,[9] the *Myojo Subaru* group,[10] members of the *Seitōsha*,[11] dramatists,[12] writers new to the literary world,[13] *Baibunsha* members,[14] and critics.[15] The literary column of the *Jijishinpo*, March 1915, gave the following review: "The undertaking of this enterprise is indeed a testimony to the revolution in our intellectual world. Shall we call it a footstep in a lonely valley or something unheard of in previous ages? There are no words to describe it. It is a masterpiece which will retain its value in the literary world for many years to come as the greatest product of the Taishō Restoration."

Yet there were some literary people who, despite their own progressive inclinations, did not approve of Kocho's candidacy. Miyake Setsurei, for instance, wrote in the *Tōkyō asahi shimbun*, February 15, that in politics Baba Kocho and others "are not, I think, complete amateurs. But they do make me uneasy, in that without becoming representatives they cannot practice their

[7] Matsuo Takayoshi, "1915 no bungakkai no aru fukei to saibannen no Sōseki," *Bungaku* (October, 1968).

[8] Suzuki Miekichi, Morita Sōhei, Komiya Toyotaka, Nōgami Toyoichirō, his wife Yaeko.

[9] Masamune Hakucho, Tayama Katai, Tokuda Shūsei, Hasegawa Tenkei, Katawami Shin.

[10] Yosano Tekkan, his wife Akiko, Kitahara Hakushu, Yoshi Isamu.

[11] Hiratsuka Raicho, Itō Nōe.

[12] Osanai Kaoru, Mayama Seika, Nagata Kideo, Matsui Shōyō, Okamoto Kidō, Akita Ujaku.

[13] Sato Haruo (Chōkō's disciple), Kubata Mantarō, Kanō Sakujirō.

[14] Sakai Toshihiko, Morita Yūshu, Yasunari Sadao.

[15] Uchida Rōan, Wadagaki Kenzo, Tanaka Suiichirō, Naruse Mukyōku, Nakazawa Rinsen.

72

fundamental beliefs and ideals." The anarchist Ōsugi Sakae, who was friendly with both Baba and Ikuta, pointed out in an article, *"Kojinshugisha to seijiundō"* (Individualism and Political Movements), appearing in the April 1915 issue of *Waseda bungaku*, that although the "pioneering movements" of Baba, Ikuta, and Yasunari were commendable, from a syndicalist viewpoint these men were uncritical of parliamentary government itself. The total absence of the names of the *Shirakaba* group from the collection indicates the coolness with which that group looked upon Baba's candidacy. It can also be considered a manifestation of the care with which the group avoided becoming deeply involved in political criticism.

Despite an atmosphere of general derision engendered by contemporary journalism, and although well aware of the criticisms already mentioned, the majority of the 81 contributors to the *Gendaibunshū* did venture to display their sympathy with Kocho's activities. Here we are primarily interested in the first essay of the collection, Natsume Sōseki's *"Watakushi no kojinshugi"* (My Individualism). In the eleventh volume of the most authoritative edition of Soseki's works, Iwanami Shoten's 1966 publication, *Sōseki zenshū*, it is noted that this essay, originally a manuscript of a speech at the Peers School (*Gakushuin*), appeared in the March 22, 1915, issue of the *Hojinzasshi*. Yet the *Gendaibunshū* was released ten days prior to this, on March 12. The date is substantiated by advertisements in various newspapers, and it is quite clear, therefore, that the first appearance of Sōseki's famous essay was in the *Gendaibunshū*. According to the collection's introductory remarks, which explain that the position of the essays represents the order in which authors agreed to contribute, Sōseki led the rest of the writers in the service of Baba Kocho. This fact becomes especially significant in conjunction with our earlier observation that Sōseki's name appeared at the head of Kocho's letter of endorsement. It should provide us with a strong clue for approaching the essential political thought of Sōseki's later years.

What was it, then, that brought Sōseki into this undertaking? The first thing that comes to mind is the overture by Sōseki's disciples, Ikuta Chōkō and Morita Sōhei.[16] When they requested

[16] I refer to Chōkō as Sōseki's disciple because the point is emphasized by historians of Japanese literature. On this point see the essay in *Bungaku* cited above.

his support of Kocho, Sōseki surely knew that Ōsugi Sakai and some socialists had already given their endorsement. It is also certain that Sōseki knew of the heated exchange between Chōkō and Abe Yoshishige regarding the relationship of social- and self-improvement which was running in the *Yomiuri shimbun*. His support of Kocho was an act based on a consideration of these conditions; he did not simply embrace the proposal made by Sōhei and Chōkō. All Sōseki's disciples and critics would agree that he was neither so rash nor unworldly as to go along with these men without knowing the ideas upon which they were acting. Even more light is shed on his position if we notice that Abe Jirō and Abe Yoshishige, both of whom were criticized by Chōkō, were not contributors to *Gendaibunshū*. At least at this stage Sōseki stood on the side of Chōkō and his sympathizer Sōhei.

A second fact to be considered is the personal relationship between Sōseki and Kocho. We learn from six of Sōseki's letters in the *Zenshū* and from Kocho's memoirs that they were in fact quite close from 1907 on. Still, we might wonder if Sōseki supported Kocho merely out of friendship. If other men with whom he is presumed to have been similarly friendly, Uchida Rōan or Togawa Shukotsu, had been candidates, would he have taken the same attitude? Sōseki's contribution to *Gendaibunshū* and his signing of Kocho's endorsement constituted, with only slight exaggeration, a political commitment. As was mentioned previously, in literary circles of the time there was a mood unfavorable to Kocho's candidacy, and even Miyake Setsurei raised objections; therefore, Sōseki's commitment seems clearly to indicate his political attitude. His endorsement of Kocho was an act in support of his own political convictions.

Sōseki's contribution of this particular essay, "*Watakushi no kojinshugi,*" further attests to the inclinations we have been discussing. Another item of considerable interest is that the stage on which Sōseki gave his famous speech on November 15 of the previous year was the *Gakushuin*, an educational institution for the children of the nobility and the rich, a group toward which he had so clearly shown an aversion in his earlier *Nihyakutōka*. Having requested that he not be introduced by his title, Doctor of Letters, Sōseki appealed as an individual commoner to the children of the privileged classes to exercise self-control in matters of political and financial power. He concluded with an affirmation that "compared to individual morality, national morality is by far an inferior thing." It seems fair to suppose that Sōseki's contribution of this manuscript to the *Gendaibunshū* prior to its appearance in the *Gakushuin's* journal *Hojinzasshi* was a candid expression of his sympathy to others in opposition to power.

Insofar as Sōseki supported and encouraged the demands of Baba Kocho's very progressive democracy, the political thought of his late years seems unexpectedly radical. If one reads his fiction, letters, diary, and other writings composed during 1905–1906, however, there is nothing at all unexpected about it. There is simply a confirmation that the passion of ten years before had not yet disappeared from his heart.

Sōseki's pronouncements of ten years earlier distinctly show him attempting to preserve the individual's character and rights in the face of control by an absolutist emperor system and the *zaibatsu*: "It used to be a world in which anything could be done with the influence of His Majesty. It is now a world where the impossible is impossible *even with* His Majesty's influence. Next will no doubt come an age when things are impossible *because of* His Majesty's influence.[17] In his novel *Wagahai wa neko dearu* this sentiment, already famous as a fragment, becomes a speech of Dokusenkun in almost exactly the same form.[18] "It is easy to be respected by one's contemporaries. It is enough to be born into the Imperial family, or as nobility, or into wealth, or power. If one becomes any of these he is soon respected. In a hundred years, however, there is no one who will respect him."[19] Then in *Nihyakutōka*, Kei-san, whom Sōseki describes as a character meant to be a model for modern youth, says: "That French Revolution was only natural. As violent as the rich and the nobles were, it's natural that it turned out as it did."[20] What is of special note here is that Sōseki was denying Meiji society while he was still in it.

Until recently this was a world in which a government minister could do anything, however willful. Therefore even today people think a man who becomes a minister can do whatever he wishes. Since everything under the influence of Iwasaki

[17] *Zenshū*, 13, 170. [18] *Zenshū*, 1, 516.
[19] *Zenshū*, 13, 196. [20] *Zenshū*, 2, 599.

[head of Mitsubishi *zaibatsu*] has until now turned out just as planned, today people also think nothing impossible with that influence. Both ministers and the Iwasaki people are considered identical. . . . Looking from a distance at the past forty years, they seem but a moment. Don't people realize the so-called elder statesmen will be reduced to beings no bigger than *fleas*? The work of Meiji is beginning now. Up to now it has been a world of luck, a time of preparation. If there is such a thing as a truly great man, one who should be called a hero of the Meiji era, he will appear hereafter. Those who do not recognize this, who think the forty years of Meiji a period of great success for the undertakings of the Restoration, and who see themselves alone as meritorious and exemplary retainers are sick with stupidity, pride, and madness. There is not one person in the past forty years who could be a model. I am certainly not so cheap as to take you [ministers and Iwasaki] as models.[21]

It is difficult to discover as thorough a contemporary disavowal of the achievements of the Meiji *genrō* and *zaibatsu*. In his novel *Nowake*, Sōseki has Shirai Doya speak in this same vein and conclude that the forty years of Meiji were "either the senile past or the juvenile." The author then goes on to have him condemn a world in which money is omnipotent.[22] Sōseki made a well-known remark to Suzuki Miekichi during this period (October 26, 1906): "I want to write literature with a passion like that of the Restoration patriots." This passion was the same that sought to destroy the control of the privileged classes. In *Nihyakutōka*, completed shortly before this letter, Keisan is obviously saying the same thing: "The principal aim of us who live in this world is, I suppose, to beat to death the monsters of this civilization—nobility and wealth—and to give some consolation to the common man who has neither money nor power."[23] Three days before his letter to Suzuki, Sōseki wrote in a letter to Kano Kokichi: "I am judging as criminals of society those agents who give rise to unpleasantness and unhappiness, and I am working to overthrow them. It is not only for myself: it is for the world, for the Emperor, for society in general that I am working to destroy them." That Sōseki's attitudes did not alter after he went to work for the *Asahi shimbun* is known from a letter to Nakamura Shigeru

[21] *Zenshū*, 13, 194.   [22] *Zenshū*, 2, 793.   [23] *Zenshū*, 2, 630.

dated August 16, 1907, at which time he was still writing *Gubi-jinso*: "I hear that the poor are eating things like thinly sliced raw potatoes with their rice and barley. Thinly sliced potatoes are what monkeys eat. This is a miserable world. The people are working diligently from morning to night, but look at that Iwasaki giant! There are some guys who spend all their time interfering with (no, planning) other people's work and eat pure rice three times a day. Sōseki's work is to attack in writing these immoralists."

Sōseki's mission of damning with his pen the despotism of the emperor system and the *zaibatsu* gave rise to a feeling of natural solidarity with the socialists. The following is a letter to Fukada Kosan, a professor at Tohoku University, dated August 12, 1906:

> Thank you for taking the trouble to send me the clippings from the *Miyako shimbun*. Although I won't join in the demonstration against the increase in train fare, since I agree with the protest I have no objections. Since in certain respects I am also a socialist, when I appear in the newspaper in the same category as Sakai Kosen it doesn't startle me in the least. Especially of late I've come to expect anything. Nothing that appears in the newspapers can surprise me.

Judging from this letter, there was an article in the newspaper stating that Sōseki had joined the railroad boycott begun on August 10 in opposition to a fare increase planned for September 11 by Tokyo's three railroad companies. It had troubled Fukada Kosan and he had sent the clipping to Sōseki. Shirai Doya's speech in *Nowake*, cited earlier, took place in fact at a meeting called to seek assistance for the families of "men taken in on suspicion of instigating the train-smashing incident the other day."[24] The Japan Socialist Party's boycott movement against the city trains developed at first into a mass meeting of citizens whose anger then exploded on September 5 into three nights of destruction. Arahata Kanson, Yasunari Sadao, and Yamaguchi Koken— members of the Japan Socialist Party—were arrested on suspicion of inciting the incident. When in the novel Shirai Doya's wife remonstrates with him, saying, "Certainly it's a fine thing to help the family of a man like that, but we'll be in trouble if you're mistaken for socialists," he shakes her off and boldly sets off for the meeting: "I don't care if we are, who cares about nationalism

[24] *Zenshū*, 2, 788.

or socialism. All I want is social justice."[25] In the upsurge of democracy following directly on the Russo-Japanese War—as exemplified by the anti-peace movement, the universal suffrage movement, and the opposition to fare increases by the Tokyo trains[26]—Sōseki unquestionably joined the socialists on the same battle-line, and it seems apparent that the socialists were aware of his political attitude. Shortly after the fifth chapter of *Wagahai wa neko dearu* was published in October of 1905, Sakai Toshihiko sent Sōseki a picture postcard bearing a photograph of Engels. He wrote: "When I read with pleasure your newly published piece, I thought it fitting to send you a word of comment. After getting your new 'Neko' I spent three nights in succession reading it to my family. I sensed the same flavor in it as with Sanma's *Ukiyoburo*."[27] Conscientious as Sōseki was, we may infer that he sent an acknowledgment to Sakai, and that he did have direct contact with this eminent socialist. It is worthwhile keeping in mind that the letter to Fukada Kosan as well as *Nowake* were written after he had probably come to know Sakai.

Sōseki's identification with the socialists disappears from the surface of his works after he joined the *Asahi shimbun*. Nevertheless, it is easy to detect in his diary fierce revulsion against this bureaucratic despotism: the story of the *genrō* Itō and Yamagata's stealing a huge sum of money from the Imperial Household Agency (June 17, 1909); the story of the swindling of the Asano family of their family treasures by Inoue Kaoru, another *genrō* (July 22, 1911); Sōseki's statement of June 10, 1912, which shows his position as a truly democratic, constitutional monarchist: "The Imperial Household is not an assemblage of gods. If they are approachable and friendly to the people they will appeal to our sympathy and receive our love and respect. That is the best way to protect them, to *keep them* longer."[28]

[25] *Ibid.*

[26] See Matsuo Takayoshi, *Taishō demokurashi no kenkyū* (Tokyo, 1967), p. 79ff.

[27] *Zenshū*, monthly report No. 1, "From the Editing Room."

[28] Emphasis added. Komiya Toyotaka, *Natsume Sōseki* (Tokyo, 1953), III, 153ff. attests that "Sōseki earnestly revered the Emperor Meiji," and "there is no question but that the death of Meiji society accompanying the demise of the Emperor who symbolized it left in Sōseki an emptiness which was extremely difficult to fill." There is not enough proof however. Komiya perfunctorily acknowledges that *Kokoro* is fiction, but in reality ignores this fact. Sōseki's state of mind in so far as we can plumb it through the immedi-

In *Sorekara* Sōseki not only shows his contempt for businessmen with political affiliations and his interest in socialists, but also takes a hard look at the paradox of "the imperialism of 'first-class' Japan"—without real strength, but attempting to compete with England and the United States by invading Korea and China. "Japan is like a frog imitating a cow; her stomach will eventually burst."[29]

Sakai Toshihiko's association with *Hankyō* was more than likely influenced by Sōseki. Sōseki had surely heard a great deal about Sakai through Chōkō and Toyotaka. Komiya Toyotaka was born in Toyotsu, Fukuoka prefecture, as was Sakai, and they had often met during their student days at the home of Toyotaka's uncle, Shirakawa Riyo, and elsewhere. Sōseki once made reservations for a party given for the writers of *Hankyō* on March 14, 1914, before its publication, but for some reason he was unable to attend. If he had been present he would probably have joined his disciples in chatting with Sakai and appeared in the same photograph as they did. Sōseki's status was such that he could have appeared with Sakai without the slightest unnaturalness. Mori Ōgai records in his diary for April 17, 1915, that he attended memorial services for Hiraide Osamu, a member of *Subaru*, and "saw Sakai Toshihiko for the first time." Sōseki probably never did meet Sakai, but it is easy to suppose that his feelings toward him were antithetical to Ōgai's.

In the spring of 1915 Sōseki demonstrated in action the political position he had laid bare in his writings ten years before. He joined in the forefront of a movement of support for Baba Kocho,

---

ate sources of his diary and letters was by no means as exaggerated as Komiya says. A look at the unusually painstaking entries in the diary between May and October of 1911, and again between May and October of 1912 shows that he did not demonstrate as much interest in the Emperor's death as he did in the Republican Revolution of 1911 in China. It was on the death of his daughter, Hinako, not his emperor, that he wrote "there are cracks in my spirit." In fact, the only items we find concerning the death of the Emperor (July 30) are comments on the accession and funeral ceremonies, which he found interesting and imposing. But on August 2 he did not hesitate to go swimming at Kamakura. He did indeed write a message of condolence for the Emperor Meiji (in the magazine *Hōgaku kyōkai*), but his reverence was limited to that accorded the constitutional monarch of a democracy, in the English fashion. Many of his fragmentary notes and diary entries indicate that Sōseki's view of the Emperor agreed fundamentally with the organic theory of Minobe Tatsukichi and others.

[29] *Zenshū*, IV, p. 402.

who had been urged by the liberals among Sōseki's followers, in response to Sakai's endorsement, and who had put forth the principles of an unusually progressive democracy. He placed himself on the battle-line shared by liberals and socialists in the literary world. Sōseki's sentiments at the time of his comments regarding his treatment by the press were exactly the same at this time, ten years later.

Some will no doubt incline to a refutation of this argument: "This view of Sōseki is too far-fetched. His support of Baba Kocho was a mere formality. In none of his works, including his diary and letters, has he left any evidence." That may in fact be so, in a nearsighted way. He did not participate in the speeches given in support of Kocho, and he did go off to Kyōtō before election day. But Sōseki was more than anything else a writer. The expression of his political intent had been fulfilled already with the signing of Kocho's letter of endorsement and his contribution of "*Watakushi no kojinshugi.*" To be sure, he did not use his political experience as material in *Michikusa*, much less the preceding novel, *Garasuto no naka*, on which he was working during the campaign. But what of his final work, *Meian*, of a year later? Asukai Masamichi, in his refreshing effort, "Concerning *Meian*" is of the opinion that Sōseki "worked his way consciously and unconsciously from the social indignation of *Nowake* to the problems of 'social class.'"[30] This interpretation acquires greater validity when Kocho's campaign is taken into account. The socialist Kobayashi, who is depicted in *Meian* as a threat to the hypocritical lives of the bourgeoisie and petty bourgeoisie, seems to be a reflection of certain socialist literati with whom Sōseki was able to become reacquainted during this election—particularly the brothers Yasunari Sadao and Jirō. One also senses the shadow of Kocho behind Uncle Fujii, Kobayashi's teacher in *Meian*. Fujii's role as a friend of the bourgeois Okamoto, moreover, bears a resemblance to that of Kocho, whose nephew by marriage was the prominent businessman Toyokawa Rohei.

There is of course no way of knowing how *Meian* was to end. But the author was the same Sōseki who had criticized militarism in *Tentoroku* just before writing it. There is no evidence anywhere that the story could not have developed to give Kobayashi and Fujii important roles, and one must wonder what Sōseki would have written had he been blessed with a longer life. The

[30] *Jinbungakuho*, 23 (1967).

conjecture that he had already ceased writing novels and was enjoying himself with poetry and painting seems less logical than the assumption that he would have gone even further into the problems of the family and social class.[31]

In the election of March 25, 1915, Kocho suffered a disastrous defeat, receiving only 32 votes. For a man who had carried out practically nothing like a campaign, however, this was a natural outcome. A question may arise as to the whereabouts of the 81 votes of the *Gendaibunshū* contributors. There existed at the time a voting requirement of a ten-yen direct national tax: consequently almost none of the general run of writers with only irregular incomes had voting privileges. Kocho's candidacy nevertheless reflected the tide of Taishō democracy in its purest form. Moreover, seen amid the clamorous debate over the candidacy of writers, the contributors to *Gendaibunshū* appear as supporters of Kocho's political stance. The mustering of so many personalities within the two weeks between February 13 and March 1 is probably an unprecedented event in the history of Japan's literary world. As Noyori Hideichi points out in the postscript to *Gendaibunshū*, it was certainly "clear proof that the literary world was a step ahead of society's tendencies."

It is significant that this election was publicly endorsed by the socialists, for the first time, and that it was encouraged by liberals who, for the sake of their own democratic goals, were compelled to join forces with them. Taishō democracy was promoted by the cooperation of these two groups from its earliest period, as were the Association for Labor Unions and the Alliance for Universal Suffrage (*Rōdōkumiai Kiseikai* and *Futsōsenkyo Kisei Dōmeikai*). This relationship continued fragmentarily during the Russo-Japanese War and expanded at its end into the suffrage movement and the fight to preserve the right to a livelihood (opposition to Tokyo train-fare increases, the movement of the people of Okayama prefecture against the construction of a harbor at Ujino, movements against irrational taxes). The liberals who had protected or cooperated with the socialists of *Baibunsha* or *Kindaishisōsha* survived even into the "winter" following the Great Treason incident.[32] This cooperative relationship was a funda-

[31] Kataki Junzo, *Natsume Sōseki* (Tokyo, 1966), p. 158.
[32] For the analysis in detail, see my *Taishō demokurashi no kenkyū*.

mental characteristic of early Taishō democracy, from the Russo-Japanese War to the First World War, and it was precisely this which virtually disappeared after 1919.[33] Ikuta Chōkō and Noyori Hideichi as well as Sōseki, in this sense must be numbered among the representative figures of early Taishō democracy. Considered in this manner, it would seem that many of the studies of Sōseki to date should be altered with respect to his political ideas.

Both Kataki Junzo and Eguchi Kiyoshi maintain that Sōseki's anti-capitalism was based on his feudal concepts.[34] Needless to say, their claims stem from an unclear understanding of Marxism and their ignorance of Sōseki's historical background. Even Miyai Ichiro's recent *The World of Sōseki* (*Sōseki no sekai*), which is an impressive effort among the overwhelming abundance of Sōseki materials, is weak in an understanding of Sōseki's political thought. Miyai cites a letter Sōseki wrote to his father-in-law, Nakane Shigeichi, from London on March 15, 1902:

> The failure of civilization in Europe today is clearly based on the extreme gap between the rich and the poor. I am afraid this imbalance has a tendency to starve or freeze to death many promising human resources every year, or leave them without any education. It turns rather to implementing the common ideas of very ordinary rich men. . . . If we tend toward the same conditions in Japan (and I believe we are tending toward them at present), it will be a matter of grave importance for the future development of labor's literacy and intelligence. Although I believe that Karl Marx's theories have faults, even simply as pure rationalizations, it is quite natural that such teachings should appear in a world like the present one.[35]

Taking this as his authority, Miyai comments:

> Sōseki criticized civilization with a keen insight and a fierce propensity for freedom which formed the very roots of his thinking. Herein he was able to hold unique, penetrating, and unexpectedly advanced views. The foundation of his social standing, however, was conservative, and he never, throughout

[33] Matsuo, "The Development of Democracy in Japan."
[34] Kataki, *ibid.*, p. 23, and Eguchi, Kiyoshi, "Sōseki sanbo yawa," in *Waga bungaku hanseiki* (Tokyo, 1953).
[35] Miyai Ichirō, *Sōseki no sekai* (Tokyo, 1962), p. 47.

his life, was able to say more, politically or socially, than he does in the letter to Nakane.[36]

Sōseki's letter does indeed take the view of the ruling class. But at a time when Japan's imperialism was finally becoming established, apart from a handful of socialists there were very few people who could be judged as progressive as Sōseki, who had early pointed out the contradictions of the imperialist trend. Even a man like Kinoshita Naoe, for example, in an 1897 article on universal suffrage recognized those reasons as "the prevention of the disastrous gap between rich and poor," "the stimulation of the flagging and inert spirit of the people, and the consequent formulation of bold plans for expansion." The Alliance for Universal Suffrage was able to take a historically progressive position because its main direction of attack was toward "millionaire politics and an oligarchy" which "looked upon the majority of the people as slaves."[37] The tone of Sōseki's early discussions is indisputably of the same quality as Kinoshita Naoe's. It seems clear also, from the materials cited earlier, that after the Russian-Japanese War Sōseki's point of view definitely shifted from that of the ruling class to that of a subject. One wonders how Miyai would interpret the fierce thrust of Sōseki's earlier letter: "Sōseki's work is to attack in writing these immoralists." It is difficult to justify his taking Sōseki to task for being socially conservative "throughout his life."

As a final and indispensable consideration in discussing Sōseki's political views I want to touch briefly on the meaning of his association with the newspaper *Asahi shimbun*. Both the Tokyo and the Osaka branches of the *Asahi* played an enormous role in the Taishō democracy movement and it is no accident that Sōseki joined this organization as an influential member. It is common knowledge that Sōseki's decision to join the newspaper was, apart from the material conditions offered, influenced by the character of the Tokyo branch's editor-in-chief, Ikebe Sanzan.[38] Yet there seems to have been more under consideration than simply the generosity of Sanzan's personality, which reminded Sōseki of Saigo Takamori. That "character" also includes intel-

[36] *Ibid.*
[37] Futsūsenkyo Kiseidōmeikai, *Shuisho* (Tokyo, 1900).
[38] Ara Masahito, *Hyōden Natsume Sōseki* (Tōkyō, 1967), p. 85.

lectual worth seems obvious. After the Russo-Japanese War the *Asahi* rapidly deepened its anti-clan government hue, and the impulse for this trend resided in two men who had the full confidence of the newspaper's president, Murayama Ryōchei: in Osaka, Torii Sōsen, and in Tokyo, Ikebe Sanzan. Both of them had originally come from Kuga Katsunan's newspaper *Nippon*.

Among those who inherited the mantle of Katsunan's nationalism, but who now strongly pushed to the forefront its democratic rather than its statist aspects, were, in addition to Sōsen and Sanzan, Matsuyama Chūjirō, Hasegawa Nyōzekan, Hanada Daigorō, and Maruyama Kanji. It has been my belief for some time that one of the sources of Taishō democracy was Katsunan's nationalism. One of the men who received a stipend from *Nippon* was Sōseki's intimate friend Masaoka Shiki. It must be fully taken into account that Sōseki received strong nationalistic influences through both Shiki and *Nippon* and that these influences formed his political thought. The man who urged Sōseki to join the *Asahi* was Torii Sōsen; the man who was directly in charge was Ikebe Sanzan; Sōseki's response to this treatment was by no means accidental. Objectively speaking, it was the *Asahi shimbun* alone which sustained fully the emotions that had blazed up within Sōseki: "I want to see how long I can survive by becoming the embodiment of the future's youth, by becoming a part of society"; "I . . . am striving to overthrow [the criminals of society] . . . for the sake of society in general."[39] In response to Sōseki's misgivings—"I do not think my works are suited for newspapers"—Ikebe Sanzan wrote, "I earnestly hope and believe that your distinction will benefit in the future from the spread of the *Asahi* and will gain a wide audience." Neither Sanzan's hope nor his belief were betrayed. The several hundred thousand readers of both the Tokyo and Osaka papers were not, as Ara Masahito has assumed, "upper-class intellectuals." They were a youthful intelligentsia which had developed and accumulated rapidly after the Russo-Japanese War. They were the widespread and avid readers of Sōsen's editorials criticizing clan cliques and of Sōseki's novels, which took as their motif the search for a common human morality. This social layer was the characteristic bearer of Taishō democracy.

Many people tend to be misled by Sōseki's idea of "follow heaven, leave the self" (*sokuten kyoshi*) into treating him unnec-

[39] Letter to Morita Sōhei, January 3, 1911.

essarily as old and out of date. If he had lived to be sixty, he would have seen universal suffrage and the Peace Preservation Law. Had he lived only five more years, he would probably have confronted the Russian Revolution, the rice riots of 1918, the resignation of the Sōsen group as a result of the Hakuko incident, and the upsurge of democratic mass movements following the First World War. How would Sōseki, "ally of the new," have taken these events?

GAIL BERNSTEIN

Kawakami Hajime: A Japanese Marxist in Search of the Way*

JAPAN'S RAPID industrialization is a well-documented success story. The Japanese leadership responded with remarkable alacrity to the military threat of the West and, using the West's capitalist economic system as a model, succeeded in industrializing within several decades after the Meiji Restoration.

The technical superiority of Western civilization was easily visible: tangible evidence lay in Commodore Perry's ships, whose guns had pointed at the Shogun's castle. Less comprehensible, however, was the value system that had generated the West's material power. Although Fukuzawa Yukichi enthusiastically located that source in the spirit of individualism, not all Japanese shared his optimism. In particular, they questioned the implications for society as a whole of the seemingly selfish behavior that would derive from the West's emphasis on individualism. Such slogans as Sakuma Shōzan's "Eastern morality, Western technology" conveyed the desire of the early Japanese Westernizers to retain traditional moral codes while accepting only the material side of Western society.

In their concern for the spiritual dimension of modern life, some intellectual leaders turned back to neo-Confucian ethics; others experimented with the Westerners' religion of Christianity; still others floundered between the two, seeking new moral values to accompany the new industrial age. To all these seekers, their world was in danger of becoming a nightmare of irreconcilable dualisms: the West and Japan, technology and morality, science and ethics. Was it possible to follow Sakuma Shōzan's formula in the twentieth century?

Such conflicts were etched deeply onto the mind of Kawakami Hajime who, as a former samurai and a student of classical eco-

* I should like to express my gratitude to Professors Charles H. Hedtke, Michael P. Sullivan, Alfreda E. Meyers, and Darline G. Levy for their careful reading of this manuscript in its various stages, and for the many valuable suggestions they made.

nomics, carried within himself many of the symptoms of this tension. He tried unsuccessfully to find a resolution of it in Marxism.

Kawakami was forty years old when in 1919 he announced his decision to embrace Marxism. One of the earliest Japanese Marxists, he became one of the most influential. His background in European economic thought, his prestige as a professor at Kyoto Imperial University, and the sheer volume of his publications contributed to his reputation as a scholar and to his power to influence the minds of young intellectuals. Inspired by Kawakami's dedication to Marxist studies, young students came to the university in order to study under his tutelage. Some of these young disciples later joined the radical student movement, becoming martyrs to the communist cause. "I must take practical action," a Tokyo Imperial University student exclaims, in a novel about student life in the 1920's: "After graduating, I'm going to Kyoto to receive instruction from Dr. Kawakami."[1]

Yet the irony of Kawakami's life was that the students he inspired to revolutionary activity were more certain of the "truth" of Marxist theory than he, and more convinced than he ever was that they must engage in revolutionary practice. There was something incongruous about a zealous young radical passionately announcing his decision to become committed or "engage in practical [i.e., political] activity," and then going off to attend the lectures of Dr. Kawakami. The radicals' hero was a frail, soft-spoken scholar, so wrapped up in his research that he rarely left the confines of the campus. While students were fighting the police in the streets of Kyoto, he was thrashing out the meaning of Marxism in the quiet of his study.

Despite Kawakami's reputation as an authority on Marxism, and even despite his own fervent commitment to Marxist studies, he could never fully accept the Marxian world view in its entirety, as his students willingly did. Nor could he simply reject Marxism. Instead, he remained locked in a love-hate attitude toward Marxism that distorted his interpretation of it and prevented him from finding fulfillment in it. What drew Kawakami to Marxism linked him to the younger generation; what prevented him from total acceptance of Marxism set him apart from that generation. A bridge between two generations and two dif-

[1] Fuji Tomio, quoted in *Nihon no hyakunen*, vi, *Narikin no tenka* (Tokyo, 1962), p. 183.

ferent views of the world, he would be remembered after his death more as a prophet of "absolute unselfishness" than as an authority on scientific socialism.

The transitional character of Kawakami's values is reflected in this irony. What first attracted students to Kawakami's side in the early 1920's was his humanist philosophy, the very element in his thought most vulnerable to attack from more thorough-going Marxist thinkers. Tanaka Seigen, who read Kawakami's *Tale of Poverty* when he was a middle-school student, was touched by the book's theme of unselfish love and moved by its humanism. He was drawn to the study of communism and materialism after reading Kawakami's stories of the "self-sacrificing Russian Bolsheviks."[2] Tanaka later in his life led bands of militant Communists in street fights with the police.

Yet Kawakami himself was reluctant to join the activists' movement. His life style and mode of thought remained more Confucian than Marxist. He was inclined to preach morality rather than revolution; he preferred books to action; and, in rare moments of leisure, he practiced calligraphy and poetry-writing, the traditional arts of the educated samurai. Standing before his students, dressed in his long kimono, he seemed strangely out of place in the hurly-burly of Japanese politics in the 1920's.

It is only natural that Kawakami's early theoretical leadership was soon supplanted by that of younger, more committed activists of a far more revolutionary persuasion. Kawakami's scholarly perseverence, which had commended him to students in the earlier 1920's, guaranteed that he could not remain a hero to more action-oriented radicals of the later Taishō period. Nor could these radicals accept his stubborn adherence to a humanist vocabulary that, they soon realized, owed more to traditional Japanese morality than to Marx. His goals of "hearing the Way" and of living according to the ethical imperative of absolute unselfishness were as out of place as his kimono in the new politics of the Taishō period. Kawakami was slow to learn that politics was not the moral vocation of an elite, but the struggle for power by the masses, and that the way to reform society was not to reform men's hearts but to change their economic institutions.

Why did Kawakami bother with Marxism at all? First of all, he viewed Marxism as a science of the distribution of wealth. He

[2] Rodger Swearingen and Paul Langer, *Red Flag in Japan* (Cambridge, Mass., 1952), p. 39.

saw in Marxism a way of continuing the economic development begun under the capitalist system, while eliminating the twin evils he had identified in the capitalist system, poverty and selfishness. He was also drawn to Marxism because he believed that the altruistic ethics of socialism echoed his own moral teachings of absolute unselfishness, and that therefore Marxism provided a way to reconcile his version of ethics and modern economics.

Marxism, however, actually forced Kawakami to abandon his commitment to absolute standards of morality and to think instead in entirely new categories: class war, class ideology, exploitation. What is more, Marxism, in its Leninist interpretation, also forced him to abandon his aloof scholarly detachment in favor of direct political action.

Kawakami eventually acquired the new Marxist vocabulary and even accepted the Leninist dictate of uniting theory with practice: in 1932 he joined the Japanese Communist Party. But he learned these lessons only with great difficulty. His road to Marxism was tortuous. His struggles with intellectual opponents, with students, with himself; his agonizing sessions with Marx's *Capital*; and his successive conversions and about-faces—all document the torment of his indecision. If Kawakami's commitment to Marxism signaled his modernity, his doubts about Marxism revealed his lingering traditionalism.

Toward the end of his life, when his prison sentence gave him time for reflection, he decided that he was a "special" Marxist.[3] Kawakami's "special" Marxism locates him as an intellectual in a transitional age whose deepest spiritual needs Marxism ultimately failed to satisfy. This failure is ironical, because Kawakami was one of the foremost exponents of Marxism in the Taishō period.

It is important to realize that Kawakami was barely familiar with socialism when he announced his decision to propagate it in 1919. His commitment preceded understanding: only after his dramatic declaration of faith did he set out to examine exactly what it was he had enthusiastically embraced.

Two of the key concepts in Marx's materialist conception of history—class warfare and class ideology—were never fully as-

[3] *Gokuchū hitorigoto*, quoted by Sumiya Etsuji, "Shakai kagakuteki shinri to shukyōteki shinri no tōitsu," *Kiyo*, v, 24 (1962).

similated into Kawakami's thought processes in the first four years of his socialist studies. Although he devoted the first ten issues of his journal, *Research in Social Problems* (*Shakai kagaku kenkyū*), to an exposition of historical materialism, he showed scant knowledge of the dialectic mode of thought. Since his major interest lay in Marxian economics, he concentrated on Marx's critique of the operation of economic laws in capitalist society, ignoring the more basic philosophical underpinnings of Marx's economic theories. His interpretation of the evolution of social-ism was essentially "idealistic": not the play of "contradictions" within society, but the play of ideas within the minds of men had contributed, in Kawakami's explanation, to the dawn of the socialist era.

This interpretation governed Kawakami's lectures on economic theory at Kyoto Imperial University and formed the basis of his *Historical Development of Capitalist Economics* (*Shihonshugi keizai no shiteki hatten*), published in 1923. Here he described Marx as the last in a long line of economic theorists beginning with Adam Smith. The heroes of the book were John Ruskin and John Stuart Mill, whom Kawakami treated as forerunners of so-cialism, because they had led the fight against classical econom-ics by repudiating the private-profit motive. Mill had made the important discovery that the distribution of wealth, unlike its production, depended on the laws and customs of society, and not on certain "iron laws" of nature. He had shown that it was possible for the government to intervene in order to effect a more equal distribution of wealth, because the question of how income was distributed depended ultimately on how men believed it *should* be distributed.[4]

Thus, Kawakami explained the evolution of socialism by the moral awakening of economists, rather than by the working of the laws of history. Socialism, for him, was an idea, a moral breakthrough that had permitted a subsequent "scientific" break-through in economics. He did not attribute moral philosophies to any particular class, nor did he consider the emergence of social-ism to be an outcome of contradictions within the economic order.

This tendency to ignore the materialist basis of moral ideas points up the traditional Japanese side of Kawakami's charac-

[4] See Robert L. Heilbroner's discussion of J. S. Mill's importance in *The Worldly Philosophers* (New York, 1965), pp. 107-109.

ter. In the light of his personal preoccupation with moral values, his eagerness to view socialism as the product of human conscience, rather than class warfare, is understandable. But having professed to being a Marxist, a realist, and a student of historical materialism, how could Kawakami confidently publish a history of classical economic thought which featured bourgeois heroes in leading roles and ignored the material circumstances of their existence?

The answer lies in Kawakami's belief in the existence of two truths, a scientific truth and a moral truth. Although he had converted to Marxism, he did not yet comprehend the doctrine of historical materialism, and, therefore, he did not yet appreciate the all-embracing nature of the Marxian world view. For this reason, he did not recognize the total intellectual commitment demanded of him as an adherent to Marxism, any more than he recognized the political commitment demanded of him. Rather than choose between the idealist and materialist views of history, he accepted both, straddling two mutually exclusive philosophies.

Kawakami's blindness was revealing. It exposed him as an outmoded humanist struggling to impart his values to the new, modernizing Japanese society. Whereas he called himself a Marxist, others labeled him a "seeker of the Way" (*kyūdōsha*). Kawakami suffered from what another Marxist, Sakai Toshihiko, once diagnosed as the "difficult-to-renounce disease of humanism."[5] More accurately, both the Marxists and Kawakami were humanists. The trouble was that Kawakami's brand of humanism differed from the Marxists' in several important ways. Both sought to rescue men from impoverishment so that they would be free to become truly human. But their definitions of the truly free human being radically differed.

Marx dreamed of a society of "whole men," "well-rounded men," freed physically from economic bondage and spiritually from their own acquisitive urges. These were not specialists, assembly-line button-pushers. Rather, enjoying the full "totality of human activities," they could find fulfillment in self-gratifying, creative work.[6] They would no longer be alienated from the

[5] Sakai Toshihiko, "Gendai shakaishugi no mottomo osorubeki kekkan," *Kaihō*, 1 (June, 1919), quoted by Furuta Hikaru, *Kawakami Hajime* (Tokyo, 1959), p. 121.

[6] Richard Tucker, *Philosophy and Myth in Karl Marx* (London, 1961), p. 198.

products of their labor. Marx gives us, in *The German Ideology,* a brief picture of life in Communist society. In that society,

> where nobody has one exclusive sphere of activity, but each can become accomplished in any branch he wishes, society regulates the general production and thus makes it possible for me to hunt in the morning, fish in the afternoon, rear cattle in the evening, criticize after dinner, just as I have a mind, without ever becoming hunter, fisherman, shepherd or critic.[7]

In contrast, Kawakami summed up his goal in Confucian words: "hearing the Way." Human life was for him a journey toward that state of moral perfection in which "one wants to do what one ought to do." Where Marx spoke of freeing men from class masters, Kawakami spoke of liberating them from their selfish desires. Where Marx spoke of self-fulfillment, Kawakami talked of self-sacrifice. Ultimately, their differences reflect the philosophical traditions which nurtured them. Marx's spirit of individualism betrays the influence of the French Enlightenment; Kawakami's altruism demonstrates the subtle imprint of traditional Japanese morality.

Kawakami's vision of moral or religious truth reflects many of the dilemmas of value and objectives evident in his philosophical and political concerns. He arrived at this definition of truth in 1905, several years after graduating from Tokyo Imperial University. Absorbed in a period of intense religious probing, he had separated from his wife and child, resigned from his teaching position, and considered joining a religious sect called the Garden of Selflessness (*Muga-En*). At this time he experienced a sudden flash of enlightenment which he described in Zen Buddhist terms: "I directly confronted death."[8] To this unforgettable experience he attributed his resolve to live a life of absolute selflessness, by eliminating all personal desires in the total dedication to the public good.

The young Hajime's religious retreat signified his quest for certitude in an uncertain age. The experiences of his early life

[7] *Ibid.,* p. 197.

[8] "Omoide," *Kawakami Hajime chosakushū* (Tokyo, 1964), ix, 235. Hereafter referred to as *Chosakushū*.

provide a key to the understanding of this search for absolute standards of morality and the concern for social problems. Kawakami's childhood development paralleled the growth of the new Japan; when he reached maturity, he suddenly became aware of the complexities of the modern world. Coming of age at the turn of the century, when the Meiji goal of an independent nation was close to fruition, he was abruptly confronted by the need for a new ethic to guide the new independent nation in the modern world.

Kawakami's training in patriotic nationalism began at an early age. Born in 1879, the son of a low-ranking samurai, he was exposed throughout his childhood to the nationalist sentiment still smoldering in his home prefecture of Yamaguchi, the former Chōshū *han*. Even as a boy he was drilled in the virtues of self-sacrifice. Yoshida Shōin was his boyhood hero, and examples such as Shōin's of selfless dedication to the nation stirred in the young Hajime a desire to achieve high office in the service of the new Japan.

Hajime in his student days at Tokyo Imperial University was in many ways typical of that breed of young, ambitious Meiji students, often of samurai background, who clamored for what they believed to be their birthright, a position in the higher reaches of the bureaucracy. They were patriotic and politically minded, and their careers were virtually assured once they had gained admittance to the Imperial University, the pinnacle of the nation's educational system and the training-ground for future statesmen. Their training in science, law, foreign languages, or, as in Kawakami's case, economics, qualified them for high office; their elite consciousness, nurtured by their class origins and reinforced by their specialized Western education, made them unwilling to accept anything less. They were encouraged by the popular slogan of the day, "rise in the world" (*risshin shusse*), to believe that their own careers and the fate of Japan were identical.

It was during his years at the University that Kawakami first began to question this equation of personal success with national goals. He discovered that behind his idealistic zeal to serve the nation lurked a hunger for personal advancement that did not seem selfless at all. "I came to realize that the path of economic studies which I had chosen in order to raise my status was, in the end, nothing but . . . the search for my own fame and profit, and the very opposite of absolute unselfishness."[9] These doubts about the motives behind his studies soon began to haunt the young Hajime; he became extremely sensitive to all manifestations of his egoistic nature, and acutely aware of the need to find some moral standard to govern his seeming endless desires. "So, for the first time, doubts concerning human life—doubts about how I must regulate my own life—were planted in my heart."[10]

Kawakami's spiritual questioning arose out of his sense of anomie. We can identify at least three reasons for his feeling of rootlessness. One may be "growing pains." Deprived for the first time of the security of his family and friends, he had been rudely plunged into the Westernized environment of the capital city. Samurai of an earlier period lacked the freedom and mobility which the modern age offered Kawakami; this freedom, however, brought with it a full measure of anxiety. An innocent abroad, he instantly confronted personal and emotional problems which, at the age of twenty, he was ill-equipped to handle and which combined to leave him frustrated, depressed, and at loose ends. That great flood of ambition that had carried through his many years of schooling seemed suddenly to have dried up, just as he was reaching for the top rung of the ladder of success.[11]

What is more, the evidence suggests that by the turn of the century there was no longer room on that top rung for the many ambitious candidates for political office, and although outstanding graduates of the Imperial University were still rewarded with high positions in government, Kawakami's own prospects were somewhat dimmed by his failure to achieve superior grades and probably, too, by his inability to cultivate important people. What awaited him was a petty desk job or perhaps an obscure teaching position, with little opportunity for the personal glory he dreamed of obtaining in the service of the nation.

The third and perhaps most important cause of the young Kawakami's confusion was his discovery of the social problems accompanying Japan's rapid industrialization. These social problems called into question his own career goals, and damped his early enthusiasm for Westernization. He suspected that his coun-

[9] "Omoide," *Chosakushū*, IX, 223.
[10] *Ibid.*, 218-219.
[11] Herbert Passin's term, in *Society and Education in Japan* (New York, 1965), p. 117.

trymen, freed from the restraints of the feudal class structure and emboldened by the Western ethos of individualism, were hurtling toward the goal of industrialization following nothing but their selfish desires for wealth. Was not such "selfish" individualism the cause of the poverty that beset Japan's modernizing society? Out of the young Hajime's anomie a new conception of his social role gradually developed. Such vocal critics of society as Tanaka Shōzō, a Diet representative, and Kinoshita Naoe, a journalist, awakened in Kawakami a social consciousness and suggested new goals to which he should devote his life: he would become a "social repairman."[12]

Kawakami's attempt to become a moral spokesman for his age was perhaps modeled on the samurai's traditional role as moral exemplar, but his search for moral guidance in the writings of Europeans such as Count Leo Tolstoy suggests the inadequacy of the old samurai texts in the modern world. The young Hajime's compulsion to create an absolute standard was symptomatic of the fact that, for him, caught in a rapidly changing society, no such absolute existed.

This lack of a moral code to suit the changed conditions of modern life explains why Kawakami was struck so forcefully by the words of the Sermon on the Mount: "Give to him that asketh thee and from him that would borrow, turn not thou away." Christ's words, Kawakami recalled, "penetratingly moved my heart and pierced my soul with their powerful force."[13] Soon after reading the Sermon, Kawakami literally followed Christ's words by donating all his clothes to the victims of the Ashio Copper Mine disaster.[14] Thirty years later, when he was imprisoned for his Communist Party activities, he wrote. "You might as well say that my being here at the age of sixty stems from those passages in the Bible."[15] The Sermon's message thus provided the

---

[12] Letter to Katayama Sen, in *Rōdō sekai* (September, 1902), 329-330.

[13] "Kakuhitsu no ji," *Shakaishugi hyōron*, first ed. (Tokyo, 1906), reprinted in *Gendai nihon shisō taikei*, XIX, *Kawakami Hajime* (Tokyo, 1964), p. 137.

[14] The Ashio Copper Mine incident became a *cause célèbre* through the efforts of Tanaka Shōzō and Socialist and Christian groups who rallied to the aid of farmers in the vicinity of the copper mine in Tochigi Prefecture when they learned that poisonous wastes from the mine, dumped in a nearby river, had laid waste the entire river valley, ruining the farmers' crops.

[15] Tsunoda Ryusaku, William Theodore deBary, and Donald Keene (eds.), *Sources of the Japanese Tradition* (New York, 1958), p. 823.

new moral standard which Kawakami needed: absolute selflessness.

The experience of the "great dying" was the culmination of
this search for moral truth, and was sparked by Kawakami's
doubts about whether he could put Christ's words into practice
in his professional life: "Should I . . . be an instructor in economics or should I . . . resign my position and engage in the education of the poor?" he asked himself. "Should I chase after fame
or wait upon benevolence? Should I seek profit or obey duty
(*gi*)?"[16] The moment of enlightenment, when he "directly confronted death," represented the resolution of this dilemma. It represented the death of his ambitious, striving ego and the birth of
a new self-image—the unselfish social reformer who would use
his professional training in economics to serve society.

Kawakami referred variously to his new ethical imperative as
"hearing the Way," "absolute unselfishness," (*zettaiteki hiriko-
shugi*) the "public instrument of society" (*tenka no kōki*). What
all these terms meant to him was the unswerving dedication to a
public cause. His lifelong search for the proper public cause to
which he could dedicate himself led him to assume many roles:
patriotic defender of the Japanese nation, prophet of selfless love,
explicator of Marxism, and, finally, champion of communism. In
his later years, he himself recognized what all these roles had in
common: "With an enthusiasm that makes me wonder whether
I wasn't mad, I engaged for a short while in religious movements.
This was even before I put my heart and soul into the study of
Marxism. That frenzied energy of the old religious movement
once again was devoted wholeheartedly to Marxist research."[17]

Kawakami thus saw a continuity in his life from these early
years of passionate searching for moral standards to his later
years as a Marxist. If there was one central theme, it was the
pursuit of truth: "Whenever something appears before my eyes
as the truth, no matter what sort of thing it is, I hang on with a
firm grip. . . . As long as it remains the truth for me, I will sub-
mit to it with a single-mindedness of purpose and a humble
heart—unconditionally, absolutely, thoroughly. . . ."[18] Kawakami's professional life as an economist was thus informed by his
earlier years as a religious seeker. The serious doubts he held in

[16] "Omoide," *Chosakushū*, IX, p. 223.
[17] *Gokuchū nikki*, Sec. 69, quoted by Sumiya Etsuji, p. 14.
[18] *Chosakushū*, VI: *Jijoden*, p. 64.

1900 about modernizing society motivated his economic studies and make his eventual rejection of capitalism in 1919 more understandable.

In the decade between his appointment to Kyoto Imperial University, in 1908, and his decision to spread socialist teachings, in January, 1919, Kawakami forged his reputation as an authority on classical economics. His attitude toward capitalist economic development, however, was far from unambiguous. He was exhilarated by the material progress which industrialization had bestowed upon Japan. He welcomed the umbrellas, the wristwatches, and all the other items of technical ingenuity that inundated Japan, and considered industrialization to be more than a necessary evil. Capitalism had not only preserved the independence of Japan; it had raised the nation to a higher level of material development.

Two factors diminished Kawakami's delight in Japan's progress into the modern world. One was his discovery of the social problems accompanying the new economic system: the "gap" between rich and poor. The other was the ethics of self-interest on which industrialization was based.

How did the classical economists justify economic man's behavior in moral terms? Adam Smith's blueprint for the "wealth of nations" guaranteed success provided that individuals were permitted freely to gratify their economic desires. By assuming an "identity of interests," he could argue that society's welfare was actually best served by each man's pursuit of his own "enlightened self-interest." Thus, self-interest operated, paradoxically, in the common interest (as long as the market was unencumbered by governmental regulation or interference), and seemingly selfish behavior actually contributed to the prosperity of society.

Although Kawakami tried to comprehend this explanation, he remained unconvinced that individuals were morally justified in snatching at opportunities to enrich their material existence. This skepticism again reveals his cultural bias: "Long ago," he wrote, "we said samurai, farmer, artisan, and merchant, and the merchant was the most lowly fellow [referring to the four-class system of the Tokugawa period]. . . . Nowadays . . . the merchant spirit is in style." Consequently, in the present world, Kawakami lamented, "whenever anyone opens his mouth, the first thing he asks is not whether something is right or wrong, but whether it is profitable or not."[19] The bitter fruit of industrialization was that it elevated profiteering to the plane of virtue.

Moreover, Kawakami remained unconvinced that capitalism operated in the common interest. There were an alarming number of dissonant notes in what was supposed to be the naturally harmonious society of free-enterprise society. During his days as a university student Kawakami had become acquainted with the problem of poverty. But it was not until he took his first trip to Europe, in 1914, that he realized that poverty was not simply the blight of less-developed countries like Japan, but was endemic to the capitalist system. Poverty existed, he discovered, even in the world's wealthiest nations, such as England, where he had lived for a short while in the home of a poor cultivator. Musing on his experiences abroad, Kawakami could only comment how odd it was that "in the various enlightened countries of the West, where the use of . . . machines is the most widespread, an extremely large number of people are poor."[20] Capitalism was thus a mixed blessing. Despite its inadequacies, however, it provided the only model for industrialization available in Kawakami's lifetime, and, therefore, he sought to work within it, compensating for its inadequacies with moral reform.

Could the capitalist economic system operate without the profit motive? Or, as Kawakami posed the question, was selfless behavior incompatible with the modern money economy? In the *Tale of Poverty* (*Bimbō monogatari*), which Kawakami published in 1916 after returning from Europe, he argued that it was possible to cure poverty within the capitalist system by replacing the profit motive with an altruistic ethic.

Kawakami offered an explanation of the causes and cure of poverty that demonstrated the vital link between ethical behavior and the just operation of the capitalist system. He argued that the cause of poverty was actually insufficient production caused by the demands of wealthy people for luxury goods. These wealthy persons had diverted society's productive forces to frivolous ends. As a result, luxury items were readily available, but there were not enough of the daily necessities. He suggested, therefore, that the rich should refrain from buying luxury goods,

[19] *Jisei no hen* (Tokyo, 1911), pp. 105-106, reprinted in *Chosakushū*, VIII.
[20] *Bimbō monogatari* (Kyoto, 1917), p. 127.

so that manufacturers would be forced to produce necessities for the poor. Wealthy consumers were urged to practice frugality and producers were enjoined to act like public servants, by managing their business enterprises as though they were "making a profit for everyone."[21] This theory was somewhat naive, coming from the pen of an authority on classical economics. Such moral panaceas scarcely differed from the suggestions of Tokugawa thinkers writing a hundred years earlier. What Kawakami had done was to blend a modern analysis of economic problems of supply and demand with a traditional cure—moral reform.

Kawakami's outmoded theory of the causes and cure of poverty may be explained by the dilemma he faced as a classical economist with humanist inclinations. Committed to furthering Japan's industrialization, he was also committed to solving the problem of poverty. Trapped between these two goals of national productivity and social welfare, he tried to alter the distribution of wealth simply by changing the capitalist ethos of individualism rather than by changing the capitalist institutions of production. While retaining private property and the emphasis on production goals, his solution replaced the selfish profit motive with an ethics of selflessness. In this way, Kawakami hoped to eradicate the two related defects of the capitalist system, poverty and selfishness.

The Tale of Poverty represents Kawakami's last major effort before turning to Marxism to preserve his ethics of selflessness while encouraging industrialization. It is therefore a major stepping-stone along his road to Marxism. Perhaps the most important point about *The Tale of Poverty* is that, although in 1917 Kawakami considered it to be "my greatest work to date,"[22] he abruptly stopped its publication in 1919, resolving to "wash my hands of bourgeois economics and prepare to study Marxian economics."[23]

A combination of forces drove Kawakami to repudiate his theory of poverty. Crucial to his decision to study socialism was the criticism he received from his former pupil, Kushida Tamizō (1885-1934), who was rapidly assimilating the new, "scientific" theories of Marxian economics that began entering Japan around

[21] *Ibid.*, p. 280.
[22] Quoted by Sumiya Etsuji, *Kawakami Hajime* (Tokyo, 1962), p. 155.
[23] Quoted by Furuta Hikaru, *Kawakami Hajime* (Tokyo, 1959), p. 117.

this time. Kushida challenged Kawakami's entire explanation of poverty, arguing in his newly acquired Marxist vocabulary that the cause of poverty lay not in the consumption of luxuries by the wealthy, but in the exploitation of the workers by the capitalists. Consequently, he reasoned, the basic solution of the problem rested not in the reform of individual morality, but in the reform of distribution. The solution, in other words, was the reconstruction of social organization. Instead of urging ethical self-awareness on the part of the wealthy, one should seek economic self-awareness on the part of the workers, because the capitalist profit motive could be eliminated only by reconstructing class organization on the basis of the workers' class-consciousness.[24]

On the level of economic philosophies, Kushida's criticism trapped Kawakami between the economics of production (capitalism) and the economics of distribution (socialism). The first served national interests; the second, social problems. In terms of methods of reform, Kushida's criticism caught Kawakami between moral reform and political action. Which one should he defend? Which economics was scientifically valid? Depressed by the decision confronting him so late in his career, Kawakami viewed himself as a prisoner awaiting sentence: "sitting here in prison . . . I greet the spring of my fortieth year."[25]

His need for decision signalled his arrival at a parting of the ways. Decision was demanded, moreover, by evidence of social upheaval which seemed to indicate the awakening of the mass of the people to the need for social reform. Kawakami's intellectual struggle reflected not the quest of an academic but the concern of one who had all along contributed almost inadvertently to that awakening by exposing the problem of poverty to the general reading public.

Events in the latter half of 1918 tipped the scales of Kawakami's precarious balance between capitalist and socialist economics. The nation-wide Rice Riots of late summer, sparked by an inflationary rise in rice prices, provided impressive proof of the seriousness of the economic problems confronting the nation. Kawakami's urging the government to give the people "ideals

[24] "Kawakami Kyōju no 'Shasi to hinkon' o yomite," *Kokka gakkai zasshi* (May, 1916), reprinted in *Kushida Tamizō zenshū* (Tokyo: 1935), I, 112.
[25] "Miketsukan," *Chosakushū*, IX, 381, originally published in *Osaka asahi* newspaper, January, 1918.

and hope"²⁶ was typical of his moral approach to economic ills. The government responded instead by trying to suppress the Osaka *Asahi's* newspaper coverage of the riots. One reporter was arrested for suggesting, through the traditional Chinese metaphor of a white rainbow, that the government's collapse was imminent. In October 1918, the liberal faction of the paper resigned in protest over the White Rainbow affair, and Kawakami, whose series of articles on the Rice Riots had appeared in the *Asahi*, also severed his connections with that newspaper.

The White Rainbow affair appears to mark the moment of Kawakami's conversion to Marxism. Having given up his affiliation with the *Asahi*, he felt he had also "lost the stage from which to speak to the people."²⁷ His journal, *Research in Social Problems* (*Shakai kagaku kenkyū*), became his more radical pulpit. This was his own journal, established so that he might "use to the greatest extent possible . . . my position as a university professor in order to propagate socialism."²⁸ The dramatic events of 1918 had thus confirmed Kushida's argument: the cure for poverty was not moral reform, but institutional change. A new system of economics was necessary.

Kawakami's "conversion" to Marxism signified his acceptance of scientific means to achieve his moral ends. Marxism was a new road to the same objectives. His conversion amounted to little more than the recognition of the need for men to change the economic institutions of capitalist society in order to achieve a more just distribution of wealth. Frustrated by his failure to stage reform by his old moralizing approach, he turned to Marxism as a cure for poverty. Marxism thus offered Kawakami an alternative to capitalism, promising both the unhindered development of industrial power and the fair distribution of wealth. The appeal of Marxism was further enhanced by its reputation as the latest and most scientific learning from the West. Kushida, the bearer of this latest learning, proved invincible as an intellectual

²⁶ Kawakami wrote a series of articles on the Rice Riots which was published in the *Osaka asahi* newspaper, between August 19 and August 28, 1918.

²⁷ Ouchi Hyōe (ed.), *Kawakami Hajime kara Kushida Tamizō e no tegami* (Tokyo, 1947), p. 51, hereafter referred to as *Tegami*.

²⁸ "Omoide," *Chosakushū*, chap. 212, quoted by Ōuchi Hyōe; "Kaidai," *Bimbō monogatari* (Tokyo, 1946), p. 189.

adversary, if only because Kawakami himself was as yet unfamiliar with Marxist thought. What was important to Kawakami was that Marxism was a science, originating in the West, and dedicated to social reform.

Although he had vowed at the time of his conversion to rally young people together around Marxian socialism,[29] Kawakami's major objective after that time was not to foment revolution, but simply to study Marxian economics, to determine whether or not its scientific laws were indeed valid. To this task he devoted the remainder of his life. He successfully tried to attract students to the discipline of economics by arousing in them a sense of responsibility for the cure of poverty and instilling in them the belief that the cure most probably lay in Marxian economics.

But, if Kawakami had abandoned moral reform in favor of institutional change, he had by no means banished moral issues from the realm of relevant discourse. The problem of morality seemed to persist in his thinking, not only as an end for action, but as an end in itself. His interest in the science of Marxism was colored by his primary commitment to morality. Kawakami's interest in men and their moral ideas explains why he continued to dwell lovingly on the biographical details of the economists he introduced in his lectures and published works even after his conversion. This interest also explains why he encouraged aspiring economics students to read the writings of John Stuart Mill. What fascinated Kawakami, as a recent convert to Marxism, was why the new economics of distribution had emerged from the solidified mass of classical economic theory to liberate men at last from submission to the "iron laws" of capitalist production. He was absorbed in describing how the personal histories of the precursors of socialism, such as Mill, had led them to turn against classical economics. His popular series of lectures narrated the triumph of "altruistic ethics," and neglected the analysis of economic forces.

Kawakami sought to create a new society based on the altruistic principles of Mill and guided by the scientific knowledge of Marx. These two men represented the two sides of Kawakami's personality, and symbolized the dualism that had haunted his life: humanism and scientism. In his loyalty to both men, Kawakami tried to close the gap between them. This relentless effort

[29] *Jijoden*, p. 136.

to reconcile morality and economics was the Sisyphean task he inherited as an intellectual in a transitional age, bridging two cultures and two different definitions of truth.

It was not until the middle of the 1920's that Kawakami abandoned his unorthodox version of Marxism in favor of the materialistic world view of his critics. Not until the end of the 1920's did he exchange his academic detachment for ideological commitment. Again it was Kushida Tamizō and also Fukumoto Kazuo (b. 1894) who pushed Kawakami in a more radical direction. Kawakami would probably have remained a moderate socialist reformer had not Kushida thrust the demanding logic of Marxism before him. Fukumoto's criticism pushed him even further, prodding him on to revolutionary practice. Kawakami credited both men with pointing him in the right direction, and spoke disparagingly of himself as a "sandwich man," a mere popularizer of "vulgar" Marxism: "the many essays concerning Marxism which I had come to write up until this time [around 1926] were all very far from a true understanding of Marxism."[30]

Kawakami's *History of Capitalist Economics*, published in 1923, reflected his doctrinal ambivalence, and Kushida's vehement denunciation of the book one year later forced Kawakami to reexamine his interpretation of Marxism and to master the doctrine of historical materialism. Kawakami never forgot how Kushida, "pounding vigorously on the big desk,"[31] delivered his furious attack on Kawakami's understanding of Marxism, singling out the keystone of Kawakami's ambivalence—his faith in the "moralistic denial of private interests." Kawakami's appeal to men's generosity and sense of justice, Kushida argued, completely ignored the economic basis of those sentiments. Socialist economics itself had evolved out of the development of economic forces and represented the interests of the proletarian class. Men's existence determined their consciousness. All morality was class morality. Accepting this criticism—indeed, "reeling back before its force"—Kawakami told Kushida, "I'm beaten. You've got the better of me. I must correct my scholarship again."[32]

[30] "Omoide," *Chosakushū*, IX, 182.   [31] *Jijoden*, pp. 115-118.
[32] *Ibid.* For Kushida's criticism of Kawakami, see Kushida Tamizō, "Shakaishugi wa yami ni mensuru ka hikari ni mensuru ka," *Kushida Tamizō zenshū*, I, 178-218, originally published in *Kaizō* (July, 1924).

In the years following this attack, Kawakami believed that he
had reached a complete understanding of Marxist theory: "After
the publication of the *Historical Development of Capitalist Economics* . . . I solved my 'twenty-year-old exercise—contempla-
tion—concerning selfish activity.' By this I mean I finally separated religion from the world of science."[33]

Kawakami's acceptance of "science" did seem complete. The
studies which he published after 1924 showed an increasing
familiarity with Marxist categories of thought. These studies were
free of references to such ideas as absolute truth or absolute
unselfishness, and to heroes such as Mill and Ruskin. Beginning
in 1927, Kawakami based his lectures on economic theory on
Capital's description of the laws of capitalist society.

Although Kawakami succeeded in separating "religious truth"
from "scientific truth" in his formal research, he still could not
discard altogether that belief in the separate reality of the inner
life that he had held since early manhood. The moment of enlightenment he had experienced in his youth served as a constant reminder that outside history there existed another realm
of reality which escaped Marxian economic analysis. To this extent, science yielded to personality. Kawakami made merely a
formal peace with his Marxist critics. He remained ensnared by
what Marx or Lenin might have called the myths of idealism.
But perhaps Marx and Lenin were heartier souls. Marx never
understood the inner conflicts that tortured his own romantic
contemporaries. His mind, writes Sir Isaiah Berlin,

> was made of stronger and cruder texture; he was insensitive,
> self-confident, and strong-willed; the causes of his unhappiness
> lay wholly outside him. . . . His inner life was tranquil, uncom-
> plicated and secure. . . . [He] looked upon moral or emotional
> suffering, and spiritual crises, as so much bourgeois self-indul-
> gence . . . like Lenin after him, he had nothing but contempt
> for those who, during the heat of battle, . . . were preoccupied
> with the state of their own souls.[34]

There was no room for a moralist like Kawakami in Marx's dis-
passionate science.

Yet Kawakami's final resistance to Marxist science was expressed in a subtle fashion. Prevented by the discipline of scien-

[33] *Jijoden*, p. 125.
[34] *Karl Marx* (New York, 1959), pp. 154-155 and p. 272.

tific socialism from allowing his subjectivism to spill over onto the pages of economic analysis, he took to using the introductions to his Marxian studies to explain to his readers the course of his long, painful road to Marxism. The autobiography was his final effort to reintroduce his ethics (and himself) into his scientific research. Begun as a narrative of how he "entered the gates of Marxism," it trailed off into a description of his spiritual wanderings. The story of Japan's social revolution was subordinated to the story of Kawakami's spiritual quest. This tendency to glorify his own inner struggle at the expense of the class struggle led to the unorthodox meaning he ascribed to his political activities on behalf of the proletarian movement. Kawakami defended his reluctant decision to engage in revolutionary practice in the terms of his old vocabulary of selflessness.

Kawakami's baptism in the turbulent waters of class warfare resulted from Fukumoto's criticism of his Marxian studies. Fukumoto challenged Kawakami on two counts: the first, that he did not understand dialectical materialism; the second, derived from the first, that he failed to perceive the essential connection between theoretical formulation and practical activity.[35] To verify his mental construct of the world, Fukumoto argued, the Marxist must interact with that world. For Fukumoto, the "Japanese Lenin," this meant that the scientific theories of Marxism had to be tested on the battlefield of revolutionary practice.

Kawakami was little inclined to agree. Economics had been an academic pursuit with him for so long, and objectivity and scholarly caution had become such an ingrained habit, that he hesitated to accept the Leninist theory of knowledge without careful scrutiny of it. "I do not scorn those men who throw themselves into practical movements," he explained, "but I think that by remaining outside, I can avoid the pitfalls that practitioners are prone to, and keep a scientific detachment while observing the facts."[36] This intense dedication to scholarship in the service of society was Kawakami's way of making his professional life morally meaningful. With a similar intensity, he noted in his autobiography, he had pursued religious truth in his university days. But now he was informed that such academic fervor was

[35] Furuta Hikaru, *Kawakami Hajime*, pp. 140-141.
[36] *Shakai kagaku kenkyū*, XL, sec. 2, quoted by Fukumoto Kazuo, *Yuibutsu shitan no tame ni* (Tokyo, 1928), pp. 348-349.

not sufficient to attain any of his goals: he could neither discover the truth, nor change society, nor, for that matter, morally justify his life without actively participating in the revolution.

Fukumoto's argument could not be ignored. Arriving home from Germany in 1924, his steamer trunk filled with the works of Lenin, Fukumoto could lay claim to being the carrier of the most up-to-date and authentically scientific Marxist learning. His special vocabularly soon became popular among enthusiastic student followers, who were impressed by his alleged mastery of dialectical materialism.[37] His message, however, was a simple one. Following Lenin's example, he called for the unity of theory and practice, and with that end in mind, set out to revive the recently dissolved Communist Party. With the original party-founders in jail, the young newcomer rapidly succeeded in gaining leadership of the Communist movement.

Fukumoto's expertise quickly disqualified Kawakami as a theoretical guide, undermining his influence over the students. Yet Kawakami was not easily won over to the activists' side. Consistent with his scholarly scruples, he began to study Soviet Marxism, mulling over Fukumoto's criticism for two years before agreeing with him in 1927 that "in human praxis alone lies the criterion of the truthfulness of any theory."[38] Political action thus became the logical, though disagreeable, conclusion of his search for scientific truth.

Allegiance to scientific truth, however, was not the sole source of Kawakami's decision to engage in revolutionary practice. Not all Japanese Marxists found it necessary to become politically engaged. Even Kushida, Kawakami's theoretical adversary, urged him to avoid the political arena: "Working shut up in your study is definitely not opposed to Marxism," he told him. "I think you, of all people, should do just that."[39] Fukumoto's exhortations had been convincing, but a deeper and more powerful force than "scientific consciousness" propelled him into action.

Kawakami participated in the proletarian movement to prove that he was modern. The symbol of his modernity was the two-piece Western business suit he wore in place of his Japanese

---

[37] Furuta, *Kawakami Hajime*, p. 140.

[38] *Shakai kagaku kenkyū*, LXXVIII (March, 1927), 18.

[39] Ōuchi Hyōe and Kojima Yūma, "Kawakami Hajime to Kushida Tamizō," appendix to Kushida Tamizō, *Shakaishugi wa yami ni mensuru ka hikari ni mensuru ka*, pp. 290-291.

kimono when he appeared at political rallies or spoke before labor union groups. But his tortured justification of his political activity in ethical terms exposed him as an antique, dressed like a revolutionary but still more concerned with the motives of his behavior than with the outcome of the class struggle.

Political action provided Kawakami with a new definition of ethical behavior; it was a modern equivalent of his old moralism. Revolutionary practice commended itself to him precisely because it was such a difficult and unpleasant road for him to follow:

> The work most suited to me was the translation of *Capital*; involvement in such things as the proletarian movement did not suit me. More than anyone else, I myself best understood this.
>
> Yet I could not rest at ease in a life absorbed in the literary work I loved best of all, closeted peacefully in my study, shutting my eyes to the movement before me. Someone engaged in translation has the right to excuse himself on those grounds. But no matter how necessary I told myself the work was, I could not be completely at ease throwing myself into it.[40]

With these words Kawakami disclosed the sense of obligation that had driven him into the political fray. Just as, in his youth, he had repudiated the "selfish" motives behind his academic study of classical economics and joined the Selfless Love movement, so now, thirty years later, he left his sequestered study of Marxism, to join the Communist movement. It is striking testimony to the continuity of Kawakami's life and the transitional quality of his Marxist thought, that he celebrated his membership in the Japanese Communist Party as the culmination of a lifelong exercise in selflessness.

All the conflicting forces at play in Kawakami's personality met in the Japanese Communist Party. Through his martyred participation in the party he simultaneously completed his long evolution as a Marxist and as a "hearer of the Way." He satisfied his scientific consciousness by engaging in revolutionary practice, but in so doing he also fulfilled his ethical imperative of self-denial. While officially stamped with the seal of authenticity as a bona

[40] *Jijoden*, pp. 166-167.

fide Marxist, he privately acted out his own commitment to the ethics of absolute selflessness. Membership in the party, which resulted in imprisonment, thus represented for Kawakami the reconciliation of the moral and scientific truths he had pursued throughout his life.

Like a man with one foot on each bank of a river, Kawakami tried to bridge two cultures and two views of learning. On one side lay the traditional view of learning as moral cultivation. On the other side lay the demands of the modern social sciences for a value-free body of knowledge. To stay on the first side, Kawakami had to renounce the scientism that modernity implied; to cross over to the other side, he had to surrender the moralism that tradition demanded. But he was compelled by reason to join these two opposites.

It was Kawakami's frantic task as a Westernizer to acquire in one lifetime familiarity with a range of learning that European thinkers in a number of countries had accumulated over a period of several generations: British economics, German Marxism (and the Hegelian philosophy that preceded it), and Russian communism. The account of his academic career, strewn with discarded ideologies, economic theories, and philosophic systems, reads like an internalized mental crusade: "In the history of economic thought," he observed, "I have discovered my own mental history."[41]

Yet Kawakami's significance in the intellectual history of modern Japan was more than as a transmitter of Western thought. All the while that he was racing to absorb this Western thought, he was also trying to fit it into his own view of the meaning and purpose of learning. His significance thus lies in his role as a transitional figure between two views of knowledge and also between two definitions of proper political behavior. Students translated his ethical preachments into violent political activism, disturbing their mentor, who was actually calling for compassionate government leadership. Kawakami had been shocked to learn that the young man who had attempted to assassinate Crown Prince Hirohito in 1923 had been stimulated by one of his articles on the selfless heroes of the 1905 Russian Revolution.[42]

[41] Letter to Kushida Tamizō, February 4, 1918, in *Tegami*, p. 62.

[42] The article, "Dampen," appeared in the April, 1921, issue of the magazine *Kaizō*. Although this issue had been banned, the would-be assassin came across a copy of it two years later. For a brief description of the assassina-

With T. S. Eliot he might have protested, "That is not what I meant at all. That is not it, at all."[43]

Few appreciated the function of Kawakami as a bridge between two generations better than his Kyoto Imperial University students. One of his favorite students, Iwata Yoshimichi, used the following words to inform Kawakami of the radicals' decision in 1925 to separate from his leadership and follow Fukumoto: "A raging current lies before us. From now on we must link arms, leap in, and cross to the other side. We cannot expect you to lead us. You seem to have tasks to perform on this side of the bank."[44]

In his exhausting race to keep up with the flow of new "scientific" learning from the West, in his exaggerated reverence for that learning, and in his almost pathetic attempt to be modern and Japanese at the same time, Kawakami exemplifies the trauma of Japan in transition. Torn by questions of value and identity, and struggling to integrate the "Japanese essence" into modern society, Kawakami's life captures the torment of twentieth-century Japan.

---

tion attempt, known as "the Toranomon incident," see *Nihon rekishi daijiten,* xiv. For Kawakami's reaction, see "Omoide," *Chosakushū,* ix, 332.

[43] "The Love Song of J. Alfred Prufrock," *Collected Poems, 1909-1935* (New York, 1936), p. 16.

[44] Furuta, *Kawakami Hajime,* p. 146.

Between Politics and Culture: Authority and the Ambiguities of Intellectual Choice in Imperial Japan

"I hate politics and the belief in politics, because it makes men arrogant, doctrinaire, obstinate, and inhuman."
—*Thomas Mann*

"True politics will start only with the Second Coming of Christ."
—*Uchimura Kanzō*

WHEN Thomas Mann denounced the inhumanity of politics in his massive defense of unpoliticality during the First World War (*Betrachtungen des eines Unpolitischen*), he could have been echoing a sentiment to which Japanese intellectuals such as Uchimura Kanzō, Kōtoku Shūsui and Takayama Chogyū had already given forceful expression.[1] But the occasions were different, and the difference instructive. Against the claims of modernity Mann hoped to provide a defense of bourgeois values. The war dramatized the new modernity, with its emphasis on mass orientations and cultural dilution, and in response to this challenge Mann argued for the preservation of the essential identity be-

[1] I should like to express my gratitude to former students at the University of California, Berkeley (1968-1969) and at the University of Wisconsin, Madison: Robin Radin, Tony Namkung, Eiji Yutani, Linda Kelso, Earl Kinmonth, and Robert Stoppert. At California I first raised some of the questions touched on in this paper in a seminar on Japanese history, and at Wisconsin I organized a seminar around some of the themes. With the unfailing patience of my graduate students I was able to bring some clarity to ideas that had been expressed originally in the vaguest form, and organize my perceptions a bit more coherently than they had appeared in the first draft of this paper. Above all else, I owe them deep thanks for their willingness to participate in areas that can best be described as the edge of history. Impressionistic, theoretical, employing at all times what "objective" historians call soft data, we were able to confirm, each in our own way, the often-forgotten truism that history is, after all, an art which is always the construct of the historian and which always imitates reality.

tween public and private realms and the necessary tension between public expectation (politics) and the claims of inner life (culture). Of course, the specific objects of his attack were what Burckhardt earlier called the "terrible simplifiers" who, in putting their art and intellect into the service of politics, had denied the special quality of middle-class culture which autonomy alone confers, and destroyed the delicate balance between art and politics. For Mann insisted that middle-class society had established the separation of public and private, culture and politics, business and art, as a necessary condition of civilized life. It was precisely this separation, he believed, that produced those humanistic values which the war now called into question. The requirements of a civilized humanity (*bildung*) demanded a social arrangement by which the artist could remove himself from the contagion of a daily life dominated by practical considerations and compromises. Yet in such an arrangement the nature of public expectation provided guarantees for this kind of withdrawal, while privatization served to check the possible excesses of public demand. The artist could choose to act in the world of politics or through his art he could instruct men how they ought to feel. Bourgeois society in Europe, at the turn of the century, offered the illusion of both possibilities, but Mann expressed fear over the possible destruction of the middle ground between public and private, the total separation of the two, and the final submergence of art into politics.

If the war inspired Mann to defend the sanctity of middle-class life, and ultimately to universalize its values, his defense also disclosed a prophetic understanding of what constituted modernity and the kind of challenge to consciousness it raised. Modernity, as World War I so clearly impressed upon him, meant both the establishment of a mass society and the corporate state, and it meant either the total separation of public and private or, at the very least, the shrinkage of private space and the corresponding growth of the public sector. It surely meant the destruction of that middle ground—politics—which, it had been believed once, linked private to public in a tension and mediated between the individual and the state, preventing excesses on both sides. Finally, modernity, for Mann, portended even worse things, in the destruction of that civilization which had given the world the most humane and liberal values, and its replacement by a culture dominated by mass consumption and political totalism.

Ironically, Japanese intellectuals and writers reached the same conclusions a full generation before Mann and the First World War. As early as the 1890's Japanese intellectuals began to record a sense of futility over the apparent separation of private and public, the destruction of politics as a means of mediation, and the meanings such an event might hold for a modernizing society. In pursuit of what Kitamura Tōkoku (1868-1894) called the "inner life," its sanctity, and its importance for culture before the claims of public order, not only did a generation of Japanese disclose anxiety over the failure of inherited assumptions about society and politics, but their perceptions, taken together, offer the surest index we have to the crisis of political consciousness and conscience that marked Japan's passage into modernity. Thomas Mann believed that the ability to eschew politics was a necessary prerequisite to art and the creation of culture; Japanese intellectuals discovered that modern political arrangements provided no guarantee for individuals to act outside politics except, perhaps, the opportunity for varieties of sublimation of which artistic activity was simply one.

The occasion which prompted Japanese intellectuals to worry about the separation of public and private values was the late Meiji reform of the 1890's (the Constitution of 1889, the Imperial Rescript on Education of the same year, and the Civil Code of 1896); the purpose of such concern was to provide a defense of the inner life as a means of arresting what they conceived to be the progressive shrinkage of the realm of private activity. The defense centered on the effort to dramatize the importance of the private realm as a necessary counterbalance to the world of public requirements. It dissolved into an acceptance of public requirements as a condition of the existence of the private realm and defining its content. Yet what this development revealed was that politics as a mediation between private and public not only had disappeared but, more importantly, had never existed in any form other than a vague promise. What started as a celebration of the political importance of individualism ended as the argument that "unpoliticality," the rejection of politics, was a necessary requirement to the preservation of individualism. Individualism defined by public values gave way to individualism defined by private values; interiority—the claims of the inner life—gave way to private interest.

In transforming society into what Marx called a "national household," the Meiji government substituted conformism for action as the principal mode of human behavior, and bureaucracy and administration for the state. The structure of late Meiji social life is well known. The government reinstated communal (*kyōdōteki*) arrangements patterned after the relationships found in the family because these were known to be non-political. Thus, the non-political and non-public character of late Meiji reforms found expression in the form of a "family-state" (*kazoku kokka*), whose members were to be related to each other as if they belonged to the same household.[2] Sameness, needless to say, was the desired end; social conformism defined the mode of behavior. Specifically, men either became public in their demeanor, and sought to satisfy publicly sanctioned goals, such as the pursuit of "success and careerism" (*risshin shusse*), or, as contemporary literature began to dramatize, they became entirely private, removed (like Futabatei Shimei's anti-hero Bunzō or Natsume Sōseki's artist in the "Grass Pillow" [*Kusamakura*]), from all external associations.[3] Yet when men become entirely private it means, according to Hannah Arendt, that they are being "deprived of seeing and hearing others, of being seen and heard by others."[4] Bunzō in the *Ukigumo* embarks upon an interminable monologue with himself, and the hero of the *Kusamakura* is satisfied in the knowledge that "no good friend is living beyond the distant hills." Under such conditions people become imprisoned in the subjectivity of their singular experience, like Kitamura Tōkoku in his last years.

Moreover, living a totally private life results in a deprivation of the reality that comes from being seen and heard by others. Politically, of course, it means being deprived of the possibility

[2] See Ishida Takeshi, *Meiji seijishisōshi kenkyū* (Tokyo, 1954) and Kawashima Takeyoshi, *Ideorogi to shite no kazoku seido* (Tokyo, 1957) for full analyses of the formation of the Meiji state, as an expression of law and as perceived by theorists.

[3] On the question of *risshin shusse* I have learned a good deal from Earl Kinmonth, who is currently preparing a dissertation on the subject. Natsume Sōseki's ironic novel *Sore kara* is still the best late Meiji guide to the subject, and Isono Fujiko has written about the question more recently in the article "Ie to jigaishiki" in *Kindai Nihonshisōshi kōza* (Tokyo, 1960), VI, 81-92.

[4] Hannah Arendt, *The Human Condition* (New York, Anchor, 1959), pp. 53ff.

of action and achievement. (Takayama Chogyū, as we shall see, offered the aesthetic life as something more than food, shelter, clothing, and indeed politics itself.) Many of the characters who inhabit the world of late Meiji fiction, it should be recalled, are men who do not act. They choose to *behave*—either in the private world of art, culture, and sexuality or in the public world of career and officially sanctioned conduct. Total privatization in the world of late nineteenth-century Japan meant concealment and the concomitant that if men do not appear to others they do not, in fact, exist.[5] Whatever they do or think is without importance to others, and what is important to others is of no interest to them. From this idea arose the consistent trivialization of experience and of consciousness itself in the confessional novel (*shishōsetsu*). For the only alternative Japanese society offered was a totally public life, lived under conditions of complete visibility and exposure in the fulfillment of publicly sanctioned goals. The narrow corridor between these alternatives—complete concealment and complete visibility—offered a precarious sanctuary at best. But it was here that the impulse to *act* was satisfied by art, the creation of culture, active negation of politics, and violence.

The consequences of this crisis, what Marx elsewhere called the "socialization of man," and the growing separation of spheres was recorded in the perceptions of intellectuals and writers with greater frequency after 1890. Yet such perceptions of this socialization of man revealed a genuine crisis of consciousness; they disclosed the classical Marxian disjunction between a change in circumstances and a change in human activity. Perceptions led to the search for alternatives, and alternatives were made more urgent by the discovery of new conceptions of personality and the popularization of bourgeois ideas of individualism. The search led to sublimation, which established "unpoliticality" as a condition for defending intimacy, for creating art and culture, and for achieving universalistic ideals such as those of justice, humanity, freedom, and benevolence. Here, in this *fin de siècle* world of late Meiji and early Taishō, men discovered that what a European like Mann was to defend as a free choice (sanctioned by middle-class society)—to act or not to act politically—was in Japan no choice at all. The situation was reversed, and to refuse

[5] *Ibid.*, p. 54.

to act politically was the precondition to freedom, individualism, art, and culture, and the surest guarantee of their continuation.[6]

From the beginning Meiji leaders reserved the right to determine ideology in Japanese society. The eighteenth-century nativist Motoori Norinaga and a generation of late Tokugawa ideologues had shared the belief that the creation of ideology was a political act and should always be in the possession of the leadership. After the Restoration the new leadership reinforced this belief and resorted to the device of the imperial rescript (used earlier in the heated *bakumatsu* debate over politics) to introduce change and to meet unexpected moments of crisis. In its late Tokugawa incarnation the imperial rescript had come to be identified with emergencies; it had also grown out of a dialectic between politics and ideas in which the Emperor was increasingly associated with political authority (as against his traditional sacral and ethical role).[7] In this politicization of a sacerdotal and ethical Emperor, political activity was identified with the Imperial realm. The idea was a refinement of Motoori's conception of a divinely appointed political realm, in which rulers were really functionaries while the ruled were subjects who refrained from voluntarily engaging in independent political activity because of their love and respect for the Emperor. "Those who are below," he wrote tersely in the *Uiyamabumi*, "must always follow the dictates of the top, whether good or bad."[8] This relation between an Emperor and his functionaries who inspired submission among the ruled was later reformulated in the creation of an Emperor's subjects (*shimmin*). In this connection Motoori also emphasized the separation of the private world, what he called "self-reliance," from external affairs. Certain activities must be removed from politics. Observations of eighteenth-century urban life and his own defense of scholarship prompted him to emphasize "real

[6] This conception of "unpoliticality" is the reverse from that argued by Tatsuo Arima in his recent book, *The Failure of Freedom* (Cambridge, Mass., 1970). See also Kamishima Jirō, "Meiji shūen," in Hashikawa Bunzō and Matsumoto Sannosuke (eds.), *Kindai Nihon seiji shisōshi* (Tokyo, 1971), I, 384-424.

[7] I have dealt with this question elsewhere; see H. D. Harootunian, *Toward Restoration* (Berkeley and Los Angeles, 1970).

[8] *Motoori Norinaga zenshū* (Tokyo, 1902), IV, 600-605.

things" (*jijutsu*)—a world in which learning was free from political necessity. If politics and learning were separated, he argued, men would be able to pursue real facts which would, in turn, revitalize the spirit of free inquiry and mutual criticism. This celebration of private scholarship not only liberated learning to make "self-reliance" a condition of its practice but also freed politics from relying on scholarship. Again, Motoori put it best when he wrote: "Scholars are supposed to inquire into and clarify the Way only; they are not supposed to involve themselves in conducting the Way."[9] He could have been offering this bit of advice to Japanese in the late Meiji period.

This relationship between ruler and ruled was retained in the Meiji period and served as the principle informing all Imperial rescripts. Morality and ideology, expressions of official anxiety, were delivered to the masses as a statement from the Emperor; its contents always came as an "August Banner of the Finest Brocade," and all who served under this banner were obliged to follow its most recent request.[10] A special feature of this device was the reminder that an Imperial announcement was essentially a moral statement. Since the very act of issuing a moral directive reflected the intimate identification between Emperor and polity, rulership and absolute power, the ruled were constantly reminded of their exclusion from politics and discouraged from engaging in any kind of exercise, interpretative or otherwise, that might alter the original meaning of the rescript. This kind of identification simply precluded the possibility of free interpretation, because the act of interpretation itself would have been equivalent to participating in the political process. So careful was the early Meiji leadership that it ultimately permitted only the most simple word-for-word recitation of the rescript, prohibiting even the attempt to employ synonyms. The example of the late Tokugawa period was still close, and the memory of too many manipulations of Imperial decrees vivid. To be political really meant, then, involvement in the Emperor's realm, and a political act in this sense carried with it the charge of lese majesty. The Imperial rescript was the perfect device for a leadership that had made of the Emperor a principal who authenticated politics and who was

[9] *Ibid.*

[10] In constructing this paradigm I have relied on the very suggestive article by Sumiya Mikio, "Kokumin-teki buijon no tōgō to bunkai," in *Kindai Nihon shisōshi kōza* (Tokyo, 1960), v, 9-42.

absolute authority; an Emperor without whom politics is possible yet who makes politics by "direct" involvement.

The behavioral expectations of the ruled were guaranteed by reifying a traditional relationship between private and public.[11] Underlying this construct was a conception of a public personality whose inner self corresponded to required outer behavior, and whose meaning was disclosed in the exercise of duties corresponding to his public role. Nothing was more important for this conception of personality than the ethical education of the whole person. But moral training promised inactivity and a reverent quietism toward the social order; the guidelines for actual behavior were marked out by accumulated precedent relating to a whole range of publicly accepted situations. Throughout the Tokugawa period neo-Confucians had worried about the relationship between inner necessity (*shisei*) and publicly approved conduct (*kei*).[12] In the end they papered over the distinction with a kind of mystical good faith; inner goodness, they believed, disposed men to behave properly in the external world. This act of faith was possible because they viewed the outer world not as a polity but as an ethical realm.

Yet the great eighteenth-century thinker Ogyū Sorai refused to entertain such illusions about human behavior.[13] Ogyū identified the realm of outer activity as politics—changing the changeable—and established an appropriate division between personal (*watakushi*) and public (*ōyake*). In this differentiation he saw the possibility of conflict. He raised the question first in an exegetical work in 1717, called the *Discrimination of Names* (*Benmei*), in which he called attention to the inherent tension between public and private. Although his purpose was to restore the true meaning to original pre-Confucian concepts which time had obliterated, his examination echoed the eighteenth-century experience. "Public is the opposite of private. Where there is mass cooperation [consensus] this is called public. Where there is the person [working] by himself, this is called private. In the Way of the lords, since there are multitudes of men who work

[11] See Maruyama Masao, *Nihon seiji shisōshi kenkyū* (Tokyo, 1954), pp. 106-138.

[12] See Sagara Akira, *Nihonjin no dentō-teki rinrikan* (Tokyo, 1965), pp. 14-32; and his *Kinsei no jukyō shisō* (Tokyo, 1967), for a systematic analysis of the tension between *kei and makoto* (*shisei*) in the Tokugawa period.

[13] Tahara Tsuguo, *Tokugawa shisōshi kenkyū* (Tokyo, 1967), pp. 239-268.

together, there is also the fact of men doing things by themselves."[14] Quoting the *Shu-ching*, Ogyū firmly established the priority of the public. The Way is steady, and there are no factions or bias. "Where there is the public, there is joy and pleasure." In answer to the traditionally rhetorical question, "Even though a man is lord, will he not act privately?" Ogyū answered: "Those who rule the earth and realm and revere the public, this is the Way that is above men."[15] Later Ogyū incorporated the datum of contemporary experience and specified the importance of maintaining the primacy of the public order. In serving their interest, he argued, men might go against the claims of public expectation.[16] To provide safeguards Ogyū politicized the neo-Confucian vision of order (making an ethical realm political). In an effort to deal with contemporary experience for which "orthodoxy" failed to take account he separated morality from politics, and ethics from history, and transformed a moral ruler who ruled by virtue of his innate goodness into a politician who ruled by personal initiative and power and who relied on new social codes, institutions, and laws. Yet, recalling the stern language of the *Benmei*, Ogyū did not identify the ruler's action with private activity. Once he made this new distinction he reformulated the differentiation between public and private into what he called public interest and private views. "Private views," he argued, or "views which stem from the heart" might easily go against the requirements of public interest which are constantly changing to meet new conditions.[17] Sung writers, he wrote earlier, had argued that the public and heavenly principles (*tenri*) were identical, while private emanated from human desire (*shikyoku*), and although this interpretation was rejected by his contemporary Itō Jinsai, Ogyū remained silent.[18] But his attitude was clear and was revealed in his revised vision of loyalty. In this new version he questioned first the structure of loyalty which, by his time, thinkers had romanticized as an expression of the loftiest moral behavior. Summoning the famous example of the Forty-seven Rōnin, retainers who had decided to avenge their lord's humiliation,

[14] Inoue Tetsujirō (ed.), *Nihon rinri ihen* (Tokyo, 1902-1903), VI, 69-70.

[15] *Ibid.*

[16] See Maruyama, pp. 75-76, 106-130.

[17] *Ibid.* Also, Kamishima Jirō, *Kindai Nihon no seishinkōzō* (Tokyo, 1968), p. 103.

[18] Inoue (*Benmei*), p. 74.

Ogyū argued that their deed was simply an example of private action. It was neither loyal nor motivated by a concern for the public interest. That they should be punished he never questioned, but that such private activity was seen as an instance of unselfish motives by contemporaries was a dangerous threat to political order.[19]

Unlike his neo-Confucian contemporaries, who saw the private simply as evil and sought to suppress it, Ogyū never precluded the possibility of private behavior. By his time it was a reality that no longer could be ignored. Yet in separating public and private and establishing their respective claims he sought to provide a means by which to manage the excesses of private views. He assigned priority to the public, which was the realm of politics, rules, rewards, rites, and punishments, while to the private he consigned behavior and activity that would not in any way impinge upon the public.

The Meiji masses were also allowed a measure of privatization. But they too were ultimately required to submerge personal interests in larger political demands. This inheritance prompted the publicist Fukuzawa Yukichi to denounce the primacy of political values altogether. In his essay "On Private Rights" (*Shikenron*), October, 1888, he complained about the weakened idea of a privatized individual and the subordination of middle-class liberal rights to the larger political considerations of the rights of the state.[20] "The people of Western nations," he charged, "know about the importance of the position of the individual, the self, and understand the significance of private rights which correspond to the self. Even though we have entered into the circle of political power in order to defend the nation, in our country we have not yet seen the development of private rights. Only the theory of governmental political power has prospered."[21] By the time Fukuzawa delivered his complaint, Meiji officialdom had gone a long way toward defining the relationship between public and private in the manner Ogyū Sorai had proposed a century and a half earlier.

The ideology of leadership was associated with the public; it

[19] Maruyama, p. 75.

[20] See Maruyama Masao, "Chūsei to hangyaku," in *Kindai Nihon shisōshi kōza* (Tokyo, 1960), VI, 407-414.

[21] Keio Gijuku (ed.), *Fukuzawa Yukichi zenshū* (Tokyo, 1961), XI, 381-382.

was official and political and was called *ōyake* or *kō*.[22] The permissible range of private or personal behavior among the masses was called *watakushi*, private, personal, I. Public expectation—*ōyake*—stressed the primacy of political goals and imparted to the masses high standards of expected behavior. *Ōyake* was always associated with high-sounding purpose: public tranquility and order, fairness, and the "consultation of public opinion (*kōgi*)"; *watakushi* was identified with irregular dealings, bad faith, selfishness, personal feelings, and private desires. Despite the apparent cross-purposes operating in this relationship, it is essential to emphasize the fact that *watakushi* was a necessary adjunct of *ōyake*. No conflict was intended. But in the inevitable encounter between the realms, individuals were admonished, as a kind of moral imperative, "to dissolve the personal and honor the public (*messhi hōkō*)."

The word *kō* (the Chinese word *k'ung*) was rendered into Japanese as *ōyake*. But *ōyake*, despite its acquired Chinese associations, originally meant *ōtaku*, large residence, Imperial palace or the Emperor's house. Even in its Japanese usage the term *ōyake* never meant open, public, though Ogyū Sorai earlier added this sense to it. The sociologist Aruga Kizaemon has argued that *ōyake* in the Tokugawa period referred to group responsibilities and obligations (*giri*), and *watakushi* referred to the individuals of the group and their prosecution of these duties.[23] Such duties never called into question the conscience of the individual, but applied to the group as an entity. Moreover, *watakushi*, in this sense, never carried with it the Western sense of individualism; a personality equipped with ego and self-awareness.[24] Let us remember that by Ogyū's earlier definition, *ōyake* represented a consensus and people performing together, and *watakushi* referred to people working by themselves, perhaps as members of a group. Even so, it is important to note that both *ōyake* and *watakushi* emphasized exteriority rather than interiority.

---

[22] Sumiya, pp. 12-14.

[23] *Aruga Kizaemon sakusho* (Tokyo, 1967), IV, 177-248.

[24] See Odagiri Hideo, "Nihon ni okeru jigaishiki no tokushitsu to shokeido," in *Kindai Nihon shisōshi kōza*, VI, 11-65. Also Minamoto Ryōen's brilliantly suggestive *Giri to ninjō* (Tokyo, 1969), pp. 2-67. Although it is Minamoto's purpose to track down the elusive roots of humanism in Japan, I think he provides information for its absence.

The original meaning of *ōyake* was probably closer to the idea of something official. Nativists and *bakumatsu* ideologues saw it as synonymous with the Emperor's realm, while those things associated with the "large residence" and those persons involved in its management were official. Despite the political changes introduced by the Meiji Restoration this sense of identification between *ōyake*—the Emperor's realm—as the arena of official political activity was consistently maintained. Morality, leadership, and ideology—the right to act in the political sphere—were entrusted to "charter" members of the group which had reinstated the Emperor in the Restoration. Behind this idea lay the assumption, recently popularized by nativists, that the realm belonged to the Emperor alone and since it was official, it was the only area in which politics could be enacted; it was public but not open. Politics came to mean managing the Emperor's realm, and those who worked in this capacity became Imperial functionaries. In this arrangement there was no provision for political activity outside the structure of Imperial officialdom. People were permitted personal lives, a measure of freedom in thought, behavior, and feeling insofar as such activity did not interfere with public-official demands. In Meiji Japan this freedom usually was limited to the world of entertainment and art, business and leisure; later in the 1920's it included consumption.

Meiji bureaucrats agreed early that a combination of talent and practicality was necessary to realize the demands of official duties in public service. It was already a principle of proper bureaucratic performance to maintain the separation between *ōyake* and *watakushi*. In fact, preserving this distinction had become a moral imperative among the rank-and-file administrators. Practicality and ability, it was believed, would always dispose men to serve the public interest and suppress private desire. Inoue Kowashi saw this differentiation between public and private as the emblem of bureaucratic talent and ability, and warned that where there were officials who simply pursued self-interest, "there will be a steady deterioration in these areas, customs will be thrown into disorder and, bending to the lure of financial emoluments, they will be separated from the people."[25] Inoue's identification of *ōyake* with talent and ability (*jinzai* and *jitsugaku*) suggests another possibility. One enters the public realm as a functionary, to perform specifically assigned duties, not to

[25] Sakata Yoshio, "Meiji no kanryō," *Jinbun gakuhō*, xxiv (1967), 16-17.

act independently or to change things. It was in this sense that Meiji leaders saw practicality, not theory, as the best preparation for an official career; it was also in this context that they denounced the rhetoric of government critics as amateurish and empty.[26]

In order to give coherent expression to the relationship between public and private on a national scale, Inoue put *ōyake* into a framework of conduct (*tatemae*) and represented *watakushi* as contemporary reality (*jissai*). In this new formulation *tatemae* was the structure of permissible conduct, and *jissai* referred to the actual performance of conduct. In this way Meiji officialdom was able to minimize the tensions between public and private and the possibility of conflict. The juxtaposition of *ōyake* and *watakushi* had always raised the specter of conflict, and the tear-drenched plays of Chikamatsu and novels of Bakin were still close enough to the early Meiji period to provide vivid illustration of the possible varieties of such conflict.[27] In this transformation, framework (*tatemae*) was supposed to impart values which people were expected to observe in their actual conduct (*jissai*). The national vision and corporate goals of the Meiji state—*fukoku kyōhei*—which all were enjoined to share and to serve in the early decades of the new era, the establishment of an official national morality in the Imperial Rescript on Education (1889) and the Civil Code (1896) represent the ideological and substantive framework of publicly sanctioned behavior. Actual performance within this framework—service to the public interest—was to be the solemn duty of the subject. Yet in establishing this kind of structure Meiji leaders were in fact legislating reality, what it was to constitute and how it was to be perceived. Behavior which did not correspond to official reality could be considered unreal.

Though it is true that politics as a mediating element between public and private, state and individual seemed to disappear sometime during the decade between the Sino-Japanese war (1894-1895), and the Russo-Japanese war (1904-1905), it had never really served as a powerful alternative to governmental

[26] Matsumoto Sannosuke, *Kindai Nihon no seiji to ningen* (Tokyo, 1967), pp. 19-20.

[27] Minamoto, *Giri to ninjō*, pp. 98ff.

power. Some writers have argued that the wars had effectively destroyed the delicate balance between *minken* and *kokken*.[28] But politics, in view of the paradigm of thought and action, could never serve as a mediate zone between public expectation and private choice; it could never be independent of the conception of an official Imperial realm. And politicians, whom Tokutomi Sohō denounced as "specialized politicians" (*semmon no seijika*), were in fact functionaries who could play no other role. As functionaries—specialists—they correctly perceived as their major task simply seeing that the system which they served functioned as it should; it was not their job, as it is for party politicians in the West, either to change something within the structure or to promote some private interest.

In any case, the relationship between public and private was formalized in the 1890's. There was only a shift, not a qualitative change, in the structure of the relationship. The separation that existed between the two was merely made more explicit. If anything changed, it was the private realm. It was expanded and its area of activity was more closely defined. Yet this change was accompanied by a sharper separation between public and private than had existed before. If the private sphere was expanded and elevated in importance, greater avoidance of politics was a condition of this new status. Moreover, the private was given sharper expression with the adoption of new theories of personality, self, and individualism made possible by Christianity and new conceptions of literature and culture. But rather than equipping the private sphere with new techniques for political action, these new theories of self merely reinforced the traditionally unpolitical character of *watakushi*, by emphasizing interiority over exteriority. This is perhaps one reason why such concepts as individualism, freedom, and liberty could never lead to concrete political action. In fact, the reverse occurred. As the area of private activity was given sharper focus, intellectuals began to argue that in order for a man to be really himself, to be an individual, he had to be free from politics, from the external world of public affairs. For, if one was truly free, then he was also free to create art, culture, and philosophy. Yet to be free, to be an individual, required turning inward, embarking on an "inner emigration," to lead what Hölderlin called a life "on my blessed island." To turn

[28] Maruyama Masao, "Meiji kokka no shisō," *Nihon shakai no shiteki kyūmei* (Tokyo, 1949), pp. 181-236.

123

outward, to seek individualism and freedom, to enter public life—the highest human achievement in Western political rhetoric—where visibility guaranteed one's individuality, was never a possibility in modern Japan. To have turned outward in search of one's individuality would have risked conflict with public expectations and the state.

Even Christianity in Japan, despite its conception of the autonomous self, provided confirmation of this "inner migration" with its vocabulary emphasizing interiority, the kingdom within, soul, conscience, etc.[29] Japanese Christians such as Uemura Masahisa and Kozaki Hiromichi were careful to stress the fundamental unpoliticality of these new values leading to an autonomous self.[30] Christians invariably saw non-involvement in political affairs as a necessary condition for achieving true individuality. Thus, it was not surprising when Tokutomi Sohō, in describing his plunge into politics, emphasized the act as an expression of samurai discipline, self-sacrifice, and the suppression of personal desire. For, in entering the public-political realm one loses rather than gains both his freedom and his individuality; one enters a state of unfreedom, since freedom can exist only outside the political-public realm, in nature and within oneself.

Although discovery of the inner life was prompted largely by Japanese Christian theologians seeking to construct a new personality, it was the writer-critic Kitamura Tōkoku who gave this new conception its most coherent expression. Kitamura not only brought many of these new concerns together, but, in exploring the relationship between politics and culture, he was able to express a response and a mode of action that Japanese intellectuals were to follow down through Mishima Yukio.[31] The singular importance of Kitamura's thought was the perception that politics as mediation was no longer an available choice. Because of their class affiliation, Kitamura and a younger generation of

[29] Takeda Kiyoko, *Ningen-kan no sōkoku* (Tokyo, 1959), pp. 65-104.

[30] Irwin Scheiner, *Christian Converts and Social Protest in Meiji Japan* (Berkeley and Los Angeles, 1970), pp. 100-126.

[31] There are no really good studies on Kitamura Tōkoku. This does not mean that there is a paucity of literature on him. He has been the subject of countless literary studies, yet few have seen him as a datum in modern Japanese intellectual history. And with the exception of Shimazaki Tōson's fictionalized account of Kitamura in the novel *Haru* there is nothing that relates the torment of personality to his perceptions of reality.

Japanese raised after the Restoration had found in the liberal movement (*jiyū minken undō*) the promise of an arrangement which might establish a permanent mediation between the individual and the state.[32] Yet this hope was intimately associated (historically in Europe and late nineteenth-century Japan) with bourgeois aspirations not to only find for themselves a place in the developing society but also to discover the most effective means by which to secure this position permanently. Kitamura recognized only late in his intellectual career that despite rhetorical promises the liberal movement itself had operated on the basis of the official conception of the relationship between public and private. The men who had been leaders in the movement wanted what those in government already possessed. But Kitamura and his generation, I believe, came to hold a different vision, rooted in the hopes of an emerging middle class. Once he perceived this break in the mediations between state and individual, he turned to the other side of bourgeois ideology—to individualism and the "inner life." In turning to the private he was assisted by Christianity and its conceptions of personality and interiority. Yet it is important to emphasize that Kitamura's celebration of an unmediated individualism and the authority of subjective experience and feeling reflected the failure of class aspirations. However, it also served as a constituent element in the formation of a critical social theory that not only rejected order and the structure of authority but denied present reality for an indeterminate future ideal. As the promise of *shimin* faded into the reality of *shimmin*, as the values of the bourgeoisie were eclipsed by those of the Imperial subject, Kitamura retreated from the external world to the reaches of inner space, where as an autonomous individual he would create culture.

In 1884 and 1885 Kitamura, like so many of his young contemporaries, showed a consuming interest in the major political

---

[32] Irokawa Daikichi, *Zōho, Meiji seishinshi* (Tokyo, 1968), pp. 53-88; 107, 144-155, and Tōyama Shigeki, "Nihon kindaika to Tōkoku no kokumin bungaku," *Bungaku*, xx (1952), pp. 1-8. It has also been argued that a very significant aspect of the *minken* movement, represented by rustic gentry (*gōshi*), sought to preserve the original Restoration promise of sectionalism before the encroaching claims of centralization. I would add that the turn to self, individualism, and the autonomy of personal authority grew out of this failure to establish politics as a mediation between sectional and central interests and as the only way to preserve the integrity of local autonomy.

issues of the day. Political fervor was extremely high among the young, who believed in the mediating possibilities of political action. Society offered no higher calling than a political career: no hope was brighter than the promise to change the world. In this excitement Kitamura, a university student at the time, confessed that the great ambition of the times was not to indulge in some sort of meritorious deed but to become a great politician in order to restore the prosperity and greatness of the Orient.[33] Behind this lofty goal was the more immediate purpose, recently popularized by Tokutomi, of redressing the social and economic imbalance within Japanese society. Whatever pain this task inflicted, Kitamura wrote nobly, it would be nothing to that already experienced by Asia's masses. It should be pointed out that this cosmopolitanism was consistent with middle-class aspirations for general social improvement. "I wanted to endeavor in politics as Christ did in religion."[34]

His ambitions were soon to dissolve into studied indifference. Kitamura's abandonment of a political calling was complex, yet it owes more, in the final analysis, to his perception that politics as mediation was no longer a possibility than to youthful disenchantment and its resulting psychological disjunctions.[35] Almost overnight he found himself resenting politics and politicians. "During these years [late 1880's] I gradually came to hate above all else the degraded state of affairs in the political world."[36] He not only questioned the motives of those who entered politics but also rejected the notion that politics could in fact achieve anything noteworthy. There were those who "did not conceal their eagerness to listen . . . to discussions produced by saké," and little more could be said of the radicals who were eagerly joining Ōi Kentarō.[37] It was in this period that Kitamura separated himself altogether from "the tyranny of politics," dissociated himself from companions and sympathizers of the political enterprise, and

[33] *Nihon gendai bungaku zenshū*, ix, *Kitamura Tōkokushū* (Tokyo, 1968), p. 225. (Hereafter *KTz*.)

[34] *Ibid.*

[35] There seems to be a generally agreed-upon explanation that Kitamura was a "romantic" and this mysteriously accounts for his "psychological disorientation." Of course, there is implicit in this explanation a theory of personality that is never explicitly articulated nor intellectually defensible. The explanation brings to mind Prime Minister Satō's public condemnation of Mishima Yukio's spectacular suicide as the deed of a madman.

[36] *KTz*, p. 226.   [37] *Ibid.*, pp. 61-62; also p. 23.

announced that his hope was "to be carried off quietly to become involved in discourse dealing with climbing mountains." This expression of indifference to politics was also prompted by a growing belief (reminiscent of Yoshida Shōin's earlier exhortations) that political activity served only the achievement of meritorious deeds and personal aggrandizement but nothing more. Politicians were "destroyers of the family," "tyrants" interested only in showy fame and glory. Here, Kitamura argued that fame and glory were products of the mob and the evils of worldliness.[38] His attack would lead him on an uncertain path in search of the "ordinary man" (symbolized in his later work by the unpolitical commoner of the Tokugawa period), who might provide an example of a "heroic humanity" to stand in direct opposition to contemporary worldliness.

While Kitamura admitted that he must "understand the wrongness of such [political] delusions" as the possibility of changing things, he continued to believe (in the late 1880's) in the possibility of finding a way to mediate between the claims of the self and the demands of public necessity. Despite his seemingly swift denunciation of politics his rejection was not complete. For a moment he thought that the real problem was philosophical. "I wanted to become a great philosopher; I wanted to destroy the newest philosophical doctrine popular in Europe at the time—the survival of the fittest." He wrote that for a while he thought along these lines, totally obsessed throughout 1885 with its possibilities. "What madness. . . . I lost all hope and was plunged in such despair that I became mentally ill." His mind emptied, Kitamura began to wander around the country, and "became an appreciator of the landscape."[39] His wanderings served as the occasion for him to look anew at art and beauty. "In this time, in this time," he wrote in a poem, "there is still time for beauty/ Yet, who now will grieve for the times/ Even though mountains, rivers, plains, villages, pavilions, castles are adornments left behind/ We see nothing with our eyes."[40] This sensitivity to beauty as a vanished ideal accompanied a discovery of humanity in all its manifestations. The event marked his decision to become "a student of human emotions." To complete this spiritual odyssey,

[38] See Kano Masanao, *Shihonshugi keiseiki no chitsujo ishiki* (Tokyo, 1969), pp. 384-385, for a perceptive analysis of Kitamura's conception of political malaise.
[39] *KTz*, p. 226.   [40] *Ibid.*, p. 184 (*Hōrai kyoku*).

Kitamura turned to Christianity. "I fell from the ladder of ambition completely," he confessed in 1888, "but from this I was able to find a new happiness in life."[41] Perceiving the impossibility of achieving class ambitions, he turned inward; public failure would be transmuted into private success, for the Kingdom is not without, but within.

Kitamura's conversion to Christianity dramatized not only the separation he was experiencing from "worldly affairs," his present, but also a separation of politics from culture. This estrangement he would establish as the indispensable condition for creativity and art. Although Christianity offered the language for a new conception of individualism, it did not really change the relationship between public and private. It merely reinforced the separation and provided *watakushi* with finer definition. Kitamura's acceptance of Christianity was not the occasion for his abandonment of the external world of politics; it was merely confirmation of his commitment to interiority. In this moment he moved completely away from an earlier ambition to become a Japanese Victor Hugo and create a political literature, to what he now considered the more demanding task of becoming a "novelist of human emotions."

Uchida Roan, a contemporary, saw in this shift a new mode of socio-cultural criticism: "It was thought until recently," he wrote in his *Omoidasu hitobito*, "that no way of success was available other than politics. But the youth of the realm have discovered the new world of literature. They have rushed into literature haughtily as a means of arousing and waking us up."[42] Yet it was a natural route. Failure to change the political world led to criticism of it. Kitamura, who gave coherent expression to this experience, represented less a simple rejection of the "outside world" (*jissekai*) than an accommodation to the terms of *watakushi* which offered separation from the realm of public morality and politics. In a sense he saw literature and art as a new mediation between individual and state.

Kitamura's "inner migration" established a new hierarchy of human values. Civil society and the state were superseded by the true virtues of inner perfection and the profundity of the world of the mind. The role of the intellectual, in this instance

[41] *Ibid.*, p. 226.

[42] Quoted in Matsumoto Sannosuke, *Kindai Nihon no seiji to ningen*, p. 18.

the creative personality, was defined in contrast to the activist, but he was safely removed from the "lesser" sphere of action. Under this arrangement the intellectual was in fact free to conduct his affairs, and could do so under all political conditions. The full implications of such an arrangement, in which private virtues were not related to public expectation, permitted the individual to take part in the social and political process by remaining indifferent to it. These processes remain external and such externality is really the pledge and promise of individuality. It is what Ralf Dahrendorf has called the "liberalism of illiberalism."[43] In abandoning a world seen for one unseen, Kitamura repudiated the present for the future; yet in rejecting reality he sought out an abstract ideal.

In his new commitment to the solitary self Kitamura was prompted to abandon whatever belief he may have had in the prevailing structure of authority. Here the possibility of uniting the self to the outer world—society—threatened to dissolve into unmediated egoism. Aware of his isolation, Kitamura tried, in "On the Inner Life," 1893 (*Naibu seimeiron*) to employ the older concept (used by nativists such as Motoori Norinaga) of *nasake*, a sympathy which enjoins men to move others, in place of self (*jiga*), in the apparent hope of overcoming the inherent egoism and selfishness in it. He tried to argue that it was an inner quality—*nasake*—which has inspired great art and thus transformed the world.[44] But Kitamura lost sight of how to expand the self to "transform the outer world." "The body grieves," he wrote, "it is difficult to conform to the times/ In the end we become an army of demons who expire in the present."[45] If "conformity to the times" was impossible the only alternative was to turn inward. Elsewhere he equated selfhood with stillness. "Things swirl around us (*ware*) and the time to separate the self is in the

[43] Ralf Dahrendorf, *Society and Democracy in Germany* (New York, 1969), p. 291.

[44] *KTz*, pp. 118-119. In the essay, " 'Katsuragawa' o hyoshite jōshi ni oyobu," Kitamura examines the meaning of *nasake* as a kind of mediation between the self (*jiko*) and nature. "When one looks at things [in nature]," he wrote, "it isn't without *nasake*." Elsewhere in the essay, he announced that "*nasake* is a kind of electricity that moves men." And in the "Tokugawa jidai no heiminteki risō," *KTz*, p. 57, he compares Western European chivalry with Japanese chivalry, and argues that the former is really egoistic while the latter was informed by *nasake*, a sense of reaching out.

[45] *Ibid.*, "Hōrai kyoku," p. 184.

rustling wind. . . ."⁴⁶ Throughout the sentimental "Music of the Elysian Fields" (*Hōrai kyoku*) Kitamura persistently repeats such expressions as "*onore*," "*ware*," "*jiga*," etc., and discloses his obsession about the singular self in nature, and repose, quiescence, composure as necessary conditions of creativity.⁴⁷

Kitamura, like Sōseki in most of his novels, argued that final authentication of human life can be offered only by the subjective affirmation of the self. In the end, he wrote on numerous occasions, we have only ourselves and our own experiences. "The times are similar to a blank sheet of paper," he wrote in the *Hōrai kyoku*, "which the self faces." Humanity, before it can subscribe to social norms, must first be honest to itself.⁴⁸ And in a Hegelian mood he identified the self with the Spirit: "All changes in material things are the result of the Spirit; history records the movement of the Spirit."⁴⁹

If the condition of Kitamura's servitude was isolation, its consolation was the realization of self-reliance. He seemed to draw strength from a quickened awareness that his conception of self was clearly at odds with social expectations. Only the self validated decisions, not society. But this individualism did not lead Kitamura into the land of political radicalism. Ironically, it kept him away from it. Instead, his consciousness negated the real world for an unrealized ideal in the future. It was this isolation, this repose and composure, which revealed the Spirit. And the Spirit was the only reality—it was free and it gave shape to the phenomenal world. "Things that are reflected in the eye, heard by the ear, will show the inner shape and sound of the self."⁵⁰ The free self is the Spirit. Yet what this metaphysical concern for the Spirit did was to prompt Kitamura and his friends in the Literary World (*Bungakkai*) to concentrate on the life of the individual (*kojin no iemochi*). Unlike his Christian contemporaries Uemura and Kozaki, Kitamura sought to liberate humanity from any dependence on the Deity (a substitute for society) and elevated the autonomous movement of the "heart which is the life inside the life of humanity itself."

⁴⁶ *Ibid.*, "Meiji bungaku kanken," p. 93.

⁴⁷ See, for example, *ibid.*, pp. 185, 190-191, 199, 203, 204ff.

⁴⁸ See Kano, p. 395; Kitamura Tōkoku, "Sō to hi," in *Heiwa*, vⅢ (1892); *KTz*, pp. 187, 191.

⁴⁹ *Ibid.*, "Meiji bungaku kanken," p. 93.

⁵⁰ *Ibid.*, p. 191.

It has been argued that Kitamura's awareness of the individual's life of freedom was inspired by a prior commitment to
greater freedom for woman and the idea of free love.[51] His conception of free love was platonic, to be sure, but disclosed a consciousness of feminine bondage in late Meiji times. But the structure of authority had not really precluded this concern. "In the
long run," he advised, "we can go no further than the freedom
of each individual."[52] What did this mean? For one thing it led
to the expression of a political view. Consistent with his celebration of individualism, Kitamura saw politics in the wider context
of culture. In the *Meiji bungaku kanken* (1893) he wrote that
the "recent misfortunes in the Orient" had resulted from not having known, since antiquity, "the freedom of the Spirit." Echoing
an earlier plaint of Fukuzawa's, Kitamura declared that in the
Orient there had been only political systems, which were different from its religions. These religions had failed, and since the
beginning there had been a complete absence of "the free spirit."
Religion in Asia had always been removed from politics. Unlike
Christianity, it had failed to have a mediating effect on governments. "Nations that have not pursued [the freedom of the spirit]
must always deteriorate and, without fail, disappear from history." But in "pursuing the freedom of the Spirit" people will
become "objects separated from politics," not religion. He warned
that in countries that do not exchange religion for politics, thinking will result either in "extreme idealism" or "extreme practicality." "Today," he continued, "though political organization
in Japan has permitted the freedom of one individual, it has
not acknowledged the freedom of the masses. Moreover, though
religious organizations in Japan have permitted a subjective freedom of the spirit, the community enjoys this freedom in a life
that is unrelated to anything. Freedom of the community is not
permitted from any other point of view."[53] Only the most privatized freedom was possible in Japan, which itself might "disappear
from history."

It had not always been this way. Kitamura applauded the
Restoration as a great revolutionary event which "severed class
ties so basic to Oriental community organization."[54] But, he noted,
the great tasks which the Restoration promised were only half

[51] See, for example, Kōsaka Masaaki, *Japanese Thought in the Meiji Era*
(Tokyo, 1958), pp. 280-283.
[52] *KTz*, p. 95.   [53] *Ibid.*, p. 94.   [54] *Ibid.*

131

accomplished. Community freedom was still off in the future and "the intellectual world is still suppressed." Fearful of "foolishness," he asked which way the Japanese would go, and answered that after a hundred years "scholars will be perplexed why [Japan] chose at the crossroads a route leading to patriotism which, lingering today, is an inheritance of the older order."[55] In *Nationality and Thought* (*Kokumin to shisō*) Kitamura amplified the theme of a lingering past and its effect on the present. Here also, he anticipated Takayama's explicit rejection of history. Past and present are always in conflict with each other, but the past must "encapsulate the destiny of the present and launch it on its course, in darkness and seclusion." The present lasts for only a short time but "clings to the edge of hope." In one there is death, in the other life. Between death and life, past and present, "a people ride on the carriage of time and rotate, from one to the other, on the long road."[56] In the world, he argued, "movements are not expressed by time, nor are arrivals announced by a voice." They occur automatically and are first perceived subjectively, and they are prompted by the "mental disposition or genius (*genki*) of a people."[57] This genius resides in the recesses of national life, "hidden in the deep valleys of the mountains," and it is not a thing that "changes in a day and a night." It is this genius, he added, that unifies the movement which is so "indispensable to a people."[58]

At this time, Kitamura asked, what specifically will unify the "mental disposition" among the people? There are many among us, he replied, who know how to be loquacious, who can teach equality, plan for the welfare of many, who can promote the progress of humanity and reveal its destiny. "There are many," he continued, "who are suitable for achieving such goals"—recalling his earlier political ambitions to lead a movement. "As for me I am, in this manner, a believer in individualism. I am a devotee of democracy."[59] To the contemporary conception of the subject Kitamura juxtaposed an ideal citizenry, individualistic in its determination—humanity committed to preserving the autonomy of its will against the claims of the state. "The people" (*kokumin*), he charged, "are individuals but possess a unified will. This will is the idea that pursues liberty. . . ." Yet it should

[55] *Ibid.*
[57] *Ibid.*, p. 114.
[59] *Ibid.*

[56] *Ibid.*, p. 113. "Kokumin to shisō."
[58] *Ibid.*

be noted that Kitamura was not raising the standard of political action. His plea for preserving the autonomy of human will was a chant against the contemporary image of the subject; his effusive celebration of the dignity of humanity a lament for vanished possibilities. Nevertheless, Kitamura was hopeful. "It would be heroic," he mused, "if democracy should lead to basic reforms suitable to the needs of our people. We have not yet discussed its merits or demerits. Rather we have gotten no further than trying to puzzle out the manner in which the public will ignore its importance."[60] Changes could be brought about, but they depended upon the "genius of the people," which, he admitted, was hidden. When he advised that this genius "does not retreat with conservatism, advance with progress, but possesses a profoundly firm foundation," he was, in effect, repeating what he had written earlier about the precincts of the self. His call for the "highest form of government for individual humans" as any arrangement that would not exceed the consensus made possible by "the will of freedom" was simply a plea for preserving the integrity of the self and the claims of individualism.[61] Of course, beneath this lofty rhetoric, Kitamura was no doubt defending bourgeois rights, but it is important that he linked this defense to his amplification of the private realm.

Much of this concern for individualism was dramatized by his plunge into abstraction and idealism. Yet it was precisely in this mode that Kitamura, cut off from contemporary reality, began to disclose the broad outlines of a new kind of cultural criticism. Rejection of objective reality as unworthy of the autonomy of subjective feelings obliged him to turn first inward and then outward beyond his present. The future is the crucible in which the self will realize its fullest promise, "the genius of the people" its destiny. Neither the present nor the Meiji past could stand close analysis. "On the surface," he wrote, "Meiji civilization has shown measurable progress. But how many people have enjoyed it? How many families have a warm fire when snow falls from the sky . . . ? How much flesh has been supplied to amuse the [feudal] lords who are back in power?"[62] Kitamura's perception

---

[60] *Ibid.*

[61] *KTz*, pp. 114-115; *Naibu seimeiron*, pp. 106ff.

[62] *Ibid.*, p. 132. "Jizen jigyō no shimpō o nozomu." In a rather beautiful poem Kitamura wrote in the *Bungakkai*, XIII (1894) the same sentiment is expressed in terms of the "lonely butterfly" and the "flower at the edge of

of the shapes behind outward forms lay at the basis of an anti-presentist conception of the world. This conception included a criticism of contemporary norms which led to an open rejection of the bureaucratic formalism of Meiji society. What bothered Kitamura most was the elevation of law and legal power as the norm regulating external life. In such an arrangement only the public life really mattered—the outward form of life preceded all other considerations. For Kitamura, and many of his contemporaries, rejection of the present prompted, as I have suggested, a turn inward, to the self, but this turn also induced a repudiation of the structure of authority. He abandoned the authority of external norms for the authority of personal experience. The resulting removal from society also inspired a spirit of wandering which, I believe, Kitamura was the first to dramatize.

For Kitamura the vision of the artist wandering along the edge of the present provided an excellent point of view from which to develop a critique of civilization. Alone in nature, he discovered beauty, to be sure, but also love. Love served as the basis of the formation of an ideal world, free from external norms, authority, and structure. A romantic's dream, this ideal world was juxtaposed to the real world of law and legal power—the present—what he called the civilization of Meiji. He argued that "love is the key to life and life comes only after love. . . . After experiencing love the feeling for the pathos [*aware*] of nature, for the beauty of the landscape, is no longer superficial."[63] Love reinforced the sense of self and dramatized the enormous distance between the individual and social reality.

Separation from external reality promised the discovery of humanity. On the one hand it liberated the individual from the state; on the other, it disclosed to the individual the true movement of nature, sensitizing him to its rhythm reflected in humanity. Here is what Kitamura meant by an awareness of the inner life. He had unleashed a "demon" within humanity, which promised to set free the affections of men and women, the sentient, the childlike, the madman, and the eccentric. Such liberation

the field." "Isn't that what we ought to grieve most, the fate of the flower at the edge of the field? Even though it receives its beauty from the same heavens that confer beauty on other flowers, there are many who fail to grieve for it because it is covered with the dust of the road and withered in debris. How strange. . . ."

[63] *Ibid.*, "Ensei shika to josei," pp. 26, 27.

allowed men to "look at the things which transcend nature with the eyes of the inner life, the eyes of a reconstituted life."[64] It was precisely this unadorned emotionalism which Kitamura found in nature that formed the basis of a true humanity, distinct from structure and norms which tend to distort what is natural. Such a vision validated the mission of the wanderer, alone in nature, seeing it truly for the first time. Man and nature, spirit and landscape were linked in an intense relationship which taught Kitamura the languages of the passions but also made him an exile in his own land. "This is what I meant," he wrote in "On the Inner Life" (*Naibu seimeiron*), "when I said 'leave the flesh, forget reality.'" Such experience heightened the sense of self. It also obliged Kitamura to exchange realities. In the end the ideal world of the future, to which he took flight in his repudiation of contemporary authority as a banished seeker of democracy, became reality itself.

It was this perception of the inner life that drove Kitamura to conclude that the only real world is the world of human inwardness. The "palace in the heart" and the "palace in the recesses of the palace" is what he called the "fundamental life."[65] What is within is for all to see, as art. Imagination, inspiration, and sympathy—products of this inner world—are the true reality. The so-called real world is a failure. Yet this is precisely the world which, earlier, Kitamura had tried to change with the mediation of politics. The world, now, is only imagination and poetry.

In "On the Inner Life" Kitamura turned again to the reverse side of phenomena. Just as he earlier denounced the Meiji achievement as counterfeit, so now he argued that a distinction must always exist between "outer civilization" and "inner civilization." Outer civilization he identified with the claims of Christianity, and saw it as "living thought," as against the "non-living thought" of Buddhism. It was an inheritance, he observed, that Asia might not overcome.[66] The confrontation between living thought and non-living thought represents the "great collision between Eastern and Western thought." Despite appearances and a commitment to the forms of an outer civilization, the "inner civilization" still persists.

In seeking evidence of this modern dilemma in Japan, Kita-

[64] *Ibid.*, p. 110. "Naibu seimeiron."
[65] *Ibid.*, pp. 108, 110.   [66] *Ibid.*, p. 107.

mura also cited the example of Confucianism, which, in his day, appeared as a powerful carry-over from the Tokugawa period. Humanity does not exist for the sake of meeting external social obligations; human character is not formed simply by the require-ments of public morality and ethics. Confucianism was a practi-cal morality, he wrote, but it failed to teach man about life and suppressed all awareness of truly human instincts such as love and other emotions.[67] Although Confucianism arbitrarily distrib-uted rewards and punishments, a "true theory of rewards and punishments must be established according to the experience of the heart—that is, from the standpoint of the inner life."[68] Toku-gawa Confucianism, in the 1890's in process of being reified, de-stroyed self-reliance and obliged men to see only the exterior, not the interior, reality. But interior reality is everything: "The work of the greatest philosophers and poets does not emanate from outside the inner life. . . ." Summoning, elsewhere, the example of the "unpolitical poet Emerson," he argued that in the end all that really mattered was humanity.[69] "But humanity . . . is not an external fact; it is the inner life. It is here that all hope is lodged, and from the inner life that all power originates. All work, wealth, and industry are connected with it. It is divine, eternal, immortal."[70]

But it was not enough: Kitamura, who saw the inner life of the self extending beyond the self to create and transform the world, found himself imprisoned on his "sacred island." If the relationship between private and public was in fact one of dis-tance, if separation was the condition of their common existence, then it was virtually impossible for the self to reach out sympa-thetically to move others and to change the outer world. In a sense Kitamura had seen this dilemma earlier, in an essay called, predictably, "My Imprisonment" (*Waga rogoku*), where he de-scribed the terms of being imprisoned in the self.[71] Hope lin-gered, and he often cited the examples of Emerson, Saigyō, Bashō, creative souls whose art had transformed their worlds. Yet in the end all he had was what he had had in the beginning of his odyssey—the self separated from the external world of

[67] *Ibid.*, p. 108; also "Meiji bungaku kanken," pp. 95ff.
[68] *Ibid.*, p. 108.   [69] *Ibid.*, p. 109.
[70] *Ibid.*, p. 175. "Emerson."
[71] *Ibid.*, pp. 7-9. "Waga rogoku." Actually this conception of imprison-ment of the self appears throughout most of his late writings.

politics and power. The good bourgeois till the end, Kitamura tried to find mediation through the common world of things. His last testament disclosed his sense of isolation and, perhaps, failure. The wanderer remained alone in nature, yet even nature remained distant:

> It is evening. I am stretched out before a window. The place is a village by the sea. Well along in autumn, the skies are clear. All things and shapes impress me as being serene. But it is as if I am being laughed at for my insincerity . . . as if I were being sneered at and belittled for my lack of power, ability and understanding. . . . Yet what of me who is a particle of earth and who has great difficulty in understanding her [nature]?
>
> The moon is late tonight and has not yet risen. When I look up at the darkened sky there are an infinite number of stars scattered above my head. In turning to myself, I see my body, and when I look inward and observe the inner self, I am amazed by the great distance separating me from nature [*kare*]. Immortality and indestructibility belong to her, while age, sickness, and death are my possessions. In face of her brightness, beauty, and freshness, shouldn't I be embarrassed [*tanzen*] by my weaknesses? . . . Yet when I change my mental set neither nature nor I exist. There is only the infinite and remote heavens with their innumerable blinking lanterns.[72]

In the end not even the self was enough. Kitamura Tōkoku committed suicide in 1894—at the age of twenty-six—offering up his life as a testimony to sincerity, as compensation for failed aspirations and personal anguish. Yet in committing himself to personal destruction he bequeathed to his generation—and beyond—what Kinoshita Naoe regarded as the most dramatic, if not ironic, testimony to the claims of privatization. But this is not to say that Kitamura's achievement could lay claim only to momentary dramatic significance. More than any other intellectual, before and after the event, he saw the conflict between state and society, public and private, and sought to overcome its restraints by finding a mode of accommodation. In the end, exhausted by his efforts, he offered the ideal version of a bourgeois society which, he believed, had first been revealed in the consciousness that had liberated Japan from the despotic control of

[72] *Ibid.*, pp. 128-129. "Issekikan."

Tokugawa feudalism. The "revolution" this consciousness unleashed degenerated into merely a stage of political transition
which smothered these "new democratic impulses."[73] But in pro-
jecting the model of a bourgeois society Kitamura, ironically, was
simply satisfying the boundaries fixed by the Meiji paradigm.
Indeed, rather than offer either alternatives or opposition, he
defined with great detail and clarity the area of privatization
(*watakushigoto*) permitted by arrangement of authority.

Kitamura Tōkoku's life ended on the eve of the Sino-Japanese
War. In all probability he would not have opposed the war, but
he also would not have approved of it. He might have seen how
the war, rather than upsetting the delicate balance between public and private, really reinforced the separation of spheres. Kitamura achieved something more than irony.

In opposing culture to the world of politics, the isolated individual to public social community, rejection of politics to political mediation, composure to action, he established some of the
most enduring guidelines for thought that twentieth-century
Japan was to know. He also imparted to art and thought the
very same middle-class values he hoped society would nourish
and elevate to organizing principles. Just as Kitamura sought to
equip the private space with a new conception of personality
and purpose, so his younger contemporary Takayama Chogyū
(1871-1902) tried to create an imaginary universe which might
correspond to the structure of authority established after the
Sino-Japanese war.[74] Unlike Kitamura, who suffered from the
ambiguities of middle-class individualism in his search for media-

[73] *Ibid.*, pp. 134, 147.

[74] Takayama Chogyū, like Kitamura Tōkoku, suffers from a paucity of
studies devoted to the relationships between writing, personality, and intellectual history. Although there are fewer literary studies on Takayama, they
usually categorize him as an original literary critic, while the historians have
seen him simply as a new breed of nationalist that cropped up after the Sino-
Japanese war and called themselves Japanists even though they differed
from the earlier variety. I have found useful Hashikawa Bunzō, "Takayama
Chogyū," in Asahi Janaru (eds.), *Nihon shisōka* (Tokyo, 1963), II, 162-
178; Irokawa Daikichi, "Meiji bunka no dansō," in Rekishigaku kenkyūkai,
Nihonshi kenkyūkai (eds.), *Nihon rekishi kōza* (Tokyo, 1963), V, 211-240;
and the provocative essay by Yasuda Yojūrō, one of the leaders of the *Nihon
roman-ha* and a writer who identified with Takayama, in an article called
"Meiji no seishin," in *Bungei* (April-June, 1937).

tion, Takayama made of this individualism a datum in, and an accommodation to, the social life of Imperial Japan. The difference is significant. Although Kitamura had already noted the failure of politics as mediation, by the time of Russo-Japanese War even nature as a mediator had disappeared. Writers and intellectuals, as Takayama was to dramatize, had only themselves, and beyond themselves the abstract conceptions of humanity served by justice, love, and benevolence.

In a sense Takayama reflected the lyric mood that flourished briefly in the wake of the Sino-Japanese war. It was from this lyricism that he formulated his project, and from which he would construct his imaginary universe. It marks his work *The Lay Priest Takiguchi* (*Takiguchi nyūdō*) which he acknowledged to be more a lyric exercise than a historical novel.[75] However, the importance of this piece was in its story: a warrior who, because of feudal political restraints, fails to win the woman he loves and desires, renounces the world and withdraws into a Buddhist monastery, where he ultimately takes his life. Although the theme bears more than a passing resemblance to the *giri-ninjō* conflicts informing Tokugawa drama, Takayama's novel is explicitly political in its consequences. Lyricism in the late 1890's was, I believe, an attempt to conceal the hard social and political realities after the Sino-Japanese war. Yet it revealed a loss of youth, beauty, and history.

In contrast to the lyricism, naive conception of man in nature, and unearthly platonic love of Kitamura, Takayama is almost a realist.[76] Moreover, Takayama, from the beginning, was unconcerned with the egoism inherent in the new conception of individualism that dogged Kitamura to the end of his life. Although he decided to portray Saitō Tokinori (his priest-hero) as a helpless creature caught and destroyed by passion, his is, nonetheless, a much fuller vision of man than Kitamura's.[77] Takayama's defense of sensuality and passion, a political act in itself, was to dramatize his growing interest in psychology and the vital im-

[75] Nihon Gendai Bungaku Zenshū (ed.), *Takayama Chogyūshū*, VIII (Tokyo, 1967), pp. 122-241. "Takiguchi nyūdō." Hereafter, *TCs* (1967).

[76] In this connection we might recall Kitamura's rather sickly conception of platonic love in the "Ensei shika to josei" and his violent condemnation of the sexual practices of the commercial classes during the Tokugawa period in the "Tokugawa jidai no heiminteki risō."

[77] See "Takiguchi nyūdō," in *TCs* (1967), pp. 215, 220ff.

139

portance of instinct and emotion which he would later amplify in his "On the Aesthetic Life" (*Biteki seikatsu o ronzu*). Finally, Takayama, in this early story about thwarted sensuality, emphasized the conflict between private impulse and public expectation, and confirmed the claims of self, instinct, and passion over politics more explicitly than Kitamura had ever done.

The route to the "aesthetic life" was not direct. In the wake of the lyricism of the 1890's Takayama momentarily plunged into a defense of cultural nationalism (*Nihonshugi*) and imperialistic expansion. Many have seen in this division a "conversion" (*tenkō*) which contrasts sharply with his later turn to aestheticism.[78] Far from being a conversion, Takayama's Japanist phase was consistent with his later aestheticism, for in both cases the leitmotif was an aggressive, indeed Darwinian, egoism. A nation following its own impulses and defining, by force, its own stature in the international community was really no different from the individual acting on his own instincts and the authority of personal feeling. Just as stronger nations must always devour weaker peoples, so the creative personality must always overcome the masses.

It is true, of course, that this patriotism owed something to

[78] I have found the idea of *tenkō*, as used by Japanese historians especially, a rather thin concept. If it implies a theory of personality, they ought to make explicit its fundamental principles; if it represents a theory of social change, we should expect a much more comprehensive explanation. A theory of social change has been suggested by Tsurumi Shunsuke and his associates in the three-volume work on *Tenkō* but I suspect that their initial purpose is to track down (and possibly destroy) left wingers who recanted during the late 1930's but who returned to the left after the war. As an ideological device *tenkō* might satisfy certain emotional needs which only the Japanese can judge. But as a serious concept in intellectual history, it falls short because it fails to explain—beyond a rather simpleminded determinism—the sources of conversion. Yet in recent Japanese history it has become almost an emblem of intellectual respectability that a writer or a thinker underwent a sudden conversion. The effects have been confusing, and lives are seemingly chopped up much in the manner of advertisements seeking to show the subject before and after they have taken or used the product. Worse, I fear, the deployment of *tenkō* really diverts historians from ever investigating the changes in a thinker as manifestations of earlier dispositions; that is to say, more than likely so-called intellectual changes represent no conversion at all but rather a consistency with earlier assumptions. The alleged conversion does not represent a change in the thought of a man but rather a dramatic turn in his consciousness of problems. His perspective on reality might in fact change, but the equipment he has brought to his perceptions remain intact.

earlier experiences. When he was fifteen years old (1885) Takayama wrote in his diary how he exulted in "commemorating, this
month, this day, the memory of the former Emperor Kōmei and
all the Emperors' ancestors and parents."[79] He asked himself,
perhaps naively, "haven't we flourished" by knowing of filial
piety? Despite these precocious expressions of nationalism Takayama's promotion of Japanism between 1897 and 1898 owes more
to the historic circumstances of the Japanese state after the Sino-
Japanese war. The pages of the influential magazine *Taiyō*, Takayama's favorite forum, were filled with denunciations of "internationalism" and "humanism"—Western concepts—as well as
effusive declarations supporting the primacy of the Japanese
state. Just as Takayama discredited the earlier call (Tokutomi,
Kitamura, Miyake Setsurei) to broaden the revolutionary promise
of the Restoration in order to elevate the masses socially and economically, so he also discouraged any sympathy for weaker peoples, at home or abroad. Domestically and internationally, he
urged, only the fittest survive, the strong will always crush the
weak.

Expansion of the state ultimately serves the interests of the
individual. "The goal of life is to have complete happiness," he
wrote in *Taiyō*, presaging his later writing. "Complete happiness
is nothing more than the full development of human life. The
state is formed to establish the family and to organize society.
But it is never more than the expedient by which such goals are
accomplished."[80] The values of the state are not absolute; rather,
it is the principle of individualistic utility and happiness in an
emerging capitalist society that takes precedence over all other
considerations. Takayama saw the state simply as a stage in the
achievement of this kind of individualism leading to "human
happiness." Ultimately, the goal of social life, which the state
must serve, was the realization of bourgeois values such as individualism, self-interest, utilitarian practicality, and "unpoliticality." If the state precluded political participation from the masses,
this fact should be used as a datum in the effort to secure the
guarantee of such values. If, on the surface, there seemed to be
a contradiction between Takayama's conception of human happiness as ultimate goal and state authority as expedient means, it
was ameliorated by the sympathy he expressed for the political

[79] *Chogyū zenshū* (Tokyo, 1904), III, 7. Hereafter *Cz.*
[80] *Taiyō* (June, 1897).

values of the new Imperial Japan. The state was guarantor of individualism, and individualism would lead to the realization of human happiness.

But Takayama was troubled by this belief. By 1899 he was ready to write off the state he had earlier praised, and actually expressed his disenchantment with contemporary writing. He condemned, as symptoms of general malaise, both writers of the day, who failed to develop "a truly national literature portraying national character," and politicians who were simply corrupt and hypocritical.[81] Earlier he had complained of how ugly and degenerate Tokyo seemed to him. It was, as he put it, the capital of crime. Just as Paris inspired the newest and latest cultural and intellectual fashions, Tokyo was noted only for its originality in varieties of crime, which then spread over the rest of the country.[82] The social circumstances of the times matched contemporary political conditions. In the essay "New Japan," he rejected both as deceptions. The new Japan, he complained, was "internally where the great figures . . . are disappearing. New personalities, educated in the atmosphere of the new Japan, are taking hold of the reins in such areas as politics, law, literature, and religion." It is a Japan, he added, which is trying to dissolve the family system through a civil code, where traditional morality and pieties are disappearing, "labor unions are emerging and colonialism is justified in the name of national self-interest."[83] Takayama asked his generation to locate its determination and aspirations. His own answer was gloomy. The state had not really fulfilled its obligation to provide human happiness. Rather, Japanese society, as a result, had become a "prosaic society," where the pursuit of money and profit prevailed over all other considerations.

In response to a contemporary dispute over succession to the Honganji Temple, Takayama cut a wide swath in his denunciation: "The contemporary political world is corrupt and degenerate. That there are religious men who attempt to bribe corrupt politicians is a monstrous outrage."[84] Less hope was promised by the intellectual world, which had been consistently indifferent to such conditions. Even the younger scholars, he wrote, were "like young old and worn-out people. Not one of them holds a

[81] *Cz*, IV, 459, 465. "Meiji no shōsetsu."
[82] *Ibid.*, pp. 410ff.   [83] *Ibid.*   [84] *Ibid.*, p. 589.

fresh ideal or troubles himself over the renovation or reform of the times."[85] In a seminal essay called the "Litterateur as Cultural Critic" (*Bummei hyōka to shite no bungakusha*), 1901, Takayama exposed contemporary literary quarrels, so fashionable among the young, as a wasted expenditure of energy. "In our literary world are there many who really understand such circumstances [alluding to Mathew Arnold's dictum that 'poetry is a criticism of life']? I really doubt that there are. I have heard of a prominent novelist who got drunk in the streets and brawled with a ricksha man. But I have not yet heard of one who has opposed contemporary civilization and poeticized new and fresh ideals."[86] They might call themselves poets and novelists, but they were only "play-acting." Their minds were not open to human impulses, they heard nothing with their ears, saw nothing with their eyes.

In flight from these conditions Takayama, like Kitamura before him, turned for sanctuary and consolation to an ideal vision beyond the present. Part of this drift was already apparent in a series of letters he wrote in 1900-1901 to his friend Anezaki Chōfū.[87] He reflected on how recently he had "fermented and changed." Because of illness (he died soon thereafter) he was willing to admit to the possibility of a psychological pathology. "I cannot believe that [this change] is other than a natural development in my spirit. I will not argue with the fact that it is a kind of individualism clothed in romanticism. I had advocated Japanism earlier and it was something that celebrated the supremacy of the state. Even today there is no reason why I must destroy this position. But it is a fact of my life that such a principle is no longer adequate."[88] Takayama was correct in his self-estimate; he had not undergone an intellectual conversion, nor had he seen any fundamental contradictions between his earlier commitments and his new interests. The meaning of this confession concerning an intellectual change was further amplified in the following self-criticism: "Ah, in order for me to overcome my weaknesses is it not important to declare as an article of personal belief that it is a deficiency of my character that I do not know

[85] Quoted in Kōsaka, p. 309.
[86] *TCs* (1967), p. 276. "Bummei hihyōka to shite no bungakusha."
[87] These letters are in Gendai Nihon Bungaku Zenshū, ed. *Chogyūshū*, XIII (Tokyo, 1928), pp. 313-315, 316. Hereafter, *Cs* (1928).
[88] *Ibid.*, pp. 301-302.

143

that I do not know?"[89] Elsewhere, he confessed that he felt that he was becoming a "madman," that he was living more intensively than ever before the life of the spirit.

Takayama's self-criticism and retreat from the world of public affairs was also expressed in the metaphor of Nichiren's struggle with political authority. Returning to the themes of the *Takiguchi Nyūdō*, he found in religion, especially that of Nichiren, a means by which to organize his despair. For Takayama, Nichiren put personal ideals over public expectations, the claims of privatization and self over politics. "He was a supreme egoist who was willing to sacrifice the state for his own beliefs."[90] In the late essay called *Nichiren shōnin to Nihonkuni* ("Nichiren and Japan"), 1902, he argued that Nichiren actually valued truth over the state and that as a result of this conviction he was willing to "approve of the destruction of the state itself." Nichiren was a man for the ages, he wrote, an individualist who overcame the present "to follow the dictates of his heart, independently, freely."[91] If he opposed the authorities of his day it was not out of any political impulse—he was beyond politics—it was for reasons which satisfied his instincts. His act expressed only his own personal sovereignty and possessed no other meaning, even though it resulted in political consequences. Kitamura had earlier noted how important it was to say "yes" and "no" as an expression of personal autonomy; Takayama elevated the authority of personal feeling into a supremely human act that conferred identity.

Takayama's apparent abandonment of the outer world was no abandonment at all. His interest in individualism and the self had marked his thinking from the beginning. Yet his sentimental self-criticism and apotheosizing of Nichiren simply dramatized the importance of developing a truly whole individualism, free from the corruption of politics. The culmination of this effort was hinted at in his "Litterateur as Cultural Critic," but reached maturity in his last major essay, "On the Aesthetic Life" (*Biteki seikatsu o ronzu*) which, above all else, gave coherent expression to the imaginary universe that bourgeois intellectuals conceived of in vague and incomplete form in the late Meiji period. Moreover, Takayama's individualism, according to Ishikawa Takuboku, was second to none in its consciousness of established authority, and was the first voice advocating the self among

[89] *Ibid.*, pp. 309-310.   [90] *Cz*, IV, 921.   [91] *Ibid.*, p. 934.

Meiji youth.[92] But, it should be recalled, unlike Kitamura, Takayama harbored no fears about the egoistic excesses of this individualism. In a sense his call for the "aesthetic life" resembled
the German quest for self-perfection, the development of culture
rooted in the experience of life and possible only when it is free
from the corrupting influences of the lower orders of human
affairs—politics, compromise, expediency, and mediocrity. Expressing the claims of middle-class autonomy, Takayama, like
Nietzsche, came to argue that culture could be created only by
the artist liberated from mundane political affairs. In a sense this
conception of self-perfection was simply a modern version of the
older *Humanitäts* ideal of Herder and Humboldt which saw in a
cultivated humanity (the rising bourgeoisie) a check to political
excesses. The idea came to Takayama through his reading of
Nietzsche. The *Übermensch* inspired Takayama's conception of
"overcoming the present"; Kitamura's wanderer became meta-
morphosed into the new image of Nichiren.

In any case, it was the celebration of intuition and the liberation of private emotion from unnatural moral obligations that
prompted Takayama to offer the aesthetic life, not as an alternative to public expectation, but as the noblest expression of privatization. His angle of vision was, perhaps, more limited than
Kitamura's, and humanity was restricted to the uncommon few
who created culture, but he was not dogged by Kitamura's uncertainties. There were good historic reasons for Takayama to
offer a defense of the aesthetic life in which the creative self
would produce culture pure and whole. Writers and intellectuals
experienced in the late 1890's a profound disillusionment when
they saw the final achievement of public nationalism.[93] Specifically, it was the firm delineation of public affairs (*ōyakegoto*)
established by the Ordinance on Assembly and Political Societies
of 1890 and the Civil Code, including the Peace Preservation
Law and the Administration Performance Law in 1900, which
dampened the hopes and aspirations of Meiji intellectuals.

The Peace Preservation Law, for example, aimed at keeping
the emerging labor unions in check. Its stated purpose was to
"manage . . . organizations and/or societies involved in public

---

[92] *Ishikawa Takuboku zenshū* (Tokyo, 1929), IV, 4ff; 552-553.
[93] See Kano Masanao, pp. 440-454; also, Kamishima Jirō, "Meiji shūen,"
pp. 383-424.

affairs."[94] The effect of the Civil Code and its ordinances was to identify politics and public affairs. In doing so the Meiji state permitted its complement—the area of "private affairs" (*watakushigoto*). The Administration Performance Law sought to regulate the management of the Peace Preservation and Police Laws. Control of this kind reached into virtually every nook and cranny of Japanese life[95] and permitted the government to promote schemes in the national interest. In the early twentieth century the phrase "for the sake of the country" became a familiar cliché that could justify virtually any kind of activity. Kitamura feared the worst and dedicated his efforts to defining the private sphere.

It was the formalization of authority that obliged writers and intellectuals to abandon the conviction that art should illuminate, educate and criticize and forced them to return to the inner life. If the outer world could not be transformed by art and thought, then art and thought must be completely liberated from the outer world to achieve the promise of its purity. In a sense this path was already being cut by Takayama Chogyū, who intended his "discovery" of passion and the power of personal intuition to liberate some men—the uncommon man—the artist from the humdrum affairs of everyday life. In his essay on the "Litterateur as Cultural Critic" he argued, like Kitamura before him, that true creativity must be separated from the petty, the commonplace, the vulgar. Great art is produced by the inner resources of the "genius," who by will and creative energy will overcome civilization itself if he is to affirm the meaning of his life.[96] Yet in transcending civilization the creative personality will act also as its critic. Takayama's exploration of the creative self and the requirements of personal freedom posited politics, the world of public affairs, as a kind of necessary evil which should be left to the common, the vulgar, and the mediocre. Unlike Kōtoku Shūsui and Uchimura Kanzō, who actively recorded their lack of faith in politics and politicians and acted on the conviction that they were an unnecessary evil, Takayama, according to Ishikawa Takuboku, was always a bit oblique in his discussions of state power.

In his revised pantheon of culture heroes Takayama installed

[94] Kano, *Shihonshugi keiseiki* . . . , p. 444. Also, Okawada Tsunetada, "Meiji seinen no seiji ishiki," in Hashikawa and Matsumoto, pp. 379-380.
[95] Kano, pp. 414, 444.
[96] *Cs* (1928), pp. 235-238. "Tensairon."

Nietzsche next to Nichiren and announced that his life and thought were an inspiration for Japan. Nietzsche ignored the claims of science, disregarded history altogether, and penetrated the deepest mysteries of life. His perceptivity, Takayama wrote, owed little to his being a philosopher, as some suggested; rather "he was a great poet and the reason for his greatness lay in the fact that he was a great *Kulturkritiker* [sic]."[97] Elsewhere, in an article entitled "An Admirer of Nietzsche" (*Nietzsche no tambisha*), Takayama equated the autonomous creative personality, who is above society, with the genius. Only the most extraordinary are free of the common. Genius alone validates experience, enriches life, and is the "sole source of consolation and inspiration." More important, the genius "pursues the means by which to deal with the times, to construct an ideal world beyond the world in which fools live. I am inspired in my hopes . . . by the achievement of the genius."[98] In this class of genius Takayama relocated Nichiren, alongside Nietzsche, Heine, and Goethe.

The achievements of Japan's recent past were crippling. Civilization was a forgery. The founders of the new order in Japan were victims of history. History, Takayama learned from Nietzsche, disregards the instincts of creative men. It is the enemy of creativity and suppresses the impulses. It equalizes the human species, disregards differences, and prevents the development of genuine individual freedom. "History eats up genius."[99] Nietzsche, because of his belief in personal independence, sought to deny historicism. He saw it as responsible for producing all those ideologies pledged to weakness and human mediocrity, such as socialism, liberalism, democracy. In combination, these ideologies have contrived to promote the false goal of humanity, which is simply the material well-being and equality of the masses. But the masses ought not to be seen as the "diadem of civilization." For when they are, when it is believed that civilization exists for the masses, "we are committing a great error."[100] The masses exist only for the sake of the *Übermensch*, the genius in the creation of cultural life. These extraordinary personalities do not acknowledge the ideals of humanism (*jindō*) but repudiate all inherited social, educational and political forms that might interfere with their project. "What they cherish most is not history,

97 *Ibid.*, p. 260. "Bummei hihyōka to shite no bungakusha."
98 *Ibid.*, p. 224. "Nietzsche no tambisha."
99 *Ibid.*, p. 260.   100 *Ibid.*

147

ideals, truth, society, or state, but the self (*ware*)." Once more Takayama turned to the example of Nietzsche. His greatness lay in his role as cultural critic who, for the sake of the individual, struggled with history to eliminate alleged truths which "classify all life under mores, customs, inheritances, hearsay, and circumstances." He struggled with a science which reduced life to statistics, heredity, and environment; with contemporary psychology which sought to understand the mysteries of the inner life as a datum of exterior observation "but failed to engage impulse and instinct," and with current philosophy, which has been preoccupied with questions of epistemology but negates the instincts, motivation, and sensation.[101] Opposed to herd civilization, Nietzsche proclaimed an "eccentric individualism" and, in a swipe at the emerging mood of naturalism, Takayama added that the song Nietzsche sang was not of mountains and rivers but rather of the mysteries of life which he alone was able to understand.

Takayama's celebration of the creative personality was founded on a conception of active unpoliticality, an active rejection of politics.[102] Politics and the public world of official expectation were debilitating and, in the final analysis, proved to be little more than a prison. But the masses belonged in this prison; modern civilization was a confirmation of this belief. The uncommon man must stand against the equalizing values of democracy and socialism which sought to make all men alike, as aristocracy stood against the lower orders, as the strong against the weak, heroism and creativity against humility and complacency. It might be noted, in passing, that Takayama's celebration of individualism, a bourgeois phenomenon, was made to seem as an elaborate defense of aristocratic values. What this transformation of bourgeois values into aristocratic values revealed was a further intensification of middle-class individualism. Georg Lukacs has argued, in his discussion on realism, that in modern society there seems to be a sharp division between "man as a private individual and man as a social being. . . . On the surface the two seem sharply divided and the appearance of an autonomous, independent existence of the individual is all the more pronounced, the more . . . modern bourgeois society is developed. It seems as if the inner

---

[101] *Ibid.*

[102] See Maruyama, "Meiji kokka no shisō," pp. 220ff; "Chūsei to hangyaku," pp. 450-452.

life, the genuine 'private' life, were proceeding according to its own autonomous laws and as if its fulfilments and tragedies were growing ever more independent of the surrounding social environment. . . ." Moreover, as consciousness of the inner life intensifies, connection with the outer world is manifest "only in high-sounding abstractions. . . ."[103]

Takayama's uncommon man lives according to his inner-most needs, drives and impulses. Resembling some of the heroes he wrote about, his uncommon man is driven by passion and biological instinct, seeking personal gratification and sensual pleasure. A natural man, he is able to realize the promise of his passions and instincts only if he considers himself free of responsibility to established moral conventions and conventional intelligence.[104] It was in this linking of privatization to the primacy of natural drives that Takayama produced his most coherent statement on the claims of the unpolitical inner life.

In 1901, on the edge of an illness that would soon claim his life, he wrote his revealing "On the Aesthetic Life." He invited the uncommon man—the artist—to stop worrying about the outer life, and to start pursuing impulse and intuition as a means of achieving the pure aesthetic. Morality and intelligence belonged to the external world and regulated its activities. Privatization meant realizing an aesthetic life, which was the highest value man could attain. In this aesthetic life nothing was more important than the "gratification of instinctive desires."[105] Morality suppressed instinct and desire; it usually was an abstraction of a concrete instance from an earlier time which later was established as a norm for "good" and "profitable" action. Yet it was unnatural. When Kusunoki Masashige, in the fourteenth century, gave up his life for the Imperial cause at Minatogawa, Takayama asked, what ideal of goodness informed his act and how could we distinguish between means and ends in his heart? Dying in this manner was Kusunoki's personal choice and satisfied his highest needs. It was not an act that was inspired by "established morality" but one that "emanated from his own heart." Men in the past, as in the *sengoku* period, chose death out of private impulse and choice, not to satisfy an external code of morality.

103 Georg Lukacs, *Studies in European Realism* (New York, 1964), pp. 8-9.
104 *Cs* (1928), pp. 206-208. "Biteki seikatsu o ronzu."
105 *Ibid.*, p. 206.

Their acts were as natural as "the chirping of a bird and the flowing of a stream."[106] Moral action stressed consciousness, deliberation and cooperation but the existential action of men like Kusunoki, Sugawara Michizane and the *sengoku bushi*, was as "instinctive as a floating cloud." Originally natural and instinctive, such acts were historicized and transmuted into external norms which, ironically, sought to eliminate the incidence of naturalness and instinctive expression. Takayama claimed that he understood the reasons behind the transformation of an existential act into a historical norm. Most people were in need of guidance; the masses craved management. But the uncommon man must be free of such constraints, free, in fact, to experience the moments of his life existentially, naturally.

Only the aesthetic life promises an alternative. In the preface to "On the Aesthetic Life" Takayama posed the question, "Why ask about the aesthetic life?" and answered, "Because it is a life and physical existence more superior to food and clothing." Uncertain about the purpose of life, Takayama was more confident in his understanding of human goals. "Having been born, our goal, it goes without saying, is to become happy."[107] Although he had uttered this plaint earlier, during his Japanist infatuation, at that time, he had linked "the sufficiency of the self and human happiness which derives from this" to the mythopeic conception of *kokutai*.[108] The effort to identify state nationalism with "happiness according to the needs of the self" and "the goal of human life" ran aground and plunged Takayama into a bitter dispute with the Christian publicist, Uchimura Kanzō. Uchimura's position was to see "anti-statism" and "anti-nationalism" as the only conditions of human well-being. In a sense, Takayama came around to this position in 1901. By that time he had stripped human happiness of its earlier association with mythopeic statism and relocated it in a radical and unmediated individualism. Less than marking a departure from his earlier patriotism, the decision anticipated the political criticism he was to disclose in one of his last confessional essays, "Contemplative Record" (*Seishiroku*) in 1902.

But what, then, is happiness? Takayama asked. "As far as I'm concerned it is nothing more than the gratification of instinct. . . . Then what is instinct? It is the basic necessity of human life. That

[106] *Ibid.*   [107] *Ibid.*, p. 207.
[108] See Irokawa Daikichi, "Meiji bunka no dansō," pp. 228-229.

which satisfies the basic needs of the human character is what I call the aesthetic life."[109] Takayama's Darwinism remained intact. What had been dropped was the necessity to justify instinct in terms of the mythology of the state. Tsubouchi Shōyō, who among late Meiji writers had been attacked most repeatedly by Takayama, argued in his "Nondescript Conversations" (*Umano-hone jingen*) that Takayama's new incarnation made him an "enemy of humanism" and that it represented merely a more recent expression of the egoism of his earlier writings. As a good liberal, Tsubouchi intuited that Takayama's conception of the aesthetic life was "distasteful selfishness," and revealed a contempt for the masses. It was the "selfishness of a corrupt, imperialistic bourgeoisie."[110] But Takayama was no more bourgeois than Tsubouchi. When Tsubouchi attacked Takayama for harboring a conception of "discriminatory individualism" and "a false individualism," he was attacking a middle-class theory of personality no more arbitrary than the one he himself held. The difference was, I believe, that Takayama had a surer grasp of political realities than Tsubouchi; unlike Tsubouchi, he had already recognized the impossibility of meaningful political and social action, and shifted the ground of argumentation to other possibilities.

Although morality was important in distinguishing humans from the lower orders of life (this was a neo-Confucian hangover), Takayama wrote, "the supreme pleasure of life is, after all, in the gratification of sexual desire." Where human sexual desire differed from animal passions was in man's consciousness of love, which was one of the most important ingredients of the aesthetic life. Knowledge and morality, while separating men from the animal kingdom, also served to "assist in the expression and continuation of basic instincts." In fact, Takayama argued, knowledge and morality were the means to achieving the ends defined by the instincts. The distinction is crucial. "Instincts are the lord, knowledge and morality the retainers."[111] Following this metaphor, Takayama argued that morality and knowledge were always external and public, while the aesthetic life was internal, private, and personal. "We must talk about the aesthetic life as

[109] *Cs* (1928), p. 206. "Jōgen."
[110] *Masamune Hakuchō zenshū* (Tokyo: 1965-1968), vi. "Tsubouchi Shōyō," pp. 418-422. Also, Irokawa, p. 238.
[111] *Cs* (1928), p. 208.

151

something that authorizes the sovereignty of feelings, not as a thing that enriches men with money and political power."

If knowledge and morality were changeable according to the times, relative to periodic necessities, then the values of the aesthetic life were absolute and its attainment was limited to the few. For those who were able to "transcend morality and knowledge today," the reward was freedom, autonomy, and an exhilarating sense of liberation from the mundane and the expedient. Here is Takayama's substitute for the state, but the state had already provided the space for an "aesthetic life." The achievement of freedom by the extraordinary few was not a political or social freedom. It was a personal freedom. Implicit in this conception was the tacit agreement that if the state allows an area of private space in which the artist is free to create culture, to lead a private and irregular life, and to hold unorthodox views in literature and philosophy, he will also, in turn, abstain from politics and criticism of the state. This agreement explains Takayama's spectacular reluctance to take a public stand against the government's censorship of the avante-garde magazine *Myōjō* for its decision to print a picture of a nude.[112] He was asked by the editor of the magazine, Yosano Tekkan, to protest the violation of freedom of press and personal expression. His reply was limp but eloquent and, I think, instructive. Takayama was really less concerned with intellectual freedom than he was with taste. In a letter to Yosano he condemned the government's censorship of the magazine not as an infraction of basic liberties but as an offense against the readers and editors of the *Myōjō* who, he believed, were cultivated and sophisticated enough to appreciate the aesthetic quality of the illustrated nude. Takayama also argued that it was time for the government and the masses to distinguish between great art and vulgar art.

But Takayama also knew that cultural creativity was a higher form of political criticism. Of course, humanity itself was incapable of reaching such heights, and he never extended this invitation to the masses. The creative personality should not be troubled, either, with the business of eking out a living. The masses worry about nothing else. The beggar who struggles for bread

[112] In response to Takayama's inept defense of literary freedom, Mori Ōgai quipped that he (Takayama) was "kiba no nai Niichi" (Nietzsche without teeth).

152

was not qualified to enjoy the freedom offered by the aesthetic life. "We must not worry about life and provisions," Takayama announced. Although the poor should never be anxious about where their food and clothing will come from next, it was pointless to be sorrowful about the downtrodden and those who have lost hope. As a necessary evil, the state, Takayama first believed, was obliged to serve the best interest of humanity, since humanity was largely incapable of serving itself. Later, in his "Bundle of Deep Emotions" (*Kangai issoku*), 1901, he raised doubts about the state's performance, and in "Nichiren and Japan" he explicitly called attention to the failure of the state to provide "complete happiness." But none of this really affected the uncommon man who was self-sufficient, who knew, in fact, that the "kingdom is always in the heart" and it was the aesthetic life that made possible the experience of the joys "and bliss in this kingdom."

Takayama's conception of individualism, like Kitamura's theory of self, was an attempt to define the space allowed for "private affairs." It offered neither a mode of opposition to the claims of the state nor a theory of action. Yet it is important, I think, to stress how both men identified the possibility of individualism in private affairs with the few. Only the uncommon few, free of political commitments, will be able, as Thomas Mann wrote in *Tonio Kröger*, to commit their fullest energies to artistic activity, which is the symbol of all genuine culture, and indeed of any profession seeking to realize the promise of solid bourgeois values such as composure and self-discipline. These uncommon few, Mann wrote of Gustave von Aschenbach in *Death in Venice*, are "the spokesmen of all who labor at the edge of exhaustion" and who are, in the final analysis, "the heroes of the age." However, Takayama, unlike Kitamura, never worried about the excesses of the self. Kitamura, it might be recalled, disclosed profound anxieties about an isolated self that cannot reach out to move others; Takayama accepted the reality of an unmediated self and declared, "I am an egoist."[113] In a slightly self-critical pose Takayama argued that although he had been denounced as an egoist, in the end there was nothing outside the self. Only the self conferred identity. Religion was useless in the search for meaning. It "has made selflessness (*muga*) the great path of humanity. Since selflessness doesn't reveal the higher conditions

[113] *Cs* (1928), p. 212. "Seishiroku."

of our existence, I don't understand why I should respect religion."[114] Not even the state or society, which he approved of, offered any sense of self. The state was really "our master. It doesn't offer much support to subjects." Though it was proper to render unto Caesar what was Caesar's, "we cannot forget that it is we, ourselves, who promise the spiritual foundation of our existence." Lives had meaning for state and society, but a distance had to be maintained. "I believe firmly that we should live in the world, but it should be remembered that the individual does not exist within state and society. State and society exist within the individual. We have to conduct our spiritual lives under these conditions."[115]

Takayama's celebration of the unmediated self reached widely into Japanese society. Its long-term effects are evident among writers in the virtual obsession with the self, the creative personality, and the aesthete in isolation. His formulations might also explain why so much fiction has been confessional and introspective. Conversely, so much energy poured into confessional novels has weakened, if not undermined, the impulse to write biography and autobiography. Moreover the romantic embellishments which Takayama and Kitamura employed became, if Japanese literature is evidence, intimately associated with efforts to explicate the self. All heroes in Japan are romantic. Finally, it might offer some explanation as to why the problem of individualism ultimately became the subject of serious academic philosophic discourse (Abe Jirō's conception of personalism; Nishida Kitarō and Miki Kiyoshi on the self; etc.) and why, more importantly, intellectuals and writers, when they turned to the task of criticism, limited their activities either to self-criticism (the I-novel) or to expansive cultural criticism (Watsuji, the *Nihon Roman-ha*, Kobayashi Hideo) but rarely or never politics. In either case the "contemporary has been overcome," but in scaling such heights Japanese writers have said, I believe, acutely important things about contemporary politics, perhaps as an exercise in sublimation, resembling those of late Tokugawa nativists such as Motoori Norinaga. While being explicitly unpolitical they, in both cases, have been no less political. Yet the most important long-term legacy of the achievement of Kitamura and Takayama was to provide the means for writers and intellectuals to operate safely in the officially sanctioned space relating to "private affairs," to

[114] *Ibid.*, p. 215. [115] *Ibid.*, p. 216.

154

turn inward and probe the dimensions of their personal existence and experience as a necessary condition of their freedom.[116] In doing this they had exchanged the claims of the inner life for the pursuit of private interest.

[116] Cf. Arima, *op. cit.*, Chapter 1; pp. 99-172.

Aspects of the Proletarian
Literary Movement in Japan

ON JULY 24, 1927, Akutagawa Ryūnosuke, one of the most gifted story-tellers of modern Japan, committed suicide, leaving behind an enigmatic note attributing his radical action to a "vague uneasiness" (*bonyari-shita fuan*). Countless explanations have been offered by scholars and critics to account for the sources and nature of this death-causing uneasiness, explanations ranging in emphasis from private reasons to public and social ones, or sometimes a combination of the two. Of the more convincing hypotheses, one that links Akutagawa's behavior to his position in the literary world of late Taishō Japan seems most relevant for our purposes. It would appear that, despite his enormous talents and the high praise of his peers, Akutagawa was assailed by doubts about his worth as a writer and his status in the literary arena. This lack of confidence was aggravated and intensified by fresh movements which trumpeted the need for revolutionary changes in Japanese literature. The advocates of these changes unceremoniously dumped Akutagawa's works in a pigeonhole labeled "established literature" (*kisei bungaku*), whose special province was the uniquely Japanese "I" novel, a species of writing derived from Japanese-style naturalism that by and large restricted its compass to an excursion, lyrical if well done, into the feelings and incidents surrounding the author's life. Although Akutagawa himself in fact never indulged in this genre of fiction, he was nonetheless regarded as old hat by the youthful avant-garde and ignominiously relegated to past history. Perhaps he would not have felt the sting so acutely had the push for the new and modern in literature been only a quickly passing phenomenon. To his dismay and misfortune, however, the newfangled movements grew stronger and more vocal by the day and, even worse, their exponents began to produce works good enough to compete with those of the so-called established writers, who in the main withdrew into a defensive silence. Akutagawa's somewhat reluctant recognition of the literary talents of

Nakano Shigeharu, a fast-rising poet, novelist, and essayist of the proletarian school, is often cited as evidence to show his exaggerated fear of an imminent literary eclipse.

The newcomers' challenges to "the establishment" mirrored the concerns of the more recent literary movements in the West. The late Taishō–early Shōwa era was a period when, as the novelist Takami Jun has accurately observed, the time gap that had always existed in Japanese borrowings from Western literature was largely closed, so that Western literary trends were now almost simultaneously reflected in comparable movements in Japan.[1] There was a difference, however, in that a single Japanese school was likely to accommodate the interests of several different movements in the West. The following remarks of Yokomitsu Riichi—a retrospective view of the period in question—furnish a picture of the multiple concerns, as well as the spirit, which propelled the school that he led. Ideas that nurtured such diverse movements as, for instance, futurism and automatic writing are discernible.

In the midst of the great metropolis spread out like an unbelievably vast stretch of burnt ruins, a speed demon known as the automobile began to loiter about for the first time. Shortly a sound-emitting monster called the radio made its appearance, and then a bird-shaped object, the aeroplane, started coursing through the skies. These were embodiments of modern science that came into existence for the first time in our country soon after the earthquake. The sensibilities of the youths witnessing the successive manifestations of these latest contraptions of modern science amid the burnt ruins could not help but be altered in some fashion. . . . No longer able to endure the dull style of naturalism with its entangled emotions, I began a revolt. At the same time I necessarily had to commence the cultivation of a morality and a sense of beauty for the new age.[2]

Yokomitsu's "revolt" consisted largely of introducing a literature of new sensibilities, attuned to the machine age that had now engulfed Tokyo, no less than it had New York, London, and

[1] *Shōwa bungaku seisui shi* (Tokyo, 1958), I, 32ff.

[2] Quoted in Nakamura Mitsuo, Usui Yoshimi, and Hirano Ken, *Gendai Nihon bungaku shi: Gendai Nihon bungaku zenshū, bekkan 1* (Tokyo, 1959), pp. 328-329.

Paris. Philosophically, his subject was the mechanization of man brought on by industrialization centered in mammoth cities that bred a chilly, impersonal mode of life. Artistically, this concern was reflected, at least partly, through a rhetoric, often brilliant and startling, that recorded the immediate sense impressions of man to stimuli from the complex, kaleidoscopic world about.

While Yokomitsu's quarrel with the established writers hinged on the latter's failure or indifference in catching the human response to the vibrant tempo and mood of modern urban life, demonstrated as much through a scintillating, new style and form as in subject matter, the criticism aimed at the old-timers by another self-styled avant-garde group, the proletarian writers, was rooted in the question of the content of literature. Indeed, though Yokomitsu's faction and proletarian writers together opposed the established literature, they never became handshaking comrades in fighting their common enemy because of their divergent views on literary priorities. In fact, they ended up bitter enemies, as a continuation of Yokomitsu's recollections indicates:

> Just at that moment [when I began my revolt against naturalism] . . . historical materialism as the first positivistic theory to appear in our country had come to assault the spiritual realm. The incursions of this thought became fiercer by the day, and it swept over the world like a cloud obscuring the sun. We of the artistic group arrived at the fate of pointing our arms, hitherto aimed at the stronghold of naturalism, toward this unexpected, formidable foe.[3]

The attack of the proletarian writers on the established literature was based on its lack of a political or social conscience. The mainstream of Japanese literature since the advent of naturalism in the early part of the twentieth century showed a studious neglect of themes of a distinctly social or political cast. This literature preferred instead to confine its subject matter to a revelation of the author's life, the self-centeredness being no doubt a symptom of the writer's constant search for a personal identity, a search made possible and even necessary by the discovery of the conscience. If these works—confessions of aberrant sexual impulses, contemplations on the inner life, accounts of family squabbles, descriptions of trivial incidents, and the like—held any social or political criticism, it was only implicit and heavily

[3] *Ibid.*, p. 329.

muted; the range of the author's experience and interests encompassed the family at most, and rarely extended into society at large. This narrowly individualistic stance in the works of the established authors, devoid of social or political commentary, was to be replaced, at least in theory, by a much wider social concern in the works of the newly-risen proletarian authors.

While the mainstream writers remained silent on social and political matters, the theme of literature and society, or literature and politics, was not totally ignored, as small coteries of authors of a socialistic hue wrote works espousing their cause. Before them, in the 1880's, literature and politics had formed a productive alliance, making the so-called political novel the dominant genre of fiction of that period. Politics as conceived in these political novels, however, was quite different from politics as interpreted by the later proletarian writers. As the noted political scientist Maruyama Masao has astutely observed, politics as reflected in the work of the Meiji political novelists was preponderantly weighted on the side of national concern.[4] Though they indeed clamored for civil rights, for the rights of the individual, their overriding concern was for the enhancement of Japan's place in the international community. On the other hand, politics was understood by the proletarian authors largely in domestic terms; for them, politics meant the contention among social classes within the country. It is perhaps possible to say, then, that while the political novelists of the Meiji period were engaged in the pursuit of a national identity, and the apolitical naturalist writers who followed them sought a personal identity, the proletarian writers of the 1920's sought a class identity within their own society.

The genesis of the proletarian literary movement is to be found in the socialistically inclined literature of the 1900's and 1910's, but the movement proper is said to have started with the establishment of the magazine *Tane-maku hito* in February, 1921, giving it the organizational focus that it needed. The fortunes of the movement were inextricably bound with those of Marxism, which was readily accepted among many intellectuals in Japan after the success of the Russian Revolution. Why Marxism was embraced with such relish is a question that has occupied the attention of many writers. Though the reasons for the turn to Marxism were undoubtedly as varied and complex as were the numbers

[4] *Nihon no shisō* (Tokyo, 1961), pp. 71ff.

of converts, it seems incontestible that there was a strong faddish element in not a few of the conversions. In a fictional work evidently based on his own experiences and acquaintances in the Society for the Study of Marxist Arts at Tokyo University, Takami Jun presents an assemblage of obstreperous and haughty young men who, in their zeal for the new and exciting, are swept up by the tide of Marxism. But when the waters begin to recede, they are all too willing to give it up with but few qualms. Only a very few, truly devoted to Marxist ideals, are ready to meet dire ends in defense of their beliefs.[5]

Although recognizing the faddish component in the appeal of Marxism, the critic Honda Shūgo also sees more serious reasons for its attraction. He points out that Marxism, with its seemingly scientific and thus infallible approach to the problems of human society, appeared to have the answer to the questions that troubled the intellectual who had just recently witnessed war, panic, unemployment, and the triumphant establishment of socialism in the Soviet Union.[6] Too, as Robert Scalapino notes, in the minds of many Japanese intellectuals, who were smarting from a sense of inferiority due to the late modernization of their motherland, Marxist theory seemed to assure for Japan quick progress toward equality with the advanced nations of the West.[7] Moreover, Marxism was allowed to go unchallenged because a lack of tradition and achievements in the social sciences left the intellectual world without any alternative theories. Honda also believes that the outlawing of the Communist Party enhanced its appeal by shrouding it in mystery. To a good number of intellectuals, therefore, communism was free of evil and exemplified the supreme ideal that promised omnipotence and beatitude.[8] Not to be discounted in winning converts among those genuinely sensitive to the existing social inequities is the humanitarian concern which Marxist doctrine apparently embraced, with its promise of the liberation of the proletariat. The critic Hirano Ken, for example,

[5] In *Gendai Nihon bungaku zenshū*, ILVI (1955), 267-349. The work originally appeared in *Nichireki* (February-July, 1935); *Jimmin bunko* (March-September, 1936).

[6] *Tenkō bungaku ron* (Tokyo, 1957), pp. 133-134.

[7] In the 2nd part of his two-part article on Marxism in Japan, appearing in *The Japan Times*: the 1st part entitled "Marxism in Japan now losing prestige," August 8, 1962, p. 6; and the 2nd part entitled "Younger generation begins to turn away from Marxism," August 10, 1962, p. 7.

[8] Honda, pp. 133-134.

sees the conversion of such literary figures as Chūjō (Miyamoto) Yuriko deriving from this humanitarian spring.[9]

From its very inception, the proletarian literary movement was strongly influenced by left-wing political thought and activities within Japan and, though it was essentially domestic, by both political and artistic pronouncements issuing from Russia, as has been the case throughout the world. The multitudinous organizational and theoretical controversies that rocked the Japanese literary movement from its beginning in 1921 to its total collapse in 1934 were invariably generated from these two outside sources. This situation—peculiar, in the annals of Japanese literature, to the proletarian literary movement, leads Maruyama Masao to conceive of the relationship between literature and politics in this period in the image of a race, with literature desperately trying to catch up with political thought and activities.[10] Indeed this somewhat comical image is not without foundation.

The organizational splits and realignments which marked the literary movement were in almost every case motivated by events outside its artistic purview. To begin with, the stimulus for the founding of *Tane-maku hito* came from the formation of the Japan Socialist League in December, 1920. In one of the early issues of the magazine, the leaders, headed by Komaki Ōmi and Kaneko Yōbun, proclaimed their intention to work for modernity, revolution, and internationalism, clearly revealing their interest as much, if not more, in political and cultural affairs as in literature per se.[11] After the great earthquake of September, 1923, which occasioned an all-out government attack on the socialist movement, *Tane-maku hito* was followed in June, 1924, by another magazine, *Bungei sensen*. Then, when Komaki, Kaneko, Aono Suekichi, and other supporters of this magazine, encompassing all shades of left-wing writers, were organized into the Japan Proletarian Literary Arts League in December of 1925, the inspiration once again came from without. The major impulse this time originated in the meeting of proletarian writers in the Soviet Union, which opened in conjunction with the Fifth Gen-

[9] Discussed in Takami, *Shōwa bungaku*, p. 122.
[10] *Op. cit.*, pp. 77ff.
[11] October, 1921, issue. See Kurahara Korehito, *et al.* (eds.), *Ninon puroretaria bungaku taikei* (Kyoto, 1955), I, 324.

eral Meeting of the Comintern in Moscow in July, 1924. The international appeal to proletarian writers formulated at the meeting had been relayed to Japan's *Bungei sensen* as well, furnishing a powerful motive for the creation of the League.

The political coloration of the League took on a decidedly Marxist tinge when it became dominated by such youthful members as Nakano Shigeharu, Hayashi Fusao, Kaji Wataru, and Tani Hajime of the Society for the Study of Marxist Arts, a student organization at Tokyo University. Gaining control of the proceedings of the Second General Meeting of the League held in November, 1926, these impetuous young radicals in effect ousted the non-Marxists, and renamed and reorganized the League into the Japan Proletarian Arts League (JPAL).

The expulsion of the non-Marxists, sounding the death-knell for the proletarian arts movement as a loose common front of anarchism, syndicalism, and bolshevism, did not presage a period of calm activity for the JPAL, as differences in political viewpoint continued to plague what was supposedly an organization for art. The first schism occurred just six months later, when Fukumoto Kazuo's political theory was injected into the arts movement. In essence, Fukumoto's views, which at the time were successfully challenging Yamakawa Hitoshi's older and more practicable theory, emphasized the study of Marxist theory and contended that a thoroughgoing knowledge of Marxist writings should be a sine qua non for membership in the Japanese Communist Party.[12] Adherents of Fukumotoism in the League accused their comrades of falling into self-intoxication through vain adherence to the arts and failing to develop the socialist political struggle of the masses. To them *Bungei sensen* appeared to be playing court to bourgeois literary circles, a cardinal sin that had to be stamped out completely in order to make the literary movement one wing of the entire proletarian political battle. Plainly, the pro-Fukumoto group under Kaji and Nakano refused to recognize the independent character of the arts movement and insisted that all be dissolved into the political fight in the narrow sense.[13] On the other hand, non-Fukumotoists such as Aono and

[12] Rodger Swearingen and Paul Langer, *Red Flag in Japan: International Communism in Action 1919-1951* (Cambridge, Mass., 1952), pp. 15-26, *passim*.

[13] See the following articles by the pro-Fukumoto group, all reproduced in vol. I of Hirano Ken, *et al.* (eds.), *Gendai Nihon bungaku ronsō shi* (Tokyo,

Hayashi, while fully acknowledging the instrumental value of the arts movement in the political struggle, wished to retain for it its special character.[14] A rapprochement between the two groups was impossible, and finally Aono and Hayashi,[15] together with Kurahara Korehito and others, left the JPAL to form the Worker-Farmer-Artists League (WFAL) in June, 1927.

In November of the same year, scarcely six months after its organization, the WFAL itself suffered a rupture. The cause was the issuance of the "1927 Thesis" or "Bukharin July Thesis" which had censured both Yamakawaism and Fukumotoism for their "dangerous deviations."[16] In the ensuing months, followers of Yamakawa tried to regain some of the territory that they had lost to the Fukumotoists. Reverberations from this joust in the left-wing political world were felt in the WFAL where staunch supporters of Yamakawa such as Aono resided. The dissension within the WFAL, therefore, was between those who aggressively supported the social-democratic theory of Yamakawa and those who leaned closer to the political views of the JPAL, which favored Fukumotoism. Members leaving the WFAL, including Hayashi and Kurahara, established the Vanguard Artists League

---

1957). (1) Tani Hajime, "Waga kuni puroretaria bungei undō no hatten"—first published in *Bungei sensen* (October, 1926). (2) Kaji Wataru, "Iwayuru shakaishugi bungei o kokufuku seyo"—first published in *Musansha shimbun* (February 5, 1927). (3) Nakano Shigeharu, "Kesshō-shitsutsu aru shoshi-minsei"—first published in *Bungei sensen* (March, 1927).

14 See the following two articles by Hayashi Fusao, also included in Hirano, *et al.* (eds.), I. (1) "Shakaishugi bungei undō"—first published in *Bungei sensen* (February, 1927). (2) "Tēze ni kansuru gokai ni tsuite"—first published in *Bungei sensen* (March, 1927).

15 Although Hayashi was an original member of the Society for the Study of Marxist Arts and was of the same generation as Nakano and others, he remained relatively untouched by Fukumotoism because his introduction to Marxism had come earlier than the advent of Fukumoto. Hirano Ken suggests that Hayashi's split with Nakano, Kaji, and Tani originated with the former's superiority complex; already known as a rising writer, Hayashi did not wish to align himself with unknowns. See "Kaisetsu," in Kurahara, *et al.* (eds.), II, 419.

16 Swearingen and Langer, p. 26. Yamakawaism was criticized for its refusal to recognize the "evident need for an independent, disciplined Communist Party," and Fukumotoism for "going too far in the opposite direction and thus exposing the Party to the danger of isolation from the masses." A bourgeois-democratic revolution to eliminate such residues of feudalism as the Emperor and the land-owners was to be the immediate aim of the Party. A successful revolution would be possible once this stage was attained.

(VAL) in November, 1927. Shortly thereafter, however, the VAL dissolved itself into the All-Japan Federation of Proletarian Arts, commonly known as NAPF from the initials of its Esperanto name, when it was formed in March, 1928, uniting into one body the members of the VAL and the JPAL. This last move too was engendered by political, not artistic, motives. The government crackdown on the Communist Party of March 15, 1928, provided the stimulus for those with similar views to band together. It was also with the establishment of NAPF that the proletarian arts movement assumed a strong communist direction.

NAPF, which far overshadowed the WFAL in its activities and in fact captured the hegemony of the literary world for the proletarian literary movement, underwent one final organizational mutation before its demise in 1934. The reorganization, purely internal in nature, renamed the Federation as the Japan Proletarian Culture Federation, ordinarily referred to as KOPF. The basis for the change was the thesis concerning "the role and mission of proletarian cultural and educational organization" which was settled upon in the Agit-Prop Council at the Fifth General Meeting of the Profintern in Moscow in August, 1930.[17] On his return, the Japanese representative to the meeting, Kurahara, was eager to put into practice the new instructions and adopt the trends emanating from the capital of the socialist world. Under the KOPF set-up, the various culture groups under its aegis were encouraged to combine as far as possible with international organizations. Thus, the Japan Proletarian Writers' League, for example, became the Japanese branch of the International Union of Revolutionary Writers in February, 1932.

If the organizational aspects of the proletarian literary movement were affected by pronouncements from Russia, so were the attempts at building a theoretical framework for creative activity. The race image is particularly apt here, as Japanese theorists hurried to assimilate the latest theoretical thought coming out of Russia. This reliance on Russian effusions is evident everywhere in the numerous theoretical controversies that punctuated the course of the literary movement, but a look at only a few of the highlights should amply illustrate the point.

[17] For an explication of this thesis, see "Kaisetsu," in Kurahara, *et al.* (eds.), vi, 369-371.

In September, 1926, Aono Suekichi, who ruled supreme as theoretician, produced an essay entitled "Shizen seichō to mokuteki ishiki" (Natural Development and Conscious Purpose) an application of Lenin's political views, expressed in *What is to be Done?*, about the literary movement. It was in a sense an extension of an earlier article of July, 1925, called " 'Shirabets' geijutsu" (Scientific Art),[18] where he advocated that more social phenomena be scientifically investigated and analyzed for the creation of a more comprehensive literature. In the new essay, Aono explained what he meant by consciousness of an objective:

> For the proletariat to seek expression by describing the life of the proletariat merely amounts to individual satisfaction, and does not entirely constitute class conduct that is conscious of the objective of the struggle by the proletarian class. . . . That is to say, only when one is led by class consciousness does one's art become art for the sake of class. Only at this point does the proletarian literary movement arise, and indeed has arisen.[19]

Although the writings of Hirabayashi Hatsunosuke, the leading theoretician in the days of *Tane-maku hito*, had revealed distinct Marxist leanings, it was this work by Aono, insisting on class consciousness of a socialistic objective, that guided the Japanese proletarian literary movement along Marxist lines. It also caused considerable confusion because, although he discussed the consciousness of an objective, he scarcely elaborated on how it should be manifested in literary works. His essay, in short, was little more than political theory which could not become literary theory or the theory of a literary movement in any practicable sense.

Kurahara Korehito, who supplanted Aono as the foremost theorist of the movement after the founding of NAPF, was even more inclined toward borrowing from Russian writings. Obviously his period of study in the Soviet Union had left indelible impressions on his mind. Indeed, Kurahara's first statements on artistic method were not much more than transplanted theory, the officially endorsed viewpoint on realism adopted by the Russian Association of Proletarian Writers (RAPP). Little challenge to Kurahara's stand appeared, as, characteristically, the members of NAPF bowed to the specter of authority.

[18] Published in *Bungei sensen*.
[19] In *Gendai Nihon bungaku zenshū*, LXXCIII (1957), 78. First published in *Bungei sensen* (September, 1926).

In his "Puroretaria rearizumu e no michi" (The Road to Proletarian Realism) of May, 1928, Kurahara attempted to lay down the methodological principles for the composition of proletarian literature. Beginning with a definition of realism, pronounced as the artistic attitude of a rising class in contrast to idealism, the artistic outlook of a degenerating class, Kurahara went on to point out the difference between proletarian realism and bourgeois realism. First, bourgeois realism was a position of individualism. Naturalistic literature, which had its beginning in the individual, sought in him something eternal and absolute, and found it in his biological nature. Man, however, is a social being and, apart from his society and age, his basic original nature adds up to mere abstraction. The proletarian writer must discard the method of tracing social problems back to man's nature, and acquire the method of looking at all human problems from a social point of view. Second, proletarian realism must demonstrate a class viewpoint: the proletarian writer must see and describe the world with the eyes of the proletarian vanguard. Without this viewpoint, the world cannot be seen in its entirety or in the process of development. Society is constantly on the march, and the impetus for change comes, not from class harmony, but from class struggle, which constitutes the true pattern of society. Kurahara concluded by urging an objective attitude toward reality, but added:

> What is important for us is not that we distort or embellish reality with our subjectivity, but that we discover in the midst of reality that which corresponds to our subjectivity—the proletarian class subjectivity. Only thus will we be able to make our literature useful in the proletarian class struggle.
>
> That is to say, first, to look at the world "with the eyes" of the proletarian vanguard, and second, to describe with the attitude of a strict realist—that is the only path to proletarian realism.[20]

To supplement this article, Kurahara wrote "Futatabi puroretaria rearizumu ni tsuite" (Proletarian Realism Revisited) in August, 1929, in which he argued that proletarian realism alone had the method of looking at reality from the world view of the proletariat. "That method is materialistic dialectics. Materialistic

[20] *Ibid.*, p. 165. "Puroretaria rearizumu e no michi" first appeared in *Senki* (May, 1928).

dialectics teaches us to recognize in what direction this society will advance, what is essential in this society, and what is incidental. Based on this method, proletarian realism selects what is essential out of the endlessly complicated social phenomena, and proceeds to describe this from the viewpoint of the direction in which it necessarily advances."[21] In essence, proletarian realism handled society in action, and meant the artistic description of "that which is inevitably leading to the victory of the proletariat." Plainly then, it could not be a truly objective realism because of its prior commitment to a particular standpoint.

There is some question over the sagacity of imposing upon the Japanese literary movement artistic theories that were developed in the Soviet Union where conditions were quite different. At any rate, Hirano Ken sees in Kurahara's first essay on proletarian realism the seeds for the development of a communist direction in the movement, leading it away from a broadly based literary movement to one concentrated in an elite capable of "looking at the world 'with the eyes' of the proletarian vanguard." According to Hirano, under the circumstances of the time the only element in the socio-political spectrum that could be characterized as a vanguard was the illegal Communist Party.[22] Later Kurahara, having joined the Party in September of 1929, contributed to the communization of the movement with an article called "Nappu geijutsuka no atarashii nimmu" of April, 1930. Reviewing the actual products of NAPF artists of the past months, Kurahara readily acknowledged that considerable advances had been achieved; artists had successfully responded to such slogans as "draw closer to the masses" and "describe the life of the laborers and peasants." However, there was one important ingredient missing and that, Kurahara pointed out, was "a clear communist viewpoint distinctly differentiated from the social-democratic viewpoint." The reason for this deficiency was the fact that NAPF writers had failed to solve the question of how to express adequately their left-wing views. Kurahara offered these recommendations to overcome the problem:

First, it is possible by taking as the theme of our artistic activity those subjects which our artists, our country's prole-

[21] Quoted in G. T. Shea, *Leftwing Literature in Japan* (Tokyo, 1964), p. 239. This article was first published in *Senki*.
[22] Nakamura, Usui, and Hirano, p. 368.

tariat, and their Party are facing at the present time. . . . In present-day Japan where the fighting proletariat is making the strengthening and broadening of the Party which stands at the head of the mass struggle its central subject, the entire concern of proletarian writers and artists must also proceed along this line. In this way, for the first time, can we become true bolshevist communist artists, not vague "proletarian artists."[23]

The artist need not restrict his materials to the activity of the vanguard, Kurahara added; indeed, the more diverse the subject matter the better. However, he continued: "If the artist is a communist . . . first, he in all likelihood will not be able to handle subjects which are completely separated from the needs of the proletariat and their Party, and second, he will probably approach his subject from the 'viewpoint of the vanguard' which connects all problems with the proletariat's revolutionary subjects of the period."[24]

The frenetic pitch and romantic fervor with which the controversies in the proletarian camp were debated attracted the attention of the entire literary world, and the years around 1927-1928 witnessed the conversion of many bourgeois writers to left-wing literature, especially from the "modernist" ranks. To name but a few of the more notable converts, Kataoka Teppei, Takeda Rintarō, and Takami Jun all turned rather suddenly to left-wing literature. Before their apostasy, they had reflected the newer trends in Western literature and art such as cubism, futurism, and dadaism, and had in a sense created a "revolution in literature." With the phenomenal upsurge of Marxist literature in and around 1927-1928, however, the "revolution in literature" was transformed into "revolutionary literature."

Not all the bourgeois writers flocked to the Marxist camp, of course. Indeed, Yokomitsu, the bellwether of "modernist" literature, remained a staunch foe of Marxism, and in 1928 engaged in a major dispute with the proletarian writers which later critics have labeled the "controversy on formalism." The starting point for Yokomitsu's attack was an assertion by Kurahara that

art is technique as well as ideology, and form as well as content. If it is a fact that form is determined by content, then it is also a fact that a form does not arise spontaneously from

[23] In Kurahara, *et al.* (eds.), IV, 305. First published in *Senki*.
[24] *Ibid.*, p. 306.

content. The form of an artistic work arises only as a development of past form that has been determined by new content. This is the only true principle of artistic development as viewed from the Marxist standpoint.[25]

The statement, Yokomitsu sardonically implied, showed Kurahara to be a false Marxist. By equating form with object and content with subject, Yokomitsu interpreted Kurahara as meaning that subject determines object, in antithesis to the time-honored principle of materialism that object creates subject.[26] Critics from among both the formalists and the Marxists joined the debate, but there could never be an acceptable solution since the concept of form and content held by the two sides differed so markedly. As the expert on Marxist literary theory, Kurahara presented the Marxist attitude in the characteristic rhetoric of the school. The content of art, Kurahara held, could not be found outside man's social activities. At every moment of his historical progress, man faces certain social needs which are ultimately determined by the progress of productivity, and these needs in human society constitute the content of all man's social activities, such as politics, economy, religion, philosophy, science, etc. Thus, the objective content of art may take the shape of and appear concretely as art, but it is never created for the first time by artistic form, since the content of art existed before art was born. As for the form of art, it is determined by the progress of productivity, which ultimately defines the form of labor of a given society in a given period. It changes with the development of productivity, and at the same time the scope of the potential form of art broadens. "The form of art," Kurahara summed up, "is determined in the dialectical interaction between the social and class necessities which constitute the content of art and the possibilities in form which have been created beforehand by the process of productivity."[27] Marxist litterateurs were thus not uninterested in the question of form, and indeed it would have been impossible to ignore at any rate. But they accorded primacy to content, specifically to social content; the modernists emphasized form.

[25] "Geijutsu undō ni okeru 'sayoku' seisanshugi," in Hirano, *et al.* (eds.), I, 315. First published in *Senki* (October, 1928).

[26] "Bungei jihyō," in Hirano, *et al.* (eds.), I, 366. First published in *Bungei shunju* (November, 1928).

[27] "Puroretaria geijutsu no naiyō to keishiki," in *Gendai Nihon bungaku zenshū*, LXXVIII, 181-184. First published in *Senki* (February, 1929).

If the race image is carried a step further, it is possible to see that within the proletarian literary camp itself there was a race to bridge the distance that separated creative works and literary theory. More accurately, authors found themselves in the disquieting position of perpetually trying to keep pace with the newest trends in left-wing literary thought and to realize these in their works. Buffeted by changes in theory and organizational set-up from time to time, writers found that what they had produced to satisfy one set of principles at a certain time would be criticized as obsolete or misdirected shortly after. In a short story by Tateno Nobuyuki called "Yūjō," where the principal characters are obviously modeled after Kurahara and Kobayashi Takiji, the most famous of the proletarian writers, the latter at one point is shown changing the course of a story being serialized in a magazine in order to accommodate Kurahara's new policies and criticisms. He rationalizes nonchalantly, "I write incorporating criticisms which I think are correct. . . . So long as the work moves in a positive direction, some disjointedness is justified."[28]

Aono Suekichi's "Shizen seichō to mokuteki ishiki" of September, 1926, mentioned earlier, should probably be singled out for nurturing the race image between theory and creative efforts. In specifying that, in contrast to simple proletarian literature, the proletarian literary movement was one to implant consciousness of an objective, Aono called for works that went beyond mere spontaneous expressions of discontent and resentment among the proletariat and would place the literary movement as an active participant in the over-all class movement of the proletariat.

Hayama Yoshiki's novel *Umi ni ikuru hitobito*,[29] though not written under the direct prompting of Aono's essay (the manuscript of the novel was completed some three years earlier), actualized in many ways the theory laid down in Aono's article. It elevated the creative aspect of the proletarian literary movement to a level matching its theory. The story takes for its background the economically prosperous period of the First World War, and for its setting a coal steamer plying between Muroran and Yokohama; it describes with stark simplicity the figures of the crew members who battle against overwhelming odds. In the

[28] In Kurahara, *et al.* (eds.), vii, 278. "Yūjō" first appeared in *Chūō kōron* in August, 1934.

[29] In *Gendai Nihon bungaku zenshū*, xxxviii (1954), 5-98. Published by Kaizōsha in November, 1926.

menacing storm that greets the ship on its departure, an apprentice sailor toiling with the steering gear is severely injured, but the ogreish captain throws him into the forecastle and leaves him unattended for days. With repeated acts of extreme callousness, bestiality, and exploitation by the captain, the anger and indignation of the crew members mount in intensity, and in the process their resentment crystallizes into a realization of the need for organized action. Once united, they formulate a plan to strike en masse until their demands for increased wages, an eight-hour day, and better medical treatment are met. The captain, eager to get the steamer to Yokohama in order to keep a rendezvous with his mistress on New Year's day, accedes to the ultimatum. It is a Pyrrhic victory for the crew members, however, for what awaits them at the dock is arrest by the Water Police for mutiny.

Umi ni ikuru hitobito received lavish praise by some Japanese critics when it first appeared in November, 1926, and even today it is numbered among the best of its genre. If only for its epoch-making role in the development of proletarian literature, it deserves special commendation. The historical significance of the work lies in the description of the gradual awakening of the workers to the truth of the class struggle underlying their individual grievances and the advantages of uniting and organizing to present a common front for their demands. It is notable for introducing into Japanese literature consciously revolutionary characters, especially in the person of Fujiwara, one of the several heroes. Where the novel achieves its greatest success, however, is in its gripping and earthy descriptions of exploited men at work, fighting both the gross atrocities of their captain and the harsh, wintry elements. Hayama catches the rough-and-tumble language of the sailors with a keen ear for dialogue, and for the most part he effects a style that well matches his subject matter. The short, choppy sentences exude a primitive sense of beauty entirely befitting the theme of the story. The thoroughly legitimate concern for a more humane order emerges most forcefully from these powerfully graphic accounts. The novel is also not without some technical sophistication as Hayama employs the crippled apprentice sailor as a kind of symbol to the others of their own fate, unless they join together and resist the inhuman treatment.

Nonetheless, the novel is by and large technically awkward, betraying everywhere the undisciplined hand of an inexperienced writer. It starts out promisingly as an objective narration in the third person, but before long it gives way to a subjective narration in the first person plural, and in the latter part of the book the author completely loses control of his point of view as he intrudes embarrassingly with asides and addresses directed to the reader. He apologizes at one point, "Like a drunkard, I proceed unsteadily, going over the same ground again and again"; but quickly he justifies his method, "But this is because I'm a seaman and not a novelist. Really, to write about such things, indeed just to 'write,' is no easy task."[30] That the job is almost too onerous is made all too plain not only by the shifting point of view but by the selection and employment of flashbacks, some to fill in the background of characters, others to provide what the author believes to be pertinent information.

Almost by definition proletarian literature is committed to depicting the proletariat in a sympathetic light while painting the capitalist in demonic colors. *Umi ni ikuru hitobito* amply displays this bias. The captain of the ship is purely and simply a villain of the darkest sort with absolutely no redeeming human virtues. On the other hand, Hayama makes an earnest attempt to invest his workers with at least two- if not three-dimensional qualities. If he had failed here, of course, his novel would have altogether lost its raison d'être, since its purpose is to picture a group of mindless seamen slowly becoming infused with a class consciousness. The transformation of the group from men of low self-esteem, each concerned only with his own limited well-being, into proud workers with a strong class identity is done realistically and convincingly in the main. There is, however, a jarring note or two. Ogura, a young man aiming to join the legion of the bourgeoisie by becoming a captain some day, turns rather suddenly into a committed fighter for the proletariat when a prostitute for the working class lectures to him about class loyalty and class pride. Humbled and deeply moved by the sermon, Ogura becomes one of the driving forces in fomenting the strike.

Fujiwara, an obvious projection of the author himself, emerges as the conscious leader of the strike. Described as having given up a parasitic student life to seek out "real" life as an apprentice in a factory where he had become engaged in socialist activities, Fujiwara is the only one experienced in labor disputes and the

[30] *Ibid.*, p. 73.

labor movement and he coolly proceeds to organize the sailors. He would not be an unbelievable character if the facts of history did not disclose him to be an anachronism. The story is laid in 1914, and Fujiwara is clearly a figure based on Hayama of about 1920-1923. His labor-movement activity and ideological thinking, described in a flashback to his earlier life, are products of the 1917 Revolution in Russia and the labor movement in postwar Japan. Thus he has little organic connection with the reality of the war period.

The concept of a race between politics and literature became more acute with the formation of NAPF and the communist direction given the cultural movement by the young left-wing intellectuals. At the general meetings of the Japan Proletarian Writers' League, one of the bodies within NAPF and later within KOPF, repeated references were made to the lag between literature and the actual political fight of the proletariat. For instance, at the second meeting, held on April 6, 1930, at which time the bolshevization of the arts movement was determined upon, it was concluded "that the literary arts movement is several steps behind the rest of the proletarian movement, that Marxist elements are comparatively few in both the content and form of proletarian literary works, and that to achieve a truly strong proletarian literature, 'a Marxist consciousness must throb in every corner of a work.' A class work will be produced for the first time only when the writer acquires a penetrating Marxist viewpoint."[31] The lag between theory and creative works was suggested in indicating the deficiencies in novels of the past year: failure to treat such topics as industrial rationalization, reduction of working hours, the unemployment problem, and mass struggles in farming and fishing villages.

One of the most celebrated writers to come into prominence during the early part of the NAPF-KOPF period was Tokunaga Suano, lauded particularly because of his rise from the worker class. His *Taiyō no nai machi*[32] of 1929, which won instant fame, answered in a limited sense Kurahara's constant entreaty for proletarian works of sweeping scope. Based on Tokunaga's personal experience as a worker and an organizer of a union at the Haku-

[31] Shea, p. 217.
[32] In *Nihon bungaku zenshū* (Tokyo, 1961), xxxvi, 211-380. First serialized in *Senki* from June to November, 1929.

bunkan Press in Tokyo, *Taiyō no nai machi* is a novel that describes the large-scale strike which erupted at the press in 1926 and eventually ended with the defeat of the union.

Tokunaga utilizes a multi-dimensional approach in delineating the configurations of the strike, embracing the viewpoints and actions not only of the workers and their families, both as individuals and groups, but of the capitalists and government officials as well. The numerous scene-changes in many ways anticipate, in the novel form, the recent motion-picture technique of rapid cuts. The camera eye sees the leaders of the strike planning their tactics, watches the mob spirit mount among the strikers as negotiations drag on, catches brutal scenes between the police and workers, spies on the company president as he fortifies himself with a system of alignments to meet the challenge, and follows the ramifications of the strike into outlying districts. The strike ends in failure when the company president fires the 2,700 workers en masse and hires scab labor to resume operations. With their leaders gone, except for a young radical group determined to carry on the fight, the strikers are ready to call a truce.

Tokunaga handles the multi-sided approach with considerable skill, giving the work a breadth and depth never before achieved by a proletarian work. The various viewpoints concerning the strike are hardly objective, however, as they are filtered through the author's own subjective proletarian consciousness. The president, Ōkawa, comes off little better than does Hayama's captain—he is the incarnation of evil itself. Still, as Ōkawa strengthens his position through an alignment with Baron Shibusaka, head of the Mitsubishi interests and a member of the Diet, and as he bullies the mediators into submission by intimating the striking union's communist connections, we get at least a picture, if not an altogether true one, of behind-the-scenes capitalist machinations.

The multi-dimensional approach can usually be artistically successful only in a novel of considerable length where there is ample room to elaborate on the variety. *Taiyō no nai machi* is not a short work by the standard of proletarian fiction, but it is hardly a *Tale of Genji* or a *War and Peace*. The diffuse, episodic, and shallow quality that works of this nature are prone to is increasingly evident in Tokunaga's novel as time and again he merely sketches outlines of peoples and events rather than endowing them with dramatic fullness.

If there are any dominant characters in the novel, Takae would be foremost among them. Aggressive and even manly in her behavior, she is a pillar of strength among the women in fostering the will to continue the strike. A renegade who reads Marx, she is thoroughly wedded to the cause, shunting aside as feudalistic notions the objections of her invalid father who speaks of obligation (*on*) to the company. In many respects, Takae becomes the prototype of the female proletarian vanguard: fearless and sexless, she is respected by all her male peers, but becomes the bedmate of none. O-Kayo, her sister, is the exact opposite—quiet, gentle, and feminine. Jailed for participating in a strike meeting, O-Kayo, pregnant by her lover, a fellow striker, comes down with beriberi, which eventually kills both her and her unborn child. Tokunaga, like Hayama, fails to curb his melodramatic instincts as he lets the mourners drape the union banner over her coffin as one of them intones sonorously, "Oh, sleeping comrade, you whose lifetime has been hapless and unfortunate, we shall forever keep in the depths of our hearts the memory of your splendid life. We shall mourn for you."[33]

Tokunaga himself has criticized the novel not on artistic grounds but for its political naivete. He has admitted, first of all, that because of his ignorance concerning the nature of the Japan Communist Party and especially its relation with the Japan Worker-Farmer Party, he failed to describe the political aspects properly in the work. Secondly, he notes that he was unable to describe critically the propensity toward Fukumotoism which was part of the central strike in the novel.[34] Indeed, the connection of the plant union with other bodies such as the parent union, the Worker-Farmer Party, and the Communist Party is left entirely vague, and what Tokunaga refers to as the controversy over Fukumotoism is revealed only in the split in union leadership between those who would make concessions to end the strike and those who would hold out to the bitter end.

Another author making his debut in the early NAPF-KOPF period and eventually winning the reputation of being the finest writer in the history of Japanese proletarian literature was Kobayashi Takiji. If his works are not of the first order artistically, they at least reveal Kobayashi's indefatigable effort to explore new themes and methods for the cause of proletarian literature. Perhaps more than any other author, he constantly strove to incor-

---

[33] *Ibid.*, p. 360.   [34] See Shea, p. 282.

porate and actualize the latest trends in proletarian literary theory in his novels and short stories, and obsequiously accepted the criticisms directed at his works from the higher echelons of the Writers' League, particularly Kurahara. If Kurahara was a pawn to the dictates issuing from the Soviet Union, Kobayashi was even more a servile follower of Kurahara's commands.

Kobayashi's best-known work is undoubtedly *Kanikōsen*,[35] which earned him not only national but a limited international recognition through a partial English translation. The novelette takes as its theme the capitalist invasion of the fishing industry as seen in the operation of a crab-canning ship which lies outside the scope of both the factory and navigation laws of the country. It is a powerful story in terse, raw language, about how the proletariat, represented by the working men on ship, is gruesomely maltreated by the capitalists, symbolized in the figure of the malevolent superintendent Asakawa. The plot, similar in bare outline to Hayama's *Umi ni ikuru hitobito*, builds up to a climax at the end when the men finally rise in a strike. The strike, however, is quashed by the Navy, which has been summoned by Asakawa, revealing to the men that the Navy too is a tool of capitalism.

In *Kanikōsen*, Kobayashi intended to expose not only the brutality of the capitalists but also their hand and influence in the government and its imperialistic designs. The superintendent's summons for loyalty and diligence from the workers, for instance, is made in the name of the national effort to bolster Japan's international position. The mission of the ship is not simply to catch crab, Asakawa roars, but also to broaden and strengthen the international prestige of the nation. He later contrives to fish secretly in Russian waters under the protection of the Japanese Navy. But Kobayashi's attempt to unmask the tie between the capitalists and the government and its larger implications is not always successful or clear, for the exposition comes only in fragmentary comments.

The difficulty of embodying political ideas in believable incidents and live characters—a difficulty experienced not only by Kobayashi but by all the proletarian writers—is perhaps no more obvious than in an improbable scene, ostensibly included to

[35] In *Nihon bungaku zenshū*, xxxvi, 21-96. First serialized in *Senki* from May to June, 1929.

strengthen the communist character of the work. A group of men is washed ashore on Russian territory when their fishing boat encounters a gale. There they are befriended by some Russians who epitomize the glories of the proletarian way of life. In an unintentionally funny scene, the men are indoctrinated with communist ideology through a Chinese interpreter speaking faltering Japanese.

"You—have no money."
"That's right."
"You—poor folk."
"That's right."
"So—you proletariat. Understand?"
"Yeah."

The Russians began walking about with smiles on their faces. Now and then they would stop and look in their direction.

"Rich man—he kill you. (He puts his hands to his throat to show a man being choked.) Rich man—he get big. (He gestures to indicate a man growing fat.) You—no matter what, no good—you get poor. Understand? Japan, bad. Working people, this. (With a scowl on his face, he poses as a sick person.) People who not work, this. (He walks around in a bossy manner.)"

The young fishermen were amused by the antics of the Chinese. They began to chuckle saying, "Yeah, that's right!"

". . . Russia, this country—all working people. No people who not work. No sneaky people. No people who choke you. Understand? Russia not country to be scared of. Everybody tell lie about Russia."

Vaguely the men wondered if this was the so-called "fearful bolshevization" often spoken of. But they got the impression that if this was "bolshevization," it was something perfectly "reasonable." They were inescapably attracted to it.[36]

After only two days, the men return to the mother ship with the design of propagating the new learning.

Kobayashi was far more impressive in depicting scenes of wanton brutality. There is something almost masochistic in these descriptions, and ironically the ghastly tortures that he detailed so skillfully foreshadowed the manner of his own death shortly

[36] *Ibid.*, pp. 46-47.

after. What is likely to remain with the reader are just these harrowing scenes rather than the jejune political ideology of the work.

The novelette employs a methodological approach deserving attention. As one means of connoting the whole social structure of contemporary Japan under the capitalist regime, Kobayashi deliberately refrained from telescoping his view on any specific individuals and opted for group portraiture. The approach involves an avoidance of personal names, leading to the awkward technique of referring to characters as "the ex-student," "the scolder," and so forth. The workers remain nameless, but the evil capitalist superintendent is given a real name, Asakawa. The result is that Asakawa stands out in bold relief and the workers merge into a horde of nonentities, an effect perhaps unintended by Kobayashi.

After completing the manuscript of the novel, Kobayashi wrote a letter to Kurahara in which he outlined as one of his aims a description of a group of workers without the depiction of the character and psychology of any one individual.[37] But Kurahara had reservations about the success of such a method, and questioned whether the proletarian writer must necessarily bury the individual in order to describe the mass. Kurahara's answer was that the materialistic view of history never denies the role of the individual in history or society; it denies the concept of the bourgeois superman, the individual opposing society. The problem was not one of the individual or the group, but of establishing the individual within the group. If *Kanikōsen* had described the character and psychology of individuals as representatives of various classes, Kurahara concluded, it would have been an even better work.[38]

In his last work, *Tō seikatsusha*, of April-May, 1933, Kobayashi portrayed the life of a Party member, a proletarian vanguard, working in a factory cell.[39] The material for the novelette is based on the author's own experience as a cell worker since his arrival in Tokyo from Hokkaidō in March of 1930, after which time he became an active member of the Writers' League and subse-

[37] Kurahara Korehito, *Kobayashi Takiji to Miyamoto Yuriko* (Tokyo, 1953), p. 65.

[38] *Ibid.*, pp. 48-49.

[39] In *Nihon bungaku zenshū*, xxxvi, 133-208. The work was first published posthumously in *Chūō kōron*, April-May, 1933.

quently of the Agit-Prop Section of the Japan Communist Party. *Tō seikatsusha* details the underground life and work of Sasaki, the "I" of the story, who directs a number of his comrades working in a factory that manufactures parachutes. The story revolves around their endeavors to popularize the revolutionary movement and mobilize the entire working force in a general strike to protest the firing of the temporary laborers. In the process, Kobayashi paints with considerable force the inherent dangers involved in such work. The constant need for vigilance against detection, the determination to conquer the sense of constriction, and the willingness to sacrifice a personal life—inevitable concomitants of such activities—are convincingly portrayed. Kobayashi also weaves into the story the hardships imposed upon the mother of the hero, who must endure not only the solitary life without her only son but also harassment and contempt from neighbors and police. Intermittently, the author obtrudes with "political" remarks or he directs criticism at Fukumotoism for its sectarian proclivities, and drops names such as Lenin and Marx. He also entertains the political idea that the workers must be made conscious of the connection between war and their own work. The strike that the cell workers have been planning ends in failure as a result of a company ruse, but Kobayashi still closes the novelette on a note of ultimate victory.

Shortly after the war, critics such as Hirano Ken and Ara Masahito pointed to Kobayashi's "contempt of man" in his treatment of Kasahara, the woman Sasaki marries. They expressed surprise that Marxist literature, which ostensibly fought for the liberation of the masses, should reveal an underlying current of apathy toward man's well-being.[40] In the novel, Sasaki marries Kasahara purely for convenience—to have a source of support and shelter. He tries to draw her into the revolutionary movement, but she remains indifferent. When she loses her job as a typist, on suspicion of harboring a communist, Sasaki persuades her to become a lowly waitress, the only work available. She accuses him of making her a sacrificial pig, and bickers about lack of attention. She nonetheless accedes to his wish, but as Sasaki becomes busier in his work and finds that Kasahara's help is inconsequential, he finally abandons her.

As interesting as this much-discussed question of the end's justifying the means is the form of the work. *Tō seikatsusha* is an

---

[40] See Shea, pp. 351-357.

"I" novel, the form which proletarian writers had castigated only a few years earlier as "bourgeois." The recourse to this form might be regarded as a symbol of the defeat of the proletarian literary movement which, by the time of the publication of *Tō seikatsusha*, was decidedly reaching its nadir. The Manchurian Incident of September, 1931, indicating a swing toward nationalistic sentiment in the country, was followed by ever-increasing efforts by the government and police to wipe out left-wing activities. The fear of arrest caused a panic among KOPF members, resulting in a drift away from the movement which spread widely by the fall of 1933. This external problem was compounded by internal dissension within the organization as certain elements began objecting to the extreme politicization of the literary movement. The Writers' League, which had lost most of its leading figures, finally decided to dissolve itself in March, 1934, bringing to a spiritless end the one single organization of Japan's revolutionary literature.

On February 20, 1933, Kobayashi Takiji was bludgeoned to death at the Tsukiji Police Station. The death of this writer, whose hectic career, combining a dynamic political activism with a profession in creative writing, epitomized the ideal life for a proletarian author, presaged the collapse of the proletarian literary movement. Thus, the heyday of the movement was marked by two deaths: the suicide of Akutagawa in 1927, signaling its rapid ascent, followed by Kobayashi's murder in 1933 signifying its swift decline. Its best days lasted but some six years at most, and if in fact the rise of proletarian literature was a factor in Akutagawa's gnawing sense of doom he need not have worried with such disastrous consequence.

Nonetheless, during this brief period the proletarian literary movement managed to gain predominance in the literary world, a feat possibly unmatched in the histories of proletarian literary movements in other capitalist countries. Despite its meager artistic accomplishments, it did succeed in leaving a number of legacies for the future of Japanese literature. Through their preoccupation with the idea of a class struggle and a class identity, proletarian authors brought to Japanese belles-lettres a social and political consciousness hitherto avoided by writers of the naturalist lineage. The social dimension that naturalist writers in the

West had provided for their own literature had to be supplied to Japanese literature, not by their Japanese counterparts, who fashioned a naturalism distinctly their own, but by the proletarian authors. It must be acknowledged that the social outlook of this literature was severely limited, embracing as it did a strictly class-struggle viewpoint, and the political themes advanced were often simplistic and crudely integrated into the works. The grand works encompassing sweeping social vistas that were envisioned by some critics were never realized. Still, proletarian literature made evident the possibility of and even the need for social and political themes in Japanese literature, thus broadening its once narrow scope. Perhaps a more fruitful literary achievement of proletarian literature, if not altogether a positive one, was its depiction of violence. Never before in the history of Japanese literature had scenes of torture, murder, and exploitation been described with such morbidly realistic but entirely fascinating detail.

Of course the failures of proletarian literature are far more pronounced than its accomplishments; its triumphs were as much the stuff of sound and fury surrounding its organizational and theoretical debates as of artistic creativity. Its literary bankruptcy is not altogether surprising, for the primacy of politics was recognized from the very beginning of the movement and the noisy discussions were probes into how best literature might be fitted into the larger revolutionary struggle. Hampered by a constant necessity to keep pace with the demands imposed upon them from outside, thus stifling their imaginative and creative powers, proletarian authors could hardly have been expected to produce works of lasting artistic value.

The creative method adopted for proletarian literature was a realism derived from dialectic materialism which presumably taught scientific objectivity in observing social phenomena. But of course this realistic approach was no more scientific or objective than the traditional realism, as it was distorted by a class-struggle viewpoint. Within the bounds of this realism, proletarian writers attempted a number of methodological innovations, among them group portraiture and the multi-dimensional approach, but these were only partly successful. Their likeliest contribution rested in a new literary content, but even here the potentially great subject of the proletariat was circumscribed by their peculiar class subjectivity which, in turn, led to a penchant for treating the workers and peasants with soapy sentimentality. In the end, what the authors produced were generally thinly clad works on strikes, exploitation of the masses, vanguard activities, and the like, containing a curious mixture of the new and the old. The new content, consisting of a proletarian consciousness representing what was supposedly the most up-to-date in social thought, was clothed in the old-fashioned garb of melodramatic characters and incidents.

The Bureaucratic Role
in Japan, 1900-1945:
The Bureaucrat as Politician

O<small>NE</small> T<small>HEME</small> which runs consistently through the literature on modern Japanese history is the major role played by bureaucratic development in the development of the political system. This concern with the role of the bureaucracy stems from the predominant position in politics and government it held and maintained after 1868. There is no question that the bureaucracy and its leaders, through control over decision-making and administration, fashioned and implemented those reforms which laid the foundation for Japan's development as a powerful nation-state. In this process the bureaucratic leaders between 1868 and 1900 created a highly centralized state characterized by bureaucratic domination and the spread of the bureaucracy into almost every aspect of Japanese life.

The rapid growth of the bureaucracy early resulted in the necessity of defining more clearly the boundaries of the bureaucratic structure and the nature of the bureaucratic role. The vast increase in the operations and services performed by the bureaucracy required structures of recruitment and role allocation which could supply an adequate number of administrators with sufficient understanding of the new political, legal, social, and economic reforms. To this end, between 1885 and 1900 the leaders of the bureaucracy instituted a series of reforms which created a new civil bureaucracy. From these reforms emerged a new bureaucrat whose role was formally characterized by those aspects which Max Weber described as "legal-rational." Yet at precisely the same time there emerged a new political role—that of the ex-bureaucrat-politician. Beginning, perhaps symbolically, with Itō Hirobumi's acceptance of the Seiyūkai's presidency in 1900, political-party recruitment of ex-bureaucrats became characteristic of Japanese political life and an apparent consequence of the bureaucracy's dominant position.

The ability of the bureaucrat to be both an efficient administrator and a party leader presents a problem which has not yet been adequately resolved. The problem stems from the widespread belief that the norms of the high-ranking bureaucrat and the party leader conflict and make it difficult if not impossible for the bureaucrat to act as a politician.[1] This belief rests on the assumption that in relatively well-developed political systems, where bureaucracies are capable of successfully implementing change and providing ever larger numbers of services and operations the bureaucratic role will be characterized by the key aspects of the Weberian legal-rational bureaucracy. In this type of bureaucracy, roles are: 1) allocated on the basis of achievement-oriented criteria directly related to administrative performance; 2) defined on the basis of specialized and differentiated activity; 3) integrated and maintained through the existence of a relatively well-defined and protected lifetime career as set forth in an implicit or explicit lifetime career contract.[2] The norms of performance of specialized tasks over a lifetime would seem to preclude the existence of both motive and opportunity for the bureaucrat to engage in a second career. This would appear to be especially so in the case of a political-party career in which the norms are ostensibly focused on the ability to bargain, compromise, and unify various interests represented in the party. While these are achievement-oriented criteria they do not require specialized training, nor are the role-activities of the political leader highly specialized and differentiated. Career commitment certainly exists among political party leaders but the lifetime career contract cannot exist as a norm since there is no formal structured assurance of continued employment even if adequate service is given. Generally, then, the norms and life-style of the political party leader do not appear to be of the type which would appeal to the high-ranking civil servant in a legal-rational bureaucracy of the kind which seemed to have emerged by 1900.

The emergence of the ex-bureaucrat-politician after 1900 thus

[1] See, for example, David E. Apter, *The Politics of Modernization* (Chicago and London, 1965), pp. 169-170. Lucian Pye, *Aspects of Political Development* (Boston and Toronto, 1966), pp. 81-82. Joseph LaPalombara, "Bureaucracy and Political Development: Notes, Queries and Dilemmas," in Joseph LaPalombara (ed.), *Bureaucracy and Political Development* (Princeton, 1963), pp. 52-53.

[2] Max Weber, *The Theory of Social and Economic Organization*, trans. by A. M. Henderson and Talcott Parsons, ed. by Talcott Parsons (New York and London, 1947), pp. 329-340.

raises the possibility that actual bureaucratic role norms did not conform to the formally stated legal-rational norms. If this was in fact the case, what then were the norms of the bureaucratic role and which aspects of these role norms made possible the emergence of the bureaucrat-politician role? Essentially it is to this aspect of bureaucratic development and its effects on political development that this analysis is directed.

More specifically, this problem may be restated as: *what norms with regard to the key aspects of role allocation, definition, and integration characterized the bureaucratic role, and which of these norms created both opportunity and motive for high-ranking civil servants to engage in political party careers in the period after 1900?* The analysis of the norms relating to role allocation, definition, and integration-maintenance are of primary significance because they govern the structure of the bureaucratic role. That is, they determine eligibility, recruitment, advancement, boundaries of activities, length of service, and terminal reward for adequate service. Furthermore, the presence or absence in a predominant fashion of: 1) bureaucratically related achievement orientation norms with regard to role allocation; 2) specialization and differentiation with regard to role activity; and 3) careerism with regard to role integration-maintenance are of critical importance in determining the relationship of the bureaucratic role to other roles. Thus, for example, if non-bureaucratic norms such as birth or participation in a revolution are the basis for recruitment because they confer wisdom and high status, then it is possible for political parties to share the same criteria for leadership recruitment. Since the criteria for recruitment are the same in both cases and are not directly related to bureaucratic or political party functions, the distinction between bureaucrat and party leader will be blurred and the bureaucrat may see no real objection to or conflict in pursuing first one then the other career, or both at the same time. Much the same is true in the case of specialization-differentiation. If role boundaries in the bureaucracy are relatively diffuse, generalized knowledge and experience rather than expertise will predominate as the basis for determining role boundaries. In this sense again the bureaucrat may see no real distinction between the activities and knowledge required of him by the bureaucracy and political parties. Finally, if there is a relative absence of careerism and career contract the bureaucrat will have no security of tenure or terminal reward for service, and will be likely to seek other opportunities such as graft or other seemingly more secure or remunerative careers. Consequently, in order to answer the basic question to which this study is directed, the emphasis is placed here on the determination and analysis of data concerning the presence or absence of the key Weberian legal-rational norms regarding role allocation, definition and integration-maintenance.

Viewed in this context, the analysis of the bureaucratic role has a number of significant implications for our understanding of the nature of Japanese politics and political development. First, such an analysis will provide us with a clearer and more substantive picture of the nature of bureaucratic development and the bureaucratic role in the period of Japan's full emergence as a powerful nation-state. Second, this analysis should go a long way toward explaining, in a specific manner, the nature of the relationship existing between bureaucracy and political parties in the period 1900-1945. This in turn may help us to a better understanding of the behavior and function of the political parties in this period and why they were unable to dominate the political structure. Finally, more broadly, Japan may be viewed as a case study of bureaucratic role development in a society undergoing the process of modernization. In this context the analysis may provide data for the comparative analysis of bureaucratic development and its role in political development generally.

Since we are concerned with changes in role norms, the analysis is centered on data related to the backgrounds of upper civil servants in the period 1900-1945. The group selected for analysis was determined by the following criteria: 1) the group had to be within the highest civil service rank (*chokunin* rank); 2) the group had to be included in the permanent civil service throughout the entire period of the analysis; 3) it was thought desirable to select a group which performed both "line" and "staff" functions since this would avoid any possible bias present in a group performing only one of these types of functions; 4) finally, there had to be adequate reportage and evidence of the recruitment of members of the group to positions in political parties.

The one group which appeared to meet all of these requirements was that of the prefectural governors. The governor was a permanent civil service officer of *chokunin* rank for the entire period 1900-1945. The office was one which carried with it both line and staff functions, since the governor was not only a high-ranking member of the civil service carrying policy-making responsibilities but also the chief local official responsible for the implementation of policy at the local level. The governors as a group are consistently reported as having participated in political party activities and as having held a wide range of party positions.[3] The prefectural governor thus appears to be an excellent focus for this analysis. A simple random sample of 25 per cent or 135 was selected from the total population of 540 who held the office in the period 1900-1945.[4]

Categories of data for the analysis of the backgrounds of this sample were derived from a set of propositions concerning bureaucratic role norms which emerged from the following analysis of the historical changes in the formal structure of the bureaucratic role between 1868 and 1945.

Role allocation norms. Prior to 1887 there existed no general formal criteria for recruitment and advancement in the upper civil service. However, between 1887 and 1899 there emerged a series of reforms which had the following consequences: 1) the establishment in 1887 and strengthening in 1893 of a civil service examination system which distinguished between a lower and an upper civil service; 2) the establishment of an upper civil service examination based on extensive knowledge of jurisprudence and various types of law such as administrative, civil, commercial, and constitutional law requiring the equivalent of a university degree in law; 3) practical elimination, with some important exceptions, of entry into the upper civil service by means other

[3] See, for example, Tetsuo Najita, *Hara Kei in the Politics of Compromise: 1905-1915* (Cambridge, Mass., 1967); Kuribayashi Teiichi, *Chihō kankai no hensen* (Tokyo, 1930); Masumi Junnosuke, *Nihon seitōshi ron* (Tokyo, 1966-1968), II, 1-56, IV, 165-208; Mitani Taichirō, *Nihon seitō seiji no keisei: Hara Kei no seiji shido no tenkai* (Tokyo, 1967); Shinobu Seizaburō, *Taishō seijishi* (Tokyo, 1952), IV, 1025-1071.

[4] The population was determined on the basis of all those who were appointed by the central government as governors of officially designated prefectures in the period from January 1, 1900, to September 30, 1945. The incumbents were determined by use of the following sources: Ijiri Tsunekichi, *Rekidai kenkanroku* (Tokyo, 1925); Naikaku Insatsukyoku, *Shokuinroku* (Tokyo, 1886-1945).

than examination; 4) the establishment of prior upper civil service experience as the major criterion for appointment to the highest ranks of the civil service.[5] Out of the various ordinances defining the structure of the upper civil service examination system there emerges a picture of a higher bureaucracy trained primarily in law and oriented toward performance as the criterion for recruitment, and experience as the criterion for advancement. On the basis of the existence of this formal structure we would expect that for the vast majority of those in the sample:

1) the basic criterion of eligibility for recruitment will be a university education in law;
2) birth in a family belonging to the traditional political elite will be of little significance since entrance into universities was formally based on universalistic criteria;
3) origin in middle- and high-income families will be characteristic since adequate preparation and maintenance at university requires relatively high income;
4) passage of the upper civil service examinations will be the criterion for recruitment into the upper civil service;
5) advancement will be based on seniority and experience as reflected in a consistent pattern of length of service and number of offices held prior to appointment as governor.

Role definition norms. Prior to the creation of the upper civil service structure in 1887-1899 there existed no formally defined or delimited areas of administrative activity. Men could and did

[5] The civil service examination system is defined in the following statutes (all references are to the *Collected Statutes* (*Hōrei zensho*)): Imperial Ordinances 37, 38, Cabinet Ordinances, 8, 19, and 20, July 23, 1887; Imperial Ordinance 57, November 5, 1887; Imperial Ordinance 58, November 7, 1887; Cabinet Ordinance 25, December 1, 1887; Imperial Ordinances 63, 64, December 24, 1887; Cabinet Ordinance 28, December 28, 1887; the revisions of 1893 are contained in the following: Imperial Ordinances 126, 183, 187, 197, October 31, 1893; Imperial Ordinance 54, May 24, 1894; Cabinet Ordinance 2, May 7, 1894; Foreign Ministry Ordinance 7, June 22, 1894; Imperial Ordinance 7, January 18, 1918; Imperial Ordinance 15, March 28, 1929; Imperial Ordinance 1, January 6, 1941. The major ordinances defining appointment, advancement, discipline, and dismissal are as follows: Imperial Ordinance 183, November 30, 1893; Imperial Ordinances 61, 62, 63, March 28, 1899; Imperial Ordinance 261, July 31, 1913.

hold positions in a variety of administrative areas despite the growth of structural specialization in the two decades after 1868.[6]

The various civil service appointment regulations passed between 1887 and 1899 created apparently clear distinctions between the upper and lower civil service roles and established a degree of role specialization within the upper civil service structure. More specifically, these regulations formally excluded from appointment to the upper civil service, with some exceptions, those without prior service in the upper civil bureaucracy or those who had not passed the upper civil service examinations.[7] This was accomplished by limiting appointment to the lower ranks of the upper civil service (*sōnin* rank) after 1893 to: 1) those who had passed the upper civil service examinations; 2) those who had at least 3 years' service (2 years after 1899) as an upper civil servant, or; 3) former and present officials who had served 3 years (2 after 1899) as judges, procurators, or diplomatic and consular officials.

Appointment to the highest ranks (*chokunin* rank) was limited by the 1899 regulation to: 1) former and present *sōnin* officials of the highest grade; 2) former *chokunin* officials with at least one year's service in *chokunin* rank; 3) former *chokunin* officials who had passed the upper civil service examinations or had 2 years' service as *sōnin* rank officials; 4) former *chokunin* judges or procurators who could be appointed to the Ministry of Justice; 5) former and present *chokunin* professors who could be appointed to the Ministry of Education; 6) flag officers who could be appointed to the Army and Navy Ministries.[8]

While these regulations did not prevent the appointment of officials who had not taken the examinations, they did limit the upper civil service career to those who had acquired a level of administrative expertise as reflected in either passing the exami-

---

[6] See Bernard S. Silberman, "National Development and the Evolution of the Legal-Rational Bureaucracy," in Hayden V. White (ed.), *Uses of History* (Detroit, 1968), pp. 260-262.

[7] *H.Z.*, Imperial Ordinance 183, November 30, 1893. Imperial Ordinance 61, March 28, 1899.

[8] *H.Z.*, Imperial Ordinance 61, March 28, 1899. In 1913 two changes were made in the appointment regulations: 1) *sōnin* diplomatic and consular officials were added to the list of those eligible for appointment as *chokunin* and 2) upper civil commission approval was required for the reappointment of ex-*chokunin* officials. *H.Z.*, Imperial Ordinance 261, July 31, 1913.

nations or prior upper civil service experience.[9] This development was largely the result of the establishment of different examinations for judges, procurators, and diplomatic-consular officials and limiting the appointment of former *chokunin* procurators, judges, professors, and flag officers to their respective ministries.[10] The combination of separate examination tracks and limitations on *chokunin* appointments in various ministries established specialized criteria which would largely exclude other upper civil servants from these areas of administrative activity. By 1900 it could be said that the formal structure of the bureaucracy recognized the upper civil service as a specialized and differentiated role. Within this role there had also apparently emerged specialized areas of activity indicating the development of functional specificity as a criterion for defining role activity throughout the entire upper civil service. To the extent that normative behavior coincided with formal requirements we should expect that:

1) the great majority of those in the sample will have been recruited from the ranks of the upper civil service;
2) the great majority will have served most of their careers in the Home Ministry which supervised prefectural administration;
3) the great majority will have been recruited from those whose service had been spent primarily in prefectural administration.

Careerism. If we view careerism as the commitment to a single role as the predominant focus of adult lifetime activity, then the role structure must exhibit at least three characteristics—relative

[9] The exceptions to these appointment regulations were relatively few. The following upper civil service positions were open to free appointment for the years indicated: Chief Cabinet Secretary (1900-1945), Vice-Ministers (excluding Army and Navy Vice-Ministers) (1913-1924), Superintendent General of Police (1913-1934), Chief of Home Ministry Bureau of Police (1913-1934), House of Peers Chief Secretary (1913-1934), Lower House Chief Secretary (1913-1934), ministry counsellors of *chokunin* rank (1913-1924), ministerial private secretaries and other private secretaries (1910-1945). The pertinent ordinances are as follows: *H.Z.*, Imperial Ordinances 162, April 27, 1900; No. 288, June 22, 1910; No. 262, July 31, 1913; No. 188, August 12, 1924; No. 80, April 7, 1934.

[10] *H.Z.*, Dajōkan Ordinance 102, December 26, 1884; Law 6, February 8, 1890; Ministry of Justice Ordinance 3, May 15, 1891; Imperial Ordinance 187, October 31, 1893; Imperial Ordinance 213, November 24, 1893; Imperial Ordinance 61, March 28, 1899.

security from dismissal on the basis of extraneous considerations, absence of other primary occupations, and some reward for adequate lifetime service. These characteristics were included and structurally defined in the civil bureaucracy in the period 1884-1899. Relative security from dismissal on the basis of extrabureaucratic considerations was formally provided for through the promulgation of the Civil Service Discipline Ordinance and the Civil Service Status Ordinance of 1899. The Status Ordinance limited causes for dismissal to those which were thought to make adequate bureaucratic performance impossible, i.e., criminal conviction, insubordination, physical or mental incapacity, surplus personnel, and reduction of the number of permanent officials. In order to protect those dismissed for the latter two reasons such officials had to be placed first on the inactive or "seconded" list. An official placed on this list could be reappointed at any time and could not be completely dismissed until he had been on the list, receiving full pay, for two years. Two years having passed, he was then required to retire but was eligible to receive all the retirement benefits of his rank and length of service.[11]

Protection from unfounded accusations of incompetence or incapacity was set up by the Disciplinary Ordinance. Under its provisions machinery was provided for hearing and handing down decisions on charges brought against higher civil service officials. To establish further protection against nonbureaucratic influences, the disciplinary committee members had to be drawn from the ranks of the permanent upper civil service.[12] These statutes made it almost impossible for an official to be dismissed outright but they did provide a means for removing higher officials from any specific office, an operational necessity whenever ministerial changes occurred.

The creation of a retirement-pension system established the means for rewarding adequate career service. As first defined in the pension-retirement ordinance of 1884 the system put into effect a full retirement pension at the age of 60 with at least 15 years' service. Ministers of state and their equivalents were eligible after two years' service at that rank. The basic pension was 60/240 of the annual salary at time of retirement plus 1/240 of the annual salary for every year after 15 years up to a maximum

---

11 *H.Z.*, Imperial Ordinance 62, March 28, 1899.
12 *H.Z.*, Imperial Ordinance 63, March 28, 1899.

of 35 years. The highest retirement pension was thus 1/3 of the annual salary at the time of retirement after 35 years of service.[13]

The revision of 1890 completed the development of the pension-retirement structure and it was to remain basically unchanged until after World War II. The major change brought about by the 1890 revision was to make the requirement of fifteen years' service the major criterion for eligibility for full pension. Eligibility for full pensions was also extended to those forced to retire because of age, service-acquired disabilities and reduction of permanent personnel.[14]

The pension-retirement system would appear to have created the basis for a "career contract" by its encouragement to pursue the civil service career over a relatively long period. When this was combined with the restrictions on random dismissal it might be said that the civil service career had formally come into existence and that careerism, in the Weberian sense, was a characteristic of the upper civil service after 1900. In view of the existence of this structure we might therefore expect that for the great majority of those in the sample:

1) careers in the upper civil service will be relatively long, taking up the greater part of adult lifetime activity;
2) there will be no participation in second careers following retirement from the upper civil service career.

In sum, it would appear that by 1900 the Japanese civil bureaucracy had evolved into a structure in which roles exhibited the major characteristics of the Weberian legal-rational type. The propositions outlined above should therefore all be true. On this basis we may also suggest the following proposition concerning the recruitment of upper civil servants to positions in political parties: *the often-made observations regarding the recruitment of significantly large numbers of upper civil servants into politi-*

[13] *H.Z.*, Dajōkan Ordinance 1, January 4, 1884. Some provision for retirement had been made as early as 1878 in the case of prefectural governors. These, however, did not apply to the upper civil service as a whole nor were specific terms of service required. Payments were in lump sum and equal to less than one year's salary. *H.Z.*, Dajōkan Ordinance 35, August 3, 1878.

[14] *H.Z.*, Law 43, June 20, 1890. The law was again revised in 1923 primarily to increase benefits to 1/3 of annual salary at the time of retirement plus 1/150 of the annual salary for every year over 15 years up to a maximum of 40 years. The highest pension benefit after 1923 was thus equal to 1/2 of the annual salary after 40 years' service. *H.Z.*, Law 48, April 13, 1923.

cal party positions are basically incorrect and therefore we will find that significantly few of those in the sample will have been recruited to positions in political parties in the period 1900-1945. The analysis which follows attempts to test these propositions by examination of those categories of data indicated by the propositions.[15]

We may begin the analysis by examining the propositions relating to the norms governing allocation of roles in the upper civil service. The first of these suggests that the basic criterion of eligibility for recruitment will be a university education in law and jurisprudence. That this was indeed the case is reflected in the data presented in Tables 1 and 2. Over 96 per cent of those

TABLE 1

University Education of Prefectural
Governors—1900-1945

Education	N	%
University	130	96.3
Non-university	5	3.7
Total	135	100.0

TABLE 2

University Specialization of Prefectural
Governors—1900-1945

Specialization	N	%	
Law	89	66.0	Law Curricula
Political Science	34	25.0	
Economics	2	1.5	
Agriculture	1	0.75	
Engineering	0	0.0	
No Degree	5	4.0	
N.A.	4	3.0	
Total	135	100.0	

[15] The biographical data for this analysis were derived from a large number of sources of which the major ones are: Heibonsha (ed.), *Dai jimmei jiten* (Tokyo, 1957-1958), 10 volumes; Igarashi Eikichi, *Taishō jimmei jiten* (Tokyo, 1914); Ishin Shiryo Hensankai, *Gendai kazoku fūyō* (Tokyo, 1929);

Silberman

appointed as governors from 1900 to 1945 had university educations. Furthermore, of those attending university 91 per cent were graduates of the legal faculties of their universities.[16] We may conclude that the actual norms governing eligibility closely conformed to the formal requirements of the structure of recruitment. Although the criterion of eligibility for recruitment seems to have been a university education in law, it has often been noted and suggested, in regard to upper civil servants, that university education and education at Tokyo Imperial University were synonymous. Tabulation of data on university attended confirms these observations (Table 3). The number recruited from

TABLE 3

University Attended by Prefectural
Governors—1900-1945

University Attended	N	%
Tokyo Imperial	115	85.0
Kyoto Imperial	10	7.0
Hitotsubashi	2	1.5
Hosei	1	0.75
American-European	2	0.75
No Degree	5	4.0
Total	135	100.0

Tokyo Imperial University far exceeds that possible on a purely random basis. The bias is underscored when it is noted that there was a larger number of recognized universities than are represented in the sample, Waseda and Keio Universities being the most notable absentees. Consequently, we may conclude that it was not any university education in law but rather an education

Osaka Mainichi Shimbunsha (ed.), *Gendai jimmeiroku* (Osaka, 1926-1935), 10 volumes; Jinji Koshinjo (ed.), *Jinji koshinroku* (Tokyo, 1903, 1908, 1911, 1915, 1918, 1921, 1925, 1928, 1931, 1934, 1937, 1939, 1941, 1943, 1948, 1951, 1953, 1955, 1957); Asahi Shimbunsha, *Asahi nenkan* (Osaka, 1920-1945), 26 volumes, Kaneko Nobuhisa, *Hokkaidō jimmei jishō* (Sapporo, 1923); Noyori Hideichi (ed.), *Meiji Taishō shi: jimbutsu hen* (Tokyo, 1930), volumes 13-15; Okamoto Takeo (ed.), *Shiga ken jimbutsu shi* (Ōtsu, Shiga Ken, 1930); Matsuda Gensuke (ed.), *Bōchō jinshi hatten kan* (Yamaguchi, 1932). In addition to these, a large number of regional biographical dictionaries, prefectural histories, and biographies were also used.

[16] In the pre-war university system political science and law were taught in the same faculties.

in law at Tokyo Imperial University which became and remained the basic criterion of eligibility. This would seem to suggest that although bureaucratically related training was normative, the acquisition of this training at one or two universities conferred a special social status which became an equally important criterion for eligibility. In this sense an extra-bureaucratic criterion, although achievement-oriented, played a major role in determining eligibility for recruitment and advancement in the upper civil service.

Access to university education was ostensibly universalistic. That is, there were no formal ascriptive restrictions on entrance to universities. Therefore, we should expect to find that birth in a family of traditional elite origins, a major criterion for eligibility prior to 1900, will be of little significance.[17] The data on pre-1868 social-stratum origins of the sample (Table 4) indicates that

TABLE 4

Pre-1868 Social Strata Origins of
Governors by Pre-1868 Social Strata

Social Stratum in Pre-1868 Social Stratum	N	%
Traditional Political Elite	65	48.0
Commoners	62	46.0
N.A.	8	6.0
Total	135	100.0

this expectation is unfulfilled. Almost half of the group (48 per cent) came from former elite families. The representation of this group in the sample is far larger than their distribution in the general population. The traditional elite population in 1868 is usually set at about 5 per cent of the total. Assuming that despite large increases in the population after 1868 the traditional elite population and their descendants remained the same proportion of the total, then this group is most certainly over-represented in the sample. Yet, because of the large number of those of commoner origin in the sample, traditional elite origin cannot be said to be a criterion of eligibility, recruitment, or advancement. The

[17] Bernard S. Silberman, "Criteria for Recruitment and Success in the Japanese Bureaucracy, 1868-1900: 'Traditional' and 'Modern' Criteria in Bureaucratic Development," *Economic Development and Cultural Change*, 24, 2 (January, 1966), 160-161.

over-representation of those of traditional elite origin may perhaps be explained by reference to a major requirement for obtaining a university education—sufficient economic resources to support a long and costly educational career. Those from former elite families would be more likely to have the means to finance costly preparatory and university education because of their higher social and educational status. The possession of both education and status made it possible after 1868 for former elite families to acquire governmental positions through which they could maintain relatively high economic status.[18] The Meiji settlement of elite family stipends in lump-sum payments may also have contributed to the maintenance of high economic status in comparison to the vast majority of the society. The significant differences in pre-1868 social status should then be explained by common economic status of descendants of commoner and elite families. Data on income of family origin was not ascertainable. Instead, economic status was approximated by ranking father's occupation. Tabulation of this data indicates that an overwhelming majority (86.5 per cent) came from higher- and middle-income occupation groups (Table 5). Economic status thus

TABLE 5

Economic Status of Families of Origin of
Prefectural Governors—1900-1945

Economic Status	Traditional Political Elite		Commoner		Total	
	N	%	N	%	N	%
High-Income	19	15.0	34	27.0	53	42.0
Middle-Income	35	27.5	22	17.0	57	44.5
Low-Income	0	0.0	0	0.0	0	13.5
Total	65	51.0	62	49.0	127	100.0

Social Strata Unknown = 8

appears to have become a major qualification for achieving eligibility reflecting the reduced significance of pre-1868 elite family status and ascriptive criteria generally.

The patterns of recruitment or appointment to the upper civil service after 1900 confirms the predominance of performance-

[18] H. D. Harootunian, "The Progress of Japan and the Samurai Class," *Pacific Historical Review*, 28 (1959), 255-266.

oriented bureaucratic norms. From 1900 on, passage of the upper civil service examination clearly became a criterion for actual appointment to the upper civil service. Between 1900 and 1945 only 6 per cent of those in the sample were appointed as governors without having passed the upper civil service examinations (Table 6).

TABLE 6

Passage of Upper Civil Service Examination by
Prefectural Governors—1900-1945

	N	%
Passed Examination	127	94.0
No Examination	8	6.0
Total	135	100.0

Experience in a number of offices prior to advancement as governor was a normative pattern and thus apparently a criterion for advancement. For the great majority (82 per cent) in the sample began at the lowest ranks of the upper civil service and moved through 6 to 10 offices prior to appointment as governor (Tables 7 and 8). Length of service, or seniority, also may be considered as a major criterion for advancement. Only one man was appointed as governor with fewer than 10 years of service, and 79 per cent had between 11 and 20 years of service prior to advancement as governor (Table 9). Advancement to the highest ranks of the civil service thus followed a pattern of appointment at the lowest ranks of the upper civil service followed by advancement through usually 6 to 10 *sōnin* offices over a period of at least, and commonly more than, 10 years. We may conclude from this that advancement was based primarily on the bureaucratically oriented criteria of experience and seniority.

Generally, with regard to the norms of allocating bureaucratic roles we may conclude that bureaucratically related achievement-oriented criteria predominated and governed the recruitment and advancement structure. Eligibility, recruitment, and advancement required relatively well-defined patterns of performance. Only one pattern of role behavior may be considered as extra-bureaucratic in character—attendance at and graduation from Tokyo Imperial University. However, the heavy predominance of men in the sample who possessed this qualification im-

TABLE 7

Level of First Office Held by
Prefectural Governors—1900-1945

Level of Office	N	%
Lower Civil Service hanin Ranks	0	0.0
Upper Civil Service sōnin Ranks 8-6	111	82.0
Upper Civil Service sōnin Ranks 5-3	13	10.0
Upper Civil Service chokunin Ranks 2-1	0	0.0
Military Service	0	0.0
N.A.	11	8.0
Total	135	100.0

TABLE 8

Number of Ministries served by Number of
Offices Held Prior to Appointment as Governor

Number of Ministries	Number of Offices Held													Total	
	1	2	3	4	5	6	7	8	9	10	11	12	NA	N	%
1	0	0	2	1	6	16	28	20	13	9	6	3	12	116	86.0
2	0	0	0	0	1	5	3	1	1	3	3	2	0	19	14.0
3	–	–	–	–	–	–	–	–	–	–	–	–	–	–	0.0
4	–	–	–	–	–	–	–	–	–	–	–	–	–	–	0.0
Total	0	0	2	1	7	21	31	21	14	12	9	5	12	135	100.0

plies that it was perhaps not only a criterion of eligibility for recruitment but a criterion for advancement as well. The restriction of the pool of eligibles for recruitment and perhaps advancement to this group does not appear, however, to have resulted in the vitiation of bureaucratic effectiveness. It well may be that this common experience functioned to integrate the bureaucracy as a social organization by producing homogeneity of outlook and values and thereby contributed to its effectiveness.

If we turn now to the question of specialization and differentiation, analysis of the pertinent data confirms the view that these aspects were characteristic of the bureaucratic role after 1900. Using the number of ministries in which the members of the sample served as a key indicator of the level of specialization and differentiation, we find that the data strongly suggest that

TABLE 9

Years of Service by Number of Offices Held Prior to Appointment as Governor

Years of Service Prior to Appointment	Number of Offices Held Prior to Appointment												NA	Total N	%
	1	2	3	4	5	6	7	8	9	10	11	12			
0-5	—	—	—	—	—	—	—	—	—	—	—	—		0	0.0
6-10	—	—	1	—	—	—	—	—	—	—	—	—		1	.75
11-15	—	—	1	—	5	10	14	9	2	2	—	—		43	30.3
16-20	—	—	—	1	2	10	13	10	10	9	6	3		64	47.5
21-25	—	—	—	—	—	1	4	2	1	1	3	1		13	10.0
26-30	—	—	—	—	—	—	—	—	1	—	—	—		1	.75
31-35	—	—	—	—	—	—	—	—	—	—	—	1		1	.75
Over 35	—	—	—	—	—	—	—	—	—	—	—	—		0	0.0
N.A.													12	12	9.0
Total	0	—	2	1	7	21	31	21	14	14	9	5	12	135	100.0
			(1.5)	(1.75)	(5.1)	(15.4)	(23.0)	(15.4)	(10.0)	(9.0)	(6.5)	(3.7)	(9.0)	(100.0)	100.0

X² = 124.632   P < .001

career specialization was characteristic of the upper civil servant. Only 14 per cent of the sample spent any portion of their careers in a ministry other than the Home Ministry (see Table 8). None of these had served in more than two ministries, that is, the Home Ministry and one other. Furthermore, of the 19 men who had served in more than one ministry 15 had done so only in the first 5 years of their career. Much the same pattern emerges when the basis of analysis is the question of how many in the sample spent over half their careers in prefectural administration. Tabulation of this data shows that 97 per cent (131) did so before appointment as governor.

From this evidence we may conclude that after 1900 the upper civil service role was characterized by specialized and differentiated administrative activity. The area in which the upper civil servant was free to pursue his career was limited for the most part to the ministry in which he first served. Within this ministry his career, or the major part of it, was likely to be restricted to one specific area of administrative activity. In this sense specialization and differentiation were the criteria for defining the boundaries of role activity.

With regard to the norm of careerism we should expect, in view of the formal restrictions on random dismissal and the existence of a retirement-pension system, that career service was relatively long. Tabulation of these data (Table 10) suggests that this was the case. The median length of service was 23 years and the mean average was 25.4 years. When this is compared with a similar group for the years 1868-1899 (Table 10) the lengthening of career service is clearly significant. For this earlier group the median was 14 years and the mean average was 17.6 years.

When we consider the length of service careers, it would appear likely that retirement would come sufficiently late in life to preclude the participation of significant numbers in post-service careers. Compilation of the data testing this thesis indicates that it is false. Both the median age and mean average at retirement are surprisingly low, 48 and 50 respectively (Table 11). Although the life expectancy of this group is unknown it was probably greater at age of entrance into the civil service than was either the median or mean age at retirement. It was, of course considerably less than the mandatory age of retirement (60). The considerable number of years left for active full-time service would thus seem to supply sufficient opportunity to engage in a

TABLE 10

Length of Service by Period of Appointment

Length of Service in 5-year intervals	1868-1899 Appointees	1900-1945 Appointees
1-5	18	0
6-10	15	3
11-15	5	0
16-20	4	28
21-25	11	47
26-30	10	17
31-35	5	12
36 & over	3	2
N.A.	9	26
Total	80	135
Median	14 years	23 years
Mean	17.6 years	25.4 years
$X^2 = 66.691$	$P < .001$	

post-service career. The early age of retirement also indirectly provides motivation for such careers by combining opportunity with relatively low pension benefits. Since the highest benefits a member of the sample could obtain in the whole period between 1900 and 1945 was half of the annual salary at time of retirement after 40 years of service, the benefits at the median age would equal, at best, no more than 2/5 of the annual salary at retirement.[19] This would appear to be a drastic reduction, coming at an age when financial commitments were likely to be at their highest. School- or university-age children and style of life associated with high bureaucratic position would create considerable pressures toward seeking added sources of income or second careers. The pressures would be especially acute in periods of inflation such as those during and immediately after World War I and again in the late 1930's and early 40's. If both opportunity and motive were present we should expect, contrary to the original thesis presented, that a significant number of the sample engaged in post-service careers. The data in Table 12 indicates quite clearly that this was the case. More than 2/3 (68 per cent) of the group had some type of post-service occupation. Of these 28 per cent entered politics at the national and/or local level,

[19] See n. 14.

TABLE 11

Age of Retirement of
Prefectural Governors—1900-1945

Age in Five-year Periods	N	%
20-24	0	0.0
25-29	0	0.0
30-34	3	2.0
35-39	0	0.0
40-44	16	12.0
45-49	48	35.5
50-54	42	31.0
55-59	15	11.0
60-64	5	3.5
65-69	0	0.0
70-74	0	0.0
N.A.	7	5.0
Total	135	100.0

Median = 48 years
Mean = 50 years

TABLE 12

Post-service Occupations of
Prefectural Governors—1900-1945

Post-Service Occupation	N	%
Business-Industry	30	22.0
Politics—Local & National	38	28.0
Law Practice	6	5.0
Government Advisor	8	6.0
Volunteer Activities	11	8.0
No Occupation	11	8.0
N.A.	31	23.0
Total	135	100.0

22 per cent entered into business careers, and 8 per cent into volunteer activities. These data bear out the widely made observations concerning the recruitment of former high-ranking civil servants into political parties. Perhaps more striking, however, is the fact that recruitment of former high-ranking civil servants was almost equally common in business. From this we can conclude that business organizations shared with the political parties a functional relationship to the bureaucracy. Only such a relationship could have produced similar structural

effects in the form of a common leadership-recruitment pattern. We may also conclude that careerism in the sense of a lifetime-career contract and a commitment to one role did not develop in the Japanese civil bureaucracy at the highest levels of the upper civil service despite legal protection of office and career.

Still unresolved, however, is the question of why retirement should have come at such a relatively early age. One explanation might be the reduction of career chances as a consequence of the emergence of specialization and differentiation as the norms for defining career activity. From 1900 on, the tendency for careers to be restricted not only to one ministry but to one area of administrative activity within a ministry meant that with each advancement there were fewer offices to which to advance. At the *chokunin*-governor level they would be few indeed. For the great majority of this period there were never more than 10 or 12 offices to which a governor could be advanced.[20] Since there were 47 governors as well as others in staff positions competing for these offices it is clear that the great majority of those at this rank would either have to be retained at their positions or forced into retirement. Analogous situations must have existed in other ministries as careers became more functionally specific. Retention in office, especially at the higher levels, would appear to be excluded as a possible norm, for several reasons. First, the relatively rapid changes in cabinets which occurred after 1900 would have brought great pressure to change the highest-level policy-making bureaucrats.[21] Second, there would have been pressure from within the upper civil service for promotion from lower ranks. Since rank at the lowest level of the upper civil service was the first office of appointment, it did not represent any career promotion. Failure to provide advancement from this position within a decent interval would inevitably result in low morale, inefficiency, and an increased tendency to use extra-bureaucratic influence to obtain promotion. Furthermore, as the data in Table 9 indicates, 59 per cent of this group spent more than 16 years in *sōnin* rank before being appointed as governors—a figure that indicates that service at the lower ranks was not by any means short nor promotion excessively rapid, and suggests that there

[20] These included 6-10 bureau chiefs, the Inspector-General of Police, and the vice-minister.

[21] There were 33 cabinets in the period 1900-1945 for a mean average of 1.4 years per cabinet.

was pressure for promotion from below which would tend to make for shorter service at the highest ranks. In effect, the delimitation of offices because of specialization combined with both internal and external pressures for rapid turnover of the highest officials would lead us to expect that service in the highest ranks would be very short and leave no alternative to retirement. This seems to be borne out by the data on length of service as governor shown in Table 13. The median length of service was 2.5

TABLE 13

Length of Service as Governors of
Appointees—1900-1945

Length of Service as Governor	N	%
1	20	14.8
2	39	29.0
3	20	14.8
4	13	9.6
5	7	5.0
6	7	5.0
7	5	3.7
8	4	3.0
9	2	1.5
10	7	5.0
11	4	3.0
12	1	0.7
13	3	2.5
14	0	0.0
15	2	1.5
16	1	.7
17	0	0.0
18	0	0.0
19	0	0.0
20	0	0.0
Total	135	100.0
Median	2.5 years	
Mean	4.3 years	

years and the average was 4.3 years. We might conclude, therefore, that the relatively early age of retirement of this group was a function of the delimitation of offices and the pressures for high rates of turnover at the highest levels of the upper civil service.

To the extent that this is true, the often-repeated observation that the rapid turnover of high officials, especially governors, was due primarily to the rise of political parties and their ability to politicize the bureaucracy does not appear to be completely correct. The "rationalization" of the bureaucracy itself in the form of increased functional specificity and differentiation between upper and lower civil services was of equal and perhaps greater importance. To test this view more empirically, the length of service of those appointed in the years 1932-1945 was tabulated. This 14-year period was one in which we might assume that party power was weakest in the whole 46-year span of the analysis. Consequently, if political party power was primarily responsible for shortening high-ranking careers, then in this period the median and average length of service as governor should be longer than that of the group as a whole. The tabulation in Table 14 indicates that this is not the case. The median for this group is 1.5 as opposed to 2.5 years for the whole group, and the mean is 2.3 as opposed to 4.3 for the entire group. The more significant correlation would appear to be with the number of cabinets. During this 14-year period there were 14 cabinets with an average life of one year and a median of 9 months, and therefore the high rate of turnover in this period would seem to be a consequence of the high rate of cabinet changes (42 per cent of the total number of cabinets 1900-1945). We may tentatively suggest that although party power may have influenced the rate and age of retirement of high officials it did not play a major role in determining these characteristics.

The political parties may have been responsible, while in office, for introducing another criterion for advancement—openly stated party sympathy and identification. To what extent party identification became a norm for advancement is not clear. The data (Tables 7-9) on the criteria for advancement, however, do not indicate any significant differences in the rate of advancement. In Table 9, where length of service is related to number of offices held prior to appointment as governor, the high level of significance between these two variables suggests the absence of extra-bureaucratic qualifications for advancement to this level. If party identification was relevant to advancement, either it was apparently limited to advancement to the next highest offices or the parties voluntarily chose to seek party identification only from those who possessed the necessary bureaucratic qualifications for

TABLE 14

Length of Service as Governors of
Appointees—1932-1945

Length of Service as Governor	N	%
1	5	15.5
2	10	31.0
3	4	12.5
4	5	15.5
5	1	3.0
6	2	6.0
7	2	6.0
8	1	3.0
9	1	3.0
10	0	0.0
11	1	3.0
12	0	0.0
13	0	0.0
14	0	0.0
15	0	0.0
16	0	0.0
17	0	0.0
18	0	0.0
19	0	0.0
20	0	0.0
Total	32	100.0 (98.5)
Median	1.5 years	
Mean	2.3 years	

service in a number of offices and seniority. At any rate it does not appear that political party influence played a significant role in delimiting upper civil service careers. The absence of career-ism among high-ranking upper civil servants, ironically enough, seems to have been a consequence of the rationalization of the bureaucratic role and structure.

The analysis presented here suggests a number of general con-clusions. It is clear that the reorganization of the civil service between 1885 and 1900 was not merely a formal or superficial one. From this restructuring emerged a new and different kind of bureaucrat. From no later than 1900 the bureaucratic role was allocated and acquired largely in terms of performance-oriented criteria. Furthermore, these criteria were directly related to bureaucratic requirements. The new bureaucrat had to acquire the equivalent of a university education in law and jurisprudence simply to be eligible for recruitment. He had to show proof of his mastery of law by passing a difficult series of examinations before entrance into the upper civil service. Advancement was based primarily on seniority and experience in a number of lower offices. There thus appeared to be close conformity between actual behavior and the formal established norms for the distribution of bureaucratic office. At the same time, however, the fact that a vast majority of the group examined in this analysis received their education from one university suggests strongly that this had become a major qualification for eligibility, recruitment, and perhaps advancement as well. While this criterion was performance-oriented it was not directly related to the performance of bureaucratic functions unless graduates of Tokyo Imperial University were always of superior intelligence and better-trained than graduates of other universities. Graduation from Tokyo Imperial University would thus seem to confer status beyond that derived from the acquisition of legal and jurisprudential expertise. All graduates, especially those from the legal faculty, would share an outlook as well as an experience.

The emergence of this pseudo-social class helps to explain the relative absence of tension and conflict in the transfer of power from the preceding bureaucratic generation, who were united on the basis of common origins in the traditional political elite and their participation in the Restoration. The opening of the civil service to those of diverse social origins might well have produced conflict. However, the restriction of eligibility to those who were trained at Tokyo Imperial University and, one step removed, to those trained to gain admittance to Todai produced a social class in which socio-economic origins were largely dissolved. The focus of this new class was the high value placed on bureaucratic service and status and the common training experience. The identity of these values with those of the preceding bureaucratic generation diminished the possibility of generational and role conflict.

The emphasis on legal and jurisprudential training was also an indication of a major change in the goals of the bureaucracy after 1885. The major aim and function of the bureaucracy was to administer rather than innovate. The stress laid on legal training was an effort to provide the greatest possible uniformity in the implementation and administration of the Meiji reforms and to guard against the imposition of new reforms which would go beyond the intent of the existing legal structure. The shift in organizational goals was reflected in the bureaucrat's attitudes toward the role of the bureaucrat in politics. He saw himself as the defender of the system against selfish group interests. Innovation of any kind thus had to be carefully scrutinized, and abandoned if it ran counter to what the bureaucrat conceived to be the intent of the legal structure. The legalistic conservatism of the bureaucrat was at the basis of his belief that the continuity and integrity of the state was the highest value. This led him to resist all attacks on the legal structure of the state but also left him willing to sacrifice other values and goals to this end.

While emergence of bureaucratically oriented criteria for training, recruitment and advancement provided the means for meeting the demands for uniformly trained personnel it also, I would suggest, created new inner tensions which had dysfunctional consequences. The absence of any objective criteria for advancement other than experience and seniority raised the problem of determining who among the eligibles with relatively equal rank, experience, and seniority should receive promotion. Considerable research in organizational behavior suggests that this is a source of tension and consternation for those competing for higher office. One of the common methods of relieving this tension and insecurity is to seek close ties with a superior who is responsible for or could influence promotion. On a formal level this means passing on to one's superior information that is favorable to oneself and tends to confirm the superior's beliefs in his own efficacy and ability as an administrator.[22] This in turn is likely to lead to the creation of informal ties of loyalty and obligation and the establishment of coalitions or cliques aimed at relieving the insecurity surrounding promotion.[23] Although sufficient information is lacking I would suggest that the proliferation of cliques in the new

[22] For the description and analysis of communications in formal organizations see Anthony Downs, *Inside Bureaucracy* (Boston, 1967), pp. 76-78, 112-131. Albert H. Rubenstein and Chadwick J. Haberstroh (eds.), *Some Theories of Organization* (Homewood, Ill., 1960), pp. 229-322. Peter M. Blau and W. Richard Scott, *Formal Organizations* (San Francisco, 1962), pp. 116-139.

[23] Downs, pp. 67-77.

bureaucracy after 1900 was in large part due to the conditions created by the establishment of bureaucratic criteria for promotion. As we might expect, the heads of such cliques were bureau chiefs who had the most influence over promotion and from whom the vice-ministers were chosen.[24]

These cliques or coalitions were both functional and dysfunctional. By providing a means for reducing tensions and competition between individuals they contributed to cohesiveness within a ministry or bureau. They could be dysfunctional to the extent that, all other aspects being equal, promotion depended on personal loyalty rather than competence, thereby reducing the efficiency of the organization. As one reached the highest strata of office, this situation was likely to result in the search for informal relationships outside the bureaucracy which would ensure promotion or a second career. Under party cabinets, this situation would appear to explain why high-ranking civil servants increasingly sought party identification.

We may also conclude that the ability of the political parties to penetrate the bureaucracy after 1900 despite office protection was largely the consequence of the elimination of extra-bureaucratic criteria for appointment and advancement. The substitution of seniority and experience for traditional elite status, participation in the Restoration, and *han* social relationships completely undermined the stability and autonomy of bureaucratic leadership. The old bureaucrat could and did rely on a whole web of social relationships which made him relatively independent of his immediate superiors. The new bureaucrat was for the most part cut off from these sources of promotion because they could not be made permanent. This is not to say that family influence and social ties ceased to be of importance, but their significance diminished with the increasing dependence on organizational norms. The decreased significance of extra-bureaucratic influence made the new upper civil servant dependent on his immediate superior for promotion on the basis of criteria which were never clearly delineated. At the highest ranks the civil servant was almost completely dependent on the cabinet minister's good opinion of him. As a consequence, whenever a ministerial post was held by a party member the highest-ranking civil servants seeking promotion were likely to admit to party sympathy and identification. In the same way, seniority and experience being equal, pro-

[24] Uzaki Yukichi, *Choya no godaibatsu* (Tokyo, 1912), pp. 98-104.

motion was likely to depend on clique identification under non-party ministers. In this respect party and clique identification were responses to the desire to reduce the tensions and ambiguity surrounding promotion.

The absence of emphasis on technical expertise as opposed to the generalist legal training which high-ranking civil servants acquired reflects the major concern and needs of the governmental structure after 1885. The massive legal reforms of the early Meiji period, which affected almost every aspect of Japanese life, required a bureaucratic corps capable of making uniform judgments. Although technical expertise became increasingly available it was not viewed as being of equal importance. The major aim was to avoid the possibility of chaos which might ensue from variations in interpreting and administering the reforms. The pre-eminence of this concern among the bureaucratic leaders at the end of the nineteenth century is clearly evident in the following quotation from Itō Hirobumi's "Instructions Addressed to the Governors of Cities and Prefectures," of September 28, 1887:

> Administrative affairs ought to advance hand in hand with the march of social improvement. Since the Restoration the condition of society has been greatly changed with the downfall of the feudal system and the mode of living has assumed an entirely new character and is now in a career of striking progress. Now in this transition from the old to the new order of things, we inevitably find many forces in a stationary and un-progressive state, while other elements and antagonistic tendencies may be found perpetually conflicting with each other, thereby preventing a harmonization of social life. . . . Under these circumstances those engaged in the work of administration ought to make stability and permanence their object. . . . were the scheme of administration planned during the last 20 years to be left to take care of itself, what would become of the future of our nation?[25]

Thirteen years later the same concern was expressed, but now as a sigh of relief by Yamagata Aritomo. "We have reached the point where laws are already highly developed, where there is

[25] As quoted in W. W. McLaren, "Japanese Government Documents," *Transactions of the Asiatic Society of Japan*, XLII, Pt. 1 (May, 1914), 324-330.

little room left for arbitrary decisions by officials, and where at least administration is becoming a specialized technique."[26]

The concern for administrative stability and uniformity was primarily along lines of administrative area of activity rather than along lines of technical expertise. It is further evident that the higher status of the generalist norm became institutionalized, since only a few in the sample could be properly described as technical experts. Certainly by the 1920's the importance of uniformity in training had diminished. Increasing urbanization and industrialization had created a need for technical expertise which was as great as if not greater than the need for uniformity. Despite this need and despite increases in specialist technical offices and training, advancement remained restricted to those with generalist training and administrative area specialization.

The higher status accorded the generalist may also, perhaps, have contributed to the bureaucracy's difficulty in dealing with the major problems of the 1920's and early 1930's. The implicit invidious distinction between the specialist and the generalist may have led the latter to look with suspicion and disdain on the advice and recommendations of the expert. Meanwhile the expert would and apparently did create cliques whose function may have been to use their expertise to resist their generalist superiors, thus creating further conflict and reduced efficiency.[27] Nevertheless, it can be said that the existence of specialization and differentiation along lines of administrative area of activity rather than technical expertise did provide the basis for the bureaucracy's ability to supply services for mass consumption throughout this period. Well-versed in the intricacies of a distinct area of administration, the post-1900 bureaucrat was able to perform with considerable efficiency—an efficiency which may well have been lacking in the technical expert.

Ironically, the emergence of the legal-rational norms of achievement and specialization, when combined with the cabinet system, conspired to undermine the norm of careerism for the highest-ranking civil servants. Promotion on the basis of seniority

---

[26] As quoted in Ōkurashō Insatsukyoku, *Gikai seido nanjūnenshi: kenseishi gaikan* (Tokyo, 1963), p. 34.

[27] The conflict between specialist and generalist is described briefly in somewhat different terms in Masumi Junnosuke, *Nihon seitōshi ron*, iv, 209-218.

and experience required a consistent pattern of promotion at all ranks in order to maintain morale and a constant flow of personnel into the bureaucracy. The number of offices available as advancement occurred was delimited by specialization and the hierarchical character of administration. Unable to aspire to high office in other ministries, the bureaucrat was forced to compete for fewer and fewer offices as he advanced toward the apex of ministerial administration. For those reaching the highest ranks the pressure for promotion from below would inevitably lead to further promotion for only a very few and retirement for the majority. The rate of turnover for higher officials was increased by the institutionalization of cabinet government. With cabinet changes came new ministers who appointed their own bureaucratic policy-makers. For those who had been successful in reaching the top positions this meant retirement at a relatively early age. Success, in this case, was likely to be fatal for long careers.

The major consequence of early retirement age was the creation of both motive and opportunity for the pursuit of a second career. Clearly aware of the pressure from below, of the scantiness of retirement pensions, of the inevitability of cabinet changes, the high-ranking bureaucrat was forced into actively seeking relationships leading to second careers or passively accepting the opportunity when it was presented. In either case the bureaucrat had to prepare himself for the transition. In order to acquire a post-retirement position, avenues of communication had to be opened, relationships had to be established, and evidence of good faith and utility had to be presented. We can only conclude that these activities led to the performance of favors and favorable interpretation of laws for special interests. For the political parties this situation clearly resulted in their ability to manipulate voting, to have public works projects granted to specific areas in order to build party strength, and to withhold such projects in areas where the opposition was strong. For business it meant public works contracts, subsidies, favorable financial and labor policies, as well as other forms of economic favoritism. The total effect was the vitiation of the value and norms of careerism and a reduction in administrative rationality and efficiency.

The development of this pattern of behavior indicates the major reason for the active recruitment of ex-bureaucrats into political parties and business. The necessity of influencing high-ranking bureaucrats in order to gain favorable legislation and favorable implementation of existing laws resulted in influence's becoming a criterion for leadership in parties and business organizations. The former high-ranking bureaucrat best understood the intricacies of the administrative structure as well as of the bureaucratic mind. He possessed avenues of communication and relationships with his former colleagues which could not be duplicated by non-bureaucrats.

The emergence of this criterion further indicates the degree to which political parties and business organizations developed and functioned as interest groups. What the full effects of this emphasis on interest-group function were on the structure and development of the Diet parties requires thorough investigation and analysis. We can, however, tentatively suggest that the interest-group relationship of the Diet parties to the bureaucracy was primarily responsible for the persisting inability of the former to develop as autonomous structures. So long as the upper civil servant continued to be legally protected from random dismissal and replacement by party politicians he possessed an autonomy which forced the parties into patterns of manipulation which required them to recruit former bureaucrats. The peculiar combination of protected career but unprotected tenure at the highest levels of the bureaucracy had the effect of institutionalizing the recruitment pattern, thus reinforcing the manipulative and influencing character of the parties. The continued presence of bureaucrats-cum-politicians formed an effective barrier to the development of policies of open confrontation through mass organization.

Without the weapons of political appointments and confrontation the parties had a pitiably small arsenal with which to achieve control of decision-making. Limited power over the budget, power of promotion, the promise of second careers were weapons of manipulation, not of domination. The use of these weapons did indeed result in the politicization of the bureaucracy, but in informal and particularistic terms rather than in formal legal and universalistic terms. In these circumstances the power of the political parties shifted continually, depending on their ability to manipulate a bewildering and intricate chorus of personalities within the bureaucracy. We are led to the conclusion that this well-known characteristic of Japanese politics in the post-1900 period is not solely or even primarily due to the so-called tendency of Japanese to view power in terms of the manipulation of complex webs of social relationships. Rather it appears to be the consequence, in large part, of the unrestricted development of the bureaucratic role along legal-rational lines. This development forced the parties even when they were ostensibly in power to use manipulative techniques which by their very nature could not be formalized or legalized. The politics of manipulation was given permanence by the recruitment of bureaucrats and ex-bureaucrats who would not and could not undermine their claims to party leadership by attacking the conditions which made their leadership possible. In this fashion, if the bureaucracy was politicized the parties were bureaucratized.

On a more general level this analysis suggests several conclusions with regard to the relationship of bureaucratic role development and political development. The Japanese case indicates that the emergence of rational-legal bureaucratic role norms does not, at certain stages of development, lead to increasing specialization and differentiation in political roles. Rather, the emergence of such norms may lead to the maintenance of close ties between bureaucracy and political parties, with the subordination of the latter. This type of development appears to be the consequence of the unrestricted development of legal-rational norms which emphasize the legal and actual protection of career but at the same time make career fulfillment impossible at the highest levels of office. The key word here is "unrestricted." The legal, formal, and actual protection of the bureaucratic career from outside interference is likely to occur when, in the initial stages of "political modernization," the bureaucracy has no effective opposition. The bureaucracy at this time establishes its right to dominate politics by virtue of its leader's role in overthrowing the previous regime and/or leadership. Eventually, with the disappearance of this generation the perpetuation of bureaucratic primacy must be legitimized by success, and claims to expertise, and efficiency. To achieve this end, legal-rational norms are instituted, with great emphasis being placed on careerism and the protection of the bureaucrat from random dismissal. In this situation political parties are unable to prove that other means of allocating decision-making roles may be equally efficient and successful. Ostensibly possessing a monopoly on expertise and efficiency, and committed to values and norms which do not represent "selfish" interests, the bureaucratic role becomes untouchable. The parties are thus reduced to manipulation if they wish to exert any power in the decision-making process. Hence the bad name of politicians in many developing societies, where they are viewed as corruptors. To manipulate and influence, parties are forced either to recruit ex-bureaucrats or to engage in the politics of mass confrontation. When parties utilize the former technique the line distinguishing politician from bureaucrat becomes and remains ambiguous. As a result non-bureaucratic organizations do not become autonomous. They remain tied to the bureaucracy through the necessity of recruiting part of their leadership in terms of the criterion of influence. These exbureaucratic leaders reject policies which might lead to confrontation and independence. Both bureaucracy and political parties become corrupted by the politics of manipulation. The bureaucrat seeks a second career while the politician seeks to manipulate. Politics takes place at an informal and particularistic level. Decision-making no longer has a clearly defined structural focus or locus. In this context responsibility is also no longer clearly determined. Maruyama Masao's description of this process in Japan may be applied to this type of development generally. "Ex-politician-bureaucrats presently became ex-bureaucrat politicians, until finally there was a deluge of bureaucrats-cum-officials, who were not really politicians at all. The autocratic sense of responsibility receded; and no democratic sense of responsibility arose to take its place."[28]

Under severe crisis this type of decision-making process tends to dissolve. Bureaucrats and politicians seek to avoid responsibility as the crisis introduces new variables and actors which makes the process of manipulation and compromise ever more difficult. Politics thus tend to be very unstable despite the fact that the various structures continue to exist and function. The major weakness of such systems is not the incapacity of the bureaucracy or the sudden collapse or conversion of political leaders. The weakness lies in the inability to create formally defined structures for allocating decision-making roles—an inability that is traceable to the bureaucratic role and structure and its relationship to other political roles and structures. In short, where unrestricted development of legal-rational norms occurs in the bureaucratic role it tends to produce a structure which claims autonomy and primacy because of its efficiency, universalistic values, and commitment to national rather than special interests.

[28] Maruyama Masao, *Thought and Behavior in Modern Japanese Politics* (London, 1963), p. 128.

215

When this occurs, as in the case of Japan, political parties cannot confront the bureaucracy directly without leaving themselves open to charges of selfishness and self-seeking. The parties are thus forced to remain subordinate, and from this lack of equilibrium evolves the pattern of politics exemplified by the Japanese case.

Finally, we may conclude from the Japanese case that the development of legal-rational norms in the bureaucratic structure does not lead necessarily to a high level of political development if by this term is meant a political structure capable of meeting ever-growing demands and challenges without serious structural crises and breakdowns. The development of such norms may lead to structural imbalances and thereby impede the development of a stable political system capable of absorbing change. It well may be, as one political scientist has suggested, that high levels of political development can be reached in the long run only when there are limitations placed on the development of legal-rational norms in the bureaucratic role and structure.[29]

[29] Fred W. Riggs, "Bureaucrats and Political Development: A Paradoxical View," in Joseph LaPalombara (ed.), *Bureaucracy and Political Development*, pp. 122-130.

Taishō Democracy as the Pre-Stage for Japanese Militarism

Between the two world wars Japan lived through two distinct periods which were in sharp contrast to one another. The first period, just after the First World War and through the 1920's, was characterized by rather liberal trends, often summed up by the phrase "Taishō Democracy." The second period, the 1930's, was marked by the war in China, militarism, and "super-nationalism." Throughout these two periods the Meiji Constitution was not changed, nor, by and large, were the institutional structure of the state nor the greater part of the bureaucratic oligarchy which had persisted since the Meiji era. In other words, what makes the contrast between the 1920's and 1930's is not a difference in the structure of the regime, but a change in the influential groups within that regime and a marked shift of policies, social trends, and cultural atmosphere. In the 1920's, Japan participated in the League of Nations, concluded agreements with other powers on disarmament, introduced universal male suffrage, started administration by majority party rule, and was intellectually open to Western political thought and ideology. In the 1930's she withdrew from the League of Nations, launched military aggression on China, and, finally, dissolved political parties and trade unions and organized a military garrison state which attacked Pearl Harbor.

Was this a conversion of a nation or did it merely indicate a new stage of that Japanese imperialism which had its origins in the Meiji period? Those who emphasize the contrast are inclined to idealize the term "Taishō Democracy" and consider the war years from 1931 to 1945 a national conversion or rather an unfortunate accident or nightmare which had best be forgotten. Hence, the success story of Japanese modernization. Those who underline the continuity of the Meiji oligarchy throughout the Taishō and Shōwa eras until 1945 are inclined to minimize the extent of liberalization which did take place in the 1920's within the traditional framework of the state and society. In doing so they obscure, in part, the origins of militarism insofar as it was a reaction to Taishō liberalism, and underestimate the heritage from the Taishō era evident in the post-Second World War period. In fact, what occurred between the 1920's and 1930's in Japan can be described as a continuity in structure with a radical change in function. The very fact that there was a liberalization of policies without changing basic political institutions made possible the reverse, an extreme militarization of the state without changing its structure. The purpose of this paper is to explain with a schema, first, why there was liberalization in the 1920's and second, how this particular type of liberalization almost inevitably led to an aggressive imperialism.

When the First World War broke out, Japan, like the United States, grasped the opportunity of profiting from the war as a major supplier to the belligerent countries. Industrial production was almost doubled during the period between 1914 and 1919. The average profit rate for industry, which in the first half of 1914 was 40.8 per cent, rose during the three-year period 1917-1919 to 55.2 per cent. During this time, in areas like shipping, shipbuilding, and mining, the profit rate even rose as high as 160 to 200 per cent.[1] This industrial expansion during the war was immediately followed by a period of successive depressions. The depressions affected mostly small enterprises, but not really the large companies.[2] It is easy to see that the business leaders who had become powerful during the war and depression years tried to extend their influence to the political sphere and supported liberal politicians in opposition to the excessive *dirigisme* of the Meiji oligarchy. The party leaders did come to represent to a large extent the interests of business: by promoting international cooperation with an eye to securing foreign markets; by trying to cut the military budget in order to attain a certain economic stability; by compromising the liberalism of the middle class with universal suffrage and a relatively liberal educational policy in

[1] Inoue Harumaru, "Dokusen-shihonshugi no kakuritsu," *Nihon rekishi, gendai II* (Tokyo, 1963), pp. 101-138.

[2] This is true particularly for the large *zaibatsu* systems. For example, before the war, Mitsui controlled 11 companies and Mitsubishi 12. In 1927, even before the great depression, Mitsui controlled 97 companies and Mitsubishi 65. Inoue, *ibid.* If the war period meant industrial expansion, then the 1920's meant, *par excellence*, the concentration of industrial power into the hands of *zaibatsu*.

218

the interest of social order, and perhaps with the intention of isolating the working class from the rest of the population.

Industrial expansion, on the other hand, led to a concentration of the population in urban areas, creating not only a large number of factory workers, but also the new middle class: civil servants, white collar workers, professional people.[3] These groups were better off than factory workers; they were relatively well educated and were sensitive to the political and social messages supplied by the mass media which were quickly developing.[4] It was the middle class who demanded and gained male universal suffrage, one of the political landmarks which distinguished the 1920's from the previous period.

From 1914 to 1919, the number of factory workers nearly doubled. At the same time, the real wage dropped sharply because of wartime inflation, and recovered the pre-war level only at the end of 1919.[5] Needless to say, the 1920's were from the beginning characterized by a large amount of unemployment. Little of the enormous profit from the war reached the working class, who first suffered from low wages, then inflation, and then from the threat of unemployment. They thus had little or no hope of escaping misery in crowded urban industrial areas, and some workers protested, petitioned, went on strike, demonstrated in the streets, and often clashed with the police. For the first time in modern Japan, labor conflict became a social problem of importance.

Thus the liberal trends in the 1920's were closely linked with Japan's industrial expansion and its effect on national life. On the other hand, some other aspects of the government's policies and

[3] More detailed information can be found in "Zōdaisuru shin-chusan-kaikyū" in Minami Hiroshi (ed.), *Taishō bunka* (Tokyo, 1965), pp. 183-195.

[4] Kato Shūichi, "Political Modernization and Mass Media" in Robert Ward (ed.), *Political Modernization in Japan and Turkey* (Princeton, 1964), pp. 236-254.

[5] Japanese occupation of the Shantung Peninsula and the Twenty-One Demands provoked the May Fourth Movement (1919), a boycott of Japanese goods, and the entente between the Nationalists and Communists (1924-1927). The latter led to the Japanese intervention in Shantung. The same pattern of action and reaction was repeated in the 1930's. To use modern terms, the "hawks" justified themselves always by the situations which they themselves created.

As for the sharp contrast between Japanese and American policies toward China in the 1920's, a good account is given in Mitani Taichirō, "Tenkanki (1918-21) no gaikō shidō," *Kindai Nihon no seiji shidō, seijika kenkyū, II* (Tokyo, 1965), pp. 293-374.

intellectual currents were predominantly affected by the new international situation created by the First World War: the retreat of the European colonial powers from Asia, Wilson and the League of Nations, and Lenin and the October Revolution. Emerging from the war as a world power, Japan quickly reacted to every new international trend.

It did not take long for the Japanese government to see the excellent opportunity of extending its influence over the Asian continent, when all great powers were engaged in the European war and, with the exception of the United States, no longer able to afford large-scale military operations in Asia. Japan occupied the Shantung Peninsula in 1914, sent an ultimatum, the Twenty-One Demands, to China in 1915, militarily intervened in Siberia (1919-1922), renewed intervention in Shantung (1927-1928), launched semi-military operations in Manchuria such as the murder of Chang Tso-lin (1928), not to mention all the aggressive acts after 1931. It is true that Japanese leaders were divided in opinions concerning the policy toward the continent, with the army often acting independently from the rest of the government. But they were unanimous in two respects: everybody in the government was aware of the much weakened position of the European powers in the Far East and the imminent American opposition to Japanese advancement; almost none accurately evaluated the rising tide of Chinese nationalism and its grave implications. It was in the liberal 1920's, not in the militaristic 1930's, that the vicious circle of Japanese foreign policy started: a hard policy was adopted, creating a situation whose solution seemed to require even harder measures.[6]

Although aggressive toward China, the governments of the 1920's were compromising toward the Western powers. Nitobe Inazō, for example, as vice-secretary of the League of Nations, tirelessly preached for international peace and cooperation. In 1922 Japan signed the Washington Treaty, giving up her gains in Shantung and agreeing to naval disarmament. She later reduced the size of the army by four divisions (1925) and finally signed and ratified the London Treaty of Naval Disarmament (1930). All these compromises were made not only under the pressure of financial difficulties, which were, to be sure, serious in those depression years, but also under the pressure of liberal public opinion, inspired by the international atmosphere, whose emblem was Wilsonian idealism.

[6] *Ibid.*

The Japanese liberalism of the 1920's had spokesmen at different levels. To mention a few: Hara Kei, as the majority party leader, spoke out against armed adventures on the continent, despite pressure from the military oligarchy. Ozaki Yukio and Inukai Tsuyoshi fought vigorously in the House of Representatives, as well as in the streets, demanding universal suffrage, majority party rule and disarmament. Yoshino Sakuzō in the university, perhaps the most influential theoretician of democracy of the time, preached eloquently for government for and by the people. The founders of the *Shinjinkai* among the students at Tokyo Imperial University who enthusiastically supported Yoshino argued also in favor of international cooperation, liberal education, and freedom of expression against all kinds of police control. Yoshino's supporters were not confined to students, nor to academics, but extended to leading journalists such as those who were active in the leading national newspaper *Ōsaka Asahi*. It should be noted also that liberal intellectuals succeeded in creating, at least in the cities, an anti-militaristic feeling among the population without which the reduction of the army divisions, for example, might not have been possible.[7] Arishima Takeo, a Christian novelist, wrote in 1918, "War and peace are matters that are freely decided by a handful of capitalists";[8] Akutagawa Ryūnosuke was sarcastic about the Imperial army in the late 1920's, saying, for example, that "army officers are like children: both like glittering metal decorations."[9] In fact, during the Siberian intervention, the number of draft-dodgers mounted to over a thousand in one year, a record figure in Japanese army history.

As for the October Revolution in Russia, neither the government nor the intellectuals were slow to respond, although in dia-

[7] Ugaki Kazunari, *Ugaki nikki* (Tokyo, 1954), p. 32.

[8] Arishima Takeo, "Mushakōji-Kunie," *Chūō kōron* (July, 1918).

[9] Akutagawa Ryūnosuke, "Shuju no Kotoba." First published in *Bungei shunjū*, 27 (1925). Akutagawa's sarcasm was directed not toward the regime itself. In that sense, he was a Japanese counterpart of Kurt Tucholsky in the Weimar Republic. About the latter, Golo Mann pointed out, "*Die hellsichtige Bosheit, mit der Kurt Tucholsky die Republik verspottete, alle ihre Lahmheiten und Falschheiten.*" And also: "*Die radikale Literatur gehörte nicht zur Republik, wohl aber zur republikanischen Zeit, in der allein sie in den Zeitschriften und auf dem Theater so laut zu Worte kommen konnte.*" Golo Mann, *Deutsche Geschichte 1919-1945* (Berlin, 1961), p. 48. This remark is valid for Akutagawa and some other writers in Taishō Japan. A decade later it became clear in Tokyo and Berlin alike that army officers were not similar to children and social democrats were not the worst government Germany could expect.

metrically different ways. Alarmed by the Communist advance, the government promptly sent the army, as we have already mentioned, against the Soviet forces in Siberia. At home, strikes were ruthlessly suppressed, as were socialist organizations. Further safeguards against the Left were created by passage of the notorious Peace Preservation Law in 1925, which was quickly revised in 1928 to raise the maximum penalty from ten years' imprisonment to death, and created the Special Police Force for the control of subversive ideas and activities. It is to be noted that when the coalition government of political parties presented the bill for the revision of the Peace Preservation Law to the 55th Diet (1928), the bill could not be passed because of strong opposition inside and outside the Diet, so that the government was forced to resort to an emergency Imperial Ordinance in order to promulgate it. The government which was based on the first general election with universal manhood suffrage feared communism so greatly that it felt obliged to impose this oppressive law and ignore all parliamentary opposition.

On the other hand, encouraged by the success of the socialist revolution in Russia, the Japanese Communist Party was founded in 1922. Under severe oppression by the police, this underground party, once dissolved and rebuilt, was until 1945 unable to organize a large number of factory workers, let alone the farmers. But it was from the party as the core that Marxist ideas began to penetrate steadily into the intellectual and artistic milieu of students, academics, creative writers, and avant-garde theater groups. Quite a few of them belonged to the party, and all of them were aware of the invisible organization, if not as the center of their intellectual life, at least as something which they had to confront seriously. The Marxist leaflets, literary magazines, novels of "social realism," theaters of "agitating propaganda," translated works of Marx and Engels all flourished, either underground or legally, with many lines crossed out by censorship. In the divided socialist parties and labor movement the Marxist leaders gradually gained ground, taking the place of older leaders with Christian or anarchist backgrounds.[10] Marxism, however, was the emblem of an intellectual rather than a political movement, without much influence on the majority of the people,

[10] In the 1920's Japanese social democrats remained in contact, at least intellectually, with their colleagues in power in the Weimar Republic who in turn expressed themselves often in Marxist terms—for example, Hilferding.

somewhat like Christianity, particularly Protestantism, in Meiji Japan.

The question of why Marxism captured the imagination of Japanese intellectuals is a complicated one. However, a few points can be made here. In the first place, the effects of the depression did not spare college graduates; it created for the first time in modern history unemployment among highly educated Japanese and contributed heavily to their political radicalization. Second, Marxism was the first and only comprehensive theory of history and society that Japanese intellectuals had ever encountered. It was an excellent instrument indeed, not necessarily to change, but to interpret, the world, particularly a world in which depressions, police brutality, and the misery of the working class seemed unavoidable. Finally, the "liberalism" of the type of Yoshino Sakuzō—he himself called it government for people (*mimpon-shugi*) as distinguished from sovereignty of people (*minshu-shugi*)—demanded better policies, but not a change in the structure of the government.[11] Consequently, those who

[11] Yoshino carefully made clear again and again that he had no objection to the Meiji Constitution, nor particularly to the Imperial prerogative. Certainly he was aware of the close relationship between the function and the structure of a government. But he was "realistic" and trying to be "constructive" within a given situation; thus, although he was successful in the short run, his efforts were totally in vain in the long run. He was successful because he concentrated on what he could do rather than what he might dream to do; he was unsuccessful because "democracy" in any sense could not long survive in that system which had originally been designed not for the ruled but for the rulers. The contradiction inherent in the "realism" of Yoshino Sakuzō was this: an argument which pretends to accept a system, in order to assure its improved functioning, works to perpetuate the system in which the room for improved functioning tends to become narrower. A choice which looked absurd yesterday was to be accepted as a given condition by "realism."

Toward the outside world, Yoshino not only preached cooperation with Western powers for peace and disarmament, but also showed his understanding of the May Fourth Movement in China, and particularly of the tide of nationalism in Korea. In fact, it was Yoshino who brilliantly exposed the popular fallacy about the Korean uprising (1918) in which the benevolent character of Japanese colonial policy was assumed and the reason for the vehement revolt of the Koreans was ascribed to the intervention of subversive agitators from outside (at the same time supposed to be Christian missionaries). Yoshino argued that, even if foreign agitators might have been involved, they would have been unable to arouse the population unless the dissatisfaction of the mass had already reached the point of explosion, and

223

saw the incompatibility between the desired policies and the structure of the government were not satisfied with Yoshino's "liberalism." They were attracted by the program of the Communist Party for abolition of the Emperor system, total disarmament, radical land reform, universal suffrage, and equality between men and women. When viewed closely this program was nothing but a series of fundamental demands for "bourgeois democracy," which, except for the abolition of armed forces, had long been realized in most countries of the Western world, notably in the United States, and which were to be imposed, in the case of Japan, by the Allied Powers after the surrender in 1945. Thus one of the striking paradoxes of Taishō liberalism was that the liberals were operating under such oppressive conditions that the fundamental ideas of political liberalism could not even be suggested in public, let alone put forward in a practicable program. In order to be consistent as a liberal, it was necessary to be a Marxist.

Economic expansion during the First World War, on the one hand, and the post-war international situation, on the other, combined to create in Japan, as a kind of reaction to Meiji society, a new situation which had much in common with German historical development in the same years. In both countries authoritarian regimes had succeeded in the industrialization of the country; in both countries super-nationalistic military states emerged in the postwar years. The parallelism may be taken further: both were subjected to depressions which intervened in the "weak rings of world capitalism"; both had repeated ministerial crises, demonstrating the inability of the political parties to rule; both had a new middle class, frustrated yet continuing to adhere to the concept of obedience to authority; in both countries the Marxist intellectuals who strove for the destruction of the regime rather than its consolidation, were isolated, and the people reacted perhaps in similar ways to the Versailles Treaty and the disarmament treaties. The difference, however, was no less important than the similarity. From the legal point of view Japa-

---

that the real problem lay not with foreign agents, but with the colonial policy itself.

On the other hand, however, Yoshino's attitude remained ambiguous regarding the policy toward China: "We should understand Chinese nationalism, but Japan's special interests on the continent should be recognized." He even hesitated to condemn the Twenty-One Demands. The basic line of Japan's China policy was not contested even by Yoshino.

nese political institutions did not change in the 1920's, while in Germany the constitution itself was completely democratized after the First World War. While the Japanese economy still rested largely on agriculture, the Weimar Republic was already far advanced in industrialization. Fundamental differences can also be detected in sociological aspects: in Japan Confucian values and large families constantly functioned to bridge the urban and rural population, while in Germany values were individualistic and the atomization of urban society was in progress. If the common aspects of the two states led to "fascism" in both cases, these differences generated, so to speak, the two different types of fascism: the one from below led by an ex-corporal, the other organized from the top by the military establishment.

In the midst of the controversial policies of the Japanese governments of the 1920's, the legal structure of the power of the traditional oligarchy was hardly affected. Institutions such as the *genrō* (elder statesmen), the Imperial Household Ministry, the Privy Council, and the House of Peers were not substantially changed. The Emperor was the sacrosanct authority under whose name those institutions, responsible to him, not to the people, could operate freely, by interpreting at their will the supposed Imperial orders. In this system the House of Representatives had little power. The Prime Minister was chosen not by the House, but by the *genrō*. The Privy Council and the House of Peers held broad constitutional powers enabling them to reject any act of the House of Representatives. The cabinet, in the name of the Emperor, had the power to dissolve the Diet, intervene in elections, control information, and limit free speech and free assembly. Besides this, the cabinet could modify laws over the heads of the House of Representatives through the promulgation of Imperial ordinances. At the same time, the army, of which the supreme command was one of the Imperial prerogatives, had to a great extent independence from the cabinet, let alone from the House of Representatives. The leaders of the armed forces could appeal directly to the Emperor without consulting the rest of the administration ("direct access to the throne"). Moreover, the army was able to influence policies of the cabinet by threatening to withdraw the Minister of War, a post to which, in the 1930's only generals and lieutenant-generals on active duty could be appointed. These arrangements also held true for the Imperial Navy. Despite male universal suffrage, cabinets of majority party

225

leaders, and the important role of public opinion in political life, "Taishō democracy" by contrast with the Weimar Republic, seriously challenged neither in action nor in ideas[12] the basic legal structure of oligarchical powers which had operated and would continue to operate until 1945 under the cover of the absolute authority of the Emperor. Built into this system were all necessary devices for the army to control the whole political apparatus, when the wind would blow in a different direction in the late 1930's.

Not only was the legal system in Japan of a traditional order, but the economic structure retained a strong traditional caste as well. Despite expansion during the war, Japanese industrialization was not so far advanced as, for example, that of Germany. As late as 1928, for example, Japan was producing less than 1/7 of the German yield in steel, and even during the Pacific War Japan never achieved the German level of steel production of 1900.[13] In the 1920's more than half of the Japanese working population were engaged in the agricultural sector (51.7 per cent in 1920),[14] while in the Weimar Republic agricultural workers accounted for less than 1/3 (ca. 30 per cent in 1925).[15] The high concentration of the rural population in Japan inevitably meant, by contrast with the production per acre, a very low level of productivity per capita. Small farmers often had so much difficulty in paying the heavy taxes that a large number of them were expropriated, and the tenants were forced to pay nearly half of their crops to the landowners. It is obvious that these conditions made Japanese agrarian economy particularly vulnerable to de-

[12] See the case of Yoshino Sakuzō as a representative liberal thinker, in footnote 1. Communists of course challenged the whole system in idea, but not in action. They were too isolated to exert an important influence on the course of political events in the country.

[13] Annual steel production (million tons) in Japan: 0.56 in 1920, 1.97 in 1928, 5.60 (the highest figure during the Second World War) in 1943; in Germany, 7.4 in 1900, 13.0 in 1910, 9.7 in 1924, 14.5 in 1928. Japanese figures are from Moriya Funio: *Keizaishi, Nihon gendaishi taikei* (Tokyo, 1961), pp. 240, 75, 385; German figures from Gustav Stolper, Kurt Hausser and Knut Borchart, *The German Economy, 1870 to the Present* (New York, reprinted in Fritz Ringer [ed.]), *The German Inflation of 1928* (London & New York, 1969), p. 53, and Eugen Varga, *Die Krise des Kapitalismus und ihre politischen Folgen* (Frankfurt, 1969), p. 129.

[14] Ōuchi Tsutomu: *Nōgyōshi, Nihon gendaishi taikei* (Tokyo, 1960), p. 118.

[15] Fritz Ringer (ed.), *op. cit.*, p. 156.

pressions. Moreover, when the market was firm, silk was the most profitable cash crop for Japanese villages. When the price of silk dropped in the United States, the major market for Japanese silk export, it meant a disaster to the "silk area" of the country.

Depressions in the 1920's thus affected the agrarian sector more than industry in Japan, and depressions led to a dramatic drop in industrial production in other major powers, such as the United States and Germany. In 1932, just before Hitler came to power, unemployment in the Weimar Republic reached the record figure of six million,[16] the index of industrial production (1928 = 100) dropped sharply to 61.2 per cent. In the same year Japan had half a million unemployed workers[17] with the index of industrial production already recovered to the 1928 level (101.0 per cent).[18] It is understandable, as many historians have suggested, that six million people in German towns, disillusioned by the decade of Social Democrats, were awaiting their Godot who turned out to be Hitler in 1933. This was not the case in Japan. Here another type of "fascism" was to be fomented in connection with the misery of the villages rather than with the unemployed mass in urban industrial centers.

Thus "liberalism" did not seem to affect in any significant degree some of the traditional aspects of Japanese society. The status-conscious hierarchical structure, in which such values as loyalty and obedience of the lower to the higher were much emphasized; the importance of belonging to small groups, such as village communities, in which the relationship between members tended to be "diffuse" in the Parsonian sense; particularly in the rural area, the tradition of the large family—of which paternalistic interventions were expected to be extended even to quite distant relatives—all appeared to have remained relatively untouched.

In this regard it is important to note that the army had its own system of ranks relatively independent of the hierarchy of status in the society outside. Family background was thus no great dis-

[16] Many historians refer to the same figure. To quote one, for instance, Helmut Heiber, *Die Republik von Weimar* (Munich, 1966), p. 228.

[17] Ōuchi, *op. cit.*, p. 167. Generally speaking, no exact assessment of unemployment is available. The figure 480,000 which Ōuchi gives is based on the official statistics, which exclude the half-employed, particularly those in the agrarian sector.

[18] Indices of industrial production in Germany and Japan are quoted from Varga, *op. cit.*, p. 222.

advantage for the sons of farmers and small landowners. The Imperial Army was a good place to try their luck in moving upward in social status. Besides it was generally believed that traditional virtues, such as loyalty and obedience, a habit of sober life and preparedness for hard work, were preserved more in the rural population than in the new middle class in the cities who were considered Westernized and therefore "weakened." Recruiting, in fact, a large number of officers from the rural area,[19] the army felt itself closely linked with the farmers. When depressions violently shook village life in the late 1920's and early 1930's, the army saw the danger at its very root. The radical idealists among the officers were alarmed and reacted, together with civilian extreme rightists of the *nōhonshugi* (agrarian idealists), in a series of attempted coup d'état.[20]

The high concentration of agrarian labor made of the Japanese villages a great reservoir, not only of soldiers, but also of factory workers and indeed of a great many other kinds of laborers. As is well known, rural Japan supplied a host of cheap labor to expanding industry. The majority of the workers in Japanese cities were not really separated from their native villages to which they could return in case of need. They had strong family ties and were integrated in the village community, which was always prepared to accept the prodigal sons. Under these conditions it was only natural that a considerable part of the unemployment in the cities was, so to speak, absorbed by the rural communities, thus reducing the number of the unemployed on the official statistics tables. In the years which followed the Great Depression, the differences between Japan and Western countries such as Germany were not merely in the numbers of people without jobs, but also in the social effect of unemployment, which was in Japan much attenuated by traditional values and the structure of society. Like their counterparts in the Weimar Republic, the Japanese middle class were living through the economic instability and political alienation of the 1920's. But unlike the Germans,

---

[19] During the period 1920 to 1933 approximately 40% of the first-year students of Rikugun Shikan Gakkō (the Military Academy) came from the families of farmers, while about 10% came from military officers' (including retired officers) families. Fujiwara Akira, *Gunjishi: Nihon gendaishi taikei* (Tokyo, 1961), p. 157.

[20] This view is shared by many historians, for example, Hayashi Saburō, *Taiheiyō sensō rikusen gaishi* (Tokyo, 1951).

Japanese were neither alone nor free. They were bound, and at the same time supported, by their relatives and integrated into the paternalistic system of one group or another. There was no "fear of freedom" (Erich Fromm), nor the basis for an "institutionalization of the fear" (Fritz Neumann), which might have generated something like the Nazi regime. If something was common to the new middle class in both countries, it was certainly not the fear but the inferiority complex vis-à-vis the traditional elites: the complex of the common people which was finally to find its outlet in ugly uniforms and hysterical outbursts of anti-intellectualism. The majority of the intellectuals were disgusted with the trend and did not effectively fight it; the minority of them enhanced it by their obscurantism, in Germany and in Japan alike.

Taishō Japan created an urban mass society, with a relatively high level of education and with a quickly developing system of modern mass communication media, thus preparing the ground for the participation of the masses in politics, but at the same time opening the way for the manipulated mass society of the future. In this respect neither Japan nor Germany was unique in the 1920's. There was, and is, no industrialized society without conflicting trends, one toward democracy, another toward a manipulated society. What really distinguished Japanese society in the 1920's from the Western world was the very fact that the participation of the mass in politics still rested largely on votes in elections which were not much more than mere formalities.

In the first place, the membership of Japanese political parties was extremely limited in number, even in the case of the party having a majority in the House. Functional in elections, perhaps efficient in intra-parliamentary maneuvers, political parties were merely organizations of the representatives without involvement of the mass. Small socialist parties held a grip on some trade unions, but unions accounted for only a tiny section of workers. There was practically no tie other than a thin thread of symbolic votes between the parties and the majority of the people.[21] No

---

[21] A comparison between the Kapp Putsch and the Japanese military coup of February 26, 1936 is to be seen in Fujiwara Akira, "Tennōsei to gumbu," *Shisō* (July, 1961), pp. 16-22. This is in sharp contrast with the Social Democrats in the Weimar Republic who could respond to a military coup d'état by calling workers to a general strike, the "Kapp Putsch" in 1920. When the rebel battalions occupied the central part of Tokyo in 1936, the government

political party in power during the pre-World War II period in Japan was ever in a position to appeal to the masses at a crisis of the regime.

In the second place, the function of the parties itself was very much limited in scope. Institutionally, through the system of the Meiji Constitution, as we have already noted, through the marked factionalism of the major parties, and through the absence of the tradition of participating individuals, political parties were extremely weak.

Finally, there was no powerful mass organization in Japan between the two wars. From 1911 to 1936 trade unions increased in number, then declined and disappeared during the Second World War. The same was true for the total membership. Even as late as 1936 less than half a million Japanese workers were organized.[22] Despite the growth in number of strikes and demonstrations by workers after the Great Depression workers were not supported by the great mass of Japanese society. With perfect self-confidence the government ruthlessly oppressed the isolated minority of strikers and demonstrators. The people who could not effectively exert pressure on the government through the political parties were also unable to influence the situation through extraparliamentary channels.

Deprived of the possibility of participation in politics in the system, the Japanese urban mass had no other choice than desperate revolt or resignation. The former was typical in the case of the "Rice Riots" which broke out in 1918 when the price of rice went up because of wartime speculation. In one sense the riots were a revolt of the urban masses against authority.[23] They were completely spontaneous, occurring all over the country, violent, utterly unorganized and without any leadership. They were

tried to control the situation by appealing to the Emperor and the loyal generals, not to the people.

[22] Iwao F. Ayusawa, *A History of Labor in Modern Japan* (Honolulu, 1966), p. 154.

[23] It may be interesting to note some common aspects between the Rice Riots and the mass protest against the ratification of the revised Security Treaty. In 1960 hundreds of thousands went into the streets but no leadership was capable of canalizing the mass movement into radical social change. The only result was the resignation of Premier Kishi, who was succeeded by a relatively liberal leader, Ikeda. The Ikeda Cabinet continued the military alliance with the United States and a few months later dissolved the House of Representatives, winning in the election which followed.

crushed within several weeks by the army, and the only immediate result was a change of cabinet, from one led by the authoritarian General Terauchi to one headed by the leader of the majority political party, Hara Kei. Hara's government went quickly ahead with the policy of intervention in Siberia. Resignation and the feeling of helplessness now manifested itself in popular songs, novels, posters and illustrations, and some types of cabaret and musical shows. Songs written in minor keys with lyrics comparing the singer to the "withered *susuki* leaves" in the desert plain, or the drunkards who could forget their troubles only by indulging in saké in cheap bistros became a dominant theme in popular music. The same syndrome is reflected in the enthusiasm with which such novels as "The Mountain-pass Daibosatsu," a long best-seller in which a solitary *samurai* without office, nihilistic, superhumanly strong, kills many for no specific reason, thus taking on the society as a whole. The most popular artist of the period was an illustrator for magazines, Takehisa Yumeji, who portrayed almost exclusively dainty other-worldly girls with large dreamy eyes, apparently suffering from tuberculosis, for whom the real world was too much. In the theater the Takarazuka Revue was an extraordinary success. It presented revues and musical comedies, all its programs being played by girls acting in both female and male roles and most of the melodies being taken from the Paris music halls of the *belle époque*. An escape from reality was thus offered in connection with a bit of perverse sex. In the same fashion when the fifteen-year war started in Manchuria, the Japanese, reduced to an apolitical mass, were easily manipulated into an escape from reality by being offered an exciting illusion of participation in a military garrison state.

By way of contrast, the German middle class played a different role. It was not merely manipulated, but it actively helped to generate a regime of its own style. Rootless in the industrial cities, sandwiched between the people in power and the organized workers, its members had to survive years of inflation and depression more disastrous than Japan's. The German urban mass were not resigned but angry. They hated the Republic, from which they were so bitterly alienated, and which they could so easily identify with all the evils of the Versailles Treaty.[24] What fol-

24 Theodor Geiger writes about the middle class: "A class denies with disgust that it is a class and conducts a bitter class struggle against the

lowed is well known. Hitler started his movement with his para-
military brownshirts, fanatic and violent, marked by hatred of the
existing social order. Then, in the process of seizing power, he
shrewdly remolded his party by eliminating those extremists who
could not forget their initial fanaticism against established
authority, and, instead of defying it, negotiated an alliance with
the most conservative elements of the republic: the army generals
and the industrialists of the Ruhr.[25] What remained was to bring
about full employment by expanding the war economy and
canalizing the frustrated mass into a collective *Rausch* by stag-
ing the pageants in Nürnberg. Hitler's power was *generated* by
the lower middle class and efficiently *supported*, with or without
enthusiasm, by bankers and industrialists.

The years of the 1920's did not prepare the Japanese grass roots
population to generate a political movement of its own, but only
to accept the militarization of the whole state, the initiative for
which came from the long established authority of the Imperial
Army. Keeping the structure of power as such, trying to impose
partly liberal, partly imperialistic policies, the government in the

---

reality and idea of the class struggle." *Die Klassengesellschaft im Schmelz-
tiegel* (Köln-Opladen, 1949), p. 168. On this Ralf Dahrendorf comments:
"Whether class struggle or not, the root of this extremism (Nazism) is insecurity of social position; its standard bearers are the least educated and
intelligent groups of the middle class." Ralf Dahrendorf, *Society and Democracy in Germany* (New York, 1967), p. 373.

[25] Hitler seized power in 1933; one year later he executed Roehm and
other extremists of the S.A., and Georg Strasser, a Nazi fanatic. Finally he
dissolved the S.A. and eliminated General von Schleicher, the strongest of
the opposition among the army leaders.

About the middle-class standard bearers of the Nazi ideology, Claude
David noted: "*Le programme du parti, on se le rappelle, était hostile aux
trusts et voulait sauvegarder les positions de la classe moyenne. . . . Mais
cela ne dura pas: en fait, la petite bourgeoisie fut, plus que jamais, éliminé
au bénéfice du grand capital.*" Claude David, *L'Allemagne de Hitler* (Paris,
1961), p. 91.

As for the alliance between the Nazis and industrialists, the question is
open as to when it began and to its degree of intensity. Well-known early
supporters of the Nazis among the business leaders were Schacht, Thyssen,
and Kirdorf (mines in the Ruhr). When twenty industrialists sent a petition
to Hindenburg on November 19, 1932, asking for the nomination of Hitler
as premier, the list did not include Krupp, Siemens, or Duisberg (I. G. Far-
ben). A short account of the subject can be found, for example, in Nishi-
kawa Matao, "Hitler no seiken shōaku," *Shisō* (February, 1967), pp. 97-112.

1920's bitterly frustrated the army, while at the same time it provided no device for checking the scope of the army's reaction.

The army had fought a purposeless war in the frozen wastes of Siberia among a hostile population and had finally been forced to withdraw without achieving anything—and, what was worse, the people of Japan did not even seem to care. Then came the abolition of four divisions despite the protest of the Army General Staff. Although the money saved by the reduction in divisions was largely used for development of tanks and airplanes, the army was still infuriated by the loss of these four divisions. In 1928 it wanted to intervene in North China in order to stop the advance of the Kuomintang Army, but the government did not approve of such action. Just when the Great Depression endangered the army's social basis itself and officers were increasingly alarmed, the government signed the Treaty of Naval Disarmament in London (1930) despite the unanimous protest of the Naval General Staff. The army and navy retaliated by charging a violation of the Imperial prerogative of supreme command. This attempt at civilian control of policy created a violent reaction at various levels of the military. Immediately after the ratification of the treaty, Prime Minister Hamaguchi was assassinated and a number of secret societies made up of young officers were formed.

During the 1930's, these frustrated officers, colonels and majors, together with civilian elements of the extreme right, repeated attempts to stage military coups d'état. All the coups failed to seize power but all succeeded in intimidating the established institutions—military and civil—so that the general line of government policy shifted gradually but steadily to the direction they desired; a military garrison state. The army leadership and the civil bureaucracy were frightened by the coup attempts and, although opposed to political party control, did not hesitate to use the imminent threat of a coup as a trump card against "liberal" factions of the government. The last and largest of the coup attempts occurred on February 25, 1936, when young extremist officers, commanding some 1400 soldiers, assassinated several cabinet ministers, occupied the governmental quarter of Tokyo, and demanded a military government personally presided over by the Emperor. The coup failed, but the leadership of the army exploited the occasion, not only to increase its pressure on the gov-

233

Kato

ernment, but also to eliminate the most radical elements in the army.

Another legacy of Taishō democracy was a standing army in Manchuria, the Kwantung Army, whose strength rose from about 10,000 in 1931 to 164,000 in 1935.[26] Given relatively weak civil control over the army in Tokyo, the General Staff of the army abroad tended to evolve plans for military contingencies which did not require the approval of the on-the-spot government. Thus on several occasions in the 1930's the army forced the civil government to accept a *fait accompli* with regard to Manchuria and China.[27] Seen from the outside, Japan appeared to be invading China with imperialistic intentions. Seen from the inside, however, most political leaders felt that Japan was being dragged into the swamp of war as part of some inevitable process.[28] As the war in China grew, it affected the national economy on the one hand, and the balance of power in the political structure on the other. As a consequence the army gained increasing influence over political decisions. The leadership of the army used not only threats of coups by young officers in order to intimidate opposing opinions, but also protected its freedom of action by appealing to the Imperial prerogative and extending its influence over the cabinet by its right of choosing the Minister of War.[29] In other

[26] Fujiwara, *op. cit.*, pp. 165, 167. When the Pacific War broke out in 1941, the Kwantung Army alone disposed of over 700,000 soldiers, 1,000 tanks, 5,000 artillery and 1,500 war planes. Okada Takeo, *Konoe Fumimaro* (Tokyo, 1959), p. 155.

[27] Even before the war in Manchuria, the army acted without approval of the government. The sending of more troops to Siberia than was decided in the Governmental Committee for Foreign Policy in 1910-1919 and the murder of Chang Tso-lin in 1928 are well-known examples.

[28] This was typical for the first Konoe Cabinet (June 1937-January 1939). The Government kept saying in effect that Japan's purpose was solely to protect China from the Communist danger, that Japan wanted no territory but the prosperity of all the people in Asia, that the Japanese Government was prepared for negotiations at any time, but Chiang Kai-shek had rejected any discussions, and that military operations were just to prove to Chiang and his friends that their attempt to take over China by military force would fail. The army, on the other hand, declared that the victory was just around the corner at every stage of the fifteen-year war on the continent.

[29] Long is the list of the cases in which the army acted against the will of the nominated premier through the choice of the army minister. In 1932, the Saitō Cabinet was forced by the army to keep General Araki as army minister; in 1936, the Hirota Cabinet could not complete the list of ministers for a long time because of the opposition of the army; in 1937, General

234

words, it was not by changing, but by fully utilizing, the institutions which Taishō democracy had not modified, that the army gradually rose to power in the 1930's.

Threatened by extremist army officers, as well as by terrorists of the far right, the alliance of business leaders and party politicians were unhappy about intervention by the army in political decisions and objected to military adventurism on the continent. However, they could not contest the basic aim, or the principle, of the army: protection of the empire by way of the Chinese continent. The reason for this was twofold: first, they agreed fundamentally with the army that Japan's economic future was tied to China; second, they could not reject the Imperial authority in whose name the army was acting.[30] Given such a situation, the possible policies from which the government could choose became fewer and fewer, until the day came when most leaders felt that there was no alternative to the attack on Pearl Harbor. The urban middle class were not in a position to offer any effective resistance, lacking, as we have observed, an organization of their own for political action. The same was true for the factory workers. On the other hand, farmers and small landowners tended to support the military against the alliance of industrialists and political parties. As for the Marxist intellectuals, they were powerless, since they had no significant ties with the working class. At the same time many of them were imprisoned, many were forced into conversion; some compromised, sometimes too little, sometimes too much, hoping, mostly in vain, to exert influence on the course of events inside the governmental organizations.[31] A few remained faithful to personal convictions, concentrating on academic work or cultivating small tracts of land; none of them

---

Ugaki could not assume the premiership because no general (nor lieutenant-general) on active duty would agree to be included in his Cabinet; in 1940, the Yonai Cabinet dissolved because the army withdrew the army minister from the Cabinet.

[30] At the beginning, the active supporters of militaristic expansionism were not the *zaibatsu*, but new industrialists, particularly those involved in production of arms. The *zaibatsu* joined later to share in the profits. The reactions of Japanese business leaders to militarism were not much different from those of their German counterparts to the Nazis.

[31] Just to mention a few typical cases: socialists like Miwa Jusō, a Marxist philosopher, Miki Kiyoshi; and such liberals as Rōyama Masamichi, Ryū Shintarō, Sasa Hiroo, joined the *Shōwa-Kenkyūkai*, a sort of brain-trust for Prime Minister Konoe Fumimaro, in 1940.

in the late 1930's were appealing to the masses. The liberals had more opportunities of appealing to the educated mass in the cities but did so without contesting the core of Japanese imperialism: internal oligarchy, bureaucratic domination, and aggression toward China. They simply could not bring themselves to reject the Imperial symbol or to challenge those who controlled it—a challenge which they had not issued even during the golden days of the Taishō democracy.

The history of Japan between the two wars must be understood not as a shift from a democracy (of the British type) to a fascism (of the Nazi type), but as a shift from a phase of liberalization to another phase of bureaucratization and militarization within a political structure which had not basically changed. The cause of liberalization was primarily the First World War and its impact on the Japanese economy. To a considerable extent we may conclude that the militarization which followed was mainly a function of liberalization of attitudes but not of the political structure which characertized the 1920's.

Failure to bring about fundamental changes in the relationship of the political parties to the civil and military bureaucracies allowed the "liberalism" of "Taishō Democracy" to disappear when it failed to provide solutions to Japan's critical problems.

The Failure of Economic
Expansionism: 1918-1931

It has been customary to talk of "Japan in transition"—between the turn of the century and the Pacific War—in terms of the search for national purpose and cultural identity. After the successful consummation of the initial stages of modern transformation, it is said, the nation staggered into the twentieth century with little preparation to accommodate the spiritual cost of modernization. The Japanese themselves were self-conscious about the crisis, the "agony" of modern life, as they sought to define their individual and collective existence in such a way as to establish a meaningful relationship between self, the small community, the metropolis, the nation, and the world. In Japan's external affairs, in particular, aimlessness and inconsistencies in foreign policy objectives after the two cardinal questions facing the country, treaty revision and Korea, had been solved, have been noted as the emerging characteristics after the Russo-Japanese War. With the passing of the Meiji oligarchs, it is generally pointed out, consensus on foreign policy questions gave way to "dual diplomacy" and to "people's diplomacy," both lacking in a precise definition of basic objectives.

There is little doubt that the search for national identity in a changing world characterized Japan's external affairs in the first four decades of the twentieth century. But it would be wrong to conclude that after the settlement of the treaty revision and the Korean questions there no longer were serious diplomatic issues that concerned the entire nation. Far from it. Korea and treaty revision, after all, were specific issues which could be solved pragmatically. Their solution required no real imagination and no great agonizing. What came after the settlement of these practical issues was far more serious and pregnant with far-reaching implications. Most critical was the question of the economic expansion of Japan. The Japanese were united in the view that the healthy and continued growth of the country was an absolute imperative, and that this was what made civilized nations powerful. Given an image of the world dominated by expanding populations, economies, and armaments, the question was not whether to expand, but how. The Japanese were aware of the distinction between economic and forceful expansionism, between informal and formal empires. During the Meiji period writers and officials often spoke of "peacetime war" (*heiwa no sensō*) among nations and emphasized the utmost importance of economic expansion. They were avid readers of Western treatises on the subject, and they developed Japan's equivalent of the great European debate on colonialism, faithfully reflecting the century-old controversy between the champions of Adam Smith and David Ricardo on one hand and of Friedrich List and John Bernard Bayles on the other.[1] By the last years of the Meiji period, advocates of laissez-faire expansionism, earlier represented by Fukuzawa Yukichi and Taguchi Ukichi, were in a distinct minority. The Japanese came to regard with admiration such exponents of formal imperialism as R. Mayo-Smith and P. Leroy-Beaulieu.

Like their Western counterparts, Japanese neo-mercantilists called for the creation of dependable markets and sources of supply abroad by means of active emigration, colonization, and trade protectionism. While these activities were preferably to be promoted through peaceful methods, the use of force was by no means excluded. The nation's army and navy were considered necessary tools of economic expansion, and forceful territorial acquisitions were often considered desirable to accomplish the goal.[2] The essence of Meiji expansionism was best summed up in Gotō Shimpei's favorite phrase, "the policy of military preparedness under the guise of non-military activities" (*bunsō-teki bubi seisaku*). Economic activities were to serve the nation's political purposes, and overseas Japanese and their investments and enterprises could be utilized for military ends in times of need.[3]

A small group of Japanese, on the other hand, remained convinced of the wisdom of peaceful expansionism. Kayahara Kazan, for instance, pointed out in 1911 that Japanese expansion overseas should take a peaceful, industrial form. Otherwise the nation would not prosper but would be left behind the advanced na-

[1] See Kuroda Ken'ichi, *Nihon shokumin shisō-shi* (Tokyo, 1942), pp. 196ff.

[2] *Ibid.*, pp. 224ff.

[3] Gotō Shimpei, *Nihon shokumin seisaku ippan—Nihon bōchōron*, Nakamura Akira (ed.), (Tokyo, 1944).

tions of the West.[4] From this time on he repeated ever more loudly that the Japanese must learn the art of economic expansionism since this was what the Western peoples were doing, and since this was precisely why they were superior to the Japanese. They must learn, he said, how to outgrow their warrior ethic and become businessmen to compete against Western businessmen. This entailed rationalism and universalism, the traits in which they were woefully deficient. But unless they developed these traits the Japanese would never win the "peacetime war." In short, they must become "world citizens." "Our life must be made cosmopolitan. Our commerce, industry, and agriculture must become internationalized. We must go and live everywhere in the world."[5]

For such views to be widely accepted, a new conception of international relations had to be introduced. The Japanese had to visualize themselves as participating in a liberal, capitalist, internationalist world order rather than a world of power politics, armament competition, and territorial aggrandizement. Rejecting a closed mercantilist system and electing the universalism of multilateral trade, they had to be persuaded that peaceful economism was the only legitimate method for solving national problems and that they could pursue the new goal without fear of diplomatic isolation. Above all, the Japanese had to convince themselves that an economistic foreign policy would in fact pay and would not be incompatible with other objectives such as security, prestige, and national identity.

The impetus was provided by the experience of World War I. Although the new economic foreign policy never completely replaced the idea of forceful expansionism, the years between the Versailles Peace Conference and the Manchurian Incident witnessed the fruition of economistic thinking. This was the time when the Japanese were willing to try to integrate themselves into the liberal international order and to avow that they belonged to the world, that they were world citizens as well as Japanese subjects. In this sense these years marked a distinctive phase in the growth of the modern Japanese consciousness. Rather than dismissing the period as one in which the Japanese merely paid

[4] Kayahara Kazan, *Kazan bunshō* (Tokyo, 1912), p. 180.
[5] Kayahara Kazan, *Chijinron* (Tokyo, 1913), pp. 209, 219; Kayahara, *Kokuminteki higeki no hassei* (Tokyo, 1918), p. 58.

lip-service to the rhetoric of internationalism while carrying on their old ambitions, we should study it as a period in which they seriously entertained a cosmopolitan image of the world. The internationalist outlook lasted but briefly, but this was not entirely the fault of the Japanese. The very short life-span of the pre-World War II cosmopolitanism tells much about the international environment in which "Taishō democracy" had to operate.

Shortly before the end of World War I the *Ōsaka mainichi* editorialized on the need for "internal development and external expansion." The Japanese could not again dream of aggressive expansion abroad, it said, but they must plan peaceful expansion through emigration and economic enterprises. If the world was truly entering a period of equality, freedom, peace, and internationalism, no nation or individual should be denied an opportunity so as to expand peacefully.[6] Here was a clear indication that the assumptions and aspirations of a new world order were taking hold of Japanese consciousness. Ideas which Kayahara had been advocating were suddenly gaining acceptance. "The chiming of the clock announcing the arrival of the year 1919 is the sound of the trumpet initiating a new war, a peaceful struggle among nations." This editorial, appearing in the January 1, 1919, issue of the *Ōsaka mainichi*, could be duplicated elsewhere. Observers agreed that the Japanese had been good and efficient warriors, but now that an era of peaceful competition had arrived, they must do all they could to win this struggle.

The realization that the familiar framework of power politics was passing, however, dawned only slowly upon Japan's leaders. One of the earliest documents reflecting such a realization is a record of the meeting of the Foreign Policy Advisory Council in November, 1918. On two occasions members of the council debated Japan's response to President Woodrow Wilson's Fourteen Points. They had been enunciated in January but it was only with the armistice in Europe that the Tokyo government recognized the need to define its attitude toward them. The debate indicated general reluctance to endorse the Wilsonian principles in toto. For instance, on Wilson's call for the abolition of secret diplomacy, the council agreed that this was unrealistic and Japan need not bind itself to such a principle. On the freedom of the seas the

[6] *Ōsaka mainichi*, August 2, 1918.

consensus was that Japan should act with its ally, Britain, in defining questions of maritime commerce and shipping. On the issue of disarmament the council approved of a Foreign Ministry draft statement that "it is totally unrealistic to expect that any satisfactory solution will be found to the question. Moreover, it will be disadvantageous for us to be restricted in our armament. However, our representatives should if possible avoid giving the impression of opposing peace or humanitarianism but should go along with the general trends [at the peace conference]." Concerning the disposition of the former German colonies the Japanese government felt no need to reconsider the position it had already reached, namely, to insist upon the retention of Tsingtao and Germany's insular possessions in the Pacific. Finally, the council responded without enthusiasm to Wilson's call for a League of Nations. There was skepticism about the workability of such a league, and the fear was also raised that it would be an instrument by the major Western powers to maintain the status quo.[7] As revealed here, the general response of Japan's leaders to Wilson's new diplomacy was one of disbelief and skepticism, coupled with the cynical view that the United States was advocating these goals in order to serve its self-interests. Nevertheless, there was the feeling that Japan was being put on the defensive; now that the United States was enunciating new principles, it seemed necessary for the nation to redefine its policies so as not to invite diplomatic isolation in the postwar world.

It was primarily through Japan's plenipotentiaries at Paris, Baron Makino Shinken and Prince Saionji Kimmochi, that the Hara Cabinet gradually came to take a more serious view of the new diplomacy. Makino, in particular, clearly reached the conclusion, shortly before his departure for Paris, that international affairs were definitely entering a new phase. As he reminded his colleagues in the Foreign Policy Advisory Council, "Today it is a worldwide trend to honor pacifism and reject oppression. Everywhere in the world the so-called Americanism is advanced, and conditions have definitely altered from the days of the old diplomacy." As he saw it, the new diplomacy was guided by the principles of "fair play, justice, and humanitarianism." This not only was a reflection of moral concern for world peace, but it also was accompanied by a trend toward economic interdependence

[7] Itō Miyoji, *Suiusō nikki*, Kobayashi Tatsuo (ed.), (Tokyo, 1966), pp. 294-310.

among nations. From Makino's point of view, Japan had no choice but to identify itself with these trends in the world. Otherwise Japan would become isolated politically and economically. Whether it liked it or not, the nation would be obliged to follow the developing trends. Therefore, it would be far better to seize the initiative and become one of the active promoters of the new order, supporting the emerging League of Nations and discarding the old practices of particularistic diplomacy. This was the essence of international cooperation. In China, particularly, Makino would advocate a complete overhaul of existing Japanese policies and the establishment of a new relationship based on justice and reciprocity. This could be brought about by such means as the abolition of extraterritoriality, withdrawal of foreign troops, and return of Boxer indemnity monies to China. Japan should positively cooperate with other nations, especially the United States, so as to restore the world's confidence in her and emerge as a great power in the new era of peace. These ideas were put down in writing and presented to the council as Makino prepared to leave for the peace conference.[8]

The response of some members of the council to Makino's statement showed that they were still reluctant to endorse his sweeping ideas. Inukai Ki asked if Makino were foreclosing the possibility of any further territorial expansion. "Are you saying that apart from economic relations Japan should desist from expansionism?" Inukai asked. Makino did not explicitly reply in the positive but observed that such seemed to be the trends of the times. Itō Miyoji, who remained skeptical of the new diplomacy throughout the interwar years, asserted, "No matter how much we are guided by the principles of fair play and justice, there will always be a possibility of territorial expansion under certain circumstances. This will be inevitable for a growing and expanding nation like us." The proposed League of Nations, too, might become an instrument of the Anglo-Saxon nations to impede Japan's legitimate expansion. Whereas Makino urged less particularistic policies in China, former Prime Minister Terauchi Masatake insisted that Japan and China had special relations due to geographical proximity and that Japanese policy toward China should not be guided by the same principles that applied to Japan's relations with other countries. Terauchi was totally out of

[8] *Ibid.*, pp. 326, 334-335.

sympathy with the new diplomacy's attack on geographical particularism and said that Japan should continue to "guide" China. To all these criticisms, standard platitudes of the language of Japanese imperialism, Makino persisted in responding by conjuring up an image of fundamental changes in world affairs and diplomatic thinking abroad. Prime Minister Hara and Foreign Minister Uchida Yasuya on the whole agreed with Makino, though rather lukewarmly.[9]

The division between proponents of the new diplomacy and skeptics was serious, but no attempt was made at this time to bridge the gap. Once they were in Paris, Makino, Saionji, and others became even further imbued with what they took to be the spirit of the new age. They were ready to accept the mandate principle concerning the former German islands, the League of Nations, and a compromise solution on the Shantung question which entailed a virtual pledge to restore the Tsingtao leasehold to China in due course. The records of Foreign Policy Advisory Council meetings indicate the unhappiness of Itō, Inukai, and others over the plenipotentiaries' failure to insist more resolutely on Japan's rights and their seeming eagerness to capitulate to Wilson's demands. It was with difficulty that Hara and Uchida persuaded the rest of the council to accept what the Japanese representatives had done in Paris.

By the time the peace conference was concluded, some of Japan's influential leaders had come to accept a certain image of the postwar world order. It was apparent to them that the nation would be inhibited from insisting on exclusive political arrangements and using military force to acquire territories. The emphasis from now on was on obtaining, preserving, and extending economic rights and interests. The diplomacy and economic expansion were to be conducted within the framework of international cooperation, in particular cooperation with the United States, the country viewed as the initiator of the new order.[10] To some, America embodied the spirit of the age. According to the political theorist and commentator Yoshino Sakuzō, President

[9] *Ibid.*, pp. 336-343.

[10] See Mitani Taichirō, "Tenkanki (1918-1921) no gaikō shidō" in Shinohara Hajime and Mitani Taichirō (eds.), *Kindai Nihon no seiji shidō* (Tokyo, 1965), pp. 293-374. For a superb description of Wilsonian "liberal-capitalist internationalism," see N. Gordon Levin, *Woodrow Wilson and World Politics* (New York, 1968).

Wilson was able to achieve as much as he did in Paris against all odds because he was supported by the awakened moral consciousness of people everywhere in the world. For Japan to go against the trends would not only antagonize the United States but also incur the hostility of world public opinion. Japan must now discontinue the selfish policy of expansion and concentrate on an orderly extension of national life.[11]

"How do you define 'economic rights'?" asked Inukai. "There can be no clear distinction between political rights and economic privileges," replied Itō.[12] Such views revealed that the old notion of "rich country, strong army" died hard. These men, Yoshino insisted, did not realize that history had entered a new stage. Old slogans and concepts had outlived their usefulness, and the time had come to recognize that the world would now be governed by the principles of freedom, equality, fraternity, and peace.[13] It remained to be seen how such beliefs would shape behavior, and to what extent the Japanese would adapt themselves to their image of the new international order. "All we can say," remarked Foreign Minister Uchida, "is that the extension of economic rights will depend upon our ability."[14]

Although the United States failed to join the League of Nations the thrust of postwar American policy never diminished, and the Washington Conference revealed its determination to continue the Wilsonian task of putting an end to the diplomacy of particularism in East Asia. In Japan, Hara was assassinated, and Makino, Saionji, and others retired from policy-making positions. But foreign policy was entrusted to professional bureaucrats and party politicians, who on the whole accepted the new emphasis on economism and internationalism. In his New Year's message, Prime Minister Takahashi Korekiyo repeated, in 1922, the by then familiar cliché that the World War had "brought about fundamental changes in the foreign policies of the powers." They had recognized the impossibility of plotting expansion through force and the need to cooperate with one another to promote justice in international relations. However, he went on to say,

[11] Yoshino Sakuzō, "Kokka seikatsu no isshin," *Chūō kōron*, 35 (January, 1920), 117-156.
[12] *Suiusō nikki*, p. 594.   [13] Yoshino, "Kokka seikatsu."
[14] Itō, *Suiusō nikki*, p. 594.

competition among nations could not be stopped. "Armed competition has become obsolete, but economic competition is growing in intensity." The Japanese people must redouble their effort to produce and sell superior merchandise at competitive prices. By doing so they would be contributing to the common welfare of mankind as well as to happiness and development at home.[15] At the termination of the Washington Conference commentators agreed that the armament race had come to a halt and the era of economic competition had begun. They called on the people to concentrate on productive activities. Now that the old policies had been buried in Washington, the powers were expected to break their particularistic, imperialistic principles and instead to promote the internationalization of economic relations. This would greatly benefit Japan, but only if the Japanese outgrew their mental habit of emotionalism, irrationalism, and traditionalism.[16]

It is revealing that some, at least, of the military were coming under the influence of such ideas. In a top-secret memorandum of which only twelve copies were circulated, Matsui Iwane of the intelligence division of the General Staff wrote in 1923 that, in the post-Washington Conference world, to use old methods of expansion was out of the question. "We must substitute economic conquest for military invasion, financial influence for military control, and achieve our goals under the slogans of co-prosperity and co-existence, friendship, and cooperation." Japan's spheres of influence should be thrown open to foreign enterprise, and Japan must desist from interfering in Chinese domestic affairs. But the nation should use its economic resources to expand its interests in China, Manchuria, and the Maritime Province.[17] Within the navy Katō Kanji, whose intransigence in 1930 was to damage the foundation of cooperative foreign policy, praised the achievements of the Washington Conference as evidence that mutual trust among nations was rising, the spirit of cooperation was influencing their policies, and the progress of civilization was making peace a reality.[18]

[15] *Tōkyō asahi*, January 1, 1922.

[16] Horie Kiichi, "Buryokuteki kyōsō kara kokusai keizaiteki kyōsō e," *Chūō kōron*, 37, 2 (February, 1922), pp. 20-30; Sugimori Kōjirō, "Kokusai mugunbi to seisan rikkoku e," *ibid.*, pp. 85-88.

[17] Matsui Iwane, "Hokuman taisaku shiken," mimeographed, June 1, 1923.

[18] *Tōkyō asahi*, March 2, 1922.

245

There was not the slightest doubt that Japan must continue to expand, but the stress was now almost entirely on economic expansionism. Foreign Minister Shidehara Kijūrō once defined the basic aim of diplomacy as the acquisition of equal opportunity for the Japanese abroad as they engaged in business activities. Their "freedom of action" brought economic benefits to the home country, and the task of foreign policy was to see to it that the Japanese enjoyed such freedom while they traded, settled, or established factories overseas. Japanese policy must seek to "develop opportunities for expansion for our nationals abroad," in Shidehara's words.[19]

The expansion of Japanese export trade was, of course, the basic policy objective of Foreign Minister Shidehara. The United States was the best customer, and friendly relations with America were a profitable proposition, given the fact that the latter consistently purchased 40 per cent of Japanese exports in the 1920's. Because of the apparent stability of the American economy, no particular effort seemed needed to direct the flow of goods to the United States. The Republican tariffs were uncomfortably high, but they were more detrimental to the growth of European exports to the United States than a hindrance to Japanese-American trade. The American market was the one factor that could be taken for granted by the promoters of Japan's economic policy.

Japan's trade policy therefore turned to other areas of the world in order to increase exports. Shidehara's whole China policy can be characterized as an attempt to reduce obstacles in the way of selling more goods to China. He worked assiduously to block Chinese schemes to raise import duties. Since the bulk of Japanese exports to China consisted of cotton fabrics and cheap miscellaneous items, even a small increase in import duties would make Chinese native goods competitive with them. During the Peking Tariff Conference (1925-1926) the Tokyo Foreign Ministry agreed to the grant of "Washington surtaxes" to China: 2.5 per cent on ordinary goods and 5 per cent on luxuries. Moreover, Japan joined other conferees in expressing readiness to restore tariff autonomy to China after January, 1929. These concessions, however, were hedged around by many conditions. Japan would insist that a special tariff treaty be concluded between the two

[19] Matsuoka Yōseki, *Dai-gojūku gikai ni okeru kokumu daijin ni taisuru yo no shitsugi* (Tokyo, 1931), p. 114.

countries simultaneously with the restoration of tariff autonomy to China, and that the grant of interim customs surtaxes be coupled with the levying of excise taxes upon native Chinese products. Obviously, these steps were designed to minimize the effect of increased customs charges upon Japanese imports. The stand was maintained throughout the rest of the decade. The slogan "co-existence and co-prosperity" signified for the Japanese Foreign Ministry a policy of expressing sympathy with China's "national aspirations" but also of "maintaining our trade with China, planning the economic development of our people in China, and promoting economic cooperation between the two countries," as a 1927 memorandum stated. Once China was unified by the Nationalists in 1928 it was extremely difficult to resist trends toward a complete overhaul in Chinese foreign trade relations. It was a measure of Shidehara's modest success and a testimony to his perseverance that the Chinese-Japanese tariff treaty of 1930 stipulated a conditional exercise by China of tariff autonomy so as to levy only minimal duties upon most Japanese merchandise until 1933.[20]

Shidehara was equally concerned with extending Japanese trade to south Asia and the Middle East. Under his leadership Japan successfully concluded a tariff agreement concerning French Indochina, putting an end to decades of discrimination against Japanese exports, and vigorously protested against measures taken in India to curtail the importation of Japanese cotton goods. Bankers and steamship companies were encouraged to open trade channels in Turkey, Egypt, and other areas of the Middle East, and Japanese trade marts were also opened. Consuls in the Balkans and the Middle East met periodically to achieve the same goals. Obata Yūkichi, ambassador to Turkey under Shidehara, is said to have been the first to promote vigorously Japan's economic diplomacy in the Middle East. He persuaded exporters in Kobe, Osaka, and Nagoya to send merchandise samples to Istanbul so as to have them exhibited. Although the amount of total Japanese exports to Turkey, consisting mainly of textiles and miscellaneous items, was a mere 4.5 million yen in 1926, less than one per cent of the total figure, this was an important beginning. Upon Obata's suggestion the Foreign Ministry

[20] Akira Iriye, *After Imperialism, The Search for a New Order in the Far East 1921-1931* (Cambridge, Mass., 1965), pp. 68ff, 116, 271ff.

organized a conference of Japanese chiefs of mission in the Middle East and the Balkans in 1926 to discuss further specific means of promoting Japanese business in these areas.[21]

The protection and extension of investments abroad was another aspect of the economic foreign policy. Here the focus remained on China since Japanese capital was not abundant and investments in that country were considered a vital part of Japan's trade relationship with it. A major concern of policy-makers was with the protection of Japanese cotton mills in Shanghai, Tientsin, and elsewhere. The incentive to Japanese textile manufacturing in China was provided by the availability of cheap labor. The cost of labor in China was estimated to be about half that in Japan, and the textiles manufactured in China did not have to pay import duties at a time when the Chinese were demanding tariff revision and ultimate autonomy. The acquisition of raw cotton was also being systematized, and Indian cotton was being brought to Shanghai by a pool of chartered ships. In 1925 the Japanese cotton mills in China organized an association to protect their joint interests, to be headed by the veteran diplomat, Funazu Shin'ichirō.[22] Foreign Ministry officials met periodically with the association's representatives and jointly mapped out their strategy to cope with the rising tide of Chinese radicalism. It is quite possible that the textiles manufactured by Chinese labor at Japanese factories in Shanghai competed with those imported from Japan, but most of these factories were branches of the establishments in Osaka and other manufacturing centers, and the Foreign Ministry extended its protective shield both to Japanese export trade and to investments in China.

There were many legal problems involved in the extension of business activities in China. One was the question of extraterritoriality. Because there existed legal and practical obstacles in the way of foreigners' ownership of land and residence in the interior of China, the Japanese were concerned with obtaining specific rights to reside and travel freely in the interior of China, in particular Manchuria, and to engage in trade and manufacturing. There was willingness to abolish extraterritoriality if the Chinese

[21] Nishi Haruhiko, *Kaisō no Nihon gaikō* (Tokyo, 1965), pp. 36-41; Shidehara Kijūrō (Tokyo, 1955), pp. 334-335; Ujita Naoyoshi (ed.), *Obata Yūkichi* (Tokyo, 1957), pp. 354-358.

[22] Nakamura Takahide, "Go-sanjū jiken to zaikabō" in *Kindai Chūgoku kenkyū* (Tokyo, 1964), VI, 110ff, 168.

would grant these rights to Japanese and if foreign lives and property could be adequately protected. What Japan wanted most was some guarantee that its nationals could peacefully and freely engage in business, travel, and if possible lease or own land in China and Manchuria.[23]

Another obstacle was the continued existence of unpaid Chinese debts, public and private. Most of the wartime loans to China, including the Nishihara loans, had been either entirely unsecured or inadequately secured, and the Japanese government and creditors had tried unsuccessfully to have them refunded before they would undertake further indirect investments in China. There was the fear that the Chinese might turn to foreign borrowing before redeeming their existing debts, and one of the goals of Shidehara's foreign policy was to persuade China to earmark portions of its tariff revenues for refunding purposes. He was particularly insistent that the Washington surtaxes be granted to China only on condition that the latter use part of the increased customs receipts for this purpose. The "debt consolidation question" remained one of the thorniest in Japanese-Chinese relations during the 1920's and revealed the Tokyo government's determination to clear obstacles in the way of investments in China. Earlier the dispute would have been settled through coercion and resulted in the setting up of customs receivership or the grant of further concessions to foreigners. No such steps were now considered, and the only lever Japan had was the threat that it would extend no further loans until the outstanding debts had been repaid.[24]

It is illuminating that Japanese businessmen in China at least initially accepted the language of economic expansionism. The influential *Peking shūhō* (*Peking Weekly*), reflecting moderate Japanese opinion in China, often asserted that business activities must be dissociated from militaristic methods and that Japanese expansion must be based on purely economic ties with China. The stationing, after 1924, of a commercial attaché, a financial attaché, and a transportation attaché at the Japanese legation was welcomed as a sign that the government was determined to assist the enterprises of the nationals. In Manchuria, a Japanese newspaper insisted that Japanese should pursue the economic and cul-

---

[23] See Japanese Foreign Ministry Archives, File PVM 65, for documentation on the extraterritoriality question.

[24] Iriye, pp. 241-242, and *passim*.

tural development of Manchuria, to be entirely divorced from militarists and *rōnin*. Ex-diplomat Matsuoka Yōsuki, working for the South Manchuria Railway, asserted in 1923 that Japan aimed only at peaceful industrialization, not at militarization of Manchuria.[25] Such expressions revealed that the Japanese in China were identifying themselves with the postwar emphasis on economic interdependence and international harmony.

Outside China there was particular interest in investment in the Russian Far East. One of the reasons for Japan's willingness, in 1924-1925, to resume diplomatic relations with Russia was its interest in obtaining concessions in North Sakhalin. The Yoshizawa-Karakhan negotiations in Peking dragged on as long as they did primarily because of this issue. Japan was intent upon perpetuating its operation of North Sakhalin coal mines and oil fields, but the Soviet Union was determined to restrict such rights. The question was complicated as some other countries, notably the United States (the Sinclair Oil Company), held certain concessions in the area. Oil was the price the Japanese government demanded in return for withdrawing the troops from North Sakhalin, and it at first asked for the right to mine all of the oil fields, whereas Russia would grant only 20 per cent. It took Yoshizawa's negotiating skill to persuade Karakhan finally to agree on allowing 50 per cent of the oil fields to be operated by Japanese. Soon afterwards ambassadors were exchanged between the two countries, the North Sakhalin Oil Company was founded, and detailed arrangements were worked out for operating the mines.

Overseas emigration as an aspect of economic diplomacy deserves a fuller treatment since this problem has not been adequately treated by historians. Before 1945 the Malthusian nightmare was a shared perception of all Japanese. Malthus' population theory had been introduced to Japan as early as the 1870's, and since then various interpretations and criticisms of it had periodically appeared in print and made its tenets widely known to Japanese readers. While demographers differed as to the applicability of the Malthusian theory to Japan, and while there were not even accurate estimates of population figures, the vision of an overcrowded country became fixed by the late 1880's, when writers began calling for massive emigration as the only sensible solu-

[25] *Peking shūhō*, April 24, October 1, November 13, 1922; April 6, 1923.

tion. This was really a perversion of Malthus, who never considered emigration as a dependable cure for the population crisis. In Japan, in contrast, an endlessly expanding population was taken as a given and even desirable factor, and writers concentrated on reducing population density by overseas expansion and settlement.[26]

Anxiety over an increasing population was particularly acute after World War I, now that forceful territorial expansionism and colonization had become unacceptable. Since the use of force was now rejected, peaceful emigration had to be pushed with vigor. While some advocated artificial birth control as a more workable alternative, most opposed it not only because of its questionable morality but because the concern was not with population growth as such, which was considered a good thing for a healthy nation, but with per capita arable land, food, and income.

By the 1920's there had emerged a group of experts on emigration and colonization problems. Men like Nitobe Inazō, Yanaibara Tadao, and Kayahara Kazan spoke and wrote extensively on these subjects. Here it will be illuminating to mention the views of Tōgō Minoru, a member of the Diet in the mid-1920's. He had studied under Nitobe at the Sapporo Agricultural School and had written a thesis on Japanese colonialism in 1906. In it he declared that it was absolutely necessary for Japan to undertake further colonization. "If the nation is to develop its power, expand its race, and become predominant over the world," he asserted, "it is imperative to seek territories overseas and colonize. The acquisition of territory might be achieved through peaceful means or through war, and wars would have to be faced as unavoidable necessities in order to protect our race." Such language was no longer spoken in the 1920's. Now Tōgō stressed the humanitarian and peaceful impact of Japanese expansion. In a 1927 talk he said that it was in the interest of world peace and the happiness of humanity for Japanese to migrate to less crowded areas and assist in their development. It was in fact the mission of Japan, a country without space, to try to equalize her opportunity in the world by insisting on the right of population mobility. "The more our population increases," he said, "the more our Japanese race will be contributing to the cause of humanity."[27]

[26] Yoshida Hideo, *Nihon jinkōron no shiteki kenkyū* (Tokyo, 1944).
[27] Tōgō Minoru, *Nihon shokumin-ron* (Tokyo, 1906), p. 237; Bureau of

Although the vocabulary used on the two occasions differed, the basic reasoning remained essentially the same: the notion of population growth out of proportion with available resources and production. In 1906 Tōgō had written, "If we are to secure food sufficiently and permanently for our endlessly expanding population, we must establish agricultural colonies abroad." Twenty years later he said that Japan, without sufficient land and food-stuff but with abundant people, must combine its resources with those of other countries which were territorially vast but thinly populated. Now that imperialism was "out of fashion," Japan had all the more reason to insist on its right to migrate to those countries which had engaged in colonization in the age of imperialism. Moreover, Japan should never relinquish its hold upon the existing colonies. Even though Koreans and Taiwanese seemed to be coming under the influence of the idea of self-determination, it was really in their interest to remain within the Japanese empire, which would promote the well-being not only of the mother country but of the native population.[28]

Since it was out of the question to acquire additional colonies, the thinking turned inevitably to noncolonial overseas settlement. In 1927 there were about 618,000 Japanese abroad on a more or less permanent basis. This was less than one per cent of the total population of the country, exclusive of Koreans, Taiwanese, and the native tribes of Karafuto. Of this number over 133,000 were in the United States, and nearly 125,000 in Hawaii. Brazil had almost 50,000 Japanese, and Peru 11,000. Together with other parts of North and South America, the Japanese population east of the Hawaiian islands numbered over 346,000, or more than half the overseas Japanese. The Philippines, Southeast Asia, and the rest of Oceania had over 34,000 Japanese. In contrast to these figures, the Japanese population on the continent of Asia was not impressive: 48,000 in China proper and 184,000 in Manchuria. These constituted less than 40 per cent of the total number of Japanese abroad. Moreover, the bulk of the Japanese in Manchuria was made up of the personnel of the Kwantung Army, the South Manchuria Railway and its holdings, and parasitic wage-earners and merchants who worked for these establishments. This

Social Affairs, Ministry of Home Affairs, *Ishokumin mondai kōshūkai kōenshū* (Tokyo, 1927), pp. 354ff.

[28] Tōgō, *Nihon shokumin-ron*, p. 201; *Kōenshū*, p. 357; Tōgō Minoru, *Shokumin seisaku to minzoku shinri* (Tokyo, 1925), pp. 340ff.

was true of the colonies as well: about 2 per cent of the population in Korea (500,000) and 5 per cent of that in Taiwan (180,000) were Japanese, and most of the 170,000 people in Karafuto were from Japan proper, but most of them worked directly or indirectly for the colonial establishment. For instance, the majority of Japanese in Korea were colonial administrators, small bureaucrats, teachers, troops, commercial enterprises connected with them, and their families. Relatively few were there as permanent colonists. Agricultural settlers from Japan proper numbered only 38,850 in 1925. The *Tōyō Takushoku Kaisha* (Asia Development Company), founded in 1905, had hoped to establish 300,000 Japanese agricultural households in Korea, but as of 1924 only 3,939 such units existed. This was because few Japanese farmers wished to resettle in Korea where they would have to compete with hard-working native peasants. The same was true of Taiwan.[29]

The truth is that by the 1920's it had become apparent that a surplus population in Japan, the existence of which was accepted as axiomatic, had not found its outlet in East Asia. Notwithstanding Gotō Shimpei's earlier boast that a million Japanese would be found on the Asian mainland within 20 years after the Russo-Japanese War, Japanese had rejected emigration and colonization in this region as an attractive prospect. Korea and Taiwan were already crowded with native populations, and in Manchuria competition with Chinese labor was severe. In all these areas it was estimated that the natives could subsist on half the amount Japanese would need to live.

Japanese officials and emigration experts were thus much more interested in encouraging agricultural settlement in Oceania, Southeast Asia, and South America. The national and prefectural governments earmarked funds for public relations purposes to disseminate information on emigration to these areas. In 1923 the central government participated in 27 public lectures on emigration by sending its staff as speakers, and the number increased to 52 in 1925 and 267 in 1930.[30] In 1918 the *Kaigai Kōgyō Kaisha* (Overseas Development Company) had been organized, amalgamating some existing emigration companies. It sought to combine emigration and investments so as to create enclaves of Japa-

[29] Ministry of Colonial Affairs, *Takumu yōran* (Tokyo, 1932), p. 327; *Kōenshū*, pp. 30-31.
[30] *Takumu yōran*, p. 563.

nese enterprises overseas. It operated a plantation in Brazil, providing land to several thousand Japanese settlers.

The Japanese government was particularly interested in promoting emigration to South America, especially Brazil. As a diplomat who spent many years in that country noted, the United States would be the most nearly ideal place for emigration; Australia, Canada, and South Africa would also be desirable areas. But they all had anti-Japanese policies. Manchuria, Malaya, Java, Sumatra, and Borneo were possibilities, and there were no legal obstacles in the way of Japanese settlement, but the competition presented by Chinese and Koreans was too keen. This left only Mexico, Peru, Colombia, Bolivia, Argentina, and Brazil. Even these, however, except Brazil, had physical and racial characteristics of society and economy which made it difficult for Japanese to settle. Brazil seemed the only country where they could succeed with only a small amount of initial capital. This type of thinking was behind the government's policy of systematic encouragement of emigration to Brazil. After the great earthquake of 1923 its victims were given the entire cost of the ocean voyage to Brazil. Others, too, became eligible for subsidies for the voyage. In order to protect actual and potential emigrants a law was passed in 1927 designed to create an organization of Japanese immigrants in Brazil so that they could act as a corporate entity. The Social Affairs Bureau of the Home Ministry likewise extended monetary incentives to emigrants, and various prefectural governments organized "overseas associations" to disseminate information and promote interchange among prospective emigrants. In 1928 a school was opened in Kobe to undertake orientation of those going to Brazil. This was in accordance with a 1927 ordinance for creating temporary housing for departing Japanese. The creation of the Ministry of Overseas Affairs (*Takumushō*) in 1929 was a culminating development, calculated especially to encourage emigration to Brazil.[31]

Outside South America, Southeast Asia and Oceania began to assume a position of importance in the 1920's. In 1927, for example, 18,041 Japanese migrated overseas, of whom 2,660 went to the Philippines, 475 to Malaya, and 248 to the Dutch East Indies. The Philippines were considered a particularly important area for Japanese settlement and investment, as the United States gov-

[31] Fujita Toshirō, *Nanbei no shokuminchi* (Tokyo, 1924), pp. 173-174; *Brazil ni okeru Nihonjin hatten-shi* (Tokyo, 1941), i, 56ff.

ernment interposed no restrictions upon Japanese immigration. In 1930 there were nearly 20,000 Japanese in the islands, mostly engaged in the cultivation of flax. They operated over 40,000 acres of flax fields, chiefly owned by Japanese firms. The Japanese people had become familiar with the South Seas during the war, and there was a growing interest in business expansion in the region. The Colonial Bureau of the Ministry of Colonial Affairs dealt with the South Seas as well as Taiwan, Manchuria, and Sakhalin.

Government agencies and publicists continued to urge Japanese to stay permanently overseas instead of drifting back to Japan. Writers were agreed that the shiftlessness of the Japanese abroad was one reason why their total population had remained so small. Ishii Itarō, chief of the third (emigration) section of the Foreign Ministry's Commerce Bureau, remarked that unless the Japanese overseas interested themselves in assimilation and acclimatization, their expansion could not be expected. "One defect of the Japanese is to seek quick success. This tendency has been destructive of any chance for Japanese expansion abroad. . . . Once you go abroad you must be prepared to stay and die there. Be patient and do not hurry, but try slowly to build up your economic base, and only then will Japanese emigration succeed."[32] Fujita Toshirō, several years a consul in Brazil, urged the Japanese immigrants to that country to obtain citizenship and assure themselves of the political rights citizenship brought. Many Japanese, he wrote, seemed to think it was unpatriotic and even disloyal to acquire another country's citizenship, but actually it was a patriotic duty to do so. Otherwise there could be no permanent and stable development of a Japanese community in Brazil.[33] As a necessary condition for permanent settlement abroad, another writer spoke of the need for Japanese women to emigrate. Only when they accompanied men and established family units could they enjoy stable home life and win the trust of the people among whom they settled.[34]

The emphasis on permanent emigration was in accord with the internationalistic thinking of the time. Japanese emigrants were viewed by some observers not as colonizers, the spearhead of imperialism, but as agents of international cooperation and world

[32] *Kōenshū*, pp. 117ff.
[33] Fujita, pp. 162-163.
[34] Naniwa Masaharu, *Nanbei fugen taikan* (Dairen, 1923), pp. 91-92.

peace. "Co-existence and co-prosperity" must be the aim of emigration policy, said Moriya Sakao, chief of the Home Ministry's Social Affairs Bureau which dealt with emigration matters. "While we send out our emigrants," he said, "we must try to spread our civilization, especially our spiritual heritage, in the world and contribute to world peace and the welfare of humanity." Conversely, Yanaibara Tadao asserted that through overseas Japanese there would be created "little Japans" everywhere which would be harbingers of change for their home country. The new Japan would come through the efforts of Japanese communities abroad; it would transcend the existing parochialism and contribute greatly to the creation of a new world.[35]

It is evident from these statements that the Japanese had something far more in mind than trade, investment, and emigration. Some thinkers such as Nitobe saw the postwar framework of economic foreign policy as providing an opportunity for the Japanese to become "world citizens," to find their existential meaning in the contribution they could make to world peace and civilization. As one writer put it, the Japanese should "leave the islands" and, turning their swords into ploughshares, dedicate themselves to the service of mankind, to the enrichment of human culture.[36] At a time when distances among nations were contracting, said Nitobe, common traits were destined to develop in all the countries. Their habits, mores, and attitudes would become closer, and in the end all peoples would learn to view one another as human beings instead of classifying them in categories. The Japanese, because of their East Asian heritage and absorption of Western civilization, were in a unique position to advance the cause of human unity.[37] Similarly, Ukita Kazutami wrote, it was the mission of the Japanese to be active abroad "without presenting a menace to other countries, obeying their laws, assimilating their habits, and to contribute as world citizens to the development of industry and dissemination of culture." The world was becoming one, and therefore Japan must identify its interests with international peace, amity, and progress. They would be served when the Japanese ceased to be narrowly nationalistic and became one with other peoples.[38]

[35] *Kōenshū*, pp. 43, 110.
[36] Sugimori, "Kokusai mugunbi," pp. 87-88.
[37] Nitobe Inazō, *Tōzai aifurete* (Tokyo, 1928).
[38] Ukita Kazutami, *Nichi-Bei hisenron* (Tokyo, 1925), p. 139.

Such high hopes sound hollow against the realities of the 1920's. Despite governmental efforts Japanese emigration figures remained low, and nowhere except in South America were Japanese automatically accepted. Even in Brazil restrictionist moves were emerging. In fact the 1920's saw an intensification of interethnic rivalries, demolishing one corner of the international economic order envisaged by the Japanese. Thus, the question of emigration provides a good transition to the discussion of factors inhibiting Japan's peaceful expansionism.

The Japanese experienced their first difficulty regarding their idea of peaceful expansionism during the Paris Peace Conference. The fact that they accepted the League of Nations without a racial equality clause should not be taken as evidence of their casual attitude toward the question. Some observers then and since have argued that racial equality was merely a bargaining point to be traded against the much more crucial issue of Shantung. Although in effect this is what happened, the debate in the inner councils of the government and in the press in Japan clearly indicates that racial equality was taken as an essential ingredient of the emerging new diplomacy.

The Foreign Ministry's first reaction to Wilson's proposal for a League of Nations was that it would be an instrument of the white race for perpetuating their domination over the world. Should such an organization be devised, a memorandum noted, "we must try as much as we can to reduce the disadvantages that we will face from the existing racial prejudices."[39] The new world order was unthinkable without some progress in bringing about racial equality.

For the Japanese plenipotentiaries in Paris this problem at first overshadowed all else. They had been instructed to couple Japan's acceptance of the League of Nations with some suitable guarantee of racial equality; otherwise it was feared that the League would become an instrument by the West to perpetuate its domination. Makino, accordingly, drafted a statement on racial equality and sought its acceptance as a clause in the League covenant. The draft statement said that the member nations would try "as much as possible to grant *de jure* and *de facto* equality" of treatment to foreign subjects in their respective territories and not to discriminate on the basis of race or nationality. According to Makino's reports, Colonel Edward M. House gave

[39] Itō, *Suiusō nikki*, p. 286.

his endorsement to the idea, but the British delegates were adamantly opposed, apparently fearing hostile reaction from the Dominions. The Chinese were the only delegates who went so far as to express some "sympathy" with the Makino statement. After President Wilson's return from the United States, he, too, came to object to the Japanese proposal. On March 20, 1919, the Japanese delegates asked for instruction in the event their efforts failed.[40]

Foreign Minister Uchida thought that since the United States Senate was very likely to reject the League, Japan should persist in its insistence on a racial equality provision. If it was impossible to insert such a clause in the League covenant itself, at least a statement on racial equality should be appended to it or to the minutes of the Peace Conference. If none of these proposals was acceptable to the other nations, Japan should threaten to refuse to sign the covenant. It is interesting to note that those who were most skeptical of the new diplomatic order, such as Itō Miyoji and Inukai Ki, were unimpressed with the urgency of the problem and objected to the threat suggested by Uchida. Prime Minister Hara, however, supported the foreign minister.[41] In the end, of course, the Japanese delegates at Paris had to satisfy themselves with making a speech and having it inserted in the minutes of the Conference. The Japanese government decided to accept such a solution and bent its last energies to a satisfactory settlement of another question, the German rights in Tsingtao.

The defeat of the racial equality clause, however, had a profound repercussion on Japanese opinion. Without the West's acceptance of the principle of equality of treatment, the emerging world order seemed to hold out little hope for Japan. The West, it seemed, had denied Japan the right to peaceful and economic territorial expansion. How Japan should behave in such a seemingly hostile world, in which it appeared to be completely isolated, became a major concern of opinion-makers as well as of officials. During the Paris debate on the racial equality question, representatives of the political parties, reserve officers' organizations, the press, and other groups jointly sent a telegram to Georges Clemenceau, Peace Conference chairman, urging the adoption of the principle of racial equality. The Japanese press almost invariably supported the principle and urged its accept-

[40] *Ibid.*, pp. 403, 433.   [41] *Ibid.*, pp. 443ff.

ance as part of the structure of the new peace. When President Wilson was reported to be reluctant to endorse the Japanese proposal, he was condemned as hypocritical and selfish. Watanabe Minojirō, editor of the *Ōsaka mainichi*, expressed a typical reaction when he summoned up latent pan-Asianism and called on the readers to "awaken" the Asians and bring about "a defensive union" of all Asia.[42]

Despite such outbursts, Japanese opinion was impressed with the image of the new international order and was ready to subscribe to the rhetoric of internationalism. It was a rare journal which did not contain, in the early 1920's, an article talking of international cooperation and economic interdependence. But, paradoxically, the more the Japanese came to accept the language of economism the more sensitive they became to all instances of racial discrimination. Racial equality was for them a sine qua non of the new diplomacy as they understood it. The introduction and final passage of the Japanese exclusion law in Congress in 1923-1924 gave some Japanese final proof that the postwar world order had failed to found itself upon racial equality. They came to regard the entire fabric of the postwar international system as unjust and against Japan's interests. A number of right-wing, anti-American associations were organized around this time to protest against the government's continued acceptance of peaceful policy and to propose radical alternatives based upon more particularistic principles. Continental expansionism, temporarily overshadowed by postwar internationalism, re-emerged, as did cultural parochialism, one writer even calling for the abolition of the use of the English language in Japan. Gotō Shimpei, quick as usual to sense trends in popular thinking, asserted that in order to "compete with the United States, the mightiest nation in the world, defend ourselves from its insults, and bring about long-lasting prosperity, we have no alternative but to strengthen our base on the Asian continent." America's racism seemed to call for a pan-Asianist response. Many Japanese in China thought that the Chinese sympathized with Japan, and regarded her humiliation as Asia's humiliation. Japan should not hesitate to go to war

[42] Oka Yoshitake, "Paris heiwa kaigi ni okeru America gaikō to waga kuni yoron," in Saitō Makoto (ed.), *Gendai America no naisei to gaikō* (Tokyo, 1959), pp. 280, 290; Watanabe Minojirō, *Koritsuteki Nihon no kōei* (Osaka, 1921), p. 158.

against the United States, declared a *Peking shūhō* editorial, since justice lay with Japan.[43]

In talking of racial equality the Japanese themselves were guilty of hypocrisy. In Japan foreigners were prohibited from owning land. Koreans and Taiwanese had to obtain permission to go to Japan, and they had no votes in their homeland. There was racial segregation in schools in the colonies, and Chinese laborers were virtually excluded from Japan. The era of Taishō democracy saw no change in these practices, and the Korean massacres of 1923 exposed the depth of Japanese racism even while the Japanese were denouncing discrimination in the West. As the Chinese minister in Tokyo remarked, "Only if the Japanese do away with restrictions on the entry of Chinese laborers can they speak with justice and humanism when they protest against America's closing of its door."[44]

It nevertheless remains true that the principle of equality among races, in particular between Japanese and Westerners, was not a cynical device to be used to cloak Japan's own mistreatment of its minorities. Neither was it a smoke-screen to blind foreign observers' eyes to postwar expansionism. Racial equality with the West was considered important because it was taken as an index of the West's sincerity in implementing the new world order in which it was professing its faith. As the *Asahi* said, this order was founded upon peace, which in turn was derived from economic interdependence among nations, more specifically "the freedom to obtain essential raw materials and to resettle surplus populations." Only if the major countries cooperated in this direction could there be peace and happiness in the world. Should the United States, the strongest and richest nation, forsake such cooperation, it should realize that it was preparing mankind for another war. The Americans, declared a joint statement by 15 newspapers in Tokyo, ought to know that the legislation excluding Japanese immigration was a slap in the face of "the citizens of the entire world" who desired peace.[45]

The immigration crisis, however, might in itself not have been

[43] Shibukawa Genji, "Nani o osoruruka Nihon," *Chūō kōron*, 39, 8 (July, 1924), pp. 33-40; Gotō Shimpei, "Nichi-Ro-Shi kankei no konpongi" (unpublished), dated 1924, Gotō Shimpei Papers (Tokyo Institute for Municipal Research).

[44] *Tōkyō asahi*, April 22, 1924.   [45] *Ibid.*, April 18, 19, 21, 1924.

considered a blow to Japan's peaceful expansionism if in other ways international cooperation and economic interdependence had been continued. For a while after 1924, moderate opinion in and out of government held to the belief that despite setbacks the new world order was still on its way to being consolidated. In the middle of the crisis the *Asahi* editorialized that though the United States had betrayed the "spirit of the Washington Conference" Japan would still adhere to it.[46] When the dire predictions of some pessimistic businessmen that Japanese-American economic relations would seriously deteriorate did not prove accurate, many came to accommodate themselves to the new situation. So long as the United States continued to supply Japan with raw cotton and capital loans, purchase its silk, and act within a cooperative framework in China, the immigration question could be regarded as a regrettable blunder by an otherwise progressive nation, not as something to necessitate an entire re-orientation in Japanese policy and thinking. The last years of the 1920's were to show, however, that the gap between image and reality, between aspiration and achievement, grew wider and wider until the Japanese came to believe that international cooperation and peaceful expansion were possibilities which existed more in their imagination than in reality and that their conceptual framework of postwar diplomacy had been based on wrong premises.

In December, 1930, Shigemitsu Mamoru, consul general at Shanghai, wrote a memorandum asserting that international cooperation as regarded China had broken down. Chinese affairs, he wrote, "have lost their quondam simplicity in which the powers could cooperate and solve various issues to their satisfaction." This was because of China's radical nationalism and the apparent lack of interest in cooperation on the part of Britain and the United States. Nine months later Shigemitsu reiterated the argument in a 686-page memorandum entitled "Revolutionary Diplomacy." "Japan must cope with East Asian matters on its own responsibility and at its own risk," he asserted. The history of the world in the postwar period seemed to indicate that Japan must protect its interests through its own efforts. No other method

[46] *Ibid.*, April 25, 1924.

was feasible in the face of China's revolutionary diplomacy.[47]

The breakdown of international cooperation vis-à-vis Chinese nationalism was a theme repeated throughout the 1930's to justify Japan's unilateral action in China. It is doubtful if there had really been a framework for cooperation among Japan, the United States, Britain, and others during the 1920's. International cooperation may have been merely a rhetoric which existed in the imagination of the Japanese. Much depends on what was meant by "cooperation." If it meant the powers' acting together in consultation with each other regarding Chinese matters, there was cooperation throughout the period. On such matters as the abolition of *likin*, revision of the laws governing extraterritoriality, the protection of foreign lives, and the implementation of other provisions of the Washington treaties, the governments of Tokyo, Washington, and London regularly exchanged views, and their representatives in Peking functioned as a body to represent the rights of the treaty powers. At the same time, each power had its own interests to protect and its own conception of how to safeguard them. They might do so within the framework of collaboration with other countries, or they might act unilaterally without regard to the policies and sensitivities of others. Much would depend on one's perception of the stability, durability, and workability of cooperation as against unilateralism.

Since international cooperation is a product of faith, what matters is that the Japanese thought, for a few years after the Washington Conference, that the concept was a viable one. They began to lose faith in it after about 1925. As the Japanese saw it, cooperation among the powers began to break down in the mid-twenties when they thought that other nations were willing to forsake cooperation in order to establish an advantageous position for themselves in China. When, at the end of 1926, the British government issued a "Christmas message" expressing its friendly and accommodating attitude toward Chinese nationalism, Japan's Foreign Ministry was shocked and embittered. It thought that Japan should have been consulted, and the Ministry complained to London accordingly. The protest was ignored.[48] A few months

[47] Shigemitsu to Yano, December 30, 1930, Japanese Foreign Ministry Archives, File PVM 70; Shigemitsu's memo, December, 1931, Japanese Foreign Ministry Archives, File PVM 46.

[48] Debuchi to Shidehara, March 5, 1927, Japanese Foreign Ministry Archives, File PVM 43.

later, during the Nanking incident, Britain expressed an interest in cooperating with Japan, but the Tokyo government took this as an opportunistic proposal reflecting London's interest in cooperation only when its relative position in China was weakening.[49] The United States, too, appeared intent upon expressing its sympathy with Chinese nationalism and entering into new arrangements with China to expand American trade without consultation with other treaty powers. America's pro-Chinese policy, complained Consul General Yada Shichitarō at Shanghai in the summer of 1928, "will obtain the Chinese people's gratitude for the United States and be likely to turn them to disliking and cursing us."[50] As the United States was the first major power to grant *de facto* recognition to the Nationalists and sign a new commercial treaty with them, there was a bitter feeling in Japan that the convener of the Washington Conference was unilaterally breaking up the cooperative formula of the Washington treaties.

Officially the Japanese government continued to talk as though cooperation still existed. Arita Hachirō, appointed chief of the Asian Bureau of the Foreign Ministry in the spring of 1928, frequently recorded his belief that "in order to win final victory in China, Japan must cooperate with the powers, in particular Britain and the United States."[51] Shidehara Kijūrō, appointed foreign minister for the second time in the summer of 1929, actively sought to revive the spirit of joint action with the powers. The successful consummation of the London Naval Conference was a symbolic fruit of the effort, and he tried to approach the Chinese question in the same spirit of cooperation. Nevertheless, by 1931 it was obvious that the United States, Britain, and Japan were working at cross-purposes in China. There was little mutual consultation on the tariff and loan questions and no joint strategy to cope with the revolutionary diplomacy of the Nationalists especially as it applied to Manchuria.

The growing conviction that the alleged cooperation did not in fact exist encouraged those in Japan who had remained skeptical of the new diplomacy. They would base Japanese policy on the indisputable ground, as they saw it, of Japan's special position in China. Whether other nations recognized the fact was

[49] Matsui to Tanaka, June 2 and 9, 1927, *ibid.*
[50] Yada to Tanaka, rec. July 30, 1928, Japanese Foreign Ministry Archives, File PVM 32.
[51] Arita's memos, April 1928, and July 13, 1928, *ibid.*

immaterial. Japan must base its policy on fact, not fiction, and its special interests in China were a solid fact in the thinking of these critics. They would call for a shift from universalism of the new diplomacy back to the particularism of the old diplomacy. The idea that cooperation had failed and that Japan must boldly resort to unilateral action provided a convenient ideological excuse for the military expansionism of the 1930's.

Even without positive cooperation with America and Britain, and even with racial prejudice in Western countries, the Japanese might have retained their faith in the new order if the reality of external economic relations had come close to the expectation dictated by the idea of peaceful expansionism. Here again trends in China were such as to bring into question the fundamental assumptions underlying postwar foreign policy. This is not an appropriate place to describe in detail the course of Japanese-Chinese relations in the 1920's. Suffice it to note the frustrations felt by the Japanese in China and Manchuria as they engaged in peaceful business and agricultural activities. If Japanese were unwelcome in Western societies, at least they could freely go to China. But their rights in China were much more restricted than those enjoyed by the Japanese already in North and South America. For instance, less than 2 per cent of the Japanese in Manchuria were engaged in agriculture, forestry, or fishing, and one fundamental obstacle to further Japanese settlement, as they saw it, was the uncertainty of land tenure in Manchuria. Although a treaty of 1915 had given Japan a right to create "commercial ports" in the interior of Manchuria in which land could be leased for agricultural purposes, no such leaseholds had come into being because of legal, practical, and tax obstacles placed in the way by Chinese authorities.[52] As noted earlier, the problem of relinquishing extraterritoriality was bound up with the issue of foreigners' right to reside and engage in business in the interior of China, and much diplomatic effort was directed toward settling the dispute as a way of facilitating Japanese emigration and settlement. All such efforts, however, had produced no real results by the end of the 1920's. The Chinese became if anything more and more uncompromising, and after 1930 they began ousting Korean tenant farmers from their agricultural settlements in Manchuria.

[52] Bureau of Commerce, Ministry of Foreign Affairs, *Jinkō mondai o kichō to shite Man-Mo takushokusaku no kenkyū* (Tokyo, 1927), pp. 81ff.

Finally, peaceful expansionism seemed, by 1930, to have failed to vindicate itself as the nation, never having recovered from the postwar recession, entered a period of acute social and economic crisis. Falling prices, curtailment of business, growing unemployment—these seemed to be the end-products of a decade of the new diplomacy. Voices began to be heard more and more loudly saying that the nation needed a new foreign policy.

"It is a good thing to talk about economic foreign policy," asserted the ex-diplomat Matsuoka Yōsuke in the Diet in January, 1931, "but we must have more than a slogan. Where are the fruits? We must be shown the benefits of this approach." He felt that Shidehara's policy had brought about no solution to the mounting economic crisis of the nation. Japan, in the midst of a crisis at home, had to demand "its rights to a bare existence." The only way out was a frankly forceful expansionism. As Matsuoka saw it, there was nothing peaceful about international economic competition. Going back to the vocabulary of neo-mercantilism, he considered trade a form of warfare and believed that the nation had the obligation to protect and extend its economic interests abroad, by force if necessary. "The economic warfare in the world," he declared, "is tending to create large economic blocs." Japan must follow suit if it were to survive. The only solution, according to Matsuoka, was the creation of a bloc embracing Japan, Manchuria, Mongolia, and the Maritime Provinces. It is suggestive that for Matsuoka as for Shidehara economic issues were at the base of foreign affairs. The only difference was in their perceptions of the world which persuaded one to urge avoidance of, and the other to duplicate, the use of force.[53] It was the difference between believing in an open economic relationship among nations and visualizing fierce competition among exclusive national entities. By 1931 all indications seemed to suggest that the neo-mercantilistic world-view of Matsuoka was more realistic than Shidehara's rational, laissez-faire image, which had apparently failed to produce tangible results.

The *Sakurakai* (Cherry Blossom Society), organized by reform-minded army officers in 1930, declared its opposition to a foreign policy which had "catered to the wishes of the foreign govern-

[53] Matsuoka Yōseki, *Tōa zenkyoku no dōyō* (Tokyo, 1931), pp. 2ff; Matsuoka, *Shitsugi*, pp. 11ff, 96-97.

ments and exhibited no zeal for expansion." It was unfair to criticize the government for a lack of expansionistic policy. Throughout the 1920's Japanese policy had aimed at peaceful economic expansion. It had tried to preserve existing rights and interests abroad, encourage migration, expand export trade, cultivate new investment opportunities, and raise the level of national well-being at home. It failed.

To say so is not to assert that the failure of postwar economic expansionism was a failure of the policy alone. Certainly factors little connected with foreign policy frustrated further expansion of economic interests. For instance, despite the absence of legal obstacles, a mere handful of Japanese desired to settle in South America or southeast Asia. Pleas by publicists and government agencies for more emigrants and permanent settlers revealed how hard it was to persuade the people to leave their homes on more than a temporary basis. There was little interest in acquiring citizenship of another country. Japan simply was not a country of emigrants, and it took the strong governmental-military backing of the 1930's to bring about a massive Japanese settlement in what emerged as the Great East Asian Co-Prosperity Sphere. Nor is there evidence that the Japanese overseas became less competitive and narrowly nationalistic in the 1920's than earlier. A writer who toured China in 1923 wondered why the Japanese, who prided themselves on being a first-class people at home, exhibited so many ugly traits once they were abroad. In China, particularly, Japanese residents tended to be highly conscious of their national and ethnic identity and were among the first to oppose the policy of cooperation with Western powers. Kayahara Kazan, long a critic of Japanese abroad, saw no need to change his views. His trip to China in the mid-1920's confirmed him in the view that the Japanese carried their parochial life-styles with them wherever they went.[54]

The disappointingly slow progress of Japanese foreign trade, another index of the failure of economic diplomacy, was also in part attributable to domestic politics. Despite the profession of faith in the international economic system, the Japanese economy was never fully integrated into it. Many industries which ordinarily would have lost out in foreign competition were protected by the government's financial policy, including periodical emer-

[54] Norisugi Yoshinao, *Chūkaminkoku ni manabu* (Shanghai, 1923); Kayahara Kazan, *Tōkai igo Kayahara Kazan bunshū* (Tokyo, 1929).

gency relief loans, and by the gold embargo which continued to be in effect long after its imposition during the war. The rate of foreign exchange fluctuated, to the detriment of the stability of the yen. The value of the yen fell, to the temporary advantage of Japanese exports. This was one reason why there was pressure to resist the restoration of the gold standard at the prewar rate of exchange. However, the government could have repealed the gold embargo and devalued the yen at the same time, thus reintegrating the Japanese economy with the world capitalist economy but also enabling Japanese goods to retain their competitive advantage. But when Japan did go back on gold in 1930 the prewar rate of exchange was maintained, with the result that the prices of imports fell, those of exports had to be reduced to retain the earlier competitive position, general purchasing power dropped, and the gold reserve dwindled fast. Finally, the great earthquake and its aftermath necessitated the import of large quantities of goods for reconstruction of cities and factories, as well as emergency relief loans to banks and commercial establishments. All these developments burdened the economy with trade deficits and tardy industrial rationalization.

Critics of postwar economic expansionism were wrong in ignoring these factors and attacking the structure of peaceful foreign policy. It cannot be denied, however, that the conceptualization of the postwar international system by the architects of peaceful expansionist policy was basically unrealistic and romantic, producing high expectations but no results to correspond to aspirations. They envisaged a world where nations pursued their enlightened self-interests, bent their resources to the promotion of welfare at home and peace abroad, and harmonized their interests through peaceful methods. This was a world where particularistic tendencies, whether of geography or of race, were replaced by universalistic economic values. It was the world of "liberal-capitalistic internationalism."

The reality was far different. It was a world which did not tolerate unrestricted economic expansionism, whether peaceful or forceful. It was a world characterized as much by a Lothrop Stoddard as by a Norman Angell, as much by an Ortega y Gasset as by a Pitirim Sorokin. Racism was rampant, and the League of Nations was dormant. Of the two countries that were supposedly the key to Japan's economic advancement, the United States maintained a consistently high tariff policy while China was clamoring for tariff autonomy. Britain was taking steps toward imperial rationalism, with preferential tariff agreements detrimental to Japanese cotton exports. It was difficult to count upon the good will of other nations to protect Japanese merchants, fishermen, and agriculturalists abroad. Informal imperialism never worked when the informal imperialists aroused the nationalism of the colonial and semi-colonial populations. After all, the United States, the symbol of the new order, was freely using force to protect its interests in Nicaragua, Haiti, and Santo Domingo. Underneath the surface impression of disarmament and perpetual amity, the armies and navies of all the powers were continuing their build-up and revising their war plans.

If Japan's proponents of economic foreign policy had a naive vision of the world, it was not entirely their fault. In many capitals statesmen hailed the coming of a new era and substituted power politics with a simple formula of Calvin Coolidge's: "Who's gonna fight us?" Above all, there was confidence in an economic system which would forever serve as a lubricant in international affairs. As Thorstein Veblen observed, "commercial nationalism, after the pattern of mid-Victorian times," was the basis of the postwar world order in which the "vested interests of property" were to be safeguarded.[55] Middle-class capitalistic values were viewed as spreading to cover the entire earth, and as industrialism advanced an era of cosmopolitan harmony was pictured to be dawning.

Many in the West saw the anomaly of economic internationalism existing side by side with political nationalism. The allegedly cosmopolitan character of capitalism had failed to produce a corresponding internationalism in the political arena. Some observers, moreover, were aware that the capitalist system had been confronted with an entirely new challenge in the shape of the Bolshevik revolution. Few, however, foresaw the rapidity with which the whole Western economic system would collapse. In *The Day After Tomorrow*, published in 1928, the American Philip Gibbs wrote, "The genius of the human mind which has investigated so many secrets of Nature with such marvelous skill, is not incapable of reshaping its own destiny and frustrating the evil forces which are threatening the future life of mankind. [We] have the possibility within ourselves for improving our minds and our manners. Upon that possibility depends the fate of civiliza-

[55] Editorial in *Dial*, July 12, 1919.

tion and all that makes life good to us."[56] This type of subdued optimism reflected the return of confidence in the West after the devastation of war.

It is not surprising, then, that the image of a peaceful and prosperous world and the ideological framework of economic expansionism should have continued to exist in Japan despite all the evidence disputing their soundness. The new diplomacy seemed to make sense in the light of the "trends of the time." It provided one tangible conceptualization of the postwar world which appeared to be a workable alternative to the old diplomacy of power politics and formal imperialism. Because it promised more than it delivered, the idea of peaceful economic expansion became suspect and was ultimately cast away once the dissatisfied public came to identify the nation's social and economic ills with the basic orientation of Japanese foreign policy.

"Europe is very far from being a graveyard," wrote Joseph Conrad in 1924. "One need not be very optimistic to see that. So it seems to me. But it may be the illusion of a solitary man. I do not know what may happen tomorrow, but I hope I shall be allowed to keep that illusion to the end of my life."[57] This "illusion" could no longer be kept after the turbulent and disheartening events of the 1930's. But it was shared by the makers of postwar Japanese policy. It was an illusion born of wishful thinking, whose cost was all the greater because it was a world-wide phenomenon. The failure of economic expansionism was not simply a Japanese failure. It was also a global failure. The Japanese who fancied themselves to be "world citizens" were no better or worse than the citizens of other countries.

[56] Philip Gibbs, *The Day After Tomorrow* (New York, 1928), p. 126.
[57] Quoted by John Strachey, "Is Europe Dead?" *Spectator*, May 31, 1924.

JAMES B. CROWLEY

A New Asian Order: Some Notes
on Prewar Japanese Nationalism

CLIO, IN THE modern manner, sings her sagas in many verses. This multiplicity is readily apparent in the telling of the Pacific War, its origins and its effects. Here there is no necessity to linger on the ironies and paradoxes of that story. In 1941, Imperial Japan presented itself as the liberator of Asia, the slayer of the European colonial dragon; the United States became the advocate of the Four Freedoms and the knightly champion of human freedom and democracy; and the European nations, without sufficient armor, invoked the battle cry of bygone jousts, vowing that they would never abandon the ramparts of empire. If each of these standpoints possessed some truth, they did not tell the whole story. In defeat, moreover, Japan, in many ways, had slain Western colonialism; and, in victory, the United States learned that the demise of Japanese militarism ushered in no era of peace and stability. Clio must wonder about the victors and the vanquished. Presently she may relate with confidence that the Pacific War was neither a momentous but isolated episode in Asian history, nor was it exclusively a Japanese-American affair. It was one part of a drama which commenced with the intrusion of the Occidental nations into Asia, and this drama has not yet ended. The Pacific War was not the first confrontation between an Asian and a Western nation, nor was it the last of such confrontations.

As a racial conflict, this war merits greater attention. Western explanations and interpretations of Japanese aggression in the 1930's and 1940's no longer seem fully persuasive, however valid they may have been for an earlier generation. Prewar Japan was not a fascist country, at least not by European standards. The Meiji constitutional system functioned throughout the 1930's and it sustained a rule of law. No mass revolutionary movements flourished and no single political party monopolized public authority. Japan spawned no Hitlers or Mussolinis, and its government was at least as democratic, as legally responsible, as those in China and the Soviet Union. Japan, moreover, was not part of an international fascist scheme to divide and rule the world, the Axis alliance notwithstanding. Still, authoritarian orientation in domestic affairs and aggressive expansionism were hallmarks of the 1930's. The problem is not to deny or to rationalize these aspects of Japanese behavior. They are indisputable facts. The problem is to recognize and understand the distinctive racial-cultural hues in Japan's prewar policies. These, we may suppose, are apt to be slighted by appraisals rooted in American assumptions, especially by attitudes nurtured in the midst of conflict and occupation.

This essay focuses on one aspect of prewar Japan, namely, the political and ideological process which produced the concepts of a New Asian Order and the Co-Prosperity Sphere. The focus, inevitably, is on the domestic or Japanese standpoint, one which ignores the meaning of this mission for other countries. This focus provides no apology or rationalization for Japanese actions. It assumes the grim reality of the violence, physical and emotional, wrought on China, the Philippines, Malaysia, Indonesia, Burma, and other Asian nations by the Japanese. My purpose, however, is not to evaluate the "reality" of Japan's New Order, nor is it my intention to present a comprehensive discussion of Japanese foreign and domestic policies. The prime concern is restricted. By reappraising some aspects of the quest for the New Asian Order, we may gain one more clue to an understanding of modern Japanese history. This may be of some interest in interpreting the road to Pearl Harbor, a subject of major importance to American historians. It may also engage the attention of those concerned with the study of Japanese nationalism, a subject of interest to all historians intrigued by the phenomenon of Asian nationalism, past and present.

In 1932, during the Shanghai incident, a pamphlet materialized which purported to be Japan's secret plan of conquest. First Manchuria, then China, eventually the world. This spurious document—the Tanaka Memorial—commanded wide notoriety. As the years unfolded, it seemed, from afar, that the Tanaka Memorial was a master blueprint of conquest. Actually, few Japanese dreamed, in 1932, of war with the Anglo-American sea powers or of expansion into Southeast Asia.[1] Other issues and aspirations

[1] For a review of Japanese policy in the early 1930's see, James B. Crowley, *Japan's Quest For Autonomy: National Security and Foreign Policy, 1930-1938* (Princeton, N.J., 1967), pp. 82-244.

seemed more pertinent. The Soviet Union was moving into Outer Mongolia and augmenting its Maritime forces. Japan had just overrun Manchuria and was engrossed in creating its client state, Manchukuo. The most pressing issue was the confirmation of this latest step, to charm or compel Russia, the Great Powers, and China into a *de facto* recognition of Manchukuo. China, fractionalized by warlord cabals and the anti-Communist campaigns of the Nanking government, offered no real threat to Manchukuo. The Soviets posed a credible threat but they were not prepared to contest Japan's infringement of Soviet rights and interests in Manchuria. If the sea powers had formed an alliance, they could have forced Japan out of Manchuria, but England and the United States were plagued by acute domestic difficulties, and were not prepared to play the role of policeman in Chinese territory. Neither Russia nor England nor the United States invoked the threat of retaliation. Instead, the sea powers articulated the "non-recognition" principle and Russia acknowledged the *de facto* presence of Manchukuo when it negotiated the liquidation of its interests in the Chinese Eastern Railway.

Japan formed Manchukuo. It thereby isolated itself—hated by the Chinese, feared by the Soviets, and censored by the Anglo-Americans. Withdrawing from the League of Nations, Japan marched under the banner of a "Japanese Monroe Doctrine." The nation had started on an endless quest, the search for a military-industrial base sufficient to render this "Monroe Doctrine" a viable international principle. Not in 1932, nor in any subsequent year, would Japan realize a strategic capability adequate to guarantee the security of the empire against the Soviet Union and the Anglo-American fleets. The commitment to Manchukuo and Asian Monroe Doctrine, nonetheless, became the "immutable" national policy. The consequence was fateful indeed. Japan had to expand her army and her navy and wage an open-ended armaments race with two of the richest nations in the world. Moreover, she had to build up *both* her army and maritime strength, while the Soviet Union could concentrate on land forces, the United States on naval power.

This configuration of power politics and Japanese security instilled apprehension and determination; apprehension about the future and determination to forge ahead with an independent foreign policy. The Manchurian venture became the point of no return. After Manchukuo, the Washington Treaty System was rejected in favor of a Monroe Doctrine embracing Manchuria, Inner Mongolia, and North China. Within the sacred islands, this mission was not portrayed as an aberration or as a sordid imperialistic undertaking. Rather, the nation's new course was cast against "the trends of the times."[2] In Japan, cooperation with the sea powers, as well as the propriety of party cabinets, became passé; but in Europe, too, the Versailles settlement and the Weimar Republic had been outmoded by Hitler's New Order. The principles of economic liberalism, disarmament, and free trade were denied in Manchukuo and Japan, and elsewhere. Fascist Germany and Communist Russia both pursued programs of armament and a managed economy. The United States implemented a diplomacy of economic nationalism and the formation of a Pan-American trade union, and England sought refuge in a sterling trade bloc. Against these manifold responses to the world depression, many Japanese regarded the commitment to Manchukuo as one facet of a world-wide movement toward regional political-economic blocs, not as the behavior of an international renegade.

Although Japan's new orientation was projected against global trends, configurations peculiar to East Asia were identified. Japan, like Germany, was regarded as a "have-not" nation which, like Germany, would clash with the status-quo orientation of the "have" nations. In contrast to Germany, Japan faced the interrelated challenge of Chinese nationalism, the semi-colonial right of the Western powers in China, and the Soviet intrigues in Mongolia and China. As many Japanese assessed the context, Communist Russia and the capitalist powers would, for divergent reasons, jointly promote Chinese resistance to Japan's Monroe Doctrine. Japan, in short, faced a hostile international environment and this hostility intensified the sense of mission behind Manchukuo. By abandoning her political links with the League and by reaffirming its passionate anti-Communism, Japan transformed the Japan-Manchukuo alliance into the prologue of the new Asia. "It has," noted one critic in 1933, "muffled the beat of the wardrums, first heard some one hundred years

[2] For a fuller discussion of this theme, James B. Crowley, "Prince Konoe and His Brain Trust, The Shōwa Kenkyūkai," in James W. Morley (ed.), *Dilemmas of Growth in Prewar Japan* (Princeton, N.J.), 1972.

ago, which sounded the hegemony of the Caucasians."[3] This racial note, with its inherent imperial overtones, accentuated the dilemma and paradox of Sino-Japanese relations. How to gain the friendship and cooperation of the Chinese, the sine qua non for Japan's Monroe Doctrine? Japan's actions, first in Manchuria, then in North China, had channeled Chinese nationalism against the preemptive threat of Japanese force and away from the semi-colonial rights of the powers and of the Soviet deeds in Mongolia.

The tense North China scene, the impending naval armaments race, and the growing Soviet forces dictated some adjustments in policy. By 1936, one heard at the policy-making level some voices talking about the "South Seas."[4] In particular, Japan's naval authorities, as well as those in political and economic circles who were dismayed by the assertive continental policy, articulated the so-called *hokushu nanshin* doctrine, "defend the north, advance to the south." By accepting the status quo in North China, these voices reasoned that Japan could concentrate on economic development, especially in the chemical and heavy-industry sectors. At the same time, Japan could enlarge the fleet for two diplomatic functions. First, with operational capability extended to the Celebes, Japan could bring pressure on the European powers to open up their colonies to Japanese investment. Second, the powers would be forced to recognize Japan's Monroe Doctrine and this, in turn, would compel China to seek an accommodation with Japan. This viewpoint permeated the "fundamental principles of National Policy" decided in August, 1936.[5] These principles, according to the Tokyo Tribunal, "set out in the utmost clarity the principles which were to guide Japan, both in her relations with other nations and in completing her internal preparations for war."[6] Without endorsing this evaluation, we may note that this national policy called for the status quo in North China, the promotion of a "Mongolian independence movement," and the enlargement of both services. For our purposes, it is most significant because the South Seas were, for the first time, explicitly internalized as an objective in national policy. And, it should be noted, this goal was advanced as an

[3] Dai Tōa Bunka Library, Shōwa Kenkyūkai Collection (DTBSKC), Takahashi Kamakishi, *Nippon wa doku e yuku ka?* *(yōkō)*, March, 1937, 25.

[4] Crowley, *Japan's Quest* . . . , pp. 284-289.

[5] International Military Tribunal Far East (IMTFE), *Exhibit 979.*

[6] IMTFE, *Judgment*, 119.

alternative to the aggressive China policy of the preceding year. Understandably, this initial reference was vague. "Footsteps" were to be taken to secure access to the resources of the South Seas; and the government affirmed that "we must make our progress gradually and peacefully." In essence, as of August, 1936, the empire wanted no war with China or with any country. The desire was to stress the development of the Japan-Manchukuo military-industrial complex to the degree that this would enable the empire to reconstruct Asia with a spirit of co-prosperity and co-existence based upon the Imperial Way. The South Seas were not considered essential to the new Asia, but access to this region was viewed with increasing interest.

At this time, the Japanese government estimated that the requisites for the next ten years of economic development would be satisfied by the Japan-Manchukuo bloc. Even the Kwantung army, which had been coveting North China, concluded in June, 1937, "The resources for national defense will clearly be met with the resources of Manchuria and East Hopei."[7] Economically, the nation's policies were not, therefore, greatly affected by the presumed necessity of additional resources. Politically, however, the government was divided by opposing assessments of the Nanking government. Many groups, especially the field armies, deemed Chiang Kai-shek "one more warlord." These people, contemptuous of Chiang's army, were, in General Tōjō's words, more than willing "to deliver a blow first of all upon the Nanking regime in order to remove this menace at our rear."[8] Others, including the general staff, thought the Nationalist government viable and judged any Sino-Japanese conflict to be the wrong war, at the wrong time, with the wrong enemy. The Soviet Union, not China, seemed the most pressing strategic threat to the empire. This ambivalent estimate of Chiang's government, moreover, was enveloped by a set of orientations which would ultimately serve as the base point for the New Asian Order.

After the Sian incident, Japanese specialists on China reevaluated the China scene. Most concurred with the judgment of the Foreign Ministry that "an agreement was reached at least on one point—namely, to resist Japan."[9] This premise, however, induced no fundamental alteration in policy. Surprisingly, it failed to sustain the belief that Chinese animosity was exclusively, or even

---

[7] Crowley, *Japan's Quest* . . . , p. 321.
[8] *Ibid.*, p. 321. [9] *Ibid.*, p. 310.

primarily, generated by Japanese behavior. The basic difficulty was attributed to the Western powers, particularly Britain.[10] As many Japanese appraised the situation, China was in the stage of semi-colonialism; the Nanking regime was unifying the nation by a tenuous alliance with Western capitalists and the Communists against Japan; and the Chinese Communists were building a fortress in Yenan. The ultimate success of this policy hinged on Great Britain, for, without British support, Chiang would be forced either to yield to the Communists or to cooperate with Japan on behalf of his domestic economic program and his long-term struggle with the Communists. With this syndrome, Sino-Japanese cooperation—based on the promotion of bourgeois nationalism and anti-communism in China—became contingent on Japan's ability to sever Chiang's dependence on the Western (capitalist) powers. The problems were manifold. Britain was concerned with safeguarding her China interests. She was not worried by the Chinese Communists or by the growing power of the Soviet Union, but she was apprehensive about Italy and Germany. Diplomatically, this posed the added issue of the Anti-Comintern Pact. Unless Japan would torpedo this agreement, any *de facto* British support for Japan's position in North China and Manchuria remained unlikely. As one critic reflected in June, 1937, "from the British standpoint there is no possibility of an Anglo-Japanese alliance if a German-Japanese pact exists."[11] From the army's perspective, however, this pact was invaluable. It restrained the Soviets and supported Japan's thrust into Inner Mongolia. On the eve of the Marco Polo Bridge incident, one expert on international affairs mirrored the thoughts of many: "The status quo is impossible." Japan could not expand into the colonial regions of the powers by means of a "free trade" or "open door" passport, nor could she gain British support for a Japanese Monroe Doctrine in China.[12]

When Prince Konoe assumed the premiership in June of 1937 (first Konoe Cabinet: June 4, 1937-January 5, 1939), he emphasized domestic affairs as the most pressing concern. There was, despite the Sian incident and the abortive efforts at a detente with Britain, no desire for or anticipation of a war with China.

[10] Crowley, "Prince Konoe . . . ," *op. cit.*
[11] DTBSKC, "Ippan gaikō iinkai dai ikkai kaigō yōroku," June 29, 1937, 21.
[12] *Ibid.*, pp. 22-23.

Within a month, however, the Marco Polo Bridge incident escalated into a major conflict. Over the objection of the army General staff, moreover, the Konoe Cabinet, in January, 1938, declared that Japan would "annihilate" the Nationalist government. This decision flowed from several considerations, not the least of which was a grave underestimation of Chiang's ability to resist. By springtime, the premier's advisors recognized that the government had misread Chinese nationalism, "overlooking the possibility of total Chinese resistance and miscalculating that the war would readily produce the internal political disintegration of China."[13] Seeing things as they were, however, did not lead to the rejection of the "annihilation" policy. On the contrary, what emerged was the impulse to redefine Japan's policy to move from the negative policy of annihilation to an affirmative one which sought to reconstruct China.

Three distinct but related problems confronted Japan: to wage a war of attrition against Nationalist China; to organize a political regime which would capture nationalist sentiment; and to undertake a diplomacy designed to cut "outside" assistance to Chiang's forces. The China Incident became a total war. In this context, many Japanese advanced the concept of an East Asian Confederation (*tōa renmei*); a Japan-Manchukuo-China bloc based upon the principles of the kingly way (*ōdō-shugi*) and cooperativism (*kyōdō-shugi*).[14] By Japanese definitions, these terms were "traditional" principles of East Asian culture and were, therefore, not synonymous with Western (imperialistic) principles. These principles were, of course, self-serving and self-deceiving. The incident had come full circle. Chinese nationalism received verbal homage, but Chiang Kai-shek became a symbol of reaction and bourgeois nationalism while the provisional regimes, resting on Japanese bayonets, were, by virtue of the kingly way and cooperativism, to become midwives for the New China. The China conflict became the hope, not the bane, of Sino-Japanese relations. "The major problem [noted one position paper] is to promote Japan's future in East Asia. The various problems connected with this task will be influenced by the means utilized in the reconstruction of Sino-Japanese relations. From this standpoint, it is imperative that this incident be han-

[13] DTBSKC, *Tōa seiji kenkyūkai*, "Shina jihen' kentō (yōyaku)," May 27, 1938, 2.

[14] Crowley, "Prince Konoe . . . ," *op. cit.*

dled in some fashion."[15] Precisely in what fashion was the crux of the question.

The Cabinet and the nation were divided over the China Incident. The premier and the War Ministry favored an alliance with Germany, the expulsion of England from North China, and the organization of a new central government in China under Wang Ching-wei. The Foreign and Naval Ministries opposed any Axis alliance or any frontal assault on the treaty rights of England. And the general staff, worried by the scale of operations, preferred some type of armistice and accommodation with Chiang's government. Rather than confess past errors, the government eventually chose to rationalize continued hostilities. Part of this compulsion included a new approach to Southeast Asia and of its relationship to the resolution of the China Incident.

This new attitude became visible with Miki Kiyoshi's essay, "The World Historical Significance of the China Incident."[16] One of Japan's most distinguished philosophers, Miki was, in 1938, an advisor and speech-writer for Premier Konoe. Many of his ideas were soon mirrored in the premier's explanations of national policy. In reference to Asian history, Miki reasoned that the China conflict marked the beginning of the twentieth century. At the same time, Miki stressed, Asia should not follow the pattern of twentieth-century Europe. Liberalism and nationalism, for example, had been the driving forces of modern Europe but, with the First World War and the Great Depression, liberalism had been "reduced to its final extremity." Henceforth, liberalism could no longer furnish a unifying influence on world events. In conjunction with this development, Miki added, communism had failed in Weimar Germany and flourished in semi-colonial Russia. It was, therefore, no answer to industrialized societies like Japan. Still, Europe was witnessing an ideological confrontation between liberal democracy and communism; and the European cauldron of nationalism, liberalism, and communism had brewed fascism. In essence, Miki said, twentieth-century Europe had created a clash of ideologies which would lead to another world war and, in the process, to the degeneration of fascism, liberalism, and communism.

[15] DTBSKC, *Gaikō iinkai tōgi: shuyō yon*, "Jihen shūshū ni tomonau ippanteki gaikō seisaku," July 7, 1938, 3.

[16] DTBSKC, uncatalogued, Miki Kiyoshi, *Shina jihen no sekai-shiteki igi*, July, 1938.

Asia and Japan, ventured Miki, should transcend this peril. To this end, Japan and all Asia would have to articulate a system of values and ethics distinct from those conceived within Western civilization. Asia should form its own union of nations, and "we must do something which will link this [China] incident with the unification of Asia." As Miki diagnosed the problems involved, four axioms were apparent: 1) the world was pluralistic, composed of several cultures; 2) these cultures were not to be evaluated by European standards; 3) European civilization was in the process of committing suicide and no longer acted as the driving force in Asian affairs; and 4) given the bankruptcy of Europe, Japan's mission was "the unification of the Asian nations, based upon mutual cooperation, under Japanese leadership." Japan obviously needed Chinese cooperation, and that would be forthcoming, Miki insisted, only if Japan cast aside colonial and imperial sentiments in favor of social and political principles leading to the common advancement of all the Asian races and the expulsion of Western imperialism from Asia. This perspective, in effect, implied that Japan could not settle the China Incident unless it denied its imperialist aspirations by championing the liberation of all Asian colonies.

Although few governmental or military leaders concurred with this sentiment in 1938, by November of that year Prince Konoe proclaimed the purpose of the China Incident as the building of a New Asian Order.[17] China, Konoe sighed, had been "the victim of the imperialistic ambitions and rivalries of the Occidental powers." Japan was "eager to see a new order established in East Asia—a new structure based on true justice." This encompassing crusade, one giant-step beyond the Japanese Monroe Doctrine, sanctioned the quest for a regional bloc based upon "Asian" cultural and political norms. It accelerated, as well, the momentum toward totalitarianism at home and force as the arbitrator of this New Asian Order.

Konoe's démarche implied a long-range threat to the colonial system of Southeast Asia, as well as a direct assault on European treaty rights in China. The New Order rhetoric, if anything, stiffened Chiang's resistance. Furthermore, as of this date, the Japanese government still predicated its economic plans in terms of the Japan-Manchukuo-China bloc. Even if the resources of the

[17] Royal Institute of International Affairs, *Documents: 1938* (London, 1940), pp. 348-349.

South Seas had been an integral component of national planning, Japan's naval leaders were unwilling to seek battle, particularly in the midst of the China conflict. This naval constraint precluded the formation of an Axis alliance in 1938-1939. Indeed, the cabinet met 75 times on this subject, the naval minister at each meeting vetoing the proposed alliance. Apart from the combined strength of the powers, Japan's naval strategists advanced two reasons dictating neutrality toward European affairs—namely, in case of a war, the sea powers would sacrifice their interests in China and, in order to gain positive Japanese cooperation, they would grant access to the resources of Southeast Asia. The army general staff, on the other hand, pressed for an Axis pact, citing its benefits vis-à-vis Russia. With the alliance, Japan would be able to concentrate greater forces in China and terminate that war quickly. This interservice conflict ended abruptly with the Nazi-Soviet Pact. Neutrality toward Europe and the New Order in China remained the public pillars of national policy.

The shock which the Nazi-Soviet deal provoked in Western circles had no counterpart in Japan. The nation, observed Professor Rōyama Masamichi, was seeking "positive independence" in Asia, not the "semi-autonomy" afforded by the Washington Conference Treaties.[18] This mission appeared to be enhanced by the Nazi-Soviet Pact. "For the first time there is, in actuality, a direct relationship between the New [European] Order and the structuring of the East Asian Order on the basis of the Asian Cooperative Theory." In particular, Hitler's diplomacy signified the demise of the Anglo-Saxon theory of international relations. In Western Europe, Rōyama reflected, nations were organized on the "fusion of democracy and nationalism," but Eastern Europe was composed of nations containing various nationalities. Moreover, East Europe was a region of "late-developed" nations which lacked effectual democratic institutions. Since the Versailles system had ignored the peculiar conditions of East Europe, there emerged, in reaction, "new anti-capitalistic economics, represented by the communistic totalitarianism of the Soviet Union and by the fascist absolutism of Germany and Italy." Russia and Germany, Rōyama added, had both articu-

---

[18] Rōyama Masamichi, *Tōa to sekai* (Tokyo, 1941), especially chapter III, "Sekai shinjitsujō no tembō," which originally appeared in the November, 1939 issue of *Kaizo*.

lated "a domestic ideology which is also a universal ideology." Both, in effect, offered a view of society and interstate behavior alternative to that articulated by the European democracies and, irrespective of the ultimate configurations of European war and diplomacy, Rōyama foresaw the appearance of large regional political-economic-ideological blocs. Each bloc would be led by a great power and each bloc would confront the dual problem of interstate relations among its members and of relations among blocs. This dual responsibility demanded a set of values which "transcends nationalism and capitalism" at the domestic and regional level. Since the League had failed in this assignment, the Nazi-Soviet Pact suggested one answer—the formation of a regional geopolitical sphere in which "cultural nationalism" and a "self-sufficient" bloc economy were esteemed. This, in turn, would resolve the "economic and security problems faced by late-developed nations." Japan, in short, needed to form an Asian regional bloc and to offer a "domestic ideology which is also a universal ideology."

This proclivity for rationalizing Japanese escapades on the mainland in terms of global trends was linked with an increasing focus on the resources of Southeast Asia. Although official policy still projected a Japan-China-Manchukuo bloc, the realities of the China scene stimulated reveries about the South Seas. "It goes without saying," in the view of one group of officials

> that the first consideration for the formation of the East Asian Economic Bloc must be the national defense material requirements of Japan, which is the leading and nucleus nation of the [East Asian] Bloc. . . . It is natural that Japan spread into the South Seas region in order to acquire the resources essential for national existence between two Super-Powers—the Soviet Union and the United States. . . . For the countries of the South Seas, it will also be profitable to incorporate themselves into the East Asian Economic Bloc.[19]

By December, 1939, Aoki Kazuo, the head of the Cabinet Planning Board, affirmed the necessity "to establish a self-contained

---

[19] This rationale, including the quotations cited, is sharply etched and criticized by Kishi Kōichi, "Taiheiyō sensō e no michi to shite no nan'po seisaku kettei to Shōwa Kenkyūkai," *Tōyō kenkyū,* 7 (February, 1964), pp. 27-34.

economy here, namely, to knit the East Asian countries into a great economic bloc."[20] Self-sufficiency, obviously, encompassed the southern region. Still, despite the historical, geopolitical, economic rationales being conjured up on behalf of southern expansion, the Cabinet confined policy to the "resolution" of the China Incident and "neutrality" toward the European conflict.

Some voices of protest challenged the inflationary vocabulary of the New Asian Order. Former Ambassador Debuchi, speaking in the House of Peers, ridiculed the "bloc economy" concept as a "castle in the air."[21] The sentiments expressed by Aoki Kazuo, Debuchi contended, obscured "the problems concerning the market for our manufactured goods, as well as our actual capabilities to supply funds and materials to the continent." Such thinking, Debuchi feared, would be the overture to "Nazi catchwords such as *Liberstraum* [sic] or *Wirtschaftram* [sic]. But the 'East Asia,' as implied in the famous Konoye statement which first enunciated the idea of a 'new order,' included the countries of Japan, Manchukuo, and China, excluding the South Seas." Ambassador Debuchi's concern was quickly vindicated, as the Overseas Minister General Koiso responded to his remarks in simple language: "Since it was impossible to expect a perfect autarchy . . . among Japan, Manchukuo, and China, it was inevitable for Japan to rely on the South Seas for the supply of needed materials for the realization of the new order in East Asia."[22] In the Lower House, Saitō Takeo blasted the China policy, not the unfolding southern policy.[23] Since 1931, Saitō noted, Japan had followed a program of expansion which had produced isolation and huge budgets. The government had also taken on the fantastic burden of trying to subjugate China proper. This was a "vain endeavor" which had thrust the nation into "a never-ending competition of armament expansion." Konoe's New Order démarche, Saitō ventured, bore no relationship to reality: "It is a dream. . . . War is not a struggle between the just and the un-

[20] *Contemporary Opinion* 327 (April 25, 1940), Translation of Debuchi article appearing in the May issue of *Gaikō jihō*.

[21] *Ibid.*

[22] *Contemporary Opinion* 328 (May 2, 1940), Translation of Iizawa Akiharu article appearing in the May issue of *Kokusai chishiki*.

[23] To my knowledge, the only complete text of Saitō's speech is in the archives of the Self-Defence Agency, War History Division, *Kihon kokusaku kankei*, III, "Saitō daigishi ensetsu ni tai suru shoken."

just. It is an out-and-out power struggle." To Saitō, Japan lacked
sufficient power. "The nation must cease questing after noble-
sounding dreams and face realities." The most operative reality
in Japan, however, was expressed in the retort of the war minister who insisted that the New Asian Order was "an ideal possible to realize. . . . A million Japanese troops in China are inspired by this conviction and one hundred thousand have died
for it."[24]

This passionate reaction soon led to the "eradication" of Saitō's
speech from the official Diet proceedings and then to the expulsion of Saitō from the Diet. As one ministry phrased the charge
against the venerable parliamentarian: Saitō had denied the
"purpose of this sacred war." He had "cast doubts" among the
people and lent "assistance to Chiang Kai-shek." He had deni-
grated "the racial ideals and racial character of the state"; he had
seen the China Incident "as being substantively the same as wars
waged by Caucasians"; and he had portrayed "the painful endeavors and sacrifices of our military personnel as meaningless."[25]
Indeed, in Saitō's frame of reference, "the China Incident is an
aggressive war; . . . the *hakko ichiu* spirit is synonymous with
the spirit of control by force; and the Imperial rule is government by the strong." Few were prepared to credit these thoughts.
It was easier to banish the heretic. Saitō's speech became the last
public censure of the New Order, a fate which symbolized the
degree to which the China Incident had become a holy crusade
on behalf of a New Asia under the benevolent Kusonosuki sword.

The basic assumption of Saitō's presentation was, ironically,
shared by the Supreme Command.[26] Questioning the sagacity of
an endless conflict on the mainland, the army general staff preferred an enclave syndrome in South and Central China, a withdrawal to key coastal cities, and a consolidation of North China
and Inner Mongolia. Once accomplished, the government could
claim "victory" and wait for the enemy to negotiate. This proposal was countered by the field armies and the China Affairs
Board, both of which voiced confidence in the war of attrition
and lamented "outside" assistance as the factor which permitted

[24] Newspaper clipping: Hugh Byas Collection, Sterling Memorial Library,
Yale University, New Haven, Conn.
[25] "Saitō daigishi . . . ," *op. cit.*
[26] Imai Kiyoshi, *et al.*, *Nihon rekishi: gendai* (Tokyo, 1963), IV, "Taiheiyō
sensō," pp. 162-163.

Chiang's government to resist. By closing the "back door" to Chungking, total victory would be attained. Given the "immutable" national policy and the reaction to Saitō's speech, the opinion of the general staff remained one view contending with those favoring more of the same in China. At this time, however, the naval general staff reassessed its position toward Germany. This shift, apparent before the spring blitzkreig of 1940, would spell the downfall of the Yonai Cabinet (January 16, 1940-July 22, 1940) and the quest for a Greater Asian Co-Prosperity Sphere by the second Konoe Cabinet (July 22, 1940-July 18, 1941).

Until the spring of 1940, Japan's naval strategists had viewed Anglo-American relations through the China Incident, not in terms of Southeast Asia. Consequently, they had, in the fall of 1939, adopted a cautious tone toward Southeast Asia, in the hope that Japan would be able to facilitate investment and trade with the Dutch East Indies, Indochina, and Thailand by a policy of neutrality toward the European war. In April, 1940, the naval general staff advanced a new concern which cast Japanese-American relations and the dynamics of the European war in a different perspective.[27] Essentially, the general staff assumed that: 1) the United States, not the European powers, stood in the way of a peaceful advance into Southeast Asia; 2) the United States had undertaken a crash program in order to gain naval hegemony in the Pacific by March, 1942; and 3) Japan, in order to cope with American naval power, would have to gain control over the resources of the Dutch East Indies. Not anticipating the Nazi blitzkrieg, the general staff viewed the East Indies in terms of three basic tenets. First, Japan must not allow any "change in the current political and economic status of the Dutch East Indies"; second, Japan should not "precipitate war with England or the United States"; and, third, if the Anglo-American countries were to "consolidate their economic and strategic position against Japan, we must be prepared for the worst contingency— *viz.*, the opening of war with England and the United States and taking military initiatives against the East Indies."

Anxious to avoid war, the general staff reasoned that the government should announce unilaterally its opposition to any change in the status quo of the Indies and adamantly resist any

---

[27] Dai Tōa Bunka Library, Commander Ogi Collection (DTBCOC), *Gaikō mondai, gunreibu dai-sanbu,* "Beikoku kongo no taiNichi dōkō handen," April 15, 1940.

American protectorate over the East Indies. "In this circumstance, if the European war develops to Germany's advantage, British influence in the Dutch East Indies would decline and Japan's influence would automatically increase." They further insisted that the government should recognize that any alternative program espoused by the United States "will necessarily lead to war." As they interpreted American policy, the Vinson naval program was directed not against Germany but by the wish "to restrain the expansive development of Japan" and to buttress "its non-recognition" policy toward Japan's advance in China. Seen this way, the Roosevelt administration planned "a strong deployment of the American fleet in the Pacific in conjunction with an accelerated build-up of personnel, bases, and airfields in the Pacific Islands." Three conclusions flowed from this evaluation: 1) Japan must "anticipate the perfection of American armament for war against Japan"; 2) the United States "has adopted, with special reference to our economic advance into the Dutch East Indies, an attitude which does not preclude the use of military force"; and 3) "henceforth, Japan's diplomacy should be basically the employment of means which will prevent an American obstruction of our national policy." Speaking in homely terms, the general staff remarked that "only the United States can pull the chestnuts of the Dutch East Indies out of the fire." To eliminate this option, Japan would have to take a belligerent stance, including closer diplomatic ties with Germany. "By so strengthening Japan's international position, the United States would hesitate to take either the decisive step of going to war with Japan or the prerequisite to this step, namely, a freezing of Japan's economic assets."

Although Japan's naval strategists now looked with favor on stronger ties with Germany, Japan did not seek a military alliance. They wanted to "help intensify the European war" and they lamented that the United States was not apt to become directly involved in the European war because this "would force the United States to moderate its open-door policy" in Asia. In short, their obsession was no longer the fear of being dragged into the European war. It was the fear of emerging United States naval power. Once the United States had gained the strategic advantage, the Western powers could maintain their control over the resources of Southeast Asia. Japan presumptively, therefore, needed the resources of the East Indies, not to win the China

285

war but to be able to keep abreast of the American rearmament program. Among its limitations, this viewpoint failed to recognize American policy as a global strategy, not a regional strategy. It did not grasp the fact that the United States considered its policies toward Europe, the colonial possessions of the Western powers, and Nationalist China as indivisible strands of one global policy, nor did it perceive that Germany's success in Europe would strengthen, not weaken, American defense of Southeast Asia. In this view, Japan was currently the dominant naval power in the Pacific; England, France, and Holland were absorbed in a European conflict; and the Dutch East Indies were vulnerable and negotiable in the marketplace of international politics. Once the United States built its fleet, it would apply sanctions and it would "naturally" launch operations against Japan. The only alternative was a strident diplomacy toward the East Indies and, if this failed, "hostilities were inevitable."

This new concern with the Dutch East Indies was only tangentially related to the China Incident, or to the quest for a New Asian Order. And the fears it embodied were vindicated with the Nazi blitzkreig. In April, the United States declared that any change in the Dutch East Indies, except by peaceful means, "would be prejudicial to the cause of stability, peace, and security . . . in the entire Pacific Area."[28] With these words, and the passage of the Stark naval program, the American government had placed a diplomatic umbrella over the Southeast Asia area. To the naval general staff, this signified war. On June 21, the War Ministry and the army general staff presented "A Draft Set of Principles to Cope With the Changing World Situation."[29] Here three principles seemed clear: 1) Germany would dominate Europe; 2) England, with American assistance, would seek to protect its life-line to India and Australia; 3) once American naval powers were perfected, England and the United States would form "a solid security-economic bloc embracing Southeast Asia."

As a parallel to this shift in strategic thinking, Prince Konoe called for a "renovation" in foreign policy and a domestic "new order" program. Only Premier (Admiral) Yonai questioned the "epoch-making" significance of Hitler's success in Europe and he

[28] Julius Pratt, *A History of United States Foreign Policy* (Englewood Cliffs, N.J., 1955), p. 648.
[29] Tanemura Seiko, *Daihon'ei himitsu nisshi* (Tokyo, 1952), pp. 17-20.

was curtly driven from office in favor of Prince Konoe. Within four months, the Konoe government signed the Axis alliance, granted *de jure* recognition to Wang Ching-wei's regime in China, and proclaimed the building of a Greater Asian Co-Prosperity Sphere as the new national mission. Underlying this decision was the concern with the South Seas. Self-evidently, a thrust in this direction, as the cabinet noted, meant an "inevitable and a natural deterioration of relations with the United States."[30] And, as the General Staff observed, the new policy signified a change to "measures for the southern advance from the present policy [which] places emphasis on the China Incident."[31] As Premier Konoe saw it, the world was destined to be divided into regional blocs. In Asia Japan's task was the construction of an Asian bloc on the principles of an eradication of European colonialism, of a joint defense against communism, and of the mutual advancement of the livelihood of the Asian races. Most pertinent, in Konoe's judgment, was the strategic imperative of the Co-Prosperity Sphere. The United States and the Soviet Union were becoming super-powers, and Japan, for its own safety, would need the resources of Southeast Asia in order to keep pace with these powers. Although this policy risked war, it could be realized "peacefully" by an Axis alliance. As Konoe phrased his logic before the Privy Council, "A humble attitude will only prompt the United States to become domineering. Therefore, a demonstration of our strength is necessary."[32] The demonstration, of course, was the Axis alliance.

Despite Konoe's public and private rationale for the New Asian Order and the Axis pact, the navy general staff, some three weeks before the alliance was sealed, stated that England had weathered the Nazi onslaught.[33] The war was not over; it was "a long-term conflict. England hopes, by obtaining American assistance, and, if possible, American intervention, that this will generate unrest in German-occupied territory and change the policy of the Soviet Union." Assuming that Roosevelt would

[30] Ministry of Foreign Affairs, Japan, *Nihon gaikō nempyō narabina shuyō bunsho, 1840-1945* (Tokyo, 1955), II, 436-437.

[31] United States Department of the Army, Office of Military History (USDAOMH), *Japanese Monograph 146*, appendix 3, 46.

[32] *Ibid.*, pp. 29-30.

[33] DTBCOC, Catalogued as *Document 699* (Memo of the naval general staff to the cabinet, dated, September 28, 1940).

win his third term as President, the naval staff ventured that the "United States might intervene and end the stalemate." In different words, Japan's naval leaders were not dazzled by Germany's triumph. As important, they were also unwilling to abandon the advocacy of a southern advance. Indeed, they wistfully hoped for an American move against Germany on the premise that "if the United States intervened in the European war, it would be necessary for her to direct her military, naval, and air power toward Europe." In order to keep this option alive, Japan's naval leaders restricted the Axis pact so as to give Japan the right to decide on war or peace if the United States were to go to war against Germany. These naval leaders also recognized the short-term disadvantages of an Axis pact, namely, it would "provoke the United States into strengthening its position in the Pacific . . . and into coordinating joint responsibility with England for the security of British territory in the South Pacific." Of course, these sentiments were not shared by all other cabinet officials. Premier Konoe expected Britain's defeat; War Minister Tōjō argued that the pact would stabilize the Soviet border and allow greater concentration of forces against Chungking; and Foreign Minister Matsuoka reasoned that Japan and Germany shared a common destiny, common victory or common defeat. Confronted by these opinions, Naval Minister Yoshida collapsed, unable to reconcile the claims that an Axis alliance would both weaken and augment American power in the Pacific, and that American intervention in the European war was unwelcome and desirable. Cabinet policy, however, was capable of this feat and the Pact was signed.

Basic to the Axis pact was the primacy of the southern policy and basic to the southern advance was the Dutch East Indies. Speaking to this issue, the Cabinet, on August 29th, noted: "We now face an emergency situation in which we have no choice but to seek necessary resources in the Southern region, particularly in the Dutch East Indies, in order to cope with the malignant scheme of the United States. For this purpose, we must not only have closer economic relations with the East Indies but we must, as well, firmly establish our political leadership over this Dutch territory."[34] Ideally, the Cabinet wanted the Dutch officials to voluntarily join the Asian Co-Prosperity Sphere and to

[34] DTBCOC, "Tai Rai-in kōshō hōshin-an," *Naikaku kettei*, August 29, 1940.

ask that Japan provide military security for the East Indies. These desires, if incorporated into explicit demands, however, would "drive the Dutch East Indies into the Anglo-American camp, with whose support they may refuse our demands. Since we cannot counter this move, . . . we would incur a loss of national prestige." Thus, the Cabinet chose to present "limited" requests, anticipating "that diplomatic negotiations will go through many complications and offer no optimistic prospects of success." Nonetheless, the Cabinet decided "to state its frank views" and it believed these sentiments were best articulated as follows: "The current unrest throughout the world and the contentions between nations were, beyond any doubt, born from the unfair distribution of resources due to an irrational territorial division of the world. . . . Holland must, therefore, open its rich resources for the welfare and the prosperity of the East Asian people and thereby benefit all the people of the world."[35] In its own way, this cabinet decision reflected the inconsistency of the new national policy. Japan sought control over the East Indies but would not go to war for this objective, and yet it was prepared for negotiations "which offer no optimistic prospects of success." This strange blend of ambition and caution would eventually make the Axis alliance a diplomatic whirlpool, drawing Japan into conflict with the United States.

The priority on the southern advance, the speeches heralding the Axis alliance, and the rhetoric proclaiming the inevitable end of European colonialism, were still not girded by precise operational and occupational plans and policies. Oddly, by December, 1940, hopes were pinned on the negotiations with the Dutch officials and a move into Indochina by means of an accommodation with Vichy France. At this time, the Cabinet Planning Board prepared "A Draft Policy for Public Opinion With Reference to the Dutch East Indies."[36] Its simplicity attests to the haste and superficiality characteristic of the government's "South Seas" program. The East Indies were to be assured that "our southern advance . . . is to their advantage because the [present] Dutch policy set up artificial barriers to the material expansion of the Japanese people and, consequently, is hindering the co-prosperity of Greater Asia. This action is irrational and selfish." The

[35] *Ibid.*
[36] DTBCOC, "Rai-in mondai ni kan suru yoron shidō hōshin-an," *Jōhō-kyoku dai-ichibu*, December 20, 1940.

Anglo-Americans would be advised that "our southern advance is a natural result of their economic suppression. We must, moreover, endeavor to impress on them that their threat of military intervention will not thwart our efforts to obtain those resources which are a matter of life and death to Japan." By December, 1940, the Cabinet Information Board stated, "The Greater Asia Co-Prosperity Sphere now comprises the South Seas region, as well as Japan, Manchukuo, and China. This change was dictated by the necessity to shake ourselves free from our economic dependence on the United States and the British Empire by securing economic self-sufficiency in order to counter their economic strangulation of Japan."[37] With this axiom now operative within the government propaganda agency, the "underlying philosophy" of the co-prosperity idea gained increasing importance. In particular, noted the Information Board, care should be taken to avoid any "image" of aggression or of "exploitation of the underdeveloped nations." If Japan were seen as avaricious, the native races would not "identify their aspirations for national independence with Japan's help. If, in the depths of their hearts, they believe that Japanese assistance would mean merely the replacement of the Dutch flag by that of the rising sun, they would regard it as useless to run the risk of allying with Japan." Still, although the threat of force was to be avoided, "the southern advance, in time, will become a matter of life and death in our national policy." For the present, the official propagandists elected to hawk the southern advance "as the one vista of hope" in the "gloomy domestic and foreign situation confronting the empire."

The futile discussions with the Dutch soon overcast this vista of hope. The sale of raw material declined monthly, almost in direct ratio to the expansion of the Amercian navy; the American fleet remained anchored at Pearl Harbor; and the Roosevelt administration transparently sustained Dutch resistance. This pressure on Japan became, within the Supreme Command, "an encirclement" of Japan, and control over the Indies, Indochina, and Thailand became "requisites for self-defense and self-existence."[38] By April, the chiefs of staff agreed that Japan should

[37] *Ibid.* Quote is from the appendix which is a policy draft dated December 12.

[38] USDAOMH, *Far East History Source File,* "Important National Policy Decisions," Appendix VIII. Also, *Nihon gaikō . . . , op. cit.,* II, 495-496.

go to war "when the encirclement of Japan by the United States, alone or in alliance with Great Britain, the Netherlands, and China becomes so restrictive that the situation becomes intolerable from the standpoint of national defense."[39] Clearly, the nation was running against the clock of American armament production, a fact that provoked bitter assessments of American policy. The central problem, to some officials, was the influence exerted by "fanatical crusaders" like Secretary Cordell Hull, who divided the world between "Christians and heathen nations."[40] From this viewpoint, Japan's plight was blamed on "an obstreperous State Department which holds firmly opinionated ideas about international diplomacy. It has now reached the point presumably whereby no nation should make any move without the prior approval of the State Department." The American strategy was plain enough: first, slowly close off the supply of strategic materials; second, gain naval superiority; and, third, force Japan out of China and Manchuria. "Success of the American policy would compel Japan, as in the past, to kowtow to the United States. With the sentinel of the Far East in economic chains, the Orient would once again become the playground of Western economic imperialists." This thought was almost unbearable. Better to resort to arms on behalf of the resources of Southeast Asia because, if successful, Japan would then be able to translate economic power "into political and social power, as has been done in the past by Western nations. Racial equality would thus become an established fact."

With this sentiment, Japan's policies became almost psychotic. "Life and death," "racial equality," "encirclement," and "strangulation" provided a set of slogans which increasingly rationalized the southern policy in terms of "national" considerations which prismed international politics through a dangerously particularistic filter. The will to act, however, did not materialize until Germany's invasion of the Soviet Union. With the outbreak of this conflict, Foreign Minister Matsuoka and General Tanaka Shinichi, Operations Chief of the general staff, ardently lobbied for a northward strike to exterminate the Soviet Bear. This viewpoint was repeatedly overruled, and Matsuoka was removed from his portfolio. The acrimony of this debate, however, was

[39] *Ibid.*
[40] DTBCOC, *Kaigunshō chōsaka kaichō kenkyū shiryō (toku) A dai yongō,* "Beikoku sansen o chūshin to suru gaikō tembō," February 22, 1941.

such that the army general staff demanded a "clear-cut resolution for war with England and the United States" or an "acceptance" of the northern campaign.[41] In late June, Admiral Nagano,
the naval Chief of Staff, finally affirmed his commitment to the
southern policy, including the resolution for hostilities. Officially,
on July 2, the government decided that "regardless of whatever
changes may occur in the world situation, Japan will adhere to
the established policy of creating a Greater Co-Prosperity
Sphere."[42] The southern region became indispensable "for self-
existence and self-defense" and "to attain this objective, we will
not hesitate to engage in war with England and the United
States." We should note that this decision antedated the oil embargo on Japan and that it was adopted with a conscious realization that an embargo might be a counter-move to Japan's advance in South Indo-China. In different words, the Vinson-Stark
naval programs, combined with the demand for a fish-or-cut-bait
decision on the southern policy, pushed the Supreme Command
and the government into the resolution for war.

The oil embargo confirmed American willingness to risk war
over the resources of Southeast Asia. "The government," noted
former Foreign Minister Arita Hachirō, "wants, on the one hand,
a readjustment of relations with the United States. . . . On the
other hand, it is dominated by the wish to spread its economic
and other influences into the southern region upon the construction of the Greater East Asia Co-Prosperity Sphere. This is a contradictory policy."[43] Responding to Arita's observation, Premier
Konoe confessed, "I quite agree with what you say."[44] The contradiction persisted and, on September 6, the government decided to prepare for war and to wage peace negotiations. This
famous Imperial Conference set the deadline for negotiations as
early October, after which time the government would go to
war.[45] This decision was pegged to the southern policy, not simply or primarily to the China Incident. Access to the resources
of the Indies and a freezing of the level of American forces in
the Pacific were basic conditions. They were, in fact, the central

[41] *Nihon gaikō . . . , op. cit.*, II, 531-532.
[42] *Ibid.*
[43] Hayashi Shigeru, *Taiheiyō sensō* (Tokyo, 1967), p. 226.
[44] *Ibid.*, p. 227.
[45] USDAOMH, *Japanese Monograph 147* (rev. ed., 1964), appendices 3
& 4.

reasons for the southern policy. Japan's naval leaders could not tolerate the expansion of American power, even though they understood, better than anyone else, that Japan could not defeat the United States. The best Admiral Nagano offered the Emperor was the "foundation for a long war" and the belief that this fate was better than the alternative of deference to American superiority. In Nagano's words, "The government has decided that if there were no war, the fate of the nation was sealed. Even if there is war, the country may be ruined. Nevertheless, a nation which does not fight in this plight has lost its spirit and it is already a doomed nation."[46] If the nation's fate was not literally at stake, Japan's existing naval superiority—the sine qua non for the nation's continental policy since 1931—was. This persuaded the naval authorities in favor of war. Others were seduced by the quest for "self-sufficiency," for "racial equality," and for the "sacred" China policy.

The fatalistic tone of Nagano's thoughts found echoes at other levels. The task force on "ideology" organized by the Naval Ministry, for example, voiced its dismay with the "contradictions" contained within the concepts *hakko ichiu* ("eight corners of the world under one roof," or "universal peace") and the "benevolence" of the Imperial Rule as the guiding principles of the Co-Prosperity Sphere.[47] These terms seemed limited to a Japanese audience. "Don't we have," asked one naval officer, "any 'slogan' comparable with the universality of America's 'democracy'?" The question was nettlesome. One advisor suggested a redefinition of *hakko ichiu* to mean "universal brotherhood," but soon all agreed that "although we say 'universal brotherhood,' it probably means that we are equal to the Caucasians but, to the peoples of Asia, we act as their leader." With some resignation, the naval advisors branded *hakko ichiu* "not for export," but, domestically, it seemed capable of "instilling our people with self-confidence." Following the September 6 decision, the naval advisors on intellectual matters again thrashed out the problem of ideological warfare and again they lamented that "the traditional chauvinism of the National Learning School" was characteristic of the nation's view of *hakko ichiu*. "We must," they insisted, "have a slo-

[46] Nakayama Masai, *Ichi gunkokushugisha no chokugen* (Tokyo, 1956), p. 180.

[47] DTBCOC, *Kaigun kenkyū shizai F dai ni go*, Watsuji Tetsurō, "Shisō kokubō ni tsuite," June 27, 1941.

gan which possesses both scholarly substance and popular appeal." The need, however, was not the father of the answer. In fact, the task force was given the duty of "working out concrete ideological measures to be incorporated in explanations of the Imperial declaration of war." This assignment was slanted to the domestic audience—that is, "It is to be hoped that we can discover some ideological means which will persuade the people to devote themselves willingly to the national course [of war]."

By early October, the fatalistic sense of an inevitable and terrifying confrontation with the United States had become so pronounced that questions about national objectives were openly ventilated. In a discussion of national objectives and foreign policy, for example, one academic advisor to the Naval Ministry confessed his perplexity and apprehension as follows: "I would like the concept of the Greater Asian Co-Prosperity Sphere clarified here and now. Although I have read tons of articles about it, I have not been able to grasp its meaning because the theory is full of contradictions. . . . The Greater Asian Co-Prosperity Sphere is not a reality, nor is it capable of becoming so. We are deceiving the world."[48] Such expressions may have alleviated some of the tension accompanying the movement toward war with the United States. Nonetheless, the resolution for war remained operative and, by November, the Naval Ministry was soliciting a series of position papers which could provide reasons for a declaration of war on the Anglo-American powers. In this context, the metaphor of life and death seemed most appropriate. As Professor Yabe Teiji put it in early September, "It must be presented to the people as a matter of life and death, not in terms of the New Asian Order."[49] The validity of his logic hinged in part on the rationale of a preventive war and on the sense of "encirclement" by the Western nations.

Although the drift toward war was undeniable, the government tried to avert open conflict. In September and October, Prince Konoe grasped at the lure of a summit conference with Roosevelt and, when it was withdrawn, Konoe resigned, unwilling to bear the responsibility for war. His successor, General Tōjō, stoically accepted the responsibility; he also mobilized one

[48] DTBCOC, *Gaikō Kenkyūkai*, Minutes of the October 7 meeting of this group.
[49] DTBCOC, *Sōgō Kenkyūkai*, Minutes of the session held on September 19, 1941.

last diplomatic overture. This, as is well known, was the "Plan A" and "Plan B" set of terms for a peaceful resolution of Japanese-American relations. Because of American preoccupation with China, these last-minute discussions have been seen as a shift in Japan's policy away from the southern advance and back to the earlier attitude toward China. Cordell Hull's memo, which ingenuously included the demand that Japan withdraw from China and Manchuria, tended to reinforce the conviction that the two nations were going to war over China. In one sense, this was true, as Tōjō's government was talking about a detente confirming, for the present time, Japan's China policy—that is, a tacit acceptance of Wang Ching-wei's regime. Still, the base point of Plan A and Plan B was the guarantee of complete access to the Dutch East Indies. Without this proviso, war was inescapable, irrespective of any accommodation over China. By rejecting both basic conditions—China and the Indies—Hull's memo unified the cabinet and the Supreme Command behind the decision for war. The American insistence on Japan's withdrawal from Manchuria and China made it crystal clear that the United States, by force or by diplomacy, was resolved to set aside the foreign policy which Japan had pursued since 1931. To the Americans, this seemed both legal and moral, a reaffirmation of the Kellogg-Briand Pact and the Nine Power Treaty. To the Japanese leaders, Hull's principles signified American determination to reduce Japan to a second-class power, to restore the *status quo ante* of 1930, and to maintain, under the mantle of international justice, the superiority of the Occidental nations over Southeast Asia, China, and Japan.

These sentiments were articulated in the public documents of Imperial Japan. On December 7th, the Japanese note to the American government observed, among other things: "It is a fact of history that the countries of East Asia for the past hundred years or more have been compelled to observe the *status quo* under the Anglo-American policy of imperialistic exploitation and to sacrifice themselves to the prosperity of the[se] two nations. The Japanese government cannot tolerate the perpetuation of such a condition."[50] The same day, in Japan, the Imperial Rescript on the war interpreted the "trend of affairs" in bleak

[50] United States Department of State, *Papers Relating to the Foreign Relations of the United States, Japan, 1931-1941* (Washington, D.C., 1943), II, 786.

terms: "Our Empire, for its existence and self-defense, has no alternative recourse but to appeal to arms and to crush every obstacle in its path."[51] The existence of the Empire had been fused with the vision of the Asian Co-Prosperity Sphere, a concept which had crystallized less than eighteen months earlier during the euphoria of Hitler's sweep through Western Europe.

Without recapitulating the thematic structure of this paper, and without considering the pertinence of European, Soviet, and American diplomacy to Japan's foreign policies of the 1930's, some simple reflections seem proper. First, Japan was a major actor, or initiator, in Asian affairs, and this role was possible, in large measure, because of American disarmament policies of the 1920's. By allowing Japan to gain a commanding naval presence in the western Pacific, the American government had sacrificed effective constraints on Japanese policy. Second, Japan's thrust into Manchuria was not the act of a renegade or feudalistic government. Japan, at that time, was the first of the colonial powers in Asia to face the simultaneous challenges of a viable nationalism in an area of major colonial investment and interests, of Soviet military power, and of the linkage among the Comintern, communism (Lenin's theory of imperialism), and a nationalist movement directed against colonial and semi-colonial privileges. Its response—Manchukuo—ultimately proved futile. But, then, the European powers who endorsed the "nonrecognition" doctrine in the League would later discover the futility of their maneuvers to retain their colonial and imperialistic advantages. Manchukuo, in brief, may have been a tragic mistake, a stupid mistake, but Japan was not the only nation that would seek to promote its own security and well-being by creating "client" states and by trying to crush nationalistic opposition by force. Third, the hubris, the drive for equality with the Occidental powers, which distinguished Japan's diplomacy of the 1930's, was not peculiar to that decade. This illusive search for "equality" began with Perry's Black Ships and, in several respects, the notion of an Asian bloc of nations—the Co-Prosperity Sphere—was a reification of the closed-door policy of Tokugawa Japan; Japan was to be the modern day *bakufu*, or military-civil leader; and

[51] Robert Butow, *Tojo and the Coming of the War* (Princeton, N.J., 1961), p. 409.

the member-nations were to be outer retainers, paying political and economic homage to Japan in return for regional security and economic well-being.

The New Asian Order was self-serving. However persuasive it may have been within Japanese society, this concept manifestly misconstrued or misunderstood the phenomenon of nationalism and the limitations of national power. Reassessing Japan's policies in 1946, Tokutomi Iichiro conceded two propositions.[52] Japan's "folly" had been unsurpassed. Westerners could validly "laugh and jeer" at Japan's inept diplomacy and stupid policies. Not even Hiroshima and Nagasaki, however, had compromised Tokutomi's conviction that Japan had gone to war for its survival and its self-respect. The war, in his eyes, had been "an explosion of dissatisfaction and discontent with the unfair treatment the world powers accorded to Japan as an independent state." Clio, we may suspect, will subsequently credit this sentiment in her recitation of the Pacific War. Japan was not the only Asian nation to become possessed by a sense of "encirclement," nor was it to be the only Asian power to articulate a diplomacy based upon racism and economic weakness. Nor was it the only Asian nation to be an "outcast" from the community of nations and a popular symbol of aggression and violence. As importantly, if Clio were to glance at the present scene, it is reasonable to assume she would observe that Japanese nationalism is still powered by the passion for "equality" with the Occidental powers.

This compulsion for equality is as volatile today as it was forty years ago. Despite ideological differences, the dominant Western powers are both heirs to European culture and civilization; they are both primarily Caucasian nations; and both have been former antagonists of Imperial Japan. It is possible that Japan, confronted with these considerations, may again formulate its sense of cultural identity and national purpose in terms of an Asian setting, with a modern version of the tarnished Co-Prosperity Sphere. To the extent this is possible, the historians of prewar Japan must recognize that the roots of the New Asian Order lie deep in the psyche of Japanese nationalism, in the drive to be free and independent of the dictates of the major Occidental powers. Conceivably, Asian historians may eventually share Hayashi Fusao's view that the Pacific War was one phase of an

---

[52] IMTFE, *Defence Document* 632 [Tokutomi deposition, February 20, 1947].

Asian Hundred Years' War to drive out the Occidental invader.[53] In any case, "racial equality" will have many permutations in Asian affairs and the mission of building a New Asian Order may be considered as one of its distinctive permutations.

[53] *Daitōa sensō kōteiron* (Tokyo, 1964-1965, 2 vol.).

The Japanese Economy, 1911-1930:
Concentration, Conflicts, and Crises

$\mathbf{D}$URING THE past two decades, while Western students of the Japanese economy have been examining Japan's two success stories—the Meiji period, to discover how an Asian nation successfully embarked on modern economic growth, and the post-1945 years to explain the "miraculous" recovery and rapid growth—the Taishō and the early Shōwa periods remained little examined. There are several obvious reasons for this neglect. The most important among them undoubtedly has been economists' concern (preoccupation?) with "economic development." It thus was natural for the Taishō period[1] to yield the spotlight to the more dramatic events of the Meiji years and the rapid postwar growth. Second, the Taishō period is difficult to analyze. It includes: the First World War and its massive and pervasive impact; the nationwide Rice Riots of August, 1918; the Great Kantō earthquake of 1923, which literally leveled Tokyo; the bank-runs of 1927; increasing labor unrest; and increasingly visible, far-reaching effects of the colonialization of Taiwan and Korea on the domestic economy. These are what economists call "exogenous" factors which bedevil researchers attempting to analyze the period with the more commonly used theoretical apparatus and tools of analysis. In an examination of the Taishō period, however, those exogenous factors are dominant elements which must be viewed as the principal forces of the Taishō economy.

Another difficulty of an entirely different nature is the lack of useful Japanese sources from which a Western student can begin his investigation. Unlike the well-researched Meiji period and the extensively analyzed postwar years, much of the available Japanese literature on the Taishō economy is patently Marxist or was written by *keizai hyōronka*, journalists specializing in economic matters.[2] We should perhaps add as yet another difficulty

---

[1] Throughout this chapter, the phrase "Taishō period" refers to the period between 1911 and the early Shōwa years before the Depression.

[2] Those Japanese works which merit close attention are not many. Al-

the complex interactions between multifaceted, swiftly changing socio-political configurations and the rapid transformation of the economy during this relatively brief period. Economists should be conscious of these interactions as the exogenous factors if they hope to comprehend the period fully.

These difficulties and the relative neglect of the period, however, are challenges to the students of the Japanese economy. The importance of the Taishō period in its own right and as a period crucial to the better understanding of the Meiji years and the pre- and postwar Shōwa years requires no emphasis. The Taishō period, after all, is an important segment of the hundred years of Japan's industrialization.

The main purpose of this chapter is to shed light on an aspect of the Taishō economy as a part of a concerted effort now under way to rectify the neglect this period has suffered. The aspect to be examined could be called oligopolization of product and capital markets, or the rise of zaibatsu power and its implications. As will be shown, along with the dramatic increase in industrial output during the First World War and the prolonged recession of the 1920's, the Japanese economy underwent rapid oligopolization and cartelization in its industrial and capital markets. And it was during this period that the dual structure, with all its implications, emerged.[3] To put it another way, it was during the Taishō period that the zaibatsu acquired all the attributes usually associated with this term and a highly skewed distribution of economic power became an ingrained characteristic of the Japanese economy.[4]

---

though most are Marxist in basic outlook, the following are the better economic histories of the period. Takahashi Kamekichi, *Meiji-Taishō sangyō hattatsu shi* (Tokyo, 1929); M. Kajinishi, T. Ōuchi, K. Ōshima and T. Katō, *Nihon ni okeru shihonshugi no hattatsu,* 2 vols. (Tokyo, 1951); M. Kajinishi, *Shōwa keizaishi* (Tokyo, 1951); Tsuchiya Takao, *Zoku Nihon keizaishi gaiyō* (Tokyo, 1939); Oshima Kiyoshi, *Kyōkōshi* (Tokyo, 1949); Takahashi Kamekichi, *Nihon kinyū ron* (Tokyo, 1931); and Tōyōkeizai Shimpōsha (ed.), *Kinyū 60 nenshi* (Tokyo, 1924).

[3] An excellent discussion of dual structure is found in Watanabe Tsunehiko, "Industrialization, Technological Progress, and Dual Structure" in L. Klein and K. Ohkawa (eds.), *Economic Growth, the Japanese Experience since the Meiji Era* (New Haven, Conn., 1968), pp. 111-134.

[4] The two dominant characteristics of zaibatsu are: (1) well-knit, tightly controlled relationships among the affiliated firms by means of holding companies, interlocking directorships, and mutual stockholdings; and (2) ex-

Questions to be asked then are: in the context of Japanese economic growth, how should the rapid concentration of economic power and the emergence of a dual structure be evaluated? Why and how did the zaibatsu gain such power during the period? What were the implications of this increased concentration of economic power on the course of Japanese economic growth during the Shōwa years? Answers to these questions are no less important in understanding the growth of the Japanese economy than are accurate evaluations of increases in productivity, technological changes, and accumulation of capital during the period.

However, before proceeding to attempt to answer these questions, let us briefly survey the major economic features of the period as these features are directly relevant to our examination and will be helpful in providing a basic background for understanding the rapidly evolving Taishō economy. The remainder of the chapter will present the facts of economic concentration, the increasingly dominant but changing roles of zaibatsu and their implications for the economy.

On the strength of forces gathered during the initial period of modern economic growth, 1890-1905, and mostly due to the First World War boom, Japan became a full-fledged industrial nation during the Taishō period.[5] The Japanese economy, seen on the eve of the Manchurian invasion in 1931, was significantly different from that found after the recession following the Russo-Japanese War. During the decade 1910-1920, the real net domestic product grew by 61.5 per cent. The figure declined to 33.4 per cent during the following recession-ridden decade of the 1920's.[6] The Ohkawa estimate of GNP stands at 13,652 million

---

tremely great financial power in the form of commercial bank credit, which is used as the central leverage to extend control in all industries. For elaboration of these characteristics and the other attributes and activities of the zaibatsu, see my "Zaibatsu, Prewar, and Zaibatsu, Postwar," *The Journal of Asian Studies*, xxiii (August, 1964), 539-554.

[5] H. Rosovsky and K. Ohkawa, "A Century of Japanese Economic Growth" in W. W. Lockwood (ed.), *The State and Economic Enterprise in Japan* (Princeton, N.J., 1965), pp. 77-83.

[6] Hugh T. Patrick, "Japanese Government Macro-Policy: Failure in the 1920's, Success (of a Sort) in the 1930's," Yale Growth Center Discussion Paper, No. 50, p. 2.

yen in 1925, the last year of Taishō, and at 10,583 million yen in 1931, compared to 4,148 million yen in 1912.[7]

The index of real output of mining and manufacturing increased from 100 in 1909 to 140.2 in 1914, 276.1 in 1919, 293.6 in 1924 and 435.4 in 1929.[8] The number of industrial factories nearly doubled during the period and employment quadrupled in heavy and chemical industries and tripled in light industry. The index of the total firm capital rose rapidly from 100 in 1909 to 160.9 in 1914, and jumped to 487.0 in 1919 and to 895.0 in 1924. The index in 1929 was an amazing 1,029.0.[9] By any measure, the sharp increase of industrial output was the most dominant feature of the Taishō period.

Japan's international trade increased sharply during the Taishō period, as seen in Table 1. Thanks to the First World War, Japan

TABLE 1

Indexes of Export and Import, 1911-1925

(1911 = 100)

	1911	*1913*	*1915*	*1917*	*1919*	*1921*	*1923*	*1925*
Export	100.0	141.4	158.3	358.3	469.1	289.1	323.7	515.3
Import	100.0	142.0	103.6	201.6	423.0	314.2	385.8	500.7

Source: Bank of Japan, *Hundred-Year Statistics of the Japanese Economy* (Tokyo, Bank of Japan, 1966)

became, for the first time and practically overnight, a major supplier of industrial goods in the world. This unexpected good fortune made Japan, which was a debtor nation of 1.1 billion yen at the end of 1914, a creditor nation of 2.77 billion yen by the beginning of 1920.[10] Table 2 tells the story of this unusual transition.

However, as seen in gold flows and balance held abroad, the strong trade balance accumulated during the war quickly dissipated following the end of the hostilities in Europe. The main cause of this dissipation was the unfavorable terms of trade

[7] K. Ohkawa, *et al.*, *The Growth Rate of the Japanese Economy Since 1878* (Tokyo, 1957), pp. 130, 247.

[8] The output index in T. Ouchi's *Nihon keizai ron* (Tokyo, 1962), p. 168, was deflated by the wholesale index of the Bank of Japan, in *Hundred Year Statistics of the Japanese Economy* (Tokyo, 1966), p. 76.

[9] Ouchi, *Nihon keizai ron*, p. 168.

[10] M. Kajinishi, *Zoku Nihon shihonshugi hattatsu shi* (Tokyo, 1957), p. 8.

TABLE 2

Summary Balance of Payments of the Japanese Empire[a]
(in millions of yen)

I. Balance on	1908-1913	1914-1919	1920	1921	1922	1923
Current Account[b]	—1142.4	3035.0	— 79.3	—246.2	—181.5	—447.9
1. Trade Balance	— 706.5	1197.5	—500.1	—442.0	—336.1	—617.7
2. Invisible Balance	— 435.9	1837.5	420.8	195.8	154.6	169.8
II. Changes in Foreign Exchange Reserves[c]	167.7	1700.7	—126.7	— 74.7	—238.5	—171.1
3. Gold Flows	— 59.7	603.8	407.5	132.5	1.1	— 0.1
4. Balance Held Abroad	227.4	1096.9	—280.8	—207.2	—239.6	—171.0

[a] Japan Proper, Taiwan, Korea, South Sea Mandated Islands.
[b] Minus indicates net inflow.
[c] Minus indicates net decrease of reserves and outflow of gold.

Source: Taken from Hugh T. Patrick, *Japanese Government Macro-Policy: Failure in the 1920's, Success (of a Sort) in the 1930's*, Yale Growth Center Discussion Paper No. 50. (April 1968.) p. 27.

which confronted Japan at the end of the war. As long as the war lasted, Japanese goods and services (shipping) could be sold at inflated prices, but these favorable terms of trade, which fluctuated between 82.3 (1918) and 99.9 (1919) on the basis of 1913 = 100, stood in 1921 at a high of 142.0 and even as late as 1929 the index still stood at an uncomfortable 106.6.[11] Roughly speaking, this was due to (a) the rapid inflation caused by the war; (b) a rise in the costs of production due to excess capacity and an increased nominal wage; multiplication of factories which were inefficient by international standards of peacetime; and (c) various devaluation measures undertaken by European nations. These facts are crucial for our later analysis. In fact, because of them, the latter half of the Taishō period can be characterized as a period of conscious deflation and of the rationalization of productive capacities under the strong guidance of the government seeking to stave off the deteriorating balance in international trade.

While the war lasted, the agricultural sector enjoyed its favorable effects—high prices and rising income—but it then sank into the long "agricultural stagnation" of the 1920's. Increases in

[11] Patrick, "Japanese Government Macro-Policy . . . ," 33 (see Table 2).

prices during the war were sharp because of increased demand and a reduction in imports of rice caused by tie-ups of ocean-going bottoms used for exports. The price of rice in 1920 stood at 376 compared to the 1900 base of 100, that of silk at 278, soy beans at 285, and wheat at 272.[12] Although reliable agricultural income data are difficult to obtain, Minami has estimated that the daily wage in agriculture rose from .73 yen in 1910 to .83 yen in 1915 and to 1.18 yen in 1920, all expressed in 1934-1936 prices.[13] The productivity of agriculture also rose visibly as a result of the increased use of fertilizer, improved seed, and new equipment of various types.[14]

The agricultural sector, however, went into a long slump during the 1920's. Agricultural income continued to decline from the peak of 1920 and was not to return to that level until after the end of the Second World War.[15] There were several reasons for this. The most significant was the importation of rice from Korea and Taiwan. Rice imports, which amounted to about 300,000 tons at the outbreak of the war, increased to 456,586 tons in 1922, and were as high as 771,086 tons in 1925.[16] Most of the rice came from Korea, where the price was approximately 10 per cent below the domestic price throughout the 1920's.[17]

The recession in the industrial sector, of course, contributed to the farmers' woes. Increasing unemployment in industry meant that the excess farm population could not be absorbed, at least for the time being. While labor productivity was rising in the agricultural sector, the total labor force in agriculture remained essentially stable at 14,235,000 persons in 1920, 14,103,000 in 1925, and 14,192,000 in 1930.[18] The rate of exodus from the agri-

---

[12] Kajinishi, *Zoku Nihon . . .* , p. 75.

[13] Minami Ryoshin, "The Turning Point in the Japanese Economy," Yale Growth Discussion Paper No. 2 (April, 1967), 18.

[14] For a detailed discussion, see Y. Hayami and S. Yamada, "Technological Progress in Agriculture," in L. Klein and K. Ohkawa (eds.), *Economic Growth*, pp. 135-161.

[15] Minami, "The Turning Point . . . ," p. 18.

[16] The Bank of Japan, *Hundred-Year Statistics*, pp. 287-288.

[17] The Ministry of Agriculture and Forestry, *Beikoku yōran* (Tokyo, 1935). The data in this source show that rice imported from Korea was usually more than twice the amount imported from Taiwan except in 1925. For comparisons of prices of domestic and Korean rice, see M. Kajinishi, *et al.*, *Nihon shihonshugi no botsuraku: I* (Tokyo, 1960), p. 253.

[18] Kajinishi, *et al.*, *ibid.*, p. 255.

cultural sector declined from 1.21 per cent of the total labor force in agriculture to .89 per cent during the 1921-1925 period and .85 during the 1925-1930 period.[19] There were visible signs of increasing concentration of land distribution, small to middle-sized farmers suffered disguised unemployment and falling real income in spite of their efforts to commercialize agriculture.[20] Prices of agricultural products tended to lag behind the general price level. As seen in Table 3, the ratio of agricultural prices to

TABLE 3

Ratio of Agricultural Prices to General Price Level

Year	1920	1921	1922	1923	1924	1925	1926	1927
Prices of all goods	110.0	85.1	82.9	84.1	87.4	85.5	79.5	72.0
Agricultural prices	91.5	70.3	81.0	85.5	84.4	90.6	78.6	69.3
Ratio	83.2	82.5	97.8	89.7	96.7	106.1	99.0	96.3

Source: M. Kajinishi, *et al.*, *Nihon shihonshugi no botsuraku* (Tokyo, 1960), I, 251.

the general price level remained below 100 during the 1920's, except for 1925. The sample budget study of farm households (Table 4) indicates the declining living standards of farmers during the 1920's.

Depressed conditions in the agricultural sector resulted in a rapidly spreading organized movement of small-to-medium tenants against landlords. The movement began with group petitions by tenants to landlords for rent reduction in 1921 and became a full-fledged movement of farmers involving non-payment of rents and opposition to the curtailment of tenancy for non-payment of rents. The number of cases of various group activities engaged in by tenants against landlords exceeded 2,700 cases by 1926, and in April of that year the left-wing Japan Farmers' Party

[19] Minami, "The Turning Point . . . ," p. 29.

[20] In 1908, 46.2 per cent of all agricultural households possessed less than five *tan*, but this had increased to 49.6 per cent by 1927. On the other hand, households owning 5-10 *tan* declined from 26.1 to 24.5 per cent of the total during the same period. The giant landholders owning more than 500 *tan* increased from 2,600 to 4,000 also during the same period. For these data and descriptions of the activities described in the text, see Kajinishi, *A Revised History*, pp. 84-89. Kajinishi, *et al.*, p. 263, observed that: "As the pressure of recession mounted on such basic products as rice and cocoon-raising, farmers had to rely increasingly on diversification in their attempts to maintain the income level."

Yamamura

TABLE 4

Farm Budgets, 1921-1927 (yen)

	Net Income from Farming and Subsidiary Earning	Farm Family Expenditures	Outstanding Debt
Owner Cultivators			
1921	1,138	1,184	469
1922	912	1,156	242
1923	1,058	1,140	63
1924	1,358	1,392	(114)*
1925	1,396	1,530	204
1926	1,174	1,383	605
1927	1,095	1,320	545
Tenants			
1921	597	642	190
1922	529	715	170
1923	682	727	60
1924	724	821	38
1925	965	890	(28)*
1926	707	928	387
1927	711	885	426

*These are savings.

Source: The Ministry of Agriculture and Forestry, *Wagakuni nōka keizai no hensen ni kansuru shiryō* as quoted in M. Kajinishi, *Zoku Nihon shihonshugi hattatsushi* (Tokyo, 1957), p. 84.

(*Nihon Nōmintō*) was organized uniting several growing farmers' organizations.[21]

Labor during the Taishō period shared little of the prosperity of the war boom and showed none during the prolonged recession of the 1920's. Although no authoritative index for real wage is available for the period before 1926, the consensus seems to be that real wages failed to rise even during the height of the World War I boom. One source puts the index of real wage of factory workers at 95 in 1916, 83 in 1917, 78 in 1918, 94 in 1919, with 1912 equal to 100.[22] If we observe the sample real wage by occupation, they are as shown in Table 5.

We note that real wage indeed declined during the prosperous years of the First World War boom due to the sharp increase in

[21] Kajinishi, *Zoku Nihon . . .*, p. 105.
[22] Sekine Etsuro's data cited in Kajinishi, *ibid.*, p. 94.

306

TABLE 5

Index of Real Daily Earnings by Occupation
1911-1926, 1911 = 100*

Year	Carpenter	Day Worker (Male)	Silk Reeling (Female)	Blacksmith	Tailor
1911	100.0	100.0	100.0	100.0	100.0
1912	99.0	97.8	115.6	95.7	98.9
1913	100.0	99.3	103.6	98.3	97.6
1914	102.4	98.8	115.0	104.3	97.6
1915	105.4	95.9	107.3	96.2	96.4
1916	82.6	82.1	83.3	86.4	82.6
1917	74.2	79.6	77.0	83.4	73.2
1918	76.7	92.9	70.1	81.8	69.7
1919	88.7	102.1	83.9	95.3	73.9
1920	114.9	130.7	107.7	112.1	95.4
1921	150.4	167.2	145.7	143.2	144.8
1922	168.9	186.4	163.6	147.8	143.9
1923	170.8	183.3	147.8	151.8	144.8
1924	170.1	176.1	146.1	142.2	148.4
1925	167.9	177.8	151.0	149.4	139.2
1926	185.6	193.8	172.4	169.4	150.2

*Lacking more comprehensive and reliable data, these indexes are presented merely to convey general patterns of changes. To obtain the index, daily nominal earnings were deflated by the wholesale price index compiled by the Bank of Japan. This can, during an inflation, overstate real wages, but no reliable consumer index for the entire nation is available for the period.

Source: Bank of Japan, *Hundred-Year Statistics*, pp. 73, 76.

prices. Real wages rose during the 1920's, but these indexes must be considered against backgrounds of rapidly rising unemployment and falling real cash earnings of workers at private factories, as shown in Table 6, during the period between the late Taishō years and the early Shōwa years.

Perhaps a more meaningful way to evaluate these changes is to observe that the category of payment classified as "payment of employees" rose from 100 in 1920 to 114.1 in 1925 and 11.2 in 1929, while GNP grew from 100, to 137.4 then to 143.1 during the same period.[23] Reflecting this prolonged recession, unemploy-

[23] The Bank of Japan, *Hundred-Year Statistics*, p. 31. Other categories of distributed personal income are proprietors' income and income for agriculture and forestry.

ment, and stagnant real cash earnings, Japan witnessed a sharp acceleration in the amount of labor unrest after 1917 as seen in Table 7.

TABLE 6

Indexes for Number of Workers Employed and
Worker Real Cash Earnings at Private Factories
(1926-1944)

	Number of Workers Employed			Real Cash Earnings		
Year	Total	Male	Female	Total	Male	Female
1926	100.0	100.0	100.0	100.0	100.0	100.0
1927	94.8	97.7	92.0	102.1	101.2	99.4
1928	90.4	97.2	83.8	105.3	103.3	99.8
1929	91.1	98.6	83.8	103.9	102.6	96.4
1930	82.0	91.3	73.0	98.7	97.3	87.4
1931	74.4	81.0	68.0	90.7	92.0	77.4
1932	74.7	79.0	70.6	88.1	92.7	70.9
1933	81.9	87.0	76.8	89.2	95.1	68.4
1934	91.3	98.4	84.3	91.2	96.3	67.3
1935	99.9	108.6	91.4	91.1	95.4	66.5

Source: Bank of Japan, *Hundred-Year Statistics*, p. 74.

TABLE 7

Number of Strikes and Factory Workers Involved
1914-1923

Year	1914	1915	1916	1917	1918	1919	1920	1921	1922	1923
Cases	50	64	108	378	417	497	282	246	250	270
Involved (1000)	7.9	7.9	8.9	57.3	66.5	63.1	36.4	58.2	41.5	36.3

Source: From the annual volumes of *Teikoku tōkeinenkan*

The government began to repress the strikes in 1920 and the leadership of an increasing number of technically illegal labor unions moved toward the left in political ideology.[24] The first Factory Act, enacted in 1911, was prevented from coming into effect until 1916 by the determined political maneuverings of employers. The act excluded all workers employed in establish-

[24] For a detailed discussion, see Kajinishi, *et al.*, *Nihon shihonshugi* . . . , pp. 225-246. The Japanese Communist Party was organized in 1922.

ments employing fewer than 5 persons, and it was relatively easy to evade the application by various means. Thus, as late as in 1925, only about 50 per cent of the labor force came under the protection of the law. Although the act did not limit the number of working hours for males, it prevented females and those under 16 years of age from working in excess of 12 hours per day. Even this, the only potentially meaningful provision, lost much of its effectiveness since the law provided that employers could extend the legal maximum by two hours during the first fifteen years following its enactment.[25]

One event closely connected with rising prices and stagnant-to-falling real wage was the nation-wide Rice Riots which occurred in August, 1918. When rice prices soared from 23.78 yen (per *koku*) in January to 31.29 yen in July and then to 41.06 yen in August, wage earners, especially low-wage earners who had been faced with increasing difficulties, finally took to looting and burning rice warehouses and vandalizing the homes of rice merchants.[26] This sharp increase in price was caused by the speculation of rice dealers, who hoped for an increase in rice prices during the summer because of the anticipated expedition of Japanese troops to Russia and by sharply reduced imports of rice due to a sudden shortage in ocean-going bottoms. The riots took place in 33 cities and 201 towns and villages. In several instances, the army had to be called out to quell the disturbances. One estimate placed the number of individuals involved at 700,000, and in fact over 6,000 persons were indicted.[27] By 1930, all these increasingly politically oriented activities by wage-earners and farmers became targets of vigorous suppression.[28]

[25] Kajinishi, *Zoku Nihon* . . . , pp. 89-90. Hazama Hiroshi, *Nihon rōmu-kanrishi kenkyū* (Tokyo, 1964), p. 302.

[26] Kajinishi, *Zoku Nihon* . . . , p. 99.

[27] *Ibid.*, pp. 99-104. A detailed discussion, supplemented with ample data, on the Rice Riots is found in Yoshinaga Mitsusaza, *Iwayuru komesōdō no kenkyū*, The Ministry of Justice, Research Material on Ideology series, No. 51, 1939.

[28] There are several good histories on farmer-labor movements. The following two sources are especially useful. Ōkōchi Kazuo, *Nihon shihonshugi to rōdō mondai* (Tokyo, 1947) and Arahata Kanson, *Nihon shakaishugi undō shi* (Tokyo, 1949). A very detailed account of the repression of labor movements is found in Suehiro Gentarō, *Nihon rōdō kumiai undō shi* (Tokyo, 1951), pp. 54-69.

During the Taishō period, as the economy underwent the First World War boom and then a long recession, the dual structure emerged to stay. By 1929, as is seen in Table 8, the smallest firms

TABLE 8

Number of Firms and Capital, 1909-1929
(Firms classified by amount of capital)

Year	Less than 100,000 yen		100,000- 500,000 yen		500,000- 1 million yen	
	No. of firms (%)	Capital (%)	No. of firms (%)	Capital (%)	No. of firms (%)	Capital (%)
1909	9,724 (84.2)	163 (11.8)	1,377 (11.8)	255 (18.7)	233 (2.2)	149 (10.9)
1914	14,351 (85.1)	232 (11.3)	1,841 (10.9)	343 (16.6)	308 (1.8)	194 (9.4)
1919	17,742 (67.5)	270 (4.5)	5,007 (19.1)	513 (8.6)	1,552 (5.9)	451 (7.5)
1924	20,901 (62.4)	384 (3.6)	7,839 (23.4)	860 (7.9)	2,059 (6.0)	639 (5.9)
1929	33,217 (71.1)	631 (3.2)	8,427 (18.1)	1,442 (7.3)	2,079 (4.4)	1,130 (5.8)

Year	1 million- 5 million yen		More than 5 million yen		Total	
1909	171 (1.5)	305 (22.4)	38 (0.3)	495 (36.2)	11,543 (100.0)	1,367 (100.0)
1914	296 (1.8)	502 (24.2)	62 (0.4)	798 (38.5)	16,858 (100.0)	2,069 (100.0)
1919	1,611 (6.1)	1,538 (25.7)	368 (1.4)	3,203 (53.7)	26,280 (100.0)	5,975 (100.0)
1924	2,154 (6.4)	2,218 (20.4)	614 (1.8)	6,748 (62.2)	33,567 (100.0)	10,849 (100.0)
1929	2,236 (4.8)	3,665 (18.6)	733 (1.6)	12,797 (65.1)	46,692 (100.0)	19,666 (100.0)

Source: Tsutomu Ōuchi, *Nihon keizai-ron*, p. 174.

(those capitalized at 100,000 yen or less) constituted 71.1 per cent of all firms, but they collectively accounted for only 3.2 per cent of the total capital of all firms. This is a decline of 8.6 per cent from the relative magnitude observed in 1909. On the other hand, the largest firms capitalized at more than 5 million yen increased from 38 firms to 733, and they increased their relative share of capital from 36.2 to 65.1 per cent during the twenty years. Noteworthy also is the fact that most of this increase was achieved during the five war years.

As shown in Table 9, the gradual concentration of factory

TABLE 9

Factory Workers by Size of Firm
1910-1929
(1000 persons)

Year	Total	%	In factories employing 5-29	%	In factories employing 30-99	%	In factories employing over 100	%
1910	811	100	279	34.1	184	21.7	348	43.5
1914	948	100	279	29.4	209	22.2	461	48.6
1919	1,648	100	399	27.7	315	19.7	896	55.0
1924	1,790	100	417	23.3	306	17.1	1,056	59.2
1929	1,899	100	458	24.1	321	16.9	1,004	59.0

Source: Tsunao Inomata, *Nihon no dokusen shihonshugi to kinyūshihon no kyoko taisaku* (Tokyo, 1932), pp. 23-24.

workers (*shokko*) is another visible sign of the emerging dual structure. Although the trend is not as pronounced as that for the distribution of capital, it is clear. Firms employing over 100 persons accounted for 59 per cent of the total factory workers by 1927 while both of the other categories (5-29 employees and 30-99 employees) decreased in importance. Here too the relative share of firms employing over 100 exceeded the 50 per cent mark during the First World War.

These changes reflected a decisive shift in the industrial structure of Japan. New leading sectors were the chemical, metal, and machinery industries, which required larger units of operation and were increasingly more capital intensive.[29] The leaders, represented by larger firms in those industries and the firms in other industries, especially smaller ones, belonged to two quite distinct groups. Between the two groups, profit-rate differentials and wage-rate differentials were large and increasing from the 1920's into the 1930's.[30] The wage level in 1938, for example, in the iron and steel industry was more than twice that paid in the textile and apparel industries, and we must recall in passing that

[29] For detailed discussion, see: Yūichi Yoshinoya, "Patterns of Industrial Development" in Klein and Ohkawa (eds.), *Economic Growth*, pp. 69-79.

[30] Watanabe, "Industrialization, Technological Progress . . . ," pp. 119-133.

there existed a wide wage differential between large and small firms across the industries.

Although the more standard measures of concentration of product markets are not available until the late 1930's,[31] there is ample evidence to show that many markets became increasingly concentrated during the Taishō period. By 1929, the firms owned or controlled by the Mitsui, Mitsubishi, and Yasuda zaibatsu, along with the giant, nationally-owned Yawata, produced 93.6 per cent of the total output of pig iron, 83.1 per cent of the steel and 83.5 per cent of processed steel products. In the ammonium sulphate industry, the Mitsui and Mitsubishi firms by 1930 virtually divided the total output between them. In the cement industry, 83.1 per cent of the output was accounted for by eight firms under the control of Mitsui, Mitsubishi, and Asano-Yasuda zaibatsu. Oji Paper and Fuji Paper, both directly controlled by Mitsui, produced 65.4 per cent of the total output of paper in 1929. In sugar, flour milling, mining, and other major industries, the pattern was essentially similar.[32] The textile industry, in which the financial penetration of the zaibatsu group was weak, was one major sector of industry which was not as highly concentrated as the other industries described above. However, in this industry too, the so-called Big Six, accounting for over 40 per cent of the total paid-in capital of the industry, emerged by the end of the 1920's to lead effectively organized cartels.[33] And cartels had become very active during the Taishō period. Major cartels affecting at least 50 per cent of markets during the period are shown in Table 10. The number of major effective cartels doubled by 1931, and, together with minor cartels which were increasing in number after the mid-1920's, the industrial markets of Japan on the eve of the Manchurian invasion were dominated by cartels.

[31] See my article cited for Table 10.

[32] These observations are based on sources cited in my article in footnote 31 and in Minobe Ryūkichi, *Karuteru, torasuto, kontserun*, vol. 2 (Tokyo, 1931). All through this paper, the expressions "zaibatsu-controlled, zaibatsu firms and zaibatsu groups" are used only in those cases which are clearly identifiable, *i.e.*, connections with zaibatsu families and banks can be readily shown by amount of shareholding, interlocking directorships, or loans made. For the pre-1940 years, such identification is quite straightforward because of the evident dependence of zaibatsu subsidiaries and affiliates on zaibatsu banks and other zaibatsu firms.

[33] These are Kanegafuchi, Tōyō, Dai-Nihon, Fuji-Gasu, Nisshin and Osaka-gōdō Cotton Textile Companies. Minobe, *Karuteru* . . . , pp. 498-502.

TABLE 10

Major Cartels in Effect During the Taishō Period

Cartel	Estab-lished	Purposes: to control
1. Coal Mining Industry Federation	1921	Quantity sold
2. Cooperative Union of Pig Iron Producers	1926	Price, joint sales
3. Mutual Agreement Association of Steel-rod Producers	1926	Output types and quantity
4. Kanto Region Steel-rod Sales Association	1927	Price, product type, output, joint sales
5. Suiyōkai (Wednesday Club) for the lead producers	1921	Price, output, joint sales
6. Cement Federation	1924	Output
7. Association of Superphosphate Producers	1920	Price, output, sales region, joint purchase of raw material
8. Japan Sugar Federation	1910	Price, output, joint sales, sales region transportation costs
9. Japan Federation of Paper Producers	1880	Price, output
10. Great Japan Textile Federation	1882	Output, transportation costs
11. Silk Industry Association	1927	Quality and output
12. Japan Artificial Fibre Federation	1927	Price, output, sales region

Source: Various sources cited in Kozo Yamamura, "Zaibatsu, Prewar and Zaibatsu, Postwar," *Journal of Asian Studies*, xxiii (August, 1964), 539-554.

The banking industry was no exception to this trend toward concentration. Between 1911 and 1914, while 80 new banks were formed, 256 disappeared, of which 14 were by merger. This trend was accelerated during the war, and between 1915 and 1920, 241 banks disappeared while only 125 were newly formed. The number of disappearances by merger increased to 107 in the 1915-1920 period. During the 1921-1925 period, 395 banks disappeared, 276 by merger. Six hundred and six "new" banks were formed during the period, but most of these were former savings banks which became regular commercial banks as a result of changes in the law in 1922. However, the most pronounced wave of concentration came between 1926 and 1930, during which only 76 banks were formed while 831 banks disappeared. A surprising number, 589 out of the 831, disappeared because of mergers. The total number of commercial banks decreased from 1,615 to 878 between 1911 and 1929.[34]

The average net worth per bank rose steadily from 274,500 yen in 1911 to 2,250,600 by 1929.[35] The five largest banks, Mitsui, Mitsubishi, Yasuda, Sumitomo, and Daiichi, increased their total capital from 50,974,000 yen, 12.7 per cent of that of all commercial banks in 1914 to 282,750,000 yen, or 19.0 per cent, in 1927. The Big Five's shares of total deposits in all commercial banks increased from 22.5 to 31.2 per cent, or from 1.5 billion yen to 9 billion yen. The share of loans made by these five banks also increased from 18.4 per cent to 23.9 per cent, or 1.7 billion yen to 8.2 billion yen during the 1914-1927 period (Table 12).

We can measure the degree of concentration in an economy in many ways, but what we have observed is sufficient to establish the fact that the market structure and undoubtedly the behavior of firms in major industries, including the banking industry, was significantly different between the eve of the First World War and the beginning of the Shōwa period.

The trend toward concentration of economic power, to be fully evaluated, requires analysis of causal relationships between the trend and the several factors of technological change, labor market, international trade, and various economic policies of the government. However, a basic understanding of this trend can be arrived at by concentrating the analysis on the role of zaibatsu banks, which exerted a pervasive and dominant influence on these factors and thus on the observed trend toward concentration.

Generally speaking, it can be argued that the dominant role that the zaibatsu banks came to play during the Taishō period could have been anticipated from the unique position enjoyed at the beginning of the Meiji era by the zaibatsu families, who had accumulated wealth before the 1800's and were in a position to take advantage of the new tide of industrialization. By 1880, because of their financial power, they had established or were already major partners in the largest banks, those which were to become zaibatsu banks. The wealth and the banks provided the foundation for the rapid growth of zaibatsu economic power.

[34] Kajinishi, *et al.*, *Nihon shihonshugi* . . . , p. 137.
[35] Patrick, "Japanese Government Macro-Policy . . . ," p. 33.

The zaibatsu in effect had a head start on the others. When, in the early 1880's, the government began to sell its unsuccessful pilot plants, there were only a few in the economy who could take advantage of the bargain and wield enough power through political connections to secure this highly desirable entré into industrial activities.[36]

The zaibatsu families, both directly and through their banks, increased their industrial activities during the first "spurt" of industrialization in the 1890's and into the Russo-Japanese War boom. On the eve of the First World War, zaibatsu-connected firms were larger and financially sounder than others, and with relatively easy access to zaibatsu funds, these firms expanded rapidly, enjoying the high-profit years of the First World War. By the time the war ended, these firms had become financially independent, *i.e.*, they required little or no financial assistance from zaibatsu banks. This meant that the zaibatsu families and banks, which owned a large proportion of shares in these zaibatsu-connected firms, no longer needed to concern themselves with supplying long- or short-term loans in any significant amount to their own firms. Many of the larger zaibatsu-connected firms themselves were in a position to buy shares of their own subsidiaries or of other firms by the time the war ended.

This development now allowed the zaibatsu banks to extend their financial resources to firms which were not connected with the zaibatsu. In some instances this process had the effect of making these firms zaibatsu-connected, or zaibatsu-controlled. But, more importantly, the many firms still remaining outside of the zaibatsu groupings were now able to acquire long- and short-term loans from zaibatsu banks. Zaibatsu banks, in which deposits and capital increased rapidly throughout the Taishō period, now needed to find new markets for their funds. Since the bank-runs of 1927 and a vigorous government policy to reduce the number of banks by eliminating weaker banks had the effect of further establishing the supremacy of the zaibatsu banks, these banks had become, by the beginning of the Shōwa period, giant and efficient intermediaries for channeling capital to large industrial firms. These activities were extremely lucrative. The zaibatsu

[36] See for a typical case my detailed description of the emergence of the Mitsubishi zaibatsu in "The Founding of Mitsubishi: A Case Study in Japanese Business History," *Business History Review*, XLI, 2 (Summer, 1967), 141-160.

holding companies, anchored by their respective banks, strengthened their financial supremacy by efficiently exploiting various
types of advantages which conglomerate operations, quarter-
backed by the zaibatsu banks, could enjoy.[37]

Viewing this general description as a hypothesis, we can establish the three following propositions:

I. As had not been the case during the latter half of the Meiji
period, during the Taishō period zaibatsu-related firms required
little or no zaibatsu-bank financial assistance, especially of long-
term capital.

II. Zaibatsu banks for the first time in the 1920's began to lend
a large and increasingly significant amount of long-term capital
to non-zaibatsu firms.

III. During the Taishō period, the absolute and relative
strength of zaibatsu banks increased rapidly through increases
in capital, mergers, and as cores of emerging holding companies.

To show the validity of Proposition I, we must show that
zaibatsu-related firms depended on zaibatsu funds, especially for
long-term financing, before and during the First World War, but
after the war no longer required such assistance in any significant amount. Preceding more general observations of the desti-
nations of bank loans, several samples from the semi-annual
financial reports of zaibatsu-connected firms will be useful in
showing the transformation of the patterns of financing of
zaibatsu-related firms. These examples are representative firms
in that they were selected to reflect the financing patterns of
zaibatsu firms during the Taishō and early Shōwa periods and
were chosen from 37 major zaibatsu-connected firms for which
these data are available.[38]

[37] Detailed and well-documented case studies on how conglomerate zaibatsu operations and joint activities were used to gain maximum profits are
found in Takahashi Kamekichi, *Nihon zaibatsu no kaibō* (Tokyo, 1930).
Especially, pp. 21-22, 55-60 and 140-141.

[38] Data were obtained from their respective company histories which the
writer has been able to obtain since 1962, and from Yūshōdō Microfilms, *The
Annual Financial Reports of One Thousand Firms: 1868-1945* (Tokyo,
1962) hereafter known as Yūshōdō Microfilms. As most of the Japanese writers agree, there were about 85 firms directly controlled by the four zaibatsu
holding companies at the end of the 1920's; the sample of 37 covers about
44 per cent of these firms. The zaibatsu affiliates which are controlled by
zaibatsu subsidiaries or by zaibatsu holding companies only to a limited

As early as 1907 the Shibaura Seisakusho (Shibaura Machine-Tool Industries) of the Mitsui group had stopped borrowing long-term funds from the Mitsui and other banks, and no long-term loan was made again until 1934. Neither does the short-term loan appear on the financial reports after 1908. The firm's capital was increased from 2 million to 5 million in 1912 before the investment boom of the First World War, and it was increased again to 20 million yen in 1920. Maintaining a dividend rate in excess of 20 per cent between 1916 and 1921, it showed very little difficulty in selling shares for the purpose of expansion.[39]

The Dai-Nihon Seruroido K.K. (The Greater Japan Celluloid Company) of the Mitsui group ceased making short-term loans in 1921, and long-term loans disappeared from the reports in 1926. The long-term loans existing during the Taishō period never exceeded an amount equivalent to a small percentage of the total assets of the company. The firm increased the ratio of reserves to owners' equity (paid-in capital) from 5 to 35 per cent during the period between 1921 and 1929. Share capital increased during the same time from 12.5 million yen in 1919 to 100 million in 1921.[40]

The Mitsui Kōzan K.K. (Mitsui Mining Company) issued no bonds during the Taishō or early Shōwa years. Its capital increased from 20 million yen in 1920 to finance the expansions of the boom years. Long-term loans were made from Mitsui *Gōmei*[41] until 1918, although the amount was small and in the neighborhood of 0.5 per cent of the total assets. Between 1919 and 1929, only six loans were made from Mitsui Bussan (Trading Company) as extended advances to coal and other chemical by-products which the mining company sold to Bussan. However,

---

degree are not included in the 85 firms classified as direct subsidiary firms. See Table 11, which shows that, in terms of paid-in capital supplied by zaibatsu, the distinction between the zaibatsu firms and affiliates are relatively distinct.

[39] Data are from Yūshōdō Microfilms; also see: Kimura Yasuichi (ed.), *Shibaura seisakusho 65 nenshi* (Tokyo, 1940).

[40] Data are from Yūshōdō Microfilms, and *Dainihon seruroido kabushiki kaisha shi*, published by the firm in 1952.

[41] A legal entity organized by the Mitsui family, which owned the Mitsui Bank before 1919. But when a part of the bank shares was sold publicly in 1919, the *Gōmei* was absorbed by the bank. The Mitsui Bank, *Mitsui Ginkō 90 nenshi* (Tokyo, 1957), pp. 210-211.

these loans from Mitsui Bussan did not exceed 1.5 per cent of the total assets of the firm and steadily increasing reserves reached 12 million yen by 1929.[42]

Even the Ōji Seishi K.K. (Ōji Paper Company), which had borrowed constantly and rather heavily from the Daiichi and Mitsui banks, became much more financially independent after the war. Short-term loans disappeared after 1919 and long-term loans usually amounted to no more than 10 per cent of the total assets except twice, in 1922 when they came to just over 10 per cent and in 1927 when they were 23 per cent. Most outside capital was obtained by means of bonds which in 1916 were issued in an amount equivalent to 23 per cent of the total assets, and during most of the 1920's fluctuated within the range of 18-26 per cent of total assets. However, the firm's reserves to total-assets ratio was at a high level of 8-14 per cent compared to a small percentage of total assets during the prewar years. The reserves to owners' equity ratio also increased from 24 to 44 per cent between 1917 and 1929.[43]

Of the Mitsubishi group, the Mitsubishi Zōsen K.K. (the Mitsubishi Shipbuilding Company) relied on bond financing to the magnitude of 10 million yen against a paid-in capital of 30 million yen in 1918. The bond obligation was gradually eliminated and stood at zero in 1927. No short-term loans were seen after 1919, and only one long-term loan of 0.5 million yen was made, in 1930, against a reserve which increased from 2 million in 1919 to 5.8 million by 1930.[44] The Mitsubishi Kōgyō K.K. (Mitsubishi Mining Company) was even sounder. In 1918 it was capitalized at 50 million yen; no bonds were sold and no long-term loans were made after 1919, while reserves rose from 0.3 million yen in 1918 to 3.2 million yen in 1929.[45]

The Nisshin Seifun K.K. (Nisshin Flour Milling Company) stayed clear of long-term borrowing during the Taishō and the early Shōwa years; it borrowed only between 1922 and 1925 and in an amount equivalent to 4.2 per cent of total assets. No explicit mention is made of short-term loans. No bonds were sold

[42] Data are from the Yūshōdō Microfilms.

[43] Yūshōdō Microfilms and vol. I of the five-volume *Ōji Seishi shashi* (Tokyo, 1957).

[44] Yūshōdō Microfilms and *Mitsubishi Zōsen* (Tokyo, 1958).

[45] Yūshōdō Microfilms and Fumoto Saburo, *Mitsubishi Iizuka tankōshi* (Tokyo, 1961).

before 1930. Capital steadily increased from 1.7 million in 1914 to 4 million in 1917 and then to 12.3 million in 1925. Since the dividend rate remained well above the 15 per cent floor after 1916, with an exceptionally high 30 per cent at the height of the war boom, the firm had no difficulty in marketing its own shares for the purpose of acquiring capital for expansion.[46]

It is possible to add many more examples to convey this changing pattern of financing in zaibatsu-connected firms. Suffice it to say that in addition to these firms there were many more zaibatsu firms which depended only to a very limited extent on the long-term loans from their respective zaibatsu bank. In fact, of the sample examined, 15 firms including Mitsui Kozan, and Mitsubishi Zosen, in the Mitsui, Mitsubishi, Sumitomo, Asano, and Koga groups engaged in no long-term borrowing at all throughout the 1920's. One safe conclusion which can be drawn from these facts is that zaibatsu-related firms were financially secure by the beginning of the 1920's and required little long-term capital from their parent banks.[47]

In examining the available bank data, we can confirm the financial independence of zaibatsu firms. If we take the example of the Mitsui Bank for which information is available, we find that by 1930 only 9.8 per cent of its total loans were made to Mitsui-connected firms.[48] Although direct evidence is not available, we can conclude that all other major banks followed an essentially similar pattern. For example, for the Sumitomo Bank, loans to Sumitomo-related firms were even smaller because the group's major firms had no long-term loans by the late 1920's.[49]

Throughout the 1920's, the basic pattern was that the zaibatsu firms, because of past relationships, enjoyed a high degree of participation from the zaibatsu banks and families, even though these largest firms could easily sell shares to the public. For the

[46] Yūshōdō Microfilms and the Company's *Nisshin Seifun kabushi* (Tokyo, 1965).
[47] The firms are Nihon Cement (Asano), Koga Mining (Koga), Mitsui Bussan, Taiheiyō Coal Mining (Mitsui), Hokkai Soda (Mitsui), Mitsubishi Papers, Nisshin Steamship (Mitsubishi), Meiji Sugar Refining (Mitsubishi), Sumitomo Besshi Lead Mining, Sumitomo Steel Pipe, Sumitomo Steel Mill, Fujikura Electric Wire (Sumitomo) and Sumitomo Wire.
[48] Calculated from the data contained in *The 80-Year History of the Mitsui Bank*, pp. 421-422, and the data in the Appendix.
[49] See footnote 47, and the Sumitomo Bank data contained in Yūshōdō Microfilms.

319

subsidiary firms, zaibatsu participation in equity was limited, but these firms too were sufficiently sound to be able to float shares of their own and required few or no zaibatsu loans. The share holdings of zaibatsu families, banks, and other firms within the same zaibatsu group in 1928 were as shown in Table 11.

TABLE 11

Paid-in Capital Supplied by Zaibatsu
1928 (per cent)

Supplied To	Supplied By	Mitsui	Mitsu-bishi	Sumi-tomo	Yasuda	Ōkura	Koga	Kawasaki
Zaibatsu Firms	Honsha	90.2	69.4	79.1	32.0	81.8	73.0	34.4
	Zaibatsu Firms	0.4	8.3	1.4	16.0	5.9	16.0	19.4
	Total	90.6	77.6	80.5	48.0	87.7	89.0	53.8
Zaibatsu Affiliates	Honsha	21.3	5.0	49.5	36.0	12.1	21.0	21.5
	Zaibatsu Firms	8.1	2.7	1.9	3.0	1.5	19.0	6.3
	Total	29.4	7.7	51.4	39.0	13.6	40.0	27.8

Source: K. Takahashi and J. Aoyama, Nihon zaibatsu-ron (Tokyo, 1938), p. 162.

The proposition that the zaibatsu banks provided, during the 1920's, an increasing amount of long-term capital to non-zaibatsu firms can be easily shown. First, we must note that bonds were a much more important means of obtaining capital than were long-term loans during the 1920's. Of the 302 largest firms examined by the Mitsubishi Economic Research Institute, bonds accounted for 21 per cent of the total capital, long-term loans 7 per cent, share capital 56 per cent, and short-term capital 15 per cent. Out of 22 industries examined by the Institute, 13 industries depended more on bonds than on long-term loans.[50]

The total value of bonds sold during the 1920-1925 period was in the amount of 2,422 million yen, of which only 18.1 per cent were for zaibatsu-connected firms. The major share of the total, 41.3 per cent, were bonds floated by utility firms (electricity, electric light, etc.) and 20.7 per cent were for railway (densha) companies. These were two industries in which zaibatsu interests were extremely small. By 1930, the total value of bonds floated was 2,927 million yen, of which zaibatsu-connected firms accounted for only 15.2 per cent. The zaibatsu firms floating the

[50] Shibagaki Kazuo, Nihon kinyūshihon bunseki (Tokyo, 1965), p. 374.

bonds were smaller subsidiaries and affiliates and not major zaibatsu firms.[51]

An important point to be made is that the four zaibatsu banks held, by the end of 1929, 27.1 per cent of the total outstanding bonds. If the insurance and credit companies of the zaibatsu groups are added, the bond holdings increase to 29.1 per cent of the total.[52] After the mid-1920's, bonds were the most important negotiable papers most zaibatsu banks, insurance companies, and credit companies held. Among the zaibatsu banks, the ratio of bonds to the total negotiable paper ranged from 46.7 per cent for the Mitsubishi Bank to Mitsui Bank's 37 per cent in 1929.[53]

As noted earlier in connection with the Mitsui Bank, the long-term loans made by zaibatsu banks increased rapidly during the latter half of the 1920's. For the Mitsui Bank, the ratio of long-term loans to total assets (t/T) rose from .25 in 1911 to .44 by the end of 1930. The ratio was somewhat lower during the 1919-1924 period, but the tendency of t/T to rise is unmistakable. The ratio of t/L (long-term loans to all types of loans) rose also from .35 in 1911 to .87 by the end of 1930. This ratio rose steadily with no visible departure from the trend throughout the 1911-1930 period.[54] The Yasuda, Sumitomo, and Daiichi banks also showed similar increases in the importance of long-term loans vis-à-vis total assets and total loans.[55]

The only exception to the above is the Mitsubishi Bank, which reduced the t/T ratio from a .5-.7 range during the First World War to a .3-.4 range in the latter half of the 1920's. The long-term loans to total loans (t/L) rose to .82 by 1916 and continued to maintain a high .7-.8 range throughout the 1920's. The major explanation for the decline in the t/T ratio is that the bank in-

[51] Calculated from the data contained in the Industrial Bank of Japan, *Nihon kōgyō 50 nenshi* (Tokyo, 1957), pp. 222-223, and Nomura Securities Companies of Japan, *Kōshasai nenkan* (Tokyo, 1930), the data sections. The zaibatsu firms were identified by referring to the sources cited in footnotes 32 and 37.

[52] Takahashi, *Nihon zaibatsu . . .* , pp. 44-47.

[53] From the data contained in the bank history of each bank, and Yūshōdō Microfilms.

[54] Long-term loans are, when not defined explicitly, total loans minus call loans, short-term loans (*tōza* and *kashikoshi*), discounting of papers (*waribiki*), and other explicitly short-term loans. It goes without saying that there are difficulties involved in obtaining accurate data on repeatedly renewed short-term loans.

[55] The Yūshōdō Microfilms, and the bank histories.

creased its share-holdings during the period. The ratio of negotiable paper holding to total assets rose steadily from .08 in 1920
to .43 in 1930. As the Mitsubishi Bank's holding of the shares of
Mitsubishi-connected firms was less than any other zaibatsu
bank's holding of the shares of its respective group, the Mitsubishi bank's t/T ratio reflects the bank's increased holding of
bonds and shares of non-zaibatsu firms. However, in assessing
the loan policies of the zaibatsu banks, the conclusion that an increasing amount of long-term loans was made by them to non-
zaibatsu firms during the 1920's is warranted.[56]

To show the increasing dominance of the zaibatsu banks during the 1920's (Proposition III), we need present only a few
facts. Table 12 clearly shows that there were significant changes

TABLE 12

The Expansion of the Big Five
A Comparison of 1919 and 1927
(end of year, 1,000 yen)

Mitsui	1919	60,000	351,130	318,526
	1927	60,000	560,334	403,512
Mitsubishi	1919	30,000	233,541	208,588
	1927	30,000	470,586	230,308
Yasuda	1919	17,500	128,575	118,535
	1927	92,750	713,276	587,967
Sumitomo	1919	30,000	348,359	345,582
	1927	50,000	552,780	367,497
Daiichi	1919	14,638	374,409	362,532
	1927	50,000	520,883	365,333
Total of Big Five	1919	152,138	1,437,014	1,353,753
	1927	282,750	2,817,860	1,954,617
Total of all Ordinary Banks	1919	717,156	5,744,096	5,666,461
	1927	1,469,708	9,027,897	8,181,695
Ratio of Big Five to	1919	21.2%	25.0%	24.0%
Total of all Ordinary Banks	1927	19.0%	31.2%	23.9%

Sources: Computed from data contained in the respective bank histories.

in both the absolute and relative positions of the zaibatsu banks
between 1919 and 1927. During this eight-year period, zaibatsu
banks increased their relative share of the total deposits from 25
to 31 per cent, or from 5.7 to 9 billion yen in absolute amounts.
The market share of loans remained virtually unchanged but the

[56] From the data contained in the Mitsubishi Bank, *Mitsubishi Ginkōshi*
(Tokyo, 1954), the Data Appendix.

total amount of loans made by these banks increased from 5.7 to 8.2 billion yen. These developments are especially significant when considered against the fact that the relative share of the paid-in capital of these banks decreased from 21.2 per cent to 19 per cent (see Table 12). Another way of appraising the financial power of the zaibatsu group is to note that eight zaibatsu groups (banks, insurance companies, credit companies) accounted for 45.7 per cent of the total capital + deposits + reserves of all private banks, insurance companies and credit companies at the end of 1929.[57]

A few important factors contributed to this rapid concentration of the financial market. One was the sporadic bank runs which the banking industry experienced after the First World War and the nation-wide bank runs of 1927 which resulted from accumulated ills of "the earthquake bills" and the practice of banks acting as "organ banks." "Earthquake bills" refer to those notes which many borrowers were unable to pay because of the earthquake of 1923 and which were guaranteed to banks by the Bank of Japan. These bills resulted in limiting the scope of freedom the Bank of Japan could adopt with regard to its monetary policy. Furthermore, they contributed to the undermining of bank portfolios. Because they had to depend on foot-dragging political decisions of the government with regard to loans, banks holding these bills were gravely weakened.[58]

The "organ bank" refers to those many banks of the period which became "organs" of their specific clients. This meant that banks were often forced into the position of making unsound loans to their clients, mostly industrial firms, who were facing financial difficulties. Since the banks were committed to their clients in the sense that large loans had already been made to these firms and their bankruptcy meant the end of the banks themselves, the banks were forced to make further unsound loans. Such practices, as the Bank of Taiwan experience with

[57] The eight zaibatsu groups refer to Mitsui, Mitsubishi, Sumitomo, Yasuda, Daiichi (*i.e.*, the Big Five, involving 29 banks, 4 credit firms, 4 life insurance companies, 19 other types of insurance companies) and the Kawasaki, Yamaguchi, and Konoike groups (involving 21 banks, 3 credit firms, 7 life insurance companies, and 6 other types of insurance firms). These three groups are the second group in size to the Big Five. Takahashi, *Nihon zaibatsu* . . . , p. 39.

[58] For detailed descriptions, see Kajinishi, *et al.*, *Nihon shihonshugi* . . . , pp. 185-190.

Suzuki Shōten showed, could and did lead to nation-wide bank runs.[59]

The instability of the banking industry caused many savers to transfer their deposits to larger and better-established banks. The zaibatsu banks, which survived these crises with only an occasional run on their branch banks, naturally were the major beneficiaries of these transferred savings. Throughout the period, the government was also anxious to stabilize the financial market, and chose to promote mergers and unifications of weaker (small and/or local) banks. Beginning in 1924, the Ministry of Finance engaged in an active program of reducing the number of banks in each prefecture, of extending assistance in evaluation of assets at the time of a merger, and of helping select the best-qualified managers of newly unified banks. This program was carried on throughout the 1920's and the ministry's "persuasion" was effective in numerous instances.[60]

No less important in bringing about the highly oligopolistic structure of the banking industry was the aggressive merger and absorption measures adopted by the largest banks themselves. A typical case is that of the Yasuda Bank. In 1923, the Yasuda Bank absorbed ten other banks scattered throughout the country to create a giant bank (see Table 12).[61] It was a common practice of the larger city banks to absorb the smaller local banks and make them into branch offices.

How large was the banking industry in which the zaibatsu interest dominated? Table 13 may help to answer this question. The sum of deposits and paid-in capital of all banks rose from an amount equivalent to 64 per cent of GNP to an excess of 100 per cent by the beginning of the 1920's. The ratio of the same sum to GNP for commercial banks (excluding the government banks) rose from 44.2 per cent to 80.9 per cent, or nearly doubled, between 1911 and 1926. There is no doubt that these ratios reflect the increasing financial power of banks within the economy during the Taishō period. These ratios were higher compared to similar ratios calculated by Cameron for West European nations and the United States.[62]

[59] *Ibid.*, pp. 157-161.

[60] Kajinishi, *Zoku Nihon . . .* , pp. 49-50.

[61] A detailed description of this merger is found in the Yasuda Bank, *Yasuda Ginkō 60 nenshi* (Tokyo, 1940), pp. 225-248.

[62] We should of course allow for the fact that the latter part of the period

TABLE 13

Growth of Bank Assets, 1911-1926
(Million yen)

Year	All Banks Deposit (A)	Paid-in Capital (B)	(A) + (B) / GNP	Commercial Banks Deposit (C)	Paid-in Capital (D)	(C) + (D) / GNP
1911	1,776	480	64.0	1,256	327	44.2
1912	1,941	534	59.7	1,357	369	41.6
1913	2,110	574	63.2	1,444	392	43.3
1914	2,212	608	71.4	1,520	401	48.7
1915	2,569	622	82.2	1,700	358	53.0
1916	3,464	648	87.2	2,257	374	55.8
1917	5,148	751	95.1	3,234	437	59.2
1918	7,236	888	88.8	4,840	513	56.3
1919	8,734	1,207	73.1	5,744	717	47.5
1920	8,829	1,639	87.5	5,827	964	56.8
1921	9,494	1,747	101.8	6,445	1,045	67.9
1922	9,551	1,875	102.2	7,801	1,450	82.8
1923	9,692	1,929	98.4	7,805	1,491	78.7
1924	10,232	1,953	93.9	8,093	1,508	74.0
1925	10,821	1,918	93.3	8,727	1,501	74.9
1926	11,272	1,924	100.0	9,179	1,497	80.9

Sources: The Bank of Japan, *Hundred-Year Statistics*, p. 194, and Ohkawa *et al.*, *Japanese Economic Growth*, pp. 170, 247.

The difficulties in evaluating the Taishō period and the early Shōwa years become obvious when we attempt to summarize significant events of these years. The effects of the First World War boom, with the strong impetus it provided for the industrialization of Japan, must be considered against the prolonged recession of the 1920's. The continued development of the heavy, metal, chemical, and other industries which made Japan an industrial power must be evaluated against the Rice Riots, stagnant real wages, a hard-pressed agricultural sector, the weak Factory Act, and other "costs" to the Japanese people. The increased power of the zaibatsu banks and the emergence of a dual structure were an integral part of the Taishō economy, and in order to evaluate the role of zaibatsu banks and the effects of

covered was the recession years, and the banks tended to have on hand excess loanable funds. Rondo Cameron, "Conclusion," in R. Cameron (ed.), *Banking in the Early Stage of Industrialization* (London and New York, 1967), pp. 301-302.

the dual structure we must consider the consequences of oligopolization and cartelization on efficient resource allocation, the adoption of new technology, price levels, and the distribution of profits. This period—"the Japanese economy has displayed only one genuine contraction, the years from 1919 to 1931"[63]—is an extremely difficult segment of Japanese economic history to discuss meaningfully without introducing questions of "welfare." It is necessary to raise these questions if an economic historian is to evaluate the period which preceded the tragedies of the 1930's and the Second World War, and it is certainly desirable if we are to try to learn from history.

Before returning to the welfare-policy question, which by its nature cannot be resolved with our knowledge of the economy of the period, let us briefly evaluate, in a historical perspective, the role of the zaibatsu banks during the 1920's. If the three propositions described above can be accepted, it is important to realize that the zaibatsu banks became much more like the German type of investment banks only during the 1920's—not during the 1890's, the first "spurt" in the economic development of Japan. It was only after and to some extent during the First World War that Japanese industrialization penetrated into heavy, chemical, and other highly capital-intensive industries. The firms in these industries required long-term funds, and the zaibatsu banks were able and willing to supply them.

The dominance of the cotton-textile industry during the initial "spurt" of the 1890's meant that Japanese industrialization began from light, labor-using industries. The requirements of a large fixed capital were much less than in the type of industrialization observed after the First World War. There is sufficient evidence to show that the cotton-textile industry's dependence on the long-term capital of banks was limited since their profits were large and their internal reserves continued to increase.[64] The mining and other heavy industries which zaibatsu-connected firms began before the turn of the century were still limited and were often founded on the former government plants these firms had

[63] K. Ohkawa and H. Rosovsky, "Postwar Japanese Growth in Historical Perspective: A Second Look," in Klein and Ohkawa (eds.), *Economic Growth*, p. 26.

[64] These points were discussed in my paper, "The Japanese Case—A Test of the Gerschenkron Hypothesis," The American Historical Association, December 1968, New York.

bought. Investment banking thus became visible in the 1920's because it was the first time such services were required by the industries.

When the zaibatsu banks appeared as investment bankers, aided by the unstable conditions of the financial market and the waves of bank runs, by the policy of the Ministry of Finance to eliminate weaker banks, and by the bank's aggressive entrepreneurial policies, they quickly became the cores of holding companies. Zaibatsu banks, zaibatsu-connected firms and their satellites, and non-zaibatsu firms which began to enjoy the zaibatsu banks' maximum financial assistance occupied the upper half of the dual structure. These privileged banks and firms led the economy in providing the capital needed to continue industrialization more efficiently than before, in producing industrial goods at a larger and closer-to-optimum scale, and in remaining competitive in international markets. They became the cutting edge of Japanese industrialization when the textile industry began to fade in relative importance during the late 1920's and the 1930's.

But as industrialization continued, led by the zaibatsu, the far larger lower half of the dual structure and those who manned it not only were unable to share the fruits of the industrialization of the 1920's, but also suffered from an increasing number of ills created by it. The visibly increasing financial power of the zaibatsu sharply contrasted with the increased precariousness of the life of employees working in factories too small to hope for a membership in the select groups of oligopolists, and of farmers whose mounting frustrations could only take the form of relatively ineffectual protests. The widening disparity in distribution of income—the zaibatsu on the one hand and the factory workers and farmers on the other—was soon manifested as political instability and social unrest.

By the late 1920's, the largest firms began to adopt fringe benefit programs for factory workers, but these benefits were limited and applied to only a small fraction of the labor force. The government, instead of reacting to the signs of discontent, chose to repress the signs without curing the basic ills. The suddenly increased political orientation of the activities challenging the established political order frightened the government, especially after the successful Russian Revolution of 1917. The remainder of the developments need no elaboration. In lieu of solving the ills, the government administered the strong medicine called fascism, and it eventually killed the patient. This is not to say that the rising economic power of the zaibatsu and what it represented caused the eventual death of the patient, but it does say that the patient required a completely different medicine.

The dramatic start for industrialization which Japan made during the Meiji period contained the seeds of the developments of the Taishō years. The way in which the zaibatsu accumulated their economic power during the Meiji years and dominated the economy of the 1920's is only an example. The dual structure, oligopolization, cartelization, and increasing disparity in the distribution of wealth within the economy, and all the social and political unrest and instabilities connected with these tendencies, firmly established themselves during the 1920's. And this was to shape the Japanese economy of the Shōwa era. It took the catastrophic defeat of the Second World War to cure Japan of the "cancer" which became visible in the 1920's.

In numerous ways, and this paper covers only one aspect, the Taishō years were a critical juncture in the economic development of Japan. Was the experience of the 1920's somehow a necessary part of the pattern of economic development Japan pursued? Was it, in some sense of the term, a price which had to be paid for the success of Japan's industrialization? Were the zaibatsu inevitable unless Japan chose to grow more slowly or with some type of planning? These are the questions which should be asked now that we have become, during the past two decades, familiar with the success story of Japan. Indeed, to appraise the past one hundred years of the Japanese economy, we must ask the most important question: how well did the welfare of the population correspond to the rapidity of the Japanese economic development? A thorough examination of the neglected Taishō and the early Shōwa periods is overdue. If we are to call Japan's economic development successful in the full sense of the term, we will be well advised to know much more about the "costs" of the success.

Incentives, Productivity Gaps, and Agricultural Growth Rates in Prewar Japan, Taiwan, and Korea [*]

Gᴇɴᴇʀᴀʟɪᴢᴀᴛɪᴏɴs ᴏɴ patterns of human behavior may be shaped, confirmed, or challenged from the study of any human experiences, whether they be mean or heroic, tragic or comic, inhuman or humane. But some experiences are not given the attention they deserve because scholars may be reluctant to study them for reasons of guilt, shame, abhorrence, or interest in more immediate problems. One such case of neglect applies to the colonial rule of Taiwan and Korea by Japan. Only a scattering of Japanese, Taiwanese, and Korean scholars have interested themselves during the postwar years in the colonial areas and problems despite the fact that the colonies were of great economic and political significance to Japan and the period was one of deep-seated change in Korea and Taiwan that must be taken account of in any historical study of these countries.

The colonial period, lasting from 1895-1945, was one of rapid economic growth not only in Japan proper, but perhaps even more vigorously in the Japanese empire. Because the Japanese colonial experience ran to extremes—harsh colonial policies on the one hand and substantial economic development on the other—its study may provide important guidelines on what to do and what *not* to do. Although this paper examines the successful agricultural and economic aspects of the colonial experience, this does not mean that I approve of Japanese colonialism (or imperialism) as such, or that I believe colonialism can be tol-

[*] This paper is a part of an ongoing comparative study of the agricultural and economic development of Japan, Taiwan, and Korea. A part of this paper was originally read at the annual meeting of the Association of Asian Studies, March 24, 1968, Philadelphia, Pa.

I am indebted to a great many persons for comments and criticisms in individual discussions and in seminars in the United States (4 seminars), Japan (8), Korea (2), and Taiwan (1). I am grateful for research assistance to Y. Kido, R. Nakamura, and L. Nakamura.

erated today for the sake of economic growth. It does mean however, that I believe that a successful policy in an area of economic activity as important as agriculture in the less developed countries merits serious study.

The approach to agricultural developments in prewar Japan, Taiwan and Korea used here is that of comparative analysis. It is an attempt to show that Japanese policies raised the growth rates of agricultural production in the colonies to levels substantially higher than that of Meiji Japan. More specifically, it examines the existence in Taiwan and Korea, at the beginning of their modern agricultural development, of lower incentives and productivities than those in Japan, the policies with which the Japanese government attempted to raise them, and the response of the colonial agricultural production to these policies.

This study terminates about the time World War II began, thus avoiding the wartime and immediate postwar period of depressed output, and also excluding the present period of vigorous growth in Korea and Taiwan. Bringing the wartime and postwar periods into the analysis is, of course, not relevant to the purpose of this paper although the recent vigorous growth of Taiwan and Korea is related to the development of the colonial period. What is being sought here are the reasons for the substantial gains in output that occurred up to the beginning of the war. That is, I am concerned with policies that overcame the inertia of the Taiwanese and Korean economies and caused them to attain growth rates that compared more than favorably with those of other nations in the interwar period. An interesting sidelight shed by this study is that the growth occurred under colonialism, which has usually been assumed to discourage modern economic growth.

The basic variable that I am concerned with in this section is land productivity—that is, changes in yield per unit area—as a measure of agricultural productivity. Conceptually, it is desirable to obtain a composite yield index of all crops, and, where it is believed desirable, a variant of this index will be used. But for comparison of yields in the three areas I shall use the paddy rice yield index because rice was the most important crop in all three countries and the most reliable and complete statistics and other information are available on it. It is assumed here that yields of other crops changed in the same direction and roughly proportionally to the change in rice yields.

When we compare Japan of early Meiji with conditions in Taiwan and Korea after their annexation by Japan in 1895 and 1910 respectively, we find that very great yield differences existed among the three areas. The main objective of this chapter is to account for these differences.

The yields presented for comparative purposes as shown on Table 1 are for Japan 2.5 metric tons of brown rice per hectare

TABLE 1

Rice Yield Per Hectare in Japan, Taiwan, and Korea
(Metric tons of brown rice per hectare)

Period	Yield in Japan[1]	Period	Yield in Taiwan	Yield in Korea[1]
	(1)		(2)	(3)
1878-82	2.47	1901-05	1.31	—
1883-87	2.53	1906-10	1.34	—
1888-92	2.59	1911-15	1.35	1.28
1893-97	2,64	1916-20	1.41	1.39
1898-1902	2.70	1921-25	1.53	1.41
1903-07	2.76	1926-30	1.65	1.49
1908-12	2.82	1931-35	1.85	1.53
1913-17	2.89	1936-40	2.02	2.05
1918-22	2.95			

Sources: Column (1) computed from J. I. Nakamura, *Agricultural Production and the Economic Development of Japan* (Tokyo, 1966), p. 92.

Column (2) computed from output and crop area data in Y. M. Ho, *Agricultural Development of Taiwan: 1903-1960* (Nashville, 1966), pp. 135-36, 149-50.

Column (3) computed from 1911-1936 data in *CNHS-SR*, 55; 1937-1938 data from *Chōsen sōtokufu tōkei nenkan*, 1938, p. 55; 1939-1940 data from *Chōsen keizai nempo*, 1941/42, p. 84.

[1] The Japanese and Korean yields are given in *koku* per *tan*. This is converted to metric tons per hectare by multiplying by conversion factor 1.5125.

in 1878-1882; for Taiwan 1.34 in 1906-1910; and for Korea 1.39 in 1916-1920. The main reason for the choice of the above dates is the availability of somewhat more reliable data. Ideally these data would be those just prior to each modern agricultural development. The yields for Japan and Taiwan can reasonably be assumed to fit this description, but this may not have applied to the Korean yield. Around 1880 Japanese agricultural inputs and methods had remained almost identical with those of the last years of the Tokugawa period (1603-1868). A possibility of increasing yields existed in the colonies because Japanese inputs and methods provided higher yields. However, except in very limited areas, the use of Japanese seeds was not possible in Taiwan because of climatic differences. Technology involving land improvement could not be immediately developed because, as a rule, it requires long-term capital expenditures. Therefore, although Japan annexed Taiwan in 1895, the yields in 1906-1910 probably approximated yields around 1895.

In Korea, however, a very substantial increase in paddy rice yields appears probable from 1910 or earlier to 1916-1920. According to one source, yields in Korea increased markedly between 1910 and 1920.[1] This seems reasonable in view of the rapid increase in the planting of higher-yielding Japanese seeds which were found to be suited to the similar climate and conditions of Korea by tests in the newly established agricultural experimental stations. In 1912, less than 3 per cent of paddy rice planted was in improved seeds. Seven years later the area planted to these tested Japanese seeds had increased to more than 50 per cent, and by 1923 improved-seed acreage exceeded traditional-seed acreage by better than 2 to 1.[2] The 5-year average yields from improved seeds appear to have been higher by 25 to 50 per cent during this period.[3]

If paddy rice yield in Korea did increase substantially from 1910 to 1920, as seems likely, then the Korean yield around 1910 was probably lower than the Taiwanese yield in 1906-1910. Indeed, the recorded 1911-1915 yield for Korea on Table 1 is 1.28 M/T per hectare, which is lower than the Taiwanese yield for any period, as can be ascertained from Table 1. Since statistical reporting was not systematically carried out at this time, a large margin must be provided for possible errors. But a lower yield in Korea is consistent with the conditions in the two countries, to be described in the following pages.

[1] Suzuki, *Chōsen no keizai* (Tokyo, 1942), pp. 57-59.
[2] Computed from K. Kohayakawa (ed.), *Hotei: Chōsen nōgyō hattatsu shi: shiryō hen* (Tokyo, 1960), p. 109. This source to be cited henceforth as *CNHS-SR*.
[3] *Ibid.*

In addition to the uncertainty regarding the Korean yield, a further question exists relating to the comparability of the yield data used. The Japanese yield is corrected for under-reporting, whereas those for Korea and Taiwan are computed directly from official data. The Japanese official yield is 1.8 metric tons per hectare, and a new recent estimate gives a figure of 1.99.[4] These estimates are also substantially above those of Taiwan and Korea, the former being about 30 per cent higher and the latter about 40 per cent. But for reasons given elsewhere, the 2.5 metric ton estimate for Japan appears to me to be the soundest.[5] The reasons for the differences presented in the rest of this section also suggest that the 2.5 estimate may be more acceptable. Thus it will be used here.

The question then is whether the Taiwanese and Korean yields are also understated by substantial amounts. If these yields were understated at all, it is probable that the understatement was substantially less than in the case of Japan, for the following reason. When Japan undertook her cadastral survey of the 1870's, some prefectures completed their surveys very early, and others, resisting the surveys, straggled. The degree of competence and accuracy with which these surveys were conducted varied widely among prefectures, with relatively more understatement for those completing their survey earlier.[6] After all prefectures had finished, it was found that a high proportion of cultivated land still remained unregistered (that is, not recorded in official land registers and therefore not subject to the land tax), and that very serious under-reporting of yields had occurred, with substantial differences in the degree of understatement. For this reason the government carried out land value reductions in those prefec-

[4] Computed from Nōrinshō, Nōrin Keizai Kyoku, Tōkei Chōsa Bu, *Nōrin ruinen tōkei hyō 1868-1953* (Tokyo, 1955), p. 24; and from M. Umemura et al. (eds.), *Estimates of Long-Term Economic Statistics of Japan Since 1868, Volume 9, Agriculture and Forestry* (Tokyo, 1966), p. 37. The latter source to be cited as *LTES* henceforth.

[5] J. I. Nakamura, *Agricultural Production and the Economic Development of Japan* (Princeton, 1966), chapter 4; and J. I. Nakamura, "The Nakamura versus the LTES Estimates of the Growth Rate of Agricultural Production," *Keizai kenkyū*, xix, 4 (October, 1968), pp. 358-361.

[6] Ōkurasho (ed.), *Meiji zenki zaisei keizai shiryō shusei* (Tokyo, 1032-1036), vii, 401. Henceforth, this will be referred to as *MZZKSS* with volume number.

tures where land was relatively overvalued by reducing the nominal (official survey) yield per *tan* and the value of rice per *koku*.[7] To avoid the cost of remeasurement and to achieve as great a degree of tax equity as possible, cultivated land would have had to be surveyed accurately and the best possible estimates of average yield would have had to be obtained.

One fundamental difference between the Japanese and colonial cadastral surveys was that in Japan peasants and the villagers measured the land area and estimated the yields, whereas in the colonies government tax officials performed these tasks. The peasants and the villagers were motivated to under-report land area and yield per unit area because the national land tax was to be a proportion of the land value, and the value of a cultivated plot was determined by the area and the yield per unit area. In the colonies, on the other hand, the government sought accuracy to avoid popular unrest that would result from tax inequities stemming from inaccurate measurement, and to avoid the costly, time-consuming, and politically destabilizing remeasurement and revaluation surveys that Japan had had to undertake because of the inaccuracy of her survey data.[8]

A number of important consequences derived from tax officials' involvement in measurement and estimation for the colonial surveys. First, they tended to take more time since the number of persons involved was much smaller.[9] In fact, for cultivated land, the Japanese survey was completed in 3 years, the Taiwanese survey required 6, and the Korean 9, despite the fact that Japan's cultivated land area was about 10 times greater than that of Taiwan and 8 per cent greater than that of Korea. Second, the methods used in measuring land were more sophisticated than would have been the case if the farmers were responsible for the measurement, because the officials were trained for the job and only those capable of using such methods would be used. Third, in estimating the yield the tax officials were armed with the coercive power of a colonial government which did not hesitate to use police power to obtain more accurate estimates.

[7] Nakamura, *Agricultural Production* . . . , pp. 194-195.

[8] *Ibid.*, p. 192.

[9] The number of persons (tax officials) involved in Korea was 7,113 [K. Kohayakawa (ed.), *Hotei: Chōsen nōgyō hattatsu shi: seisaku-hen* (Tokyo, 1959), p. 354. This source to be cited henceforth as *CNHS-SS*.], whereas in Japan at least all heads of farm families were involved—that is, some 5 million persons.

A part of the greater time required was given to informing the populace that the basis and proof of property ownership was being changed, and that land was being redistributed away from absentee landlords to the cultivators. Once these objectives were understood, accurate measurement and registration could be expected. In fact, the post-World War II land reform in Taiwan was expedited due to the accuracy of the original Japanese land surveys.[10] The 80 to 87 per cent gap between the Taiwanese and Korean yields and that of Japan requires the existence of very substantial differences in the conditions that influence yield. One such difference exists in the man-land ratio. Hectares of cultivated land per capita were 0.121, 0.200, and 0.260 for Japan (1890), Taiwan (1910), and Korea (1920), respectively. The areas in Taiwan and Korea are 65 and 115 per cent greater than those of Japan. Other things being equal, in densely populated countries the smaller the area of cultivated land per capita, the more productive each unit area must be. Other things were not as nearly equal as is desirable. The most important of these are net exports, which for Japan were negligible in 1888-1892, but for Korea were 15 per cent[11] in 1916-1920, and for Taiwan, 14 per cent[12] in 1910. However, the per capita area differences overshadow the exports in both cases. A closely related measure is that of the hectares per farm worker which are 0.328, 0.566, and 0.619, respectively, for Japan (1890), Taiwan (1910), and Korea (1920). The areas for Taiwan and Korea are 73 and 89 per cent greater than for Japan. Other things being equal, this measure provides an index of how much more intensively—and therefore productively—land can be worked, irrespective of exports.

A second factor that helps to explain the differences in land productivity appears in the use of fertilizers. The value of fertilizers consumed was 65 yen (1935-1937 prices) per hectare in Japan in 1883-1887,[13] 14 yen (1935-1937 prices) in Taiwan in

[10] A.Y.C. Koo, *The Role of Land Reform in Economic Development: A Case Study of Taiwan* (New York, 1968), p. 12.

[11] Computed from data in *CNHS-SR*, pp. 105, 115, 118.

[12] Computed from A. J. Grajdanzev, *Economic Development of Formosa* (Shanghai, 1941), p. 55.

[13] Computed from fertilizer price data in Y. Hayami, "Hiryō tōkaryō no suikei," *Nōgyō sōgō kenkyū*, XVII, 1 (January, 1963), p. 253; fertilizer price index in LTES, pp. 192-193; and cultivated land area adjusted for undermeasurement from Nakamura, *Agricultural Production* . . . , pp. 43, 48.

1910,[14] and 5 yen (1934-1936 prices) in Korea in 1918-1922.[15] Although the prices may not be strictly comparable,[16] the spread is more than sufficient to justify the conclusion that a much more intensive fertilizer use was practiced in Japan, which can be expected to account for a substantial spread in per unit area yields. Furthermore, in Taiwan multiple cropping was more heavily practiced than in the other two countries. This factor would also tend to reduce yield per crop.

The use of fertilizer is partly a function of information, but primarily it is a function of the cost of fertilizers and benefits accruing therefrom. Cost reductions and benefits over output required for household consumption result from the existence of markets, and markets begin to proliferate only when relatively cheap communications and transportation become available. In Korea, transportation facilities were of a primitive nature around the turn of the century and only local markets existed over most of the country.[17] Taiwan fared somewhat better since its development was partly determined by the existence of the nearby mainland China market and other markets to which quantities of tea, camphor, sugar, and rice were exported. In the south a "few stretches of heavy roads passed through the sugar fields" for the use of sugar growers; in the rest of the island there were almost no public roads.[18]

The quality of human capital in agriculture as measured by literacy also helps to explain the productivity gap. In Japan the level of male literacy at the end of the Tokugawa period has been estimated to have been 40 to 50 per cent.[19] Since 80 per cent

[14] Fertilizer data from S.P.S. Ho, "Agricultural Transformation under Colonialism: The Case of Taiwan," *The Journal of Economic History*, xxviii, 3 (September, 1968), p. 318; cultivated land area from Y. M. Ho, *Agricultural Development of Taiwan: 1903-1960* (Nashville, 1965), p. 51.

[15] Fertilizer and cultivated land area data from *CNHS-SR*, pp. 97, 111, 112.

[16] All valuations are in yen, which for all three countries were identical since the monetary systems of the two colonies were integrated into that of Japan. The prices are composite prices including farm-produced and commercial fertilizers, and their valuations varied in the three countries.

[17] I. L. Bishop, *Korea and her Neighbors* (London, 1898), ii, 104-105. See also H. Shikata, "*Shijō wo tsujite mitaru Chōsen no keizai,*" *Chōsen keizai no kenkyū* (Tokyo, 1929), pp. 1-286.

[18] J. W. Davidson, *The Island of Formosa: History, People, Resources, and Commercial Prospects* (1903), pp. 619-620.

[19] H. Passin, *Society and Education in Japan* (New York, 1965), p. 47.

or more of the population was rural, one-fourth or more of rural males may have been literate. More importantly, education was usually tied to the practical needs of the children. For example, the titles of readers in rural areas (dates of introduction in parenthesis) included *Country Reader* (1758); *Agricultural Reader* (1762); *Farmer's Reader* (1766); *Farming People's Reader* (1789-1800); *Increased Profits for Farmers* (1811); *Bumper Crops* (1836).[20] In contrast, in Korea education was almost entirely limited to the privileged classes. Earlier observers noted the irrelevance to the nation's needs of Korean education, which was designed to educate the youth of the upper classes in classical Chinese texts to pass the royal examination.[21] The educational system in Taiwan was similarly sterile for the most part. Schooling was confined to the children of wealthy parents, and the curriculum consisted of learning characters and mastering the classics. According to one observer, "there were none of the studies which in Western lands and in Japan are considered necessary for an educated man, and the general tendency of their training was to increase conservatism and love for ancient customs: the greatest stumbling block in the way of Chinese progress."[22]

An overriding question still remains. Why did the Japanese expend more labor and invest more in fertilizers, irrigation facilities, human capital, and other profitable inputs during the Tokugawa period than did the Taiwanese and Koreans in the precolonial period? The main reason was that the institutions and practices existing in Japan did not stifle incentives to exert greater effort and to innovate, whereas in Taiwan and Korea they did.

Incentive is dampened when particular institutions and practices permit government officials or other persons with power and authority arbitarily and frequently to seize the income and wealth of the people by various means, including appropriation through unregulated taxation.[23] On the other hand, incentive to

[20] *Ibid.*, p. 32.

[21] A. J. Brown, *The Mastery of the Far East, the Story of Korea's Transformation and Japan's Rise to Supremacy in the Orient* (New York, 1919), p. 78; Bishop, II, 207-212.

[22] Davidson, p. 602.

[23] The generic term in the economically advanced countries for these practices is corruption. In the less developed countries, they are modes of be-

produce will be high when a substantial share of the increase in output is retained by persons who make the decisions that determine the level of output. What is required for modern economic growth, then, are institutions and practices that reward effort and efficiency in both the private and government sectors. But this development assumes the existence of a reasonably honest and efficient administration. In Tokugawa Japan, despite occasional lapses, such a bureaucracy had come into existence in a number of provinces.[24]

One reason that predatory practices by government officials were not a serious problem in Japan was because the incentive to become corrupt was weaker. Perhaps the most important basis for corruption is the desire to accumulate wealth. But members of the Japanese ruling class were not permitted to accumulate wealth because accumulation by subordinates would threaten the hegemony of the Shogun or the feudal lords. The members were provided stipends on which they lived, and any surplus above subsistence needs was normally used up in forced consumption or other forms of spending expenditures forced upon them by the Shogun or the feudal lords as a means to prevent undue accumulations of wealth.[25] Because accumulation was denied them and their income tended to be adequte to their needs, the incentive to engage in corrupt practices was apparently effectively contained. It is a significant fact that whereas merchant families in Japan amassed fortunes and passed them on from generation to generation, this did not occur among samurai-administrators. An effective separation of political and economic vested interests had been in existence during the Tokugawa period.

A second reason for honesty and efficiency was the existence of a feudal system with some 300 semi-autonomous political units. Considering the feudal ideology, this meant that each unit felt itself to be surrounded by more or less competitive (and

---

havior often accepted as the norm by long usage. As such they may not be regarded as morally wrong. (This point was impressed upon me by Kenneth B. Platt, Agricultural Economics Adviser, United States Agency for International Development, who was then stationed in Korea.)

[24] See, for example, A. Craig, *Chōshū in the Meiji Restoration* (Cambridge, Mass., 1962), p. 355.

[25] Nakamura, *Agricultural Production . . .* , p. 157.

even hostile) polities. This imposed on each, to a greater or lesser extent depending upon its circumstances, a discipline and efficiency to meet the challenge of these competitive units. Such values of discipline and efficiency imply the existence of a strongly inhibiting force on corruption.

When existing social and political institutions and the need for social and political stability shape certain patterns of behavior, such behavior tends to become incorporated in a code of ethics. Thus, the samurai made loyalty to superiors, which was associated with their political function, the highest of virtues. Association with commoners, which might lead to bribery of samurai who were in positions of political power, was regarded as demeaning.[26] These moral precepts tended to reinforce the mundane bases of conduct. This constitutes a third reason for the existence of a bureaucracy that did not seriously impede growth.

Corruption in the government is not necessarily inconsistent with economic growth. If payoffs and the like are required to move frozen resources more quickly and smoothly through government red tape, then such forms of corruption may be a necessary cost of economic development, at least until the old values and attitudes can be changed. On the other hand, arbitrary and irrational, therefore unpredictable, forms of levies on wealth and income will inhibit growth because producers simply will not take action (risks) when the range of uncertainty in the anticipation of benefits (profits) is too great. When the amount (proportion) of the payroll can be anticipated, such payoffs can be treated as a cost of production as, say, a tax would be.

If property rights, including rights to income and wealth, are given greater protection, the incidence of unpredictable levies on income will decline. Then, because returns can be anticipated with greater certainty, producers will have greater incentive to produce. In practice, the response in increased production may be delayed because behavior patterns take time to change and

---

[26] The conduct of Japanese officials in Taiwan, where they regarded themselves in the position of samurai vis-à-vis the Taiwanese, who were regarded as commoners, is similar. Where corrupt practices existed, the relationship was typically between Japanese officials and Japanese businessmen, not with Taiwanese. [G. W. Barclay, *Colonial Development and Population in Taiwan* (Princeton, 1954), p. 59.] Similar behavior also occurred in Korea.

because the producers may regard the government program as another scheme to squeeze more taxes from them rather than as a measure to raise productivity by giving them a greater share of the incremental output.[27]

Recent research indicates that incentive to increase output remained strong in Japan during the Tokugawa period. Contrary to the often-repeated view that the economy stagnated in the last half of the Tokugawa period, per capita income appears to have had an upward trend in agriculture, industry, and commerce.[28] Moreover, the response of Japanese enterprises to the challenge provided by the end of the seclusion policy and to feudal restrictions indicates that the Japanese had nurtured values and attitudes which could not have been so vital a force if incentives had indeed been stifled.

In contrast, the Yi Dynasty of Korea had fostered institutions that encouraged the "squeeze" and nepotism. Officials at national, provincial, and local levels were expected to use their official positions to enrich themselves and their families—or at the least, were not discouraged from doing so. Any sign of affluence among the commoners was cause for attention by officials, who exacted from them most if not all of any increment in income or wealth above subsistence needs. As a consequence the incentive to work harder and to accumulate wealth was very low, if existent at all, among the peasants, fishermen, and other commoners. This is the basis for the superficial observation by foreigners that Koreans are lazy, when in fact the predatory practices of the *yang-bans* had drained away motivation for increased economic output.[29] Unlike the situation in Tokugawa Japan where political and economic vested interests remained separated, in Korea political power was a necessary steppingstone to the accumulation of wealth and vice-versa. Political and economic vested interests resided in the same group of people. This was the basis of corruption in Korea, and it also helps to explain the strength of entrenched interests which prevented the Yi Dynasty from adopting economic and political reforms that

[27] Farmers have good basis for suspicion. Such measures tend to increase the tax base, and taxes do tend to rise over time—particularly the local land tax.

[28] Nakamura, *Agricultural Production . . .* , pp. 76-77.

[29] For Mrs. Bishop's views on Korean energy and industry given incentives, see *op. cit.*, ii, 145.

might have made the emergence of a strong and independent Korea a more likely event.[30]

The relationship between corrupt practices and low productivity is explained by Mrs. Bishop as follows:

> Korea is not necessarily a poor country. Her resources are undeveloped, not exhausted. Her capacities for successful agriculture are scarcely exploited. . . .
>
> On the other hand, the energies of her people lie dormant. The upper classes . . . spend their lives in inactivity. To the middle classes no careers are open; there are no skilled occupations to which they can turn their energies. The lower classes work no harder than is necessary to keep the wolf from the door, for very sufficient reasons. Even in Seoul, the largest mercantile establishments have hardly risen to the level of shops. Everything in Korea has been on a low, poor, mean level. Class privileges, class and official exactions, a total absence of justice, the insecurity of all earnings . . . a class of official robbers steeped in intrigue . . . the mutual jealousies of interested foreigners . . . have all done their best to reduce Korea to that condition of resourcelessness and dreary squalor. . . .
>
> I have repeated almost *ad nauseam* that the cultivator of the soil is the *ultimate sponge*. The farmers work harder than any other class, and could easily double the production of the land, their methods, though somewhat primitive, being fairly well adapted to the soil and the climate. But having no security for their gains, they are content to produce only what will feed and clothe their families, and are afraid to build better houses or to dress respectably.[31]

Other observers with similar concern for the common people of Korea agree that corruption, misery, and official indifference prevailed. Mrs. Bishop's observations are more perceptive than most because she clearly saw that the squeeze put on the peasantry led to the deadening of incentive, which in turn reduced the country to low productivity. The latter put continuous pres-

---

[30] T. Suzuki, *Chōsen no keizai* (Tokyo, 1942), pp. 111-112. Y. Horie has stated that the separation of economic and political vested interests in Tokugawa Japan made reforms easier to adopt after the Meiji Restoration. *Meiji Ishin to keizai kindaika* (Tokyo, 1963), pp. 23-27.

[31] Bishop, II, 278-280.

sure on officials to maintain their exactions from the masses to complete the vicious circle. The society, the institutions, and the behavior patterns of the people had adjusted to these conditions over many centuries of Yi rule.

Conditions for the peasantry in Taiwan apparently were better than those in Korea—incentive sufficient to produce a surplus for export appears to have persisted. One reason for this state of affairs was that Taiwan had always remained open to foreign contact, whereas both Japan and Korea had retreated behind isolation until the latter half of the nineteenth century. Foreign contact provided increased demand for Taiwanese agricultural products and access to foreign technology—both factors that tend to increase productivity. This effect was offset by poor roads and the depredations of the *banditti*, which hindered the development of internal markets.[32]

More importantly, officials were expected to enrich themselves while in office as in Korea. This was built into the system because the salary paid the official was insufficient to maintain his family and retinue.[33] It is no surprise, then, that under Manchu rule Taiwan was regarded "as a source of speedy enrichment; and at times their exactions and misrule became so oppressive that revolts followed. A Chinese saying of those days concerning Taiwan sums up the situation: 'Every three years a disorder, and every five years a rebellion.' "[34] When Gotō Shimpei, a highly gifted administrator, took over as the chief civilian officer of Taiwan in 1898, discipline among government functionaries "was almost unknown," and the lowest-class interpreters and detectives of Taiwanese origin were said to have been drawing pay from both the *banditti* and the Japanese.[35]

These impressionistic descriptions can hardly provide a definitive statement on the relative suppression of incentives in the three countries. But the existence of institutions encouraging cor-

[32] G. L. Mackay, *Far from Formosa: The Island, Its People and Missions* (New York, 1895), p. 105.

[33] Barclay, p. 47.

[34] Grajdanzev, p. 15. See also Barclay, p. 45.

[35] S. Gotō, "The Administration of Formosa," in S. Okuma (ed.), *Fifty Years of New Japan* (London, 1909), pp. 532, 538. See also R. H. Myers and A. Ching, "Agricultural Development in Taiwan under Japanese Colonial Rule," *The Journal of Asian Studies*, xxiii, 4 (August, 1964), p. 560.

ruption in Taiwan and Korea and their relative absence in Japan, where the accumulation of wealth was denied the ruling class, strongly supports the view that differences in incentives help to account for the gap in productivity between Japan, Taiwan, and Korea during the early period of their agricultural development.

An effective economic growth policy depends on whether the expectations of the two parties to the policy—the policy-maker and the people or peoples acted on—are reasonably satisfied. The people whose behavior the government seeks to alter will expect the government to have honest and efficient administrators and attractive inducements to change. The government, in turn, if it can provide the above requirements, will expect the people to support its program. An effective policy, given these premises, requires not only a developmental policy with appropriate incentives but also effective political control.

Colonial rule may be defined simply as the governing of a country by a foreign leadership for the purposes determined by the foreign government and ultimately, if not also immediately, for the benefit of the foreign nation. The most immediate problem of such rule is effective political control over the colonial territory. It was, then, consistent with her goal that one of the first measures taken by Japan after the annexation of Taiwan and Korea was to insure control over these territories.[36] A powerful centralized bureaucracy under a governor-general—a military man at the beginning, in both cases—was imposed, backed by strong military and police presence. The proportion of Japanese officials in the central and local governments increased rapidly in both colonies, in line with the policy of achieving effective administrative control. In Taiwan, when official abuses became obvious and intolerable around 1898, the replacement of officials of the old regime by Japanese was speeded up.[37] By 1904 about 52 per cent of civil service personnel were Japanese, and this figure had increased to 66 per cent in 1930.[38] In Korea, the process of takeover by Japanese officials and police began during the protectorate years (1905-1910), and by the end of this period

[36] In Korea the take-over process started after she became a protectorate of Japan in 1905.

[37] Gotō, p. 533. [38] Koo, p. 11.

Japanese occupied about 40 per cent of all official posts. Four years later, the proportion had increased to about 70 per cent.[39]

Control over the colonies was not exercised solely by impersonal across-the-desk relationships. In Taiwan the small group *pao-chia* system was utilized by the government to maintain surveillance over and contact with the populace. Immediate contact was maintained by the police, who performed not only the police function, but also, in effect, served as minor officials who "enforced administration policy on sanitation, registration of households, tax collecting, engineering works, water control, planting windbreak forest zones, and, during World War I, even promoted the use of new rice seeds."[40] The police also served in an expanded capacity in Korea.[41]

The use of Japanese in administrative and professional posts in the colonies was a cost to Japan since it deprived her of trained personnel, who were then still in short supply. The fact that she bore this cost is a measure of the importance placed on early and certain political control and economic development of the colonies. Insofar as the colonies were poorly supplied with the type of personnel whose values, attitudes, and technical competence would help to promote economic development, the use of Japanese officials was an important factor in the growth that was achieved prior to World War II.

A second measure of great importance was the separation of economic from political vested interests. In Japan the oligarchs, a new governing elite with ultimate authority, replaced the Shogunate and the feudal lords in 1868. They used the land reform and the measures which paved the way for the reform to separate the feudal lords from their power base—their feudal domains and their samurai vassals and commoners. In the process,

[39] W. Dong, *Japanese Colonial Policy and Practice in Korea, 1905-1945: A Study in Assimilation* (Georgetown University Ph.D. dissertation, 1965; University Microfilms, Inc., Ann Arbor, Mich.), pp. 94, 222.

[40] H. Y. Chang and R. Myers, "Japanese Colonial Development Policy in Taiwan, 1895-1906: A Case of Bureaucratic Enterprise," *The Journal of Asian Studies*, XXII, 4 (August, 1963), p. 440. See also Grajdanzev, pp. 171-172, 195-198, regarding the *pao-chia* system.

[41] A. Ireland, *The New Korea* (New York, 1926), pp. 159-161. See also A. Lyman, "The Administration of Justice in Korea Under the Japanese Regime: Police Functions and Civil Liberties," *The Journal of the Bar Association of the District of Columbia*, XVI, 11 (November, 1949), pp. 489-497.

a transfer of wealth and income to the landowners took place.[42] Also elevated to a new level was the merchant class, which had become in most respects the locus of economic, but not political, power in the Tokugawa period. In Taiwan and Korea before the Japanese annexation (and protectorate for Korea) economic and political power tended to reside in the same elite group because political power made possible the accumulation of wealth, and much of the wealth consisted of fixed assets in the form of cultivated land.[43] The separation of economic and political power was accomplished by the removal of Taiwanese and Koreans from positions of political power. One consequence of the separation was the institution of land reform, which in Taiwan also helped in the separation by removing land income rights enjoyed by a class of people who may be regarded as absentee landlords. More importantly, the land reform clearly delineated property and income rights which previously, due to historical factors and the abuses of governmental authority, had not been clear.

An interesting parallel among the three countries is that the reforms were imposed from the top and that in each case the shift in the balance of economic power was away from the former ruling elite toward the commoners and, in the colonies, increasingly to Japanese businessmen and to the government. The locus of political power also shifted. Exactly where it moved is a debated point in Japan, but for most of the Meiji era power was exercised by the oligarchs. In the case of the colonies it is clear that political power was effectively taken over by the governor-general's office.

It is a matter of historical record that Japan's major economic policy in Taiwan and Korea, until late in the colonial period, was agricultural and commercial development, which was an integral part of her overall development plan for the empire. This policy

[42] J. I. Nakamura, "Meiji Land Reform, Redistribution of Income, and Savings from Agriculture," *Economic Development and Cultural Change*, xiv, 4 (July, 1966), pp. 428-439.

[43] P. Kovenock has correctly pointed out that the situation in Taiwan, which was a frontier area still in the process of settlement by the Chinese, was more fluid and that wealth did not necessarily confer political power or vice versa. But a separation of the two, as in Japan, did not exist.

derived from five important considerations: 1) Japan's growing food shortage; 2) her expanding industrial production; 3) the resource endowment of the colonial areas; 4) strategic requirements; and 5) Taiwan's and Korea's low levels of agricultural technology and productivity which led to the belief that rapid agricultural development could be achieved. Taiwan's annexation in 1895 came in the middle of the decade when Japan became a rice importer and, only a decade later, Korea became a protectorate after Japan's status as a food importer had been fully confirmed. This was also a time when some of Japan's industrial products, particularly textiles, were starting to penetrate the world market, and Taiwan and Korea promised to provide lucrative controlled markets. But more important still, in view of Japan's desire to develop her empire, was the form of the colonies' resource endowments—higher land-man ratio, lack of industrial capital, and the low level of development of human skills. The colonies not only had less population per unit of cultivated land, but offered greater possibilities for increasing the area of cultivated land and for raising the yield per unit area. Furthermore, the available human capital was complementary with other agricultural resources, but was less well suited to non-agricultural production. Strategic considerations hardly mattered during the early phase of the colonies' development because the other factors would have been sufficiently important to overshadow these.

Many of the specific colonial economic policies pursued by Japan derived directly from the experience of planning her own economic development.[44] Most important policies established in the colonies can be traced directly to their successful implementation in Japan (in many cases the policies adopted for Japan derived directly from the Western experience of growth), and in the case of Korea, their success in Taiwan as well. This generalization also applies to non-economic policies. A difference

[44] The term "planning" is not used in the current sense of programming the development of an economy. Rather it is meant that Japan believed, as Adam Smith did, that given capitalist institutions and adequate incentives and inducements from the government, the economy would grow as though guided by an "invisible hand." Thus her planning consisted of providing the appropriate institutions and inducements, including an infrastructure which would provide external economies to the private sector.

between the development plans for the colonies and those for Japan is the greater energy and force with which the former were carried out. The difference may have been partly due to Japan's greater knowledge of planning and more economically advanced state when she began her planning for the colonies and to the fact that the Taiwanese and Koreans, as subject people, required greater coercion and could be coerced more readily than could the Japanese.

An important and, perhaps, unique characteristic of the Japanese was their impatience with slow economic progress.[45] This impatience, a factor in the relatively rapid development in all three countries, was first exhibited in Japan. It was epitomized by M. Maeda, who was responsible for Japan's first comprehensive "plan" of development, which appears in that remarkable 1884 document, *Kōgyō iken*, setting forth a development program for the decade from 1885 to 1895.[46] It called for extraordinarily high production targets for a great many industrial commodities and agricultural crops.[47] These targets were not fulfilled except in a few industries; in some, the targets were overfulfilled.[48] What Maeda had in mind was what we might today call a "big push" strategy of economic growth, although his strategy was based not explicitly on the desirability of capturing external economies or developing a number of industries simultaneously, but rather on the simple desire for rapid economic

[45] Suzuki, pp. 111-112.

[46] Literally "Views on the Promotion of Enterprise." The document comprises three volumes of *MZZKSS*, volumes 18, 19, 20.

[47] *Ibid.*, vol. 18, 50-61.

[48] An article that appeared in 1967 states that the scheduled growth targets for a number of agricultural and industrial products were met and shows that, in some, overfulfillment of targets occurred. The statement would be true if the official production statistics are accurate as the authors assume. I. Inukai and A. Tussing, "*Kōgyō Iken*: Japan's Ten-year Plan, 1884," *Economic Development and Cultural Change*, XIV, 1 (October, 1967), pp. 51-71.

The consensus now seems to be that the increase in production which shows up in official statistics during the decade (the increase occurs primarily between 1886 and 1888) was a result of understatement of production in the early 1880's. In my view the understatement continued well into the twentieth century. For further discussion see Nakamura, *Agricultural Production* . . . , chapters 4, 6.

development.[49] Although the available production data render judgment on the growth of agricultural and industrial production unreliable, the development of social overhead capital took place at rates about equivalent to those Maeda had anticipated.[50]

One reason for the uneven performance of the Japanese economy in respect to the target was that there was very little direct interference in the allocation of resources except in social overhead capital formation and certain militarily strategic industries. The plan had no teeth in it, and Maeda evidently expected the incentives and inducements of government action and the many appeals to the national spirit to provide entrepreneurial incentives. The plan also failed to take account of market forces in Japan and the rest of the world. It is plain that the Japanese believed that planning should extend to the creation of appropriate environment and conditions—including the provision of social overhead capital—for economic development and that this along with the national spirit would provide the basis for growth.

Planning was more important in the colonies than in Japan. Japan's agricultural and commercial development objectives for Taiwan and Korea dictated certain government acts and expenditures. The heavy expenditures on social overhead capital (railways, roads, shipping, and communications) and agricultural development (irrigation facilities, provision of working capital, agricultural infrastructure) followed primarily from the need for a source of food, agricultural raw materials, and an outlet for Japan's industrial products. Since the long-run goals of colonial development were clear, the particular measures which had to be taken to accomplish those goals also became more evident and therefore could be pursued with greater vigor than the more ambiguous goals of earlier Japanese economic development. Given a relatively backward populace prone to resistance, and

[49] For a discussion of the "big push" strategy see P. N. Rosenstein-Rodan, "Notes on the Theory of the 'Big Push,'" in H. S. Ellis and H. C. Wallich (eds.), *Economic Development for Latin America* (New York, 1961), pp. 57-73. Maeda was aware of the pecuniary economies that would be forthcoming from investment in social overhead capital.

[50] Inukai and Tussing, p. 59, show that the expected increases were 947 and 103 per cent in railway mileage and ships, and the actual achievements were 1065 and 79 per cent respectively. See also W. W. Lockwood, *Economic Development of Japan* (Princeton, 1954), p. 14.

given Japan's impatience, the nature of military and political control which took shape was, perhaps, to be expected.[51]

To some extent the appearance of planning may have been exaggerated by the fact that the economic policies pursued in the colonies did not conflict, for the most part, with the operations of market forces except as these forces were distorted by the depression. But there is hardly any doubt that Japan planned the development of her colonies more comprehensively and effectively than she did her own development—and, for that matter, than did the other colonial powers.

A unique feature of Japan's colonial agricultural program was the development of traditional agriculture, which typically engaged in the production of necessities by traditional methods. This differs from the type of agriculture promoted by Western colonial powers, which typically tended to be commercial agriculture producing exotic industrial crops, often by heavy fixed investment on plantations, in order to supply the markets of economically advanced nations.

A second distinguishing feature was the Japanese expectation that Taiwanese and Korean land and labor productivity could be induced to rise—an expectation that was fulfilled. On the other hand, Westerners at this time either assumed that the colonial peoples had a backward-bending supply curve of effort or did not believe that the social benefits of raising productivity would offset the social costs, from their point of view (not necessarily from that of the colonial peoples). The Japanese attitudes were consistent with their knowledge of the Taiwanese and Korean peoples and cultures. No presumption existed on the part of the Japanese that the Taiwanese and Koreans were not capable of being induced to increase their productivity. That is, they believed that the latter's long-run, if not short-run, supply curves of effort were positively sloped. History has vindicated their view, since the response apparently came within a generation.

The economic consequences of these two different approaches can be substantial. The Japanese, in effect, attempted to mobilize the energies of the entire agricultural population by a process

[51] The desire for rapid and effective control of the economies is evident also in the extraordinary attention given to the collection of statistical data from soon after Japan took control. For a pertinent comment on Japan's propensity to keep records see Barclay, p. viii.

leading from an increase in land and labor productivity to the production of an increasing marketable surplus, to a growing awareness of markets for crops and for agricultural inputs and the choices they offered.[52] At this point the farmer had started to develop the values and reactions that in many respects mark him as a modern, not a traditional, man, and one better suited to assume a role in industrialization. On the other hand, the colonial peoples of Western powers tended to operate under two handicaps: 1) in plantation agriculture only a small segment of the population was directly affected; and 2) to the extent that the Western nations did not often provide sufficient incentives, the productivity of the plantation workers did not rise.

Japan had advantages over the Western nations that made her course of action more economically attractive than it would have been for them. Her foremost import requirement was rice, a product *par excellence* of traditional East Asian agriculture, thus causing her to promote increased output from traditional agriculture. The proximity of Taiwan and Korea to Japan meant lower transportation costs, better information, less resistance to colonial service by government officials, and more government confidence that strong measures could be enforced because quick military support from the home country could be relied on. Since Japan herself was a nation of islands, the integration of two more territories sufficiently close so as to cost very little extra in transportation and time presented relatively few problems. Therefore, it is possible to conceive of the integration of the two colonial economies into Japan as almost on a par with that of the islands. That is, instead of the development of export-oriented enclaves, as was typically the case for Western colonial powers, the economic linkages established between Japan and the two colonies extended to all sectors of the economies.

Productivity increase is positively related to the proportion of the increase that the producer can retain and to the degree of assurance that the return will not be arbitrarily expropriated. In all three areas similar measures were taken to make both these

[52] The process would tend to be accompanied by an increase in the level of rural education as the rural per capita income rises. But this process takes time, and in the case of Korea the farmers may have just started to acquire these by-products when the war caused a setback.

conditions more favorable. These measures, in general, established private property systems and provided other capitalist economic institutions. A principal instrument of change was the land reform.[53] The earlier Japanese land reform (cultivated-land survey completed in 1876) provided models for more thorough and accurate land surveys in Taiwan (completed 1906) and Korea (1918). Prior to the land surveys, land records had been in a more or less chaotic state in all three countries, and the surveys uncovered much concealed (unregistered or misclassified) cultivated land. The surveys and the reforms therefore were calculated to: 1) identify, classify, and register all plots; 2) determine ownership; 3) protect ownership rights; 4) simplify the sale and purchase of land; 5) achieve tax equity; and 6) to promote land improvement and utilization. In Japan, a political objective of the reform was to separate the *daimyō* from their sources of power—land and subjects. In Taiwan it was to separate the absentee landlords (*ta-tsu-fu*) from the land.[54] In Korea, while the connection between some of the *yang-ban*[55] and their rural sources of income was severed, the land reform did not cut so deeply into the economic structure as it did in the other two countries.[56]

Prior to the land reform not only were property rights uncertain, but arbitrary seizure of property and income was possible in Taiwan and Korea. Uncertainty and possibility of expropriation existed to some extent in Japan also, although they failed to stop growth in productivity. After the reforms, the requirements of a functional capitalist system established the sanctity of property, and levies on income (land tax, excise taxes, etc.) were determined by law.

The effect of economic reforms on incentives is dependent

[53] For discussion of land reforms in Japan, Taiwan, and Korea see the following: Nakamura, *Agricultural Production* . . . , Appendix A; Myers and Ching; and Okurashō, *Meiji Taishō zaisei shi* (Tokyo, 1935-1940), vol. 18, 183ff. *Meiji Taishō zaisei shi* will be cited henceforth as *MTZS*. For Korea see also Brown, *op. cit.*, pp. 363-365.

[54] They were given bonds in compensation. For details see *MTZS*, vol. 18, 209-230.

[55] A member of the Korean ruling class before the Japanese annexation of Korea.

[56] It is possible that the Japanese could have won somewhat greater support from the commoners (as distinct from the *yang-ban*), if they had boldly gone as far as, or even further than, they did in Taiwan.

largely on honest and efficient administration. Observers and scholars agree that despite some irregularities, the colonial bureaucracy was reasonably honest, efficient, and hard-working. The reasons for this are not hard to find. The police (and for that matter, other officials) were given a good salary, had automatic raises, and, in accordance with the standard Japanese practice, also had permanent tenure unless removed from office for cause. Colonial officials could also retire after only 12 years of service as against 16 years of service in Japan.[57] These conditions, unlike those that held true for pre-annexation Taiwanese and Korean officials, deterred corruption and encouraged effort.[58] One long-time observer of the colonial scene had the following to say: "In the matter of corruption, I am convinced beyond all doubt that, allowing for an occasional exception, the government of self-ruled countries is much more corrupt than that of colonial dependencies, and that, in the latter, malversation in public office is of very rare occurrence."[59] A government based on the rule of law and generally regarded as free of corruption would provide assurance to the masses of farmers and other working people that the income they had earned and the wealth they had accumulated would not be arbitrarily expropriated. This change would constitute a powerful incentive to increased effort.

We have noted that a productivity gap existed between Japan and her colonies when the new regimes took over. The process of agricultural growth in the colonies was one of narrowing this gap. We are here concerned primarily with technical change, particularly with the diffusion of superior techniques (inputs) already available in the economy but not widely known, and with the importation of foreign technology. Differences in the types and sources of agricultural inputs in the three countries help to explain differences in the rates and patterns of growth.

[57] Professor M. Miyamoto called my attention to this point.

[58] Chang and Myers, p. 440. See also Barclay, pp. 68-69. For a description of the character of colonial bureaucracy in Korea see Brown, chapters 22, 23; and Lyman, *op. cit.*

[59] Ireland, *op. cit.*, p. 11. Writers today use somewhat more restrained language. Today's scholars, who are more ready to applaud understatement than overstatement, may find the voice somewhat strident. For Korea, before and following annexation, few would deny the applicability of the statement. For Ireland's view, see *ibid.*, p. 17.

Meiji agricultural leaders sought among other things to disseminate broadly throughout Japan the best available domestic varieties of crops and the best cultivation techniques. One view is that Meiji agriculture grew rapidly because a backlog of technology from the Tokugawa period was more quickly diffused after the Meiji Restoration, as a result of the efforts of veteran farmers.[60] If diffusion of techniques by government prodding did increase output to the extent held by these writers, the implication is that: although yield-increasing innovations existed toward the end of the Tokugawa period, most Japanese remained ignorant of the fact or were aware of it but did not respond, or that such innovations were forthcoming with such rapidity that a special effort was needed to get them out to the farmers. The fact is that yield-raising innovations came slowly and, when they did arrive, were probably disseminated fairly quickly throughout the nation when they were not purely local in application. This was due to the existence of a nation-wide network of transportation and communications and a level of literacy that was, as we have already noted, exceptionally high for an underdeveloped country.[61] Some inputs, of course, remain unused until cost-benefit data are favorable. Thus the use of commercial fertilizers spread after railways and roads reduced their cost and increased the farm price of outputs. This increase came almost entirely in the twentieth century,[62] after the use of veteran farmers[63] as travelling lecturers had been virtually discontinued.[64]

[60] Y. Hayami, "On the Japanese Experience of Agricultural Growth: Review Article," *Rural Economic Problems*, IV, 2 (May, 1968), p. 86; H. Rosovsky, "Rumbles in the Ricefields: Professor Nakamura vs the Official Statistics," *The Journal of Asian Studies*, XXVII, 2 (February, 1968), p. 358. See also Y. Hayami and S. Yamada, "Technological Progress in Agriculture," in L. Klein and K. Ohkawa (eds.), *Economic Growth: The Japanese Experience Since the Meiji Era* (Homewood, Ill., 1968).

[61] The names of texts for Tokugawa period rural school children indicate the interest in agricultural improvements. *Supra*, p. 10.

[62] Hayami, "Hiryō tōkaryō no suikei," 293.

[63] "Veteran farmers" is my literal translation of *rōnō*; "superior farmers" would be a freer and more accurate rendering.

[64] At the beginning veteran farmers had been primarily used to introduce Western farming methods. S. Tobata and T. Morinaga (eds.), *Nihon nōgyō hattatsu shi* (Tokyo, 1953-1959), IX, 49. But in the 1880's, they became one of the factors in the agricultural improvement policy under a law providing for travelling lecturers in which they played an important role. (*Ibid.*, III, 310.) This law was abolished in 1893 (*ibid.*, 310), and a new law was

Criticisms of the methods of veteran farmers had begun in the 1880's, led by such men as T. Sako, J. Yokoi, and M. Fresca.[65] The decline of the influence of veteran farmers came just at the time when the agricultural colleges were beginning to turn out specialists in agriculture. The fact that the colleges were dropped at this time is related to the growing criticism of the work of veteran farmers.[66] They had been the best available personnel at the time, but when trained specialists arrived, they became expendable. The main reason for their relative ineffectiveness was that Japan's agriculture was developed almost as far as the available knowledge, technology, and economic forces permitted. More significant development required breakthroughs in technology or major changes in economic conditions. Because Japan was a pioneer in her type of agriculture[67] despite the absence of modern research and development techniques, innovations came slowly.[68]

The levels of domestic technological developments were much lower in Taiwan and Korea. The problem of whether veteran farmers would be used to disseminate domestic techniques simply did not arise. It was immediately assumed that policies used successfully in Japan and elsewhere should be applied in the colonies. Among other things, the importance of spreading information on tested seeds, fertilizers, and cultivation methods was stressed. This probably was a reaction to recommendations of untested and unsuccessful techniques by veteran farmers and others in Japan before the advent of trained specialists.

The introduction of inputs and techniques imported from foreign nations has been the source of much of the world's agricultural and industrial development. In this regard Japan was no exception. However, because Japan's leaders were enamored of

passed which instituted a new travelling lecturer system, operating under the control of the newly established agricultural experimental station, in which graduates from agricultural colleges played the leading role as lecturers. (*Ibid.*)

[65] *Ibid.*, I, 60-62.

[66] A few did play a role in agricultural development although the extent of their contribution is in controversy: e.g., N. Nakamura, D. Funatsu, S. Nara, and O. Hayashi. *Ibid.*, I, 114.

[67] S. Kawano, *Taiwan Beikoku zeizai ron* (Tokyo, 1941). An exception is the Dutch techniques in riparian and drainage works, pp. 133-136.

[68] Nakamura, *Agricultural Production* . . . , p. 86.

the wondrous machines and techniques then being used in the West, the introduction of these inputs in early Meiji was indiscriminate. As a consequence, this attempt failed except with some crops and livestock which were adaptable to Japanese conditions. More fruitful was the introduction of the scientific approach to solving problems—particularly in applied research. The main reason for the failure of specific innovations to take root was that Western innovations were designed for relatively large-scale dry-land farms, whereas the scale of Japanese farming was very small and Japan's main agricultural problem was the discovery of new inputs for small-scale, irrigated rice culture. A major difference between the Japanese and Western modes of production was that the former required more land-saving inputs such as fertilizers, improved seed, and irrigation, whereas the latter—particularly sparsely settled regions—required proportionally more labor-saving inputs such as agricultural machines, roads, and railroads.

On the other hand, foreign inputs played a much more important role in Taiwan and Korea. Given the gap in paddy rice yields per hectare (as a proxy for the yield of all agricultural crops) between Japan and her two colonies and the technological gap that it implies, the indicated policy for raising yield was to introduce yield-raising inputs from the higher yield countries. Japan's almost total failure with specialized Western inputs such as seed, machinery, and the like, understandably caused her officials to be more discriminating in introducing them into Taiwan and Korea. In fact, owing to the importance of the rice crop in these countries and the small scale of operations which places a premium on land-saving technology, Japanese techniques were usually more applicable. Specialized foreign technology that went into Taiwan and Korea was, then, mostly Japanese technology. The more general techniques, such as the use of commercial fertilizers, controlled use of water, the building of an agricultural infrastructure, the scientific method, experimental stations, and the like—some of which were derived from the West—were introduced (transmitted) and/or stimulated by Japanese agricultural specialists in both countries.

Climatic factors, however, introduced significant differences between Korea and Taiwan in measures used to increase rice production. For example, improved seed from Japan were not suitable in Taiwan except in plateau regions where the climate was nearly similar.[69] Therefore, a real breakthrough in yield did not come until 1925 after experimental stations, modelled on those of Japan, produced a high-yielding variety adapted to Taiwan's climate and to the Japanese palate.[70] Korea fared much better. Improved seed from Japan which had been tested and found suitable for Korean conditions was productively used on a rapidly growing proportion of paddy fields.

Japan, of course, had no indigenous techniques applicable to the tropical crops of Taiwan. She went elsewhere, primarily to other tropical areas, for improved varieties of sugar and other crops and for superior cultivation techniques. In fact, the attention of agricultural officials in Taiwan was first given to the promotion of sugar-cane production rather than to rice production because importation of sugar constituted a more serious drain on Japanese foreign exchange in the 1890's than rice.[71] This attention was reinforced by the fact that in the 1890's Japan had only just become a rice importer and the trend may not have been entirely clear to policy-makers[72] whereas she was a heavy and consistent sugar importer.[73]

An interesting aspect of Japan's sugar-cane farming was that it was the only case in her empire of large-scale farming and of huge initial outlays of private investment in agricultural enterprises.[74] This was in most respects a typical colonial plantation agriculture in which the plantation management supervised all aspects of cultivation, from the planting of seedlings to the harvest.[75] This was an exception to Japan's colonial policy of developing traditional agriculture, but not one that was entirely

[69] Kawano, p. 59.

[70] The rice produced was *Taichu* 65, the preeminent *ponlai* variety which was planted to 85 per cent of the area planted to *ponlai* rice. (*Ibid.*, p. 65.) This type of rice was developed from the more glutinous rice of Japan which suits Japanese and Korean taste, in contrast to most Asians' taste for non-glutinous rice.

[71] In the 3-year period of 1893-1895, the average annual value of sugar imports was 12 million yen against 5 million yen for rice. Computed from Oriental Economist, *Foreign Trade of Japan: A Statistical Survey* (Tokyo, 1935), pp. 165, 154.

[72] The erratic statistical reporting of agricultural production during the Meiji era could easily have confused policy-makers.

[73] Sugar imports accounted for 10 per cent of total imports in 1893-1895. Computed from *ibid.*, p. 165.

[74] Kawano, p. 24.   [75] *Ibid.*, p. 25.

without instruction to the farmers. According to S. Tobata, Taiwan developed better farmers than Japan did because climatic conditions offered the farmer in Southern Taiwan a choice between planting rice and sugar on paddy fields and thus made him cost-benefit conscious. This was not true for the Japanese farmer, who had no choice but to plant rice.[76]

Measures for, and costs of, the promotion of sugar-cane and rice production differed. In general, loans and subsidies to encourage sugar-cane production were given to individual growers to pay for seedlings, fertilizers, land reclamation and improvement, irrigation and drainage facilities, and the like, to promote capital-intensive large-scale operation.[77] The promotion of rice production, on the other hand, was achieved mostly through research and development, aid to agricultural associations, and bureaucratic action such as extension work.[78] Because rice was a traditional crop grown widely throughout the island, heavy and prolonged financial aid was not required to induce farmers to adopt productive new inputs. According to S. Kawano, subsidies and loans to the private sector for sugar production amounted to about 13 million yen from 1902 to about 1935.[79] This, he says, is vastly in excess of 680 thousand yen for rice-seed improvement and distribution, expenditures on encouragement of the use of green manure crops and compost, and subsidization of warehouse construction for the storage of rice.

Since Japan had relied primarily on trained specialists for administrative work, extension service, and research and development after they became available, she, quite consistently, exported the now available experts to help the agricultural development of her colonies. Although it had taken time for Japan to develop experts to man the many functions for which they were required in her economic development, Taiwan and Korea had experts allocated to them as soon as effective control over these areas was acquired. If success in economic development required the coordinated efforts of technicians, then Tai-

[76] This point was made during the course of a conversation in August, 1967, at the Institute of Developing Economies in Tokyo.

[77] Kawano, pp. 27-28.   [78] *Ibid.*, pp. 160, 28.

[79] *Ibid.*, pp. 27-28. Financial aid was given also in the form of protection from foreign competition by tariffs to rice and sugar-cane producers. However this protection was at least partly nullified for the small cane producers because they had to sell in monopsonistic market in which sugar-cane prices were closely tied to rice prices. Koo, p. 20.

wan and Korea were provided with this important input at a time when such specialists were becoming available. Further, they came under Japan's control when she had begun to appreciate the value of experts.

A comparison of Taiwanese, Korean, and Japanese agricultural output and inputs will be shown by the use of growth rates and of percentage changes because this is more meaningful for our purposes than absolute figures. A number of indicators suggest that the growth rate of agricultural output was higher in Taiwan and Korea than in Japan. Some of these have been noted earlier—for example, the incentive differences and productivity gaps between Japan and her colonies, and the efforts made to narrow them. Another is that Japan became a food importer whereas Taiwan and Korea were exporters. A third important indicator is that Japan's population grew more slowly (0.9 per cent) than those of Taiwan (1.3) and Korea (1.6).

For this statistical examination the time-periods considered for each of the three countries differ considerably. For Taiwan and Korea we are concerned with the colonial period, and actually with 1911-1915 to 1936-1940 for the former and 1918-1922 to 1933-1937 for the latter, because more reliable records are available for these years. For Japan the period selected is 1878-1882 to 1918-1922. During these periods the growth rates of agricultural output based on *official* statistics were 3.4, 1.7, and 2.4 per cent, respectively, for Taiwan, Korea, and Japan. Contrary to expectations, since similar biases in the data was assumed for all three countries, Korean growth rate computed from official statistics is lower than the Japanese rate by a wide margin. However, the Japanese growth rates have been shown to be biased upward, and the Nakamura estimates reduced them to about 1.0 per cent, which is below the Korean rate of growth estimated from official statistics. A new estimate, which is called the LTES,[80] estimates places the rate at 1.9 per cent, which is higher than the official rate.[81]

Considering the fact that the population-growth rate from

[80] LTES is a partial acronym of *Estimates of Long-term Economic Statistics of Japan since 1868: Volume 9: Agricultural and Forestry*, M. Umemura *et al.* (eds.) The estimates are from this book.

[81] For growth rate data see Table 5.

TABLE 2

Indices of Agricultural Output and Inputs in Korea, 1913-1937

Period	Suh's agricultural output[1]	Staple food crop output[2]	Crop area	Agricultural households	Fertilizer consumption[3]	Irrigated land area
	(1)	(2)	(3)	(4)	(5)	(6)
1910-12	75.4	72.3	—	90.0	—	—
1913-17	97.0	90.4	88.9	97.1	—	76.1
1918-22	100.0	100.0	100.0	100.0	100.0	100.0
1923-27	104.7	99.7	103.6	101.6	230.7	101.7
1928-32	120.3	102.6	108.1	106.2	441.3	106.2
1933-37	128.1	119.2	113.1	113.1	734.3	110.0
1939-41	137.7	—	—	—	—	—

Sources: Column (1) computed from S. C. Suh, "Growth and Structural Changes in the Korean Economy Since 1910" (Harvard University Department of Economics dissertation, 1966), II, 37. This is an index of 3-year averages.
Column (2) computed from data in *Chōsen sōtokufu tōkei nenkan*, and FAO. *Food Composition Tables for International Use* (October, 1949). See Note 2.
Column (3) computed from K. Kohayakawa (ed.), *Chōsen nōgyō hattatsu shi: shiryō hen* (Tokyo, 1960), p. 98. Land used in shifting agriculture is not included.
Column (4) computed from *ibid.*, p. 91.
Column (5) computed from *ibid.*, pp. 111-112, by using 1928-30 prices.
Column (6) computed from *ibid.*, p. 97, and *Chōsen sōtokufu tōkei nenkan 1938*, 52-53.
[1] The agricultural production by Suh is his market value of agricultural production, which includes the value of green manure crops.
[2] Staple food crop output is calculated in terms of calorie values of the following food staples: rice, wheat, barley, naked barley, foxtail millet, barnyard millet, proso millet, kaoliang, oats, corn, Irish potatoes, sweet potatoes, soy beans, and azuki.
[3] Fertilizers consumed include both farm produced and commercial fertilizers.

1920 to 1935 was 1.6 per cent in Korea, a 1.7 per cent increase in agricultural production is barely enough to meet the increasing food needs of a growing population. However, the growth rate of staple food crops from 1918-1922 to 1933-1937 according to official statistics was only 1.2 per cent per year. In the same period, net exports (exports minus imports) of staple food crops increased at a rate of 5 per cent per year, and by the end of the period was 18 per cent of total staple food crops. Significantly, the net supply of staple food crops increased by only 9 per cent during this period, a growth rate of 0.6 per cent.[82] For Korea the difference in the growth rates of population and the net staple

[82] Staple-food data computed from Table 6.

TABLE 3

Indices of Agricultural Output and Inputs in Taiwan, 1911-1940

Year	Gross agricultural output[1]	Crop area	Labor force	Fertilizer consumption[2]	"Irrigated land area"[3]
	(1)	*(2)*	*(3)*	*(4)*	*(5)*
1911-15	100.0	100.0	100.0	100.0	100.0
1916-20	115.3	106.4	99.4	159.5	118.1
1921-25	132.9	111.8	99.1	189.4	138.6
1926-30	164.3	119.4	103.5	262.9	170.9
1931-35	202.0	131.1	116.9	351.5	193.6
1936-40	230.7	138.4	125.9	503.9	219.2

Source: Computed from S. Ho, "Agricultural Transformation under Colonialism: The Case of Taiwan," *The Journal of Economic History,* xxviii, 3 (September, 1968), p. 318.

[1] Gross agricultural output is defined to include also agricultural products used on the farms including intermediate products.

[2] Fertilizers consumed include self-supplied and commercial fertilizers.

[3] "Irrigated land area" refers to irrigated land whose improvement was subsidized by the government.

food supply indicate a decline in consumption of staple crops of 11 per cent from 1918-1922 to 1933-1937. Computation of calorie availability for human consumption shows that calorie consumption from staple food crops apparently declined. But what is even more significant is that the supply seems to have been less than the minimal requirement for good health, which we will conservatively assume to be 2000 calories per person per day, although the United Nations puts requirements at about 2300 calories for Asians.[83] In 1928-1932 the average availability implied by official statistics was 1575 calories and in 1933-1937 it was 1663, as shown in Table 7. In 1918-1922 it had been 1932.

A qualification in the calorie supply data should be made. Not all sources of calories have been included. Excluded are meat, animal fat, poultry, fish, dairy products, vegetables, and fruits. In Japan in 1934-1938 these sources were computed to have supplied 7 per cent of total calories.[84] The percentage was probably lower for Korea, where average income level was lower. How-

[83] United Nations, *Compendium of Social Statistics: 1963,* p. 163.

[84] Computed from United Nations, *Food Balance Sheet: Japan 1934-38.*

TABLE 4

Indices of Agricultural Output and Inputs in Japan, 1878-1922

Period	Nakamura agricultural output	LTES agricultural output[1]	Arable land area	Labor force	Fertilizer consumption[2]	Irrigated land area
	(1)	(2)	(3)	(4)	(5)	(6)
1878-82	100.0	100.0	100.0	100.0	—	100.0
1883-87	103.9	113.3	101.3	100.4	100.0	101.2
1888-92	108.8	121.0	102.7	100.1	103.2	102.6
1893-97	113.2	126.0	104.2	98.9	109.4	103.2
1898-1902	119.8	142.2	107.5	97.7	117.1	104.7
1903-07	126.9	155.2	110.9	97.4	127.6	106.3
1908-12	135.5	165.6	115.4	97.1	152.2	108.5
1913-17	143.9	199.2	118.8	97.1	170.8	111.0
1918-22	152.6	212.7	122.4	96.6	193.6	113.0

Sources: Column (1) computed from J. Nakamura, *Agricultural Production and the Economic Development of Japan 1873-1922* (Princeton, 1966), p. 114.
Column (2) computed from M. Umemura, *et al.*, *Estimates of Long Term Economic Statistics of Japan Since 1868*, Vol. 9, 152-153.
Column (3) computed from Nakamura, pp. 43, 48.
Column (4) computed from M. Umemura, *Chingin-koyō nōgyō* (Tokyo, 1961), p. 119.
Column (5) Y. Hayami, "Hiryō tōka ryō no suikei," *Nōgyō sōgō kenkyū*, xvii, 1 (January, 1963), p. 253.
Column (6) computed from Nakamura, p. 43.
[1] The LTES index of agricultural output of Column (2) is based on the assumption that government agricultural production data are reliable from 1890. The Nakamura index assumes that government statistics understated production until 1918-22. See text or Nakamura, pp. 65-73, for explanation.
[2] Fertilizer consumption data include self-supplied and commercial fertilizers. M. Umemura, *et al.*, pp. 194-195, also compiles a fertilizer consumption series but it does not include self-supplied fertilizers.

ever, assuming a 7 per cent increase, 1575 calories rises to 1685, and the 1663 calories to 1779.[85]

There appear to be two valid propositions regarding Korean statistics. The first is that statistical reporting was relatively accurate for a short period after the completion of the cadastral

[85] Of 72 countries submitting calorie consumption data to the Food and Agricultural Organization of the United Nations, only 6 show daily per capita consumption of less than 2000 in their latest reports. However, the Economic Research Service, Foreign Regional Analysis Division, U.S. Department of Agriculture, estimates that each of the 6 consumed more than 2000 calories. Nakamura, "Nakamura Versus the LTES Estimates . . . ," p. 361.

TABLE 5

Growth Rates of Agricultural Output and Inputs in
Japan, Korea, and Taiwan

	Gross agricultural output	Crop area	Labor force	Fertilizer consumption	Irrigated land area
	(1)	*(2)*	*(3)*	*(4)*	*(5)*
Japan (1878-82 to 1918-22)					
1. Ohkawa estimates	2.4	—	—0.19	—	—
2. Nakamura estimates	1.0	0.6[1]	—0.08	1.9	0.3
3. LTES estimates	1.9	—	—0.12	—[2]	0.3
Korea					
4. (1919-21 to 1934-36)	1.7[3]	0.8	0.8[4]	14.2	0.6
Taiwan					
5. (1911-15 to 1936-40)	3.4	1.3	0.9	6.7	1.8

Sources: Row 1 computed from K. Ohkawa, *et al.*, *The Growth Rate of the Japanese Economy Since 1878* (Tokyo, 1957).

Row 2 computed from Table 4.

Row 3 computed from M. Umemura, *et al.*, *Estimates of Long-term Economic Statistics of Japan Since 1868*, Vol. 9 (Tokyo, 1966).

Row 4 computed from Table 2. Agricultural households are assumed to grow proportionately with the agricultural labor force.

Row 5 computed from Table 3, except for irrigated land area data which is taken from *Taiwan sōtokufu tōkeisho*.

[1] The Nakamura crop area growth rate is derived from the sum of upland fields, paddy fields. and double-cropped paddy fields. Although it is believed that some absolute increase in multiple cropping occurred, this increase is assumed to be offset by the increase in Hokkaido cultivated land area which accounted for 75 per cent of the total increase. Hokkaido land is single-cropped due to the short growing season.

[2] LTES estimate of fertilizer consumption is for commercial fertilizers and green manure crops only, and, therefore, being noncomparable is left out.

[3] For Korea the growth rate of agricultural output from 1919-21 to 1939-41, according to S. C. Suh's estimate of output, is also 1.7 per cent. (Computed from Table 2.)

[4] Korean labor force growth is assumed to be the same as the growth rate of agricultural households.

survey in 1918. The second is that the village agricultural associations responsible for statistical reporting underreported output by an increasing percentage thereafter. The underreporting is accordant with past Korean practice, by which local officials underreported crops in order to withhold a higher proportion of their tax revenues from the central government.[86] Underreporting has, of course, been a persistent practice in almost all socie-

[86] Bishop.

TABLE 6

Average Production, Net Exports, and Net Domestic Supply of Staple Food
Crops in Brown Rice Equivalents in Korea, 1913-1937
(unit = 1000 *koku*)

Year	Annual average production[1]	Index	Annual average net exports[2]	Index	Annual average net supply	Index	(3) ÷ (1)	Index of population
	(1)	*(2)*	*(3)*	*(4)*	*(5)*	*(6)*	*(7)*	*(8)*
1913-17	29663	90.4	2351	69.2	27312	92.9	.08	94.2
1918-22	32804	100.0	3396	100.0	29408	100.0	.10	100.0
1923-27	32701	99.7	3642	107.2	29059	98.8	.11	110.0
1928-32	33658	102.6	5310	156.4	28348	96.4	.16	117.2
1933-37	39108	119.2	7071	208.2	32037	108.9	.18	126.6

Sources: Column (1) computed from data in *Chōsen sōtokufu tōkei nempō*.
Column (3) computed from data in above *Tōkei nempō* and Oriental Economist (ed.),
Foreign Trade of Japan: A Statistical Survey (1935).
Column (5) is the difference between Column (1) and Column (3).
Column (8) computed from data in *Chōsen sōtokufu tōkei nenkan*.
[1] Annual average production is the production of staple foods (rice, barley, naked barley,
wheat, foxtail millet, barnyard millet, proso millet, kaoliang, corn, oats, soy bean, azuki, sweet
potatoes, and Irish potatoes) converted to brown rice equivalents by calorie content.
[2] Annual average net exports is the difference between exports and imports of staple foods in
brown rice equivalents.

TABLE 7

Calorie Consumption Per Person Per Day in Korea, 1913-1917 to 1933-1937

Year	Calorie consumption[1]	Index of (1)	% of requirements[2]
	(1)	*(2)*	*(3)*
1913-17	1906	98.7	95
1918-22	1932	100.0	97
1923-27	1757	90.9	88
1928-32	1575	81.5	79
1933-37	1663	86.1	83

Source: Column (1) computed from data in *Chōsen sōtokufu tōkei nenkan*.
[1] Calories computed from the total production less exports plus imports
and less seed, feed, and waste. The food crops produced include rice, wheat,
barley, naked barley, soy bean, azuki, foxtail millet, barnyard millet, proso
millet, kaoliang, oats, corn, Irish potatoes, and sweet potatoes. Exports include
rice, wheat, soy bean, *azuki*, wheat flour, and sugar. Imports include rice,
wheat, barley, soy bean, *azuki*, wheat flour, sugar, foxtail millet, corn, and
kaoliang.
[2] Requirements assumed to be 2000 calories per person per day.

ties because taxation is usually related to the volume of production, but other evidence supports the hypothesis that underreporting existed in Korea. One economist discusses a new method of calculating rice production in 1936[87] in which, by the use of extrapolation backward to 1928, the previous and official data are raised by what appears to be an average of 26 per cent.

Finally, the food supply situation in the 1930's indicates that Koreans as a whole did not suffer a food shortage. The Japanese government, following the serious rice shortages of 1918 and 1919, began to take positive steps to make colonial Taiwan and Korea the granary of the Japanese Empire, including the formulation of elaborate land improvement and reclamation programs in Korea to increase annual rice production by about 1.35 million metric tons in thirty years.[88] But the program was not fully carried out because the empire found itself with an oversupply of food, particularly rice, by the late 1920's.[89] This was, of course, associated with the world-wide glut of agricultural products that persisted between the two World Wars. The fact that there was an oversupply of food on the markets did not mean that everyone was well fed. Owing to highly unequal distribution of income, during much of this period a substantial proportion of the population went hungry in most countries of the world regardless of the development or character of their political and economic systems.

Two widely divergent estimates of prewar daily calorie supply per person in Taiwan have recently been published. The lower estimates, by S.P.S. Ho, are 5-year averages available over a period from 1910 to 1944 obtained by using total food production data. Using two different assumptions he obtains one estimate that ranges from 1760 to 1932 calories, and another from 1865 to 2208.[90] H. Y. Chang, using farm household economy and expenditure survey data, estimates daily calorie consumption to have averaged around 3,600 in the 1930's.[91] Since total production data are almost certainly understated by a substantial amount[92] and farm household survey data tend to be more accurate, the Chang estimate is likely to be more accurate.

[87] Grajdanzev, pp. 296-299. [88] *CNHS-SS*, p. 425.
[89] K. Takahashi, *Gendai chōsen keizai ron* (Tokyo, 1935), pp. 228-232.
[90] S.P.S. Ho, p. 336.
[91] H. Y. Chang, "A Study of the Living Conditions of Farmers in Taiwan, 1931-1950," *The Developing Economies*, vii, 1 (March, 1969), p. 55.
[92] Taiwanese farmers and former officials I have talked with state that underreporting was the prevailing practice. M. Cohen, Columbia University

The calorie supply computed for Japan from the official statistics shows a clear upward trend to about 1920 from a totally inadequate daily supply of 1351 calories per person in 1878-1882.[93] Then the supply declines again into the 1930's as the Korean calorie supply did.[94] Both these sets of data are derived from official statistics. The decline to inadequate supplies was probably due to an attempt by the agricultural associations, the crop-reporting agencies in the two countries, to obtain subsidies from the government by underreporting production (therefore income) during the world agricultural depression of the 1920's and the 1930's. The total production data for Taiwan also suggest that underreporting for the same purpose was taking place in Taiwan.

A second method of checking the reliability of production data is to examine for consistency the relationship between input and output. A limited number of inputs will be considered here— crop area, labor force, fertilizer consumption, use of improved seeds, and irrigated land area. Table 1 shows that the growth rates of inputs in Taiwan and Korea exceeded those of Japan in every case. Crop area increased unevenly in the three countries. It increased at the rate of 1.3 per cent per year in Taiwan and 0.8 per cent in Korea. The Japanese rate was 0.6 per cent.[95] A unit increase in Japan was probably least effective because 75 per cent of the change took place in Hokkaido, where 90 per cent of the increase in land area was in upland fields and where the short growing season precluded the possibility of double-cropping. For all cultivated fields in Japan only 24 per cent of the increase was in paddy fields.[96] In Taiwan and Korea, on the other hand, the increase in land supply occurred in a more effective form. In the former 99 per cent of the increase was in paddy fields,[97] and in the latter the paddy-field area increased by more than the area of cultivated land, the area of upland fields having declined by 1 per cent.[98]

---

anthropologist who has engaged in field study in Taiwan, states that farmers in the village he studied also indicated that they underreported output.

[93] S. Nakayama, "Shukuryō shōhi suijun no chōki ni tsuite," *Nōgyō sōgō kenkyū*, XII, 4 (October, 1958), p. 25.

[94] Table 7.   [95] Table 5.

[96] Computed from Nakamura, *Agricultural Production* . . . , pp. 43, 48.

[97] Computed from Y. M. Ho, p. 51.

[98] Computed from *CNHS-SR*, p. 97.

Labor force declined by 0.1 per cent per year in Japan but increased by 0.9 and 0.8 per cent in Taiwan and Korea.[99] These movements appear to be consistent with changes in cultivated-land areas and especially with changes in the paddy-field areas— as might be expected since no fundamental changes affecting the farm worker–cultivated-land ratio occurred during this period.

An examination of estimates of fertilizer consumption in the three countries shows remarkable differences in the rates at which consumption expanded. The rate in Japan was 2 per cent per year; in contrast, the rate in Korea was 14 per cent. In Taiwan it grew at 7 per cent.[100] All these consumption rates include self-supplied and commercial fertilizers. In the terminal 5-year periods the ratio of the values of fertilizers consumed to gross value of agricultural output was 17 per cent in Taiwan,[101] 18 per cent in Korea,[102] and 16 per cent in Japan.[103] Although a margin for error must be provided, it is probable that they will still remain roughly of the same order of magnitude in the terminal periods. If the above evidence is accepted, it can be inferred that the rapid increase of fertilizer consumption in Taiwan and Korea took place because high-yield responses continued despite the heavy application.

In the terminal 5-year periods the ratios of the values of commercial fertilizers to total fertilizers are, respectively, 60, 36, and 39 per cent for Taiwan, Korea, and Japan.[104] No estimates are available on the relative effectiveness of a unit value of self-supplied and commercial fertilizers. However, since the ratios in Korea and Japan are nearly identical, it may be reasonably concluded that this factor did not cause the effectiveness of fertilizers to differ between the two countries. If this conclusion is correct or nearly correct, then we would expect the growth rate of yield per unit area in Korea to be higher by a wide margin than in Japan because the growth rate of fertilizer consumption was 7 times greater in Korea than in Japan. It is possible, of course, that the growth rate of fertilizer consumption for Korea has an upward bias. If such a bias exists it will be due mostly to

[99] Table 5.   [100] Table 5.

[101] Computed from S.P.S. Ho, p. 318.

[102] Computed from *CNHS-SR*, pp. 111-112, and Suh, pp. 11-37.

[103] Computed from Hayami, p. 253, and M. Umemura, pp. 146-147.

[104] Computed from Taiwan Province, pp. 586, 588; *CNHS-SR*, p. 112; and Hayami, p. 253.

incomplete coverage in the early reporting of fertilizer consumption. But since observers have noted that fertilizer use was very low in Korea in the initial period relative to that in Japan, it seems safe enough to assume that a very great difference in growth rates did exist.[105]

Another cause for the rapidly rising yields in Korea is the rapid replacement of the previously used rice seed with more productive improved varieties. And since use of improved seed required heavy use of fertilizers for high yields, farmers increased its use at a high rate, indicating that farmers responded quickly to economic opportunity.

Crop area alone does not satisfactorily explain the influence of land on land productivity. Land improvement—conversion of upland fields into irrigated fields—can increase output.[106] We have noted that in both Korea and Taiwan all or nearly all of the increase in cultivated land area was in irrigated fields, whereas in Japan 71 per cent of the increase was in upland fields.[107] The increases in the area of irrigated fields were 0.3, 0.6, and 1.8 per cent, respectively, for Japan, Korea, and Taiwan.

On the basis of the above analysis the following conclusions regarding the growth rates of gross agricultural output in the three countries appear to be reasonable:

(1) The growth rate in Taiwan probably ranged tolerably close to 3.4 per cent, although it could have been higher if underreporting increased in the latter part of the period, as the data seem to suggest.

(2) If the Ohkawa and LTES estimates of agricultural output are taken, a clear inconsistency exists between the output and input growth rates of Japan and Korea. In every case, the growth rates of inputs in Korea are higher and in all cases but one decidedly higher than those of Japan. Therefore, it would appear that either the two Japanese rates are too high or the Korean rate is too low, or that both are erroneous in the directions indicated. I have concluded elsewhere that both Japanese rates are

[105] See Suzuki, pp. 127-128.

[106] For the periods under consideration, the increase in irrigated fields may be regarded as a proxy for fixed capital inputs since the little other data available are not sufficiently reliable. S. Ho, p. 318, uses irrigated fields developed under Japanese official sponsorship as the proxy—and this procedure makes better sense in most respects. I use all new irrigated land for comparability with Japanese and Korean data.

[107] Computed from Nakamura, *Agricultural Production* . . . , pp. 43, 48.

too high.[108] In regard to the Korean rate, I have suggested that the implied supply available from the official statistics is much too low, on the following grounds: a) an intolerably low calorie supply, and b) a net domestic food supply from staple-food crops growing at only a 0.6 per cent rate. In fact, the output of staple-food crops grew at 1.2 per cent in Korea, and the difference from the net supply rate is accounted for by the increase in the net exports of staple foods. For the domestic staple-food supply to have increased at the same rate as the population (1.6 per cent), the staple-food output would have had to grow at an annual rate of about 2.1 per cent.[109] On the basis that the Suh growth rate of agricultural output is 1.7 per cent, which is considerably higher than the growth rate of staple-food crops computed from official data, it is possible that a corrected growth rate of agricultural output using Suh's techniques would be in the neighborhood of 3.0 per cent. It must be stressed that these growth figures are intended to be taken only as rough orders of magnitudes rather than as approximations of the actual growth rates.

(3) On the basis of the input data (Table 5), it is not possible to conclude whether the Korean growth rate should be higher or lower than the Taiwanese growth rate. A guess is that the Korean rate was somewhat lower for the following reasons: a) Taiwanese agriculture was strongly stimulated by Japanese demand for non-competing products such as sugar and tropical fruits; b) sugar, moreover, received both tariff protection and heavy subsidization;[110] c) finally, the response of the Taiwanese farmer to economic inducements may have been greater than that of the Korean farmer who, according to one analyst, required more direct government supervision and non-economic compulsion to adopt yield-raising innovations.[111]

(4) If a growth rate of 2 to 3 per cent for Korea and 1 per cent for Japan is accepted, the growth-rate gap is very great indeed. Does such a gap seem plausible? From the data in Table 1 and Table 5 we may conclude that it is possible and likely. The rice-

[108] See my *Agricultural Production* . . . , and "Nakamura versus the LTES. . . ."

[109] This assumes that the value of staple-food supply remained as a constant proportion of the value of agricultural production.

[110] The annual growth rate of sugar production was 7.1 per cent in the 30-year period from 1906-1910 to 1936-1940. Computed from data in Y. M. Ho, p. 141.

[111] S. Tobata, *Nihon nōgyō no tenkai katei* (Tokyo, 1941), p. 95.

yield gap at the beginning of the respective periods for the two countries is very wide indeed (Table 1). The technology for raising output in Japan was being developed slowly and laboriously because she was at the innovational frontier. But foreign (primarily Japanese) technology was immediately available to Korea. The incentive gap was also very great. For the Koreans, starting from a very low base, a small rise would have an enormous impact. This probably is one of the reasons for the rapidity with which improved Japanese seeds spread in Korea immediately after the annexation. The input data, particularly the increase in the application of fertilizer, also shows that a growth-rate gap of the magnitude indicated is within the range of possibilities. Finally, agricultural infrastructure (credit institutions, agricultural extension services, experimental stations, agricultural associations, and the like) was more quickly established in Korea than in Japan during the periods under consideration.

Measured by the growth rate to the beginning of World War II, the development of small-scale, traditional agriculture in Taiwan and Korea appears to have been a success without precedent in the world. That success appears to be related to: 1) the presence of an authoritarian alien government in effective political control;[112] 2) steadfast commitment to economic development of the colonies by that government; 3) previous experience of successful economic growth on the part of that government; 4) the prior existence of low productivity and incentive levels in the colonies to be developed; 5) the provision of incentives by such measures as the establishment of a capitalist economic organization and the institution of land tax reform; 6) the proximity of the colonies to Japan; 7) the integration of the colonial economies into that of the Japanese Empire; 8) growing demand for the principal agricultural commodities (rice and sugar) of the colonies; 9) objectives of colonial economic development conforming to resource endowments within the empire; 10) the utilization of trained, imported specialists for developmental work; 11) emphasis on developing traditional agriculture, which involved most of the people in the developmental effort; and 12)

[112] For quotations of views that Taiwan today remains under an authoritarian alien government see D. H. Mendel, Jr., "Japanese Policy and Views Toward Formosa," *The Journal of Asian Studies*, xxvⅢ, 3 (May, 1969).

the presence of reasonably honest and efficient administrative personnel imported from Japan.

The above influences helped make the growth rates of agriculture in Taiwan and Korea higher than that of Japan (by a factor of 2, 3, or even 4). This made possible certain important contributions by the colonies to the economic growth of the Japanese Empire. One of these was the production of sufficient food to meet the growing needs of the empire. In the course of this growth, however, a depression was encountered which severely restricted the demand for agricultural products and caused a disastrous decline in agricultural prices. This placed a severe strain on the agricultural sector of the colonies, but may have put even greater pressure on Japan's farmers because agricultural costs were higher in Japan and her farmers had to compete against colonial rice producers.[113]

The second contribution was to provide labor to the non-agricultural sector. The majority were unskilled workers who placed no burden of cost on the industrial sector since they had been raised on the farms and their "cost of production" was paid by the farmers. The existence of a colony with a growing supply of labor helped keep industrial wages lower and permitted Japan's industries to have available for a longer period an "unlimited supply of labor." To put it somewhat differently, it helped prolong the technological dualism which is a characteristic of less developed countries. Since the colonial farms were more competitive than Japanese farms, it helped push Japanese agricultural labor, which was better prepared by virtue of education and exposure to modern values and attitudes than its colonial counterparts, into the industrial sector. But this same process helped retard the emergence of industrial labor in the colonies.

The colonies also helped the empire by providing industrial raw materials and, through their exports, foreign exchange. On the demand side, the colonies provided a market for the industrial products made in Japan as the level of income in the colonies rose over time (with a setback during the depression).

The prewar experiences in the agricultural development of both Taiwan and Korea provide more applicable immediate les-

---

[113] If Japan's farm discontent was a causative factor in her aggressive ventures of the 1930's, then it may well be argued that her original colonial experience sparked the emergence of a vicious circle in which her first colonial venture led to a further expansion of the empire.

sons for the agricultural development of the less developed countries than does Japan's experience. The initial conditions existing in the two countries were more like those that exist in present less developed countries. Furthermore, a more thorough and effective mobilization of resources and a more rapid formation of an infrastructure was achieved. In Japan, on the other hand, a fairly high level of agricultural development had already been achieved, and a great deal of the infrastructure in the form of economic and political organization and in human and material capital formation had already been laid. However, the Japanese experience cannot be slighted, for it provided important guidelines to the agricultural development of Taiwan and Korea.

The process of promoting agricultural development in less developed countries is becoming increasingly well understood. This know-how was still in its formative stage when Japanese agriculture was developing during the Meiji era, and one result was relatively slow growth of agriculture. By the time of the Taiwanese and Korean experience in agricultural development, the techniques and methods of achieving rapid growth in traditional agriculture were better developed. (The speed of growth is important because on it depends whether an economy can overcome the drag of population growth.) Rapid agricultural growth here as everywhere required the introduction of new modern inputs imported from foreign countries. This was crucially important in the case of Taiwan and Korea, whose agriculture represents the first successful attempts to develop small-scale, traditional agriculture in a relatively short period of time.

One of the more remarkable features of the Japanese Empire was the rapidity of its economic growth during the interwar period when most of the rest of the world was growing at very low rates.[114] Of the many factors responsible for this, the establishment of an integrated, expanding and (literally) free trade area in a world trade market otherwise becoming more restrictive was an expansive force.[115] The empire served itself well, in terms of economic growth, by providing on both the supply and demand sides a much larger market than would have been pos-

[114] Conspicuous exceptions were the major totalitarian states: U.S.S.R., Germany, and Italy.

[115] Despite the complaints of domestic producers about cheap foreign rice imports, the Japanese government did not reimpose duties on rice imports from the colonies. Johnston, p. 58.

371

sible otherwise. It benefited from the relative absence of two constraints which hold true in latter day common markets. One was that instead of many centers of decision there was only one—Tokyo. The other, closely related, was that Japan did not permit the niceties of a balanced regional development to trouble her—her main considerations were economic and strategic. Rather, she deliberately planned a regional dualism at first in the sense that one region (Japan) was to contain the growing industrial sector, and the other (Taiwan and Korea), the growing agricultural sector.[116] Yet, under the exigencies of economic need, the planned regionalism started to break down in the 1930's. The economic need derived from strategic considerations, to be sure, but in the present-day world, it is possible to stimulate similar economic forces through planned development.

If producers are provided with appropriate incentives, agricultural development in most traditional agricultural societies can be more effectively organized from the top and in a shorter period of time than can industrial development. The basic human capital is already available to a large extent for agricultural purposes. The problem is to introduce new country- or locally tested inputs that will increase productivity and, at the same time, to provide incentives for their adoption by traditional farmers. Some of these inputs will be lumpy and require huge capital expenditures. They may provide social returns substantially greater than private returns and therefore require heavy government investment—e.g., in transportation, communication, irrigation, administration, and education.

Through the colonial government-general Japan invested, and perhaps overinvested, in all these except education. This was in many respects a "big push" policy where the nature of the investment may have been strategically more important than the "big push" so often advocated today; that is, in the massive provision of administrative personnel and development specialists. It was

[116] Since this was a period of vigorous growth of the industrial sector in Japan, the rapid growth of agricultural production in the colonies led to the strong concurrent growth of the industrial and the agricultural sectors within the Japanese Empire. It is true that the economy of Japan and those of her colonies also grew concurrently. For a discussion of the concurrent growth within the Japanese economy see K. Ohkawa, "Concurrent Growth of Agriculture with Industry: A Study of the Japanese Case" in R. N. Dixey (ed.), *International Explorations of Agricultural Economics* (Ames, Iowa, 1964), pp. 201-212.

highly developed human capital that was in short supply. Japan provided this input, which was endowed with those values and attitudes that had helped sustain her own growth and that were relatively absent among the colonial peoples. Although there is no question that Japan grossly underinvested in formal education in the colonies, the specialists, including extension workers, were educational inputs of a kind that provided important practical and almost immediate benefits to the economy. Japan, it would seem, regarded the colonists and colonial areas as economic factors to be used to achieve certain economic objectives within the empire. From this abstract point of view, the Japanese neglect of formal education[117] (relative to education in Japan) may have been economically rational to Japan as it was to most nations of the world and, particularly, to colonial governments at that time.[118]

Finally, no single statement can be made about investment priorities for the underdeveloped countries, where there is great diversity in historical backgrounds, stage of development, resource endowments, and special economic and other circumstances. But the Taiwanese and Korean experience during the interwar period seems to confirm current doctrine regarding the greater early stress on agricultural development.[119]

[117] The increase in school enrollment was very slow until late in the 1930's, when Japan stepped up its colonial education program to "japanize" the colonists and also provide the basis for better economic performance.

[118] It is also true that two other factors may have acted as deterrents to more education: the independence movement leaders were educated men, and if Japan did not trust colonial administrators and did not employ the educated elite, they would be a source of further unrest.

[119] See above for benefits to be derived from early agricultural development.

ANN WASWO[1]

The Origins of Tenant Unrest

Examination of the origins of tenant unrest is essential to an understanding of the social dislocations accompanying modernization in Japan. The number of tenancy disputes increased rapidly after World War I, from a reported total of 256 in 1918 to over 2,700 in 1926. Tenants who had once been content to make individual rent agreements with their landlords now insisted on collective bargaining, a change reflected in the growing number of tenant unions. Mass meetings, violent demonstrations, and looting—the style of rural uprisings in the Tokugawa and early Meiji periods—were not abandoned, but tenants now employed more rational means of protest as well, organizing boycotts of local businesses run by landlords and obtaining professional legal aid. By the early 1920's a sense of crisis prevailed in official circles. Not only were tenancy disputes more numerous than industrial labor disputes; they revealed the existence of discontent in that very part of Japanese society, the rural villages, long regarded as the nation's ultimate guarantee of social stability. What caused this discontent? Why did tenants, formerly submissive and deferential, begin to challenge the authority of their landlords and to demand changes in tenancy conditions?

One common explanation of tenant unrest focuses on the poverty of tenant farmers. They were farmers "with a spade, a hand plow, and a sickle for tools, with the most primitive fertilizers, with hardly a beast of burden to ease [their] labor. . . . Debt-ridden, tax-burdened, undernourished, miserably housed, [their] wretchedness defies comparison."[2] The chief cause of their poverty, it is argued, was high rents. Although rents on upland fields

[1] The author wishes to thank the Committee on East Asian Studies of Stanford University for financial support received in connection with the preparation of parts of this paper.

[2] Wakakawa Seiyei, "The Japanese Farm Tenancy System," in D. G. Haring (ed.), *Japan's Prospect* (Cambridge, Mass., 1946), p. 163.

374

were sometimes payable in cash, rents on paddy fields were almost always due in rice, averaging roughly half the crop. Few tenants had surplus rice to sell after paying rents, and some lacked even enough for their own consumption. The higher the rents they paid, the greater the threat to their survival. When that threat became unbearable, they were forced into rebellion.[3]

Throughout the 1920's disputes involving paddy were far more common than disputes involving upland fields; over half the total number of disputes were triggered by poor harvests, and the principal demand of tenants was rent reduction,[4] facts which would appear to suggest that the high burden of rents in bad years threatened tenants with starvation and, thus, to support the view that poverty caused disputes. If this were true, however, one would expect to find a higher rate of disputes in those parts of the country where rents were highest, that is, where the tenants' standard of living was lowest and their ability to endure poor harvests least. But this was not the case. As shown in Table 1, rents exceeded the national average of 50.9 per cent of the crop in only 5 of the 10 prefectures with the highest dispute rates in the nation during the 1920's. And the same was true in prefectures with the lowest dispute rates: in 5 of the 10, rents exceeded the national average.

In terms of the actual amount of the crop retained by tenants, the relationship between high rents and rate of disputes is also unclear. In only 4 of the 10 prefectures with the highest dispute rates was the amount retained by tenants below the national average of .936 *koku* per *tan*. It was below the national average in 5 of the 10 prefectures with the lowest dispute rates.

The above figures for rents, of course, represent prefectural averages. Within a given prefecture rents varied considerably, as did the burden of local taxes and the cost of living. Even so, disputes did not always occur in those areas with higher rents. Rents in Okayama prefecture, at 56.1 per cent of the crop, were among the highest in the nation; in rate of disputes in the 1920's

---

[3] Nakazawa Benjirō, "Kosaku mondai no chiriteki rekishiteki kōsatsu," *Teikoku nōkai hō*, xi (September, 1921), pp. 31-32.

[4] Annual statistics compiled by the Ministry of Agriculture on type of land involved in disputes, immediate causes of disputes, and demands of tenants are reproduced in Nōminundōshi Kenkyūkai (ed.), *Nihon nōmin undō shi* (Tokyo, 1961), pp. 125, 15, and 121. Hereafter cited as *NNUS*. See Table 4 for the percentage of disputes involving tenant demands for rent reduction.

TABLE 1

Rent Levels and Tenancy Disputes, 1920-1930

	Dispute rate[a]	Average yield per tan (koku)[b]	Average rent paid per tan (koku)[b]	Tenant's share of crop per tan (koku)[b]	Average rent as % of yield[b]
Prefectures with highest dispute rates					
Osaka	187.8	2.180	1.061	1.119	48.7
Hyogo	92.2	2.300	1.200	1.100	52.2
Kyoto	66.5	1.968	1.049	.919	53.3
Aiichi	58.6	1.928	.970	.958	50.3
Nara	57.0	2.253	1.181	1.072	52.4
Mie	54.8	1.660	.810	.850	48.8
Tottori	52.9	1.810	.983	.827	55.3
Kagawa	51.6	1.944	.934	1.010	48.0
Gifu	51.5	1.746	.908	.838	52.0
Kanagawa	49.7	2.160	.990	1.170	45.8
Prefectures with lowest dispute rates					
Kochi	6.2	1.820	1.056	.764	58.0
Ishikawa	5.5	1.918	1.021	.897	53.2
Toyama	5.1	2.161	.950	1.211	44.0
Fukushima	4.7	2.000	.990	1.010	49.5
Yamaguchi	3.5	1.815	.909	.906	50.1
Miyagi	3.1	1.930	.910	1.020	47.2
Oita	2.6	1.727	.911	.816	52.8
Kagoshima	2.1	1.506	.890	.616	59.1
Aomori	.7	2.000	.900	1.100	45.0
Iwate	.7	2.067	1.120	.947	54.2
National average		1.908	.972	.936	50.9

[a] The dispute rate is the average number of tenants and part-owner-cultivators-part-tenants participating in tenancy disputes per 1,000 tenants and part-owner-cultivators-part-tenants in each prefecture during the period 1920-1930. In determining rank in dispute rates Hokkaido and Okinawa were excluded.

[b] Yields and rent levels cited are averages for the period 1916-1920 on single-crop paddy. The data are from Nōrinshō, Nōmukyoku, *Taishō jūnen hompō kosaku kankō*, pp. 65-67.

Okayama ranked eighteenth. But within the prefecture tenancy disputes were most numerous, and the organized tenant movement strongest, in the south, although rents were generally higher in the north.[5]

[5] *Ibid.*, p. 515.

Moreover, rents throughout most of the nation took a greater percentage of the yearly crop in mid-Meiji than in the Taishō period (Table 2). Yet few disputes occurred until after 1917,

TABLE 2

Changes in Rent Levels, 1885-1920 (national averages)

Year	Type of land	Yield/ tan (koku)	Rent/ tan (koku)	Rate of rent	Tenant's share per tan (koku)
1885		1.672	0.970	58%	.702
1908-1912	single-crop paddy	1.680	0.898	54%	.782
	double-crop paddy	2.033	1.156	57%	.877
1916-1920	single-crop paddy	1.908	0.972	51%	.936
	double-crop paddy	2.169	1.195	55%	.974

NNUS, p. 240, Table 12; based on data in Nōrinshō, Nōseikyoku, *Nōchi mondai ni kansuru tōkei shiryō*. In computing national averages Hokkaido and Okinawa were excluded.

when the share retained by tenants after paying rents increased. As a government report observed in the late 1920's, disputes did not always occur where tenancy conditions were poor or where tenants experienced unbearable poverty. Rather, they were generally more numerous in those parts of the country where tenants were the best-nourished, most adequately housed, and most prosperous.[6] That high rents caused distress among many tenants cannot be denied, but it does not appear that their distress was the cause of disputes.

Other writers emphasize the unforeseen consequences of universal education and conscription and the ideological impact of World War I and the Russian Revolution as causes of tenant unrest. By late Meiji, 6 years of schooling were required of all Japanese, rich and poor. As one writer observed in 1921, a wide variety of youth groups and conferences on farming in rural

[6] Nōrinshō, Nōmukyoku, *Kosaku sōgi no gaikyō* (Tokyo, 1928), pp. 2-3.

areas provided tenant farmers with additional opportunities to expand their knowledge. Even a poor farmer, if interested in learning, could borrow books from public libraries and read newspapers regularly. As a result, the educational gap between landlords and tenants narrowed considerably. The experience of attending local schools with the children of landlords, and in some cases of proving intellectually superior to them, increased the self-confidence of tenants and showed them that social status had little to do with ability.[7] Universal conscription, it is argued, had a similar effect. A tenant who became a sergeant in his local regiment while his landlord remained a private was not apt to remain as content with the traditional social hierarchy as his father or grandfather had been.[8]

An additional argument focuses on the ideological impact of World War I and the Russian Revolution. Until 1914 one had to travel to the cities of Japan to learn about new currents of political and social thought in the West. But with the outbreak of World War I, coverage of international events in Japanese newspapers rapidly increased. In addition to stories about the war itself, there were lengthy articles explaining democracy and socialism—and, after the upheaval in Russia, communism as well. Ideas which previously had been studied by only a handful of Japanese intellectuals now were accessible to everyone, including literate tenant farmers. Already dissatisfied with their own social and economic condition, they eagerly adopted notions of human equality and social justice. Encouraged by the knowledge that the lower classes in Europe were rebelling against privilege and aristocracy, they too, it is argued, launched an attack against their masters, the landlords.[9]

That the attitudes and aspirations of tenant farmers did change during the 1920's is clearly indicated by the increasing number of disputes. But it is difficult to trace these changes solely to the influence of education, conscription, and revolutionary ideas.

Universal education was not necessarily a liberating experience for tenant farmers. In addition to teaching skills such as reading and writing, the schools also promoted the official ortho-

[7] Hayashi Chūtarō, "Kosaku mondai ni kansuru kōsatsu," *Teikoku nōkai hō*, xi (November, 1921), p. 30.

[8] Ronald Dore, *Land Reform in Japan* (London, 1959), pp. 54-55.

[9] Hayashi, "Kosaku mondai . . . ," pp. 29-30; Dore, *Land Reform . . .* , p. 55.

doxy of the Japanese state—the divine origin of the nation and the throne, the value of harmony and cooperation, the virtue of filial piety. The local schoolmaster, usually a member of the rural elite,[10] saw to it that teachers did not introduce material which conflicted with the existing social order. As one tenant leader observed, "We are taught to be obedient to our landlords and to serve our social superiors; that it is an honor to be a soldier and pay taxes . . . that one must be resigned to poverty; that labor is divine; that it is patriotic to provide the livelihood of land-lords, capitalists, and noblemen."[11] The same writer also doubted the ability of the average tenant to put any of the skills he acquired at school to use: "Before he enters school the child of a tenant farmer takes care of younger children and watches the family home while his parents are away. Even after he begins school he still has many chores to do. . . . As soon as he finishes his compulsory education he goes to work in the fields, laboring as hard as he can, like a beast of burden. . . . When he comes home at night he is too tired to read a newspaper and goes immediately to sleep."[12]

Second, we must be careful of exaggerating the influence of military service on tenant farmers. Like the school system, the armed services also promoted patriotism, emphasizing loyalty to the Emperor and to one's superiors. What military service gave to tenants was knowledge of the usefulness of discipline and organization. That this knowledge actually caused disputes is doubtful, but clearly it helped make the tenants' actions against landlords more effective once disputes began.

Third, ideology appears to have been more important to the leaders of the tenant movement than to ordinary tenants. Competing national organizations of tenants, many led by men not tenants themselves, called for the socialization of land, the overthrow of capitalism, or, until universal manhood suffrage was enacted in 1925, for voting rights for the lower classes.[13] But the rank-and-file members of these organizations remained more interested in practical economic issues. Tenants became affiliated with a given national union for the immediate advantages it

[10] Allan B. Cole, *Japanese Society and Politics: the Impact of Mobility and Social Stratification* (Boston, 1956), p. 115.

[11] Mori Eikichi, "Kaikyū ishiki to kumiai undō," *Nōsei kenkyū*, III, 7 (1924), pp. 61-62.

[12] *Ibid.*   [13] Dore, *Land Reform*, pp. 74-77.

could offer them—legal guidance and financial aid, for example. Which of the several competing organizations they joined depended less on their support for any particular doctrine than on their personal connections with a given group of leaders.[14]

A report on rural conditions in Gifu Prefecture in the early 1920's noted that most local leaders of tenancy disputes were well advanced in years, averaging fifty or older, and poorly educated. Few had ties with political parties.[15] It is true that in one district of the prefecture former soldiers were active in the tenant movement, but on closer examination this case does not prove an especially good example of the role of conscription in providing tenants with a desire for equality of status. Roughly 13 per cent of the members of tenant unions in the district in 1920 were veterans and reservists (*zaigō gunjin*). The great majority, however, were privates.[16] That they played a role in the union movement was largely due to the efforts of Ōno Kingo, who had served as a corporal in Siberia during the Russo-Japanese War. After a second tour of duty in Siberia from 1918 to 1919, at which time he apparently became interested in socialism, he returned to Gifu and, while still a non-commissioned officer, became one of the most important organizers of the local tenant movement. He himself, however, was not a tenant farmer but a landlord's son, owning slightly more than one *chō* of land and operating a small saké shop. In addition to his political beliefs, it appears that he was motivated by intense dislike of the landlord who headed the local landlords' association, his former father-in-law.[17]

In the rural villages of Gifu Prefecture as a whole it was estimated that only 10 per cent of the population read newspapers.[18] According to police reports from a village in Fukui Prefecture where a dispute occurred in 1920, slightly more than 100 residents subscribed to newspapers, but very few tenants were included in their number; no "dangerous" intellectual magazines were in circulation.[19] Other reports noted that the Rice Riots of 1918, which revealed the effectiveness of mass action and the weakness of local police, played a greater role in overcoming the

[14] *Ibid.*, p. 77.

[15] Nōshōmushō, Nōmukyoku, *Kosaku sōgi ni kansuru chōsa* (Tokyo, 1922), I, 172-173. Hereafter cited as *KS*.

[16] *Ibid.*, p. 77.

[17] *NNUS*, pp. 138, 689-691; *KS*, I, 172, 197.

[18] *Ibid.*, p. 174.   [19] *Ibid.*, p. 234.

tenants' reluctance to challenge established authority than had abstract ideas about social justice or the evils of capitalism.[20]

Probably the greatest problem with arguments which seek to trace the origins of tenant unrest to education and conscription is that they fail to account for marked regional differences in the distribution of tenancy disputes. Education and conscription were both universal, and yet during the 1920's disputes were concentrated in southwestern Japan.

Between 1917 and 1931 58 per cent of all reported disputes occurred in the Kinki and Chubu regions; only 8 per cent occurred in the Tohoku, with even fewer disputes reported from other outlying regions of the country (Table 3). During the late

TABLE 3

Regional Distribution of Tenancy Disputes, 1917-1931 and 1932-1941

	Region	# disputes	% of total
1917-1931			
	Kinki	8,709	34.9
	Chubu	5,775	23.1
	Kanto	2,586	10.3
	Chugoku	2,011	8.0
	Tohoku	1,988	8.0
	Kyushu	1,983	8.0
	Shikoku	1,416	5.7
	Hokkaido	494	2.0
	Total	24,962	100.0
1932-1941			
	Tohoku	12,330	26.0
	Chubu	8,654	18.1
	Kinki	6,501	13.6
	Kanto	6,127	12.8
	Kyushu	4,619	9.7
	Chugoku	3,554	7.4
	Shikoku	3,230	6.8
	Hokkaido	2,680	5.6
	Total	47,695	100.0

NNUS, pp. 133-134, Tables 10 and 11; based on data in Nōrinshō, Nōsei-kyoku, *Kosaku nenpō* (1931) and *Nōchi nenpō* (1941).

1920's, it is true, the number of disputes in northeastern Japan increased, and indeed during the 1930's the Tohoku achieved the dubious distinction of ranking first in the nation in number of

[20] *Ibid.*, p. 95; *KS*, II, 128-129, 158-159.

disputes. But the spread of disputes to the Tohoku represented not a continuation of previous trends, but rather a new kind of rural unrest, caused principally by the economic distress of small landlords during the Great Depression.[21] Unlike disputes in southwestern Japan, those in the Tohoku in the 1930's were small in scale, involving as a rule only one or two tenants and a few *chō* of land, suggesting individual rather than collective action.[22] Indeed, although tenant unions were formed in the Tohoku they never rivaled those of southwestern Japan in number or membership.[23] Whereas the majority of disputes in southwestern Japan during the 1920's were triggered by poor harvests and involved tenant demands for rent reduction, those in the Tohoku during the 1930's were for the most part triggered by landlords' attempts to evict tenants, typically because they wished to cultivate additional land themselves, and involved tenant demands for the continuation of tenancy or for compensation if tenancy were terminated (Tables 4 and 5).

There were two basic differences between southwestern and northeastern Japan which explain why disputes were common in the one region during the 1920's and rare in the other. The first was level of industrialization. While the northeast remained predominantly agricultural, the southwest, which included such major cities as Osaka and Nagoya, was the most economically advanced region of the country.

Industrialization, and in particular the rapid spurt of economic growth caused by World War I, affected tenant farmers in several ways. First, the increase in urban job opportunities reduced competition for land among tenants. Where population pressure on the land was high, a landlord could always find land-poor farmers willing to cultivate his fields on almost any terms; if dis-

[21] Tobata Seiichi, *Nōchi o meguru jinushi to nōmin* (Tokyo, 1947), p. 66; *NNUS*, pp. 53-54; Nōrinshō, Nōmukyoku, *Chihō betsu kosaku sōgi gaiyō* (Tokyo, 1936), III, 13-14, 45, 46, 48, 78.

[22] Okada Munemori, "Saikin ni okeru kosaku sōgi no jōkyō to nōmin kumiai undō no dōkō," part 2, *Teikoku nōkai hō*, XXVI (July, 1936), pp. 76-79; *NNUS*, p. 63 (Table 4).

[23] Okada, "Kosaku sōgi no jōkyō," part 4, *Teikoku nōkai hō*, XXVI (September, 1936), pp. 23-25; Nōrinsho, Nōmukyoku, *Jinushi kosakunin kumiai undō no gaiyō* (Tokyo, 1928), p. 82.

TABLE 4

Principal Demands of Tenants, 1923-1941

Year	Total # disputes	Rent reduction temporary #	%	permanent #	%	Continuation of tenancy or compensation #	%
1923	1,917	1,249	65.0	582	30.3	15	0.8
1924	1,532	1,044	67.0	358	22.2	35	2.8
1925	2,206	1,444	64.0	475	21.0	173	7.7
1926	2,751	2,011	78.0	272	9.8	318	11.8
1927	2,052	1,206	59.0	253	12.4	444	21.5
1928	1,866	1,014	50.4	177	9.5	484	26.0
1929	2,434	1,339	55.0	151	6.2	728	29.8
1930	2,478	1,042	42.0	192	7.8	1,030	41.6
1931	3,419	1,609	47.0	166	4.9	1,363	40.0
1932	3,414	1,267	37.0	121	3.5	1,468	43.0
1933	4,000	1,013	25.4	127	3.2	2,305	57.8
1934	5,828	2,168	37.2	109	1.9	2,668	44.5
1935	6,824	2,616	38.2	105	1.5	3,055	45.0
1936	6,804	1,621	24.0	213	3.1	3,674	53.9
1937	6,170	1,318	21.3	230	3.7	3,509	57.0
1938	4,615	1,063	23.0	157	3.4	2,421	52.5
1939	3,578	711	19.9	230	6.4	1,645	46.0
1940	3,165	767	24.2	243	7.7	1,412	44.6
1941	3,308	867	25.6	294	8.7	1,316	38.9

NNUS, p. 121, Table 2; based on "Kosaku sōgi ni kansuru chōsa shohyō" in Nōrinshō, Nōsei-kyoku, *Kosaku nenpō* (1932) and *Nōchi nenpō* (1941). Other demands, made less frequently than the above, include: 1) extension of deadlines for paying rents, 2) less strict quality standards for rent rice, 3) payment of bonuses in cash or kind for meeting quality standards, and 4) compensation for fertilizer and other cultivating costs.

satisfied tenants demanded rent reductions, they could be speedily replaced. Where, on the other hand, part of the local population migrated to the cities, population pressure on the land declined and tenants could demand lower rents with less fear of reprisal. Reports from Saitama Prefecture, for example, noted that "many people abandoned farming recently because of the growth of secondary employment and a great increase in wages. As a result, there is a surplus of arable land, and tenant farmers have become emboldened."[24] High wages for workers in the coal mines, factories, and foundries of northern Kyushu after

[24] *KS*, ɪɪ, 77.

TABLE 5

Eviction Disputes in the Tohoku and Kinki, 1932-1941

Year	National Total			Tohoku			Kinki		
	Number disputes	Number eviction disputes	%	Number disputes	Number eviction disputes	%	Number disputes	Number eviction disputes	%
1932	3,414	1,520	45	754	467	62	383	80	21
1933	4,000	2,275	57	1,006	741	74	480	105	22
1934	5,828	2,704	46	1,253	880	70	861	141	16
1935	6,824	3,031	44	1,566	1,041	66	763	121	16
1936	6,804	3,644	54	1,769	1,319	75	573	147	26
1937	6,170	3,575	58	1,748	1,370	78	632	142	22
1938	4,615	2,562	56	1,250	954	76	512	141	28
1939	3,578	1,752	49	1,152	677	59	289	122	42
1940	3,165	1,484	47	970	563	58	270	63	23
1941	3,303	1,373	42	825	476	56	254	76	26

NNUS, p. 52, Table 4; based on data in annual editions of Nōrinshō, Nōseikyoku, *Kosaku nenpō* and *Nōchi nenpō*.

the outbreak of World War I also attracted local farmers, creating shortages of tenants in many villages and encouraging remaining tenants to engage in disputes.[25]

The increase in urban job opportunities also reduced the tenants' interest in and dependence on farming. In Aiichi Prefecture, for example, it appears that tenants engaged in disputes because they knew that if landlords refused to meet their demands they could easily find work in Nagoya.[26]

With the end of the wartime boom in the early 1920's, however, urban job opportunities declined somewhat. Many former or part-time tenant farmers were laid off as factories curtailed production; others found their wages severely reduced.[27] Those who had remained on their farms and had profited from higher prices for agricultural produce during the boom also suffered losses.[28] Few of them were worse off than they had been before the war, but after a taste of prosperity they now found their reduced standard of living intolerable. It appears that, unable to do anything about general economic conditions, they turned against their most visible and accessible oppressors, the landlords.

Moreover, despite the brevity of the wartime boom, the experience of working as industrial laborers had a lasting effect on tenants. They quickly perceived not only that they could make more money as laborers than as tenants, but also that the work-load was often lighter and the hours shorter. When they returned to tenant farming, they sought greater rewards for their labor, on which they now placed a higher value, by demanding rent reductions. Thus, although the police reports from Fukui Prefecture, quoted previously, observed that few tenants read newspapers or "dangerous" magazines, they noted that many tenants had worked in nearby textile factories and had become more "cunning" than ordinary tenants and less content with the existing tenancy system.[29] Officials in Aiichi Prefecture noted that "the basic cause of most disputes is the awareness among tenants that agricultural labor is much more troublesome than other kinds of labor and that farming itself is much less profit-

[25] *KS*, I, 412.

[26] *Ibid.*, p. 95. See also Watanabe Shinichi, "Rōdō ichiba no hatten to kosaku kankei," *Nōgyō to keizai*, IX (1937), p. 20.

[27] *KS*, II, 59.   [28] *KS*, I, 43; *KS*, II, 31-32.

[29] *KS*, I, 234.

able than other occupations. Poor harvests merely provide tenants with an immediate excuse for expressing their grievances."[30]

The second difference between southwestern and northeastern Japan was the type of landlord prevailing in each region. Although the "Meiji landlord" has become a subject of scholarly debate,[31] very little has been written about landlords in subsequent, post-Meiji years. Most analyses of tenancy disputes focus on tenant farmers; where landlords are mentioned at all they are, at best, described as impotent bystanders unable to control the progressive forces of change in the countryside. More typically, they are cast as villains whose rapaciousness fomented rebellion. Examples of villainous landlords who raised rents at every opportunity and charged exorbitant interest rates can indeed be found, but there are other features of the landlords' role in causing disputes which should not be overlooked. To a great extent, landlords, not tenants, were the agents of social change in the countryside. Where they responded energetically to modernization, tenancy disputes erupted; where they remained traditional, disputes were rare.

During the Meiji period small landlords owning less than 3 chō of land, who formed the great majority of landlords in Japan, were not easily distinguished from other villagers—in the phrase used by Japanese writers, their coloring as landlords was muted. Living simply and often farmers themselves, they gave tenants little cause for jealousy. Many of them had been owner-cultivators of small plots or even tenants in the past, slowly expanding their holdings until they acquired more land than they could farm with family labor. It was not inconceivable to tenants that they, too, by a combination of diligence and good fortune, might eventually achieve the same degree of success. Indeed, movement between the two classes, small landlords and tenants, was not uncommon.[32]

[30] KS, ii, 128. For an interesting discussion of the influence of industrialization on tenant unrest see George O. Totten, "Labor and Agrarian Disputes in Japan Following World War I," Economic Development and Cultural Change, ix, 1, part II (October, 1960), pp. 187-212.

[31] Ronald Dore, "The Meiji Landlord: Good or Bad," Journal of Asian Studies, xviii (May, 1959), pp. 343-355.

[32] One example is described in J. W. Robertson Scott, The Foundations of Japan (London, 1922), p. 376.

386

In contrast, the economic and social gap between tenants and larger landlords, especially those owning 10 or more *chō*, was readily apparent. While tenants lived in simple farmhouses, these landlords had spacious and elegant homes, often surrounded by magnificent gardens. They ate pure white rice accompanied by side dishes of fish, meat, and vegetables while their tenants ate foreign rice (*gaimai*), rice mixed with barley, and potatoes, and looked forward to small portions of fish or meat on a few special occasions during the year.[33] Able to get by on the income they received from tenant rents,[34] these landlords did not have to work; although many farmed small plots of land, they could, if they chose, live a life of almost total leisure. They married within the same status circle, entertained officials when they came on inspection trips, and were buried in the most attractive parts of village cemeteries.[35]

That tenants were aware and sometimes resentful of the comfortable life of these landlords is beyond doubt. No matter how humble and submissive they seemed, one observer noted, tenants "are still human beings and naturally harbor feelings of discontent. . . . If the walls had ears and one could listen to them talking by the fireside on a winter's evening, one would discover how oppressed they feel."[36] "I am too poor to be a Homma," a popular saying went, referring to the largest landowning family in Japan, "I can only afford to be a *daimyo*."[37]

One characteristic of landlord-tenant relationships which limited tenant resentment was their longevity. Many tenant families in the Meiji era had farmed the land of the same landlord family for generations. In some cases, whether true in fact or not, the two families claimed a common ancestry, and their economic relationship was reinforced by kinship and religious ties. Even where kinship ties did not exist, the tenant was conscious of continuing a relationship with his landlord which his father or grandfather before him had initiated and which had provided his family's livelihood for a half-century or more. Born into and

---

[33] *NNUS*, p. 29, n. 12.

[34] Araki Moriaki, "Junushisei no tenkai," *Iwanami kōza Nihon rekishi.* (Tokyo, 1962), xvi, 81.

[35] Robertson Scott, *Foundations . . .* , pp. 213-214, 306.

[36] Amano Fujio, *Nōson shakai mondai: jinushi to kosakunin* (Tokyo, 1920), p. 8.

[37] Told to the author by Seiichi Tobata.

brought up in a status of dependency, he grew accustomed to hardship and to obeying the landlord's orders. Although he might occasionally feel that the treatment he received was unduly harsh, it did not occur to him to question the landlord's right to exercise whatever power he possessed.[38]

Of equal, if not greater, importance in limiting tenant resentment, however, were the political, economic, and social functions which landlords, as a wealthy and leisured elite, performed for their tenants and the villages in which they lived. That they monopolized village offices was due not only to their superior ascriptive status but also to their ability to hold office and achieve the ends other villagers, including tenants, desired. Because most of the higher posts in village government offered little, if any, salary, while requiring a substantial expenditure of time and money, only wealthy men could afford to fill them. Moreover, the social and business contacts which landlords developed in neighboring towns and villages by means of marriage or such commercial activity as the sale of rent-rice often enabled them to win favorable settlements for their own villages in local irrigation disputes, to argue successfully for new roads and other improvements in transportation, and otherwise to promote village prosperity.[39]

Although they took over half the harvest as rent, they also provided tenants with additional sources of income which enabled them to survive from year to year. The children of tenants were employed as household servants. During the off-season and on special occasions tenants and their wives worked for their landlord—cleaning out storage facilities, picking mulberry leaves, planting and harvesting rice on the landlord's own farm, and assisting at weddings and funerals—receiving money, clothing, and food in return.[40]

The resentment tenants might feel toward their landlord's gracious style of life was checked by their awareness that upkeep and improvements on his home provided them with many oppor-

[38] Amano, *Nōson shakai mondai*, pp. 5, 9; Kondo Yasuo, *Mura no kōzo* (Tokyo, 1955), p. 49; Thomas C. Smith, "The Japanese Village in the Seventeenth Century," *Journal of Economic History*, XII (Winter, 1952), p. 15.

[39] Tobata, *Nōchi o meguru* . . . , p. 71; Kurt Steiner, *Local Government in Japan* (Stanford, 1965), pp. 414-415.

[40] Social Science Research Institute (ed.), *The Power Structure in a Rural Community; the Case of Mutsuzawa Mura* (Tokyo, 1960), pp. 2-4.

tunities for employment. Indeed, some landlords hired tenants to build their gardens during years of famine or depression.[41] Viewing the gardens later, the tenants' sense of envy was mingled with, and perhaps overwhelmed by, gratitude toward the landlords for saving them from starvation.

Finally, tenant resentment was checked by the social functions landlords performed. Besides entertaining other landlords and distinguished visitors, they also held feasts for their tenants and provided both money and equipment for local festivals, weddings, and funerals. They mediated disputes and served as go-betweens in arranging tenant marriages. A room in the landlord's home was usually available to tenants as a meeting-place and, somewhat later, for listening to the radio.[42]

In a very real sense, then, landlords were "the host plants of the land; tenants, like ivy, coil around them and are protected from the weather."[43] Tenants accepted the wealth and power of landlords not only as part of the natural order of society, but also because both were useful in assuring their own survival and well-being.

But by the 1920's the situation had changed. Many landlords ceased accumulating land and invested their capital in businesses of their own or in the stock market.[44] Just as tenants discovered that greater rewards could be derived from industrial labor, landlords found that greater profits could be made from non-agricultural investment. If, for example, a man purchased 10 *chō* of land in the early 1920's and let it to tenants at average rents, his net income after taxes would amount to 5.3 per cent of the purchase price. Had he purchased stock in Kanegafuchi Textiles instead, he would have received a net return of 10.8 per cent, roughly twice as much.[45] Still other landlords moved away from

[41] I am indebted to Ueno Kyō, Mayor of Nango Village, Miyagi Prefecture, for this information.

[42] Wagatsuma Tōsaku, "Jinushi seido to buraku seido no kankei," *Teikoku nōkai ho* xxxiii (May, 1943), p. 6; John W. Bennett and Iwao Ishino, *Paternalism in the Japanese Economy* (Minneapolis, 1963), pp. 203-204, 217-218; Social Science Research Institute, *Power Structure* . . . , p. 4.

[43] Amano, *Nōson shakai mondai*, p. 18.

[44] This subject is discussed in some detail in Saito Eiichi, "Jinushi no zaisan kōsei ni tsuite," *Shakai seisaku jihō*, No. 156 (September, 1933), pp. 64-76, and No. 157 (October, 1933), pp. 74-87.

[45] Dorothy Orchard, "Agrarian Problems of Modern Japan," *Journal of Political Economy*, xxxvii (April, 1929), p. 135.

their native villages to the cities to escape the burden of local taxes, to pursue new occupations, or simply to enjoy the pleasures of urban life.[46]

Unfortunately, these changes among landlords cannot be rigorously documented, but the available data, although confined to only a small percentage of all landlords, suggest that both absentee ownership and non-agricultural investment were more pronounced among landlords in economically advanced regions like the Kinki than in backward regions like the Tohoku. In 1924, for example, 52 per cent of landlords in the Kinki who owned 50 *chō* or more resided outside the district (*gun* or *shi*) in which their land was located; in the Tohoku, only 17 per cent.[47] Similarly, over half the landlords owning 50 *chō* or more in the Kinki and Chugoku who were listed by name in the registers of large landlords compiled in 1890 and 1898 were not included in the register of 1924; less than one-third of the large landlords in the Tohoku were not included. Some of these landlords had been forced to sell all or part of their land to cover personal debts and business losses; others had done so voluntarily, to generate capital for industrial investment.[48]

These changes among landlords did not necessarily lead to a worsening of tenancy conditions. Ireland in the eighteenth century, "the darkest chapter in the history of English landlords,"[49] has come to epitomize the evil effects of absentee ownership. The holdings of absentee landlords were divided into tiny parcels and let at higher than average rents; overseers charged tenants special fees in addition to rents for the privilege of cultivating the land they managed; farming villages remained in wretched poverty. But the effects of absentee ownership in Japan were almost exactly the opposite.

Absentee landlords usually had other sources of income and

[46] Higashiura Shōji, "Mura no zaisei to fuzai jinushi ni tsuite jirei hitotsu," *Teikoku nōkai hō*, xv (February, 1925), pp. 6-8; Toyama Shinzō, "Fuzai jinushi to kazei," *Teikoku nōkai hō*, vi (October, 1916), pp. 36-40; Kondo, *Mura no kōzō*, pp. 426-427; Dore, *Land Reform* . . . , pp. 23-24. Of local taxes, the *kosūwari*, or house tax, was especially high; house taxes were low in most cities.

[47] Tobata, *Nōchi o meguru* . . . , pp. 38-40, especially Table 18, p. 40.

[48] Shibutani Ryūichi and Ishiyama Shōjirō, "Meiji chūki no jinushi meibo," *Tochi seido shigaku*, 30 (June, 1966), p. 58.

[49] G. E. Mingay, *English Landed Society in the Eighteenth Century* (London, 1963), p. 47.

were less dependent on tenant rents than were resident land-lords. The rents they charged were often lower than prevailing rents and rarely any higher. Living at some distance from their holdings and lacking intimate knowledge of rural conditions, they were generally more willing than resident owners to meet tenant demands for rent reduction.[50]

Resident landlords bought and sold land frequently. Typical-ly, the new owners raised rents when they took possession and sometimes evicted current tenants in favor of their own. In con-trast, absentee owners rarely acquired new holdings; their ten-ants enjoyed greater security, farming the same plots for many years in succession.[51]

In general, the tenants of absentee landlords cultivated a larger area per capita than the tenants of resident landlords. According to the 1924 survey of large landlords, for example, the tenants of absentee landlords leased an average of 5.2 *tan*; ten-ants of resident landlords, an average of 4.3 *tan*.[52] Although most absentee landlords employed overseers to manage their holdings, few cases of extortion or other unfair treatment of tenants were reported.[53]

Like the absentee landlord, the landlord who invested part of his capital in business or industry was not as dependent on rental income as the non-investing landlord and was generally in a better position to grant rent reductions to his tenants. Moreover, his investments often brought immediate benefits to his tenants and the local farming population. The expansion of railroads, for example, in which landlords invested heavily, brought many vil-lages into closer contact with lucrative urban markets for their produce and made it possible for many tenants to work in nearby towns during the off-season.[54] There were indirect benefits for tenants in landlord investment as well. If, for example, landlords had not contributed to industrial development, job opportunities for the surplus rural population would have increased at a slower rate, causing greater population pressure on the land, more in-tense competition for land among tenants, and hence, even high-er rents.[55]

But even though tenancy conditions did not necessarily be-

[50] Tobata, *Nōchi o meguru* . . . , pp. 43-45.
[51] *Ibid.*, pp. 43-44.
[52] *Ibid.*, pp. 42, 44-45. (Table 10.)
[53] *Ibid.*, pp. 45-46.
[54] Robertson Scott, *Foundations* . . . , p. 283.
[55] Dore, *Land Reform* . . . , p. 48.

come worse, it became more difficult for these landlords to perform their traditional functions in rural society. Although absentee landlords might return occasionally to their native villages to visit family graves or tend to local business, they gradually became strangers to the other residents. At the New Year they might gather all their tenants together for a banquet and the distribution of gifts, but it was a ceremony devoid of past familiarity. Now their managers took care of day-to-day affairs: the selection of tenants, supervision of farming, and collection of rents. In some cases managers also handled sales of rent-rice and the landlords had little to do but pocket the profits.[56] To their tenants they became distant figures, with great power over their lives but little involvement in or understanding of local affairs.

Other landlords, increasingly concerned with their investments and national economic affairs, had less time to devote to local government. It was hard for them to compartmentalize their behavior—to compete for profits in business or on the stock exchange and still make benevolent, and often costly, gestures toward their tenants. Instead, they became increasingly impatient with the elaborate ritual of gift-giving and the many demands made upon their time and wealth. Some attempted to lease as much of their land as possible to tenants in other villages—thereby becoming absentee landlords without moving at all—to escape the personalized relations in their own communities.[57]

By the standards employed today, these landlords were modern men in both attitude and style of life. If they had a chance to sell a portion of their land at a profit, they did so readily, with no apologies to their ancestors. They sent their sons to the university to study law and economics. Some sent their daughters to high school, a trend deplored by traditionalists.[58] It was not unusual for them to be more interested in national politics than community affairs, donating money to political parties or campaigning for seats in the Diet.[59]

But their way of life, however modern it may have been, was

[56] See, for example, Okayama ken naimubu, *Okayama ken kosaku kankō chōsa sho* (Okayama, 1924), pp. 85-86, 88.

[57] Wagatsuma, "Jinushi seido . . . ," p. 8.

[58] Thomas C. Smith, "Landlords' Sons in the Business Elite," *Economic Development and Cultural Change*, IX, 1, part II (October, 1960), pp. 93-108 *passim*; Yokoi Jikei, "Jinushi no seikatsu," *Chūō nōji hō*, 63 (June, 1905), p. 2.

[59] Amano, *Nōson shakai mondai*, p. 19.

alien, and at times offensive, to their tenants and to other villagers. That several landlords in Gifu Prefecture kept mistresses in town, for example, was considered scandalous by the local population,[60] though we may question whether it was the mistress-keeping itself or the mistress-keeping in town which offended them. By failing to perform the duties traditionally expected of them, and by dissociating themselves from rural life, these landlords lost the checks on tenant resentment they had enjoyed in the past.

A tenant union leader in a village in Saga Prefecture reported in the early 1920's that it was easy to organize tenants into militant unions in *buraku* where absentee ownership prevailed, but difficult to organize tenants at all in *buraku* where landlords resided.[61] Sugiyama Motojirō, founder and head of the Japan Farmers' Union, observed in 1926 that more disputes occurred on land owned by absentee landlords than on land owned by village residents.[62] Although no comprehensive data exist on the kinds of landlords involved in disputes in the 1920's, frequent references to the involvement of absentee landlords in the case studies of disputes published by the Ministry of Agriculture tend to substantiate his claim.

In a few of these case studies inferior tenancy conditions on absentee-owned land are cited as the cause of disputes.[63] Moreover, it is possible that some tenants engaged in disputes with absentee landlords for tactical reasons. Having other sources of income and lacking the interest or ability to farm their own land, absentee landlords were, as noted previously, more willing to grant tenant demands for rent reduction than were resident landlords. Once a settlement favorable to the tenants had been reached, the tenants could then demand similar terms from resident landlords, arguing persuasively that rent levels should be the same on equivalent grades of land, regardless of ownership.[64]

But the most common reason cited for these disputes was the hostility of tenant farmers toward absentee landlords who showed little interest in local affairs. As mentioned previously, the tenants of absentee landlords usually paid no more in rent

---

[60] *KS*, i, 176.   [61] *NNUS*, pp. 114-115.

[62] Sugiyama Motojirō, "Mazu fuzai jinushi o naku seyo," *Nōsei kenkyū*, v (1926), p. 23.

[63] *KS*, i, 123, 398.

[64] *Okayama ken kosaku kankō*, p. 92; *KS*, i, 424.

than did tenants of resident landlords, while enjoying greater security of tenure. But apparently these economic advantages were not as meaningful to them as personal relations with their landlords, precisely what absentee landlords could not provide.[65]

Observers in southern Okayama Prefecture noted the absence of "feelings of friendship and intimacy" between absentee landlords and their tenants as a cause of disputes.[66] That over 60 per cent of all landlords in a village in Yamanashi Prefecture were absentee owners who did not display traditional paternalism was regarded as the basic cause of disputes.[67] Similarly, the existence of many absentee landlords who failed to provide leadership and financial aid in their village was one cause of a dispute in Aiichi Prefecture in 1917.[68]

Landlords who remained in the villages but no longer performed customary functions also experienced more disputes than traditional village landlords. In some cases tenant resentment was intensified because these landlords still claimed the prerogatives their functions had justified in the past. A report from Hyogo Prefecture portrayed most local landlords as "bigots" because they sat in chairs when their tenants came to see them but made the tenants sit on the floor.[69] In Gifu Prefecture landlords "treated tenants in the manner of feudal lords dealing with their retainers,"[70] not letting visiting tenants enter the room they occupied. But this type of behavior, now considered haughty by tenants, had been considered entirely appropriate a few years before. Indeed, Gifu tenants previously had called landlords fathers of the land (*tsuchi oya*) and treated them with all the deference due a feudal lord. The crucial difference now was that the landlords were uninterested in their tenants' affairs and did nothing to command their respect.[71] In other cases, however, it was not the haughtiness of resident landlords which aroused tenant resentment, but the very absence of landlord-tenant contact. Landlords in a village in Yamanashi Prefecture were "too intent on making money" to see their tenants.[72] All the landlords involved

[65] The reaction of tenant farmers in Japan to the increasingly impersonal treatment they received from landlords is by no means unique. For an analysis of a similar situation in an American factory in the 1950's see Alvin W. Gouldner, *Patterns of Industrial Bureaucracy* (Glencoe, Ill., 1954), especially chapters I-V.

[66] *Okayama ken kosaku kankō*, p. 314.

[67] *Ibid.*, p. 192.   [68] *Ibid.*, p. 95.   [69] *KS*, ii, 65.

[70] *KS*, i, 175.   [71] *Ibid.*, pp. 173, 175.   [72] *KS*, ii, 200.

in a dispute in Fukui Prefecture in 1920 were residents of their villages, but they were considered "absentee owners" by their tenants because they lived on the shopping streets of the villages, ran small businesses, and had no interest in farming.[73]

In contrast to southwestern Japan, in northeastern Japan economic backwardness served as a check on tenant unrest during the 1920's. Because there were far fewer opportunities for tenants to obtain part-time employment outside of agriculture, they remained more dependent on farming and less aware of its relative unprofitability.[74] If they did have off-season work, it was more likely to be in fishing or handicrafts than in industry. Therefore, they had less personal experience with full-time wage labor, and their traditional attitude toward farming—as a way of life more than as a way of making money—remained relatively unchanged. True, they had access to information about tenancy disputes in other parts of the country. As one northern landlord remarked, "One must take note of the newspapers. . . . If there is any sort of incident . . . they speedily report it. In some ways, this is admirable, but it also gives evil knowledge to farmers who themselves know nothing of such things."[75] Moreover, university students in the Tohoku, following the example set by young activists in Tokyo, made numerous attempts to organize local tenant unions and political parties.[76] But neither the mass media nor the students had much effect on tenants.

One important reason, other than the traditionalism of the tenants themselves, was the continued traditionalism of their landlords, which also had its basis in the economic backwardness of the region. Unlike southwestern Japan, the Tohoku contained few large cities to entice landlords away from their native vil-

[73] *KS*, I, 232-233.

[74] Despite migration to other prefectures, population pressure on the land remained high. The farming population of Yamagata Prefecture, one of the most prosperous in the Tohoku, actually increased between 1907 and 1938, causing a reduction of slightly more than 1 *tan* in the area of land per farm household. Yamagata ken keizaibu, *Kosaku jijō to nōmin undō* (Yamagata, 1940), p. 1.

[75] Niigata ken nōkai (ed.), *Jinushi kosaku mondai ni taisuru jinushi no iken* (Niigata, 1921), p. 27.

[76] Sunaga Shigemitsu (ed.), *Kindai Nihon no jinushi to nōmin* (Tokyo, 1966), pp. 357-358.

lages, and fewer investment opportunities, locally at least, to attract their capital from agriculture. A larger percentage of landlords than in southwestern Japan, therefore, remained in the countryside as resident landlords, living unostentatiously as a rule, often cultivating part of their land themselves, and taking an active interest in local affairs.[77] Their performance of their traditional role in village society and the frequency of their personal contact with tenants militated against the open expression of conflict.

Paradoxically, the economic backwardness of northeastern Japan and the traditionalism of its landlords made tenancy disputes more likely than elsewhere in the nation during the depression of the 1930's. Because of a harsh climate poor harvests were common, their impact intensified by the impossibility of double-cropping. Few but the largest landlords had substantial savings; what little they did possess was usually deposited in small provincial banks, many of which failed in the early 1930's.[78] Forced to sell more rice than before to pay land taxes, they could no longer tolerate rent arrears or grant generous rent reductions. Many landlords, precisely because they were experienced farmers, owned all the necessary tools, and were well acquainted with local farming conditions, thought immediately of expanding the area of land they cultivated—that is, of evicting tenants as a way out of their predicament.

The depression did not have a similar effect in southwestern Japan. Landlords there, too, found their incomes sharply reduced, but those who had left the villages or who had devoted their time to business or politics hesitated before demanding their land back. If, after all, they proved unsuccessful as farmers, they would end up with no income at all. Eviction disputes were fairly rare (Table 5). Unable to get off-season work in factories, tenants were forced to rely once more on farming for their livelihood. Competition for land increased as thousands of unemployed urban workers returned to the villages, their train fare paid by the government as a social relief measure. With a surplus of idle labor in almost every village and many families eager for land on even the most unfavorable terms, it became increas-

[77] One such landlord family, the Otaki of Yamagata Prefecture, is described in Dore, *Land Reform* . . . , pp. 30-41. See also *KS*, II, 270-271, 278, 383.

[78] Nōrinshō, Nōmukyoku, *Chihō betsu kosaku sōgi gaiyō*, III, 13.

ingly risky to engage in disputes. While tenancy disputes in northeastern Japan rapidly increased, the number of disputes in southwestern Japan rose only slightly. Compared to the previous decade, the number of disputes in the Kinki between 1932 and 1941 declined by 25 per cent (Table 3).

Tenant unrest in Japan in the 1920's appears to have originated in two principal sources, economic growth and changes among landlords, both more pronounced in southwestern Japan than in outlying regions. The desire for improved tenancy conditions arose not from despair or desperation but from prosperity, however slight and fleeting, which gave tenants the economic ability to engage in disputes and which raised not only their standard of living but also their expectations of what that standard of living should be.

The disruption of traditional landlord-tenant relations, caused in large part by the landlords' positive response to modernization, was an additional source of unrest. It was not status inequality itself which prompted disputes, but the failure of landlords to perform those time-honored and useful functions in rural society which had justified their superior status in the past. Ironically, had landlords in southwestern Japan remained more traditional, had they conformed more closely to the stereotype of landed elites in modernizing societies, shunning commerce and resisting the temptations of urban styles of life, they might have avoided, or at least postponed, the tenant challenge to their authority.

Japanese Industrial Relations
at the Crossroads:
The Great Noda Strike of 1927-1928

WOULD THE "unique" aspects of Japanese industrial relations, built on indigenous familial patterns of paternalism, prevail or would employer-employee relations be "westernized" along the lines of European and American unionism? This was not entirely clear in Japan of the mid-1920's when the problems of industrial organization became increasingly critical. Both labor and management were divided on the issue. The major division within labor was between the mass of workers who were not organized and the 4 to 5 per cent who were. The unorganized were those presumably less touched by foreign influences. The mass of workers in minuscule firms worked along with the master as part of the family. Union organization was meaningless to them. The greater the size of the enterprise, its degree of mechanization, and the urbanization of its setting, the fewer were the communication barriers to the appeals of unionism, but many other factors militated against unionism and for acceptance of prevailing managerial policies.

In contrast to the unorganized, all elements in the labor movement by the very fact of participation were presumably acting in terms of a Western model simply because labor organization had developed abroad in societies earlier and more deeply affected by industrialism. By 1925 the Japanese labor movement had become irreconcilably split between a revolutionary (Communist) and a gradualist (social democratic) approach. An earlier anarcho-syndicalist trend was fast disappearing. The revolutionaries wanted to use the discontent of the workers and the techniques of industrial relations for fundamental transformation of society. The social democrats, though divided among themselves on questions of militancy, were in agreement that they would work within the framework of the constitution and the capitalist system for the amelioration of the lot of the laboring and farming classes.[1] Their primary objective, therefore, was to organize industrial workers (and their allies, the tenant farmers), so that they could negotiate with management (or the landlords) on more nearly equal terms. The strike was to be a weapon of last resort. But this and all techniques were to be taught to the workers. Organizing for their own interests would give them self-respect and would bring about a redistribution of income that would strengthen the nation, develop democracy, and promote the economy by providing an internal consumer market.

Although there was no question of Japanese management looking upon the revolutionaries with anything other than hostility, there was a section of liberal business opinion that was willing to make ideological concessions to unionism in order to promote the development of a "sound" labor movement that would cooperate with management. Perhaps most prominent among such business leaders was the banker Shibusawa Eiichi (1840-1931) whose views were echoed and developed further by the Harmonization Society (Kyōchōkai) which he helped to found in 1919 with high-level support in government and industry. This organization was committed to the legal recognition and spread of labor unions and concomitantly to bargaining and collective agreements.[2]

The majority of Japanese businessmen, however, made little distinction between the Japanese social democrats and Communists, between the "moderates" and "radicals." They considered that the real aim of unionization was to undermine the economy and foment revolution. They also argued that Japan, with her lack of resources and her backwardness, and often the object of racial and commercial discrimination, could ill afford any redistribution of income that would inhibit her ability to compete in the world markets. But above all they appealed to the "uniqueness" and implied superiority of Japanese ethical relations which were based on an analogy with the uniquely Japanese "house" (*ie*). The management ideology that evolved from this can be called "familial paternalism."[3] In essence this meant that the

[1] See my book, *The Social Democratic Movement in Prewar Japan* (New Haven and London, 1966), p. 49, and, for splits within the movement, see chapters 5 through 7.

[2] Byron K. Marshall, *Capitalism and Nationalism in Prewar Japan: The Ideology of the Business Elite, 1868-1941* (Stanford, 1967), pp. 82-89.

[3] This is the term used, for instance, by M. Y. Yoshino, *Japan's Managerial System: Tradition and Innovation* (Cambridge, Mass., 1968), pp. 78-82.

enterprise, no matter what its size, should be characterized by virtues analogous to those that prevailed in a Japanese family: loyalty (akin to filial piety) from those below and concern (bordering on affection) from those above. Each member, from president to humblest worker, should be content with his station but do his utmost whatever his job, because each was contributing to the good of all. All should benefit in good times and at times of festivity (such as at the New Year, from year-end bonuses), but by the same token all should pull in their belts for the good of the firm when times were bad.

This type of familial paternalism underwent a subtle change from the first decade of the twentieth century to the end of the 1920's. Its emphasis gradually shifted as it softened from a strong authoritarianism to an orientation of close emotional ties, solidarity, harmony, and cooperation.[4]

In this study we shall observe the actions of a firm whose orientation had not yet made that shift. We shall see the beginnings of its concrete manifestations, however, in a range of innovations: recruitment from schools, with levels of education essentially determining employee status; security of tenure; promotional rewards based on length of service; low wages supplemented by bonuses of many different types, from seasonal ones to those accompanying accident, old age, retirement, or discharge. The system included "temporary" workers as an essential element. They provided the ballast to be discharged when the work force had to be reduced, and their existence, precarious and looked-down-upon, made the permanent workers cleave all the more closely to the company and behave in an appropriate manner, thus not only fostering loyalty to the enterprise but providing attitudinal incentive in the absence of various material incentives, such as extra pay for overtime.

The majority of managers were convinced that the adoption of "foreign" patterns of industrial relations was unwise and unnecessary. Not only would it destroy the seamless fabric of Japa-

[4] This type of ideology and its practice is thoroughly analyzed by Hiroshi Hazama, *Nihon rōmu kanri shi kenkyū: keieikazokushugi no keisei to tenkai* (Tokyo, 1964), pp. 14-43. A good exposition in English is found in Yoshino, pp. 78-82. The earlier ideology is also criticized in Koji Taira, "Factory Legislation and Management Modernization during Japan's Industrialization, 1886-1916," *Business History Review*, XLIV, 1 (Spring 1970), pp. 86-97.

nese values, but, whereas Western workers had no choice but to make demands on the basis of individual rights, Japanese workers were blessed with a tradition of paternal benevolence.[5] In the long run this view prevailed: it could be imposed on the unorganized; and the independently organized were eventually forced by the government to dissolve.

The alternatives did achieve some success before their disappearance and in this sense provided a tradition upon which the post-World War II labor movement was able to build. The militancy of the Communist-led groups caused both government and management to give some concessions to the more moderate social democrats, but the former were decisively suppressed by 1929. Thereafter, the success of the social democrats was more apparent than real, because it was achieved by substantial compromises. In the Diet elections of 1937 they won 38 seats (8.2 per cent) with almost 10 per cent of the vote, and labor union membership reached its peak with over 420,000 members, but this was only an estimated 6 per cent of Japanese workers. By 1940 both union and party movements came to a halt. While the immediate cause for their demise was the Pacific War and government repression, this does not fully explain the failure of the labor movement to attract widespread support in the preceding two decades.

An answer to this problem has recently been suggested by Robert Evans, Jr., who argues that the failure may have been related to the incompatibility of the pattern of industrial relations espoused by trade unions with that of familial paternalism, or, in his words, perhaps "unions did not prosper because they failed to provide a meaningful organization consistent with a Japanese pattern of personnel management."[6]

The case study in this essay can perhaps give us some clues toward answering this question in a more concrete fashion. It is an interesting and significant case in many respects—interesting for the variety of modern techniques used by labor and management in the conflict and for the ways in which each side utilized traditional cultural mores to legitimize their actions and further

[5] Marshall, p. 87.
[6] Robert Evans, Jr., "Evolution of the Japanese System of Employer-Employee Relations, 1868-1945," *Business History Review*, XLIV, 1 (Spring 1970), p. 125.

their own cause. In addition, it has human interest, exposing a glimpse of drama in the lives of working people in the late Taishō–early Shōwa period.

The significance of the Noda strike derives from its character, timing, and intensity. It was a test case of whether industrial relations based on union recognition would be acceptable to management and the government and whether Japanese workers were capable of responsible use of the techniques involved— possibilities that were heightened by the ideological position of the leadership of the strike. This "conservative" wing of the social democratic movement accepted the continuation of the capitalist system for the foreseeable future and sought respectability through personal contacts with persons high in the bureaucracy, in politics, and in business circles. And finally the timing of the strike, September 1927-April 1928, was significant. In the years immediately preceding, several measures crucial to industrial relations were introduced: enforcement of the Health Insurance Law of 1922; enforcement of the Revised Factory Act of 1911; repeal of Articles 17 and 30 of the Peace Police Law of 1900, which had restricted union activity; and passage of the Labor Disputes Conciliation Law. Furthermore, in the year before the Universal Manhood Suffrage Law had been passed, enabling males over 25 to vote, without any tax qualifications, thus politically emancipating much of labor for the first time, and opening the door for labor-based political parties. This law, however, was coupled with the ominous Peace Preservation Law, aimed at restricting radical leftist thought and activity. Local and national elections took place for the first time under these laws, while the strike was going on. This was thus a period when hope for a new departure in employer-employee relations and for a new role for labor in Japanese society was at its height. Perhaps equally high was fear of such a departure on the part of its opponents of labor's emancipation, as witnessed by the Tanaka Cabinet's mass arrests of actual and alleged leftist radicals on March 15, 1928, and the determination of management to crush the union in this strike, which finally ended on April 20—the longest strike in Japanese history up to that time.

The story of the strike itself is a fascinating one. Culled from the newspapers of the day, subsequent studies by people concerned, and police files, it reads like a dime novel, replete with violence, treachery, and heroism.[7] On September 16, 1927, 16 of the 17 plants of the Noda Soy Sauce Company had to close down as 1,358 of the 2,092 employees had decided to strike to secure some 7 demands for better pay and conditions. The strike was triggered by what the workers suspected was a move by the company to undermine the union. The main implicit demand, thus, was recognition of the union as the body with the right to bargain collectively.[8]

[7] The most detailed account of the strike is to be found in Matsuoka Komakichi, *Noda dai rōdō sōgi.* This is almost matched in size by Namiki Shigetarō (ed. and pub.), *Noda sōgi no temmatsu* (Noda, 1928). Namiki, who was the Noda Company's labor relations specialist, earlier edited and published *Noda sōgi no keika nichiroku* (Noda, 1928). Other materials include: Shihōshō Keijikyoku, *Shisō kenkyū shiryō, dai kyū shū: noda sōgi no temmatsu* (marked confidential [*Hi*]), (Tokyo, September, 1928), 78 pp. Appendices start on p. 29, the first 28 pp. being a report given by Kusama Tokumitsu of the Labor Section of the Harmonization Society at the Ministry of Justice on June 21, 1928); Kyōchōkai Rōdōka, *Noda rōdō sōgi no temmatsu* (n.p. [Tokyo], 1928), 91 pp.; and a mimeographed report by the Kyōchōkai Kyomuka, "Sōgi-go ni okeru Noda Kabushiki Kaisha no Kun'iku Shisetsu," *Rōdōsha kyōiku chōsa shiryō,* 22 (March 27, 1929). A contemporary book that gives special attention to the Noda strike is Machida Tatsujirō, *Rōdō sōgi no kaibō* (Tokyo, 1929); Machida was a member of the board of the Harmonization Society and was directly concerned with conciliation in the dispute. Another contemporary account is Nihon Shakai Mondai Kenkyūjo (eds.), *Noda kessen ki* (Tokyo, 1928). An eyewitness account more recently published is Yaji Kazuo, *Mukashi no rōdō sōgi no omoide* (Tokyo, 1956). A still more recently published account is to be found in Ōkōchi Kazuo and Matsuo Hiroshi, *Nihon rōdō kumiai monogatari: Shōwa* (Tokyo, 1965), pp. 101-113. A helpful recently published collection of materials is *Sōdōmei gojūnen shi* (Tokyo, 1964-1966), I, II; references to Noda include: I, 624-633, 838-841; II, 176-203, 927, 1011ff. Finally, there are the newspapers of the day; as it is the most accessible, I have gone over the bound edition of the *Asahi shimbun,* which covered the strike in great detail.

[8] Specifically, the demands were as follows:
1. A wage raise: a 10 per cent increase for male workers and 20 per cent for female workers.
2. An increase in the rate of payments for allowances for discharge, old age, and retirement: to the present rate an additional one day for every month worked.
3. Apprenticeship training for coopers and operatives in each factory: 12 apprentices to be trained in each factory.
4. A minimum year-end bonus to be equal to one month's wages.
5. A fixed period from initial employment to recognition as a skilled operative: skilled operative (permanent worker) status to be achieved in four years from initial employment.
6. Full application of the Employee Relief Provisions (*kōin fujo kitei*) to

The men with kerchiefs around their heads and many of the women, wearing baggy *mompei* trousers over their kimonos, gathered in clusters to discuss their assigned roles in the strike. A red flag was hoisted on a factory chimney. Union messengers with red arm bands darted here and there. Pickets were placed strategically through the small town of Noda in the largely agrarian prefecture of Chiba, which, though located near Tokyo, was somewhat off the well-traveled routes north and south. The group that was to visit the families of non-strikers was chosen, and those with responsibility for publicity began to plan posters, leaflets, and meetings. Others returned to their agricultural chores, as they spent only part of their time at the plant. The workers had now had 5 years of rather successful experience with trade unionism and felt a surge of power and self-confidence. The company officials, many of whom were members of the Mogi family, who owned the business, glowered at the strikers from their office windows, determined that this strike would break the union. On their part, they derived self-confidence from the preparations they had made for the showdown. They were intent on punishing the workers for abandoning the traditional respect for those in authority in the company and town.

day laborers: increase the present half the amount awarded to regular employees to the full amount.
Although not articulated at the time, the union objectives included union recognition, a collective agreement, and a closed shop. See Matsuoka, pp. 111-112 and 320-323 and Namiki, *Temmatsu . . .* , p. 12. The number of workers who went on strike was reported at 1,407 in Namiki, *Nichiroku . . .* , p. 5. The company's formal reply was as follows:
1. Concerning this, (a) instead of the 1.5 per cent each put in by management and labor for the Health Insurance Union, the company will raise its share to 2 per cent and the workers can reduce theirs to 1 per cent; (b) at the time for next year's wage raises, we will consider the matter very seriously; (c) how about putting in overtime?
2. It is difficult to accede to this.
3. It is difficult to meet your wishes on this.
4. We intend to do our best on this.
5. We will try our best on this.
6. We agree to this.
The company did not mention recognition of the right to bargain collectively. Matsuoka, pp. 112-113. The move the workers believed was aimed at undermining the union was the puzzling appearance of a second transportation agency (Motomaru Unsōten) to take over part of the work of the existing firm (Marusan Unsōten), thus threatening the livelihood of its 59 workers, who had earlier been organized by the Noda local, had demonstrated, and won a few concessions.

In the following months, the company carried out several large-scale firings, first issuing an ultimatum to return to work, so that by December 20, 1927, all those on strike were officially discharged. Work had gotten back under way in Plant No. 17 10 days after the strike started, and as time went by the other 16 plants were replenished with some 550 temporary workers. By December, 80 per cent of pre-strike production was reached with 1,350 employees at work, 300 of whom had dropped out of the strike, and of these 150 were clerks, not plant workers. On several occasions scabs were physically attacked by strikers, giving the police pretexts for arresting, for a time, all the strike leaders. The company hired ultra-nationalist bully gangs to come in and rough up the strikers.

At first the strikers followed all the textbook prescriptions for the strike situation, seeing that responsibilities were clearly allocated (the strike leader being a long-time employee, Koiwai Aisuke, who had earlier demonstrated his abilities) and seeing that local and outside opinion would receive the union local's interpretation of events in order to counter company propaganda, by means of meetings, statements, and handbills. The earlier-organized consumers' cooperative was mobilized, credit arranged, and resources pooled for living without wages. The Kyōchōkai was invited to investigate in case it should be called upon to act as conciliator. Picket lines were set up. The local theater was procured for mass meetings.

But as time passed and the company recovered from the initial strike blow, the workers' tactics became more desperate, with aspects of more traditional behavior appearing. Some violence occurred. When the police interfered with picnics, which were used to raise worker morale, the women tried shrine visits to pray for success. When teachers and their students began harassing the workers' children in the local school, the union organized a school boycott of the strikers' children. When marches to Tokyo with petitions to government people were blocked by the police, a lone worker made a dramatic appeal to the Emperor. As workers lost self-confidence, responsibility for leading the strike was moved upward several levels from the local to the Kantō (regional) Labor Federation, and finally full powers were entrusted to the experienced Matsuoka Komakichi (second in command to the internationally famous Suzuki Bunji, the "Gompers of Japan"). Finally, political, government, and business leaders (including the venerable Shibusawa) became involved in attempts at conciliation.

The settlement, which was reached on April 19, 1928, more than seven weary months after the inception of the strike, in effect destroyed the union. Only 300 of the 1,047 workers fired were allowed to return to work, although the others received discharge bonuses and livelihood maintenance. The labor songs of the strikers and their children ceased. Those who continued to work at the Noda plants were a more docile and submissive lot, but now their working conditions were much improved under the new, more concerned paternalism of the Mogis than had been the case 6 years earlier before the organization of the Noda local.

How did this strike fit in with the general pattern of strike activities at the time? Without going into a history of industrial relations in Japan, we can say that roughly from the time of the recession following the great Kantō earthquake of September, 1923, labor leaders were hesitant about embarking on disputes and if their demands were not accepted at once, they withdrew them. But in 1926-1927, according to the statistics, the number of disputes rose abruptly from 293, about what it had been for several years, to 494 in 1926 and then fell to 383, where it stayed for several years before again increasing drastically. As to their outcome—whether they ended in compromise, victory, or defeat for the workers—we can conclude that they were about evenly balanced.[9] Labor disputes generally, however, were gradually

[9] See Machida, pp. 5-7 and also the following which is adapted from a table from Machida, p. 20 of the Appendix:

Outcome of Labor Disputes, 1924-1298
Number of Incidents without parentheses
Number of Participants in parentheses

RESULTS

Year	Compromise	Victory	Defeat	Total
1924	135	66	132	333
	(19,707)	(20,609)	(23,211)	(54,527)
1925	114	52	127	293
	(10,744)	(11,922)	(18,076)	(40,742)
1926	161	139	195	495
	(14,412)	(11,999)	(40,825)	(67,134)
1927	119	109	155	383
	(13,383)	(8,345)	(25,942)	(46,672)
1928	132	95	161	397
	(21,414)	(11,558)	(13,097)	(46,252)

spreading. As the recession of 1927 deepened, strikes lessened among large-scale industry where the chances of victory were slight, and spread rather to smaller enterprises, such as Noda, where labor conditions, in most cases, were far worse and where management had badly neglected labor relations. It was here that the experience and skill of organized labor could, under the circumstances, make the best gains.

The length of disputes was also rising. In 1919 only 9 disputes ran over 11 days, but in 1920, 33 did; in 1921 and 1922, 42 did; in 1923, 65; in 1924, 88. In 1927 there were 39 that lasted over one month and 12 over 50 days. In 1928 there were 9 over 50 days. It was in this context of expanding labor unrest that the Noda strike, lasting 218 days and breaking all records in Japan until after World War II, took place.

Behind this bare-bones account of the Noda strike lies a wealth of material that can be highlighted in terms of change and continuity; it was a complex, interrelated process that can probably be presented best by examining first the company and then the union as a background to noting the significance of the tactics employed by both sides.

For some three hundred years the soy sauce breweries in Noda had been owned and operated by members of the Mogi family. New breweries had been established throughout the years by branch families. A loose form of organization had existed, based on the maintenance of family ties. In order to help members of the family who were not doing well financially, Mogi Sheiji in 1918 amalgamated most of the small breweries into an incorporated company capitalized at 8,000,000 yen. He standardized the product and labeled it all Kikkōman.[10] Within a short time this company became the largest soy sauce producer in Japan, a position it has retained to this day.

[10] Kikkōman is made up of three Chinese characters. The first two mean "tortoise shell" and the third means literally "ten thousand" or by extension "myriad." The tortoise is a symbol of longevity, which is considered good, and *man* also connotes longevity, as it is used in *banzai*, literally "ten thousand years." *Kikkō* also means by extension "hexagonal." Therefore, the trademark of Kikkōman soy sauce is the Chinese character for *man* enclosed in a hexagon. Some other marks were used by the company for cheaper types of soy sauce, though the contents were actually the same, according to a handbill put out by the Noda local. See Namiki, *Temmatsu . . .* , pp. 245-247.

Soy or soya or soja sauce—the English word derives from the Japanese *shōyu*, which comes in turn from the Chinese *chiang-yu*—stands on the table at every Japanese meal. It is as much a staple as sugar in the United States. Though a traditional condiment and food supplement, it continues to hold its own in modern Japanese cuisine. Its use has nothing to do with modernization; it is enjoyed as much by urban as by rural folk. It was, however, traditionally produced locally throughout Japan, but the rationalized methods adopted by the Mogis, together with their nearness to the ever-expanding Tokyo market, made it a business of national importance in the food industry.

Despite the large capitalization, most of the stock was owned by the various branches of the Mogi family, who were also the entrepreneurs. The family also dominated the town of Noda politically as well as economically. About 60 per cent of the population of 16,700 was dependent either directly or indirectly on the company and its subsidiaries for their livelihood.[11] Members of the Mogi family controlled the town assembly, the school board, the fire department, and the local army reservist group, as well as owning the local bank, the cinema, an inn, and a restaurant. Their economic power had a feudal tinge to it. Until the early 1920's, for example, at the marriage of a member of the Mogi family, the main street was strewn with sand as a symbol of respect for their high status.

The company's attitudes toward its employees did not change quickly, despite the reorganization of 1917 and improved methods of production. In fact, a regional newspaper on September 25, 1922, described the company's reaction to the formation of the union local: "The townspeople [of Noda] had never engaged in any higher form of collective action than the lantern procession staged at the conclusion of the World War. When the company saw them demonstrate defiantly, singing labor songs, it was as surprised as a savage on first seeing an airplane."[12]

Up until three years after the First World War, the Noda

[11] These figures are from the Noda Town Hall as of 1926; the whole table is reproduced in Matsuoka, pp. 14-15.

[12] The *Jiji shimpō* (September 25, 1922), as quoted in Matsuoka, p. 101. Modernization of the plant went on at Noda. The company was actually producing about 30 per cent of the soy sauce in Japan (that is, about 300,000 barrels per annum), but after 1925, by building the modern three-storied Plant No. 17 of steel-reinforced concrete that cost 10,000,000 yen, it was able to boost production by 30 per cent. Ōkōchi and Matsuo, p. 103.

workers led what could only be described as truly impoverished and wretched lives. They were recruited through four local bosses (*oyakata*) who got a rake-off on the workers' yearly wages which they negotiated with the company.[13] Each worker had to sign a yearly contract, or more correctly a promissory note, to work for a year, stating the name of a guarantor as well as the *oyakata*. Four-fifths of the workers lived in shabby shelters provided by the plant, where they slept in two rows and ate the poor and scanty food provided by the company. This practice grew up because most of the workers were too poor to maintain a household. Many could not afford to marry or, if already married, had to leave their wives to be supported at their parents' home. Their social status was low and most of them engaged in other, part-time work, such as farm labor. They were referred to contemptuously as soy sauce yokels (*shōyūyamono*), and among the factory foremen they were called "horses." If one was absent, it was said, "He is grazing." About 80 per cent of the workers started work in the small hours of the morning on an assigned task that might take them an average of 5 hours and then so on to their supplementary work. The other 20 per cent labored from sunup to sundown.

Most of the workers were thus not entirely dependent on their jobs at the plant. They were semi-agrarian; their farming was marginal, unable to sustain them fully. The period under discussion witnessed a transition to more full-time factory work at Noda. Even at the time of the strike many more laborers were employed than would have been needed if they had worked full-time. The work was spread thinly, a common pattern during the period. As a result of the strike fewer workers were employed but they worked full-time and thus became even more dependent on the company.

The Noda local of the Japan General Federation of Labor (*Nihon Rōdō Sōdōmei Noda shibu*) was founded on December 15, 1921, by one Koizumi Shichizō, who had come in contact with the burgeoning labor movement a few years earlier while

---

[13] For a careful study of the labor boss system, as seen before the Occupation reform took hold, see John W. Bennett and Iwao Ishino, *Paternalism in the Japanese Economy: Anthropological Studies of Oyabun-Kobun Patterns* (Minneapolis, 1963), especially chapters 3 and 4.

employed in a steel foundry in Hokkaidō where Matsuoka Komakichi was active in union organization. After that, Koizumi took
a job at a machine shop in Tokyo, which in 1921 sent him to
Noda to install some machinery. Moved by the miserable condition of the workers there, he quietly talked to them about organizing a union. While working there he injured his right hand
and was summarily dismissed without any compensation from
the machine shop, whose owner no longer considered him useful.
As a national union official, his mentor, Matsuoka negotiated
with the shop and got him a modest discharge bonus of 150 yen.
The accident was a fateful one since it now allowed Koizumi
to turn his full attention to the organization of the Noda plants.
He started the local with 300 members on December 15, 1921,
and in six months he had persuaded the rest of the workers to
join.

Koizumi may be viewed as an example of the impact of
urban modes of behavior and organization on rural society. In
this sense his activities represented an aspect of the process of
modernization in that the possibility of collective action expanded the number of alternatives available for response to
social and economic crisis by the half-peasant workers.[14] His
success seems to have stemmed in large part from his prestige as
a skilled worker who understood the new machines, as distinct
from the traditional artisan guarding the secrets of traditional
brewing methods.

It is interesting to note the relationship between the process
of modernization and the development of social tensions. First,
the company had been reorganized, streamlining management,
control, and financing. One of the major consequences was the
decision to update production and order new machinery. This
involved bringing in technicians from the outside, among whom
were men like Koizumi who were already aware of the possibilities inherent in organization. A man like Koizumi, with his urban
background and education, could not only articulate what the
workers only dimly knew about their own conditions, but he
could also point the way to change. The result was a conflict

[14] I have previously discussed this example in terms of the transmission of
modern techniques of labor conflict from urban to rural areas in "Labor and
Agrarian Disputes in Japan Following World War I," *Economic Development and Cultural Change*, issue entitled "City and Village in Japan," ix, 1,
part II (October, 1960), pp. 204-205.

which brought about major changes in the pattern of personnel management. The objective conditions for change were present; Koizumi presented one possible line of action (others might have been Communist or anarchist) and had the experience and organizational expertise to make him a successful catalyst.

At the inauguration of the union local, Suzuki Bunji, the well-known founder of the parent organization; Baba Tsunego, a labor-oriented journalist; and Matsuoka, who in contrast to the others had actually risen from a working class background, all came to give talks on the labor movement and politics. When they arrived at the Noda station, they were met by a union delegation that bowed in unison to such distinguished visitors. This poignant little scene, Matsuoka later declared, was not easily forgotten in the annals of Japanese labor history. An impressive constitution of over 80 articles was adopted, providing for the election of officials for one-year periods who would, in turn, select the union head. Majority vote was specified for the decision of issues.[15]

The parent organization, known simply as the General Federation (*Sōdōmei*), was a very political animal. It had been drawn into politics by the need to secure legislation to support the elementary rights of labor, and this had started as early as 1918 with the basic struggle for securing the vote for the workingman. This in turn produced internal struggles over political philosophy and tactics. The struggle against the anarcho-syndicalists (1921-1923), who favored "direct action" over political participation which they believed corrupted the worker, was important. Next came the controversy over whether to struggle for reform within the narrow legal and constitutional confines of the time or to struggle for revolutionary change with a wider range of tactics. These conflicts polarized the *Sōdōmei*, and as mentioned earlier, split it in May, 1925. The Noda local, having been organized by Koizumi, who had personal connections with the moderate Matsuoka and the Suzuki faction, remained loyal to it. Thus, the Noda approach to industrial relations remained at least within the realm of acceptability to important circles in business, politics, and government. This meant, also, that the local's growth and success or failure would have important repercussions on the internal politics of the labor movement.

[15] For a copy of the constitution as well as appended mutual aid provisions see Matsuoka, pp. 58-68.

In its growth the Noda local underwent several changes in name reflecting changes in organizational structure and principles. When formed, it comprised about 300 members from Plant 15 in Noda, and in the following year it took in all of the 50 workers at Plant 16 in nearby Gyōtoku Machi. In February the local changed its name from *shibu* to *rengōkai*, literally from branch to association, indicating that it would be organized along craft lines: the brewers, the tub workers, the firemen, the cask-makers, each having their own *kumiai* or local. At this juncture, however, workers in various other companies in Noda, such as the Nansei Printing Company, the Nakasō Miso Company, and the Marusan and Noda Transportation Agencies, joined the local so that the organizational principle was changed to enterprise unionism; that is, all workers in any company, no matter what kind of work they did, would be included. Once again the local changed its name to the *Noda shibu rengōkai*, with one *shibu* or branch for each company. With the increase in workers from various types of brewing (soy sauce, beer, "cida," *karupisu*, and others), the Kantō Brewery Labor Union (*Kantō Jōzō Rōdō Kumiai*) was set up over the *Noda shibu rengōkai* in June, 1923. Finally in June, 1925, the terminology was changed again, so that there would be not a branch for each factory but a *kōjō iinkai* (factory committee or works council), thus necessitating a change in the status of the Noda local from a branch association (*rengō-kai*) to a branch. The significance of this change was that it coincided with the submission to the Imperial Diet of a draft trade union bill by the Social Bureau of the Home Ministry. The *Sōdō-mei* was trying to prevent the works council system from becoming an alternative to union recognition by making the system a form of union organization and, therefore, a means toward gaining management's recognition of unions and their right to bargain collectively.[16] This plan was seen by the right-wing *Sōdōmei* leaders, such as Matsuoka, as a moderate non-revolutionary, non-Communist type of westernization, or rationalization, or industrial relations.[17]

[16] For a discussion of the *Sōdōmei's* tactics in this regard and the general significance of works councils, see Totten, "Collective Bargaining and Works Councils as Innovations in Industrial Relations in Japan During the 1920's," in R. P. Dore (ed.), *Aspects of Social Change in Modern Japan* (Princeton, 1967), pp. 223-227.

[17] The term *kōjō iinkai*, because it was attacked by leftist unions as a means for "degenerate" union officials to achieve "harmony" with manage-

Thereafter, the Kantō Brewery Labor Union developed along regional-industrial lines. By August, 1927, it contained 14 branches with 3,245 members but with the Noda branch dominating the union with 1,547 of the members.[18] In fact, this union became the most affluent member of the Kantō Labor Federation (*Kantō Rōdō Dōmeikai*), which together with the parallel Kansai organization constituted the two main pillars of the General Federation (*Sōdōmei*). The latter came to depend on funds contributed by the Kantō Brewery Labor Union, using them at times to help other unions when in trouble.[19]

This account of the growth of the local indicates that this section of the labor movement was experimenting with the various principles of trade union organization to see which accorded best with the conditions obtaining in Japan at the time. The comparatively sound financial condition of the union also shows that it was fairly successful.

During the first almost 6 years of its existence the union carried on several disputes which, although all ended in compro-

ment to management's advantage, had a moderate ring to it. The leftists' alternative to this was the *kōjō daihyōsha kaigi* (factory representatives' meetings) which encouraged a much sharper breakdown of the traditional attitudes of respect toward management. For descriptions and sources, see *ibid.*, pp. 228-230. In Matsuoka's eyes the closed shop was a necessary concomitant of collective bargaining during the "transitional" stage Japan was going through before democracy could be reached. It was necessary for two reasons: (1) without it, collective agreements could not be carried out effectively; and (2) it was necessary to keep out leftist agitators who would agitate for agitation's sake, in Matsuoka's view, and wreck agreements. Finally, he believed that in this transitional stage, it would be best that collective agreements be negotiated, supervised, and controlled by *Sōdōmei* headquarters, to avoid emotionalism, to utilize the experience of the whole movement, and to avoid premature strikes, as the Noda dispute turned out to be. Matsuoka, pp. 320-323.

[18] According to a table in Matsuoka, pp. 69-70. At least 6 other branches in the area of Gumma, Kanagawa, Tochigi, Saitama, Ibaraki, and Tokyo had reportedly been set up but had subsequently been destroyed by management.

[19] In 1928 the General Federation reported a total membership of 39,315, which like most union figures was probably greatly exaggerated. For a table of the membership in English broken down by occupation in organizational units, see Totten, "Japanese Social Democracy: An Analysis of the Background, Leadership, and Organized Support of the Social Democratic Movement in Prewar Japan" (Ph.D. dissertation, Yale University, 1954), pp. 217-218.

mises, could be considered advances for the union. Yet in the background mutual suspicion and fear remained.

The first accomplishment of the union was achieved before its formal inauguration. When the company got wind of the union's organizing intentions, it quickly set up separate company unions in each plant with names like Ten Thousand Friends' Society (*Manyūkai*), but on the inaugural day of the federation of these unions, with saké flowing and local officials present, some of the workers demanded eradication of membership restriction clauses. Koizumi mounted the platform and denounced the company union, causing an uproar. The Noda police chief stepped in to mediate; the meeting ended and the company union soon fell apart.

After the Noda local got started, the company improved food and bedding in the living quarters and then decided to tear them down and build dormitories. The union countered with the request that the money be used for loans to workers so that they could build their own homes. The company rejected the request, but as conditions improved workers married and moved out, and the new dormitories became vacant. One was then given to the girls' school and the other made into a hospital. The company did build homes for married workers and rented them out.

But in the background the tension between the company and the union remained. One incident dramatically illustrates the atmosphere of hostility. The brewery firemen demanded an end to the squeeze traditionally received by the foremen (*tōryō*). Two of the foremen convinced a former union official, who had been deposed because of his tendency to violence, that he was wronged and should kill Koizumi. To protect Koizumi, several men were assigned to guard him, but feelings ran so high that two unionists attacked the would-be assassin with samurai swords and mortally wounded him. Koizumi and 18 others were detained by the police for almost a year before being found guilty. On appeal, Koizumi and 16 of the 18 were found innocent, and the two actual attackers were given 5 years at hard labor. Suzuki Bunji, head of the national union, acted as a special lawyer in this case.

In January, 1923, the company, responding to growing tensions, hired a personnel manager who introduced several new policies: the yearly individual contracts were eliminated, a wage system calculated on an eight-hour day was established, and meal payments or allowances were ended. The movement toward greater rationalization came to include a 30 per cent work speed-up, to which the workers responded with a slow-down. The company then fired several union leaders and Matsuoka came down to negotiate—unsuccessfully. From this situation came the first strike on March 16, 1923, which lasted 28 days. After about two weeks, in desperation the union members resorted to a school boycott to protect their children from antagonism and because without income they could not afford to send them to school. Public opinion sympathized with the workers and the company was forced to accept mediation by the prefectural governor in a compromise settlement. This was the first time a school boycott had been used in Japan. Shortly thereafter it was repeated in a strike at the Osaka Iron Works and again in far-off Otaru, before being resorted to a second time by the Noda workers in the great strike—but this time with less public accord.

Conciliation in the governor's office settled another dispute in 1924 that did not eventuate in a strike. The company had revised the bonus system; the union had drawn up an elaborate counter proposal; in the settlement the company made slight concessions. In 1925, when the company fired a unionist, the union presented a set of demands which, interestingly enough, included an "end to the temporary worker system" and the setting up of "works councils" (*kōjō iinkai*) in addition to rehiring the men. The company rehired the men and the union withdrew its demands, all without intercession. Finally, in July, 1925, when the workers of the small Marusan Transportation Agency, which subcontracted for the Noda Soy Sauce Company, were all fired for having joined the union, the Noda workers demonstrated vigorously and a kind of compromise was reached, but this issue flared up again and became the spark that ignited the great strike two years later.

It is hard to generalize, about such a short period, as to the pattern of industrial relations that had developed, but we say that conciliation, when it occurred through the offices of prefectural government, tended to be less satisfactory to the company than to the union. We can also say that the improvement in the conditions of the workers clearly came through the threat or exercise of collective action by the workers.

Gradually the union built a strong "struggle fund" to which every member contributed a portion of his wages. Under Koizumi's influence, the local established a consumers' and sellers' cooperative (*kōbai kumiai*).[20] There were limits to its growth in Noda because many of its members were farmers who grew much of their own rice and vegetables. Nevertheless, it became an important source of funds for the union members during the strike.

The unions also arranged for speeches, lectures, and even study groups with the help of the *Sōdōmei*. The speakers would usually come in from Tokyo. Each summer a three-to-four-day open-air school was held. Since most of the workers usually worked in the early morning and for much less than 8 hours, they had time to participate. They accepted at face value most of what these "teachers" told them, but they did not take kindly to the explanation that they could earn more money by working longer hours, because they felt that that would lead to unemployment for some of them. In this sense the workers exhibited characteristics typical of the workers in economically underdeveloped areas in their preference for returns other than higher wages.[21] The workers were here, it seems, expressing a preference for group welfare over individual gain. At any rate these lectures appear to have opened new horizons to the Noda workers and thereby to have contributed to increasing their self-confidence and awareness.

This indoctrination, which to a certain extent amounted to a counter-ethics and a different set of data from those taught in the Japanese school system, became more institutionalized in what was called the Noda Labor School, established in June, 1925, for which a permanent structure was completed by August, 1926. Some 120 young workers—about one in every 20 from each factory—were selected for study at the school. Lectures were given on the history of the labor movement, economics, and political thought at home and abroad by intellectuals in the labor movement, some of whom later became publicists or even socialist members of the Diet.[22] The teachers had to express themselves

[20] Organization and finances of these cooperatives may be found in Matsuoka, pp. 72-79.

[21] Matsuoka, pp. 104-105.

[22] For instance, Matsushita Yoshio, author and General Federation official and later Social Democratic Party leader; Kamei Kanichirō who had studied at Tokyo Imperial, Fordham, and Columbia universities, first elected to the Diet in 1928 as a Social Democrat; Matsunaga Yoshio, lawyer, author, Diet candidate 1930, 1932, elected in 1937; Saitō Kenichi, a General Federation

clearly and simply because an analysis of the educational level of the Noda workers revealed that one out of 15 of the men and almost half of the women had not even graduated from elementary school and only one had graduated from middle school.[23] The indoctrination was aimed at the whole community. New reading material came into Noda, and the local began publishing its own paper. Subscriptions to the *Sōdōmei* organ and several of the larger daily newspapers also increased considerably. The pattern of rural isolation was rapidly breaking down.[24]

---

leader; Matsuoka Komakichi, General Federation official and Diet candidate but only elected after World War II; and Akamatsu Katsumaro, Tokyo Imperial graduate, prolific author, political maverick, elected to Diet in 1937. See Matsuoka, p. 79, and Totten, *The Social Democratic Movement in Prewar Japan*, chapter 5. A number of labor schools were set up in the 1920's by labor unions; they were usually night schools with semesters of 3 to 6 months, meeting 2 to 3 times a week; they often included a course on the agrarian movement as well. See *ibid.*, p. 394 and *Sōdōmei gojunen shi*, II, 986.

[23] Educational Background of the Noda Workers

Educational Level	Men	Women
Middle-school graduates	1	0
Higher elementary-school graduates	172	2
Elementary-school graduates	1,277	38
Those who did not go to school	118	25
Totals	1,368	65

The figures are from the Chiba Prefectural authorities in 1923, according to Matsuoka, p. 84. Figures like this suggest that we ought to be skeptical of the sweepingly high rates of literacy claimed by Japan before the end of World War II.

[24] In 1923, according to Matsuoka, pp. 84-85, the workers were exposed to the following numbers of yearly subscriptions:

Newspapers	Number	Journals	Number
Tōkyō asahi	21	*Rōdō dōmei* (organ of the *Sōdōmei*)	100
Jiji shimpō	10		
Nihon nōmin shimbun	50	*Rōdō* (organ of the Noda local)	1,600
Kokumin shimbun	60		
Hochi shimbun	8	Total	1,700
Yorozu chōhō	8		
Bōsō nichinichi	1		
Total	158		

Unfortunately we do not have later figures to show an increase over time of such subscriptions, but they probably grew and then declined after the union was broken. Nevertheless, the union helped develop reading habits and interest in politics in Japan and the world at large.

417

The formation of the local also resulted in a marked decrease in crimes and public offenses in Noda, an indication of the union role in creating social cohesion. The former *hiroshiki* dormitories had encouraged a social pattern in which the men as a group spent their pittances on saké, prostitutes, and gambling. By 1926 the union had succeeded in providing alternative uses of leisure time. The pubs with prostitutes had entirely disappeared and so had gambling, for which a man could be expelled from the union. The workers were no longer referred to as "*shōyuyamono*" but as employees (*kōin*), and new cultural activities, such as sports and social gatherings, were occupying their spare time. The whole tone and discipline of the town had undergone considerable change.

Part of the change which had occurred can be explained by the political activities of the union. The Noda Town Assembly had traditionally been dominated by the Mogi family, but with the formation of the Noda local, a focal point for opposition became available for the first time. Participating in the assembly election in April, 1924, the local was able to get all three of its candidates elected at its first try. In July, after the passage of the Universal Manhood Suffrage Act, it organized a political group, the *Chiba Minseitō*, associating itself with the party which stood in opposition to the one which the Mogis habitually supported—the *Seiyūkai*. The local party's program called for reform along class lines, promised to act only by legal means, and supported the League of Nations and world peace through coexistence.[25] When the *Sōdōmei* finally engineered the formation of the Social Democratic Party (*Shakai Minshūtō*), on December 5, 1926, the *Chiba Minseitō* dissolved itself and became a local branch of that party. Political action had, by the time of the strike, become a normative aspect of local union activities. Thus, during the strike

[25] The platform of the *Chiba Minseitō* was as follows:
1. We wish to reform all the evils of the politics, the economy, and the educational system of the present-day society from the standpoint of the proletarian class.
2. We wish to achieve our goals honestly by rational, legal means.
3. We want to cooperate with other proletarian parties to set up a single national proletarian party.
4. We wish to support reform of the League of Nations, and by maintaining world peace, promote the coexistence and coprosperity of all mankind.

Matsuoka, p. 80.

itself these assembly members started a campaign that succeeded in gathering some 3000 signatures (seals) on a petition to the governor asking that payment of taxes might be delayed to help the small business people who were suffering economically from the lack of buying power of the strikers. And again a national boycott against Kikkōman soy sauce was promoted by the Social Democrats and other campaigning proletarian party candidates as an aid to the strikers and in the hope of gaining labor support at the polls, for the strike was now receiving national publicity. The first local elections after passage of the Universal Manhood Suffrage Act of 1925 occurred in 1927 and 1928, that for the Chiba Prefectural Assembly being on January 20, 1928. One candidate was put up by the local branch of the SDP, but due to the rigors of the strike not much of a political campaign could be launched and the candidate was defeated rather badly. For the same reason, plans were dropped for putting up a candidate for the Imperial Diet election of February 20, 1928.

Despite the fact that the Noda local could not supply a candidate for the 1928 national election, the publicity received by the Noda strike was useful to the proletarian candidates in whipping up class consciousness and attacking the "reactionary" *Seiyūkai* government of General Tanaka Giichi. With this as one of the issues, the Social Democrats won 4 seats and the other proletarian parties an additional 4, gathering almost 490,000 votes, or 5 per cent of the votes cast. Among those elected were Kamei Kanichirō, who had lectured at the Noda Labor School, and Suzuki Bunji, who had addressed the local's founding ceremony.[26]

One aspect of this political participation by the Noda local and its national affiliates is that it follows the Anglo-European style of labor participation in politics. Despite the fact that the whole parliamentary process, with its bargaining and decision-making by counting noses, is antithetical to the traditional Japanese pat-

[26] Kyōchōkai *Rōdōka*, pp. 61-63. Interestingly enough, as a result of gaining 8 seats in the Diet, the proletarian representatives came very near to controlling a "casting vote" in the House of Representatives, since the *Seiyūkai* and *Minseitō* parties held an almost equal number of seats. Matsuoka wanted his party to refrain from promising to vote with the *Minseitō* on a no-confidence vote against the *Seiyūkai*, hoping that this would provide leverage to force the *Seiyūkai* into intervening favorably in the resolution of the Noda dispute. Matsuoka, however, was overruled on this tactic. This outcome indicates in a concrete way the possibilities of a political link for labor, especially if parliamentary politics had continued to thrive in prewar Japan.

terns of consensus or confrontation,[27] political activities were seen by the *Sōdōmei* and Noda local leaders as relevant. If through collective independent action it was possible to change economic and social conditions, as it had been up to this strike, it would also be possible and imperative to strive for political change. Legislation in the form of a labor union law was needed, for instance, to buttress any recognition of the unions that might be wrung from management.[28] In short, then, the development of the union in Noda had not only helped create the basis for a more rational structure of labor organization and support on the local level, it had also begun the process of politicizing the worker as a class, rather than group, participant.

The outline and a number of details of Mogi Saheiji's strategies and tactics for dealing with the appearance and rise of the union have already been described, but a closer analysis will help clarify the significance of these innovations. Mogi failed in his attempt to counter union activities by forming a company union. The general experience of management with company unions during this period in Japan was that they were apt to turn about and "bite the hand that fed them."[29] With the organizational framework set up, they could turn militant by themselves or be influenced or infiltrated by leftists, or, as in the case of Noda, become the means for solidifying sympathy for an independent union.

In August, 1922, Mogi did set up a committee to investigate problems relative to the treatment and control of employees. This resulted first in concessions on workers' living conditions, the plan to convert to the wage system on an eight-hour basis, and the decision to hire a personnel specialist, Namiki Shigetarō, which was probably the single most important decision, because he was extremely competent and possessed the determination to carry out the destruction of the union. Namiki joined the staff in January,

[27] See the discussion of this in Robert A. Scalapino and Junnosuke Masumi, *Parties and Politics in Contemporary Japan* (Berkeley and Los Angeles, 1962), pp. 5-6.

[28] For the proletarian parties' labor policies, see Totten, *The Social Democratic Movement in Prewar Japan*, pp. 212-222. For more detail on the trade union bills, see Iwao F. Ayusawa, *A History of Labor in Modern Japan* (Honolulu, 1966), pp. 219-222.

[29] Machida, pp. 211-212.

1923, as chief of the Plant Section (*kōjō kachō*). His background was in local government, having served as County Head (Gunchō) in Chiba Prefecture. Besides being mainly responsible for the various tactics of weakening the union's morale, splitting the workers, protecting the plants, bringing in strike breakers, and appealing to public opinion, he also introduced new labor policies that had lasting significance. Thus, for example, he required special standards for employee recruitment at the newest of the units at Noda, Plant No. 17. Each of its employees had to be at least a graduate of kōtō shōgakkō (that is, to have gone through the eighth grade for students not preparing for university—compulsory education at this period was supposedly 6 years).[30] When the strike came, these Plant 17 employees did not participate in it.[31] Rumor had it that upon being employed all had pledged secretly not to join the union. In any case, they remained loyal to the company. The company had been successful in instilling in them a type of elite consciousness that separated them from their fellow workers of less education. More significantly, Namiki recognized that a rational technique of recruitment could be used as a substitute for traditional tension-creating recruitment techniques.

Namiki was thus more than a simple strike-breaker. His "rationalizing" policies, combined with repressive strike-breaking tactics, enabled the company to build up 80 per cent of production during the strike. After the strike he published rather detailed accounts of the strike for the benefit of Japanese management in general.[32] In sum, the emergence of the union forced the company to undertake a program of rationalization and bureaucratization

[30] In speaking generally of this period, Professor Levine singles out recruitment of company employees directly from the secondary schools and their in-plant training as one of the two most important steps taken by management, the other being to induce *oyakata* and their workers to become employees of the firm. See Solomon B. Levine, "Labor and Collective Bargaining," in William W. Lockwood (ed.), *The State and Economic Enterprise in Japan* (Princeton, 1965), pp. 645-649. In the case of Noda, however, the *oyakata* were done away with by the union.

[31] Near the beginning of the strike, they did respect picket lines that the Noda local threw around the plant, but the management had all the strike leaders arrested by the police, and while they were being held in detention for a day the company hired trucks and transported the workers to Plant No. 17; thereafter they continued to work.

[32] See footnote 7 above for citations of Namiki's publications.

421

resulting in the rise of a rational as opposed to a traditional paternalism.

On the other hand, participation in the union contributed to the dissolution of traditional paternalism. In its labor school, at its gatherings, and in its literature, the union attempted to instill "class consciousness" in the workers. For the union leaders this meant what we might call "horizontal identification"—that is, consciousness of the common interests all workers have in relation to management. In so doing they were running counter to a social structure marked by vertically oriented norms—that is, awareness of position on a status scale held together by mutual obligations of paternalism and service. In the factory situation, "class consciousness" meant unity among the workers in articulating demands and defending gains against divisive tactics by the employers. In its vagueness "class consciousness," as the Japanese used the term, encompassed all workers and even tenant farmers. It was not a specific horizontal identification of the kind that would unite workers with special skills along craft lines. In Noda, as elsewhere, the vertical status differentiations among the workers depended not so much on their skills at the shop as on factors somewhat extraneous to production, such as their educational background, size of family, seniority, and personal connections. Thus class consciousness brought workers into conflict with *social* values, norms and goals which they had long accepted as basic to their role behavior of acceptance of authority based on status and obligations determined by status.

In the case of the Noda local, horizontal identification, in stirring empathy among other organized workers throughout the country, did help materially: donations of money and goods did arrive to help the workers continue their struggle. At the same time, of course, it tended to intensify the tensions between workers and management in such a way as to absolve the latter of their supposed traditional obligations to their employees, thus opening the way for the development of a more rational or contractual paternalism.

The company, in resisting the union, sought consistently to utilize traditionally accepted vertical identification to encourage worker dependence on management while at the same time introducing more rational practices, whereas the workers attempted to develop class consciousness along horizontal lines to promote independence and self-confidence. While the union sought sympathy from the non-propertied working people all over Japan, the company was not at all unaware of the importance of publicity and public opinion. Not only did the company provide spokesmen to the many eager reporters who flocked to Noda, but the management regularly issued statements and fabricated pamphlets as though they were from third parties, such as "a citizen" or "a worker."[33] The conflict thus took on the overtones of a contest between value systems—a contest in which the public was invited to take sides.

Symbolic of this contest was the boycott of Kikkōman Soy Sauce proposed by the union. I have not been able to determine what effect this campaign had, but the persistence of the company's opposition and its quick recovery suggests that its effect was not great.[34] Secondary effects, however, were much clearer. On the one hand, the union did receive contributions toward its "struggle fund," and toys and textbooks for the children of union members who boycotted the school. But, on the other hand, when the strike was over, those who remained discharged found that openings otherwise available were closed to them because they had participated in the Noda strike. They were in effect blacklisted over a very wide area, due to the intense publicity given to the strike. We might well conclude that, if the Noda strike represented a contest for public support, the union and the values it represented did not strike a deep chord of sympathy or support in Japanese society.

In many respects the strike took on a very personal (what the Japanese called "emotional" or *kanjōteki*) character. The company hired spies to report on strike plans and activities. The company staff and some of the higher officials made house visits to certain employee families, making promises and threats in turn. They also visited relatives of the strikers in nearby villages, such as the wives' parents, and even induced a divorce. This personal element, when intensified, erupted in violence directed

[33] See Namiki, *Temmatsu . . .* , pp. 263-269.

[34] One such handbill exposed the Company's grading system of types of sauce; see Namiki, *Temmatsu . . .* , pp. 245-247. For the General Federation–Social Democratic Party handbill, see Matsuoka, pp. 197-198; for other proletarian parties and unions supporting the strike and boycott, see *ibid.*, pp. 199-206.

against individuals. We have already noted the pre-strike killing. The union leaders worked hard to prevent violence during the strike, because they knew from bitter experience that, given the attitudes of the police, it would always be more detrimental to the side of the union. Still, some of the workers could not be restrained by union discipline. One worker threw acid in the face of a man hired by the company to engineer strike-breaking tactics and blinded him. The striker was, of course, arrested along with many others. Two other similar incidents occurred.

On the company side, although the Mogi family usually hired others to do the dirty work for them they became the objects of attacks. Company officials were never seen alone on the streets. They barricaded their homes and some sent their families away. In other strikes of the time there were cases in which an individual striker or a group would journey to Tokyo from the strike area, which might be as far away as Kyushu, to attack the absentee owner of the firm.[35]

This emotionalism shattered community harmony, so traditionally prized in Japan perhaps because of the knowledge that, when once slightly breached, it can so quickly be shattered in the Japanese context. The breakdown of community harmony was epitomized in the school boycott organized by the workers. After three months, on January 16, 1928, the strikers decided to withdraw their children from school, as they had done in an earlier strike in the attempt to dramatize the sincerity of their commitment. This time, however, they decided to set up their own school and continue their children's education.

This boycott would probably not have been necessary or effective in a less rural setting. In a real urban area the children would probably have been distributed in several districts and would probably have come from a variety of occupational backgrounds. But in Noda all were gathered in the same buildings and tended to divide into two camps: the children of the Mogi family and their supporters versus the children of the strikers; in between were the children of those townspeople who were trying to be neutral, which was difficult since shopowners, for instance, wanted patronage from both sides. The strike caused fights among the children of the contending parties and discrimination by the principal, some teachers, and the school committee,

[35] Machida, pp. 184-186.

424

who were all beholden to the Mogi family for, among other things, the gift of a new school building.

The strikers' own school was taught by six teachers sent from Tokyo by the *Sōdōmei* (including Miss Akamatsu Tsuneko, who already was prominent in the labor movement and who in postwar Japan became a Socialist Diet member).[36] At first each day began with a shrine pilgrimage to pray for the success of the strike, but this was soon forbidden by the police. Its place was taken by an oath in terms of responses. The teacher would ask, "Whom are we fighting together with?" And the children would reply in unison with their right hands raised, "Together with our parents." It went on, "Why are we fighting?" "To punish the stubborn capitalists." "When are we fighting until?" "Until the enemy is downed." "What of the future?" "It is ours!"[37]

The General Federation developed a rather elaborate survey questionnaire after the strike and had it administered to children of both strikers and non-strikers. The depth of the hatred by the strikers' children for the Mogis, capitalists, government, and police, and the degree of their identification with labor and social democratic goals was surprising. Elementary-grade students were using words like "oppression," "violence," "bias," and, of course, "capitalist."[38] The use of the boycott seems to suggest that as labor conflict appeared in the countryside it produced major changes in the social structure of the community. Associational patterns as well as behavior appear to have been markedly affected.

So great, indeed, appears to have been the cleavage in Noda that direct communication between the contending parties was almost out of the question. The dislike for confrontation even in lesser matters in Japanese life was very strong, necessitating frequent use of go-betweens, conciliators, and mediators. In this

[36] Miss Akamatsu was the younger sister of Akamatsu Katsumaro, a well-known socialist leader; Iomaro, another brother, was active in the labor movement. In 1928 Miss Akamatsu was active in the Social Democratic Women's Federation that supported the Social Democratic Party.

[37] Matsuoka, p. 222; the same words are found in a slightly different order in Machida, p. 188.

[38] The questionnaire and its results may be found in Matsuoka, pp. 127-156. For instance, 55 wanted to grow up to be "a good, upright worker," whereas only 3 wanted to be "a military general." The students apparently studied especially hard during the boycott, and they wrote many letters of thanks to sympathizers all over the country.

strike a great number of people from various walks of life came forward to offer their services, but the company refused them all. One of the first to come forward was the *Kyōchōkai*, but the company considered it too close to the *Minseitō* to be advantageous. The company also refused such right-wing nationalists as Ōkawa Shūmei whom the union found acceptable. In the end, one incident apparently was most decisive in bringing about mediation: an attempt to make a direct appeal to the Emperor.

This attempt was carried out by a single individual on his own initiative, Horigoshi Umeo, who was not only a director (*riji*) of the Noda local but also a member of the executve committee and secretary (*shuji*) of the Kantō Brewery Labor Union and a member of the Kantō Labor Federation. From the beginning he was actively involved in the dispute, being second in command of the strikers under Koizumi. He had been arrested and detained from December 25, 1927, until January 18, 1928, for demonstrating along with 70 others. Such treatment, of course, was not unusual in prewar Japan. But toward the end of the strike, he became very despondent and agitated, especially after the union had decided to withdraw all its demands and give Matsuoka full power to negotiate, and then had gained nothing from the first three meetings by February 13, 1928. He decided there was no way out but to appeal directly to His Majesty, the Emperor, and beg his judgment.

On the evenings of February 17 and 18, 1928, he secretly went to the local union headquarters in Noda and drafted a two-page memorandum to the throne, describing the plight of the 1000 fired workers and the 5000 who made up their families. He then sought an opportunity to present it directly, but in the latter part of February Imperial Princess Hisanomiya Yasuko became ill; she died on March 8. "Overcome with grief," Horigoshi decided for a time to give up his plan, but on the evening of March 16 he secretly went to the headquarters again, revised the first page to express his grief over the death of the Princess, and decided to present the memorial at the first opportunity.

According to the newspapers of March 19, the Emperor and Empress were to leave the palace by car the next day at 1:30 P.M. for Tokyo Station to proceed to the palace at Hayama. Horigoshi took the express for Tokyo the next morning, mixed with the crowd near the Marunouchi Building, and when the Emperor's car appeared, he rushed forward about 9 feet from those lining the street, squatted down on his heels with head bowed and hands raised with the petition, and cried, *"jikiso, jikiso!"* (direct appeal, direct appeal). The car sped by and he was immediately arrested, but the incident was widely reported in the newspapers and many readers were shocked that someone would have dared to appeal to the Emperor directly; Horigoshi was sentenced to six months for violating the regulations on petitioning.[39]

This direct appeal to the Emperor, which was a kind of "right" from the past, evoked a response that can hardly be imagined in postwar Japan, although the same Emperor is on the throne.[40] The response in Japanese was expressed as *"osore ōi"* or *"kyōku ni taenai"*—to be awestruck or full of dread at the thought of anything that would bother the Emperor. Both the company and the *Sōdōmei*, when issuing statements, used those words.[41]

The appeal took the company aback and it immediately announced that it was asking the *Kyōchōkai* to become a conciliator. The General Federation, while deploring the appeal attempt in its statement, drew attention apologetically to the motives involved. The strikers tried to follow up the incident with a petition campaign, but it was prevented by the police. Without this incident the strike might have gone on longer, because the unionists had already been defeated and had nothing further to lose. They had little hope of returning to work when the strike was settled, so it was just a matter of what could be saved from the situation. Matsuoka had already been given carte blanche by the union to see what he could do.

This incident may be viewed as an attempt to use traditional symbols and sanction to support the emergence of new role values and norms and to impose limitations on the company's use of repressive tactics.[42] We might go on to say that in the

[39] For the police description of this case, see Shihōshō Keijikyoku, *Shisō kenkyū shiryō*, 9 (September, 1928), pp. 70-71, as well as newspapers for that and following days.

[40] Some slightly similar response of shock was registered in Japan in February, 1961, when some rightists attacked the editor of the well-known *Chūō kōron* for publishing an article (thus bringing it to general attention) in which the author, Fukazawa Shichirō, related his dream that the Imperial family had been executed. See Yamamoto Seiichirō, "Annals of Postwar Suppression of Freedom of Speech: Part 4," *Shakaitō* (April, 1970).

[41] The General Federation's statement may be found in Matsuoka, pp. 194-195; for the Company's reaction, see Namiki, *Temmatsu* . . . , pp. 56-67.

[42] I have elsewhere discussed the use of tradition to bring about change

absence of formal rules governing the relations between employer and employee traditional norms and behavior operated in an informal structure. How conscious Horigoshi was that he was using this appeal to the Emperor as an appeal to the public we shall never know. But it seems improbable that he could have believed that the Emperor himself would have intervened in the strike, taking pity on his suffering subjects.

Nevertheless, in the negotiations that followed, the company continued to insist on the dissolution of the local among Noda workers; it also refused to rehire discharged workers and demanded exclusive company control of labor relations, but it did soften its attitude regarding payments of bonuses to discharged workers. This change of attitude was evidently brought about both by strong indications of public opinion on the side of the workers, aided by the appeal to the Emperor, and by the *Seiyūkai*—indicating behind the scenes a desire to dispose of the case before the special session of the Diet in the late spring.

A settlement was finally signed in Tokyo on April 19, 1928, between the company and Matsuoka, representing the strikers, with government officials and members of the Harmonization Society in attendance. The following day the agreement was reluctantly endorsed by the strikers at a tearful meeting in the Noda theater.

The settlement was simple. Out of the 1,047 workers fired, 300 would be allowed to return to work. Altogether a sum of 380,000 yen was to be paid by the company for discharge bonuses and livelihood maintenance for those fired, plus an additional 70,000 yen for the union to pay off its debts or use as it saw fit.

This last item is an interesting and significant one. It was usual in Japan at this time for the company to pay the union an extra sum at the conclusion of a strike to symbolize the re-establishment of personal relations. Sometimes money that was left over after paying off debts incurred during the strike would be used by the union to replenish its "struggle fund"—a custom not among those imported from the West along with most of the

in developing societies: see Totten, "Models and the Problem of Internal Legitimacy," in Willard A. Beling and George O. Totten (eds.), *Developing Nations: Quest for a Model* (New York, 1970), p. 30.

strike techniques.[43] General acceptance of this pattern suggests that it functioned as a means of dissolving and clearing away personal bitterness and as a means of restating the company's traditional obligations to workers. It is ironical, however, that the unions as organizations had come to be recognized as legitimate objects of this traditional patronage, thereby that their right to act and speak for labor was informally recognized.

Beyond the financial items, there was one more important element of the final agreement: that both sides would withdraw all strike-inspired court charges against the other, or against anyone else. The company had lodged numerous complaints, claiming property damage against the union or unionists, but the union, too, had had its resort to the courts.

At the very first general meeting of the local after the strike began, a "contract" had been drawn up and signed by all the strikers, each pledging that if he went into a Noda Soy Sauce plant to work before the strike ended he would pay the union a fine of 500 yen. Only 58 broke the pledge and returned to work as scabs.[44] On November 8, 1927, the local brought charges of breach of contract against these men and the General Federation sent down two lawyers from Tokyo to press the charge, one of whom, incidentally, was Katayama Tetsu, who became the first and only Socialist Prime Minister of Japan following the Second World War. No decision had been reached on this case before the strike ended. This use of the courts, however, is interesting in light of the general assertion that the Japanese do not like to turn to the courts for redress.[45] Clearly, as unions evolved into autonomous organizations, there was little in the way of traditional conciliation procedures that could deal with the problems of industrial conflict, and as a consequence the resort to the courts became more frequent. The legal aspects of labor and agrarian protest, in fact, had much to do with making what little

[43] Professor Suehiro once remarked, concerning this custom in prewar Japan, that it "is probably incomprehensible to a non-Japanese." Suehiro Itsutarō, *Nihon rōdō kumiai undō shi* (Tokyo, 1950), pp. 89-90. A breakdown of this disposition of the funds may be found in Matsuoka, pp. 300-306.

[44] Shihōshō Keijikyoku, p. 23.

[45] See Takeyoshi Kawashima, "Dispute Resolution in Contemporary Japan," in Arthur Taylor von Mehren (ed.), *Law in Japan: The Legal Order in a Changing Society* (Cambridge, Mass., 1963), pp. 41-50.

progress there was in the development of individual rights in the prewar period.

Out of the 745 employees who were fired, 360 soon found new employment, but only 40 of these new jobs were factory work. All the rest were in agriculture or small business. This was natural inasmuch as these employees had formerly been engaged in farming or petty buying and selling.[46] Another 185 workers had supplementary work from before; thus they could at least subsist without their Noda jobs.

It was extremely difficult for the remaining 200 who were totally unemployed to find jobs. The prefectural employment exchanges (*ken shokugyō shōkaijo*), which had recently been set up by the government, tried to find work for them but discovered that employers did not want to hire former Noda strikers.[47] The *Sōdōmei* also was largely ineffective in finding new places for these workers, even though it had a job policy committee (*jitsugyō taisaku iinkai*), which was supposed to take practical steps in helping strikers.

[46] We may wonder about some of those discharged workers who must have gone into agriculture as tenant farmers after this strike in Chiba. Did they then incite others to organize and stand up for their rights against landlords? A look at the statistics on tenant-farmer disputes for Chiba Prefecture suggests that this may have been the case.

Number of Tenant Farmer Disputes in Chiba Prefecture

Year	Number of Disputes
1917	1
1918	1
1919	3
1920	7
1921	1
1922	6
1923	13
1924	5
1925	8
1926	0
1927	7
1928	38
1929	105
1930	57

Source: Naikaku Tōkeikyoku, *Rōdō tōkei yōran* (Tokyo, 1932), p. 256.

[47] For background on these Employment Exchanges, see Ayusawa, pp. 204-209 and for socialist policy toward them, see Totten, *Social Democratic Movement* . . . , pp. 219-220.

Although blacklisting was not an uncommon occurrence in the West, the way it operated in Japan was perhaps more subtle and pervasive. Lists did not have to be made. In the first place, workers were usually hired early in life, perhaps right out of school, and they often remained with the company for the rest of their lives. Second, the web of social relationships was very tight in Japan. It was not easy to conceal participation in a strike. The whole system of recruitment laid great stress on social factors other than abilities and availability. And, finally, the question of loyalty in the Japanese sense was involved: the whole tradition of *rōnin* or masterless warriors cast a shadow on all whose ties to his superior had been broken. In the case of Noda, the widespread publicity of the strike made it all the more difficult to conceal participation in it. Nevertheless, several who had shown leadership capabilities did become active again through the *Sōdōmei* as local labor leaders in nearby areas.[48]

At the Noda Soy Sauce plants, however, management control was uncontested after the settlement. The workers were henceforth employed on an eight-hour schedule and work discipline was strengthened. After the strike was over, the company drew up a yearly plan, designating social activities for the workers on a month-by-month basis, that would be combined with nationalistic and Confucian indoctrination.[49] In order to string out and regularize pay raises, it gradually made up a clear system of

[48] In looking over a column entitled "Jimbutsu sensen" that appeared in the *Sōdōmei* organ *Rōdō* between March 1934 and August 1935, it was possible to recognize a few of the local labor leaders in Chiba and neighboring prefectures as people who had been active in the Noda labor dispute. For instance, it is interesting to note that Horigoshi Umeo, who had made the dramatic appeal to the Emperor, was still secretary (*shuji*) of the Kantō Brewery Labor Union as well as of the Chiba Prefectural Brewery Association (*Rengōkai*). He had been welcomed to his old position as secretary after being released from 8 months' imprisonment for the incident. Other executive committee members with Noda strike background included Nemoto Rokurō and Sugaya Kiyoshi. Then in Kumaya, Saitama Prefecture, where he had moved after having headed the Noda Branch during the strike, Koiwai Aisuke became the head of the Brewery Union and was elected to the City Assembly. Another activist from Noda days who was working with him was Takahashi Ukichi. There was another in the Fujioka Branch. This column was reprinted in *Sōdōmei gojūnen shi*, ii, 1011-1126; see especially 1011-1120.

[49] Kyōchōkai Kyōmuka, mentioned in footnote 7 above.

seniority-based rewards that assumed permanent attachment by the workers to the firm.

In this respect the strike resulted in rationalizing work arrangements. In fact, the old authoritarian paternalism, in which the workers were neglected, could not be reestablished. And since the pattern of cooperation based on the coexistence of union and management had been rejected, it now behooved the company to develop a new kind of paternalism, one that demonstrated in concrete terms its concern for the welfare of its workers.

The failure of the local to win the Noda strike brought about its demise. The 300 workers who were rehired were expected to withdraw from the union as soon as it had tidied up its business after the strike. The rest of the Noda strikers were no longer Noda employees, and most were scattered. The only members then left in the Noda locals were some 80 employees of the Shiraki Soy Sauce Company located in the Noda area but not affiliated with the Noda Company. These workers did not go on strike but contributed half their wages throughout the dispute to help their fellow union members. They got nothing out of the strike, and, since many of them had thus become disillusioned with the labor movement as a whole, they withdrew and the union collapsed.

The pattern of union demise after an unsuccessful dispute was the usual one in prewar Japan. The very duration of the strike and the almost six years of life of the Noda local were the exception. In effect, the success of management appears to have destroyed any commitment to the concept of labor organization among the workers. While this may have created a more docile work force, we shall never know for sure whether the company could not have dealt with the workers in a more efficient and organized fashion, if it had respected organized labor initiative and dealt with it on the basis of bargaining. The implications of such a possibility would have been enormous.

In the 1920's the pattern of industrial relations in Japan was in flux, adjusting to new conditions of industrial development and changes in cultural values. At the time, they appeared to stand at a crossroad with three directions, in decreasing orders of probability: (1) some kind of revised familial paternalism;

(2) some form of conflict-cooperation pattern based on the co-existence of organized labor and management; (3) a conflict pattern that would contribute to social, economic, and political revolution in Japan. As far as management was concerned, the overwhelming majority preferred the first possibility; a small minority, connected with advanced industrialization, considered the second more realistic and productive in the long run; presumably all opposed the third.

The very existence of the labor movement, therefore, depended in large part on how well it could provide meaningful and effective organizational structures and techniques to workers. Whether its ability to do so would be sufficient to insure its existence and growth is outside the purview of this study. My feeling is that there were plural causes for the unions' failure to prosper, including the nature and structure of the Japanese economy, the constellation of political forces, and the impact of world events.

We have examined only one case, and one case is never enough to prove any hypothesis. Nevertheless, this was a significant and symbolic case in many respects. Confining ourselves to it and to its time and place, we can conclude, it seems to me, that the pattern of industrial relations fought for here, despite its defeat in this particular strike, apparently did prove sufficiently meaningful to the leaders and many of those involved to provide them with a continuing commitment to a type of social democratic ideology, namely, that the working class can gradually improve its position under capitalism by combining economic and political struggle within the bounds of law, leading eventually to a welfare state.

In the Noda strike the workers had persisted mightily. They fought the longest strike in Japanese annals up to that time. Only 58 out of the 1,358 who went on strike broke their agreement and scabbed, and only some 250 more dropped out. The solidarity, the effectiveness of their organization, and the variety and creativeness of their tactics were astonishing, considering their rural setting. They had succeeded to a marked degree in winning public opinion and support. Most of the conciliators who came forward to offer their services were considered more likely to be an aid to the strikers than to the company, given its unbudging position. This included police, government authorities, and even ultra-nationalists. The legal situation was not entirely disadvantageous; there were resources in law sufficient to make it not entirely clear as to which side would benefit from continued litigation. In politics, there was a glimpse of leverage even in the Imperial Diet, when the social democratic or proletarian parties got a "casting vote." Even sections of the bureaucracy were more favorably disposed than was business to the enactment of a labor law that would give legal sanction to unions and collective agreements. The military was comparatively quiescent at the time, suffering from internal factional quarrels. In this environment it was not a foregone conclusion that "sound" union-management relations could not develop.

The workers proved to be innovative in their use of traditional cultural mores to legitimize their actions—with mixed success. The appeal to the Emperor is probably the most outstanding and probably the single most helpful action, despite the astonished embarrassment it caused. Group shrine visits (*jinja sampai*) were effective morale-boosters. The school boycott was in part an appeal to public opinion to sympathize with the strikers, who were forced to withdraw their children from school because community social harmony was shattered by the bias of the principal and others for the powerful Mogi family.

When social harmony had so broken down that personal violence erupted, such behavior might be termed traditional, but it would have been of no avail to the union other than frightening its opponents, unless it could appeal to some traditional value. This was not the situation in the incidents of violence at Noda. Such tactics had recently been used in several other strikes, and Noda workers had heard of them, but all involved had been apprehended and had received no support in public opinion.

The main tactics used by the Noda strikers were those sanctioned by the modern ideology of a pluralist society with models such as those of England, Germany, and to a lesser degree the United States. The strike tactic itself, though considered a weapon of last resort, was probably most outstanding, unless we classify the organization of the union in the first place as a tactic. Unequivocally more modern were the various financial supports for the strike eventually used by the Noda local. Ever since the strike of 1923, the Noda local had been building a strike fund. Each union member would deposit in a postal savings account in his own name 50 sen or more each month. A union official would keep the deposit book, allowing the individual to withdraw the funds in cases of emergency or change of employment. In this way the local built up a fund of over 100,000 yen that helped it through the 7-month strike. The local also received some 400 yen in contributions from *Sōdōmei*-related and friendly organizations. Consumer cooperatives were rather rare in Japan as aids to union finances, but the Noda dispute provided a very successful example, for its cooperative, despite some troubles, did contribute about 500,000 yen to the strike. The fact that the Noda workers lived on such a low standard helped them weather deprivations that more affluent workers might not have been able to withstand.

Many other modern tactics were used by the union. One was the collection of data about the company, which should have been a prime consideration before making the decision to strike. The union had done it to a certain extent, but then there was the question of interpretation. Matsuoka had advised against the strike in the first place because, in his opinion, the union was not yet strong enough and the company was too well prepared. He reminded the strikers of this at the final plenary union meeting when he asked for their approval of the miserable settlement he had been forced to accept from the company. If a works council, composed either of workers' representatives or of workers and staff together had been set up, it might have been possible to arrive at compromises on the demands the union actually made. The union had demanded the creation of such a works council earlier, when a union leader was fired, but, when the company rehired him, the union withdrew its demands, hoping that the company itself would eventually make some move in this direction, but it did not. A works council did not necessarily assume the existence of a union, but the crushing of the union was the company's primary goal, in any event.

The varied and numerous attempts to appeal to public opinion showed the union's consciousness of its importance. Of course, the company's equal interest in propaganda spurred them on. They published pamphlets, put out posters, hired sandwichmen, and talked with all who came to find out what the strike was about. They also helped in the political campaigns of those who brought up the issue. Finally, they used the tactic of trying to get the public to boycott Kikkōman and other grades of Noda soy sauce.

They did resort to the courts in a suit against the scabs and accept the services of *Sōdōmei*-related lawyers for defense of union members. At open meetings witnessed by police they denounced police tactics and brutality. They sent delegations to local government officials, and declared themselves ready to accept the governor's intervention for purposes of conciliation.

Despite all this, the resources of management proved superior and of course the company's finances were infinitely greater. The slight recession at the time did not affect such food staples as soy sauce as much as other, less essential goods. The company, too, took advantage of a panoply of modern techniques. Of crucial importance was its employment of Namiki as a strategist. He had the knowledge and determination to carry through a policy of destruction of the union. The company's selective firings of strike leaders and later mass firings of workers, after letters of warning, were superior weapons to those of the strike, because the supply of workers was great. The company could use its money and influence, as well as strike-breakers, to deny the workers buildings in which to have an office and hold meetings. It had political connections in high places, up to the prime minister, who was a *Seiyūkai* man and of course it had overwhelming influence among sections of the town of Noda, such as over the local school officials. Although it failed in creating a viable company union, it could use the carrot of bettering conditions without, or in spite of, the union. Finally, in the end, the company became convinced that it should indoctrinate the workers with traditional virtues. But the logic of familial paternalism meant the provision of sufficient welfare and security in return for the workers' loyalty and hard work—a rational or contractual paternalism that became the pattern of industrial relations which prevailed. In short, the labor conflicts of the 1920's resulted in the emergence of a uniquely Japanese pattern of industrial relations and organization, one which tied the welfare of the worker to his company rather than to his class compatriots. It is, perhaps, not unreasonable to suggest that the paternalism which came to dominate Japanese labor relations is in large part responsible for the fact that today Japan is rated third in the world in gross national product but, depending on the statistics used, anywhere from sixteenth to twenty-first in living standards. The repression of labor in Taishō thus continues to bear its fruit.

Conclusion: Taisho Japan
and the Crisis of Secularism

THERE IS NO reason to assume, as Marius Jansen pointed out some years ago, that the accession to the throne in 1912 of the weak-minded successor to the Emperor Meiji should have marked the beginning of a new era. Yet despite Jansen's admirable logic the name of the new emperor, Taishō, continued to be used to denote the years from about 1910 down to 1930. Like a doppelgänger or a dybbuk, the name has come to possess the field of modern Japanese history. Just as the fear of the dybbuk tells us about those who perceive it as a form of reality, so, perhaps the Taishō label tells us more about the historians of modern Japan than about the years they are seeking to retrieve. Even the most superficial examination of the postwar literature on Taishō Japan will suggest that the term is used to denote not simply a specific set of years beginning in 1912 and ending in 1926. Rather, closer examination discloses the presence of a conceptual framework for the analysis of Japanese history since the late nineteenth century.

This conceptual framework, when applied to the Taishō years, has two main themes. First, the turn of the century is seen as representing a new stage in the development of modernity in Japan, one which ended cataclysmically in the decade of the 1930's, with the drift toward militarism and adventuristic expansion. Second, it has been postulated that the major features of this modernizing process were the emergence of democratic institutions and the subsequent development of a wide range of social, economic, and political contradictions that were clearly observable in the years between 1912 and 1926. From this belief it has often been concluded that an analysis of these contradictions would in fact reveal the reasons for the failure of democracy in Japan. Essential to this theme is the assumption that the "failure of democracy" symbolized the irrational development of absolutism in Japan or, as it is sometimes put, the failure symbolized the persistence of unique traditional norms and values.

437

It is ironic, perhaps, that both Marxists and non-Marxists (mostly Americans) have shared, in their respective approaches, these conceptual and ideological assumptions. Both schools of analysis have emphasized the role of persisting "traditional" or "feudal" values as the main impediment to "rational" development, as well as the short-run utility of these values in creating a modern state. The division existing between these two schools has thus occurred largely over the question of determining the reasons behind the persistence of traditional values. Marxists have argued that the lingering of feudal values has resulted from the peculiarities of economic and class development; non-Marxists employing a modified Weberian—Parsonian—model have proposed that this phenomenon owes more to the diffuse character of Japanese social structure which, in turn, reinforces and maintains traditional values throughout the organizational context of the society.

It was the desire to reach beyond these polemics over the role of traditional values and norms that generated the conference at which the papers making up this volume were first presented. The participants were asked to come with their own conception of Taishō as it had emerged from their research on a specific topic. We expected wide differences in topics, orientations, and conclusions, and we were not disappointed. Yet despite these inevitable differences the essays share certain themes and areas of agreement. Furthermore, above and beyond the mass of new information present in these papers they also, taken together, suggest that there may be ways of viewing the Taishō experience other than simply as the battleground on which the conflicts generated by modernization were fought.

The essays in this volume do not challenge the now generally held view that Taishō as a period covered more years than those assigned to the reign of the Taishō Emperor. However, the essays suggest that Taishō did not end with the demise of the parties in the early 1930's but rather that the name is descriptive of the era between, approximately, 1900 and the beginning of the Pacific War. What is significant about this periodization is not the time span but the assumptions underlying this view. It is, I think, fairly clear that the criteria used to define the period are not related to the ideological stances that have resulted in the use of the rather vague and ambiguous measurements implied by the terms feudalism, capitalism, tradition, modernity, and growth. If the volume, as something more than its parts, is not informed by these concepts, then what conceptual outlook does it present?

On the most general level the volume is informed by a concern with the phenomenon and praxis of change in Japan. In this sense the majority of essayists appear to be more strongly motivated by the desire to explicate the nature of behavior and consciousness and the relationships between them rather than by the desire to explicate the historicity of Taishō, that is, its place in the transition from tradition to modernity. This is by no means to deny either the historical character of the essays or the presence of ideological assumptions by individual essayists. But history and historicity are, after all, two different pursuits. As Pierre Bayle, the early Enlightenment historian, suggested, the practice of history is not the elucidation of theoretical or metaphysical structures, but the elucidation of praxis. Yet if the individual essayists are not devoid of ideology, the volume as an entity has escaped historicity by approaching its subject with a degree of randomness—a conscious avoidance of "value-free" conceptual integrity. The randomness of topics, methods, and underlying assumptions made it possible to avoid some of the pitfalls of historicity and historicism.

On the most general level the essays allow us the possibility of viewing Taishō as something more than a transitional period whose character was derived from the process of change from a traditional to a modern society. There are a number of themes running through these essays that point to the possibility that Taishō history and development were not only characterized by the tensions rising from the process of industrialization but were also the consequence of tensions growing out of a revolutionary transformation, in the early Meiji period, of the conception of society; from a prescriptive conception of natural moral order to a secular voluntaristic one.

Of these themes, perhaps the most dominant is conflict. Certainly, it is no revelation that the Taishō period was one in which conflict and confrontation were persisting elements. However, if we examine the nature of the conflicts portrayed in these essays— whether they are direct confrontations between tenants and landlords, factory workers and owners, bureaucrats and politicians, or between Japan and other nations—what is striking is the marketplace character of the assumptions that appear to have generated these conflicts.

If we turn to the two essays describing direct conflict, those by Totten and Waswo, it seems clear that it was generated by expectations and organized in ways that reflected different underlying beliefs about the nature of society and the kinds of rewards due from proper behavior different from those which existed in the Tokugawa and early Meiji periods. The demands of the tenants and the Noda workers for the right to bargain as organized groups and the right to participate in the determination of their economic rewards cannot be said to have emerged from the conception of a self-evident and natural "just share." Such demands for the formalization and rationalization of relationships indicate the absence of a belief that a just share stems from proper adherence to natural relationships. Instead, they reflect a belief that labor was a possession of the individual and that a just share was a product of conscious self-determination that men were free to pursue by bargaining in the marketplace. It was this assumption of the secular marketplace character of economic life that led the tenants and workers at Noda to demand clarification and formal definition of their relationships to the economic order. To achieve a just share in the absence of one that was self-evident required new styles of organization precisely because a just share could be determined only by a continuing bargaining process. The utilization of unions was, in this sense, a reflection of the need for continuing formal organizations created by the bargaining conception of determining a just share of economic rewards. Thus, as Totten implies when he speaks of convergence, unions did not emerge as organizational adaptations for the pursuit of traditional conceptions of proper economic rewards, but as a response to a secular, contractual conception of economic relationships that produced similar organizations elsewhere.

Despite their traditionalistic rhetoric the resistance of the landlords and factory owners to the demands and expectations of their tenants and workers also appears not to have been generated by a belief in the validity of natural moral traditional relationships. As Waswo points out, much of the problem between landlord and tenants stemmed from the absentee character of landlords and their conception of the landlord-tenant relationship as a purely legal and economic one. The landlord's conception of just economic rewards thus seems to have emanated also from their commitment to a marketplace conception of a just share: that is, the belief that legal possession of the land gave them the right to determine the division of profits on a purely contractual basis. Much the same may be said of the Noda management, whose tactics in dealing with the strike, including the use of strike-breakers, thugs, and calling out the police, are far more reminiscent of laissez-faire economic assumptions and behavior than of any other. Furthermore, the labor policies that were instituted both before and after the strike by the Noda management—more rational recruitment procedures and a "rational paternalism," as Totten calls it—appear to be strategies evoked by and designed to reduce or eliminate the costs of conflict as well as of inefficient use of labor. In short, the behavior of the landlords and the Noda management appear to have been based on the very secular assumption that property rights determine the appropriateness of economic rewards and the strategies for achieving them.

One can conclude, at least tentatively, that these conflicts were not generated by traditional expectations coming into conflict with the demands of modernity. Both the rationality of organization and the specificity of demands reflect the conflict of expectations and the actuality arising from a secular conception of economic relationships. The expectations arising from a growing awareness that there were no natural limitations to the pursuit of economic freedom clashed with a reality that denied that promise and provided no means by which it might be achieved. With the increasing tempo of industrialization after 1900, the result was a steady increase in industrial and rural conflict. This was especially so after the major gains made by rural and urban labor during the World War I boom. The destruction of those gains by rising prices and repression was certainly a major factor in setting off the Rice Riots of August and September, 1918. The participation of major segments of both rural and urban populations, as well as the organization and specificity of their demands, suggests that traditional expectations played a minor role in this dramatic confrontation. Continued repression following World War I failed to eliminate the rational organization of expectations, thus indicating the degree to which secular conceptions of economic relationships had taken root in Japanese society.

The essays describing the intellectual and ideological currents of the period also reveal, I believe, the primacy of secular values as the focus of Taishō thought and action. Superficially, there seems little to connect such men as Takayama Chogyū, Yoshino

Sakuzō, Kawakami Hajime, Natsume Sōseki, and the proletarian writers. Yet they are connected in the sense that their central concerns are not focused upon attempts to bring Taishō society into accord with a moral structure based on relationships that were assumed to be a reflection of a proper natural order. Or to put it another way, they were not railing against contemporary Japanese society because it had departed from the proper order of things and relationships. Their ideological commitments were generated, as Harootunian, for example, points out, by the belief that society was in no way related to a natural order; that in fact, despite a rhetoric couched in hoary Confucian aphorisms, the social and political orthodoxy of the Meiji bureaucrats was secular, voluntaristic, and expedient in character. Moreover, they had also come to conceive of the bureaucracy's political orthodoxy as an arbitrary one validated only by the claim of a secular college of cardinals to have a monopoly on the divination of Imperial will.

It was this consciousness of the basic arbitrariness of the Meiji orthodoxy, I would suggest, that produced the search, common to all the ideologues described in the essays, for a universal source of moral behavior that could transform the public order, that would fulfill the need for and firmly establish the relationship between private moral impulse and society. For some, as Harootunian indicates, the arbitrary secularism of the administrative state was so oppressive that they sought to withdraw from the public into a private world that fed, often destructively, upon itself in the search for creative tension. For others, as Najita, Bernstein, Matsuo, and Iwamoto have indicated, this awareness that society was an object of will led them to attempt to contest the Meiji bureaucrats' conception that administrative law alone encompassed the *kokutai*—the Imperial will. In their search for moral guidelines that would properly define and mediate between personal action and public order, all these ideologues rejected, as corrupt, the politics generated by the arbitrariness of the Meiji orthodoxy. Indeed, the ideologues of Taishō, viewing politics as an arena or marketplace in which men without moral convictions sought to impose their will, came finally to reject all politics as corrupt. Here too, with the possible exception of Kawakami, apoliticality became the sole act of protest of which they were capable.

The ideologues of Taishō, one may suggest, were responding

to the revolutionary condition created by the Meiji leaders' un-
witting destruction of the Confucian paradigm of the natural
order as the basis for organizing society. By substituting Imperial
will as the sole legitimation for public behavior, order, and weal,
the oligarchs established the basis of a secular society where,
free of the limitations imposed by a natural order, men might
appeal to the Imperial will to sustain any number of proper social
orders. The oligarchs had responded to this potential anarchy
by assigning to themselves and the bureaucracy a monopoly over
the interpretation of Imperial will. So long as the bureaucracy
was dominated by men possessing the aura of greatness that
came of restoring the Emperor, the monopoly went almost unchallenged. By the turn of the century, however, the basis of
bureaucratic leadership had become training in law, which had
now become the embodiment and canon of Imperial will. In a
sense, by 1900, the Restoration had become bureaucratized. It
was this bureaucratization of Imperial will that revealed its essentially arbitrary character and led Sōseki to say plaintively and
prophetically: "It used to be a world in which anything could
be done with the influence of His Majesty. It is now a world
where the impossible is impossible *even with* His Majesty's influence. Next will no doubt come an age when things are impossible
because of His Majesty's influence." Yoshino, Kawakami, Kitamura, and the others were responding to the dilemma of modern
secular society: the problem of freedom and order.

If the autonomy of Imperial will served as the legitimation of
the secular political orthodoxy which the Meiji oligarchs created, it also served as the basis for Japan's search for great power
status. As Crowley, in his essay, puts it: "the *hubris*, the drive
for equality with the Occidental Powers, which distinguished
Japan's diplomacy of the 1930's, was not specific to that decade.
This elusive search for 'equality' began with Perry's black ships."
As Crowley and Iriye suggest, Japan's foreign policy prior to the
Pacific War was not generated by a conspiracy created in the
1920's and '30's nor by organizational failures stemming from
the persistence of "irrational" or "traditional" values. Japanese
policy was generated by a world view that had emerged out of
the Restoration. Just as society was not an aspect of a clearly
revealed self-regulating and moral natural order, neither was
the society of nations. Just as the autonomy of the Imperial will
was the condition of, and legitimation for, the creation of social

443

order—so the autonomy of Imperial will was the condition of legitimation for a proper international order. It was this conception of autonomy, freedom from the past, and natural order, that made it possible, as David Abosch so cogently pointed out at the conference, for the Japanese leaders to grasp with such rapidity the Western conception of sovereignty as the basic criterion for determining national interest and for ordering the relations among states. Moreover, I think it can be argued, as Crowley does, that it was the assumption that Japan's autonomy was a basic condition of a legitimate international order that provided the dynamism for Japan's pursuit of imperium. How else can one explain the Meiji leaders' belief that Japan, despite her history as a peripheral society and despite her lack of natural resources, could become a Great Power? Only by viewing the Restoration of the Emperor as an act of will that transcended Japanese history and denied nature as a mitigating force on Imperial will could the Meiji leaders come to view Japan's historical role as an object of will. Certainly, a people that had overcome the past by an act of will could not be expected to remain in the backwash of any power, no matter how great.

Autonomy in this context thus meant the exertion of national will to achieve a place in the world order that confirmed the Restoration as an act of will rooted in the Japanese genius and not as an insignificant historical accident. An order that did not accord Japan a position of "equality" was one that was patently improper. As Iriye and Crowley show, Japan was willing to abide by the rules of the imperial game so long as those rules did not inhibit Japan's ability to achieve and maintain equality with the Great Powers. When, however, a series of events in the 1920's and '30's—the denial of racial equality, the dissolution of the Anglo-Japanese Alliance, the emergence of an informal Anglo-American alliance, the rise of Chinese nationalism seemingly abetted by the British—all seemed to indicate a change in the rules, Japan refused to play. They abandoned peaceful economic competition as futile and a sign of weakness. Japan now engaged in a search for the basis of an order that would insure her equality—an order that eventually surfaced as the Co-prosperity Sphere.

The degree to which this attitude dominated Japanese public life in the period after 1900 is reflected as well in the two essays by Yamamura and Nakamura. These essays are significant not only because they present new information about major areas of Japanese economic development, but also because they reveal that choices about economic development did not stem directly from some inherent logic of development. Both writers make it clear that choices regarding economic development resulted in large part from the desire to maintain equality with the Great Powers. The decision to develop and exploit colonial agricultural productivity was based on the desire, Nakamura points out, to enhance Japan's economic autonomy. The pursuit of cheap and plentiful food resources was maintained even after its effects on Japanese farmers had created a major source of alienation and discontent. In the same vein, Yamamura argues that the decision to encourage cartelization and oligopolization was the consequence of the desire to increase Japan's competitive position on the world market. Although this goal was achieved, Yamamura points out, rightly I believe, that it was accomplished at the cost of repressing the demands of the masses of workers and farmers for some kind of economic justice. In effect, the government bureaucracy and big business were willing to trade off social tension and alienation for economic growth and the maintenance of empire.

The Pacific War, then, was not the consequence of the failure of democracy nor of any inherent contradictions in the process of growth. The policies that distinguished the 1930's may be viewed as the logical consequences of that new and revolutionary vision of history and society that emerged from the act of Restoration—a vision in which Imperial will and national will were synonymous and in which the autonomy of this will had to be insured both within and without Japanese society. To reject that autonomy or acquiesce in its limitation was not only lese majeste but also a betrayal of Japan's modern history and her identity.

In pursuing the theme of conflict I have suggested that the kinds of conflict described in these essays could have stemmed only from a secular conception and a view of society in which no behavior was exempted from the claims of Imperial will by virtue of its natural morality. This interpretation is, I believe, supported when the role of law in Taishō society is examined. Only such a conception would have produced a state orthodoxy expressed in terms of administrative law—a law whose legitimacy stemmed from its origin in Imperial will. In its bureaucratic incarnation this will was as arbitrary as that of any Calvinist God. Moreover, this orthodoxy possessed the potentiality of a great irony that was realized in the Taishō period. For, though its aim was the creation of a stable social order through a legal system that sought to eliminate competitors in the appeal to and divination of Imperial will, it encouraged conflict and competition. Since Imperial will and its expression in law were essentially arbitrary, they provided no guidelines for dealing with new problems or behavior. Proper behavior could be determined only after the fact—after it had occurred and been judged as acceptable (or wanting) on the scales of social order. Thus, all acts were possible unless already proscribed by law. In Taishō, the law provided no principle by which men could judge whether the acts they were engaged in were antisocial until after they had occurred. Conflict emerged as the only means of identifying proper public behavior. Even such timid warriors as Kawakami and Yoshino saw conflict as a value from which a new moral order might be derived.

Only within the realm of interpersonal relationships, where informal group values provided norms of expected behavior with regard to the everyday world, was antisocial behavior predictable, and conflict avoidable. One is led to speculate that the strength of the Japanese commitment to such groups in the modern period was directly proportional to the degree of bureaucratization of public life. In the face of a public order defined by arbitrary rules and conflict, the informal group, perhaps, offered the sole haven of emotional security and predictability.

This suggests one of the basic paradoxes of Taishō history and society. On the one hand society was presumed to be a secular voluntaristic product of man's will to achieve social order and discipline. All action was possible provided it did not interfere with order as it had been defined up to that time. But the ex post facto means of determining the relationship of acts to social order resulted in ever-increasing limitations on the ability to act. This was especially true after 1900 as urbanization and industrialization created new actors and conditions in Japanese society. Each new kind of action—strikes, political organization of the masses, investigations of new ideologies—produced new regulations. Thus, in 1925, the paradox of the demands of freedom and order in secular society reached its culmination when the Diet, under the aegis of the political parties, passed both the Universal Manhood Suffrage Bill and the most repressive Peace Preservation

Bill in Japanese history. As Kato has pointed out in his essay, it is precisely in this sense that Taishō democracy was not the antithesis of the "fascism" of the 1930's but its prelude. By fully acquiescing in the view that order was the essential requirement of society where otherwise all things were possible, the parties made inevitable the time when political party opposition itself would be viewed as detrimental to order.

If conflict is one theme common to many of these essays, the ubiquitousness and omnipresence of the bureaucracy is another. As the essays in this volume indicate, the period after 1900 saw the bureaucracy pervade almost every aspect of Japanese life—from the regulation of the family to the determination of economic policy, from the regulation of reading matter to the determination of proper thought and action. Described in this fashion, the bureaucracy appears to have been a monolithic structure. Yet, as my own essay indicates, the rational development of the bureaucracy by 1900 reduced rather than increased its autonomy. Not only was the bureaucracy subject to pressures from the outside as a consequence of its increasingly rational nature but, internally as well, differentiation and specialization gave rise to conflicts over budget allocations and goal priorities. These consequences of rational development rendered the bureaucracy less than monolithic in terms of its everyday activities and tasks.

However, as the data on the prefectural governors suggest, the bureaucracy, by virtue of its training and its commitment to rules as the organizing principle of administration, was monolithic in its conception of itself as a charismatic organization. The Meiji leaders' conception of the bureaucracy as the sole institution capable of legitimately interpreting the Imperial will provided it with a status and authority far beyond that provided by its members' expertise. The successful institutionalization of charisma in the bureaucracy is reflected in two aspects of its development: its autonomy and its rationality. The former derived its legitimacy from the bureaucracy's role as servants of the Emperor, responsible only to him. This view, held from the time of the Restoration, was formally stated in the Meiji Constitution. The bureaucracy thus was conceived as the direct extension of Imperial will and national interest. The autonomy which this relationship to Imperial will required was more than implied. The constitution made the bureaucracy the possessor of all the expressed and residual civil powers of the Emperor. The administrative structure of this autonomy was worked out between 1887 (the establishment of the upper and lower civil service examination system) and 1899 (the Civil Service Appointment, Status, and Disciplinary Ordinances). By 1900, the basic autonomy and integrity of the civil service was assured by Imperial ordinances that placed the power of determining eligibility, recruitment, appointment, tenure, and discipline in the hands of permanent senior civil servants. Despite the breach in integrity described in my essay, the political parties were unable to vitiate bureaucratic autonomy. At best they were able informally to politicize a small number of senior civil servants—and then only by bureaucratizing themselves.

The second characteristic of the bureaucracy's charismatic role was the commitment to law and rules not only as the organizing principle of the bureaucracy but as the basis for training civil servants. The necessity of pursuing legal training created a uniformity of pre-service socialization, and the legal-rational character of the bureaucracy created a uniformity of career experiences. Out of this uniformity emerged a bureaucratic leadership that was extraordinarily homogeneous. The use of law as the basis of both organizational structure and leadership training served also to create a leadership committed to law as the organizing principle not only of administration but of society as well. Bureaucracy and law, by 1900, had become almost synonymous: so much so that an independent legal profession can hardly be said to have existed in the Taishō period. The relationship of the bureaucracy to law symbolized and reflected the bureaucracy's special role in the interpretation and implementation of Imperial will.

The Meiji leaders' commitment to law as the basis of bureaucratic training and leadership values was neither fortuitous nor simply imitative. Essentially, it arose, one can conjecture, from their belief that social order could proceed, in the light of their own seizure of power, only from the existence of a single mechanism for the authoritative expression of Imperial will. The authoritativeness of this expression could be established on a permanent basis only by resort to formal law, and the authoritativeness of the institution responsible for law could be established only by requiring that prolonged legal-jurisprudential training be the basis of bureaucratic expertise. By the turn of the century this commitment to law produced a bureaucracy whose leadership was and continued to be homogeneous, not only in socialization and career, but also in ideological outlook. This basic homogeneity of leadership values, norms, and behavior throughout the Taishō period provided the bureaucracy with a kind of monolithic character and continuity that was unmatchable by any other political institution, with the possible exception of the military bureaucracy.

The political parties' recruitment of their highest leadership from the bureaucracy reflected the acceptance of the validity of bureaucratic values and their underlying ideology. The conflicts of the parties with the bureaucracy did not stem from differing views of the nature of political order. The parties accepted the dictum that Imperial will was the organizing principle of society and that this will was encapsulated in law. Conflict was thus essentially limited to the question of expanding the decision-making elite to include not only bureaucrats but also those former or non-bureaucrats who were committed to the same values. It was this identity of values between the major parties and the bureaucracy that led, logically, to the demise of the former in the 1930's. When they were forced to choose between national interest and the demands of party power, the political leaders, bureaucrats at heart, chose the former without the slightest demur that the dichotomy was a false one. Viewing the politics of Taishō one is led to conclude, along with Kato, that the parties failed because they were, in fact, part of the bureaucratic establishment and ideology. Reluctant to challenge the autonomy of Imperial will, the parties, in the final analysis, were reluctant to challenge the bureaucracy's monopoly of interpretation and implementation of that will by pursuing alternative ideologies and organization.

The burden of this discussion, so far, has been that Taishō history and society were dominated not by the conflict of traditional expectations with the demands of modernity, but by the tensions emerging from the secularization of Japanese society— its liberation from the strictures and limitations imposed by the belief in a natural moral order. This liberation was reflected in the emergence, by the beginning of the twentieth century, of legal-rationality, in the Weberian sense, as the focus of the organization of nearly every aspect of Japanese life. The dependence on rules or law to define not only political and economic relationships but also social relationships such as the family (the

449

Civil Code of 1898) and community (the Local Administration Ordinances of 1878 and 1888) clearly indicates that the Meiji leaders did not believe that society was based on natural relationships that were a paradigm for all social relationships. By the turn of the century not even the family was considered as a natural set of relationships but, like all other social organizations, one subject to secular determination. The penetration of bureaucratic rationality into almost every phase of Japanese life provided an ever-expanding participation in and exposure to the secular rational marketplace conception of society. It was this exposure that produced, I would suggest, a growing consciousness of the implications of and potential for self-determination inherent in a society not bound by an immutable natural order of things. With this consciousness, however, also came the belief that the promise of self-determination and -fulfillment was denied by an arbitrary bureaucratic definition of the nature of a proper social life. The gap between the promise of secular society and its actuality became evident to increasing numbers as industrialization and urbanization revealed the emptiness of the promise for the vast majority of the society. This revelation produced not only the quest for universal ideologies that might integrate the individual and society but also demands from those who had yet to share in benefits of industrialization—workers, tenant farmers, *eta,* small farmers—that the gap be closed in economic, if not political, terms. The character of Taishō history emanates, I would argue, from the paradoxes inherent in the secular conception of society—its potential for perfect freedom and harmony, on one hand, and its potential for perfect anarchy and disorder on the other. Freedom from the limitations of a transcendent natural order created in Japan, as in all societies where such limits have dissolved, enormous tensions between the claims of freedom and order, and of private and public. To the extent that secular voluntaristic conceptions of society are the hallmark of modernity, one may conclude that Japan at the beginning of the twentieth century had achieved modernity. This achievement, however, did not grow from some autonomous process of modernity. There is no reason to assume that secular notions of society are part of some inevitable process of history. It was not a product of industrialization, although industrialization and the creation of mass urban society exacerbated the tensions inherent in secularism. This was especially the case after

World War I, when external conditions and events created greater consciousness of the gap between promise and fulfillment.

If industrialization did not create the conditions and reality of the secular society in Japan, what were its wellsprings? As Weber noted in his classical analysis of the relationship between the Protestant ethic and capitalism, there is a close connection between secular notions of society and the rise of legal-rational organization of authority and social structures. The rejection of a natural moral order results in the need for a new legitimation for behavior. Rules and law become the organizing principle for determining the source of behavior, legitimacy, and authority. Without law there can be no uniformity of expectations about behavior or uniformity of behavior. Thus, organizational and social rationality stem from the breakdown of consensus about the natural character of authority and social behavior. This paradigm suggests a clue to the origins of the secular notion of society in Meiji Japan. The success of the Imperial Restoration in 1868 presented the leaders of the new government with the problem of how to establish the legitimacy of the government's authority and insure compliance to its demands. By their destruction of Tokugawa legitimacy through the appeal to higher moral authority—the Imperial will—the leaders of the new government had opened a Pandora's box. The appeal to higher moral authority created the potentiality for anarchy—any man might legitimate his search for power or the pursuit of selfish interests by the same appeal. In effect, as with the Calvinists and the Puritans, the appeal to higher moral authority as the basis of legitimacy revealed the essential arbitrariness and mutability of any political, economic, or social arrangement. The Meiji leaders could not depend on the claim that the new government represented the true natural order of politics. In their appeal to Imperial will they had implicitly argued that there was no natural order, only a natural commitment to Imperial will that superseded all existing political and social relationships. By legitimizing their overthrow of the Tokugawa on the basis of a solipsistic knowledge of Imperial will they were, in effect, claiming that there could be no limitations upon that will. There was no one natural political order. Men were free to organize society in any manner so long as it represented the Imperial will to create a stable, harmonious, and independent social order.

The potentiality for political and social disorder that the leaders of the new government had created broke upon them as they faced the problem of insuring the legitimacy of the government and its right to demand obedience. In the face of a possibly infinite number of appeals to Imperial will the Meiji leaders had to create, as did Calvin in Geneva, an administrative and social orthodoxy. They had to create a bureaucracy with both a monopoly of authority and the right to interpret Imperial will. This could be accomplished in the context of 1868 only by creating a single integrated structure of authority in which loyalty to the Emperor was the primary criterion for officeholding. At the same time, the lack of any consensus on what constituted his will created the problem of insuring adherence to authority and uniform implementation of decisions. For government administration, the result was increased use of formal rules that were defined as expressions of Imperial will. On a broad social level the result was the reliance on law as the expression of Imperial will to define not only proper political but also proper social and economic behavior. Within the first decades of the Restoration, law and Imperial will had become synonymous, and neither was open to question as the organizing principle of society. In essence, the successful Restoration of Imperial will in 1868 resulted in the rejection of a natural moral order of relationships and replaced it with one based on formal, defined relationships whose legitimacy had its source in the Imperial will. In this sense, all social relationships derived their legitimacy and appropriateness from the existence of that will as revealed in the law.

This commitment to Imperial will as the sole source of legitimation for expected behavior suggests also the source of the Meiji leaders' commitment to the market economy and the value of competitiveness. The appeal to Imperial will denied the possibility of any natural hierarchy of political, social, or economic status. Before the awesome majesty of the Emperor there were no "great men"—only subjects. Distinctions among men could be based only on ability and the willingness to utilize this ability in the service of the Emperor. The competitiveness of ability could be the only means for assigning power, wealth, and status. In the political marketplace the reward was bureaucratic office; in the economic marketplace the reward was wealth. To receive these rewards was to receive them as gifts from the hands of the Emperor, thus creating a burden of obligation that required the subordination of individual will. In the end, all achievement could be and had to be legitimized by the slogan "for the good of the nation."

If, indeed, the notion of society as secular was derived from the act of Restoration and the problems of legitimacy and authority it created, this derivation suggests why the tensions of secularity were resolved in favor of the claims of public order. From the very beginning of the *Ishin*, secularity and its potentialities were identified as deriving from the condition of the autonomy of Imperial will. So long as this remained a basic assumption, the claims of self-determination and fulfillment would always be rejected or subordinated in favor of public Imperial claims of order and discipline. Since law was the concrete expression of Imperial will, the bureaucracy's legal expertise enabled it to maintain its identity with the Imperial symbol. The political parties had no such legitimacy or identity and, therefore, could be no more than beggars at the doors of power. Their only alternative was to reject the concept of Imperial autonomy as the source of law and find a new source for law. Neither by training nor social class were the party leaders capable of such revolutionary acts. Ironically enough, it was their commitment to the rule of law that led the party leaders to eschew mass politics and accept the primacy of public demands over those of privacy. One can only conclude, along with Najita, Harootunian, and Kato, that "Taishō democracy" and "Shōwa fascism" were not two distinct phenomena but were patterns of behavior stemming from shared assumptions about the nature of politics and society.

Finally, the role of the Imperial will as the condition of secular society in Japan suggests the validity of the concept of what has come to be called civil religion. It was the apotheosization of the Emperor as the supreme and arbitrary source of political and social values that freed Japanese society from the bonds of natural relationships and natural discipline. Religious values thus become fused with political values so that the latter came to perform the function of maintaining social values. Although this shift may seem paradoxical, the point is made, perhaps, by remembering that it was the Calvinist and Puritan conception of a just but arbitrary God that was largely responsible for the emergence of secularism in seventeenth-century Europe, and it was the emergence of this secularism that created the crises of modernity in Europe in the succeeding two centuries.

453

In Japanese personal names the family name appears first: Yoshino Sakuzō; Kawakami Hajime. Americans of Japanese descent use the Anglicized form with the family name last: Tetsuo Najita is indexed as Najita, Tetsuo.

455

Index

Yoshino's interpretation of, 42-43, 55, 63, 64, 223n

Meiji period, 217-18, 223, 299, 345; agriculture, 330, 331, 353, 355, 371; early, 19, 20, 439, 440; end of, 3-5, 7, 12; expansionism, 238-39; ideology, 15, 17-22, 27, 31-32, 112-22, 442-44, 447-48, 450-52; Kitamura's analysis of, 133-34; late, 13, 17, 18, 20, 21, 112-14; Natsume Sōseki's writings on, 75-76, 78-79, 113n; tenant farmers, 374, 377, 386-87; zaibatsu, 314-16

Meiji Restoration, 115, 121, 131-32, 141, 207, 209, 353, 443-45, 451-53; Restorationist Revolution (Bo-shin War, 1868), 5, 11

middle class: in cities, 228-31; culture and politics of, 111, 125, 138-39; in Germany, 231-32; liberalism and, 218-19; in militarization of state, 235

Middle East, Japanese trade with, 247-48

Miki Kiyoshi, 154, 235n; "The World Historical Significance of the China Incident," 278-79

militarism, 232-36; beginning of, after World War I, 220; democracy related to, 217-36; economic policy and, 264; in nationalism and expansion, 217, 271, 272, 277, 280, 283; opposition to, 221, 235-36

Mill, John Stuart, 46, 90, 102, 104

Minami Ryoshin, 304

Minobe Tatsukichi, 64, 79n

Mishima Yukio, 126n

Mitsubishi Bank, 321-22

Mitsubishi Economic Research Institute, 320

Mitsubishi Kōgyō K.K., 318

Mitsubishi zaibatsu, 71, 312, 314, 319

Mitsubishi Zōsen K.K., 318, 319

Mitsui Bank, 319, 321

Mitsui Bussan, 317-18

Mitsui *Gōmei*, 317

Mitsui Kōzan K.K., 317, 319

Mitsui zaibatsu, 312, 314, 317, 319

Miwa Jusō, 235n

Miyai Ichiro, 82

Miyake Setsurei, 5, 21, 42, 72-74, 141

Miyako Shimbun, 77

Mogi family, 404, 406-08, 418, 424-25, 434, 420

Mogi Sheiji, 407

Mongolia, 265; Inner, 273, 276, 283; Outer, 272

Monroe Doctrine, Japanese, 272-74, 276, 279

Mori Ōgai, 26-27, 79, 152n

Morita Sōhei: in *Hankyō*, 69; in politics, 70-71, 73-74

Moriya Sakao, 256

Morris, William, 22

Moscow: Comintern meeting (1924), 162; Profintern meeting (1930), 164

Motoori Norinaga, 115-16, 129, 154

Mountain-pass Daibosatsu, The, 231

Movement for Constitutional Government (1912-1913), 43

Muga-En (Garden of Selflessness, sect), 92

Mugaen (periodical), 69

Murayama Ryōchei, 84

Mushakoji Saneatsu, 7

Mussolini, Benito, 51

Mutsuhito, Emperor, *see* Meiji

Myōjō (periodical), 152

Myojo Subaru group, 72

Nagano Osami, Adm., 292-93

Nagoya, 247, 382, 385

Najita, Tetsuo, 442, 453

Nakae Chōmin, 22

Nakamura, James I., 358, 444-45

Nakamura Shigeru, 76-77

Nakane Shigeichi, 82-83

Nakano Shigeharu, 157, 162

Nakasō Miso Company, 412

Nakazawa Rinsen, 71

Namiki Shigetarō, 420-21, 436

Nanking incident, 263

Nansei Printing Company, 412

with Axis, 280, 287-89; Japanese anticipation of, 284-95; Japan's role in, 270-71; U.S. in, 270, 284-88, 290, 295

Yabe Teiji, 294
Yada Shichitarō, 263
Yamagata Aritomo, 9, 67, 78, 210-11
Yamaguchi Koken, 77
Yamakawa Hitoshi, 162, 163
Yamamoto Gombei, 68, 69
Yamamura, Kozo, 444-45
Yamanashi Prefecture, tenant unrest, 394
Yanaibara Tadao, 251, 256
Yasuda Bank, 321, 324
Yasuda zaibatsu, 312, 314
Yasunari Jirō, 80
Yasunari Sadao, 69, 71, 73, 77, 80
Yawata zaibatsu, 312
Yenan, 276
Yokoi, J., 354
Yokomitsu Riichi, 157-58, 168-69
Yomiuri shimbun, 74

Yonai Mitsuma, 284, 286
Yorozu chōhō, 9, 71
Yosano Tekkan, 71, 152
Yoshida Shōin, 93, 127
Yoshida Zengo, 288
Yoshihito, Emperor (Taishō), 4, 6-8, 437
Yoshino Sakuzō, 17, 29-66, 221, 223-24, 226n, 243-44, 441-43, 446; Christianity, 33, 61-62; custom and function, views on, 44-51; democracy, views on, 29-31, 39-41, 51-52, 61-62; Hegel's influence on, 33-35, 48-49, 54, 62; individualism, views on, 35-36, 38, 53-54, 58-61; nationalism, views on, 32-33, 36-41, 49-51, 62; on Russo-Japanese war, 36-38
Yoshizawa, 250

zaibatsu (cartels), 300-01, 312-28; banks, 312n, 313-27; Meiji period, families, 314-16